Lecture Notes in Computer Science 2633

Edited by G. Goos, J. Hartmanis, and J. van Leeuwen

T0189045

Springer

Berlin
Heidelberg
New York
Hong Kong
London
Milan
Paris
Tokyo

Fabrizio Sebastiani (Ed.)

Advances in Information Retrieval

25th European Conference on IR Research, ECIR 2003
Pisa, Italy, April 14-16, 2003
Proceedings

 Springer

Series Editors

Gerhard Goos, Karlsruhe University, Germany
Juris Hartmanis, Cornell University, NY, USA
Jan van Leeuwen, Utrecht University, The Netherlands

Volume Editor

Fabrizio Sebastiani
Istituto di Scienza e Tecnologie dell'Informazione
Consiglio Nazionale delle Ricerche
Via Giuseppe Moruzzi, 1, 56124 Pisa, Italy
E-mail: fabrizio@iei.pi.cnr.it

Cataloging-in-Publication Data applied for

A catalog record for this book is available from the Library of Congress.

Bibliographic information published by Die Deutsche Bibliothek
Die Deutsche Bibliothek lists this publication in the Deutsche Nationalbibliografie;
detailed bibliographic data is available in the Internet at <http://dnb.ddb.de>.

CR Subject Classification (1998): H.3, H.2, I.2.3, I.2.6, H.4, H.5.4, I.7

ISSN 0302-9743
ISBN 3-540-01274-5 Springer-Verlag Berlin Heidelberg New York

Springer-Verlag Berlin Heidelberg New York
a member of BertelsmannSpringer Science+Business Media GmbH

http://www.springer.de

© Springer-Verlag Berlin Heidelberg 2003
Printed in Germany

Typesetting: Camera-ready by author, data conversion by DA-TeX Gerd Blumenstein
Printed on acid-free paper   SPIN: 10924907   06/3142   5 4 3 2 1 0

Preface

The European Conference on Information Retrieval Research, now in its 25th "Silver Jubilee" edition, was initially established by the Information Retrieval Specialist Group of the British Computer Society (BCS-IRSG) under the name "Annual Colloquium on Information Retrieval Research," and was always held in the United Kingdom until 1997. Since 1998 the location of the colloquium has alternated between the United Kingdom and the rest of Europe, in order to reflect the growing European orientation of the event. For the same reason, in 2001 the event was renamed "European Annual Colloquium on Information Retrieval Research." Since 2002, the proceedings of the Colloquium have been published by Springer-Verlag in their Lecture Notes in Computer Science series.

In 2003 BCS-IRSG decided to rename the event "European Conference on Information Retrieval Research," in order to reflect what the event had slowly turned into, i.e., a full-blown conference with a European program committee, strong peer reviewing, and a (mostly) European audience.

However, ECIR still retains the strong student focus that has characterized the Colloquia since their inception: student fees are kept particularly low, a student travel grant program is available in order to encourage students to attend the conference (and encourage student authors to present their papers personally), and a Best Student Paper Award is assigned (conversely, ECIR has no best paper award).

In terms of submissions, ECIR 2003 has been a record-breaking success, since 101 papers were submitted in response to the call for papers, which amounts to a 94% increase with respect to ECIR 2002 in Glasgow and a 260% increase with respect to ECIR 2001 in Darmstadt. All papers were reviewed by at least three reviewers. Out of the 101 submitted papers, 31 were selected as full papers for oral presentation, and 16 were selected as short papers for poster presentation. Students are very well represented, since 20 out of 31 full papers and 13 out of 16 short papers involve a full-time student, which means that the traditional student focus of the Colloquium has been well preserved.

The contributions in these proceedings are indicative of the wide range of issues being tackled in current IR research, and include both theoretical and experimental work in several media (text, hypertext, structured text, multilingual text, spoken text, images, and music) and in several tasks (search, retrieval, clustering, categorization, both content-based and collaborative filtering, summarization , information extraction, question answering, topic detection and tracking, and visualization), either in centralized or in distributed environments, and tackling either effectiveness or efficiency issues.

I want to thank, first of all, the authors who submitted their papers to ECIR 2003, and thus contributed to the creation of a strong, high-quality program, which allowed us to look forward to an exciting conference. I am also deeply indebted to all the colleagues who accepted to serve on the Program

Committee and to all the colleagues who acted as additional reviewers; thank you for all the good work, and also for meeting the tight reviewing deadlines imposed by the ECIR 2003 schedule. Many thanks also to Karen Spärck Jones and Alberto Del Bimbo for accepting to give the ECIR 2003 keynote speeches; to Keith van Rijsbergen, Maristella Agosti, Ayse Göker, Kees Koster, Peter Ingwersen, and Alan Smeaton, for accepting to join what promises to be a very interesting panel; to Sándor Dominich, Pia Borlund, and Joemon Jose for accepting to be on the Best Student Paper Award Committee; to Ayse Göker and the BCS-IRSG Steering Committee for their support; and to Richard van de Stadt, of Borbala Online Conference Service, for making the Cyberchair conference management software freely available, which greatly simplified all the tasks connected with the submission and the reviewing of the papers.

I am extremely grateful to the companies and institutions who sponsored ECIR 2003: Elsevier, the Associazione Italiana di Informatica e Calcolo Automatico (AICA), the European Information Retrieval Specialist Group of the Council of European Professional Informatics Societies (CEPIS-EIRSG), Libero, Fast Search & Transfer, Canon Research Europe, Microsoft Research, Sharp Laboratories of Europe, IBM Research, and DataPort–AppleCentre. Their generous contribution allowed the Organizing Committee to keep the registration fees low and to enable a strong student grant program.

Finally, I want to extend a special word of thanks to the people who helped me in the organization of the conference: to Patrizia Andronico, who designed the ECIR 2003 official poster and website; to Francesca Borri, who took care of local arrangements with professionalism and much more beyond the call of duty; to the ECIR 2003 webmaster Claudio Gennaro, who painstakingly dealt with all the system issues related to the management of Cyberchair; and to our student volunteers Henri Avancini, Leonardo Candela, and Franca Debole, who helped at various stages of the organization. It is thanks to all of them if the organization of ECIR 2003 was not just hard work, but also a pleasure.

January 2003   Fabrizio Sebastiani

Organization

ECIR 2003 was organized by the Istituto di Scienze e Tecnologie dell'Informazione of the Consiglio Nazionale delle Ricerche (CNR, the Italian National Council of Research), with the collaboration of the Istituto di Informatica e Telematica of the CNR, and under the auspices of the Information Retrieval Specialist Group of the British Computer Society (BCS-IRSG).

Organizing Committee

Chair:	Fabrizio Sebastiani, National Council of Research, Italy
Web & Graphic Design:	Patrizia Andronico, National Council of Research, Italy
Local Arrangements:	Francesca Borri, National Council of Research, Italy
Webmaster :	Claudio Gennaro, National Council of Research, Italy

Program Committee

Fabrizio Sebastiani, National Council of Research, Italy (Chair)

Alan Smeaton, Dublin City University, Ireland
Alessandro Sperduti, University of Padova, Italy
Andreas Rauber, Vienna University of Technology, Austria
Arjen de Vries, Centre for Mathematics and Computer Science, The Netherlands
Avi Arampatzis, University of Nijmegen, The Netherlands
Ayse Göker, Robert Gordon University, UK
Barry Smyth, University College Dublin, Ireland
Carol Peters, National Council of Research, Italy
Claudio Carpineto, Fondazione Ugo Bordoni, Italy
David Carmel, IBM Research, Israel
David Harper, Robert Gordon University, UK
Djoerd Hiemstra, University of Twente, The Netherlands
Dunja Mladenić, Jožef Stefan Institute, Slavenia
Edda Leopold, Fraunhofer Institute, Germany
Eero Sormunen, University of Tampere, Finland
Fabio Crestani, University of Strathclyde, UK
Gabriella Pasi, National Council of Research, Italy
Gareth Jones, University of Exeter, UK
Gianni Amati, Fondazione Ugo Bordoni, Italy
Giuseppe Amato, National Council of Research, Italy
Gloria Bordogna, National Council of Research, Italy

Best Student Paper Award Committee

Additional Reviewers

Alexei Vinokourov
Athanasios Kehagias
Behzad Shahraray
Bernardo Magnini
Birger Larsen
Carlo Meghini
Caspar Treijtel
ChengXiang Zhai
Claus-Peter Klas
Donna Harman
Erik Thorlund Jepsen
Eugenio Di Sciascio
Fabio Aiolli
Fabio Paternò
Franca Debole
Franciska De Jong
Franco Scarselli
Gilles Hubert
Giorgio Satta
Giuseppe Attardi
Gregory Grefenstette
Henri Avancini
Henrik Nottelmann
Isabelle Moulinier
Janez Brank

Jean Pierre Chevallet
José Maria Gómez-Hidalgo
Jurij Leskovec
Leonardo Candela
Lynda Lechani
Marc Seutter
Maria Elena Renda
Marie-France Bruandet
Massimiliano Pontil
Michelangelo Diligenti
Monica Bianchini
Natasa Milić-Frayling
Nicola Orio
Norbert Gövert
Paolo Ferragina
Renée Pohlmann
Ryen White
Simon Tong
SK Michael Wong
Tassos Tombros
Thorsten Joachims
Tony Rose
Victor Lavrenko
Yoshi Gotoh

Previous Venues of ECIR

2002 Glasgow, UK
2001 Darmstadt, Germany
2000 Cambridge, UK
1999 Glasgow, UK
1998 Grenoble, France
1997 Aberdeen, UK
1996 Manchester, UK
1995 Crewe, UK
1994 Drymen, UK
1993 Glasgow, UK
1992 Lancaster, UK
1991 Lancaster, UK

1990 Huddersfield, UK
1989 Huddersfield, UK
1988 Huddersfield, UK
1987 Glasgow, UK
1986 Glasgow, UK
1985 Bradford, UK
1984 Bradford, UK
1983 Sheffield, UK
1982 Sheffield, UK
1981 Birmingham, UK
1980 Leeds, UK
1979 Leeds, UK

Main Corporate Sponsor

Gold Sponsor

Sponsors

Table of Contents

Collaborative Filtering and Text Mining

Text Representation and Natural Language Processing

Formal Models and Language Models for IR

Machine Learning and IR

Text Categorization 1

Usability, Interactivity, and Visualization Issues in IR

Text Categorization 2

Architectural Issues and Efficiency Issues in IR

Posters

Document Retrieval:
Shallow Data, Deep Theories;
Historical Reflections, Potential Directions

Karen Spärck Jones

Computer Laboratory, University of Cambridge
William Gates Building, JJ Thomson Avenue, Cambridge CB3 0FD, UK
sparckjones@cl.cam.ac.uk

Abstract. This paper reviews the development of statistically-based retrieval. Since the 1950s statistical techniques have clearly demonstrated their practical worth and statistical theories their staying power, for document or text retrieval. In the last decade the TREC programme, and the Web, have offered new retrieval challenges to which these methods have successfully risen. They are now one element in the much wider and very productive spread of statistical methods to all areas of information and language processing, in which innovative approaches to modelling their data and tasks are being applied.

1 Introduction

Two ideas have played a crucial role in automated information retrieval. They are not in themselves computational ideas, but computers were necessary to make them work. Specifically, computers made them so much easier to apply that the quantitative changes in information management that followed automation have become qualitative ones.

Many things about information and searching for it are quite timeless (though they may not be recognised as such in shiny current computing contexts). But the two very simple ideas that pervade modern retrieval systems have effected an information revolution. One of these ideas is taking words as they stand. The other is counting their stances. It is not merely sufficient, it is necessary for document or text retrieval to respect the actual words that people use. It is thus also essential for effective retrieval to respond to the ways words are distributed in documents: the relative frequencies with which words occur and cooccur mark topics and their significance in texts.

Stated thus, these ideas may appear banal, and just what *any* approach to indexing and searching requires. But the latter has not historically been the case, and working out the consequences of these simple ideas has been the distinguishing feature of automated retrieval since research on it began fifty years ago. These two ideas, obvious though they now seem, were important novelties in the context of traditional library classification in the 1950s. The innovative retrieval work associated with them that began in the 50s and grew in the 60s

F. Sebastiani (Ed.): ECIR 2003, LNCS 2633, pp. 1–11, 2003.

provided the base for current Web search technology, and the wholly new information world that many take this to represent. In this paper I will look at the way these ideas have evolved, and try to identify critical points in this evolution both in the past and, now, for the future.

2   Innovative Ideas

The stimulus for new thinking about indexing and searching in the 50s came from the growth of, and increasing specialisation in, the scientific literature. Traditional subject classification schemes were too general, too rigid, and too prescriptive to support effective retrieval from collections of scientific papers. Indexing had to be more fine-grained, more flexible, and more reflective of the documents themselves.

The researchers of the 50s responded to these needs with a whole range of notions and tools. These included: using given text words and phrases, however specialised, for indexing, as opposed to independent category labels (Taube et al. 1952); defining topics at search time by postcoordination, rather than at file time by precoordination (also Taube et al.); choosing indexing vocabularies to reflect file topic distributions, not external structures (Mooers 1951); exploiting numeric data to refine topic characterisation (Luhn 1957); and developing formal models for retrieval based on statistics and probability (Maron and Kuhns 1960). The important point about all of these proposals is that they lent themselves to automation even, already, in the pre-computer form of punched card manipulation, as with Taube and Mooers, but more strikingly, using early computers, in Luhn's work (see Schultz 1968).

Much of this early work was concerned, in one way or another, with classification. The presumption was that indexing and retrieval depend on classification, whether of what there is 'out there' or of what is said about this. Though the world of information was changing with a growing and richer literature, it was still a world of information; and since manipulating information depends on classification, it seemed that what was called for was new views, and methods, of classification. The novel ideas about retrieval just mentioned were therefore seen as grist for classification mills.

The UK-based Classification Research Group (1969) was especially active in investigating ways of shaking up traditional approaches to information description and classification so as to make indexing more responsive to document realities, especially subject specialisation and rapid scientific and technological change; but their presumption was still that constructing classifications and indexing with them would be manual rather than automatic. The more radical research on classification that flourished on both sides of the Atlantic in the late 50s and early 60s focussed on automatic methods of classification, and hence of indexing. This research embraced the new ideas about derivative indexing, grounded in the texts of the documents themselves, in a much more wholehearted way, since classification was based on bottom-level distributional data about words.

The work done at the Cambridge Language Research Unit in the UK illustrates this development very well (Needham and Spärck Jones 1964). It sought to apply general, formal classification techniques to text vocabularies, characterised by their document occurrences, in order to obtain thesaurus classes of words with similar document distributions. The members of a class could be substituted for one another in searching to obtain query-document topic matches, while the classes themselves could be freely combined in postcoordinate fashion.

This period of research on statistically-based indexing and classification was a very exciting time, as Stevens 1965 and Stevens et al. 1965 show. The work both in this specific area and more generally in novel approaches to indexing and classification was thoroughly international, with many European contributors, for example to the Elsinore Classification Research Conference (Atherton 1965).

This was also the period when Salton's research at Harvard and then in the thirty-years of SMART work at Cornell began (Salton 1968, 1971). This too started by seeking to automate then-conventional forms of indexing and searching but, particularly through working with abstract texts, gradually moved to placing more emphasis on non-conventional techniques like term weighting. Bely et al. (1970)'s very sophisticated work on automatic controlled-language indexing using SYNTOL also indirectly encouraged simpler techniques, since the elaborate indexing devices they used were not especially effective for retrieval. This work is more properly seen as a pioneering project on information *extraction*.

In all of the statistically-based studies, automation was critical in making it possible both to deal with volumes of data (though these were trivial by modern standards), and to apply procedures consistently and objectively: manipulating numerical data about text words is something computers are much better at than humans.

Even more importantly, automation made it possible to do very large numbers of systematic and controlled experiments to evaluate methods of indexing and searching. The Cranfield projects (Cleverdon 1967, Spärck Jones 1981) were pioneering efforts in system evaluation and, as Cleverdon noted, while essentially manual, sought to simulate machine objectivity. But even though the number of studies, e.g. of different indexing devices, was very impressive, it was evident from the subsequent SMART work that with automatic indexing and searching, far more extensive tests across different environment variables or system parameters could be done.

The work on relevance feedback done both at Cornell from the 60s and in Cambridge a little later (Salton 1971, Spärck Jones 1980) illustrates the gain from automation, both for retrieval itself and for research on retrieval. Of course human searching involves the use of relevance information; but the specific feedback methods, just like those for term weighting (or classification), are wholly unsuited to human implementation and wholly suited to machine application. At the same time, the enormous volume of experiments with different weighting strategies and formulae since the late 60s could never have been carried out without automated test rigs.

Though automation for cataloguing and catalogue searching, as done by the Library of Congress and OCLC, and for systems for the journal literature, as exemplified by Medlars or Inspec, appeared in the later 60s, this did not immediately lead to radical innovations in the nature of indexing. The scientific literature systems continued with manual indexing and subject-based description, though this was now done with specialised thesauri and controlled languages rather than the older universal classification schemes. The first move towards more modern approaches appeared with the ability to search eg actual title words in MEDLINE, rather than only descriptor fields, though with Boolean not ranking searches. In these operational systems the advantage of automation came primarily from the 'administrative' convenience it provided through access to large databases, rapid searching, and so forth.

The Science Citation Index, on the other hand, showed automation is a more original light, since citation indexing constituted a new type of indexing and could never have been done on a large scale without computers. Moreover, though the indexing did not exploit frequency data in the style adopted for term weighting, it did show the importance of quantitative data referring to documents.

3   Development and Consolidation

Research in the 1970s and 80s continued to develop and test the new approaches of the 60s to indexing and searching using text words and statistical data. This work did not make much impact on the large-scale bibliographic search services, which very reasonably concentrated on other issues of user importance, like rapid document delivery. Moreover even where full-text files were in question, as with legal systems, queries remained in the Boolean mode. But at Cornell and e.g. Cambridge and City University in the UK, work on both theory and practice for statistically-based methods continued. This was successful in further developing appropriate formal models for retrieval, as in Salton 1975, van Rijsbergen 1979, and Robertson and Spärck Jones 1976, and in extending the range of experiments that confirmed the value of these approaches (e.g. Salton and Buckley 1988). These tests included not only ones to compare variations on statistical methods, but ones that suggested that they could compete successfully with conventional controlled indexing (Salton 1986). Research in this area was indeed now extended to enrich at least some conventional bibliographic services, as in Biebricher et al. 1988.

Moreover, though the 70s were the heyday of AI claims for the superior merit of symbolic approaches to information and language processing, as Salton pointed out (Salton 1995), whatever AI might offer other tasks, it had never been demonstrated superior to statistical approaches for the general retrieval case. Similarly, though continued attempts were made to show that 'proper' language processing, i.e. syntactic and possibly also semantic parsing, was required for better retrieval performance, this was not supported by the test results. Rather, insofar as compound index terms, as opposed to single words, were of use, so-called statistical phrases defined by repeated word tuples were just as effective as ones obtained by explicit parsing (Salton et al. 1990, Croft et al. 1991). This is the analogue, for complex concepts, of frequency as an indicator of concept significance for simple terms. Even where some explicit language analysis was involved, as in stemming, this could be much simpler than the full-scale lemmatisation needed for other information processing tasks (Porter 1980).

The one area that remained surprisingly intractable was full-scale automatic classification, whether of terms or documents. Quite apart from the problems of identifying appropriate class definitions and viable classification algorithms, straightforward attempts to group terms to obtain a thesaurus, or to cluster documents to focus searching, could not be shown to deliver significant general improvements in retrieval effectiveness. Thus document grouping enhanced precision but with serious damage to recall (Croft 1980). Similarly, it had earlier appeared that term classes were only of any value at all when they were confined to very strongly related terms and were applied to promote extra, rather than substitute, term matches (Spärck Jones and Barber 1971).

It instead became more clear, during the 80s, that in classification as in other aspects of indexing and searching, the desired effects could be achieved by indirect rather than direct means. Thus the aim of classification, whether of terms or documents, was to bring objects with similar distributional behaviour together since the groupings obtained would, when tied to query terms, be correlated with document relevance. The whole effect of relevance feedback, especially when used to expand rather than just reweight index descriptions, is to pick up classes of terms that are motivated by shared relevant document distributions. It is true that in using known relevant documents for feedback a system has more pertinent information to exploit than in the original classification case; but the performance gains that have been consistently demonstrated in the 90s for so-called blind relevance feedback, where documents are only assumed, not known, to be relevant, illustrate a form of indirect indexing, albeit one more focussed than the earlier ones.

From one point of view, the 1980s marked time. The mass of experiments done showed that the initial ideas about the value of statistical facts for retrieval had justified staying power, but had barely affected operational systems apart from some relatively tentative initiatives (Doszkocs 1983). This was partly for the same reasons as before, namely that operational services had many other goals than just ratcheting up precision and recall, but also because, though research experiments became bigger, the service databases grew very rapidly and it was far from obvious that the research methods or results would scale up.

On the other hand, better tools for other applications, like natural language processing for text editing and database query interpretation, made it possible to conduct more far-reaching tests of language processing for retrieval, as in phrasal indexing (Salton et al. 1990), even if the results were negative.

But the 80s were significant from a rather different point of view for retrieval. This was the period when the computing community in general concentrated on user interaction and the form of human/computer interfaces, and when established literature services began the shift from professional intermediary to end-user searching. This naturally stimulated the retrieval community to address the implications for the user's search skills, or rather lack of them. But while this most obviously led to proposals for expert system interfaces (Belkin et al. 1983), it also provided a rationale for search devices which minimise user effort while maximising the payoff from information the user is uniquely qualified to provide, as in relevance feedback exploiting statistical data.

More generally, it is clear that for retrieval, the 80s were the period before a major earthquake. The underlying plates were moving and changing shape. End-user computing was growing and taking a different form; computing power was rapidly increasing; the internet was giving remote access to files and processes a quite new convenience and utility; machine-readable full text was coming on stream; related areas like natural language processing were moving to corpus-based data extraction both for resources like lexicons and in tasks like message interpretation; AI was recognising the legitimacy of statistical approaches to knowledge characterisation and capture, and developing machine learning techniques. Thus while the retrieval innovations of the previous decades were being consolidated, the larger information world was being remade. The question is thus how these innovations have fared in this new world.

4 New Situations

The innovations of the 60s and 70s have in fact fared very well. The 1990s have been payoff time for statistically-based retrieval. Given the underlying shifts in the context it only needed the two earthquake triggers supplied by the Text REtrieval Conferences (TRECs) and the Web to bring the retrieval strategies previously confined to the research laboratory out onto the operational stage.

The design, scale and range of the TREC effort on retrieval evaluation have made what can be done with the text-derived and statistics-driven work of previous research quite clear; and the Web has provided new applications to exploit this. Early Web search engines were not tied down by the prior commitments and presuppositions of the bibliographic services. Their builders were open to ideas from computing research, so statistical techniques were applied in system design, for example in AltaVista, and they have a key role, albeit in a different form, in Google.

The TREC evaluations themselves, over more than a decade, tested indexing and searching devices far more thoroughly than ever before (TREC-2, 1995, TREC-6, 2000, Voorhees and Harman, in press). With world-wide participation, and very significant contributions from Europe, they have also brought multilingual operations into the hitherto English-centred evaluation world. As importantly, their data and findings have stimulated extensive further work, both along existing lines (e.g. Spärck Jones et al. 2000), and in newer ones (e.g. Dumais et al. 2002).

In 'mainstream' retrieval, TREC has confirmed earlier beliefs and findings on the value of the 'basic' statistical strategies, albeit with some development in scaling up to very large files. TREC has continued to cast doubt on the added value, for ad hoc topic searching, of structured classifications and thesauri or (to use the currently fashionable term) ontologies, whether manually or automatically constructed, and on the value of sophisticated natural language processing for retrieval. More importantly, in the TREC Web track experiments, where the older research ideas have been applied to far more challenging and timely data than before, these methods have maintained their standing. These experiments have shown that hyperlink information, the Web's real indexing novelty, does not imply better performance, for topic searching, than ordinary content terms, though it is helpful for the more specific task of finding homepages (Hawking and Craswell 2002). The TREC tests as a whole also show that statistical methods, especially when enhanced by simple feedback, can bootstrap respectable performance from a poor initial request. This matters because the user's contribution and effort are important for effective retrieval, but cannot be guaranteed present. It is also worth noting that TREC confirmed early on that statistical retrieval strategies developed for English applied elsewhere, for instance to Chinese (Wilkinson 1998)

The TREC experiments have served to endorse not only the computational technologies applied, but also the IR theories underlying them. In general, the established statistically-based approaches - the Vector Space Model, the Probabilistic Model, the Inference Model - have performed well, and much alike, not surprisingly since they tend to use the same facts about about terms and documents in similar ways. The older Boolean Model has barely figured in TREC, and tests with a Non-Classical Logic Model have so far been limited. The most interesting recent development has been the introduction, or rather import, of a new model, the so-called Language Model. Language Modelling has performed well in TREC, and has stimulated new debate on appropriate models for retrieval (Croft and Lafferty, in press).

This model, like others, is a probabilistic one. Initially developed and established as highly effective for speech recognition (Young and Chase 1998), it has been applied in appropriate forms to a range of language and information processing tasks including translation and summarising, as well as retrieval (Brown et al. 1992, Banko et al. 2000, Knight and Marcu 2000, Berger and Lafferty 1999, Miller et al. 1999, Ponte and Croft 1998, Hiemstra 2002).

If we take all retrieval models as characterising the relation between a query and a (relevant) document, we can relate the Language Model to the other previous statistically-based models as follows. The Vector Space Model treats this relation as an object proximity relationship (Salton et al. 1975, Salton 1975). The Inference Model views the query document relation as a connectivity one (Turtle and Croft 1990). The Non-Classical Logic Model takes the query document relationship as a proof one, with the document proving the query (van Rijsbergen 1986). The Probabilistic Model has a generative relation from a query (along with relevance) to a document (Robertson et al. 1981, see also Fuhr 1989, Kwok 1995).

In the Language Model there is also a generative relationship, but the other way round, from the document to the query, i.e. the query is thought of as derived from the document (and relevance), in the same sort of way that in speech the heard sounds are generated from a word string. The other tasks to which the LM has been applied are given an analogous generative or derivational characterisation, though is not always very intuitive, so in translation the *source* text is seen as generated by the desired target text, and in summarising the full document is seen as generated by the desired summary text. In all of these applications of Language Modelling the task process is one of recovering the unknown original, given a more or less corrupted or defective received version; the system learns to do this by extensive training on prior instances of pairs, e.g. in the summarising case of full texts and their human abstracts, in the retrieval case of relevant documents and queries.

Language Modelling, like Vector Space Modelling for instance, is a quite general, abstract approach to information characterisation and processing, with many potential task applications. Whether it is superior to others as a theoretical foundation for retrieval, and if so in what way, is still a matter for argument (Croft and Lafferty, in press). But as technology it has shown its power, in both speech and other cases, to exploit large masses of training material very effectively, and to allow good probability estimation. It has also, in TREC, performed very well so far, as well as though not consistently and significantly better than, the best of the other models. Thus what its overall contribution to retrieval systems will be is not yet clear.

What the recent work on Language Modelling has emphasised, however, is first, the value of the very large training data sets that are now available for system development and customisation. The work on machine learning, text mining, and the like which has been done in the last decade has shown how valuable such large data resources are in building description (and hence discrimination) systems, whether as data extraction feature sets, categorisation rules, or grammars. Further, it appears that very heterogenous data, hitherto thought of as a source of confusion rather than clarification, can be readily digested, to very nutritious effect, by such learning systems. Though document collections of familiar kinds are more varied than is often recognised, the sheer variety of the Web has been seen as a challenge rather than opportunity for indexing and search techniques. In fact, as operational systems such as Autonomy's suggest, the range of material in a large file can promote, rather than undermine, the characterisation of topics and concerns for effective information management.

The recent work on Language Modelling has also, by being applied to multiple tasks, reinforced the other important development that TREC has helped to foster, for example through its filtering and question-answering tracks, namely making progress with multi-task systems. While those engaged with document retrieval in earlier decades recognised that documents might be sought for a variety of purposes, and information services might accommodate multiple tasks so that, for example, it might be possible to request a document be translated, advances in information and language processing are now stimulating genuinely integrated, and hence truly flexible, multi-task systems. These can take advantage on the one hand of of common formal models and computational techniques, as illustrated by Language Modelling, applying them to different component tasks. But they can also take advantage, on the other hand, of techniques and resources developed for particular purposes and simply incorporate them in larger systems. This is manifest in the wide application of stemmers, part of speech taggers, named entity recognisers and the like.

The Mitre MiTAP illustrates this most recent progress towards multi-task systems very well (Damianos et al. 2002). It exploits a range of devices, and components, developed across the whole information and language processing field, and supports a range of tasks including retrieval, translation and summarising, within the framework of a single convenient interface, in a substantial, fully operational system. It is not, of course, just a statistically-based system: it incorporates parsing, for example. But it makes use of statistical as well as symbolic methods, most obviously in its retrieval sub-component, but also, and more interestingly, elsewhere. Thus as one small example of the way that text-statistic notions dating back to the 1960s have found a modern home, the MiTAP summariser uses *tf*idf*-type weighting.

References

[1] Atherton, P. (Ed.) *Classification research*, Copenhagen: Munksgaard, 1965.
[2] Banko, M., Mittal, V. and Witbrock, M. 'Headline generation based on statistical translation', *ACL 2000: Proceedings of the 38th Annual Meeting of the Association for Computational Linguistics*, 2000, 318-325.
[3] Belkin, N. J., Seeger, T. and Wersig, G. 'Distributed expert problem treatment as a model for information system analysis and design', *Journal of Information Science*, 5, 1983, 153-167.
[4] Bely, N. et al. *Procédures d'analyse sémantique appliquées a la documentation scientifique*, Paris: Gauthier-Villars, 1970.
[5] Berger, A. and Lafferty, J. 'Information retrieval as statistical translation', *Proceedings of the 23rd International ACM SIGIR Conference on Research and Development in Information Retrieval*, 1999, 222-229.
[6] Biebricher, B. et al. 'The automatic indexing system AIR/PHYS - from research to application', *Proceedings of the 11th Annual International ACM SIGIR Conference on Research and Development in Information Retrieval*, 1988, 333-342.
[7] Brown, P. F. et al. 'Class-based n-gram models of natural language', *Computational Linguistics*, 18, 1992, 467-680.
[8] Classification Research Group, *Classification and information control: papers representing the work of the CRG from 1960 to 1968*, London: The Library Asssociation, 1969.
[9] Cleverdon, C. W. 'The Cranfield tests on index language devices', *Aslib Proceedings*, 12, 1967, 173-193.
[10] Croft, W. B. 'A model of cluster searching based on classification', *Information systems*, 5, 1980, 189-195.
[11] Croft, W. B. and Lafferty, J. Eds.) *Language modelling for information retrieval*, Dordrecht: Kluwer, in press.
[12] Croft, W. B., Turtle, H.R and Lewis, D. D. 'The use of phrases and structured queries in information retrieval', *Proceedings of the 14th Annual International ACM SIGIR Conference on Research and Development in Information Retrieval*, 1991, 32-45.

[13] Damianos, L. et al. 'MiTAP for biosecurity: a case study', *The AI Magazine*, 23 (4), 2002, 13-29.

[14] Doszkocs, T. E. 'CITENLM: natural language searching in an online catalogue', *Information Technology and Libraries*, 2, 1983, 364-380.

[15] Dumais, S., et al. 'Web question answering: is more always better?', *Proceedings of the 25th Annual International ACM SIGIR Conference on Research and Development in Information Retrieval*, 2002, 291-298.

[16] Fuhr, N. 'Models for retrieval with probabilistic indexing', *Information Processing and Management*, 25, 1989, 55-72.

[17] Hawking, D. and Craswell, N. 'Overview of the TREC-2001 Web track', *Proceedings of the Tenth Text REtrieval Conference (TREC-2001)*, Ed. E. M. Voorhees and D. K. Harman, Special Publication 500-250, Gaithersburg, MD: National Institute for Standards and Technology, 2002.

[18] Hiemstra, D. 'Term-specific smoothing for the language modelling approach to information retrieval: the importance of a query term', *Proceedings of the 25th Annual International ACM SIGIR Conference on Research and Development in Information Retrieval*, 2002, 35-41.

[19] Knight, K. and Marcu, D. 'Summarisation beyond sentence extraction: a probabilistic approach to sentence compression', *Artificial Intelligence*, 139, 2002, 91-107.

[20] Kwok, K. L. 'A network approach to probabilistic information retrieval', *ACM Transactions on Information Systems*, 13, 1995, 324-353.

[21] Luhn, H. P. 'A statistical approach to mechanised encoding and searching of literary information', *IBM Journal of Research and Development*, 1, 1957, 309-317.

[22] Maron, M. E. and Kuhns, J. L. 'On relevance, probabilistic indexing and information retrieval', *Journal of the ACM*, 7, 1960, 216-244.

[23] Miller, D. R. H. Leek, T. and Schwartz, R. M. 'A hidden Markov model retrieval system', *Proceedings of the 23rd Annual International ACM SIGIR Conference on Research and Development in Information Retrieval*, 1999, 214-221.

[24] Mooers, C. N. 'Zatocoding applied to mechanical organisation of knowledge', *American Documentation*, 2, 1951, 20-32.

[25] Needham, R. M. and Spärck Jones. K. 'Keywords and clumps', *Journal of Documentation*, 20, 1964, 5-15.

[26] J. M. Ponte and W. B. Croft, 'A language modelling approach to information retrieval', *Proceedings of the 21st Annual International ACM SIGIR Conference on Research and Development in Information Retrieval*, 1998, 275-281.

[27] Porter, M. F. 'An algorithm for suffix stripping', *Program*, 14, 1980, 130-137.

[28] Rijsbergen, C. J. van *Information retrieval*, 2nd ed., London: Butterworths, 1979.

[29] Rijsbergen, C. J. van 'A non-classical logic for information retrieval', *The Computer Journal*, 29, 1986, 481-485.

[30] Robertson, S. E., van Rijsbergen, C. J. and Porter, M. F. 'Probabilistic models of indexing and searching', in *Information retrieval research*, (Ed. R. N. Oddy et al.), London:Butterworths, 1981.

[31] Robertson, S. E. and Spärck Jones, K. 'Relevance weighting of search terms', *Journal of the American Society for Information Science*, 27, 1976, 129-146.

[32] Salton, G. *Automatic information organisation and retrieval*, New York: McGraw-Hill, 1968.

[33] Salton, G. (Ed.) *The SMART retrieval system: experiments in automatic document processing*, Englewood Cliffs, NJ: Prentice-Hall, 1971.

[34] Salton, G. *A theory of indexing*, Philadelphia: Society for Industrial and Applied Mathematics, 1975.

[35] Salton, G. 'Another look at automatic text-retrieval systems', *Communications of the ACM*, 29, 1986, 648-656.

[36] Salton, G. Remarks at the meeting on 30 Years of Information Retrieval at Cornell: A SMART Celebration, Department of Computer Science, Cornell University, April 1995 (video record).

[37] Salton, G. and Buckley, C. 'Term weighting approaches to automatic information retrieval', *Information Processing and management*, 24, 1988, 269-280.

[38] Salton, G., Buckley, C. and Smith, M. 'On the application of syntactic methodologies in automatic text analysis', *Information Processing and Management*, 26, 1990, 73-92.

[39] Salton, G., Wong, A. and Yang, C. S. 'A vector space model for automatic indexing', *Communications of the ACM*, 18, 1975, 613-620.

[40] Schultz, C. K. (Ed.), *H. P. Luhn : Pioneer of information science*, New York: Spartan, 1968.

[41] Spärck Jones, K. 'The Cranfield tests', in *Information retrieval experiment*, (Ed. K. Spärck Jones), 1981.

[42] Spärck Jones, K. 'Search term relevance weighting - some recent results', *Journal of Information Science*, 1, 1980, 325-332.

[43] Spärck Jones, K. and Barber, E. O. 'What makes an automatic keyword classification effective?', *Journal of the American Society for Information Science*, 22, 1971, 66-75.

[44] Spärck Jones, K., Walker, S. and Robertson, S. E. 'A probabilistic model of information retrieval: development and comparative experiments. Parts 1 and 2', *Information Processing and Management*, 36, 2000, 779-840.

[45] Stevens, M. E. *Automatic indexing: a state-of-the-art report*, Monograph 91, Washington, DC: National Bureau of Standards, 1965.

[46] Stevens, M. E., Guiliano, V. E. and Heilprin, L. B. *Statistical association methods for mechanised documentation*, Symposium Proceedings 1964, Miscellaneous Publication 269, National Bureau of Standards, Washington DC., 1965.

[47] Taube, M., Gull, C. D. and Wachtel, I. S. 'Unit terms in coordinate indexing' *American Documentation*, 3, 1952, 213-.

[48] TREC-2, Special Issue on the Second Text REtrieval Conference (TREC-2), *Information Processing and Management*, 31, 1995, 269-448.

[49] TREC-6, Special Issue on the Sixth Text REtrieval Conference (TREC-6), *Information Processing and Management*, 36, 2000, 1-204.

[50] Turtle, H. R. and Croft, W. B. 'Inference networks for document retrieval', *Proceedings of the13th Annual International ACM SIGIR Conference on Research and Development in Information Retrieval*, 1990, 1-24.

[51] Voorhees, E. M. and Harman, D. K. Eds.) *TREC: Experiment and evaluation in information retrieval*, Cambridge, MA: MIT Press, in press.

[52] Wilkinson, R. 'Chinese document retrieval at TREC-6', *The Sixth Text REtrieval Conference*, (Ed. E. M. Voorhees and D. K. Harman), Special Publication 200-240, National Institute of Standards and Technologoy, Gaithersburg, MD, 1998, 25-30.

[53] Young, S. J. and Chase, L. L. 'Speech recognition evaluation: a review of the U. S. CSR and LVCSR programmes', *Computer Speech and Language*, 12, 1998, 263-279.

Annotation and Retrieval
of Structured Video Documents

Marco Bertini, Alberto Del Bimbo, and Walter Nunziati

Università di Firenze, 50139 Firenze, Italia
{bertini,delbimbo,nunziati}@dsi.unifi.it

Abstract. Live Logging and Posterity Logging are the two basic applications for video databases. The former aims at providing effective annotation of video in quasi-real time and supports extraction of meaningful clips from the live stream; the latter provides annotation for later reuse of video material and is the prerequisite for retrieval by content from video digital libraries. Both require that information is adequately structured with interchange format and that annotation is performed, at a great extent, automatically. Video information structure must encompass both low-intermediate level video organization and event relationships that define specific highlights and situations. Analysis of the visual data of the video stream permits to extract hints, identify events and detect highlights. All of this must be supported by a-priori knowledge of the subject and effective reasoning engines capable to capture the inherent semantics of the visual events.

1 Introduction

As digital video libraries are becoming more readily available to professional and home users, the problem of content-based annotation and retrieval, and the ability to access relevant data become more important.

Research in this field is motivated by the strong interest shown by broadcasters, who are interested in systems that ease the process of annotation and retrieval of the huge amount of live and archived video materials. Live (production) logging and posterity logging support the task of editing TV programs, as they enable identification of relevant shots in the broadcasters' archives. Exploitation of such valuable assets is considered a key method for the improvement of production quality in a competitive market. Systems that enable efficient indexing and retrieval by content of video segments are the tools needed to achieve the aforementioned production quality and reduction of the costs of production and archiving.

Utilizing low-level features for retrieval, generally, is not a suitable approach, since it does not match well the human perception, and user interfaces generally are quite cumbersome. Moreover the user should deal with an information-overload and spend time trying to figure out how small bits of information compose a bigger picture. While the extraction of low-level information and features

F. Sebastiani (Ed.): ECIR 2003, LNCS 2633, pp. 12–24, 2003.

can be reliably performed automatically, the aggregation of these cues and recognition of semantic information is an active research field. At present the most sensible approach to semantic video indexing and annotation is to build domain specific information systems, where the prior domain knowledge is exploited to select the low-level information needed for further processing, and to provide higher-level semantic access to information.

Typically the steps required to automatically create a video annotation include temporal segmentation of the stream into shots, detection and recognition of text appearing in captions, extraction and interpretation of the audio track (including speech recognition), visual summarization of shot content, and semantic annotation. In general, a bottom-up approach is followed, moving from low level perceptual features to a high level semantic description of the content of the video being examined.

Textual retrieval is the key method to formulate semantic level queries, since visual information retrieval systems are limited to the use of low-level features such as color, texture, shape, motion, spatio-temporal compositions. On the other hand textual queries allow retrieval of people, events, highlights and concepts.

Both annotation and retrieval are dependent on the video domain: news videos queries may include people and places, based on text extracted form captions or from speech recognition[14], while commercials may be retrieved in terms of their semiotic content [2]. Sport videos are usually annotated in terms of highlights [15]. [16] and [17] provide reviews of video analysis and indexing.

2   A Use Case: Sports Videos

This paper addresses in particular the problem of detection and recognition of sport highlights in videos. Among the many sports types, soccer is for sure one of the most relevant—at least in Europe. Within scope of the ASSAVID project[1] a number of tools supporting automatic annotation and retrieval of sports videos have been developed. By gaining insight into the current practice of broadcasters, we were able to identify relevant issues to be addressed, as well as to gain a solid domain knowledge. Broadcasters typically rely on two logging approaches: *live (production) logging*, which is typically carried out live (or shortly after the event) by an assistant producer to select relevant shots to be edited into a magazine or news program that reports on sports highlights of the day (e.g. "Match of the day" or "GrandStand"); *posterity logging*, which is performed by librarians to make a detailed annotation of the video tapes, so as to allow their reuse in the long term to provide added depth and historical context to recent events (e.g. select best achievements of a sports personality during his/her career). The first

[1] This work was partially supported by the ASSAVID EU Project (Automatic Segmentation and Semantic Annotation of Sports Videos, http://www.bpe-rnd.co.uk/assavid/), under contract IST-13082. The consortium comprises ACS SpA (I), BBC R&D (UK), Institut Dalle Molle D'Intelligence Artificielle Perceptive (CH), Sony BPE (UK), University of Florence (I), University of Surrey (UK).

```
<?xml version="1.0" encoding="UTF-8"?>
<!ELEMENT document (summary?, annotation*)>
<!ELEMENT summary (#PCDATA)>
<!ELEMENT annotation (timecode, category, value*)>
<!ELEMENT timecode EMPTY>
<!ELEMENT category EMPTY>
<!ELEMENT value (#PCDATA)>
<!ATTLIST document
    name CDATA #REQUIRED
    date CDATA #IMPLIED
    version CDATA #IMPLIED
    author CDATA #REQUIRED
    producer CDATA #REQUIRED
    producerIp CDATA #IMPLIED
>
<!ATTLIST timecode
    time CDATA #IMPLIED
    frames CDATA #IMPLIED
>
<!ATTLIST category
    name (Cue | Description | Sport | Image | Audio | Shot.Change | Text | Rating) #REQUIRED
    subname (Event | Personality | New.Speaker | Music | Sounds | Caption |
        On.Screen) #IMPLIED
>
<!ATTLIST value
    kind (string | image | time | frames | integer | float) #IMPLIED
>
```

Fig. 1. ASSAVID XML DTD

type of annotation may include subjective comments (e.g. a "good goal"), while the latter usually is based on annotation standards defined by each broadcaster. In the following chapters we report on our experience in the classification of soccer highlights using an approach based on temporal logic models. The method has been tested using several soccer videos containing a wide range of different video editing and camera motion styles, as produced by several different international broadcasters. Considering a variety of styles is of paramount importance in this field, as otherwise the system lacks robustness. In fact, videos produced by different directors display different styles in the length of the shots, in the number of cameras, in the editing effects.

2.1   XML Data Structure

The ASSAVID system comprises several subsystems that produce low and mid-level annotation for generic sports, and high-level annotation for soccer. Among the subsystems there is video segmentation, mosaicing, audio event and sport type recognition (Univ. of Surrey), video OCR and speech recognition (IDIAP), contextual reasoning engine (Univ. of Surrey and IDIAP), and the soccer highlight recognition (Univ. di Firenze). These subsystems exchange data between them, and all the annotations are to be fed into a SQL database (PostgreSQL). These two requirements led to the use of a common XML DTD, shown in Fig. 1. The data structure defined by this DTD is able to deal both with low and high level information.

TimeCode	Cue	Description	Sport	Audio	Shot Change
22:37:30.00			CloseUp : 0.917053		
22:37:30.10	three_quarters				
22:37:30.20	three_quarters				
22:37:31.05	three_quarters				
22:37:31.15	three_quarters				
22:37:31.20					1
22:37:31.22	midfield	Mosaic Duration: 80 msec			
22:37:31.25					1
22:37:32.00	right_midfield	Mosaic Duration: 1800 msec	CloseUp : 0.926974	WhistleReferee 0.857445	

Fig. 2. Automatic annotation: shot changes, visual and audio content, playfield position

22:43:05.21		Soccer highlight: Forward pass	CloseUp : 0.967876
22:43:06.00	right_midfield		
22:43:06.00		Great Pass	
22:43:06.09		Good pass by	
22:43:06.10	right_midfield		

Fig. 3. Automatic and manual annotation: playfield position and soccer highlights

Figure 2 shows several low and mid-level annotations created by ASSAVID subsystems that have been merged according to the time code. Annotations in the Sport and Audio column have numerical values that are used by other subsystems. The Cue column contains the soccer playfield positions shown, a feature used by the soccer highlight subsystem. This cue may be useful also for librarians, since some annotation standards for posterity logging comprise this information.

2.2 Automatic and Manual Annotation

Live logging is the most critical annotation process due to the strict time requirements. Often it is carried on at the location where the event is recorded by an assistant producer, and then refined. The goal of this annotation is to find the most interesting highlights of the action, and usually logs produced during this process contain subjective annotations. In this case the role of automatic annotation is to detect the highlights, to let the assistant producers concentrate on the subjective annotation, and other types of annotation that can not be automatized. Figure 3 shows the merge of the annotations of two different producers (third and fourth lines), along with automatic annotation produced by the system described in this paper.

3   Previous Work

The problem of detection and recognition of highlights in sport videos is an active research topic. Among sports that have been analyzed so far, we can cite soccer

([7], [3], [8], [9]), tennis [10], basketball ([11], [12], [6]), baseball [13], American football. We review hereafter previous work related to soccer videos. The work presented in [7] is limited to detection and tracking of both the ball and the players; the authors do not attempt to identify highlights. In [3], the authors rely on the fact that the playing field is always green for the purpose of extracting it. Successive detection of ball and players is limited to the field, described by a binary mask. To determine position of moving objects (ball and players) within the field, the central circle is first located, and a four-point homographic planar transformation is then performed, to map image points to the model of the playing field. Whenever the central circle is not present in the current frame, a mosaic image is used to extend the search context. In this latter case, the mosaicing transformation is combined with the homographic transformation. This appears to be a fairly expensive approach. In [8] a hierarchical E-R model that captures domain knowledge of soccer has been proposed. This scheme organizes basic actions as well as complex events (both observed and interpreted), and uses a set of (nested) rules to tell whether a certain event takes place or not. The system relies on 3D data of position of players and ball, that are obtained from either microwave sensors or multiple video cameras. Despite the authors' claim that, unlike other systems, their own works on an exhaustive set of events, only little evidence of this is provided, as only a basic action (*deflection*) and a complex event (*save*) are discussed. In [9] has been proposed the usage of panoramic (mosaic) images to present soccer highlights: moving objects and the ball are super-imposed on a background image featuring the playing field. Ball, players, and goal posts are detected. However, despite the title, only presentation of highlights is addressed, and no semantic analysis of relevant events is carried out.

4   Analysis of the Videos

More than 20 hours of videos were inspected, showing that producers of videos use a main camera to follow the action of the game; since game action depends on the ball position, there exists a strong correlation between camera action and the movement of the ball. The main camera is positioned along one of the long sides of the playing field. In Fig.4 some typical scenes taken with the main camera are shown.

Fig. 4. Example of frames taken from the main camera

Identification of the part of the playing field currently shown and camera action are among the most significant features that can be extracted from shots taken by the main camera; these features can be used to describe and identify relevant game events. Typical actions featured by the main camera are: *i*) pan, *ii*) tilt, and *iii*) zoom. Pan and tilt are used to move from a part of the playing field to another one, while zoom is used to change the framing of the subject. These three movements can be detected separately.

Highlights that we have been elected for thorough investigation are: *i*) forward launches, *ii*) shoots on goal, *iii*) turnovers, *iv*) placed kicks, comprising penalty kicks, free kicks next to the goal box, and corner kicks. These are typical highlights shown in TV news and magazine programs summarizing a match, even if these actions do not lead to the scoring of a goal. Moreover, penalty kicks and corners are often used to calculate match statistics. All the four highlights are part of attack actions taking place near the goal box area, and they are strictly related to goal actions. It must also be noted that for each of the these highlights there are two different versions, one for each playing field side. The system that we present can discriminate each case. Test videos were acquired from Digital Video (DV) tapes, recorded at full PAL resolution, and 25 fps. Some test videos were selected from the BBC sport video archive, while other videos were digitally recorded from satellite TV channels.

5   Playfield Zone Classification

The soccer playfield has been divided in 12 zones, 6 for each side (Fig. 5). These zones have been chosen so that the change from one to the other indicates a change in the action shown, such as a defense action that changes into a counter-attack, or an attack that enters the goal box. Moreover it must be noted that typical camera views are associated with the selected zones. In some cases the zones can't be recognized from simple image analysis (zones near the center of the playfield), but the temporal analysis solves this problem.

The features used to recognize the playfield zones are playfield lines and the playfield shape. From this features we calculate a five elements vector composed by the following elements:

- playfield shape descriptor F: six different views of the playfield are recognized. They are shown in figure 6 a);
- playfield line orientation descriptor O: playfield lines are extracted, and their directions are quantized in 32 bins. These bins are grouped to calculate the number of horizontal and vertical lines, and the number of lines whose angle is greater or smaller than $\pi/2$, as shown in figure 6 b);
- playfield size descriptor R: this descriptor signals if the percentage of pixels of a frame, that belong to the playfield, is above a threshold;
- playfield corner position C: this descriptor may assume 4 values: absence of playfield corner in the image, or presence of one of three possible positions of the playfield corner that is farthest from the camera, as shown in figure 7a);

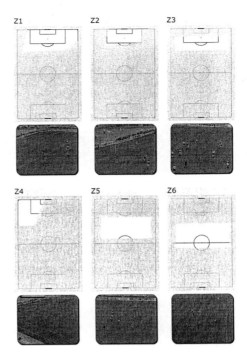

Fig. 5. Playfield zones, Z7 to Z12 are symmetrical

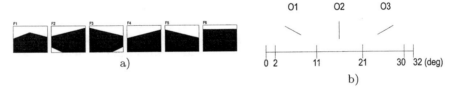

Fig. 6. (a) Playfield shape descriptor F. (b) Playfield line orientation descriptor O

- midfield line descriptor M: this descriptor is similar to the C descriptor, but it indicates the presence and type of the midfield line.

A Naïve Bayes classifier has been used to classify each playfield zone Zx. This choice is motivated by the fact that: *i)* we are interested in confidence values for each zone, to handle views that are not easily classified; *ii)* some descriptors are not useful for some zones (e.g. the C descriptor is not useful for the midfield zone); *iii)* some zones are mutually exclusive and some are not, thus it is not possible to define them as different values of a single variable.

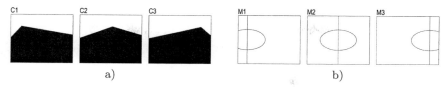

Fig. 7. (a) Playfield corner position descriptor C. (b) Midfield line descriptor M

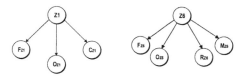

Fig. 8. Naïve Bayes networks: Z1 and Z6 zone classifiers

In figure 8 the classifiers for Z1 and Z6 are shown. It must be noted that in some cases some values of the descriptors correspond to a single value of the variable of the classifier, e.g.:

$$F_{Z1} = \begin{cases} 1 \text{ if } F = F_1 \\ 2 \text{ if } F = F_2 \\ 3 \text{ otherwise} \end{cases} \qquad F_{Z6} = \begin{cases} 1 \text{ if } F = F_3 \\ 2 \text{ otherwise} \end{cases}$$

Playfield zone classification is performed through the following steps: playfield lines and shape are extracted from the image, descriptors are then calculated and the observation values of the classifier variables are selected. The classifier with the highest confidence value (if above a threshold) is selected.

6   Camera Motion Analysis

As noted in section 4, camera parameters are strongly related to ball movement. Pan, tilt and zoom values are calculated for each shot. The curves of these values are filtered and quantized, using 5 levels for pan, 3 for tilt and zoom. Analysis of the videos has shown that conditions such as a flying ball rather than a change of direction, can be observed from camera motion parameters. Through heuristic analysis of these values, three descriptors of *low*, *medium* and *high* ball motion have been derived. Figure 9 shows a typical shot action: at time t_{start} a player kicks the ball toward the goal post. Acceleration and deceleration (at time t_{OK}) can be identified. Often zoom on the goal post can be observed.

Figure 10 shows a compact and interesting view of playfield position and camera motion (direction and speed). Figure 11 shows a form used for manual annotation, where position and direction are annotated by hand. It is interesting to see how mid-level features, used by the highlight recognition system, are also used for annotation.

20   Marco Bertini et al.

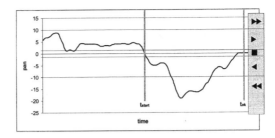

Fig. 9. Typical shot action: at time t_{start} the ball is kicked toward the goal post. Symbols on the right identifies low, medium and high motion

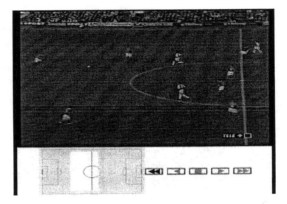

Fig. 10. Compact view of playfield position and camera motion (direction and speed)

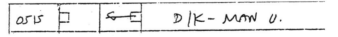

Fig. 11. Manual annotation form with playfield position and camera movement

7   Players' Position

The actual position of players on the playfield plane is computed through a transformation (estimated automatically from frame to frame) which maps any imaged playfield point (x, y) onto the real playfield point (X, Y). The planar homography is estimated using playfield lines correspondences. Players' position is instrumental in the precise classification of placed kicks. However, analysing every single player's position is not a feasible approach because of the varying number of framed players, the variations in their relative positions, the different

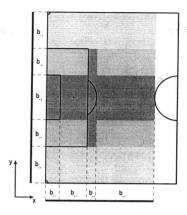

Fig. 12. For the purpose of placed kick classification, the playfield has been partitioned in a number of regions by quantizing the x and y coordinates into 4 and 5 levels, respectively. Relevance of the areas w.r.t. the problem of placed kick classification is coded by the shading (dark: very relevant; light: nor relevant)

framing terms (due to the many styles used by different directors), and of occasionally missed player detections (due to occlusions or to the poor quality of some videos). Inspection of videos and analysis of domain knowledge suggested that clustering and quantization represent a more viable solution. Experimental results confirmed the hypothesis that players' positions typically display different distributions on the playfield depending on the specific placed kick. Fig. 12 shows the relevance of different parts of the playfield surrounding the goal w.r.t. to the problem of placed kick classification: presence or absence of players in the darkest areas significantly contribute to the discrimination between the three classes of placed kicks; whereas presence or absence of players in the lighter areas are less relevant. Models for *penalty*, *corner*, and *free kick* develop upon these results.

8   Model Checking

Information provided from playfield zone recognition and camera motion analysis is used to create temporal logic models of the highlights. In fact the highlights can be characterized by the playfield zone where they happen, and how the action develops through the playfield. For instance the forward launch requires that the ball moves quickly from midfield toward the goal box. The models of all the actions have been implemented as FSM. Figure 13, 14 show two FSM, one for the goal shot and one for the turnover.

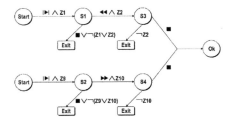

Fig. 13. Shot model: on the arcs are reported the camera motion and playfield zones needed for the state transition. The upper branch describes a shot in the left goal post, the lower branch the shot in the right goal post. If state *OK* is reached then the highlight is recognized

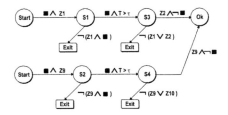

Fig. 14. Restart model: the final transition requires a minimum time length

9   Experimental Results

The system has been tested on about one hour of videos, separated in 80 sequences, selected from 15 European competitions. Tables 1 and 2 report the results:

From the results it can be noticed that those highlights that can be easily defined (free/penalty kicks and shoots on goal) obtain a good recognition rates. Recognition of shoots on goal is very good, specially if we consider that the false detection is due to attack actions near the goal box. Also the good re-

Table 1. Highlight classification results. The placed kick comprise corner, penalty and free kicks near the goal box zone

	Detect.	Correct	Miss.	False
Forward launch	36	32 (95%)	1 (0.03%)	4 (0.06%)
Shoots on goal	18	14 (93%)	1 (0.06%)	4 (0.06%)
Turnover	20	10 (50%)	3 (0.05%)	10 (50%)
Placed kick	13	13 (87%)	2 (13%)	0

Table 2. Actual highlights and their classification. The *Other* class contains actions that were not modeled. The placed kick comprise corner, penalty and free kicks near the goal box zone

Classific. result	Actual highlight				
	Fwd. launch	Sh. on goal	Turnover	C./p. kick	Other
Fwd. launch	32	1	1	0	2
Shoots on goal	1	14	0	0	3
Turnover	0	0	10	0	10
Placed kick	0	0	0	13	2

Table 3. An experiment was conducted to assess the accuracy in classifying placed kicks. The high quality of results is accounted to the precise measures of players' positions

	Detected	Correct	Missed	False
Penalty	18	17	0	1
Corner	19	18	1	1
Free kick	18	17	1	1

sult of forward launches detection is encouraging, since this highlight is usually very similar to other actions. It must be noticed that while this highlight is not important *per se*, it is linked to other important highlights, such as counterattacks. The recognition of turnovers is critical since its definition is quite fuzzy; probably adding other features such as player position would reduce the false detection. In a second experiment, we focussed on the accuracy in classifying placed kicks. For this purpose, a second test set was collected, featuring nearly 60 placed kicks—approximately 20 for each of the three classes (penalty, corner, free kick). Results are reported in Table 3, which shows that very good recognition rates are achieved (on average, around 96%). This can be accounted to the high discriminatory power attained through exact evaluation of players' position enabled by the homography, that is instrumental in the precise discrimination among the three classes.

10   Conclusions and Future Work

In this paper we have presented a system that recognizes soccer highlights using an approach based on temporal logic. The system uses the recognition of playfield zones shown in the frames, and camera motion parameters, to model the highlights. The automatic annotation allow mid and high-level queries such as the playfield location or a required highlight. Experimental results are extremely encouraging. Our future work will aim at improvement of feature extraction, extension of detected highlights (e.g. counterattack), and improvement of the retrieval system, using synthetic views of the actions.

References

[1] Y.Ariki, and Y.Sugiyama, "Classification of TV Sports News by DCT Features using Multiple Subspace Method", in *Proc. 14th Int. Conf. on Pattern Recognition (ICPR'98)*, pp. 1488–1491, 1998.

[2] C. Colombo, A. Del Bimbo, and P. Pala, "Semantics in Visual Information Retrieval," *IEEE MultiMedia* 6(3):38–53, 1999.

[3] Y. Gong, L. T. Sin, C. H. Chuan, H. Zhang, and M. Sakauchi, "Automatic Parsing of TV Soccer Programs", in *Proc. of the Int'l Conf. on Multimedia Computing and Systems (ICMCS'95)*, Washington, D.C, May 15-18, 1995.

[4] H. Miyamori, S.-I. Iisaku, "Video annotation for content-based retrieval using human behavior analysis and domain knowledge", in *Proc. Int. Workshop on Automatic Face and Gesture Recognition 2000*, 2000.

[5] R C. Nelson, "Finding Line Segments by Stick Growing", *IEEE Transactions on PAMI*, 16(5):519-523, May 1994.

[6] W. Zhou, A. Vellaikal, and C. C. J. Kuo, "Rule-based video classification system for basketball video indexing", in *Proc. ACM Multimedia 2000 workshop*, pp. 213–216, 2000.

[7] S.Choi, Y.Seo, H.Kim, K.-S.Hong, "Where are the ball and players? : Soccer Game Analysis with Color-based Tracking and Image Mosaick", *Proc. of Int'l Conf. Image Analysis and Processing (ICIAP'97)*, 1997.

[8] V.Tovinkere, R. J.Qian, "Detecting Semantic Events in Soccer Games: Towards a Complete Solution", *Proc. of Int'l Conf. on Multimedia and Expo (ICME 2001)*, pp. 1040–1043, 2001.

[9] D.Yow, B.-L.Yeo, M.Yeung, B.Liu, "Analysis and Presentation of Soccer Highlights from Digital Video", *Proc. of 2nd Asian Conf. on Computer Vision (ACCV'95)*, 1995.

[10] G. Sudhir, J. C. M. Lee, A. K. Jain, "Automatic Classification of Tennis Video for High-level Content-based Retrieval", *Proc. of the Int'l Workshop on Content-Based Access of Image and Video Databases (CAIVD '98)*, 1998.

[11] S.Nepal, U.Srinivasan, G.Reynolds, "Automatic Detection of 'Goal' Segments in Basketball Videos", *Proc. of ACM Multimedia*, pp. 261-269, 2001.

[12] D. D.Saur, Y.-P.Tan, S. R.Kulkami, P. J.Ramadge, "Automatic Analysis and Annotation of Basketball Video", *Storage and Retrieval for Image and Video Databases V*, pp. 176-187, 1997.

[13] Y.Rui, A.Gupta, A.Acero, "Automatically Extracting Highlights for TV Baseball Programs", *Proc. of ACM Multimedia*, 2000.

[14] M. Bertini, A. Del Bimbo, and P. Pala. "Content-based indexing and retrieval of TV news", *Pattern Recognition Letters*, 22(5):503-516, 2001.

[15] A. Hampapur, "Semantic Video Indexing: Approach and Issues", *SIGMOD Record* Vol 28, Special section on semantic interoperability in global information systems, March 1999.

[16] C-W. Ngo, H-J. Zhang, T-C. Pong, "Recent Advances in Content Based Video Analysis", *International Journal of Image and Graphics* 3(1):445-468, 2001.

[17] C. G. M. Snoek and M. Worring, "A State-of-the-art Review on Multimodal Video Indexing", *Proceedings of the 8th Annual Conference of the Advanced School for Computing and Imaging*, 194–202, 2002.

Improving the Evaluation of Web Search Systems

Cathal Gurrin[*] and Alan F. Smeaton

School of Computer Applications, Dublin City University, Ireland
cgurrin@computing.dcu.ie

Abstract. Linkage analysis as an aid to web search has been assumed to be of significant benefit and we know that it is being implemented by many major Search Engines. Why then have few TREC participants been able to scientifically prove the benefits of linkage analysis over the past three years? In this paper we put forward reasons why disappointing results have been found and we identify the linkage density requirements of a dataset to faithfully support experiments into linkage analysis. We also report a series of linkage-based retrieval experiments on a more densely linked dataset culled from the TREC web documents.

1 Introduction

The first generation of web search engines which have contributed to the huge popularity of the WWW were based on directly computing the similarity between a query and the text appearing in a web page and were effectively a direct application of standard document retrieval techniques. While these initial "first generation" web search engines addressed the engineering problems of web spidering and efficient searching for large numbers of both users and documents, they did not innovate much in the approaches taken to document ranking.

In the past few years we have seen most, if not all, web search engines incorporate linkage analysis as part of their retrieval operation. Anecdotally this appears to have improved the precision of retrieval yet, up until recently, there has been little scientific evidence in support of the claims for better quality retrieval, especially using the conventional TREC evaluation methodology. Participants in the four most recent TREC conferences (1999 - 2002) have been invited to perform benchmarking of information retrieval systems on web data and have had the option of using linkage information as part of their retrieval strategies. Up until TREC-2002, the general consensus was that except in extremely rare cases, and for insignificant improvements anyway, linkage information had not yet been successfully incorporated into conventional retrieval strategies when evaluated using the TREC test collection methodology. In most cases, linkage-based information was found to significantly harm conventional retrieval though improvements had been found specifically in a

---

[*] The work presented in this paper is based on research undertaken by the first author as a postgraduate student while working on his Ph.D. dissertation.

F. Sebastiani (Ed.): ECIR 2003, LNCS 2633, pp. 25-40, 2003.

homepage finding task, which was to locate homepages contained within the two TREC test collections used in 2001 and 2002.

In this paper we present a rationale as to why we believe TREC Web Track participants (including ourselves) using the TREC web-based test collections (prior to 2002) have been unable to demonstrate improved retrieval performance when incorporating linkage analysis into retrieval strategies. We begin with a brief introduction to linkage analysis in the next section and follow that with an overview of the TREC web track focusing on an analysis of the datasets employed. We follow this with a description of a densely linked subset of a TREC web collection and our experiments on this subset. Finally we will compare the characteristics of TREC datasets to our own survey of web structure and suggest the linkage requirements for any future datasets to support TREC style evaluation of linkage-based retrieval.

2   An Introduction to Linkage Analysis and Its Use in Retrieval

The "first generation" of search engine primarily utilised the content of the document when generating ranked listings. However, an additional source of latent information available to web collections is how documents are linked together and it is the study of this aspect of the web that is referred to as linkage analysis. More recent search engines utilise linkage data and are able to gather information mined from the documents themselves, as well as information from the linkage structure of the web. In most cases this linkage information is represented as a 'Connectivity' or a 'Linkage' Score for each document, which will influence final document ranking.

Generally speaking, on the WWW we can separate links into one of two broad types based on their intended function when created:

- *On-site* links are created to link documents within a particular domain and exist to aid the user in navigating within a domain, or web site. These links are not generally believed to carry much exploitable weight of human judgement.
- *Off-site* (content, or outward) links on the other hand link documents from different domains (across web site boundaries). They are found to mostly link from a source document to a target document that contains similar and, in the web page author's opinion, useful information. The requirement of on-site links to support structural navigation does not apply to off-site links.

In general we can assume that a document with a higher number of off-site in-links (where in-links are hypertext links pointing to a web page) will be a more 'popular' document than one with less off-site in-links. For the purpose of linkage analysis we are interested primarily in the number of (and the quality of) off-site citations (in-links) that a web page receives as opposed to on-site citations. If a web page receives a lot of off-site citations then we can broadly conclude that this page may be a better page than one that receives significantly fewer off-site citations. Thus in the context of linkage information for conventional web searching we should primarily be interested in off-site links as opposed to on-site links.

Given that an off-site link to a document can be seen as an indication of the usefulness of that document, a simple linkage score can be generated for each document based on the off-site indegree of that document and hence we can rank documents by off-site indegrees. Researchers at AT&T [1] have demonstrated, using their own crawled data, that incorporating indegree ranking into retrieval strategies is equally as good as incorporating other more advanced techniques for using linkage information, such as the PageRank algorithm that we will now discuss.

The best known linkage analysis technique in use on the web today is probably the PageRank algorithm [2], believed to be implemented in the Google search engine [3]. PageRank is based on a simple indexing-time process that generates a linkage score (the PageRank) for each document in the search engine's index. This PageRank score is combined at query time with other sources of evidence such as a content-only score giving a final document score used in ranking results. PageRank is based on a simulation of a random user's behaviour while browsing the web where the user keeps clicking on successive links at random. Due to the fact that a user can get caught in page loops, rather than looping forever, the user jumps to a random web page (chosen using the vector E over all web pages). E is normally uniform for all web pages.

PageRank is calculated over a number of iterations until an acceptable level of convergence of the PageRanks has been reached. The PageRank (Pr') of a document is calculated using a formula similar to the following (see formula 1), where S_n is the set of documents that link into document n, c is a constant used for normalisation, Pr_n is the current PageRank of n and E is a uniform vector over all web pages.

$$Pr'_n = c \cdot \sum_{m \in S_n} \frac{Pr_m}{outdegree_m} + (1-c) \cdot E_n \ . \tag{1}$$

Another well-known technique incorporating linkage information in web searching is Kleinberg's [4], which is similar to PageRank in that it is an iterative algorithm based purely on the linkage between documents but it has major differences, namely:

- It is executed at query time, rather than at indexing time
- It computes two scores per document as opposed to one single score. Hub scores reflect a document's usefulness as a source of links to relevant content while Authority scores represent a document's usefulness as a source of relevant content
- It is processed on a small subset of 'relevant' documents, not all documents.

The Hub and Authority scores are calculated for each document on a small subset chosen due to their rank in a content-only search run, or due to their being in the immediate neighbourhood of these highly ranked documents. The process is iterative and the Authority and Hub vectors will eventually converge, at which point the iterations can stop. Once convergence has been achieved, the documents are ranked into two groups, by hub (links to content) and authority (content) scores. A number of improvements to this model have been suggested and successfully evaluated [5].

3   Evaluation of Web-Based Retrieval: The TREC Web Track

From 1999 to 2001 a web "track" in the annual TREC benchmarking exercise has supported participants in their endeavours to find out whether the best methods in ad-hoc (conventional) retrieval also work best on the TREC collections of web data and whether link information in web data can be used to obtain more effective retrieval than using page content alone [6]. In 2002, this ad-hoc search task has been replaced by a Topic Distillation task (evaluated using the measure of precision at 10), the goal of which is to find a small number of key resources on a topic as opposed to the more conventional (ad-hoc) listing of relevant pages. Topic Distillation, although not that far removed from ad-hoc is perhaps more suited to web search evaluation.

In order to support these experiments TREC distributes test collections. TREC test collections consist of three components, a set of documents, a set of queries (called topics) and a set of relevance judgements for each query for use in evaluating the performance of retrieval. The TREC relevance judgements are incomplete (obtained using the pooling method) and are almost always binary relevance judgements.

The first TREC test collection for the web track was the WT2g collection that was used in the TREC-8 conference in 1999. This was a 2GB collection and was said to contain an "interesting quantity" of closed hyperlinks (having both source and target within the dataset). A larger collection of 10 GB of web data, known as WT10g, was used in TREC-9 and TREC-2001. Most recently an 18 GB collection (.GOV) was used for TREC 2002. We examine each collection below.

3.1   TREC-8 (WT2g)

As stated above, the TREC-8 web track used a 2GB collection called WT2g that consisted of 247,491 HTML documents. The WT2g collection is a subset of the 100GB VLC dataset, which is itself a subset of a 300 GB Internet Archive crawl completed in early 1997. Seventeen participating groups took part in the web track in TREC-8 and those that utilised the link information implemented a variety of approaches including Kleinberg's and PageRank mentioned earlier. We ourselves implemented techniques based on citation counting [7].

To the initial surprise of many participants, no participating group (save one with insignificant improvements) managed to improve precision over that attained by conventional content-only searching when linkage information was incorporated into the retrieval process. There were a number of reasons put forward to explain this [8] but the primary reason seemed to be the sparcity of linkage data within WT2g. The number of closed off-site links within WT2g is 2,797 out of 1,166,702, or 0.24% of the total [6], which we, and others, found to be insufficient to support effective linkage-based web retrieval.

3.2   TREC-9 & TREC-2001 (WT10g)

The shortcomings of WT2g led to the creation of a new collection, WT10g, which was used in the web tracks of TREC-9 and in TREC-2001. A corpus size of 10GB was chosen which comprised 1,692,096 documents. Similar to the preceding WT2g, WT10g was also subset of the 100GB VLC dataset but was extracted from the VLC in such a way that maximised the number of off-site links included within WT10g. However, the linkage density of the VLC serves to restrict the number of links that are candidates for inclusion in any extracted collection. The following diagram (Fig. 1) illustrates some of the issues related to the construction of WT10g.

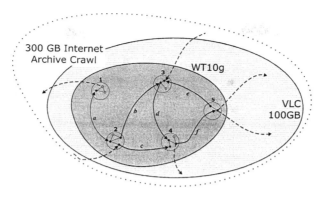

Fig. 1. Construction of the WT10g Collection

Figure 1 shows the original 300 GB crawl, the VLC 100 GB subset of that, then the WT10g subset of the VLC with websites marked 1, 2, 3, 4 and 5, and sample links. The available links in the WT10g collection would be all those contained within web-sites 1 to 5 (on-site links) as well as those (off-site links) between sites within the WT10g dataset (labeled a to f in Figure 1). The WT10g corpus contained a total of 171,740 off-site links for 1.69 million documents, averaging at 1 off site link for every ten documents. Thus any linkage-based techniques could only influence a small proportion of the documents within WT10g and once again none of the participants' experiments (22 participants in all) for TREC-9 (including our own experiments on citation analysis and spreading activation [9]) were able to illustrate any improvement in performance over content-only retrieval when incorporating any linkage-based algorithm into the retrieval process.

TREC-2001 (the 10th TREC conference) once again encouraged participants (29 in all) to partake in linkage analysis experiments using WT10g and once again linkage analysis was not found to aid retrieval performance in the ad-hoc retrieval task. This time, in addition to the conventional retrieval task, a new task was introduced to the web-track, namely a homepage finding task (essentially a known-item task) which it was hoped would better support linkage-based methods than would conventional IR experiments. Prior evaluation of such methods during construction phase of WT10g had illustrated that such a task could indeed yield performance improvements [10] and some linkage-based improvements were indeed evident in this task.

3.3   TREC-2002 (.GOV)

The .GOV collection used in 2002 consisted of 1,247,753 documents (not all HTML) from a fresh crawl of web pages made in early 2002. It was hoped that fresher web data would better reflect today's WWW. Findings for TREC-2002 illustrate that for some groups the application of linkage analysis did indeed improve retrieval perform-ance in the Topic Distillation task [11] as well as (once again) in the Named Page finding task. So what was the difference between the .GOV collection and the previ-ous collections? The off-site link density of the .GOV collection (averaging 1.98 off-site in-links for each document) was far greater than that of WT10g (0.101). This, we believe, was a primary reason for the encouraging findings.

In summary the web track in TREC has contributed in a major way to focusing attention on scientifically measuring the effectiveness of web searching but progress in actually achieving that measurement has been slow, principally, we believe, because of the test collections used. Our belief is that a dataset better capable of supporting linkage-based web IR would better illustrate the benefits of linkage-based retrieval. The .GOV collection was a step on the way but is not truly representative. The results of experiments on the .GOV collection have only recently become available and the experiments presented in this paper primarily focus on the WT10g (pre .GOV) collection. The recent findings of TREC participants using .GOV do not affect our findings presented herein in any way.

In an effort to generate a more representative collection than the then available WT10g, we generated a new dataset, based on WT10g, but which maximised the density of off-site links and this is described in the following section.

4   Extracting a Densely Linked Subset of WT10g

The creation of the WT10g dataset seriously underestimated the density of off-site links if it was to be reasonably compatible in structure to the WWW and to support faithful experiments on web searching. However, the primary advantage of using WT10g is readily available relevance judgements for 100 queries. We used the TREC-9 query set (50 queries) for our experiments. Generating a new dataset of our own to allow us to do linkage retrieval experiments would require undertaking our own relevance judgements, which is both expensive and time-consuming. Our solution was to develop a subset of WT10g (including relevance judgements) and to evaluate a content-only experiment and to compare all of our linkage experiments against this benchmark content-only experiment, using the relevance judgements.

When generating this densely linked subset of WT10g (called WT_Dense) we had two requirements for the new collection, these being:

1. To maximise the number of off-site links in the dataset, and
2. To maximise the size of the new dataset itself.

Generating a dataset to satisfy these two requirements was straightforward and we simply generated the dataset by following a three-step procedure as described below.

1. We identified all documents that are linked via all 171,740 off-site links (any document linked by a...f in Figure 1).
2. All such documents were extracted to produce a set of 120,494 unique documents.
3. All links (both on-site and off-site) between these documents and the relevance judgements for these documents were extracted from the WT10g collection. It should be noted that we are focusing on off-site links as opposed to on-site links, which we believe to be of lesser importance for linkage-based retrieval.

4.1   Comparing WT_Dense to WT10g

The composition of WT_Dense compared with WT10g is summarised below:

Table 1. Comparing WT10g and WT_Dense

	WT10G	WT_Dense
Number of Documents	1,692,096	120,494
Number of off-site links	171,740	171,740
Average off-site indegree	0.10	1.43
Number of unique servers represented	11,680	11,611
Average number of docs per server	144	10
Generality	0.15%	0.21%
Number of TREC-9 Queries with relevant documents	50	36
Average number of relevant documents per query	52	7

As can be seen from Table 1, WT_Dense contains a far higher density of off-site links, an average of 1.43 per document while keeping the generality (percentage of documents relevant to any of the topics) of the dataset similar to WT10g. However, results of a survey of web structure presented later in this paper suggest that this overage indegree figure of 1.43 still falls way below the true figures as found on the web.

As expected the number of servers represented was almost identical in WT_Dense as it was in WT10g, this is because of the inclusion of all off-site links and both the source and target of each link. The one drawback of this is that the average number of documents on each server is only 10 as opposed to 144 with WT10g. This is unavoidable as we only have 7.1% of the WT10g dataset represented in WT_Dense, but it means that we are taking the core pages, home pages and top pages from almost all of the 11,680 servers in the WT10g collection. In addition, fourteen of the fifty TREC-9 queries had no relevant documents in WT_Dense and reducing the number of queries to 36, thus reducing the number of performance comparisons. In addition, although unavoidable, the average number of relevant documents per query was reduced to 7, which we note to be well below the norm.

4.2   Experiments on WT_Dense

We ran a number of retrieval experiments (content-only and linkage based) on the new densely linked dataset using the TREC-9 topics (450-499). We used manually generated queries, which we found to produce the best content-only retrieval performance for the TREC-9 topics.

Our first experiment was a content-only experiment for which we utilised the popular BM25 ranking algorithm. The top 1,000 ranked documents for each query were used as a benchmark against which to compare the retrieval performance of our subsequent linkage-based runs. These subsequent linkage-based runs were based on re-ranking the top 2,000 documents produced in the content-only phase using algorithms based on citation ranking, spreading activation and PageRank.

Citation Ranking

This experiment was based on re-ranking all 2,000 documents from the content-only experiment using both off-site indegrees and the original content-only scores. Before combining both content and linkage scores we normalised the linkage scores so that they would be in an equivalent range to the content-only scores. Let *norm* refer to a normalised score, $indegree_n$ be the off-site indegree of n, Sc_n be the content-only score of n and α be a constant (value of 0.25) used to regulate the influence of linkage evidence (based on values used by AT&T in TREC-9 [12]), we rank by Sc'_n for each document, as shown in equation 2:

$$Sc'_n = Sc_n + \left(norm(indegree_n) \times \alpha\right) . \tag{2}$$

In the results section, this experiment will be referred to as CitationA.

It is our belief that the method chosen for combining linkage and content evidence is essential to successfully incorporating linkage evidence into any retrieval process. We have developed a technique for combining content and linkage scores, which we will refer to as the *Scarcity-Abundance technique*. Essentially this technique dynamically estimates linkage and content influence based on a broadness measure for the topic represented by a user query. The method we employ to do this examines the number of documents retrieved (result set) for each query from a content-only run. A larger result set (the abundance problem) indicates a broader query that would benefit more from linkage-based methods [4], than would a query with narrow focus and vice versa. The content-influence (*1-a*) employed is inversely proportional to the level of linkage influence (*a*). This experiment is referred to in our results as CitationB.

Spreading Activation

Spreading Activation refers to a technique that propagates numerical values (or activation levels) among the connected nodes of a graph. In the context of this experiment it facilitates a document transferring its content-only score across its outlinks. Only documents that are scored in the content-only phase have any effect on the process. The formula for calculating each document score is shown as equation 3. Let S be the set highly scored documents and S_n be the in-set of n, we rank by Sc'_n:

$$Sc'_n = Sc_n + \sum_{m \in S_n} \frac{Sc_m}{outdegree_m} . \tag{3}$$

This experiment we shall refer to in our results as SpreadAct.

PageRank Experiment

We also evaluated the PageRank algorithm (an indexing time process) as outlined earlier in this paper. We combined the linkage and content scores for our PageRank experiment using both the parameter technique (linkage weight of 0.25) as well as the scarcity-abundance technique. We will refer to this in our results as PageRankA for the parameter combination and PageRankB for the scarcity-abundance combination.

Table 2. Precision Values for the Experiments on WT_Dense

	CONTENT	CITATION A	CITATION B	SPREADACT	PAGERANK A	PAGERANK B
5	0.2389	0.2444	0.2500	0.0500	0.2444	0.2444
10	0.1833	0.1833	0.1861	0.0639	0.1833	0.1806
15	0.1611	0.1630	0.1630	0.0722	0.1630	0.1593
20	0.1500	0.1472	0.1486	0.0750	0.1486	0.1486
30	0.1167	0.1148	0.1148	0.0787	0.1130	0.1139
100	0.0444	0.0444	0.0442	0.0406	0.0444	0.0444
200	0.0246	0.0247	0.0249	0.0244	0.0246	0.0246
500	0.0114	0.0114	0.0114	0.0114	0.0114	0.0114
1000	0.0061	0.0061	0.0061	0.0061	0.0061	0.0061

4.3   Experimental Results

Our linkage experiments are based on re-ranking content-only results, giving us the ability to directly compare linkage and content-only results. Outlined below in a brief summary of our results we see that some linkage experiments actually achieved small improvements in precision (shown as bold/italic in Table 2) over content-only runs when examined at rank positions 5, 10 and 15. This is encouraging because up until these experiments, TREC participants (except one experiment in 1999) were unable to obtain any improvement in retrieval performance when using WT10g data, and although WT_Dense is not the same dataset as WT10g we are using a subset of both the dataset and the relevance judgements and when we ran similar experiments on the full WT10g dataset we did not achieve any improvement in performance at all.

Our experiments suggest that by increasing the density of off-site links within a collection one can support successful linkage-based retrieval experiments. Although the improvements are quite small and on a small collection, our findings are backed up by the recent successful results of some TREC participants using the more densely linked .GOV collection in the Topic Distillation task.

Our next step was to examine the linkage structure of the web and compare it to the TREC collections and our own WT_Dense collection. If the linkage density on the web is underestimated within these collections, then it is likely that a more representative dataset would illustrate more clearly if and by how much, linkage-based techniques can aid conventional retrieval performance. In order to evaluate this and to identify the requirements for a small-scale test collection, which faithfully models the linkage structure of the web, we conducted a survey of 5,000 web pages.

5   Examining Real-World Web Structure

We present the results of a small survey of web pages from early 2002 whose aim was to explore the linkage structure of the WWW. In order to estimate in-degree densities we had to examine all out-links from the web pages and since the web is a directed graph and each out-link is also an in-link, observing the average outdegree of each document allowed us to identify the average indegree of every document. This assumes that one does not to include any broken links in this calculation.

However, we need to know more than the average outdegree of each web page as we also need to know the average number of off-site out-links and the average number of on-site out-links which can be discovered by observation.

5.1   A Survey of Web Pages

In order to correctly identify the average in-degree (both off-site and on-site) of web pages we carried out our own survey of the linkage structure of the WWW as it is in 2002 by sampling web pages at random using a random URL generation tool.

Previous Work

Previous work has been carried out in this area, an example being the SOWS III survey of web structure, which also involved the random sampling of WWW pages [13]. The SOWS III survey was based on fetching and examining 200 documents and the findings indicate that the average number of links parsed from each document was 22.9, of which 1.3 were found to be dead, giving an average of 21.6 valid out-links from every document.

In addition to SOWS III, Cyveillance Inc. carried out experiments in 2000 [14] in order to size the Internet and they found that the average page contains 23 on-site out-links and 5.6 off-site out-links, however they did limit their processing of web pages to pages under 200KB in size.

From our point of view, we were interested examining the valid (non-broken) off-site and on-site link structure of documents in order to estimate the number of valid links that exist on the real web so we conducted our own survey.

Surveying the WWW

When generating our own sample we identified the target population as being all web pages that are reachable by a conventional web crawler. Therefore we feel that it is acceptable to base a sample on documents chosen at random from a large crawl of web data, for example, a search engine's index as opposed to truly random URL sampling based on selecting random IP addresses. From [15] we know that 8.24% of web pages are not connected into the main body of the web and if pages from these sections are not manually submitted for inclusion in a crawl, many will not be found and therefore it is acceptable that these pages would not form part of the target population. Hence, the use of crawler based sampling is reasonable and acceptable for the purposes of our experiment.

Our approach to generating random URLs required the use of a web accessible random URL generator [16]. Our sample size was 5,000 and if we examine our sample at a 95% confidence level, our confidence interval is 1.39%, which compares favourably with a confidence interval of 6.93% for SOWS III. This means that we can be 95% confident that our results are +/- 1.39% of our stated figures. One caveat with our survey is that these confidence figures assume truly random sampling and since we relied on URouLette for our random URLs, we are not sure how random our sample is and from how large a list of candidate URLs the random URLs are chosen. All sampling techniques that rely on choosing a document at random from a web crawl are only random with respect to the crawled data and thus cannot be classified as truly random. Truly random sampling would, as mentioned, likely involve some form of random IP address generation and subsequent web page selection.

Observations from our Survey

Based on our survey we are in a position to present our findings on the link structure of these 5,000 documents. We can see from Table 3 that 3,940 documents contain out-links, with only 2,706 containing off-site out-links.

We estimate the average (HTTP links only) outdegree of WWW documents to be 19.8, which is comprised of 5.2 off-site links and 14.6 on-site links. However, after downloading and examining all of the target pages (to identify broken links) from all links found in the 5,000 document sample we found that 3.2% of all out-links were broken links in that they yield only an HTTP 404 type error or equivalent.

Considering this information we can identify the following valid (non-broken) out-link structure for all documents on the web (rounded to one decimal place) as:

If we compare our findings to those of SOWS III and Cyveillance we can see that our average outdegree figure is not that dissimilar to either, with SOWS III estimating the average outdegree to be 21.6. However Cyveillance is somewhat higher at 28.6, but we must remember that Cyveillance restricts the size of documents processed and we ourselves only process valid HTTP links. Given that our findings are very similar to SOWS III (and similar to Cyveillance w.r.t. off-site links more so than on-site links) this adds weight to our findings and our belief that utilising URouLette did not affect the randomness of survey to any notable extent.

However, simply examining the average number of links within the collection is not an ideal measurement as the distribution of the indegrees will not be uniform and gives us "little insight into the topology" [17]. An additional test that we can apply to our sample is based on examining the distributions of document outdegrees. If we conclude that the distribution of outdegrees approximates a power-law distribution then this adds more weight to the accuracy of our survey.

Table 3. Basic linkage structure of documents from the random sample

Documents that contain out-links	3,940
Documents with no out-links	1,060
Documents with off-site out-links	2,706
Documents with on-site out-links	3,571

Table 4. Average document outdegree figures from our survey

Average off-site out-degree for each document	4.9
Average on-site out-degree for each document	14.2
Average out-degree for each document	19.1

5.2   Examining the Distribution of Web Page Outdegrees

It has been discovered that the distribution of web page indegrees follows closely to a power-law distribution [15], yet the distribution does not follow a pure power-law

[18], and rather we consider it to approximate a power-law distribution. We are told that the "distribution of inbound links on the web as a whole is closest to a pure power-law" while "category specific distributions exhibit very large derivations from power-law scaling" [18]. This raises issues for the generation of test collections because any attempt to influence the documents comprising a dataset in order to include some category specificity (perhaps to aid in query selection) will result in problems when trying to recreate the natural web link structure. However, test collections using the TREC methodology are non-category specific and thus we can be satisfied that the distributions of document indegrees should approximate a power-law distribution, which is indeed the case for WT10g and .GOV[17].

Power Law Distributions

Power-laws are used in mathematics when one wishes to relate one quantity to the power of another. A power-law implies that small occurrences are extremely common whereas large occurrences are extremely rare, so if applied to web page indegrees or outdegrees this means that the vast majority of web pages have a very small number of in (or out) -links and a few pages have a large number of in (or out) -links.

Power-law distributions are not just used to describe the indegrees of web pages (or computer science problems in general), rather they are common to both man made and naturally occurring phenomena [19]. From computer science we see power-law distributions in web page indegrees [15], outdegrees [20], in the number of pages on websites [21], in Internet growth models [19], and in the distributions of word frequencies in language [22].

The characteristic signature of data that follows a power-law is that when the data is plotted on a log-log scale, the distribution shows itself to be linear (with the slope based on the exponent). Were our sample of web pages to be accurate then the distributions of our outdegree calculations would have that same characteristic signature. In addition, we can calculate the correlation co-efficient, which will range from 0..1, with 1 being perfect positive correlation to a power-law distribution.

If we examine the distribution of non-broken off-site out-links in our web sample then we can see that this approximates a power-law as can be seen in Fig. 2.

If we examine the distribution of on-site outdegrees of non-broken on-site links we find a power law distribution also, although the correlation co-efficient at 0.8542 is less than that of the off-site distribution.

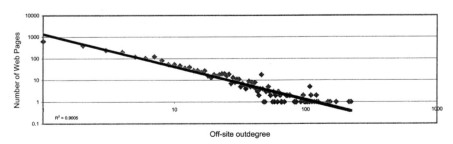

Fig. 2. The off-site outdegree distribution of our sample plotted on a log-log scale with broken links removed, including trendline (correlation co-efficient = 0.9005)

By examining the distribution of outdegrees from our sample, we have illustrated that both distributions approximate a power-law and that this is precisely what we would expect to find if our sample accurately reflected the web's structure.

We know [15] that document indegrees (including off-site indegrees) also approximate (or follow) a power-law distribution. Consequently, when building a dataset to support faithful experiments into linkage-based retrieval of web pages, the indegree distribution of links within the dataset should approximate a power-law distribution and based on our average outdegree figures from our web page sample we can identify the link density that we would expect to find in such a dataset.

6   Conclusions and Future Work

In this paper we have presented the results of experiments into linkage-based web IR using both the TREC test collections and our own densely linked subset of a TREC test collection. As a result of our disappointing findings and those of other TREC participants we examined the structure of the real web in order to identify the required linkage properties of such a representative test collection, which we present below.

Our belief is that only a collection that accurately recreates the linkage structure of the web will be able to truly answer the question of whether or not incorporating linkage evidence aids retrieval performance for web search and since we do not have such a collection more evidence is needed. We now illustrate the collection requirements.

6.1   Requirements for a Representative Test Collection

As a result of our survey of 5,000 web pages and the work of the TREC web track organisers into methods of constructing a test collection [10] we can identify the requirements for a test collection to support truly accurate investigation into linkage-based retrieval. This test collection should model real web searching, by means of:

- A sufficiently large and representative document set [10].
- A representative link structure within this document set.
- A large set of representative web queries [10].
- Sufficiently complete relevance judgments [10].
- Sufficiently high generality of the dataset so as to clearly illustrate any benefit which linkage-based retrieval techniques bring to web retrieval.

As stated above, the ideal web test collection should include a link structure that accurately reflects the true link structure of the WWW to enable meaningful experiments into linkage-based IR. This link structure can be summarised thus:

- Must have an average off-site indegree of (or adequately near) 4.9.
- Must have an average on-site indegree of (or adequately near) 14.2.
- The indegree distributions (both off-site and on-site) must approximate a power-law distribution with exponents capable of producing appropriate indegree figures.

Our findings illustrate that our subset of WT10g, WT_Dense, like the other collections used for web search experiments (even .GOV), seriously underestimate the off-site link density of the WWW. WT10g and WT2g have an even lower off-site link density than WT_Dense or .GOV so the problems with using WT10g and WT2g are even more acute.

Assuming that all out-links (with the exception of broken-links) also act as in-links then Table 5 compares the average off-site indegree figures for the TREC collections, WT_Dense and what our survey suggests to be the ideal figure.

This analysis leads us to conclude that previous and present TREC test collections have seriously underestimated the required link density of off-site links, even though the distribution of these links do follow a power law distribution [17]. Although the TREC web track has aided the research field immensely by providing a framework for experimentation, unfortunately the collections used have not supported TREC participants' experiments into linkage-based web IR sufficiently.

The recent .GOV collection is a major improvement, but still falls short of the required off-site link density while WT_Dense also underestimates the off-site link density by a factor of over three. This leads us to question if there is a certain (critical) density of off-site links required within a collection before it can support linkage experiments. Results from this year's web track suggest that an average of 1.98 off-site in-links into each document is sufficient to show improvements in retrieval performance and our experiments suggest that 1.425 may also be sufficient, but both fall short of the ideal. The benefits (or otherwise) of incorporating linkage analysis into web search will be more clearly illustrated on a more representative collection.

6.2   Future Work

One issue that we have not addressed in this paper is that of how to generate such a test collection. This is a complex issue and one that we plan to examine in the near future. Simply crawling a set of web documents is dependent on the queuing algorithm in the crawler and the results will vary greatly making it an extremely difficult task, hence our current thinking is that the dataset should be generated by carefully selecting documents from a larger collection in order to construct a small-scale representative collection, similar to our generation of WT_Dense. We refer the reader to the paper describing the construction of WT10g [10] for an example of one such process, albeit with differing requirements to those we have presented above. The size of this super-set of documents is subject to experimentation, as it must contain a high enough density of links between documents to enable successful subset extraction. Other issues such as the effects on a test collection by judiciously adding documents to meet a required link distribution and density have yet to be seen. It is with the aim of solving these problems that we continue our research.

Table 5. Comparing our sample to recent TREC collections

	WT2g	WT10g	WT_Dense	.Gov	Web Survey
Average indegree	0.011	0.101	1.425	1.98	4.916

References

[1]   Amento, B., Terveen, L. and Hill, W.: Does 'Authority' mean quality? Pre-
        dicting Expert Quality Ratings of Web Document. Proceedings of the 25th
        Annual International ACM SIGIR Conference on Research and Development
        in IR (2000)

[2]   Page L., Brin S., Motwani R. and Winograd T.: The PageRank Citation Rank-
        ing: Bringing Order to the Web. Stanford Digital Libraries working paper
        (1997) 0072

[3]   Brin S. and Page L.: The Anatomy of a Large-Scale Hypertextual Web Search
        Engine. Proceedings of the 7th International WWW Conference (1998)

[4]   Kleinberg, J.: Authorative Sources in a Hyperlinked Environment. Proceedings
        of the 9th ACM-SIAM Symposium on Discrete Algorithms (1998)

[5]   Bharat K. and Henzinger M.: Improved Algorithms for Topic Distillation in a
        Hyperlinked Environment. Proceedings of the 23rd Annual International ACM
        SIGIR Conference on Research and Development in IR (1998)

[6]   Hawking D., Voorhees E., Craswell N. and Bailey P.: Overview of the TREC-
        8 Web Track. Proceedings of the 8th Annual TREC Conference" (1999)

[7]   Gurrin, C. and Smeaton, A.F.: Connectivity Analysis Approaches to Increasing
        Precision in Retrieval from Hyperlinked Documents. Proceedings of the 8th
        Annual TREC Conference", November 16-19 (1999)

[8]   Hawking D.: - Overview of the TREC-9 Web Track. Proceedings of the 9th
        Annual TREC Conference", November 16-19 (2000)

[9]   Gurrin, C. and Smeaton, A.F.: Dublin City University Experiments in Connec-
        tivity Analysis for TREC-9. Proceedings of the 9th Annual TREC Conference"
        (2000)

[10]   Bailey, P., Craswell, N. and Hawking, D.: Engineering a multi-purpose test
        collection for Web retrieval experiments. Information Processing and Man-
        agement (2001)

[11]   Wu, L., Huang, X., Niu, J., Xia, Y., Feng, Z., Zhou, Y.: FDU at TREC 2002:
        Filtering, Q&A, Web and Video Tasks. Draft Proceedings of the 11th Annual
        TREC Conference, November 19-22 (2002)

[12]   Singhal, A. and Kaszkiel, M.: AT&T at TREC-9. Proceedings of the 9th An-
        nual TREC Conference, November 16-19 (2000)

[13]   SOWS III: The Third State of the Web Survey, Available online at URL:
        http://www.pantos.org/atw/35654-a.html. (last visited November 2002)

[14]   Murray B. and Moore A.: Sizing the Internet - A White Paper. Cyveillance,
        Inc., 2000. Available online at URL: http://www.cyveillance.com/web
        /corporate/white_papers.htm. (last visited November 2002)

[15]   Broder A., Kumar R., Maghoul, F., Raghavan P., Rajagopalan S., Stata R.,
        Tomkins A. and Weiner J.: Graph Structure in the Web. Proceedings of
        WWW9 (2000)

[16]   URouLette Random Web Page Generator, Available online at URL:
        http://www.uroulette.com. (last visited November 2002)

[17]   Soboroff, I.: Does WT10g look like the Web?. Proceedings of the 27rd Annual
        International ACM SIGIR Conference on Research and Development in IR
        (2002)

[18] Pennock, D., Flake, G., Lawrence, S., Glover, E. and Giles, C.: Winners don't take all: Characterising the competition for links on the web. Proceedings of the National Academy of Sciences, Volume 99, Issue 8, (April 2002) 5207-5211

[19] Mitzenmacher M.: A Brief History of Generative Models for Power Law and Lognormal Distributions. Allerton (2001)

[20] Faloutsos, M., Faloutsos, P., Faloutsos, C.: On Power-Law Relationships of the Internet Topology. Proceedings of ACM SIGCOMM 99 (1999)

[21] Adamic, L. and Humberman B.: The Web's Hidden Order. Communications of the ACM, Vol. 44, No. 9 (2001)

[22] Adamic, L.: Zipf, Power-laws, and Pareto - a ranking tutorial. Available online at URL: http://www.hpl.hp.com/shl/papers/ranking/. (last visited November 2002)

When Are Links Useful?
Experiments in Text Classification.

Michelle Fisher and Richard Everson

Department of Computer Science, Exeter University
{r.m.everson,m.j.fisher}@exeter.ac.uk

Abstract. Link analysis methods have become popular for information access tasks, especially information retrieval, where the link information in a document collection is used to complement the traditionally used content information. However, there has been little firm evidence to confirm the utility of link information. We show that link information can be useful when the document collection has a sufficiently high link density and links are of sufficiently high quality. We report experiments on text classification of the Cora and WebKB data sets using Probabilistic Latent Semantic Analysis and Probabilistic Hypertext Induced Topic Selection. Comparison with manually assigned classes shows that link information enhances classification in data with sufficiently high link density, but is detrimental to performance at low link densities or if the quality of the links is degraded. We introduce a new frequency-based method for selecting the most useful citations from a document collection for use in the model.

1 Introduction

In recent years link analysis methods have become popular for use in information access tasks. Many of the popular search engines [15] now use link analysis to assist their ranking algorithms. The most well known of these search engines is Google [7]; Brin et al. describe the link analysis method (known as PageRank [14]) used by Google. Kleinberg described his link analysis method called Hypertext Induced Topic Selection (HITS) in [12]. However, until recently no-one had attempted to show that link methods were actually beneficial to information access task performance. In 1999 TREC [16] started a web track with one of the key aims being to discover whether link methods were useful. Unfortunately, the TREC-8 experiments showed that combining content and link information yielded no benefits over using pure content methods [9]; in fact the performance of some participants was actually degraded when link information was included. This was in part due to a poorly collected document collection containing few cross-host links, but the more recent TREC Web Tracks, with specially engineered document collections with high link density across hosts have still not shown that links are particularly useful [8]. There have been a couple of victories for link methods: Bailey, Craswell & Hawking showed that they could be

F. Sebastiani (Ed.): ECIR 2003, LNCS 2633, pp. 41–56, 2003.

useful for site finding tasks [2], and Craswell, Hawking & Robertson also obtained good results for site finding tasks, using link anchor text information [4] rather than the links themselves. Use of link anchor text may be one of the reasons that search engines using link analysis methods, such as Google, seem to perform so well even though there is no documented performance benefit from combining term and link information.

Ideally we would have used information retrieval experiments to give the results in this paper, unfortunately there are very few adhoc information retrieval datasets available containing both text and links. The comparison of datasets shown in this paper would not have been possible with current information retrieval datasets, so instead, to give quantitative results, we have used text classification experiments.

This paper shows that link information can be useful when the document collection being used has a sufficiently high link density. The quality of the link information is also important. We use Cohn & Hofmann's Probabilistic LSI and Probabilistic HITS (PLSI and PHITS) method [3]; we repeat and extend Cohn & Hofmann's text classification experiments in [3] on the Cora [13] and WebKB [1] data sets, which are collections of automatically classified academic papers and manually classified web pages. Comparison with manually assigned classes shows that link information enhances classification when the link density is sufficiently high, but is detrimental to classification performance at low link densities or if the quality of the links is degraded. We also introduce a new frequency-based method for selecting the most useful citations from a document collection for use in the model; this has the added benefit of increasing the effective link density of a collection.

We first describe Cohn & Hofmann's joint probabilistic model for content and links, PLSI and PHITS, section 3 discusses link density measures and in section 4 we describe the document collections used in our experiments. The results of our experiments are presented and discussed in sections 5 and 6.

2   PLSI & PHITS

PLSI & PHITS [3] is a latent variable model, where the high dimensional data is projected onto a smaller number of latent dimensions. This results in noise reduction, topic identification and is a principled method of combining text and link information. PLSI and PHITS are probabilistic equivalents of the LSI [5] and HITS [12] methods appropriate for multinomial observations.

In common with the majority of information retrieval methods, we ignore the order of the terms and citations within a document, and describe a document $d_j \in \mathcal{D} = \{d_1, ..., d_J\}$ as a bag-of-words or terms $t_i \in \mathcal{T} = \{t_1, ..., t_I\}$ and citations or links $c_l \in \mathcal{C} = \{c_1, ..., c_L\}$. Note that there may be $L > J$ documents available for citation; $L = J$ when citations are made entirely within the document collection. This information can also be described by a term-document matrix N, where entry $N_{j,i}$ contains the number of times term t_i occurs in document d_j, and a document-citation matrix A, where entry $A_{j,l}$ corresponds to the number of times citation c_l occurs in document d_j.

PLSA & PHITS [3] is a latent variable model for general co-occurrence data, which associates an unobserved class variable $z_k \in \mathcal{Z} = \{z_1, ..., z_K\}$ with each observation or occurrence of term t_i and citation c_l in document d_j. The model is based on the assumption of an underlying document generation process:

- Pick a document d_j with probability $P(d_j) = 1/J$
- Pick a latent class z_k with probability $P(z_k|d_j)$
- Generate a term t_i with probability $P(t_i|z_k)$ and a citation c_l with probability $P(c_l|z_k)$.

The observed document consists of observation pairs (d_j, t_i) and (d_j, c_l), but the latent class variable z_k is discarded. Note however, that the terms and citations occurring in a particular document are associated because they are each conditioned on the particular latent class z_k. Thus terms and links occurring in a particular document are expected to be associated with particular topics associated with the document.

As shown by Hofmann [10], the joint probability model for predicting citations and terms in documents can be expressed as:

$$P(d_j, t_i) = \sum_k^K P(z_k)P(t_i|z_k)P(d_j|z_k), P(d_j, c_l) = \sum_k^K P(z_k)P(c_l|z_k)P(d_j|z_k) \quad (1)$$

$P(t_i|z_k)$, $P(c_l|z_k)$, $P(d_j|z_k)$ and $P(z_k)$ are determined by maximising the normalised log-likelihood function of the observed term and citation frequencies. Contributions from term information and citation information are combined as a convex combination:

$$\mathcal{L} = \alpha \sum_j \sum_i N_{j,i} \log P(d_j, t_i) + (1 - \alpha) \sum_j \sum_l A_{j,l} \log P(d_j, c_l) \quad (2)$$

The parameter α sets the relative weight of terms and link information. If α is 1 the model takes only the terms into consideration, while if it is 0 only citations are considered.

The Expectation Maximisation (EM) [6] algorithm, a standard method for maximum likelihood estimation in latent variable models, can be applied to find the local maximum of $\mathcal{L}$. Alternating the E and M steps increases the likelihood, $\mathcal{L}$, converging to a local maximum. Hofmann [11] introduced tempered EM (TEM) to avoid over-fitting, which is often severe for sparse data, by controlling the effective model complexity and to reduce the sensitivity of EM to local maxima. TEM is discussed in some detail since our procedure differs from that of Cohn and Hofmann [3]. A control parameter β modifies the E-step by discounting [10] the data likelihood when $\beta < 1$; $\beta = 1.0$ results in the standard E-step. To implement TEM we use the algorithm proposed by Hofmann [10]: hold out some portion of the data, perform early stopping on the held out data with $\beta = 1$. Decrease β by setting $\beta = \eta\beta$, where $\eta < 1$, and continue TEM steps while performance on held out data improves. While a lower limit of β has not been reached or until decreasing β does not yield further improvements, continue decreasing β and performing TEM steps.

Classification of an unknown test document d_{new} is achieved as follows. First, a representation in latent space $P(z_k|d_{new})$ is calculated by 'folding in'; that is, the mixing proportions $P(z_k|d_{new})$ are calculated by EM, but with the factors $P(t_i|z_k)$ and $P(c_l|z_k)$ fixed. The K-dimensional vector of mixing proportions is then used with the cosine similarity measure to find the nearest neighbour in the training documents to d_{new}. The test document is then assigned the class of its nearest neighbour, and classification accuracy is judged against the manually assigned class.

3   Link Density Measures

Document collections containing links (for example, a collection of journal articles where the links between documents are the citations, or a collection of documents from the web where the links are hyperlinks) can be modelled as a directed graph $\mathcal{G}(\mathcal{D}, \mathcal{C})$. Here the vertices $d \in \mathcal{D}$ are the documents and each edge $c \in \mathcal{C}$ is a directed link between a pair of documents. The edges each have an integer weight w_c; this weight is 1 when a document cites another document only once, but can be higher when there are multiple citations from one document to another.

A measure of the link density of a document collection could be defined in several ways, but we find the graph sparseness, Γ, measure most useful:

$$\Gamma = \frac{|\mathcal{C}|}{J \cdot L} \quad \leq \quad \Gamma_w = \frac{1}{J \cdot L} \sum_{c=1}^{|\mathcal{C}|} w_c \tag{3}$$

where $|\mathcal{C}|$ is the number of edges in the graph, J is the number of vertices or documents and L is the number of documents that can be cited. Often J and L are equal but defining them separately will be useful in later sections. Note that Γ is the fraction of non-zero entries on the citation matrix, A. The weighted graph sparseness, Γ_w, measure accounts for the weights on the edges of the graph; that is, multiple citations carry additional weight.

A further useful measure is the average number of links, ρ, that a document makes and the weighted average number, ρ_w, of links per document:

$$\rho = \frac{|\mathcal{C}|}{J} \quad \leq \quad \rho_w = \frac{1}{J} \sum_{c=1}^{|\mathcal{C}|} w_c \tag{4}$$

4   Document Collections

The WebKB Collection   The WebKB data set [1] contains 8282 web pages collected from computer science departments of various universities in January 1997

Table 1. Number of documents in each manually determined class for the WebKB dataset (left) and the Cora dataset (right)

Cora	
Class	*Number of Docs*
Reinforcement_Learning (ReinL)	354
Genetic_Algorithms (GA)	625
Theory	532
Probabilistic_Methods (ProbM)	656
Case_Based	491
Rule_Learning (RuleL)	282
Neural_Networks (NN)	1390
TOTAL	4330

WebKB	
Class	*Number of Docs*
course	907
department	176
faculty	1091
project	497
staff	129
student	1599
TOTAL	4399

by the WebKB project of the CMU text learning group. The pages have been manually classified into seven classes. To permit direct comparison with Cohn & Hofmann's experiments, we ignored the seventh 'other' category containing 3764 of the documents and also ignored web pages with non-conforming HTML. The resulting collection contains 4399 web pages, each document belonging to one of six classes (table 1). For the WebKB set we use full text indexing. In total there are 30403 terms in the index, of which we use the 500 most frequent stemmed terms that do not occur in standard stop-words lists. We found (experiments not shown here) that increasing the number of terms used yielded little benefit in classification accuracy.

The WebKB data set contains 4395 within collection links, the graph sparseness link density is $\Gamma = 2.27 \times 10^{-4}$ and the average number of links per document is $\rho = 0.999$. The weighted link density is $\Gamma_w = 2.58 \times 10^{-4}$ and the weighted average number of links per document is $\rho_w = 1.13$.

To calculate the term density and average number of terms, the Cs are exchanged for Ts and the Ls for Is in equations (3) and (4). The term density is 9.9×10^{-2} and the weighted term density is 1.8×10^{-1}. The average number of terms per document is 49.7 and the weighted average is 92.4.

2020 of the documents in the WebKB collection are not cited by any document within the WebKB collection and 2793 documents do not cite any documents within the collection.

The Cora Collection The Cora data set [13] was collected automatically by intelligent web spiders. In the whole data set there are about 37000 papers, all of which have been automatically classified into hierarchical categories such as /Artificial_Intelligence/Machine_Learning/Theory. In common with Cohn & Hofmann's work, we use the 4330 documents in the 7 sub-categories of Machine Learning, see table 1.

Terms occurring in the title, abstract, author and affiliation are used as index terms. In total there are 15753 terms; after stop-word removal, documents are indexed by the 500 most frequently occurring stemmed terms.

The document collection contains 12263 within collection links, using the graph sparseness measure it has a link density of $\Gamma = 6.54 \times 10^{-4}$ and $\rho = 2.8$ links per document. Each paper in the Cora data set may make multiple citations of the same document throughout the text, so that the edges $\mathcal{G}(\mathcal{D}, \mathcal{C})$ have weights greater than one. However, we have used only the 'references' section of the papers, in which each document is only cited once. Consequently, all edges have weight one, meaning that the weighted link density measures are equal to the non-weighted ones.

The term density is 7.2×10^{-2}, the weighted density is 1.1×10^{-1}. The average number of terms per document is 36.1 and the weighted average is 55.8.

2115 of the documents are not cited from any of the documents within the Machine Learning collection and 993 documents do not cite any documents within the collection.

It is already clear from this brief collection analysis that the Cora dataset not only has a higher link density, but also has higher quality link information than the WebKB collection. Only just over one fifth of the Cora documents do not cite any documents within the collection, whereas almost two thirds of the documents in the WebKB document collection do not cite any documents within the dataset.

5   Experiments and Results

To investigate whether link information can be useful for information access tasks if there is a sufficiently high link density in the document collection, we use the PLSI and PHITS model to gain a low-dimensional latent space representation of the data sets and then perform nearest neighbour text classification on a 15 percent held out portion of the documents. We first performed experiments on both the WebKB and Cora data sets to serve as our baseline results and then altered various aspects of the data sets and models to explore how link density and link quality affect classification accuracy.

As described in section 2, the parameter α assigns more or less weight to the content and link information of the collection. When $\alpha = 0$ the model uses just link information and when $\alpha = 1$ only term information is used. Any value in between 0 and 1 will produce a joint representation using both term and link information. The experiments below show whether using both content and link information produces better classification accuracy than using either alone.

For the TEM regime in our experiments (introduced in section 2), we use an initial value of $\beta = 1$, a lower limit of $\beta = 0.8$ and an update parameter of $\eta = 0.95$. Cohn and Hofmann used an update parameter of $\eta = 0.9$ in [3] which caused the model to stop learning too early; however, our TEM parameters allow us to improve the classification accuracy on both document collections, but also

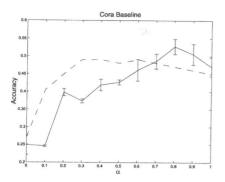
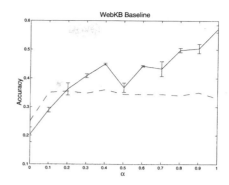

Fig. 1. Average classification accuracy and standard deviation for the Cora (left) and the WebKB (right) document collections. Dotted lines show Cohn & Hofmann's classification accuracies estimated from published graphs [3]

show that best performance on the WebKB data set is achieved using only term information.

For these experiments we use the same number of factors as there are true classes, seven for Cora and six for WebKB. Each of the figures shows the average classification accuracy over three runs with different randomly selected test sets, where accuracy is the fraction of documents correctly classified.

Figure 1 shows the classification accuracy for the Cora and WebKB document collections as the weight, α, ascribed to link and term information is varied. Classification rates obtained by Cohn & Hofmann [3], using different TEM settings are also shown. In agreement with Cohn & Hofmann, we find that the Cora documents are more accurately classified when both link and term information is utilised, although with our TEM regime, peak accuracies are achieved when more weight is given to term information ($\alpha = 0.8$) than reported by Cohn & Hofmann. However, the addition of link information ($\alpha < 1$) in the WebKB data is detrimental to classification performance. It should be noted, however, that the TEM regime used here is able to achieve substantially higher classification rates for these data than previously reported [3].

As demonstrated below, the contrasting results for Cora and WebKB collections are due to the quality and density of the link information in both of these collections. There is an almost three times higher link density in the Cora data set than in the WebKB data set. Also, the quality of the link information (i.e., citations of other papers) in the Cora set is likely to be higher because they are academic papers. The WebKB data set was collected from only a few universities and many of the links in this collection are likely to be navigation links (links to help the user navigate around a web site). As discussed by Kleinberg [12], navigational links are less likely to point at relevant information; in fact, Kleinberg went as far as to delete navigational links in his experiments. Hawkings [8]

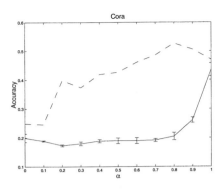
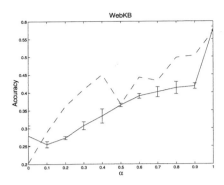

Fig. 2. Average classification accuracy using randomised link information for the Cora (left) and the WebKB (right) data sets. The baseline accuracies are shown by the dotted lines (see figure 1)

suggests that the most important type of links in a web collection are links from one host to another, links between universities are rare in the WebKB data.

5.1 Randomising the Link Information

To determine whether the link information in both datasets provided useful information, we randomised the link information in both collections. In terms of the graph $\mathcal{G}(\mathcal{D}, \mathcal{C})$ described in section 3, we kept the number of edges and the weights on the edges the same, but simply made the edges point from and to different vertices or documents.

As shown in figure 2, the classification accuracy for the Cora collection drops considerably for any $\alpha < 1$. However, the classification accuracy for the WebKB data is barely changed; the $0 < \alpha < 1$ accuracies are slightly lower and the trend with α is more linear. This indicates that the link information in the WebKB collection is ineffectual for text classification.

5.2 Diluting Link Information

To show that the main reason for the poor classification accuracy when using link information for the WebKB document collection is the low link density, we have run experiments on the Cora document collection in which we removed portions of the link information. To reduce the amount of link information in the Cora data set to the density in the WebKB data set, we randomly delete two thirds of the edges in the Cora graph. Note that this procedure reduces the quantity of links but leaves the quality unchanged, whereas the randomisation procedure reduces the quality but leaves the link density constant. The results of this experiment are shown in figure 3. We carried out the same procedure

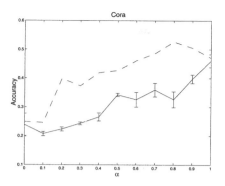 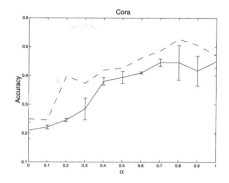

Fig. 3. Removing portions of the link information from the Cora dataset. Average classification accuracy and standard deviation when two thirds of all the link information is removed is shown on the left, ie. making Cora link densities equivalent to WebKB. The right shows the same information when only one third of the link information has been removed. The dotted lines denote the baseline accuracies (see figure 1)

a second time but this time removed only one third of the edges, resulting in the classification accuracies shown on the right hand side of figure 3.

When both one third and two thirds of the link information is removed there is no benefit to using both content and link information, supporting the hypothesis that low link density is the reason for poor accuracy in the WebKB collection, although, removing only one third results in classification rates that are only slightly below the baseline result. It is interesting to observe the resemblance between the classification rate curves for the diluted Cora data and the unaltered WebKB data (figure 1).

Also, notice that diluting the links even by two thirds results in better classification rates than when the link information was randomised (figure 2). This confirms that even small amounts of (high quality) link information are useful in the Cora data set and that misdirected links are detrimental to classification performance.

5.3 Concentrating Link Density

Although we have used an unsupervised training method, the classes of the documents are in fact known. The WebKB data has been manually classified and the Cora data was automatically classified. This class information can be used to add additional links into the collections in a manner that reinforces the true topic distributions. This is achieved by randomly choosing two documents from within the same true class and making an intra-class link between them; no additional inter-class links were made.

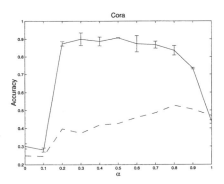 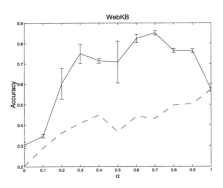

Fig. 4. The average classification accuracy and standard deviation with artificially increased link densities for the Cora (left) data and the WebKB (right). Baseline accuracies are shown by the dotted lines (see figure 1)

For the Cora data set, double the total number of original links were added in intra-class links, which has the effect of raising the intra-inter class link ratio from $9568/12263 = 0.78$ to $34094/36789 = 0.9$. The left hand side of figure 4 shows the classification accuracy achieved; clearly the accuracy has been raised over a wider range of α than in the baseline experiments, and the peak accuracy is now achieved by giving more weight (lower α) to the link component of the model.

Initially, we increased the number of intra-class links in the WebKB data set by two thirds, as with Cora, to $9674/13185 = 0.71$. However, the classification accuracy using this higher link density did not improve. To discover the reason for this, we examined in more detail the intra-class to inter-class link ratio of both document sets and the quality of the link information in both of the datasets.

Tables 2 and 3 show the numbers of links between each class. The Cora data set has a intra-inter link ratio of $9568/12263 = 0.78$, and as can be seen from table 2 the majority of links are intra-class links. It may also be observed that the matrix is roughly symmetrical, meaning that documents in class A are cited by documents in class B about as many times as documents in class B cite documents in class A. The total number of links from each class is also roughly proportional to the number of documents in that class.

In contrast the WebKB data set has much lower quality link information: the intra-inter link ratio is $884/4395 = 0.201$, the links are not symmetrical and the number of links per class is not proportional to the number of documents in that class. It is interesting to note here that the documents in the 'department' class (only 179, mostly home page documents) contain very few out links (59) but are cited the most times out of all the classes (1648).

All of the documents in the Cora data set serve the same purpose: they are all journal papers about computer science. On the other hand, although all the of

Table 2. Number of links from and to each manual class for the Cora data. The largest number of out links from each class is shown in bold and the largest number of in links to each class is underlined

	C Base	Rule L	Theory	Rein L	NN	GA	Prob M	Total Out
C Base	**924**	82	136	27	97	38	51	1365
Rule L	46	**470**	113	3	27	5	6	670
Theory	84	119	**1369**	47	181	38	140	1978
Rein L	40	12	55	**1522**	104	164	46	1943
NN	33	27	186	94	**2200**	54	174	2768
GA	20	2	31	62	56	**1724**	5	1900
Prob M	25	16	121	22	103	3	**1359**	1649
Total In	1172	728	2011	1777	2768	2026	1781	12263

Table 3. Number of links from and to each manual class for the WebKB data

	course	department	faculty	project	staff	student	Total Out
course	**258**	143	175	22	4	121	723
department	1	**31**	5	20	2	0	59
faculty	132	**488**	176	176	4	63	1039
project	4	143	186	**194**	33	129	689
staff	0	**76**	14	34	18	3	145
student	214	**767**	330	213	9	207	1740
Total In	609	1648	886	659	70	523	4395

the web pages in the WebKB data set are about computer science departments, web pages in general have more diverse functions. A department home page, for example, is for introducing the surfer to and directing the surfer around a site, whereas a staff leaf node is simply for reading.

Taking into account the differences between the data sets, we increased the intra-inter link ratio of the WebKB data as well as concentrating the link density of the both data sets. We increased the link density until the intra-inter class link ratio was the same as that of the link-concentrated Cora data, namely $33185/36696 = 0.9$. The right hand side of figure 4 shows the resulting classification accuracy. Like the Cora data, the accuracy has been raised over a wide range of α, and improved classification now results from using link information in addition to term information.

To summarise: document classification is enhanced by using link information if the links are both sufficiently dense and of sufficiently high quality.

5.4 Number of Factors

Cohn & Hofmann's experiments [3] used the same number of factors or latent classes, K (eq (1)), as the number of manually assigned classes. We investigated whether the classification accuracy was improved by using more factors.

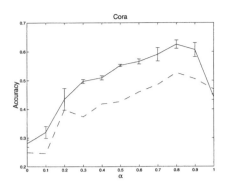
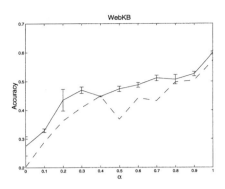

Fig. 5. Average classification accuracy for the Cora data (left) and the WekKB data (right) with 14 latent factors (Cora) and 12 latent classes (WebKB). The dotted lines show the baseline accuracies (see figure 1)

As shown in figure 5 classification is improved for both datasets when the number of factors is doubled. However, further doubling the number of factors again showed no further improvement. This indicates that the collections should be represented by more topics than indicated by the manual categorisation; one possibility is that this effect is due to multi-topic documents aswell as single-topic documents on a wide variety of subjects. It is also worth noting that the peak classification rates are achieved at the same link:content ratio (α) as with the smaller number of classes.

5.5   Selecting Citations

Until now we have considered only the links from one document within the collection to another document within the collection, so $L = J$. Here we investigate the utility of links to documents outside the collections, that is, to documents whose content is unknown; we call these *external links*. Using external links is important as they serve to increase the link density. For reasons of both computational efficiency and information retrieval performance, we use only the most frequently occurring links. This is analogous to the common practice of indexing only the most frequently occurring *terms* in a collection.

It may also be imagined that many of the frequently occurring links on the web would be *stop-links* (like stop-words for terms). These stop-links may be advertisement links or links to search engines which provide no useful information for classification or retrieval. Although stop-links could be removed, robust methods for *stemming* and detecting *stop-links* have yet to be devised. Here we use all the most frequent links.

The documents within the Machine Learning Cora data set cite 34928 documents and in total there are 91842 citations, following an approximately Zipfian

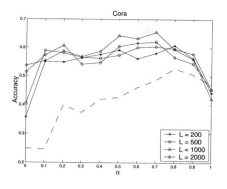
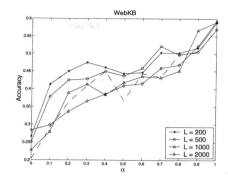

Fig. 6. Average classification accuracy for the Cora (left) and WebKB (right) data sets using the 200, 500, 1000 and 2000 most frequent internal and external links. The dotted lines show the baseline accuracies (see figure 1)

distribution [17]. As might be expected, the majority of documents are only cited once (21545 documents). 2970 documents are cited more than 5 times, 1187 documents are cited more than 10 times and only 417 documents are cited more than 20 times. As shown in figure 6, for both collections we used the $L = 200, 500, 1000, 2000$ external and internal documents that are cited most frequently from within the document collection. The details for the Cora and WebKB collections at each L are shown in table 4.

The left hand side of figure 6 shows the marked increase in classification accuracies achieved by using external links for the Cora data. Note also that best classification is obtained when more weight ($0.5 \leq \alpha \leq 0.7$) is given to link information compared with baseline ($\alpha = 0.8$).

The documents within the WebKB document set cite 53228 documents and in total there are 75958 citations. 44373 of the documents are only cited once from within the collection. 1009 documents are cited in more than 4 documents and only 264 documents are cited more than 10 times.

As shown in figure 6, the classification accuracy for WebKB using the most frequent internal and external links is not improved above the baseline. We

Table 4. Details corresponding to figure 6. *Accuracy* is the mean accuracies over all α and *internal links* is the number of internal links

	Cora				WebKB			
L	$\Gamma \times 10^{-3}$	ρ	Accuracy	Internal links	$\Gamma \times 10^{-3}$	ρ	Accuracy	Internal links
200	13.85	2.77	0.540	40/200	6.84	1.37	0.460	43/200
500	8.74	4.38	0.555	113/500	4.06	2.03	0.447	88/500
1000	6.05	6.06	0.575	218/1000	2.68	2.69	0.416	168/1000
2000	4.08	8.18	0.562	418/2000	1.77	3.56	0.412	252/2000

believe this is because, by selecting citations we were only able to double the average number of links per page and in doing this we quartered the number of documents that could be cited. The WebKB data set does not contain enough high quality link information for link analysis methods to be useful.

For the Cora collection, as the number of most frequent links is increased (and the link density is decreased) the mean classification accuracy increases until $L = 1000$, but then starts to decrease at $L = 2000$ (this decrease continues with increasing L although not shown in figure 6 or table 4). In contrast, as the number of most frequent links for the WebKB data is increased the mean classification accuracy simply decreases. This effect is due to the difference in link quality in the datasets. The high quality Cora links result in classification accuracy increases as long as the new links provide sufficient information. However, the classification accuracy can be seen to decrease when the noise provided by the new links outweighs the information. In the case of the WebKB even $L = 200$ links provide more noise than useful information. This effect is also found when selecting terms, using all terms in a collection will decrease performance because the low frequency terms add noise, so the best performance is found when a small number of the most frequently occurring terms is selected.

6   Discussion

We have investigated the utility of links and citations for information access tasks, in particular text classification. The PLSA+PHITS model [3] provides a principled probabilistic model for document-term and document-citation pairs and has been shown here and in [3] to provide improved classification performance when account is taken of the links between documents as well as the terms within them.

The results obtained here indicate better classification accuracy than those reported in [3] on the Cora and WebKB datasets. Note, however, that different numbers of terms and citations were indexed and the TEM training regime differed. Additional improvements can also be obtained by using more latent classes than the number of manually assigned classes, because the document collection pertains to a richer variety of topics than the rather coarse manual classification. Although not shown here, we found that classification is also enhanced by using a k-NN classifier instead of merely the single nearest neighbour. For both the Cora and the WebKB datasets the optimum k, (usually $k_{opt} \approx 15$), achieved an increase in classification of about 10 percent for all α. We anticipate that other more sophisticated classifiers will also be effective, although perhaps at additional computational cost.

Our experiments show that the density of links within a collection is important; indeed, diluting the links in the Cora collection diminishes the classification performance to the point where inclusion of link information always degrades content-based classification. Nonetheless, our experiments with link randomisation and link concentration, show that quality of links is also important. As might be expected, intra-class links are significant for document classification;

artificially boosting the intra-class links in the WebKB collection allows link information to enhance, rather than degrade, document classification. We have also shown that utilising links to documents external to a collection (whose content is therefore not known) can improve classification. However, the external links must be of high quality. An important area for future investigation will be the detection of *stop-links* and methods for *stemming* links.

As mentioned in the introduction, TREC web tracks have found little benefit in using content and link information over content methods alone. The TREC-8 Web Track used the WT2g collection which has already been criticised [9] for its low link density and lack of cross-host links. In fact, in 247491 documents there are only 2797 cross-host links. The overall graph sparseness is $\Gamma = 1.9 \times 10^{-5}$; that is, a factor of 34 times lower than the Cora data and 12 times lower than the WebKB data. The results presented here indicate that, at least for document classification purposes the WT2g link density is far too low to effectively augment content based methods.

Figures for the TREC-9 Web Track collection, which was specifically engineered to be representative of the Web [2], or for the Web as a whole are not available. However, it is unlikely that the density of high quality links approaches that of the Cora collection in which link information is certainly useful. Information access techniques in relatively haphazard collections such as the Web in its current form may therefore have to rely heavily on content.

Acknowledgments

Michelle Fisher is supported by a CASE studentship with BT and the EPSRC. We are grateful for helpful discussions with Gareth Jones.

References

[1] CMU world wide knowledge base WebKB project. www-2.cs.cmu.edu/ webkb/.

[2] P. Bailey, N. Craswell, and D. Hawking. Engineering a multi-purpose test collection for web retrieval experiments. Information Processing and Management, 2001.

[3] D. Cohn and T. Hofmann. The missing link O a probabilistic model of document content and hypertext connectivity. Neural Information Processing Systems, 13:430O436, 2001. T. Leen et al. eds.

[4] N. Craswell, D. Hawking, and S. Robertson. Effective site finding using link anchor information. In Proc. 24th SIGIR, pages 250O257, 2001.

[5] S. Deerwester, S. T. Dumais, G. W. Furnas, T. K. Landauer, and R. Harshman. Indexing by latent semantic analysis. J. Am. Soc. Info. Science 41, 6:391O407, 1990.

[6] A. Dempster, N. Laird, and D. Rubin. Maximum likelihood from incomplete data via the EM algorithm with discussion. Journal Royal Statisical Society 2, 39:1O38, 1977.

[7] Google. http://www.google.com/technology/whyuse.html.

[8] D. Hawking. Overview of the TREC-9 Web Track. In 9th Text REtrieval Conference (TREC-9), 2000.

[9] D. Hawking, E. Voorhees, N. Craswell, and P. Bailey. Overview of the TREC-8 Web Track. In Eighth Text REtrieval Conference (TREC-8), Gaithersburg, Maryland, 1999.

[10] T. Hofmann. Probabilistic latent semantic indexing. In Proc. 22nd SIGIR, pages 50O57, 1999.

[11] T. Hofmann and J. Puzicha. Unsupervised learning from dyadic data. Technical Report TR-98-042, University of California, Berkeley, CA, 1998.

[12] J. M. Kleinberg. Authoritative sources in a hyperlinked environment. Journal of the ACM, 46(5):604O632, 1999.

[13] A. McCallum, K. Nigam, J. Rennie, and K. Seymore. Automating the construction of internet portals with machine learning. Information Retrieval Journal, 3:127O163, 2000. http://www.research.whizbang.com/data/.

[14] L. Page, S. Brin, R. Motwani, and T. Winograd. The PageRank citation ranking: Bringing order to the Web. Technical report, Stanford Digital Library Technologies Project, 1998.

[15] D. Sullivan. Search engine watch, 2002. www.searchenginewatch.com.

[16] Text REtrieval Conference (TREC) Home Page. http://www.trec.nist.gov/.

[17] H. Zipf. Human behaviour and the principle of least effort. Addison-Wesley, 1949.

Hierarchical Classification of HTML Documents with WebClassII

Michelangelo Ceci and Donato Malerba

Dipartimento di Informatica, Università degli Studi
via Orabona, 4 - 70126 Bari - Italy
{ceci,malerba}@di.uniba.it

Abstract. This paper describes a new method for the classification of a HTML document into a hierarchy of categories. The hierarchy of categories is involved in all phases of automated document classification, namely feature extraction, learning, and classification of a new document. The innovative aspects of this work are the feature selection process, the automated threshold determination for classification scores, and an experimental study on real-word Web documents that can be associated to any node in the hierarchy. Moreover, a new measure for the evaluation of system performances has been introduced in order to compare three different techniques (flat, hierarchical with proper training sets, hierarchical with hierarchical training sets). The method has been implemented in the context of a client-server application, named WebClassII. Results show that for hierarchical techniques it is better to use hierarchical training sets.

1 Introduction

In cooperative information repositories the manual indexing of documents is effective only when all information providers have a thorough comprehension of the underlying shared ontology. However, an experimental study on manual indexing for Boolean information retrieval systems has shown that the degree of overlap in the keywords selected by two similarly trained people to represent the same document is not higher than 30% on average [2]. Therefore, to facilitate sharing of Web documents among distributed work groups in a large organization, it is important to develop automated document classification tools that assist users in the process of document classification with respect to a given set of document categories.

WebClass [8] is a client-server application that has been designed to support the search activity of a geographically distributed group of people with common interests. It works as an intermediary when users browse the Web through the system and categorize documents by means of one of the classification techniques available. Automated classification of Web pages is performed on the basis of their textual content and may require a preliminary training phase in which document classifiers are built for each document category on the basis of a set of training examples.

F. Sebastiani (Ed.): ECIR 2003, LNCS 2633, pp. 57–72, 2003.

A simplifying assumption made in the design of WebClass is that document categories are not hierarchically related. This permits the system to build either one unique classifier for all categories (e.g., a decision tree that assigns a document to one of the pre-defined document categories) or to build a classifier for each category independently of the others (*flat classification*). However, in many practical situations categories are organized into a hierarchy like the one developed by Yahoo! (www.yahoo.com). This hierarchical organization is essential when the number of categories is quite high, since it supports a thematic search by browsing topics of interests.

In this work we present an upgrade of some techniques implemented in WebClass to the case of Web documents organized in a *hierarchy of categories*, that is, a tree structure whose nodes and leaves are document categories. The upgrading of the techniques involved all aspects of automated document classification, namely:

- the definition of a document representation language (*feature extraction*),
- the construction of document classifiers (*learning*), and
- the *classification* of a new document according to the hierarchy of categories.

The paper is organized as follows. In the next section, we introduce some issues related to upgrading to the document classification techniques and we discuss some related work. In Section 3 we describe a new feature selection process for document classification, while in Section 4 we present the naïve Bayes and the centroid-based classification techniques as well as the automated threshold determination algorithm. Section 5 is devoted to the explanation of the document classification process. All these techniques have been implemented in a new version of the WebClass system, named WebClassII. Finally, some experimental results are reported and commented in Section 6.

2   Hierarchical Document Classification: Issues and Related Work

In flat classification, a unique set of features is extracted from the training documents belonging to several distinct categories [5]. The uniqueness of the feature set permits the application of several statistical and machine learning algorithms defined for multi-class problems. However, this approach is impractical when the number of categories is high. In the case of hierarchically related categories it would be difficult to select a proper set of features, since documents concerning general topics are well represented by general terms like "mathematics", while documents concerning specific topics (e.g., trigonometry) are better represented by specific terms like "cosine". By taking into account the hierarchy of categories, it is possible to define several representations (sets of features) for each document. Each representation is useful for the classification of a document at one level of the hierarchy. In this way, general terms and specific terms are not forced to coexist in the same feature set.

As for the learning process, it is possible to consider the hierarchy of categories either in the formulation of the learning algorithm or in the definition of the training sets. For instance, Almuallim et al. [1] defined a specific decision tree induction algorithm for the case of hierarchical attributes. Training sets can be specialized for each internal node of the hierarchy by considering only documents of the sub-hierarchy rooted in the internal node (*hierarchical training set*). This is an alternative to using all documents for each learning problem like in flat classification.

In the classification process, considering the problem hierarchically reduces the number of decisions that each classifier has to take and increases its accuracy. Indeed, in flat classification with r categories the classifier has to choose one of r. This can be difficult in the case of large values of r and may lead to inaccurate decisions. In the case of hierarchical classification, the problem is partitioned into smaller subproblems, each of which can be effectively and efficiently managed.

Some of these aspects have been considered in related works. In particular, in the seminal work by Koller and Sahami [7] the hierarchy of categories is used in every processing step. For the feature extraction step a category dictionary is built for each node in the hierarchy. Feature extraction is based on an information theoretic criterion that eliminates both irrelevant and redundant features. For the learning step, two Bayesian classifiers are compared, namely the naïve Bayes and KDB [13]. A distinct classifier is built for each internal node (i.e., split) of the hierarchy. In the classification step, which proceeds top-down, it is used to decide to which subtree to send the new document. There is no possibility of recovering errors performed by the classifiers associated to the higher levels in the hierarchy. Two limitations of this study are the possibility of associating documents only to the leaves of the hierarchy and the effectiveness of the learning methods only for relatively small vocabularies (<100 features).

McCallum et al. [9] proposed a method based on the naïve Bayes. A unique feature set is defined for all documents by taking the union of all category vocabularies. Features for a given category are selected by means of the mutual information at each internal node of the tree, using the node's immediate children as classes. In the learning step, the hierarchy is considered in the shrinkage technique used to improve the estimate of some probabilities. For the classification step, the authors compare two techniques: exploring all possible paths in the hierarchy and greedily selecting the most probable one as done in [7]. Results show that greedy selection is more error prone but also more computational efficient. As in the previous work, all documents can be assigned only to the leaves of the hierarchy.

Mladenic [10] used the hierarchical structure to decompose a problem into a set of subproblems corresponding to categories (nodes in the hierarchy). For each subproblem, a naïve Bayes classifier is built from a set of positive examples, which is constructed from examples in the corresponding category node and all examples of its subtrees, and a set of negative examples corresponding to all remaining documents. The set of features selected for each category can be different. The classification applies to all the classifiers (nodes) in parallel, using some pruning of unpromising nodes. In particular, a document is passed down to a category only if the posterior probability for that category is higher than a user-defined threshold. Contrary to the previous work, document can be assigned to any node of the hierarchy.

In the work by D'Alessio et al. [3] documents are associated only to leaf categories of the hierarchy. Two sets of features are associated to each category, one is positive (features extracted from documents of the category) while the other is negative (features extracted from documents of sibling categories in the hierarchy). In addition to contributing to feature extraction, the training set is also used to estimate feature weights and a set of thresholds, one for each category. Classification in a given category is based on a weighted sum of feature occurrences that should be greater than the category threshold. Both single and multiple classifications are possible for each testing document. The classification of a document proceeds top-down either through a single path (one-of-M classification) or through multiple-paths (binary classification). An innovative contribution of this work is the possibility of restructuring an initial hierarchy or building a new one from scratch.

Dumais and Chen [4] use the hierarchical structure for two purposes. First, to train several Support Vector Machines (SVM's), one for each intermediate node. The sets of positive and negative examples are constructed from documents of categories at the same level, and different feature sets are built, one for each category.[1] Second, to classify documents by combining scores from SVM's at different levels. Several combination rules are compared, some requiring a category threshold to be exceeded to pass a test document down to descendant categories. Multiple classification of a document is allowed for leaf categories, while the assignment of a document to intermediate categories is not considered. An empirical comparison based on a large heterogeneous collection of pages from LookSmart's web directory showed small advantages in accuracy for hierarchical models over flat models.

Our work differs from previous studies in several respects. First, documents can be associated to both internal and leaf nodes of the hierarchy. Surprisingly, this aspect is considered only in [10]. However, differently from Mladenic's work, we consider actual Web documents referenced in the Yahoo! ontology, and not only the items which briefly describe them in the Yahoo! Web directories (see Fig. 1). This is the situation that we expect to have in cooperative web repositories indexed by a hierarchy of categories.

A second difference is in the feature selection process for each internal category. It is based on an upgrade of the technique implemented and tested in WebClass, named TF-PF^2-ICF. Indeed, a comparison with other two well-known feature selection measures showed better results in the case of flat classification [8].

The third difference is in the development of a technique for the automated selection of thresholds both for posterior probabilities (in the case of naïve Bayes classifiers) and for similarity measures (in the case of centroid-based classifiers). The thresholds are used to determine whether a document has to be passed down to the one of the child categories during the top-down classification process.

The fourth innovative contribution is the comparison of system performances on two types of training sets definable for a given category: i) a *proper* training set, which includes documents of the category (positive examples) and documents of the sibling categories (negative examples), and ii) a *hierarchical training set*, which includes documents of the subtree rooted in the category (positive examples) and documents of the sibling subtrees (negative examples).

---

[1] Note that differently from [3], where each category is associated with two sets of features, positive and negative, here positive and negative examples are used to select a unique feature set for each category.

Finally, we define new measures for the evaluation of the system performances so to capture some aspects related to the "semantic" closeness of the predicted category from the actual one.

3   The Feature Selection Process

In WebClassII each document is represented as a numerical feature vector, where each feature corresponds to the occurrence of a particular word in the document. In this representation, also called *bag-of-words*, no ordering of words or any structure of text is used. The feature set is unique for each category and is automatically determined by means of a set of positive and negative training examples. All training documents are initially tokenized, and the set of tokens (words) is filtered in order to remove HTML tags, punctuation marks, numbers and tokens of less than three characters. Only relevant tokens are used in the feature set. Before selecting relevant features, standard text pre-processing methods are used to:

1. Remove words with high frequency, or *stopwords*, such as articles and adverbs. Stopwords have been taken from Glimpse (glimpse.cs.arizona.edu), a tool used to index files by means of words.
2. Determine equivalent stems (*stemming*), such as 'topolog' in the words 'topology' and 'topological', by means of Porter's algorithm for English texts [11].

Many approaches have been proposed in the literature on information retrieval for the identification of relevant words to be used as index terms of documents [12]. Most of them simply score words according to some measure and select the best firsts. However, techniques proposed for information retrieval purposes are not always appropriate for the task of document classification. Indeed, we are not interested in words characterizing each single document, but we look for words that distinguish a document category from other categories. Generally speaking, the set of words required for classification purposes is much smaller than the set of words required for indexing purposes.

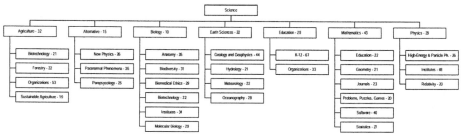

Fig. 1. A segment of Yahoo! ontology considered in this work. Numbers refer to the number of training documents selected for each category. Documents were downloaded on 12th March, 2002

For two-class problems, Mladenic [10] compared scoring measures based on the *Odds ratio* and those based on *information gain*, leading her to favor the former. For multi-class problems, as in the case of WebClassII, Malerba et al. [8] developed a feature selection procedure based on an extension of the well-known TF-IDF measure. They showed that this feature selection technique compares favorably with respect to average mutual information and odds-ratio. Here we briefly present its extension to the case of hierarchical training sets.

Let c be a category and c' one of its children in the hierarchy of categories, that is, $c' \in SubCategories(c)$. Let d be a training document from c', w a feature extracted from d (after the tokenizing, filtering and stemming steps) and $TF_d(w)$ the relative frequency of w in d. Then, the following statistics can be computed:

- the maximum value of $TF_d(w)$ on all training documents d of category c',

$$TF_{c'}(w) = \max_{d \in Training(c')} TF_d(w)$$

- the *page frequency*, that is, the percentage of documents of category c' in which the feature w occurs,

$$PF_{c'}(w) = \frac{occ_{c'}(w)}{|Training(c')|}$$

where *Training(c')* can be either a proper training set or a hierarchical training set for documents of category c'. We remark that only documents considered as positive examples of c' are used to compute both $TF_{c'}(w)$ and $PF_{c'}(w)$.

The union of feature sets extracted from Web pages of c' defines an "empirical" *category dictionary* used by documents on the topics specified by that category. By sorting the dictionary with respect to $TF_{c'}(w)$, words occurring frequently only in one long HTML page might be favored. Indeed, Web page authors usually "hide" a number of occurrences of "keywords" in the HTML code, in order to force search engines to rank that page in the first positions of the returned lists of Web references. By sorting each category dictionary according to the product $TF_{c'}(w) \times PF_{c'}(w)^2$, the effect of this phenomenon is kept under control.[2] Moreover, common words used in documents of c' will appear in the first entries of the corresponding category dictionary. Some of these words are actually specific to that category, while others are simply common English words (e.g., "information", "unique", "suggestion", "time" and "people") and should be considered as *quasi-stopwords*. In order to move quasi-stopwords down in the sorted dictionary, the value $TF_{c'}(w) \times PF_{c'}(w)^2$ is multiplied by a factor $ICF_c(w) = 1/CF_c(w)$, where $CF_c(w)$ (*category frequency*) is the number of categories $c'' \in SubCategories(c)$ in which the word w occurs. In this way, the relevant features that discriminate documents of c' from documents of its sibling categories can be found in the first entries of the category dictionary for c'. We remark that the estimation of $ICF_c(w)$ also takes into account documents considered as negative examples of c'.

---

[2] The plain $PF_c(w)$ factor was also used, but was found to reduce performance slightly. For small sets of training documents, the term $PF_{c'}(w)$ might not be small enough to reduce the effect of very frequent words in single documents.

If n_{dict} is the maximum number of features selected for a category dictionary, then $Dict_{c'} = [(w_1, v_1), (w_2, v_2), \ldots, (w_k, v_k)]$ such that $\forall i \in [1 \ldots k]$ w_i is a feature extracted from some document d in c', $v_i = TF(w_i) \times PF_{c'}^2(w_i) \times \dfrac{1}{CF_c(w_i)}$ and $k \le n_{dict}$ (with $k = n_{dict}$ when at least n_{dict} features can be extracted from training documents of category c'). The feature set ($FeatSet_c$) associated to a category c is the union of $Dict_{c'}$ for all its subcategories c' (see Fig. 2). It contains features that appear frequently in many documents of one of the subcategories but seldom occur in documents of the other subcategories (orthogonality of category features). In other words, selected features decrease the intra-category dissimilarity and increase the inter-category dissimilarity. Therefore, they are useful to classify a document (temporarily) assigned to c as belonging to a subcategory of c itself. It is noteworthy that this approach returns a set of quite general features (like "math" and "mathemat") for upper level categories, and a set of specific features (like "topolog") for lower level categories.

Once the set of features has been determined, training documents can be represented as feature vectors, where each feature value is the frequency of a word.

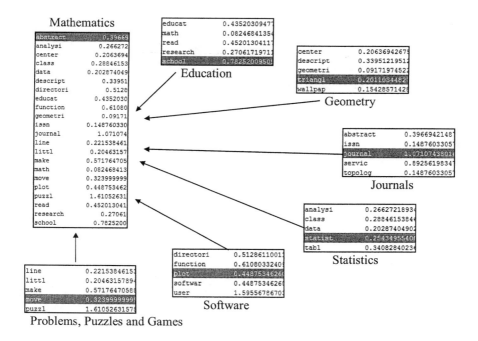

Fig. 2. Category dictionaries extracted by WebClassII for all subcategories of "Mathematics" ($n_{dict}=5$) and feature set selected for "Mathematics". Some features, like "geometri", are extracted from Web documents in German. Indeed, the collection of Web pages referenced by the Yahoo! Web directory "Science" also includes several non-English documents

4   The Learning Process

Currently, WebClassII has two alternative ways of assigning a Web page to a category:

1. By computing the similarity between the document and the *centroid* of that category.
2. By estimating the Bayesian posterior probability for that category (naïve Bayes).

Therefore, a training phase is necessary either to compute the centroids of the categories or to estimate the posterior probability distributions.

Let d be a document temporarily assigned to category c. We intend to classify d into one of the subcategories of c. According to the Bayesian theory, the optimal classification of d assigns d to the category $c_i \in SubCategories(c)$ maximizing the posterior probability $P_c(c_i|d)$. Under the assumption that each word in d occurs independently of other words, as well as independently of the text length, it is possible to estimate the posterior probability as follows (adapted from [6]):

$$P_c(c_i \mid d) = \frac{P_c(c_i) \times \prod\limits_{w \in FeatSet_c} P_c(w \mid c_i)^{TF(w,d)}}{\sum\limits_{c' \in SubCategories(c)} P_c(c') \times \prod\limits_{w \in FeatSet_c} P_c(w \mid c')^{TF(w,d)}} \qquad (1)$$

where the prior probability $P_c(c_i)$ is estimated as follows:

$$P_c(c_i) = \frac{|Training(c_i)|}{\sum\limits_{c' \in SubCategories(c)} |Training(c')|} = \frac{|Training(c_i)|}{|Training(c)|} \qquad (2)$$

and the likelihood $P_c(w \mid c_i)$ is estimated according to Laplace's law of succession:

$$P_c(w \mid c_i) = \frac{1 + PF(w, c_i)}{|FeatSet_c| + \sum\limits_{w' \in FeatSet_c} PF(w', c_i)} \qquad (3)$$

In the above formulas, $TF(w,d)$ and $PF(w,c)$ denote the absolute frequency of w in d and the absolute frequency of w in documents of category c, respectively. The likelihood $P_c(w \mid c_i)$ could be estimated according to the relative frequency, that is:

$$P_c(w \mid c_i) = \frac{PF(w, c_i)}{\sum\limits_{w' \in FeatSet_c} PF(w', c_i)} \qquad (4)$$

However, Laplace probability estimate is preferred because it is non-null even when $PF(w,c)=0$, that is when w does not occur in training documents of category c. Indeed, in Bayesian statistical inference, the assignment of a probability of zero to some parameter values of a probability distribution is considered a strong assumption, because it means it is impossible for the parameter to take on those values.

The *centroid* of a category is defined as an feature vector whose components are computed by averaging on the corresponding feature values of all training documents of the category. In order to classify a document, the centroid most similar to the document description has to be found. The similarity measure considered is the *cosine correlation*, which computes the angle spanned by two vectors (the document and the centroid). The mathematical formulations of both the centroid and the similarity measure are the following:

$$P_c(w, c_i) = \frac{\sum_{d \in Training\ (c_i)} TF_d(w)}{|Training\ (c_i)|} \qquad Sim_c(c_i, d) = \frac{\sum_{w \in FeatSet_c} P_c(w, c_i) \times TF_d(w)}{\sqrt{\sum_{w \in FeatSet_c} P_c(w, c_i)^2 \times \sum_{w \in FeatSet_c} TF_d(w)^2}} \qquad (5)$$

The cosine correlation returns a particularly meaningful value when vectors are highly dimensional and features define orthogonal directions. In WebClassII both conditions are satisfied, though orthogonality refers to the group of features extracted from each category dictionary rather than to the individual features.

The above formulation of both the naïve Bayes and the centroid-based classifiers assigns a document d to the most probable or the most similar class, independently of the absolute value of the posterior probability or similarity measure. However, we should expect that WebClassII users try to classify documents not related to any category in the hierarchy. In this case we expect a "reject" of the document. Although this problem can be operatively dealt with by adding a "reject" category, where all such documents might be collected, from the viewpoint of document classification this is not always correct. This reject category represents "the rest of the world" and the computation of a posterior probability, as well as the computation of a centroid, would make little sense.

By assuming that documents to be rejected have either a low posterior probability for all categories or a small similarity to the centroids of all categories, the problem can be reformulated in a different way, namely, how to define a threshold for the value taken by a naïve Bayes or centroid-based classifier γ. In WebClassII the value of this threshold $Th_c(c_i)$ is algorithmically determined as follows. Let $\gamma_{c \to c'}(d) = P_c(c' \mid d)$ or $\gamma_{c \to c'}(d) = Sim_c(c', d)$ depending on the classifier. In other words, $\gamma_{c \to c'}(d)$ denotes the value returned by the classifier associated to the internal node c when the decision of classifying the document d in the subcategory c' is made. Then, we define the following threshold:

$$TruePosTh_c(c') = \min_{d \in Training(c')} \gamma_{c \to c'}(d)$$

Assumed that all training documents of c' have been (temporarily) assigned to c during the classification process, it is certainly desirable to set $Th_c(c_i)$ to a value lower than $TruePosTh_c(c')$, so that all training documents of c' can be correctly passed down from c to c'. Specifically, $TruePosTh_c(c')$ is the minimum threshold that allows all training documents of category c' (temporarily) assigned to c to be passed down to the category c'. On the other hand, it is desirable to set $Th_c(c_i)$ to a value greater than or equal to the two following thresholds:

$$FalsePosTh_c(c') = \max_{c'' \in SubCategories(c), c'' \neq c', d \in Training(c'')} \gamma_{c \to c'}(d)$$

$$ParentTh_c(c') = \max_{c' \in SubCategories(c), d \in Training(c), d \notin Training(c')} \gamma_{c \to c'}(d)$$

where the first is the maximum threshold that causes a misclassification of documents belonging to siblings of c', while the second is the maximum threshold that causes a misclassification of documents of the parent category c. In other words, $Th_c(c_i)$ should be set to a value lower than $TruePosTh_c(c')$ but not too low, since it might cause the misclassification in c' of training documents belonging either to siblings of c' or to c.

Obviously, if $\max(FalsePosTh_c(c'), ParentTh_c(c')) < TruePosTh_c(c')$ we can set $Th_c(c') = \max(FalsePosTh_c(c'), ParentTh_c(c'))$
since no misclassification is committed on the training examples of c'. This is the case in which the classifier separates well all examples of c' (and its descendants, in the case of hierarchical training sets) from those of its parent and sibling categories.

In general, the above inequality does not hold, in which case the threshold is determined empirically by maximizing the $Fscore$[3]. The procedure followed by WebClassII when the above inequality does not hold is reported in Fig. 3. Input data are the following:

1. $\gamma_c(c_i) = [\gamma_{c \to c_i}(d) | d \in Training(c_i)]$ that is, the list of values taken by the classifier for all documents of category c_i (or a subcategory, in the case of hierarchical training sets);

$$\gamma_c(\neg c_i) = \left[\gamma_{c \to c_i}(d) \middle| d \in \left(Training(c) \cup \bigcup_{c_j \in SubCategories(c)} Training(c_j) \right) - Training(c_i) \right]$$

that is, the list of values taken by the classifier for each document in c or a subcategory of c different from c_i;

2. $V = \gamma_c(c_i) \cup \gamma_c(\neg c_i)$ sorted in ascending order;
3. β, that is, the parameter used in the computation of the $Fscore$.

The only output parameter of the procedure is $Th_c(c_i)$. It is determined by examining the sorted list V of classification scores and by selecting the middle point between two values in V such that the $Fscore$ is maximized.

5   The Classification Process

The classification of a new document is performed by searching the hierarchy of categories. The system starts from the root and selects the nodes to be expanded such

---

[3] $Fscore$ is a measure that synthesizes two important parameters used in information retrieval, namely *recall* and *precision*. It depends on a parameter β:

$$Fscore_\beta = \frac{(1 + \beta^2) \cdot precision \cdot recall}{\beta^2 \cdot precision + recall}$$

In this work, we follow the common practice of setting β to 1, which gives equal importance to precision and recall.

that the score returned by the classifier is higher than the threshold determined by the system. At the end of the process, all explored categories (either internal or leaf) are considered for the final selection. The winner is the explored category with the highest score. If the document is assigned to the root, then it is considered rejected.

It is noteworthy that the application of a classifier is always preceded by a change in the document representation according to the set of selected features. Since selected features are expected to be more specific for lower levels categories, the document is represented at decreasing levels of abstraction during the classification process. This automated representation change is highly desirable in hierarchical classification.

6   Experimental Results

In this section we study the performance of WebClassII on a set of Web documents. The data source used in this experimental study is Yahoo! ontology. We extracted 1026 actual Web documents referenced at the top two levels of the Web directory http://dir.yahoo.com/Science. There are 7 categories at the first level and 28 categories at the second level (see Fig. 1). A document assigned to the root of the hierarchy is considered "rejected" since its content is not related to any of the 35 subcategories.

The dataset is analyzed by means of a 5-fold cross-validation, that is, the dataset is first divided into five *folds* of near-equal size, and then, for every fold, WebClassII is trained on the remaining folds and tested on it. The system performance is evaluated by averaging some performance measures (see below) on the five cross-validation folds.

---

maxFscore := 0; $Th_c(c_i)$:= 0;

$\forall k := 1, 2, ..., |V|-1$

begin

$positive := 0; negative := 0; middle := \dfrac{(V[k] + V[k+1])}{2}$;

$\forall v \in \gamma_c(c_i)$ if ($v > middle$) then $positive := positive + 1$;

$\forall v \in \gamma_c(\neg c_i)$ if ($v > middle$) then $negative := negative + 1$;

$precision(c_i) := \dfrac{positive}{positive + negative}$; $recall(c_i) := \dfrac{positive}{|\gamma_c(c_i)|}$;

$Fscore_\beta := \dfrac{(1 + \beta^2) \times precision(c_i) \times recall(c_i)}{\beta^2 \times precision(c_i) + recall(c_i)}$;

if ($Fscore_\beta > maxFscore$) then

   begin maxFscore := $Fscore_\beta$; $Th_c(c_i)$ = middle; end

end

Fig. 3. Automated threshold definition for a category c_i. Here $|V|$ and $|\gamma_c(c_i)|$ denote the cardinality of V and the number of training documents of category c_i, respectively

Several feature sets of different size have been extracted for each internal category in order to investigate the effect of this factor on the system performance. In particular, the feature set size ranges from 5 to 50 features per category. Features are extracted using hierarchical training sets. In principle, this guarantees that it is possible to associate a feature set also to those categories that have no proper training documents, although this is not the case of this experimentation.

Collected statistics concern centroid-based and naïve Bayes classifiers trained according to one of the following three techniques:

1. flat, that is, by considering all subcategories together and neglecting their relations;
2. hierarchical with proper training sets, this is, by assigning only documents of category c to *Training(c)*;
3. hierarchical with hierarchical training sets, this is, by assigning documents of either category c or one of its subcategories to *Training(c)*.

The baseline for the comparison is represented by the flat technique.

To evaluate both flat and hierarchical classification techniques, we begin considering the macro-weighted-average (MWA) of both precision and recall measures [14]. As shown in Fig. 3, the precision for a category c, denoted as *precision(c)*, measures the percentage of correct assignments among all the documents assigned to c, while the measure *recall(c)* gives the percentage of correct assignments in c among all the documents that should be assigned to c. For the whole category space, say $\{c_1, ..., c_m\}$, the MWA of precision and recall are defined as follows:

$$precision = \frac{\sum_{i=1}^{m} precision(c_i)w_i}{m} \qquad recall = \frac{\sum_{i=1}^{m} recall(c_i)w_i}{m}$$

where the weight w_i is the percentage of documents of category c_i.

Results reported in Fig. 4 and 5 show that the flat technique always outperforms the hierarchical technique with respect to precision, while the naïve Bayes with hierarchical training sets has the best recall for increasing feature set size. Moreover, the centroid-based classifiers almost always have a lower accuracy and recall than the corresponding naïve Bayes classifiers, independently of the adopted technique (flat or hierarchical) and of the feature set size. Another interesting point is that the use of hierarchical training sets improves both performance measures independently of the method and the feature set size.

In fig. 6 the percentage of "rejected" documents is reported. All training and test documents belong to a category of the hierarchy; therefore, it would be desirable to have very low percentages of rejected documents. However, only the naïve Bayes method with hierarchical training sets have percentages below 30%. This means that the high thresholds automatically determined for the root classifier prevent most of test documents from passing down the hierarchy of categories during the classification process. For lower thresholds the rejection rate would decrease, but the system would be more prone to errors.

Intuitively, if a classification method misclassifies documents into categories similar to the correct categories, it is considered better than another method that misclassifies the documents into totally unrelated categories. Therefore, we define other three evaluation measures for a category c, namely:

1. the *misclassification error*, which computes the percentage of documents in c misclassified into a category c' not related to c in the hierarchy;
2. the *generalization error*, which computes the percentage of documents in c misclassified into a supercategory c';
3. the *specialization error*, which computes the percentage of documents in c misclassified into a subcategory c';

For each category c, the sum of the recall, the generalization error, the specialization error and the misclassification error equals one.

The MWA of the misclassification error is reported in Fig. 7. Bayesian methods, which showed the lowest percentages of rejected documents, are also the most prone to misclassification errors. However, in the case of hierarchical training sets, the increase of misclassification rate with respect to the centroid-based approach is about 7%, while the decrease of the rejection rate is above 23% with 50 features per category.

The graphs in fig. 8 and 9 show the generalization and specialization errors. The flat approaches have the lowest generalization error, since they simply ignore the relations among categories. The centroid-based method with hierarchical training sets tend to overgeneralize. This is due to the "conservative" thresholds determined by the algorithm in Fig. 3. On the contrary, all methods have a low specialization error rate.

A finer analysis of the experimental results can be performed by considering some evaluation measures level by level in the hierarchy. The average precision and recall for the seven classes at the first level are reported in Fig. 10 and 11, while statistics concerning the categories at the second level are reported in Fig. 12 and 13. At both levels, the precision of the flat technique is generally the best. At first level, the recall is better for all the hierarchical techniques, while at the second level only the naïve Bayes with hierarchical training sets has a better recall than the flat technique. Interestingly, at the first level, the methods using proper training sets perform better (in precision and recall) than the methods using the hierarchical training sets, while this result is reversed at the second level. In other words, categories at lower levels take major advantages from hierarchical training sets.

Finally, it is noteworthy that the centroid-based method is more computational efficient of the naïve Bayes only in the flat approach, while they have almost equal learning time in the hierarchical approaches. In any case, the learning time of hierarchical techniques is lower than the flat technique, independently of the method.

7   Conclusions

In this paper, the problem of automatically classifying HTML documents into a hierarchy of categories has been investigated in the context of a client-server application developed to support Web document sharing in a group of users with common interests. We studied the use of the hierarchy of categories both in the feature extraction and in the construction of the classifiers and in the classification process. As to feature extraction, a novel technique for the selection of relevant features from training pages has been presented. For the learning step, two classifiers have been considered and a thresholding algorithm has been proposed in the case of a reject class. For the classification, a graph search technique that explores all possible paths has been considered.

Experiments have been performed on a set of Web documents indexed in the Yahoo! ontology. Three techniques have been compared: i) flat classification; ii) hierarchical classification with proper training sets and iii) hierarchical classification with hierarchical training sets. Results on the Yahoo! documents show mainly that:

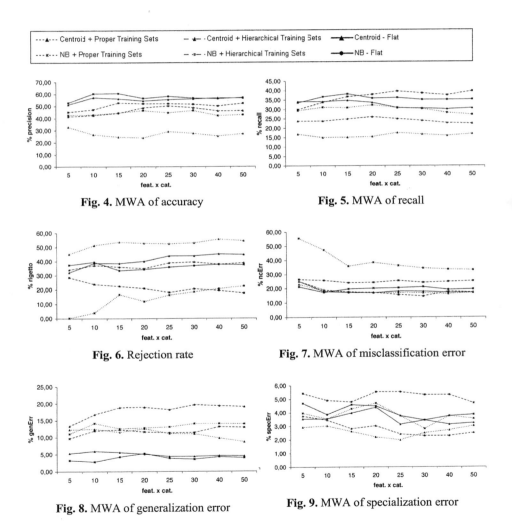

Fig. 4. MWA of accuracy

Fig. 5. MWA of recall

Fig. 6. Rejection rate

Fig. 7. MWA of misclassification error

Fig. 8. MWA of generalization error

Fig. 9. MWA of specialization error

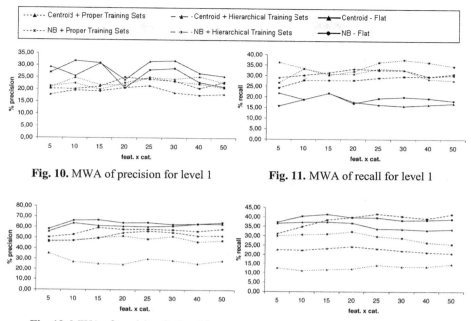

Fig. 10. MWA of precision for level 1

Fig. 11. MWA of recall for level 1

Fig. 12. MWA of precision for level 2

Fig. 13. MWA of recall for level 2

1. For increasing feature sets size, the best performances are observed for the naïve Bayes classifier trained according to either the flat approach or hierarchical training sets. Our results are comparable to those reported in [9], which is the only other work where Web documents indexed by Yahoo! ontology are actually used. However, in our study we have obtained an overall recall of 39.58% using only 875 features, while McCallum et al.'s method required about 13,000 features.

2. Bayesian methods show the lowest percentages of rejected documents but also the highest of misclassification errors. In any case, the relatively small increase of the misclassification rate is counterbalanced by the relatively large decrease of the rejection rate.

3. The lower the level of categories in the hierarchy, the greater the advantage of hierarchical training sets.

The level-by-level analysis performed in this work helped to better understand the different behaviour of the hierarchical and flat approaches. As future work we intend to investigate the relation between sibling categories in the performance evaluation as well as the application a multistrategy approach where different criteria and techniques are used at different levels of the hierarchy.

References

[1]   Almuallim H., Akiba Y., & Kaneda S.: An efficient algorithm for finding optimal gain-ratio multiple-split tests on hierarchical attributes in decision tree learning. Proc. of the Nat. Conf. on Artificial Intelligence (AAAI'96) (1996) 703-708

[2]   Cleverdon C.: Optimizing convenient online access to bibliographic databases. Information Services and Use. 4 (1984) 37-47

[3]   D'Alessio S., Murray K., Schiaffino R., & Kershenbau A.: The effect of using hierarchical classifiers in text categorization. Proc. of the 6th Int. Conf. on "Recherche d'Information Assistée par Ordinateur" (RIAO) (2000) 302-313

[4]   Dumais S.& Chen H.: Hierarchical classification of Web document. Proc. of the 23rd ACM Int. Conf. on Research and Development in Information Retrieval (SIGIR'00) (2000) 256-263

[5]   Esposito F., Malerba D., Di Pace L., & Leo P.: A Machine Learning Approach to Web Mining. In E. Lamma & P. Mello (Eds.). AI*IA 99: Advances in Artificial Intelligence, Lecture Notes in Artificial Intelligence, Vol. 1792, Berlin: Springer (2000) 190-201

[6]   Joachims T.: A probabilistic analysis of the Rocchio algorithm with TFIDF for text categorization. Proc. of the 14th Int. Conf. on Machine Learning (1997) 143-151

[7]   Koller D. & Sahami M.: Hierarchically classifying documents using very few words. Proc. of the 14th Int. Conf. on Machine Learning ICML'97 (1997) 170-178

[8]   Malerba D., Esposito F., & Ceci M.: Mining HTML Pages to Support Document Sharing in a Cooperative System. In R. Unland, A. Chaudri, D. Chabane & W. Lindner (Eds.): XML-Based Data Management and Multimedia Engineering - EDBT 2002 Workshops, Lecture Notes in Computer Science, Vol. 2490, Berlin:Springer (2002)

[9]   McCallum A., Rosenfeld R., Mitchell T.M., Ng A.Y.: Improving text classification by shrinkage in a hierarchy of classes. Proc. of the 15th Int. Conf. on Machine Learning (ICML'98) (1998) 359-367

[10]   Mladenic D.: Machine learning on non-homogeneus, distribuited text data, PhD Thesis, University of Ljubjana (1998)

[11]   Porter M. F.: An algorithm for suffix stripping. Program, 14(3) (1980) 130-137

[12]   Salton G.: Automatic text processing: The transformation, analysis, and retrieval of information by computer. Reading, MA: Addison-Wesley (1989)

[13]   Sahami M.: Learning limited dependence Bayesian classifiers. Proc. of the 2nd Int. Conference on Knowledge Discovery in Databases (KDD'96) (1996) 335-338

[14]   Sebastiani F.: Machine Learning in Automated Text Categorization. ACM Computing Surveys 34 (2002) 1-47

Hierarchical Indexing and Flexible Element Retrieval for Structured Document

Hang Cui[1,*], Ji-Rong Wen[2], and Tat-Seng Chua[1]

[1] Department of Computer Science, School of Computing
National University of Singapore, Singapore
{chuats,cuihang}@comp.nus.edu.sg
[2] Microsoft Research Asia
No.49 Zhichun Road Haidian District, Beijing, P.R.China
jrwen@microsoft.com

Abstract. As more and more structured documents, such as the SGML or XML documents, become available on the Web, there is a growing demand to develop effective structured document retrieval which exploits both content and hierarchical structure of documents and return document elements with appropriate granularity. Previous work on partial retrieval of structured document has limited applications due to the requirement of structured queries and restriction that the document structure cannot be traversed according to queries. In this paper, we put forward a method for flexible element retrieval which can retrieve relevant document elements with arbitrary granularity against natural language queries. The proposed techniques constitute a novel hierarchical index propagation and pruning mechanism and an algorithm of ranking document elements based on the hierarchical index. The experimental results show that our method significantly outperforms other existing methods. Our method also shows robustness to the long-standing problems of text length normalization and threshold setting in structured document retrieval.

1   Introduction

Traditional information retrieval treats document as the smallest retrieval unit, but in many scenarios a user may actually require part of the document with higher precision and finer granularity. Suppose a user who studies history of military operations would like to find out "what military aircrafts were used in Desert Storm". He or she may retrieve articles named *Military Aircrafts* and *Gulf War* as two of the top-ranked results, both of which contain only a part of relevant content. The user then has to scan each (usually very long) document to look for relevant information. This is a time-

---

* This work was performed when the author was a visiting student at Microsoft Research Asia.

F. Sebastiani (Ed.): ECIR 2003, LNCS 2633, pp. 73–87, 2003.

consuming process which hinders the effectiveness of information retrieval. Such an information overload is very common in typical Web searching applications.

Today, with the widely use of XML, there is an increasing demand to develop better techniques for structured document retrieval. XML provides a standard and effective way for the author to explicitly express the structure of a document. For example, our corpus from the Encarta website (http://encarta.msn.com) can be considered as a set of content-oriented XML documents. A typical structured document is represented as a collection of nodes such as sections, subsections, and paragraphs, as shown in Figure 1. We call each node as an element in the rest of this paper. The node representing the whole document, known as the root, is also considered as an element such that all nodes in the entire document tree are treated equally. The leaf nodes are made up of paragraphs. All upper-level nodes are ancestors of paragraphs, with their contents formed by those of paragraphs.

A document, especially a long one, usually covers multiple aspects of a central topic. The elements in a document can be viewed as a concept tree, i.e., the upper element represents a broader concept which covers all the concepts beneath it. Document retrieval can only be partially called *information* retrieval unless the elements expressing the appropriate level of concept can be precisely retrieved. An effective retrieval system should provide this capability without imposing too much burden on users.

In this paper, we propose a method of retrieving relevant document elements, exploiting both structural information and the statistics of term distributions in structured documents. The main thrust of this solution is to allow the retrieval of relevant document elements with arbitrary granularity using keyword-based queries. We call it a flexible element retrieval strategy. Our solution is mainly made up of two parts – a novel hierarchical index propagation and pruning mechanism and an algorithm for selecting suitable document elements based on the hierarchical index.

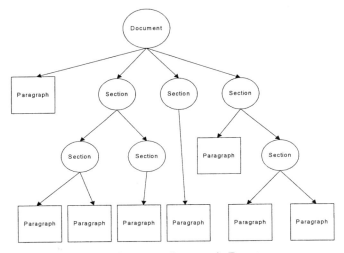

Fig. 1. Document Structure in Encarta

Comparing to existing works, we put much emphasis on the indexing phase. Applying specific indices to retrieving data with structural information has long been studied in the areas of database and IR, such as indexing semi-structured data for XML documents retrieval [12] and bottom-up indexing schemes for structured documents retrieval [11]. Previous approaches assign index terms to only the leaf nodes [10] [12] [14] [15] or fixed-length passages [3] [8] [9]. The main drawback of such a kind of indexing mechanism is that the flat index does not match the hierarchical structure of documents. It discards semantic relationships among the elements. The inconsistency between the structures of documents and indices prevents users from obtaining composite elements, thus results in many discrete passages, which leads to the tough work of assembling the resulting excerpts of text to users [15].

The essential problem for indexing structured document is that, in order to get elements at arbitrary levels, the weights for various elements against a given query must be comparable. [4] has a similar purpose in indexing and retrieving hypertext medical handbook in which related materials are represented as linked cards. In their method, the weight of a card E is determined by the TF-IDF values of all the query terms in E plus the average TF-IDF weights of all immediate-descendant elements of E. Card weights are propagated recursively from the leaf elements to the root element. This is one of the first works to index document elements by combining the content and structure information. But this method may not be practical to index a large amount of structured documents mainly due to two reasons. First, in the hypertext medical handbook model, every element has its own content and the contents of its descendant elements are only viewed as supplements to its own content. However, in the case of general structured documents, such as the XML documents, an intermediate element usually does not have its own content and it is totally made of the contents of its descendant elements. If the weight propagation technique in [4] is directly employed, the weight of a composite element without its own content will always be ranked lower than that of its descendents, because its weight is the average value of the summed weights of all its descendents. Consequently, the leaf elements will always be retrieved as best matches. Second, the propagation mechanism in [4] does not perform any pre-processing and thus the same index terms may be distributed in multiple elements of one document, which is very costly in terms of both storage space and computation time, especially when handling a large amount of documents. Moreover, the author did not give any quantitative evaluation of the proposed method. Thus it is hard to judge its effect in a real application scenario.

We approach the goal of flexible element retrieval by a hierarchical indexing mechanism, which is not only able to index the leaf nodes but also intermediate nodes, i.e. section and document nodes. Basically, we use a propagation and pruning mechanism to select index terms. From bottom up, terms that can "exactly" describe the inherent concept of an element are propagated to it while terms with too broad or too narrow meanings are pruned. Index pruning is employed to ensure that an index term appearing in an element would not appear in any of its descendent elements thus the content overlap in the text is avoided in the index. This saves much storage space and retrieval time. Moreover, this hierarchical indexing mechanism produces an index structure that is identical to the document structure. Hence we can perform document element retrieval on the index space directly. Figure 2 illustrates the process of index propagation and pruning. Assuming that we have a document named "China" with a section "History" and this section contains subsections such as "Tang dynasty", "Ming dynasty" and "Qing dynasty", etc. Then for the section "History", only terms like "history" and "dynasty" are good index terms, while for the whole document, only the term "China" is the best choice.

Based on the hierarchical index, we also propose a flexible element retrieval algorithm to rank candidate elements against queries so that suitable document elements that precisely meet user's information needs can be returned.

We conducted a series of experiments to evaluate the performance of our method in terms of precision and recall at element level. The results show that our method significantly outperforms the compared method and is less sensitive to threshold setting than the traditional passage retrieval methods.

2   Related Work

In recent years, many structured document retrieval techniques have been developed. In traditional IR community, due to the absence of explicit structural information, documents are treated as a sequence of fixed-length [3] or pre-defined [15] portions of text, which are considered as passages or paragraphs. Passage retrieval [3] [8] [9] [15] [16] is one of the early techniques aiming to retrieve and return more compact and shorter answers at passage level to the user. A passage retrieval method usually indexes the documents at passage or paragraph level, and applies the variants of TFIDF measure to rank passages, while [13] is an exception, which suggests using Hidden Markov Model to retrieve both documents and passages. More recently, researchers start to address the problem of mixing content and structure in retrieval models [2]. [12] suggests a model containing a number of useful operators that can achieve relatively high efficiency.

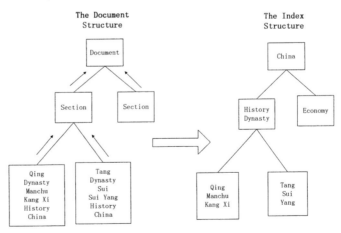

Fig. 2. Index propagation and pruning mechanism

Another group of methods, mainly developed by the database community, concentrate on retrieving specific fields of semi-structured or XML data by indexing structures and strictly defined query languages [1] [7]. In the case of XML query languages, these methods require the user to specify structured queries. However, without the knowledge of the document structure, it would be very hard for the users to formulate meaningful queries. Moreover, only the data elements whose structures exactly match the specified query structure can be retrieved.

We found there was a lack of an appropriate method that balances the trade-off between the full utilization of document structure and the convenience of common users. Some researchers attempt to address this problem. [14] explores the use of inference network to represent elements of a document at different levels so that all elements can be treated equally. However it still has difficulty in properly ranking various elements with the existence of content overlaps. [6] proposes a new way to index a bibliography repository with a hierarchical structure. Focused retrieval method of locating document components that contain relevant information is introduced in [10]. [5] describes a new query language introducing some information retrieval features, such as weighting to XML documents retrieval.

3   Hierarchical Indexing of Structured Documents

In this section, we describe the details of our hierarchical indexing strategy. For each document, we automatically establish a hierarchical index with the same structure as that of the document. Index terms are distributed across all nodes in the document tree. The basic idea of assigning an index term to an element node is that the term should characterize the concept of this element and differentiate it from the others. Thus, a rule of thumb for selecting good index terms is that the term should appear frequently and be distributed evenly in the text of an element and, its rank is high compared to its peer terms.

3.1   Term Weighting for Elements

By taking advantage of the hierarchical structure of the documents, the distribution of a term in an element can be measured by investigating the term's appearances in the descendant elements of this element. It is noted here that we consider only immediate-descendant elements of the element because we believe that the topic of an element is best supported by the elements that it owns directly. If a term is distributed evenly in a composite element's immediate-descendant elements, this term would be a good candidate index term for this element.

We introduce the concept of entropy here as a criterion to measure the distribution of a term in an element. Here we distinguish between two types of elements – the intermediate elements and leaf elements which are paragraphs. For an intermediate element, we compute the weight of a term by combining the term's intra frequency in this element and the term's distribution in its immediate-descendent elements. That is the weight of term t_i in an arbitrary composite element E_j can be defined as:

$$Weight\,(t_i, E_j) = \ln(1 + tf\,(t_i, E_j)) \times I(t_i, E_j) \tag{1}$$

where $tf(t_i, E_j)$ denotes the frequency of term t_i in the element E_j. $I(t_i, E_j)$ is the entropy measure, i.e. the distribution of the term t_i in element E_j and is defined as:

$$I(t_i, E_j) = \frac{-\displaystyle\sum_{Sub_k \in E_j} tf\,(t_i, sub_k) \times \ln \dfrac{tf\,(t_i, sub_k)}{tf\,(t_i, E_j)}}{-\displaystyle\sum_{Sub_k \in E_j} \dfrac{tf\,(t_i, E_j)}{N(sub)} \times \ln \dfrac{1}{N(sub)}}$$

$$= \frac{-\displaystyle\sum_{Sub_k \in E_j} tf\,(t_i, sub_k) \times \ln \dfrac{tf\,(t_i, sub_k)}{tf\,(t_i, E_j)}}{-tf\,(t_i, E_j) \times \ln \dfrac{1}{N(sub)}} \tag{2}$$

where sub_k stands for the kth immediate-descendant element of E_j and $N(sub)$ the number of such descendant elements.

In Equation 2, it is worthwhile to notice that term frequency varies greatly in different elements due to the great variance of text lengths. Entropy measure may encounter the same length normalization problem as in other document or passage retrieval methods. [3] [8] [9] [6] [14] [15] addressed the normalization of text length but were limited to the factor of term frequency. We compute the theoretic maximum entropy $-tf\,(t_i, E_j) \times \ln \dfrac{1}{N(sub)}$ and use this as normalization factor. It hypothesizes that all appearances of this term in a specific element are exactly equal in each of its immediate-descendant elements. The proportion of this value is used as the distribution measure of a term. It counters the negative effect of varying text lengths to some extent.

Leaf elements of paragraphs are "atomic" elements, which have no children elements, thus we simply employ the traditional TFIDF measure to compute the weight of terms in a single paragraph. A term's weight in a paragraph is defined as:

$$Weight(t_i, P_j) = \ln(tf\,(t_i, P_j)) \times \ln \frac{N}{n_i} \tag{3}$$

$Weight(t_i, P_j)$ represents the weight of term t_i in paragraph P_j. $tf(t_i, P_j)$ is the term frequency of t_i in the paragraph. N denotes the total number of documents in the corpus and n_i the number of documents containing t_i.

Term weights are further normalized to be comparable in different elements. Term weights obtained by Equations 1 and 3 are divided by the maximum weight of all terms in the same element so that all terms' weights fall into the range of between 0 and 1.

3.2   Propagation and Pruning of Index Terms

Recall that a term in an element whose weight is relatively high should be selected as the index term for this element. Specifically, the selection of index terms is realized by the propagation and pruning process. In the previous section, we derive the weights for each term in an arbitrary element. A term is propagated to an upper element if its weight exceeds a certain threshold, and meanwhile this term is pruned from these descendant elements since it may stand for a more general concept. This process is done recursively from bottom up until all the nodes in the tree are assigned proper index terms without duplications in the same branch of the index tree. Obviously, the threshold controlling the term selection should be dynamically adjusted according to the statistics of all the terms' weights in a specific element. More precisely, a term is chosen as an index term for an element if and only if its weight is above the average value plus the standard deviation of all terms' weights in this element. Our indexing propagation and pruning mechanism can be described as follows:

Algorithm 1 – terms selection (index terms propagation and pruning)

1. For each leaf element, i.e. paragraph, calculate all terms' weights for paragraphs according to Equation (3).
2. For each composite element E_j at the next upper level, calculate the terms' weights using formula (1) by measuring these terms' occurrences in this element and the distributions in the immediate-descendant elements of E_j.
3. For term t_i, if $Weight(t_i, E_j) \geq average(E_j) + std\_dev(E_j)$, then term t_i is selected as an index term of the element E_j and all the descendent elements of E_j would eliminate t_i from their index term lists. This process is called the index term propagation and pruning. Here *average(E_j)* denotes the arithmetic average of all terms' weights in element E_j and *std_dev(E_j)* the standard deviation of these weights.
4. Recursively perform step 2 onwards until the root node (i.e., the document) is reached.

This indexing solution makes full use of the internal structural information of documents. Since all terms are compared to each other at the same level and a theoretic maximum entropy value is used as the normalization factor, the negative effect of varying lengths of text in elements at different levels is minimized. Our experimental results are able to testify this. In addition, an index term of an element need not necessarily appear in all sub-elements of this element due to the nature of the measurement of the term weight. Thus more representative index terms other than just a few words in titles can be found.

4   Flexible Element Retrieval and Result Browsing

In this section, we describe the flexible element retrieval algorithm which is used to select suitable document elements. With the help of hierarchical index, the main task of the retrieval phase is online searching and ranking of candidate elements.

4.1   Path Ranking and Retrieval Process

For each document, we use a path ranking algorithm to calculate relevance values of all candidate elements against a query. A path for an element is defined as the branch containing all the ancestor elements of this element (including itself) in the document tree. According to our hierarchical indexing mechanism, an element does not share any index terms with its ancestors. Thus we say that an element is completely represented by all index terms of the elements along its path. Conversely, a path can be expressed as the element at the lowest level in the path. Therefore, the element ranking problem can be transformed to a path ranking problem, that is, to find those element paths with high relevance values to the query.

The relevance value for a path against a given query is defined as:

$$Relevance(Path_p) = \sum_{i=1}^{Q} Weight(t_i, Path_p) \times \ln \frac{N}{n_i} \qquad (4)$$

$\ln \frac{N}{n_i}$ is the IDF value of query term t_i and is used here as the query term's weight. Q stands for the number of query terms in a query. $Weight(t_i, Path_p)$ is defined as the weight of the query term t_i for path $Path_p$. We define that a term's weight for a path is its weight for the element that containing this term along the path, as is defined by Equations (1) and (3).

Given a new query, we use traditional document retrieval methods to get a list of relevant documents first in order to narrow down the search space. Then when the user selects one of the relevant documents, the system searches for all candidate elements of this document and ranks their paths according to Equation (4). The most relevant elements are sorted and displayed with the structural context to the user. The overall process is described as below:

Algorithm 2 – Path ranking

1. Find all elements that contain at least one query term.
2. Get paths for all candidate elements and merge the paths, that is, merge two paths into one if one is a part of the other.
3. Assign the weights of the query terms for elements to their paths respectively.
4. Rank these paths according to Equation (4).
5. Return the elements corresponding to the ranked paths with the ranks satisfying the pre-defined threshold in a descending order.

A long-standing problem in structured document retrieval is how to select proper elements which best satisfy the user's query needs. Usual method to solve this problem is to set a fixed threshold and the elements with ranks above this threshold are returned as the results [15]. However due to the variation in text length, the proper threshold varies with documents and queries. We use the average of all retrieved elements' ranks as the dynamic threshold. The experiments show that a more accurate element retrieval can be attained based on this dynamic threshold.

4.2   Result Browsing

Flexible information retrieval may return larger or smaller granularity results than what the user needs. Therefore a good user interface for browsing the results in the original tree structure context is crucial for improving users' query process. Figure 3 shows a snapshot of the interface of our flexible element retrieval system with a given query "Qing dynasty".

In Figure 3, we can see that total of sixteen elements are returned for the document named "China", among which there are sections and paragraphs. The top element is a section with the title "The Manchu Qing Dynasty" that is dedicated for describing the Qing Dynasty in the history of China. This section is under the 7th section of this document, whose title is "History". From the left browsing pane, we can see clearly each section or paragraph's position in the document. In comparison, when we click the first article "Qing Dynasty", we get the whole document since the entire document is rooted on this topic. In summary, the flexible retrieval system returns the most appropriate document elements to users according to their queries.

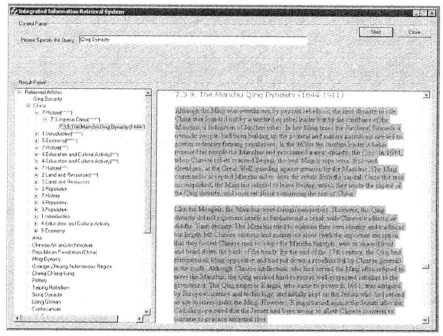

Fig. 3. The interface of the Flexible Element Retrieval System

5   Evaluation

In this section, we evaluate the performance of our proposed flexible element retrieval method and investigate the effects of threshold settings on element retrieval. The experiments are conducted on the Encarta corpus, which contains 41,942 well structured XML documents. The query set is made up of 10 queries, which can be best answered by only a part of the relevant documents. The 10 queries used in this experiment are listed in Figure 4.

```
1. History of China
2. Qing Dynasty
3. Atomic bomb in American history
4. Ford Motors in World War II
5. What is the impact of Newton on calculus?
6. What is the attitude of Microsoft to World Wide Web?
7. What is the influence of Lincoln in American history?
8. Fleet Street in London
9. Military aircrafts used in Desert Storm
10 .What missiles can nuclear submarines carry?
```

Fig. 4. Queries for element retrieval evaluation

For comparison purpose, we implemented a passage retrieval system, TFIDF Para. This system uses only pre-defined paragraphs in Encarta documents as passages while ignoring other structural information. A term's weight in a paragraph is defined by the conventional TFIDF measure [15], which is the same as Equation (3). The relevance measure between a given query and a specific paragraph is the cosine similarity between their term vectors.

Relevance judgments are made by human assessors. For each query, the assessors first select a document that is considered as most relevant. Then the relevant elements in that document against this query are judged and selected by the assessors without the knowledge of the targeting systems. Besides precision and recall, we also employ F-Value to be an integrated measure for performance evaluation.

$$F-Value = \frac{2}{1/recall + 1/precision} \qquad (5)$$

When deciding what fractions of the retrieved elements should be returned to the users as the answers, we use both fixed thresholds from 0.1 to 0.9 at the increment of 0.1 plus 0.95 and two dynamic thresholds. One such dynamic threshold is the average of the rank values of all retrieved elements for a query (Avg), and the other is Avg plus the standard deviation of these values (Std_Dev). The results obtained by these two methods with various thresholds are illustrated in Tables 1, 2 and 3 for precision, recall and F-value respectively. For the flexible element retrieval method, we test its performance on two different sets of index. Each composite element, say a document or a section, has a title, which is a good indicator for its content. In order to get more convincing results, we build the first set of index without using the titles. Experiments indicate that most of the title terms can be re-constructed by our indexing mechanism. In the second set of index, we add the title for a document or a section to every paragraph below it as index terms. For TFIDF Para system, the index utilizes the titles as is done in the second set of index.

From the above tables, we can see clearly that with the various threshold settings our flexible element retrieval method has a significant improvement in retrieval performance, especially measured by precision and F-Value, over the method of applying TFIDF measure to paragraph level directly. With respect to F-Value, the average improvement is 56.02% involving titles, and 40.89% without considering titles. In both cases of adding title terms into index terms and not dealing with title terms, the precision of the flexible element retrieval system is much better than the TFIDF Para system with the average improvement of 48.83% and 41.67% respectively. We attribute the drastic augment in precision to the high quality index terms selected by our index propagation and pruning algorithm. In addition, the flexible element retrieval method can return elements with various granularities which may be paragraphs, sections or even the whole documents depending on the specification of queries. In contrast, previous passage retrieval methods return only fixed-level passages. However, there is slight decrease in recall for some threshold settings when using the index set without adding the title terms. This is caused by our index term selection threshold, which is somehow too tight such that some proper terms are missed because their distributions in text do not meet the selection threshold. But we deem that the decreased recall can be compensated by our interface which allows users to browse in the document structure freely.

Table 1. Comparison of precision

Threshold	TFIDF Para	Flexible Retrieval (with titles)	Flexible Retrieval (without titles)	improvement (with titles) over TFIDF	improvement (without titles) over TFIDF
0.1	0.3549	0.5263	0.5059	48.30%	42.55%
0.2	0.3948	0.5318	0.5107	34.70%	29.36%
0.3	0.4374	0.5361	0.5338	22.57%	22.04%
0.4	0.5096	0.5361	0.5478	5.20%	7.50%
0.5	0.5158	0.5854	0.5800	13.49%	12.45%
0.6	0.5801	0.5902	0.6159	1.74%	6.17%
0.7	0.6482	0.6864	0.6478	5.89%	-0.06%
0.8	0.6487	0.7521	0.7521	15.94%	15.94%
0.9	0.6333	0.8212	0.7855	29.67%	24.03%
0.95	0.6167	0.7917	0.7839	28.38%	27.11%
Avg	0.4045	0.7665	0.6115	89.49%	51.17%
Avg+Sdev	0.5457	0.7790	0.6667	42.75%	22.17%

Table 2. Comparison of recall

Threshold	TFIDF Para	Flexible Retrieval (with titles)	Flexible Retrieval (without titles)	improvement (with titles) over TFIDF	improvement (without titles) over TFIDF
0.1	0.9350	1.0000	0.8667	6.95%	-7.30%
0.2	0.9350	1.0000	0.8667	6.95%	-7.30%
0.3	0.9350	1.0000	0.8667	6.95%	-7.30%
0.4	0.9021	1.0000	0.8667	10.85%	-3.92%
0.5	0.7309	1.0000	0.8500	36.82%	16.29%
0.6	0.5964	0.9500	0.8417	59.29%	41.13%
0.7	0.5571	0.9333	0.7333	67.53%	31.63%
0.8	0.3999	0.8121	0.6583	103.08%	64.62%
0.9	0.2407	0.7793	0.5833	223.76%	142.33%
0.95	0.2401	0.6377	0.5527	165.60%	130.20%
Avg	0.7456	0.9417	0.6800	26.30%	-8.80%
Avg+Sdev	0.5670	0.5839	0.5756	2.98%	1.52%

Table 3. Comparison of F-Values

Threshold	TFIDF Para	Flexible Retrieval (with titles)	Flexible Retrieval (without titles)	improvement (with titles) over TFIDF	improvement (without titles) over TFIDF
0.1	0.5145	0.6896	0.6389	34.04%	24.17%
0.2	0.5552	0.6943	0.6427	25.07%	15.76%
0.3	0.5960	0.6980	0.6607	17.12%	10.85%
0.4	0.6513	0.6980	0.6713	7.17%	3.07%
0.5	0.6048	0.7385	0.6895	22.11%	14.01%
0.6	0.5881	0.7281	0.7113	23.79%	20.94%
0.7	0.5992	0.7910	0.6879	32.01%	14.80%
0.8	0.4948	0.7809	0.7021	57.84%	41.90%
0.9	0.3488	0.7997	0.6695	129.26%	91.92%
0.95	0.3456	0.7064	0.6483	104.38%	87.57%
Avg	0.5245	0.8451	0.6439	61.14%	22.78%
Avg+Sdev	0.5561	0.6675	0.6178	20.02%	11.09%

Previous leaf nodes indexing methods make an element available against a query only if the element contains a part of the query, i.e., a relevant composite element can be retrieved with all of its descendant elements if and only if each of the descendants contains at least one query term. This is not the case in many documents so a lot of relative paragraphs containing no query terms are missed in the TFIDF Para system's results. On the other hand, TFIDF Para system introduces much noise into the final result by adding some paragraphs which do not cover the meaning of the user query but do contain some query terms. In comparison, with the index propagation and pruning mechanism, the index with the tree structure in our system can make sure of a relatively better concept matching. To a composite element, say a section, the appropriate index terms would be propagated to it even if only a part of its descendant elements contain these terms. This index structure ensures the integrity of the resulting elements.

5.1   Threshold Setting

Threshold setting is very crucial for structured document retrieval to get a set of desirable resulting elements. In previous works, the thresholds are usually fixed [15]. In our experiments, we find that using a single threshold cannot make the system always perform well for different queries since the documents vary greatly in structure and length. We explore the use of dynamic thresholds instead of fixed threshold in our experiments.

In order to see how various thresholds affect the retrieval performance, we plot the F-Values obtained with various thresholds in Figure 5. The Figure shows that the curve generated by our method, especially the curve representing the results obtained without using title terms, is much flatter than that obtained by the TFIDF Para method. The performance of the TFIDF Para method varies greatly with the changing of threshold. The highest F-Value obtained by TFIDF Para is 0.6513(at the threshold of 0.4), which is 177.96% greater than the lowest value of 0.2343 (at no threshold). In comparison, with the use of title terms, the maximum (at threshold Avg) and the minimum (at threshold Avg+SDev) F-Values of our method vary only 26.61%; and in the case of without considering title terms, the variation is only 15.13%. This indicates the fact that our method is less sensitive to threshold setting. We attribute the robustness to that our method takes full advantage of the document structure to mix the statistics of term occurrences and distributions in weighting terms.

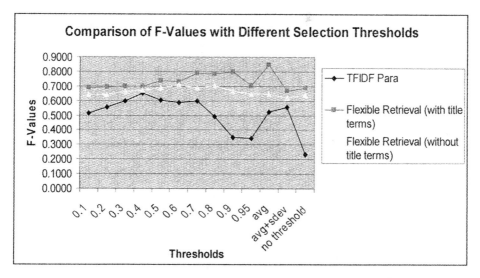

Fig. 5. Comparison of F-Values with different thresholds

Moreover, from Figure 5, it is interesting to note that the dynamic thresholds, such as Avg and Avg+SDev, can produce desirable results. When using the index set with title terms, the F-Value of the flexible retrieval system achieves the best performance when using the threshold avg. Our method using the index set without title terms can also get very good result with the threshold Avg, which is slightly less (9.47%) than the best one. But due to the sensitivity to the threshold setting, TFIDF Para system cannot be improved when using dynamic threshold. This testifies that dynamic threshold is a good alternative for threshold setting for our system since in most cases we cannot use one threshold to ensure the best performance for all documents and queries.

6   Conclusion

Passage retrieval based on structural information in documents has long been suggested as effective ways to retrieve elements of a document with finer granularity. In this paper, we proposed a new hierarchical index propagation and pruning mechanism for structured documents and realize a flexible element retrieval system based on this index structure. An index term is propagated to an upper level element in the tree structure if it represents a more general concept, which is judged by comparing its statistical information with other peer terms' weights in that element. Index terms are distributed across the whole document tree and each element has a list of index terms which can best represent the concept of that element. The flexible element retrieval method is dedicated to providing users with the most appropriate elements at any level. We conducted experiments to evaluate our method in terms of precision and recall in element level. Experimental results showed that our method significantly outperformed the method of applying TFIDF measure to only the paragraph level. It was also found that our method was not sensitive to threshold setting compared to other passage retrieval methods. Moreover, we observed that dynamic threshold is a better solution for the threshold setting for element retrieval.

Acknowledgement

The authors would like to express their sincere thanks to Dr. Wei-Ying Ma for his valuable comments and suggestions to improve this paper.

References

[1]   Abiteboul S., Quass D., McHugh J., Widom J. and Wiener J., 1996, The Lorel Query Language for Semi-structured Data, Department of Computer Science. Stanford University, California, USA, 1996.

[2]   Baeza-Yates, R., Navarro, G., 1996, Integrating contents and structure in text retrieval, ACM SIGMOD Record, 25(1):67-79, March 1996.

[3]   Callan, J., 1994, Passage-level evidence in document retrieval. In Proceedings of the 17 Annual ACM SIGIR Conference on Research and Development in Information Retrieval, Dublin, Ireland, 1994, Pages 302-310.

[4]   Frisse, M, 1988, Searching for Information in a hypertext medical handbook, Comm. of ACM, 31(7), July 1988, Pages 263-271.

[5]   Fuhr, N., Grobjohann, K., 2001, XIRQL: a query language for information retrieval in XML documents, In Proceedings of the 24th Annual International ACM SIGIR Conference on Research and Development in Information Retrieval, New Orleans, Louisiana, USA, September 2001, Pages 172-180.

[6]   Geffet, M., Feitelson, D., 2001, Hierarchical indexing and document matching in BoW, In Proceedings of JCDL'01, Roanoke, Virginia, USA, 2001, pages 259-267.

[7]   Goldman, R., Shivakumar, N., Venkatasubramanian, S. and Garcia-Molina, H., Proximity search in databases, In Proceedings of the Twenty-Fourth International Conference on Very Large Data Bases, New York, USA, August 1998, Pages 26-37.

[8]   Kaszkiel, M., Zobel J. and Sacks-Davis R., 1999, Efficient passage ranking for document databases, ACM Transactions on Information Systems, Vol. 17, No. 4, October 1999, Pages 406-439.

[9]   Kaszkiel, M., Zobel, J., 1997, Passage retrieval revisited, In Proceedings of the 20th Annual ACM SIGIR International Conference on Research and Development in Information Retrieval, 1997, Philadelphia, PA, USA, Pages 178-185.

[10]   Kazai, G., Lalmas, M., and Rölleke, T., 2001, Aggregated Representation for the Focussed Retrieval of Structured Documents, SIGIR 2001 Workshop, Mathematical/Formal Methods in IR, New Orleans, 2001.

[11]   Lee, Y., Yoo, S. Yoon, K. and Berra, P., 1996, Index structures for structured documents, In Proc. of the First ACM International Conf. on Digital Libraries, pp. 91-99, 1996, Bethesda, Maryland.

[12]   McHugh, J., Abiteboul, S., Goldman, R., Quass, D., and Widom, J., 1997, Lore: a database management System for semistructured data, SIGMOD Record, 26(3), September 1997, Pages 54-66.

[13]   Mittendorf, E., and Schauble, P., 1994, Document and Passage Retrieval Based on Hidden Markov Models, In Proceedings of the Seventeenth Annual International ACM SIGIR Conference on Research and Development in Information Retrieval, Dublin, Ireland, July, 1994, Pages 318-327.

[14]   Myaeng, S., Jang, D., Kim, M. and Zhoo Z., 1998, A flexible model for retrieval of SGML documents, In Proceedings of the 21st Annual International ACM SIGIR Conference on Research and Development in Information Retrieval, Melbourne, Australia, 1998, Pages 138-145.

[15]   Salton, G., Allan, J. and Singhall, A., 1996, Automatic Text Decomposition and Structuring, Information Processing and Management. 32(2), Pages 127-138.

[16]   Wilkinson, R., 1994, Effective retrieval of structured document, In Proceedings of the Seventeenth Annual International ACM SIGIR Conference on Research and Development in Information Retrieval, Dublin, 1994, Pages 311-317.

Construction of a Test Collection for the Focussed Retrieval of Structured Documents

Gabriella Kazai, Mounia Lalmas, and Jane Reid

Department of Computer Science
Queen Mary, University of London, London, E1 4NS
{gabs,mounia,jane}@dcs.qmul.ac.uk

Abstract. In this paper, we examine the methodological issues involved in constructing test collections of structured documents and obtaining best entry points for the evaluation of the focussed retrieval of document components. We describe a pilot test of the proposed test collection construction methodology performed on a document collection of Shakespeare plays. In our analysis, we examine the effect of query complexity and type on overall query difficulty, the use of multiple relevance judges for each query, the problem of obtaining exhaustive relevance assessments from participants, and the method of eliciting relevance assessments and best entry points. Our findings indicate that the methodology is indeed feasible in this small-scale context, and merits further investigation.

1 Introduction

With the widespread use of hypermedia and the rapid adoption of the XML markup language on the Web, there is a growing need to exploit the structural characteristics of documents for the purpose of retrieval. Structure can be found both within an individual document, e.g. a report may contain sections and subsections, and between documents, e.g. Web documents may be connected by hyperlinks. Structured document retrieval (SDR) attempts to exploit such structural information by retrieving documents based on combined structure and content information. This approach has several advantages, including improvement of retrieval effectiveness (e.g. [1], [2], [3], [4], [5], [6]), reduction of user effort (e.g. [7], [8]) and reduction of time and disorientation during the search process (e.g. [9]).

Structural information can be exploited at several stages of the information retrieval (IR) process. Firstly, it can be used at the indexing stage. At this stage, document components are identified and indexed as separate, but related, units. Secondly, structural information can be used at the retrieval stage. There have been three main groups of approaches to SDR. Passage retrieval approaches retrieve documents based on the most relevant passage(s) ([10], [4], [11]). Data modeling approaches employ data models for representation and querying with respect to document content and structure ([12], [13]). Aggregation-based approaches calculate

F. Sebastiani (Ed.): ECIR 2003, LNCS 2633, pp. 88-103, 2003.

the relevance of document parts based on the aggregation of their own representations and those of their structurally related parts ([14], [15], [6], [16]). Thirdly, structural information can be used at the results presentation stage. This may be achieved by several different methods. Related objects may be placed together in sub-lists in a traditional-style ranked document list, or grouped together into clusters. Results presentation may be focussed by presentation of selected document components only, rather than all relevant document components. This approach is referred to as *focussed retrieval*. Focussed retrieval is an aggregation-based approach to SDR that combines the browsing and querying paradigms to return the *best entry points* to a structured document. A best entry point (BEP) is a document component from which the user can obtain optimal access by browsing to relevant document components ([9], [17]).

Although SDR systems have already been built, comprehensive evaluation of these systems has not yet been performed[1]. The standard method of evaluating IR systems is by means of a test collection, and the standard measure used is that of retrieval effectiveness ([18], chapter 3). However, traditional test collections (e.g. [19]) are not suitable for evaluating SDR systems because they do not take account of the structural information in the collection, i.e. relevance assessments are made at a document level only. Furthermore, a test collection intended to evaluate an SDR system employing focussed retrieval would also require the ability to evaluate best entry points.

In this paper we discuss the requirements for constructing a structured document test collection for the evaluation of focussed retrieval of structured documents (Section 2). We describe a pilot test of the proposed test collection construction methodology performed on a collection of publicly available Shakespeare plays (Section 3). The outcome of our pilot test is the Shakespeare test collection, available for public use at http://qmir.dcs.qmul.ac.uk/Focus/resources.htm. It comprises 12 XML documents, 43 user queries, relevance assessments and BEPs. The methodology employed in our pilot test collection construction allows us to investigate test collection characteristics and user behaviour during the process of relevance judgement. We evaluate the test collection construction methodology, focussing on the effect of query complexity and type on overall query difficulty, the use of multiple relevance judges for each query, the problem of obtaining exhaustive relevance assessments from participants, and the method of eliciting relevance assessments and BEPs (Section 4). We close with conclusions and future work in Section 5.

2   Structured Document Test Collection Requirements

The aim of a test collection construction methodology is to derive a set of queries and relevance assessments for a given document collection. This aim is typically achieved by setting up an experimental study with the document collection and a set of participants. The methodology for constructing a *structured document* test collection has additional, specific requirements relating to the structural information contained in the document collection. Decisions therefore need to be made about several aspects

---

[1] The first large-scale SDR evaluation initiative, INEX (http://qmir.dcs.qmul.ac.uk/inex/) has just ended.

of the methodology before the experiment is performed. The next five sub-sections discuss the requirements for each stage of the structured document test collection construction methodology (Fig. 1) in more detail.

2.1   Documents

There are many different kinds of structure, so the first choice that has to be made is what kind of documents to include in the structured document test collection. The documents could exhibit internal structure (logical structured documents), or external structure (linked Web documents), or a mixture of the two. In the case of linked documents, the links could be either semantic or structural. The nature of the documents chosen also depends on whether a data-centric or document-centric viewpoint is adopted [5]. From the data-centric viewpoint, structured documents serve as containers for data exchange between applications. The document-centric viewpoint, on the other hand, treats documents as traditional textual units, augmented by structural data. To evaluate systems based on the data-centric view, synthetic XML data may be used; however, to evaluate content-based retrieval of structured documents, real-world documents are required.

2.2   Participants

It is normal to recruit participants who are expert in the document collection domain. It is also desirable to choose participants who have real information needs, i.e. who are motivated to take part in the experiment.

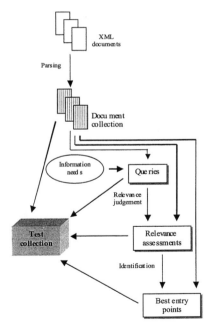

Fig. 1. The structured document test collection construction methodology

2.3   Queries

The format and topic of the queries should be representative of the variety of real user requests that users of the document collection may issue. Queries may take one of several forms, ranging from the actual search statement itself to an expanded version containing supplementary information (e.g. TREC topics [19]). The queries in a structured document test collection should also reflect the additional functionality of structured query languages, i.e. that it is possible to query by structure as well as content. According to this new criterion we can identify the following three types of queries: Content-only, Structure-only, and Content-and-structure.

Content-only queries are the standard type of query in IR. They describe a topic of interest to the user and are represented, in most retrieval systems, by keywords. The need for this type of query in a structured document test collection stems from the fact that users are often unable or unwilling to restrict their search to a specific structural unit. This provides a challenge for SDR systems, since they must not only locate relevant document components, but also identify the appropriate level of granularity.

Structure-only queries do not contain any reference to the content or topic of the information need, but pertain only to the structure of the document collection and/or individual documents. Examples of such queries are "Retrieve the section title and first paragraph of Section 2.3", and "Retrieve those web pages that are linked from this page". In this case, retrieval is based on matching between the query requirements and the structural data about the collection (structure index).

Content-and-structure queries combine topical and structural requirements. An example of such a query is "Retrieve the title and the first paragraph of sections about wine-making in the Rhine region". In this case, retrieval requires matching on both the content index and the structure index of the document collection.

2.4   Relevance Assessments

Relevance assessments are then gathered. Two principal decisions need to be made regarding the relevance judgement process: 1) Will there be one judge per query, or more than one? and 2) Will the relevance assessments be binary or multi-valued?

In addition, in a document collection with multiple structural levels, relevance assessments must be derived for each structural level. However, this cannot be achieved by the simple strategy of asking judges to judge each possible structural unit, for two reasons. Firstly, this would be incredibly resource-intensive, especially for large-scale document collections. Secondly, it would be very difficult for judges to assign accurate and consistent relevance assessments in a multiple-layer structure. A choice of structural level for relevance assessments must therefore be made. A possible choice is the smallest structural unit. Relevance assessments at the lowest structural level can allow for the automatic computation of relevance of higher structural levels by a process of relevance propagation. A *pessimistic* propagation strategy would judge a containing element relevant to a given query only if all of its contained elements were relevant. An *optimistic* strategy would judge a containing element relevant to a given query if at least one of its contained elements were relevant. This process could not easily be carried out in the opposite direction, i.e.

given relevance assessments at a higher structural level, it is usually not possible to derive the relevance of lower structural levels.

In the case of XML documents, the smallest structural element corresponds to the last elements of a containment chain [20]. In the case of logically structured documents, a paragraph or a sentence could be set as the lowest level. In the case of a web site, the individual web pages of the site could be considered as the smallest structural units.

2.5   Best Entry Points (BEPs)

An additional requirement for test collections intended to evaluate focussed SDR systems is to identify BEPs for the given queries. BEP identification should be performed by the same participants who performed the relevance judgement, since they are already familiar with the given queries. The selection of BEPs requires the use of an interface that allows the participants to browse the document structure, including the relevance assessments. The purpose of the interface is to show the context of the relevance assessments, and allow the user to form an intuitive understanding of the costs associated with finding relevant document components from potential BEPs.

The interface should support the following browsing behaviour:

1.   Next. The user moves to the next sequential unit at the same structural level.
2.   Previous. The user moves to the previous sequential unit at the same structural level.
3.   Up. The user moves up a level in the hierarchical structure.
4.   Down. The user moves down a level in the hierarchical structure.

The next section provides a detailed description of the Shakespeare test collection experiment, taking into account the factors discussed above.

3   The Shakespeare Test Collection Experiment

Our aim was to construct a focussed structured document collection by performing a pilot test, which would take into account the methodological issues discussed in Section 2. In this section, we introduce the basic elements of this pilot test. Section 3.1 describes the document collection, and Section 3.2 discusses the participants who were recruited to take part in the experiment. Section 3.3 describes the test collection construction methodology itself.

3.1   Document Collection

The document collection used as the basis of this experiment consists of 37 Shakespeare plays. This material was chosen because of the unusual characteristics of the data. This is in contrast to many of the studies on test collections, which use computer-related data and participants because of their accessibility.

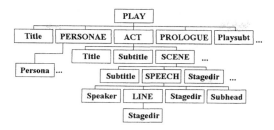

Fig. 2. Part of the Shakespeare collection's XML structure

The plays, marked up originally in XML by Jon Bosak, were downloaded from the Web (http://www.ibiblio.org/bosak/). They were then parsed to identify each piece of content enclosed by XML tags as retrievable entities. The parser assigns a unique object identification number to each retrievable XML element and stores this as an attribute of the corresponding XML tag. Figure 2 shows part of the XML document structure. The maximum depth of nested XML elements is 6.

A total of 179,689 elements were identified in the 37 plays. Twelve plays were then selected for the final test collection on the basis of participant familiarity. The twelve plays are: Antony and Cleopatra, A Midsummer Night's Dream, Hamlet, Julius Caesar, King Lear, Macbeth, Much Ado About Nothing, Othello, Romeo and Juliet, The Tempest, Troilus and Cressida, and Twelfth Night. On average each of the 12 chosen plays contains 5,096 elements, including 5 acts, 21 scenes, 892 speeches and 3,311 lines.

3.2   Participants

Sixteen students from the undergraduate BA in English Literature and Drama at Queen Mary, University of London originally signed up for the experiment. Fourteen were selected on the basis of their Shakespeare knowledge. However, three dropped out after failing to complete the first task, so the final group of participants consisted of eleven students (five first years, two second years, four third years). The time required to complete the experiment was estimated at approximately seven hours, and payment was fixed at £40, to be paid on completion of all the tasks.

The participants were asked to choose 3 Shakespeare plays with which they were familiar. A questionnaire was administered to all participants to gather data about their interest in Shakespeare, their skill in the use of electronic resources and their familiarity with their chosen plays. Five of the participants were interested in Shakespeare for personal reasons (e.g. they enjoyed the language), five for academic reasons (i.e. reasons related to their current course or their future career) and one participant was interested for both personal and academic reasons. All the students were familiar with the Internet, and all used Internet search engines on a regular basis, but only one had used a full-text poetry database before.

Participants were asked to rate their familiarity with their chosen plays on a five-point scale (1 = very well, 5 = not well at all). Ranked by familiarity on the part of the participants, the two most confident students gave a rating of 1.00 for all their plays. The least confident student scored an average of 2.83 (across all chosen plays). The average score across all participants was 1.74. Ranked by play, The Tempest was the best known play, with a rating of 1.00 from all the participants who chose it. Troilus and Cressida was the worst known play, with a rating of 3.25 across all the participants who chose it. Data about participants' familiarity with their chosen plays was collated, and 12 plays selected on the basis that 2-3 participants were familiar with each play.

3.3   The Shakespeare Test Collection Methodology

The experiment was carried out in 3 stages: obtaining queries, gathering relevance assessments and identifying BEPs.

Obtaining queries

Participants were asked to produce queries for each of their plays. They were asked to formulate queries (i.e. search statements) that addressed real information needs, and covered topics that were of interest to them and for which they were motivated to seek the answers. It was desirable to obtain queries of varying complexity, and two main types of queries were identified in this context:

1. Factual queries, where it is likely that a small number of short, simple passages will provide the answer. An example query is "How old is Juliet?"
2. Essay-topic queries, where it is likely that reference will have to be made to many, complex passages. An example query is "The character of Lady Macbeth".

An additional criterion, as discussed in Section 2.3, was that the queries contained a mixture of content-only, structure-only (e.g. 'What is the title of the second scene?"), and content-and-structure queries (e.g. including a structural condition like "at the beginning of the play").

A total of 215 queries were obtained, with an average of 18 per play and 19.5 per participant. Of this pool, 43 queries were finally selected for the latter stages of the study (Table 1). The following selection criteria were employed:

1. No more than 4 queries per play, due to the limited number of participants
2. A maximum of one factual query per play
3. Queries of varying complexity should be selected for each play

Table 1. Distribution of queries across query categories

	Content-only	Content-and-structure	*Total*
Factual	9	2	*11*
Essay-topic	26	6	*32*
Total	*35*	*8*	*43*

Relevance Assessments

In this study we used binary assessments collected from multiple judges. The obvious way of obtaining the relevance assessments would have been by employing the pooling method often used in IR research [21]. This method allows the identification of a smaller, optimal pool of document components for relevance judgement from a large-scale document collection. However, at the time of this study, only one SDR system was available to us, so the decision was taken to provide the participants with printed versions of their plays and associated queries, and ask them to highlight the relevant passages on the printed document by hand. This was considered an acceptable solution in this context, since the students were already familiar with the plays, and the document collection was comparatively small-scale. Relevant passages were described as those that they would consult (read or reference) in order to answer a given query. The participants were given one week to complete this task.

The relevant passages were treated at the lowest structural level, referred to as leaf level elements, as described in Section 2.4. As a result, we obtained 117 sets of relevance assessments, totaling 6,296 leaf level XML elements, from the 11 participants for the 43 queries. The multiple sets of relevance assessments were then pooled for each query to derive the final set of relevance assessments for the test collection. Merging the different sets of relevance assessments, we obtained a total of 4,898 unique leaf level XML elements in 43 query sets. The average number of relevant leaf level XML elements is 114 per query. Since there is only one relevant play for each query, and given that a play contains, on average, 5,096 elements, the relevant elements for a given query represent 2.23% of the play.

Best Entry Points (BEPs)

BEPs were solicited by interviewing the participants individually. An interview lasted approximately 2 hours, and was divided into 3 stages. Stage 1 (10 – 15 minutes) involved the completion of a questionnaire regarding their own background knowledge and interests, together with some questions about the tasks (Section 4). Stage 2 (20 – 30 minutes) involved the participants explaining how they had interpreted a given query and why they had judged particular texts as relevant. Stage 3 (75 – 90 minutes) involved the participants choosing best entry points for each of their queries. The BEPs were identified by consulting the pooled relevance assessments of all the participants assigned to that individual query. It should be noted that the BEPs did not have to be elements that had been judged relevant, but were, in some cases, non-relevant container or contained elements. The participants were aided in their selection of BEPs by the use of a user interface (Fig. 3) that explicitly showed both the structure and content of the plays, and clearly highlighted the elements that had been marked relevant by at least one participant. They were asked to identify the BEPs as elements that they would prefer to be retrieved by a search engine in response to a query.

Each play was viewed in an expandable / collapsible tree view. The queries were presented in a drop-down list at the top of the screen. Users could either select a query from this list, or type it into the text box directly. Once a query was entered, the tree view section of the window was updated to display the appropriate play and relevance assessments. Each higher level structural element, such as SCENE or SPEECH, could be expanded to view its lower level child nodes, or could be collapsed to hide its child nodes. By default, all non-relevant elements appeared collapsed and all relevant elements appeared expanded. Relevant elements were marked with a red arrow. Users could also scroll up and down the text.

Fig. 3. User interface for best entry point selection

A total of 928 BEPs were collected from the 11 participants for the 43 queries, in 117 sets. This number was reduced to 512 by removing duplicate elements. The BEPs for each query, as judged by each participant, were then combined to form the final set of BEPs; only elements judged as BEPs by the majority of the participants were included. This was to avoid the problem of multiple BEPs representing the same cluster of relevant elements, e.g. two individual participants choosing two different lines of the same speech as best entry points. The average number of BEPs per query in the final set was 21.58 for non-unique elements and 12.12 for unique elements.

4   Analysis

In our analysis, we focus on an evaluation of the methodology employed in the Shakespeare user study.

Firstly, we examined the effect of query complexity (factual vs. essay-topic) and query type (content-only vs. content-and-structure) on the participants' assessment of the difficulty level of the queries. As mentioned in Section 3.3, we administered a questionnaire to the participants, in which we asked them to rate each query they judged with respect to two dimensions, using a five-point scale (1 = very easy, 5 = very difficult). The two dimensions were: 1) How easy it was to understand the query, and 2) How easy it was to find the answers.

We obtained an estimate of the overall difficulty of each query by averaging the scores for the two dimensions over all the participants who judged that query. Scores were then averaged across all queries belonging to an individual query category (Table 2).

Table 2. Query difficulty for different query categories

Query category	Ease of understanding	Ease of finding answer	Average difficulty
Factual	1.20	1.55	1.37
Essay-topic	1.83	2.39	2.11
Content-only	1.60	2.06	1.83
Content-and-structure	1.96	2.67	2.31
Overall average	*1.66*	*2.18*	*1.92*

We can see that the participants generally found it easier to understand the queries than to find the answers, despite the fact that most participants reported a high level of familiarity with the plays they were using. The ordering of the query categories was the same for both dimensions, and the average difficulty reflects this. Factual queries were found to be easiest, as might have been expected from the small number of relevant objects generally required for these queries. Content-and-structure queries were found to be the most difficult, as they require both content and structural constraints to be fulfilled; this implies an increased amount of effort in identifying relevant objects.

Secondly, we analysed the feasibility of involving multiple participants in assessing each individual query by examining the degree of agreement among the multiple sets of relevance assessments and BEPs. Several studies have examined agreement between relevance assessors (e.g. [22]); however, BEP agreement has not yet been studied. Furthermore, few test collections have employed multiple relevance judges; one exception to this is [23]. We therefore measured the overlap for both the relevant object and BEP sets, where overlap was defined as the size of the intersection of the relevant sets divided by the size of the union of the relevant sets [24].

Since BEPs could be of any structural level, it was possible to examine BEP agreement directly at different structural levels; BEP agreement was also calculated across *all* levels. It should be noted that there were no BEPs at ACT level, and only one at PLAY level. However, it was not possible to make this direct comparison at different structural levels for relevance assessments, since those were made at leaf level only (97% were LINE objects). We therefore created *extrapolated relevance assessments* at higher structural levels by assuming relevance at the structural level above that of the relevance assessment on which it was based. An optimistic relevance extrapolation strategy was used [16]; for example, if one line was marked as relevant, relevance was extrapolated to the (complete) speech containing that line, and so on.

The resulting relevant object and BEP agreement data can be found in Tables 3 and 4, respectively. The data shows that (extrapolated) relevance agreement increases consistently with structural level, except for content-and-structure queries at speech level. This exception may be due to the fact that the location of relevant material is already constrained by the structural element of the query, so agreement does not show improvement at the higher structural level. Overall, participants may not always agree on the exact context of the relevant object, but tend to agree on the general area in which the relevant objects can be found. The results also show that query type and complexity do not have a strong effect on relevance agreement, although factual queries show slightly higher relevance agreement at most structural levels.

Table 3. Average relevance agreement for different query categories across structural levels

Query category	Leaf-level	Speech	Scene	Act
Factual	35%	43%	59%	84%
Essay-topic	27%	30%	68%	76%
Content-only	29%	35%	65%	80%
Content-and-structure	30%	30%	63%	73%
Overall average	*31%*	*35%*	*64%*	*78%*

Table 4. Average BEP agreement for different query categories across structural levels.

Query category	Leaf-level	Speech	Scene	Act	Play	All levels
Factual	63%	52%	67%	---	---	67%
Essay-topic	46%	62%	41%	---	0%	57%
Content-only	55%	60%	45%	---	---	62%
Content-and-structure	35%	59%	50%	---	0%	53%
Overall average	*49%*	*58%*	*51%*	*---*	*0%*	*60%*

Agreement is better for BEPs than relevance assessments for all categories at leaf and speech level. Agreement then deteriorates at higher structural levels, except for factual queries. This exception may be due to the fact that factual queries have a lower number of relevant objects than queries from other categories, so there was less potential for disagreement between participants. The general deterioration may be heavily influenced by the reduced number of BEPs at higher levels. Another, related reason for this result might be the optimistic method of relevance extrapolation employed. This implies that there will be more relevant objects at higher structural levels, and the number of BEPs at higher structural levels may thus appear artificially low in comparison.

Overall, we can see that a reasonable level of BEP agreement is achieved for all query categories across all structural levels (with the exception of PLAY), showing that the concept of BEP is an intuitive one for our participants. However, relevance agreement is rather low, especially for leaf-level elements. Although comparative evaluation of retrieval systems has proved robust in the face of quite large differences between relevance judges [24], these results show that BEPs would clearly provide a more stable basis for retrieval.

Thirdly, we examined the issue of eliciting exhaustive, rather than merely selective, relevance assessments from the participants, in order to explore whether this might explain the relatively low relevance agreement. Participants were asked directly, in the course of the interview (Section 3.3, Best Entry Points), to state, for each query they judged, whether they had made exhaustive or selective relevance assessments. Percentage exhaustiveness of relevance assessment sets was then calculated for each query, over all participants who judged that query. The results for different query categories can be seen in Table 5. It should be noted that BEPs were chosen after a full review of the associated relevance judgements and in discussion with the interviewer, and may, therefore, safely be regarded as exhaustive.

Table 5. Exhaustiveness of relevance assessments for different query categories

Query category	Exhaustiveness
Factual	48%
Essay-topic	65%
Content-only	60%
Content-and-structure	62%
Overall average	*60%*

Most of the query categories show a similar level of exhaustiveness, with the exception of factual queries. This exception can be explained by the fact that participants often stopped searching for further relevant passages once they felt they had found the answer to a factual query. These results confirm that the low level of relevance agreement may have been partially due to selective relevance assessments. This indicates that use of the pooling method for obtaining relevance assessments is strongly recommended in order to identify an optimal subset of documents for relevance judgement. Given this modification, we can conclude that the collection of relevance assessments and BEPs from multiple judges should, indeed, prove feasible in practice.

Finally, we assessed the effect of soliciting relevance assessments at leaf-level only, in order to explore whether users are influenced into choosing relevant objects and BEPs at this lowest structural level. We examined two factors, for different query categories:

1. For relevance assessments, the number of full speeches considered relevant as a proportion of the number of speeches of which at least one line was considered relevant (Table 6).
2. For BEPs, the proportion of BEPs at different structural levels (Table 7).

We can see from these results that relevance assessments usually consist of complete speeches, rather than single lines. Over all query categories, only 22.3% of the full speeches considered relevant were found to consist of a single line only. This shows that participants did not feel pressurised into choosing single lines as relevant objects. In fact, the most natural structural level for relevance assessments, from the users' viewpoint, was clearly speech level.

Table 6. Proportion of speeches considered relevant for different query categories

Query category	Proportion of speeches considered completely relevant
Factual	95%
Essay-topic	92%
Content-only	93%
Content-and-structure	93%
Overall average	*93%*

Table 7. Distribution of BEPs for different query categories across structural levels

Query category	Leaf-level	Speech	Scene	Act	Play	Other	Total
Factual	2.93 (58%)	1.67 (33%)	0.18 (4%)	0 (0%)	0 (0%)	0.30 (6%)	5.09 (100%)
Essay-topic	3.66 (41%)	4.73 (53%)	0.52 (6%)	0 (0%)	0.01 (0%)	0.03 (0%)	8.95 (100%)
Content-only	3.95 (46%)	4.21 (49%)	0.45 (5%)	0 (0%)	0 (0%)	0.06 (1%)	8.67 (100%)
Content-and-structure	1.39 (29%)	2.79 (57%)	0.35 (7%)	0 (0%)	0.03 (1%)	0.29 (6%)	4.86 (100%)
Overall average	*3.48 (44%)*	*3.95 (50%)*	*0.44 (5%)*	*0 (0%)*	*0.01 (0%)*	*0.10 (1%)*	*7.97 (100%)*

Although the total number of BEPs differs considerably according to query category, their relative distribution across structural levels is rather similar for all query categories. Overall, the majority of BEPs were selected from leaf or speech levels, together accounting for 94% of all BEPs. Speech level was the most common, with the exception of factual queries, for which leaf-level BEPs were most common. This slightly different pattern for factual queries can be explained by the nature of the queries themselves, which involve a question-answering, rather than an evidence-gathering process. The "answer" to factual queries is, therefore, likely to be contained in fewer, lower-level contexts.

These results show that the participants were not influenced by the choice of leaf-level as the basis for relevance assessments. This means that the strategy of choosing a lowest structural level, with a view to propagating relevance to higher structural levels at a later stage, is feasible as well as desirable, since it reduces the complexity of the methodology as well as the time taken to perform the experiment. Further support for the relevance judgement process could be provided in the form of an interface similar to that used during the BEP phase of this study (Section 2.5).

5   Conclusions

This paper proposes a methodology for the construction of structured document test collections. We address the additional requirements imposed by structured document retrieval, and by focussed retrieval in particular, over standard IR. We carried out a pilot test of the proposed methodology, which resulted in the construction of the Shakespeare test collection. In our analysis of the resulting data, we focussed on an evaluation of the methodology employed in the user study.

Firstly, we found that factual queries were considered the easiest, and content-and-structure queries the most difficult, due to the combination of content and structural constraints that have to be fulfilled.

Secondly, we discovered that (extrapolated) relevance agreement increases consistently with structural level for most query categories, with factual queries showing a slightly increased relevance agreement at most structural levels. BEP agreement is higher than relevance agreement at lower structural levels, but usually deteriorates slightly at higher levels. The low level of relevance agreement, compared to BEP agreement, may be at least partially due to participants employing selective, rather than exhaustive, relevance assessments. However, if the pooling method is used to obtain relevance assessments, it is anticipated that a more satisfactory level of agreement will be achieved. We therefore conclude that the collection of relevance assessments and BEPs from multiple judges is, indeed, feasible in practice, and that the use of BEPs will provide a stable basis for focussed SDR.

Lastly, our analysis showed that, in fact, relevance assessments almost always consist of complete speeches, rather than single lines. The majority of BEPs were also selected from speech level. The apparent preference for speech level is further supported by analysis of information seeking behaviour from this study [25] and from a follow-on, small-scale user study [26]. We can conclude, therefore, that participants were not unduly influenced by the choice of leaf-level as the basis for relevance assessments. This means that the strategy of choosing a lowest structural level, with a view to propagating relevance to higher structural levels at a later stage, is a sensible and feasible one.

Recent work has built on the results reported in this paper. The methodology was modified and used successfully in the INEX Initiative [27]. This involved the construction of a large-scale test collection based on a document collection of more than 12,000 scientific articles provided by the IEEE Computer Society. Ongoing work aims to identify what further adaptation is necessary to use the standard test collection evaluation methodology in the context of SDR, e.g. adaptation of recall and precision measures. Finally, further work will focus on an in-depth examination of the characteristics of factual queries, which appear to yield different results from other query categories for many of the factors we examined.

Acknowledgement

This work was carried out under EPSRC grant number GR/N37612.

References

[1]   Brin, S., Page, L.: The Anatomy of a Large-scale Hypertextual Web Search Engine. In: 7th WWW Conference, Brisbane, Australia (1998)

[2]   Silva, I., Ribeiro-Neto, B., Calado, P., Moura, E., Ziviani, N.: Link-Based and Content-Based Evidential Information in a Belief Network Model. In: 23rd ACM-SIGIR, Athens (2000)

[3]   Géry, M., Chevallet, J-P.:Toward a Structured Information Retrieval System on the Web: Automatic Structure Extraction of Web Pages. In: Pre-Proceedings of the International Workshop on Web Dynamics, London (2001)

[4]   Wilkinson, R.: Effective Retrieval of Structured Documents. In: 17th ACM-SIGIR, Dublin (1994) 311-317

[5]   Kotsakis, E.: Structured Information Retrieval in XML documents. In: Proceedings of the 17th ACM Symposium on Applied Computing (SAC'02), Madrid, Spain (2002)

[6]   Myaeng, S., Jang, D.H., Kim, M.S., Zhoo, Z.C.: A Flexible Model for Retrieval of SGML Documents. In: 21st ACM-SIGIR, Melbourne, Australia (1998) 138-145

[7]   Roelleke, T.: POOL: Probabilistic Object-Oriented Logical Representation and Retrieval of Complex Objects - A Model for Hypermedia Retrieval, Ph.D. Thesis, University of Dortmund, Verlag-Shaker (1999)

[8]   Fuhr, N., Großjohann K.: XIRQL: A Query Language for Information Retrieval in XML Documents. In: 24th ACM-SIGIR, New Orleans (2001) 172-180

[9]   Chiaramella, Y., Mulhem, P., Fourel, F.: A Model for Multimedia Information Retrieval, Technical Report Fermi ESPRIT BRA 8134, University of Glasgow (1996)

[10]   Callan, J.: Passage-Level Evidence in Document Retrieval. In: 17th ACM SIGIR, Dublin (1994) 302-310

[11]   Salton, G., Allan, J., Buckley, C.: Approaches to Passage Retrieval in Full Text Information Systems. In: 16th ACM SGIR, Pittsburgh (1993) 49-58

[12]   Burkowski, F.J.: Retrieval Activities in a Database Consisting of Heterogeneous Collections of Structured Texts. In: 15th ACM SIGIR, Copenhagen (1992) 112-125

[13]   Navarro, G., Baeza-Yates, R.: A Language for Queries on Structure and Content of Textual Databases. In: 18th ACM-SIGIR, Seattle (1995) 93-101

[14]   Frisse, M.: Searching for Information in a Hypertext Medical Handbook. Communications of the ACM 31 (1988) 880-886

[15]   Lalmas, M., Moutogianni, E.: A Dempster-Shafer Indexing for the Focussed Retrieval of a Hierarchically Structured Document Space: Implementation and Experiments on a Web Museum Collection. In: 6th RIAO Conference on Content-Based Multimedia Information Access, Paris (2000)

[16]   Roelleke, T., Lalmas, M., Kazai, G., Ruthven, I., Quicker, S.: The Accessibility Dimension for Structured Document Retrieval. In: 24th European Conference on Information Retrieval Research (ECIR'02), Glasgow (2002)

[17]   Kazai, G., Lalmas, M., Roelleke, T.: A Model for the Representation and Focussed Retrieval of Structured Documents based on Fuzzy Aggregation. In: String Processing and Information Retrieval (SPIRE 2001), Laguna De San Rafael, Chile (2001)

[18]   Baeza-Yates, R., Ribeiro-Neto, B.: Modern Information Retrieval. Addison Wesley (1999)

[19]   http://www.trec.nist.gov. TREC web site

[20]   Chinenyanga, T.P., Kushmerick, N.: Expressive Retrieval from XML Documents. In: 24th ACM-SIGIR, New Orleans (2001) 163-171

[21]   Harman, D.K.: The TREC Conferences. In: Kuhlen, R., Rittberger, M. (eds.): Hypertext - Information Retrieval - Multimedia: Proceedings of HIM 95, Konstanz, Germany (1995) 9-28

[22] Janes, J.W.: Other People's Judgments: A Comparison of Users' and Others' Judgments of Document Relevance, Topicality and Utility. Journal of the American Society of Information Science 45 (1994) 160-171

[23] Shaw, W.M., Wood, J.B., Wood, R.E., Tibbo, H.R.: The Cystic Fibrosis Database: Content and Research Opportunities. Library and Information Science Research 13 (1991) 347-366

[24] Vorhees, E.M.: Variations in Relevance Judgments and the Measurement of Retrieval Effectiveness. In: Croft, W.B., Moffat, A., van Rijsbergen, C.J., Wilkinson, R., Zobel, J. (eds.): 21st ACM-SIGIR, Melbourne (1998) 315-323

[25] Lalmas, M., Reid, J., Hertzum, M.: Information Seeking Behaviour in the Context of Structured Documents. In preparation

[26] Finesilver, K., Reid J. User behaviour in the Context of Structured Documents. To appear in: 25th European Conference on Information Retrieval Research (ECIR'03), Pisa (2003)

[27] Fuhr, N., Goevert, N., Kazai, G., Lalmas, M. (eds.): INEX Proceedings, Schloss Dagstuhl (2002)

User Behaviour in the Context of Structured Documents

Karen Finesilver and Jane Reid

Open and Distance Learning Unit / Department of Computer Science
Queen Mary, University of London, London, E1 4NS
karen@odl.qmul.ac.uk
jane@dcs.qmul.ac.uk

Abstract. This paper describes a small-scale experimental study examining user behaviour in the context of structured documents. Two variants of the same interface to support information seeking were implemented, one highlighting relevant objects and one highlighting best entry points (BEPs). BEPs are intended to support users' natural information seeking behaviour by providing optimal starting points for browsing to relevant objects. Analysis of the results from the comparative study of these two interfaces shows that the BEP interface was strongly preferred to the relevant object interface, and that appropriate usage of BEPs can lead to improved task performance. However, the study also highlighted shortcomings related to the inconsistent nature of BEPs and to BEP interface design.

1 Introduction

Document collections often display structural characteristics. Structure can be internal, e.g. sections within an individual document, or external, e.g. hyperlinks between web documents. Structured document retrieval (SDR) aims to combine structural and content information in order to improve retrieval effectiveness (e.g. [1], [2], [3], [4], [5]), support users in identifying relevant information quickly and efficiently (e.g. [6], [7]), and relieve problems caused by distance between related document components in results interfaces (e.g. [8]).

Structural information can be exploited at all stages of the information retrieval process: indexing ([9], [10]), retrieval and results presentation. This paper focusses on the last two stages, specifically: the use of aggregation-based approaches to SDR, which calculate the relevance of document components based on the aggregation of their own representations and those of their structurally related components ([11], [12], [5], [13]); and results presentation methods designed to support information seeking behaviour in the context of structured documents. There are several methods of employing structural information in results presentation, e.g. fisheye views to enable effective browsing of large documents [14]; expand-collapse functionality to support focus on, and movement between, particular structural elements of documents [15]; and use of clustering or sub-lists of related objects by web search engines (Google, Northern Light). Results presentation may also be focussed by presentation

F. Sebastiani (Ed.): ECIR 2003, LNCS 2633, pp. 104–119, 2003.

of selected document components only, rather than all relevant document components; this approach is referred to as *focussed retrieval.*

Focussed retrieval is an aggregation-based approach to SDR that acknowledges the importance of users' natural browsing behaviour, and combines the browsing and querying paradigms to return *best entry points* to structured documents. A best entry point (BEP) is a document component from which the user can obtain optimal access, by browsing, to relevant document components ([8], [16]). The use of BEPs instead of relevant document components as the basic units of the results list is thus intended to support information seeking behaviour, and enable users to gain more effective and efficient access to relevant information items.

This paper describes a small-scale experimental study that aims to examine:
Usage and effectiveness of BEPs and relevant objects in the context of task performance
User behaviour in the context of structured documents

Section 2 presents the experimental methodology employed. Section 3 analyses the main results of the study in terms of questionnaire data, composition of objects chosen during searching, information seeking behaviour, and task performance. Section 4 discusses correlations between these different elements, the relationship of our results to previous research on BEPs, and implications of our results for interface design for focussed SDR systems. We close with conclusions and further work in Section 5.

2   Experimental Methodology

In order to examine the usage and effectiveness of BEPs and relevant objects in the context of task performance, we required access to pre-defined queries, relevance assessments and BEP judgements. This section describes the focussed structured document test collection used in the study (Section 2.1), the participants (Section 2.2), the system developed for the study (Section 2.3), and the experimental design (Section 2.4).

2.1   Test Collection

The test collection used was the Shakespeare test collection, publicly available at http://qmir.dcs.qmw.ac.uk/Focus/resources.htm. The test collection is based on a document collection of 12 Shakespeare plays, which forms a subset of the complete collection of Shakespeare plays marked up in XML by Jon Bosak (available from the web at http://www.ibiblio.org/bosak/). Every individual object in the collection has a unique object ID, which is stored as an attribute of the object's XML tags. The main structural objects are PLAY, ACT, SCENE, SPEECH and LINE (Fig. 1). In addition, there is a small number of other tags, e.g. Persona, Stagedir (stage directions).

The test collection also contains 43 queries, each of which relates to one of the 12 plays. The queries are grouped on two dimensions [17]: query type (content-only or content-and-structure) and query complexity (factual or essay-topic).

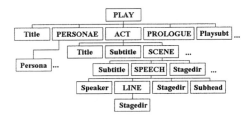

Fig. 1. Part of the Shakespeare collection's XML structure

Queries have associated *leaf-level multi-judge relevance assessments*, which are stored as attributes of the corresponding relevant objects' XML tags. Each query has been judged by 2-4 judges (average 2.75 judges per query), and all relevance assessments are at leaf-level (97% of all relevance assessments are LINE or Stagedir objects).

Each query also has a set of BEPs associated with it, which, like the relevance assessments, are stored as attributes of the corresponding objects' XML tags. BEPs are intended to support users' natural information seeking behaviour by providing entry points to the document structure, from which the user can browse to relevant document components. Unlike relevance assessments, BEPs can be at any structural level (44% of all BEPs in the collection are leaf objects, and 50% are speech objects). It should be noted that BEPs are, therefore, not always objects that have been judged relevant, but are, in some cases, non-relevant container or contained objects. For example, in the case of a long sequence of relevant lines, the first line of the sequence might be chosen as a BEP (*browsing BEP*). Alternatively, if a large proportion of the speeches in a scene were considered relevant, the complete scene might be chosen as a BEP (*container BEP*).

2.2   Participants

Eight undergraduate students were recruited from the Department of English and Drama at Queen Mary, University of London. Each participant was paid £10 on completion of the experiment, on the basis that it would last around 90 minutes. A Masters student was also recruited from the same department to mark the final task outcomes. She was paid £20 on completion of the marking.

2.3   System and Interface Development

The system to be used in the study was built using Borland JBuilder, with a Java interface. A data object model (DOM) was written to parse the XML Shakespeare play files and store them in data trees. These trees were then converted to JTree format (viewable tree structure) by the use of an adapter class. Relevance assessments and BEPs were read from the XML files and stored in arrays.

The user interface (Fig. 2) was designed to support both linear (at the same structural level) and hierarchical (moving between structural levels) information seeking behaviour in the context of structured documents. The interface is split into two main panes. The left-hand pane displays the structure of the play. Any object that is opened up by the user is displayed in the right-hand pane, e.g. if the user clicks on a speech in the left-hand pane, the contents of that speech are displayed in the right-hand pane. Direct hierarchical information seeking behaviour is supported by use of the left-hand structure pane. Linear information seeking is supported by use of the previous and next buttons in the top right corner of the interface, or by linear use of the left-hand structure pane (e.g. using the keyboard arrow keys).

Queries were pre-entered and chosen from a pull-down menu at the top of the screen. Two variants of the interface were developed, one with the related relevance assessments highlighted (in red), and the other with the related BEPs highlighted. The two interface variants were identical in every other respect.

Software logging was set up, in order to log, for each object selected by the participant, the object ID, the time at which it was selected, its structural level and whether the object was a BEP or a relevance assessment. A separate log was created for each participant session.

2.4   Experimental Design

Two queries were chosen from the 43 queries of the Shakespeare test collection. Since the aim of the experiment was to encourage and examine information seeking behaviour, the queries were chosen to be complex and have a high number of relevance assessments and BEPs. Two essay-topic, content-only queries were, therefore, selected:

Query 1:   "To what extent is Hamlet's madness a pretence?" (Hamlet)
Query 2:   "Give an analysis of the 'merry war' and witticism that pass between Beatrice and Benedick." (Much Ado About Nothing)

Table 1 shows a breakdown of the BEPs, RJs (relevant objects) and BEP/RJs (objects that appear in both the relevance assessment and BEP sets) for these two queries, organized by structural level. It should be noted that all RJs (and therefore also all BEP/RJs) are leaf objects.

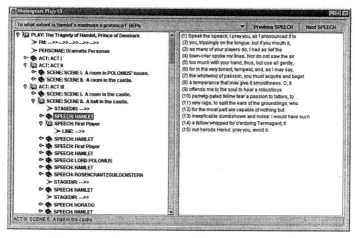

Fig. 2. Screen shot of the information seeking interface

Table 1. Breakdown of BEPs and RJs for the two chosen queries

		Structural level						
		Leaf	Speech	Scene	Act	Play	Other	Total
Hamlet	BEPs	1	23	3	0	0	0	27
	RJs	496	0	0	0	0	0	496
	BEP/RJs	13	0	0	0	0	0	13
	Total	510	23	3	0	0	0	536
Much Ado	BEPs	1	22	3	0	0	0	26
	RJs	377	0	0	0	0	0	377
	BEP/RJs	9	0	0	0	0	0	9
	Total	387	22	3	0	0	0	412

Table 2. Allocation of participants to experimental conditions

	BEP interface	RJ interface
Hamlet	Participants 1-4	Participants 5-8
Much Ado	Participants 5-8	Participants 1-4

Each participant performed both queries, one with the associated BEPs highlighted in the interface, and the other with the associated RJs highlighted (Table 2). Order of interface presentation was counterbalanced.

At the start of the session, each participant was given the chance to become familiar with the interface during a brief training session, using a different Shakespeare play; a help sheet was also issued, which explained the basic elements of the interface. The participant then had 40 minutes to perform each task, which was to write a brief answer to the question (i.e. the query itself), using the interface to find text to back up the answer (indirectly through reading or directly through referencing).

Finally, the participant was asked to fill in a questionnaire, which included questions related to background knowledge, experience of the tasks, and opinions about the interfaces.

After the experiment, the participants' answers were given to the marker, who assigned a percentage score to each answer on the basis of completeness and coverage of content.

3   Results and Analysis

This section describes the results obtained from our user study. There are 4 main sets of results: data from the participant questionnaires, analysis of the composition of the objects chosen by participants during their searching, analysis of the information seeking behaviour of participants during their searching, and task performance results in the form of percentage scores.

3.1   Questionnaire Data

The data elicited by the participant questionnaires was divided into three types: background, query-related and interface-related.

Background information concerns the participants' general familiarity with the works of Shakespeare, and their familiarity with the individual plays used in the experiment (on a scale of 1 to 5, where 1 = very familiar and 5 = not familiar at all). The average general familiarity of participants with the works of Shakespeare was 3.5 (2 participants scored 5, and none scored 1). Participants were, on average, more familiar with Hamlet than Much Ado, and more familiar with the play they used in the RJ interface task than the one they used in the BEP interface task (Table 3). Participants were also asked whether they used the internet and internet search engines. All participants regularly used both.

Query-related information concerns how difficult the participants found the queries to answer (on a scale of 1 to 5, where 1 = very easy and 5 = very difficult). Participants generally found the Hamlet query harder than the Much Ado query, and the query they performed on the BEP interface harder than the query they performed on the RJ interface (Table 4).

Table 3. Average participant familiarity with the plays

	BEP interface	RJ interface	Overall
Hamlet	3.25	3.50	3.38
Much Ado	1.75	2.50	2.13
Overall	2.50	3.00	2.75

Table 4. Average query difficulty

	BEP interface	RJ interface	Overall
Hamlet	3.00	3.25	3.13
Much Ado	3.25	2.50	2.88
Overall	3.13	2.88	3.00

Participants were also asked whether they had an idea of the answer to the questions before they started searching, and whether they had enough time to complete the task (yes/no). Participants had a prior idea of the answer in less than half of the searches performed, with considerably fewer positive answers for the BEP interface than the RJ interface (Table 5). Very few of the participants (3 of the 16 participant sessions) felt they had enough time to complete their tasks (Table 6).

Interface-related information concerns which interface the participants found easier, faster and more helpful (Table 7), and whether they had any comments on possible differences between the two interfaces. A large majority of participants judged the BEP interface as easier and faster. Most participants perceived both interfaces as being equally helpful.

Table 5. Number of participants with a prior idea of the answer to the query

	BEP interface	RJ interface	Overall
Hamlet	2	3	5
Much Ado	0	2	2
Overall	2	5	7

Table 6. Number of participants who had enough time

	BEP interface	RJ interface	Overall
Hamlet	1	0	1
Much Ado	1	1	2
Overall	2	1	3

Table 7. Number of participants expressing a preference for each interface

	BEP interface	RJ interface	No difference
Easier	6	1	1
Faster	6	0	2
More helpful	2	1	5
Overall	14	2	8

Most of the comments did not shed much light on the participants' reasons for preferring one interface to the other. However, one participant commented "The first interface *(the BEP interface)* prompted me to scan throughout more of the text, to get a better understanding of the text as a whole and a better understanding of the development of themes and relationships. Although the second interface *(the RJ interface)* enabled me to be precise about certain quotes I felt that I was bogged down in certain scenes and I wasn't able to explore the text as a whole."

3.2   Object Composition

In this section, we discuss the average composition of the objects chosen by participants in the course of their searching, analysed by query and interface, object type and structural level (Tables 8 and 9).

Most of the objects chosen by participants, across all query/interface combinations, were speech objects. In the Hamlet/RJ combination, it is noticeable that participants hit on quite a large number of BEPs too, by chance, during their session. This is mostly due to the preference of participants for browsing at speech level (rather than line level), which was also the level of most BEPs (23 of the total 27 BEPs). In the Much Ado/RJ combination, on the other hand, participants examined more leaf level objects and fewer speech objects, thus reducing the number of BEPs they found by chance. Objects of higher structural levels were rarely examined, especially in the RJ interface.

Table 8. Average composition of objects chosen by parabticipants for the Hamlet query

Hamlet		Structural level						
		Leaf	Speech	Scene	Act	Play	Other	Total
BEP interface	BEPs	0 (0%)	11.75 (12.1%)	2 (2.1%)	0 (0%)	0 (0%)	0 (0%)	13.75 (14.2%)
	RJs	2 (2.1%)	0 (0%)	0 (0%)	0 (0%)	0 (0%)	0 (0%)	2 (2.1%)
	BEP/RJs	1 (1.0%)	0 (0%)	0 (0%)	0 (0%)	0 (0%)	0 (0%)	1 (1.0%)
	Others	6 (6.2%)	64 (66.1%)	7.5 (7.8%)	1.5 (1.6%)	0.25 (0.3%)	0.75 (0.8%)	80 (82.7%)
	Total	9 (9.3%)	75.75 (78.3%)	9.5 (9.8%)	1.5 (1.6%)	0.25 (0.3%)	0.75 (0.8%)	96.75 (100%)
RJ interface	BEPs	0.25 (0.4%)	5.75 (8.6%)	0 (0%)	0 (0%)	0 (0%)	0 (0%)	6 (9.0%)
	RJs	8.25 (12.3%)	0 (0%)	0 (0%)	0 (0%)	0 (0%)	0 (0%)	8.25 (12.3%)
	BEP/RJs	3 (4.5%)	0 (0%)	0 (0%)	0 (0%)	0 (0%)	0 (0%)	3 (4.5%)
	Others	5.5 (8.2%)	39.75 (59.3%)	3.25 (4.9%)	0.5 (0.7%)	0.25 (0.4%)	0.5 (0.7%)	49.75 (74.3%)
	Total	17 (25.4%)	45.5 (67.9%)	3.25 (4.9%)	0.5 (0.7%)	0.25 (0.4%)	0.5 (0.7%)	67 (100%)

Table 9. Average composition of objects chosen by participants for the Much Ado query

Much Ado		Structural level						
		Leaf	Speech	Scene	Act	Play	Other	Total
BEP interface	BEPs	0 (0%)	11 (13.9%)	1 (1.3%)	0 (0%)	0 (0%)	0 (0%)	12 15.2%
	RJs	0 (0%)	0 (0%)	0 (0%)	0 (0%)	0 (0%)	0 (0%)	0 (0%)
	BEP/RJs	0.5 (0.6%)	0 (0%)	0 (0%)	0 (0%)	0 (0%)	0 (0%)	0.5 (0.6%)
	Others	2.5 (3.2%)	61.75 (78.2%)	1 (1.3%)	0.5 (0.6%)	0.5 (0.6%)	0.25 (0.3%)	66.5 (84.2%)
	Total	3 (3.8%)	72.75 (92.1%)	2 (2.5%)	0.5 (0.6%)	0.5 (0.6%)	0.25 (0.3%)	79 (100%)
RJ interface	BEPs	0 (0%)	3.75 (4.5%)	0.25 (0.3%)	0 (0%)	0 (0%)	0 (0%)	4 (4.7%)
	RJs	15.5 (18.4%)	0 (0%)	0 (0%)	0 (0%)	0 (0%)	0 (0%)	15.5 (18.4%)
	BEP/RJs	0.75 (0.9%)	0 (0%)	0 (0%)	0 (0%)	0 (0%)	0 (0%)	0.75 (0.9%)
	Others	2 (2.4%)	61 (72.4%)	0.25 (0.3%)	0 (0%)	0.25 (0.3%)	0.5 (0.6%)	64 (76.0%)
	Total	18.25 (21.7%)	64.75 (76.9%)	0.5 (0.6%)	0 (0%)	0.25 (0.3%)	0.5 (0.6%)	84.25 (100%)

3.3   Information Seeking Behaviour

The user logs were analysed in order to identify types of actions performed during the search process. Six main actions were identified as a result of the analysis:

- JUMPING. Participants often used this action to reach an object that was some distance away from their current object in the play's structure. Common strategies were: jumping to the next BEP or RJ (usually forwards in the linear structure, and at the same structural level); jumping to the next recognizable structural level (either forwards or backwards in the linear structure), e.g. to look at the next act; jumping to a repeat object, i.e. an object revisited by the participant several times in the course of the session; and jumping to an area of the play that the participant already knew, from their previous knowledge, would be useful.
- LINEAR BROWSING. Participants often used linear browsing at a consistent structural level, usually speech level. The majority of this behaviour was forwards, with the occasional backwards browsing to seek contextual information for the current object, often being followed immediately by forwards browsing through previously visited objects. Other common strategies were: browsing of BEPs / RJs only, and browsing using other query-related criteria, e.g. from one speech by a particular speaker to the next speech by the same speaker.
- HIERARCHICAL BROWSING. Participants most often used this action to examine the contents of the current object, e.g. to look at the relevant lines within the current speech, or to examine the container of the current object. It was noticeable that hierarchical browsing almost always involved a single structural level, e.g. browsing from line to speech, rather than multiple levels, e.g. from line to scene.
- SKIMMING. Participants occasionally moved rapidly through the structure of the play by skimming, i.e. without spending any time looking at the content. This action was rare, but was usually employed in sections of the play that consisted of a succession of individual line speeches, thus allowing the participant to gain an overview of the content while still progressing quickly through the structure.
- RANDOM EXPLORATION. This action was rarely used. The aim appeared to be to explore the structure of the play, or perhaps the functionality of the interface, usually at the start of the session.
- PAUSING. Participants sometimes paused on one object for a considerable length of time. Any pause over one minute or so usually indicated a point at which the participant stopped to make notes or record an important quotation.

The amount of time participants spent on their tasks was also analysed (Table 10). There was very little difference between interfaces, as would be expected from the fixed time limit imposed for the tasks. Participants spent, on average, slightly less time on the Much Ado query than the Hamlet query.

Table 10. Average session time (minutes:seconds)

	BEP interface	RJ interface	Overall
Hamlet	29:24	30:04	29:44
Much Ado	25:39	25:50	25:45
Overall	27:32	27:57	27:44

3.4   Task Performance

After the experiment, participants' answers were assigned a percentage score by the marker (Table 11). Scores were tested for significance using the parametric related t-test. There was found to be no effect from either of the independent variables, interface or query, at $p < 0.1$. However, it should be noted that participants were, on average, less familiar with the query they were performing on the BEP interface, found the query more difficult, and had less prior idea of the answer. We might, therefore, have expected that participants would perform considerably worse on the BEP interface than the RJ interface; in fact, they achieved a comparable average score.

Table 11. Average scores (percentages)

	BEP interface	RJ interface	Overall
Hamlet	35.00	43.75	39.38
Much Ado	48.75	37.50	43.13
Overall	41.88	40.63	41.25

It is noticeable that participants performed better on the Hamlet query with the RJ interface, and on the Much Ado query with the BEP interface. This could indicate that the two interfaces supported different types of task to differing extents; this issue is discussed further in Section 4.1.

4   Discussion

We focus on three main areas for our discussion. Firstly, we examine our results for possible correlations between task performance and background data, time spent on searching, and information seeking strategies. Secondly, we discuss links between our results and those of previous, related research. Thirdly, we examine the implications of our results for interface design for focussed SDR systems.

4.1   Correlations

We started by looking for a possible correlation between task performance and background information. We identified the best indicator of performance as whether participants felt they had enough time. The only 3 sessions where the participants felt they did have enough time were also the 3 top-scoring sessions (1st, 2nd and $3^{rd}=$). The second best indicator appeared to be whether participants had a prior idea of the answer to the query before they started searching. In 6 of the 8 top-scoring sessions, the participant stated that they had a prior idea of the answer, compared to only 1 participant in the 8 bottom-scoring sessions. Familiarity with the play did not appear to provide a very good indication of task performance for individual participant sessions, and difficulty of query an even poorer indication.

One noticeable point arising from the questionnaire data was that participants did not necessarily prefer the interface with which they obtained the better score. Of the 8 participants, 2 preferred the interface with which they had performed better on all 3 preference dimensions (easier, faster and more helpful), 3 preferred their better interface on 2 dimensions, 1 judged both interfaces the same on all 3 dimensions, 1 preferred their worse interface on 1 dimension and 1 preferred their worse interface on 2 dimensions. This reminds us that user opinions often arise from a complex mix of experience, not simply as the result of one factor.

Secondly, we looked for a possible correlation between task performance and time spent on searching. Although participants generally performed slightly better on the Much Ado query than the Hamlet query, they actually spent slightly less time on the Much Ado query. However, they did find the Much Ado query, on average, less difficult than the Hamlet query, so this may explain both the lesser amount of time and the better task performance. Participants performed comparably on the BEP and RJ interfaces, both in terms of time spent and task performance. However, they were, on average, less familiar with the query they used with the BEP interface, and found it more difficult, suggesting that the BEP interface may have saved them some time and allowed them to perform better than might have been expected.

Thirdly, we looked for a possible correlation between task performance and information seeking strategies. We attempted to determine good and bad information seeking strategies for each of the different query/interface combinations by ordering our results according to task performance, and identifying the top and bottom participant sessions for each combination. The distribution of queries and interfaces was evenly spread throughout the ordering, so this corresponded to picking participant sessions 1-4 as the top sessions, and 11 and 14-16 as the bottom sessions. Individual participants were also well distributed throughout the ordering, with one participant appearing in both the top and the bottom 4 participant sessions examined.

We started by attempting to identify good and bad strategies for the different interfaces. Good strategies for the BEP interface involved:

- Heavy use of BEPs, especially linear browsing of BEPs
- Browsing at speech level, and using BEPs of higher structural levels mainly for navigation purposes
- Using BEPs as originally intended, i.e. as starting points for browsing to relevant objects

Bad strategies for the BEP interface involved:

- Viewing more objects, but a lower percentage of BEPs
- Less discriminating browsing behaviour, i.e. continuing to browse through non-relevant objects

Good strategies for the RJ interface involved:

- Browsing at speech level, which is more efficient than browsing at line level
- Identifying and browsing long sequences of relevant objects

Bad strategies for the RJ interface involved:

- Duplication of effort by examining both line and container speech objects

We then attempted to identify good and bad strategies for the different queries. This proved to be more difficult, although there were indications that better performance with the Much Ado query was linked to focusing on local areas of the text, while better performance with the Hamlet query was linked to greater breadth of exploration.

We also found several general performance indicators, which spanned all interface/query combinations. Overall indicators of good performance were use of a consistent structural level (usually speech) for browsing, and pausing behaviour in order to make notes during the search. Overall indicators of bad performance were a high percentage of random exploration, backwards browsing, or skipping behaviour. Participants who found a lot of non-relevant material at the start of the session also tended to be less effective.

Finally, we examined the hypothesis, suggested in Section 3.4, that the BEP interface better supported the Much Ado query, while the RJ interface better supported the Hamlet query. Since the same participant group performed both these interface/query combinations, we first examined the participants' background data. This showed that the better-performing participant group had, on average, a lower familiarity with the play, thought the query was more difficult, and had less prior idea of the answer before they started searching. In addition, fewer participants in this group felt they had enough time. The two participant groups spent almost exactly the same amount of time on searching. It is clear, therefore, that background data cannot explain the superiority of one participant group's performance over the other.

We then examined the composition of BEPs and relevant objects selected by participants in the different interface/query combinations. Again, there was nothing unusual that could explain the differences, except perhaps the comparatively high number of BEPs found by chance in the Hamlet/RJ combination.

We turned, lastly, to analysis of the nature of the individual BEPs and RJs for the two queries. It appeared that the BEPs in Much Ado were often *browsing BEPs*, i.e. the first object in a sequence of relevant objects, while in Hamlet, a greater proportion of BEPs were *container BEPs*, i.e. (real or virtual) objects which contained several relevant objects. It is possible, therefore, that the use of BEPs with the Hamlet query did not provide any advantage, since BEPs and RJs were quite similar in composition. In fact, the higher proportion of container BEPs may have encouraged inappropriate browsing behaviour, i.e. participants may have browsed from container BEPs to non-relevant objects. In contrast, the nature of the BEPs in Much Ado differed substantially from that of the RJs, and appears to have succeeded in the original aim, namely to support participants in finding relevant objects through browsing.

4.2   Links with Other Research

This work builds on the Shakespeare user study carried out at Queen Mary, University of London ([17], [18]).   In this section, we discuss links with the Shakespeare study and other related research.

Firstly, we examine the concept of BEP itself.   In the Shakespeare study, the concept of BEP was shown to be an intuitive one by the comparatively high level of agreement among participants on the choice of BEP in a given context.   However, in this study we have shown that the concept of BEP is not always intuitive, since not every participant adopted the "correct" strategy for using BEPs.   This could be due to several factors:

- Interface presentation order.   Those participants who used the RJ interface first may not have realized that a different strategy was required with the BEP interface.
- The variable nature of BEPs.   Participants experiencing container BEPs early on may not have understood that later BEPs were intended as the basis for browsing.
- Participants' individual preferences for browsing (as in a hypermedia interface) or going directly to relevant objects (as in a query-based interface).

Secondly, the related issue of the effectiveness of BEPs is an important one. Although participants performed no better on the BEP interface overall, those participants who made good use of BEPs (mostly with the Much Ado query) did seem to perform better.   Participants themselves seemed to recognize the importance of BEPs, since they often returned to them during an individual session; BEPs accounted for 22% of repeat objects in the Hamlet/BEP combination, and 25% of repeat objects in the Much Ado/BEP combination.   There also seemed to be a reasonable degree of agreement between participants on which BEPs were important; BEPs accounted for 23% of overlap objects (i.e. objects chosen by at least two participants) in the Hamlet/BEP combination, and 22% of overlap objects in the Much Ado/BEP combination.

Thirdly, we examine the data concerning preference for structural level.   A study of information seeking using a document collection of software documentation, the Tess study ([15], [19]), concluded that participants preferred to enter the documentation at the level above that of relevant objects and browse downwards in the structure to examine the relevant objects themselves.   The results from the Shakespeare study [18] showed that participants preferred to browse at speech level, rather than leaf level.   The data reported in this paper confirm the Shakespeare study results.   However, this strategy may have been at least partly due to the interface design, since choosing a container speech object in our interface caused all contained leaf objects to be displayed; there was thus no benefit to our participants in browsing at leaf level.   In the Tess interface, on the other hand, only material that belonged exclusively to the container object's structural level was displayed.   Because of this difference too, we saw very little evidence in our study of hierarchical browsing behaviour for the purpose of viewing contextual information.   However, participants did sometimes use backwards linear browsing, especially from BEPs and relevant objects, in order to view the immediate context.

4.3   Implications for Interface Design

Our results have two main implications for interface design for focussed SDR systems. Firstly, there is evidence to suggest that participants sometimes failed to identify the correct strategy for using BEPs because of confusion over their dual nature as starting points for browsing and containers of relevant objects. In order to foster development of good information seeking strategies, the nature of BEPs should, therefore, be consistent within a particular interface.

Secondly, it was found that participants only looked at approximately half the BEPs (51% of the 27 BEPs for the Hamlet query and 46% of the 26 BEPs for the Much Ado query, on average). If participants had consistently adopted the approach of browsing from BEPs, this proportion could have been even lower. It therefore becomes crucial to find methods of supporting users in identifying the most important BEPs, e.g. by grouping or ordering the BEPs in some way.

5   Conclusions and Further Work

The main conclusions from our work are that participants strongly preferred the BEP interface to the relevant object interface, and that *appropriate* usage of BEPs can lead to improved task performance. However, our study has also highlighted shortcomings related to the inconsistent nature of BEPs and to BEP interface design.

Future work will examine the issue of what should constitute a BEP, particularly which of the suggested types (starting point for linear browsing or container object of relevant objects) provides more intuitive support for users' information seeking behaviour. It will also focus on identifying what factors might affect the choice of using one or other type of BEP in a particular interface, e.g. the type of queries being supported [17], or the target group of users. Results from this work can also feed into ongoing work on automatic identification of BEPs from relevance assessments [20].

Work on interface design to support information seeking in the context of structured documents is already in progress. One approach is to provide more explicit support for users in exploiting the structural information of the document collection. A current student project is evaluating the effect on information seeking behaviour and task performance of different methods of presenting the hierarchical structure of documents [21]. Another approach is to employ some form of ranking in order to support participants in identifying the most important BEPs. A current student project is evaluating the effect on information seeking behaviour and task performance of two methods of ranking: (standard) relevance ranking and ranking by informativeness. Informativeness is a subjective measure that acknowledges the prime importance of presentation order by determining the "ideal" ordering of documents [22].

Finally, many of our results are, inevitably, heavily influenced by the characteristics of the document collection. Further work will, therefore, need to be carried out on different document collections, and on collections from different domains, in order to determine the extent to which we can generalize from our results.

Acknowledgement

This work was carried out by the first author as the final year project component of a BSc in Computer Science at Queen Mary, University of London during academic session 2001/02.

References

[1]   Brin, S., Page, L.: The Anatomy of a Large-scale Hypertextual Web Search Engine. In: 7th WWW Conference, Brisbane, Australia (1998)

[2]   Silva, I., Ribeiro-Neto, B., Calado, P., Moura, E., Ziviani, N.: Link-Based and Content-Based Evidential Information in a Belief Network Model. In: 23rd ACM-SIGIR, Athens (2000)

[3]   Wilkinson, R.: Effective Retrieval of Structured Documents. In: 17th ACM-SIGIR, Dublin (1994) 311-317

[4]   Kotsakis, E.: Structured Information Retrieval in XML documents. In: Proceedings of the 17th ACM Symposium on Applied Computing (SAC'02), Madrid, Spain (2002)

[5]   Myaeng, S., Jang, D.H., Kim, M.S., Zhoo, Z.C.: A Flexible Model for Retrieval of SGML Documents. In: 21st ACM-SIGIR, Melbourne, Australia (1998) 138-145

[6]   Roelleke, T.: POOL: Probabilistic Object-Oriented Logical Representation and Retrieval of Complex Objects - A Model for Hypermedia Retrieval, Ph.D. Thesis, University of Dortmund, Verlag-Shaker (1999)

[7]   Fuhr, N., Großjohann K.: XIRQL: A Query Language for Information Retrieval in XML Documents. In: 24th ACM-SIGIR, New Orleans (2001) 172-180

[8]   Chiaramella, Y., Mulhem, P., Fourel, F.: A Model for Multimedia Information Retrieval, Technical Report Fermi ESPRIT BRA 8134, University of Glasgow (1996)

[9]   Tenopir, C., Ro, J.S: Full Text Databases. Greenwood Press (1990)

[10]   Cleveland, D.B., Cleveland, A.D., Wise, O.B.: Less than full text indexing using a non-Boolean searching model. JASIS 35(1984):19-28

[11]   Frisse, M.: Searching for Information in a Hypertext Medical Handbook. Communications of the ACM 31 (1988) 880-886

[12]   Lalmas, M., Moutogianni, E.: A Dempster-Shafer Indexing for the Focussed Retrieval of a Hierarchically Structured Document Space: Implementation and Experiments on a Web Museum Collection. In: 6th RIAO Conference on Content-Based Multimedia Information Access, Paris (2000)

[13]   Roelleke, T., Lalmas, M., Kazai, G., Ruthven, I., Quicker, S.: The Accessibility Dimension for Structured Document Retrieval. In: 24th European Conference on Information Retrieval Research (ECIR'02), Glasgow (2002)

[14]   Furnas, G.W.: The fisheye view: A new look at structured files. In Card S.K., Mackinlay J.D., Shneiderman B. (eds.): Readings in Information Visualization: Using Vision to Think, Morgan Kaufmann (1999), pp.312-330. (Reprinted from The fisheye view: A new look at structured files, Bell Laboratories Technical Memorandum #81-11221-9, October 12, 1981)

[15] Hertzum, M., Frøkjær, E.: Browsing and querying in online documentation: A study of user interfaces and the interaction process. In ACM Transactions on Computer-Human Interaction, 3(1996) 136-161

[16] Kazai, G., Lalmas, M., Roelleke, T.: A Model for the Representation and Focussed Retrieval of Structured Documents based on Fuzzy Aggregation. In: String Processing and Information Retrieval (SPIRE), Laguna De San Rafael, Chile (2001)

[17] Kazai, G., Lalmas, M., Reid, J.: Construction of a Test Collection for the Focussed Retrieval of Structured Documents. To appear in: 25th European Conference on Information Retrieval (ECIR'03), Pisa (2003)

[18] Lalmas, M., Reid, J., Hertzum, M.: Information Seeking Behaviour in the Context of Structured Documents. In preparation

[19] Hertzum, M., Lalmas, M., Frøkjær, E.: How are Searching and Reading Intertwined during Retrieval from Hierarchically Structured Documents? In: INTERACT 2001, Japn (2001)

[20] Kazai, G., Lalmas, M., Roelleke, T.: Focussed Structured Document Retrieval. In: String Processing and Information Retrieval (SPIRE), Lisbon (2002)

[21] Chimera, R., Shneiderman, B.: An Exploratory Evaluation of Three Interfaces for Browsing Large Hierarchical Tables of Contents. In: ACM Transactions on Information Systems, 12(1994) 383-406

[22] Tague-Sutcliffe, J.: Measuring Information: An Information Services Perspective. ASIS (1995)

Attaining Fast and Successful Searches
in E-commerce Environments*

Raz Lin[1] , Sarit Kraus[1], and Jeffrey Tew[2]

[1] Department of Computer Science
Bar-Ilan University, Ramat-Gan, 52900, Israel
{linraz,sarit}@cs.biu.ac.il
[2] MSRL Lab
GM R&D Center, Warren, MI USA
jeffrey.tew@gm.com

Abstract. Current online stores suffer from a cardinal problem. There
are too many products to offer, and customers find themselves lost due
to the vast selection. As opposed to traditional stores, there is little or no
guidance that helps the customers as they search. In this paper, we
propose a new approach for searching in online stores. This approach is
based on algorithms commonly used in recommendation systems, but
which are rarely used for searches in online stores. We employ this
approach for both keyword and browse searches, and present an
implementation of this approach. We compared several search guide
algorithms experimentally, and the experiments' results show that the
suggested algorithms are applicable to the domain of online stores.

1   Introduction

As on-line stores offer more and more products, it becomes more difficult for
customers to find what they need with a reasonable amount of time. As the time the
customers spend on searching for the desired product increases, the time they spend in
the store focusing on a single search increases, and thus the chances they would wish
to visit the store again in the future decreases. While in a retail store there is a
salesperson, who guides the customer during the search process and helps him find
the best product that suits his needs, such sales personnel are not available in online
stores. Thus, online stores need to use other mechanisms that will replace the
traditional role of the salesperson.

We have developed a general system for guided search in an online store (OSGS)
that assists customers in completing their purchases without wasting time. Our aim is
to provide an efficient and fast mechanism. We believe that a general system for
guided search also requires algorithms to identify the customers' profiles. This will
lead to long-term relationships with customers and will increase the store's long-term

---

* This work is supported by a grant from GM.

F. Sebastiani (Ed.): ECIR 2003, LNCS 2633, pp. 120–134, 2003.

benefits. OSGS supports both keyword search and browse search. This system should work in any domain, with minor adjustments to the algorithms and the database it uses. We have implemented and tested our system in the domain of GM's auto-spare parts. The experiments show that OSGS improves the customers' satisfaction with the search process, and reduces customer effort during the search itself. In the next section we discuss previous research in the area of recommendation systems and search engines. Section 3 describes our proposed OSGS and its implementation. Section 4 describes the experiments and our results. Finally, Section 5 states our conclusions.

2   Background

Recommendation systems recommend the customer products they think the customer would be interested in buying. They differ from our proposed system since they do not support the customer in the search process itself; they merely provide suggestions. The main technologies in recommendation systems that are commonly used to address the challenge of finding the right product for the customer are information retrieval and collaborative filtering [3, 4, 5, 6, 7, 12, 13]. Our system is not a recommendation system. We help the customer *while* he engages in the actual searching for products.   Moreover, all the systems, which use personalization techniques, typically do not combine different personalization techniques. We integrate information retrieval and collaborative filtering techniques and apply a user profile that consists of demographic profile, preferences profile and history profile.

Another way to help customers is to provide search engines to find necessary products. Most search engines provide a simple interface for either keyword search or browse search. Our system enables both.

In a keyword search, the customer provides the system with keywords and the system, in turn, provides the customer with a list of the products which best fit his keywords. The choice of the appropriate products is done using a similarity measure. The most effective one for keyword search has been established as being the inverse document frequency multiplied by term frequency (IDF*TF) [5], i.e., the inverse of the number of occurrences of the keyword in the whole collection of documents multiplied by the number of occurrences of the keyword in the document. In online stores, most stores retrieve all the documents or use some table lookup for popular keywords. Another option for assisting a user in his search is to try to improve his query by adding, deleting, and replacing the user's keywords with new ones [2, 4, 5]. This approach is not usable in a browse search, since there are no queries in browse searches. Moreover, in the domain of online stores, in general, and in auto spare parts in particular, there is little maneuvering space for identification of additional keywords other than those provided by the customer. Thus, we do not believe that applying sophisticated algorithms to the query would be of much assistance.

Browsing enables the customer to search for the product by using categories. The customer starts with the top-most level category and continues to explore new sub-categories until he finds the desired product. One advantage of this kind of search is that it allows the customer to obtain information on possible products during the search. Another advantage is *scope reduction*, i.e. reducing the range of products of interest to the customer.

In the browsing task, the customer is assumed to have incomplete, imperfect knowledge of the contents and its organization. Because of this, the browsing process is fundamentally uncertain and iterative [8]. The browsing allows the customer to search for a product even without knowing any keywords to aid in his search.

Most of the current browsing systems, such as Yahoo! and Amazon, do not personalize the browsing process. Holte and Drummond [8] describe an approach for helping users while they browse a library of software. They try to infer the customer's intention as he browses in order to limit the time involved and help perform a successful search by using the past history of the user and then suggesting other pages he might be interested in. Our system tries to infer the customer's intention by using a combination of algorithms, rather than just one algorithm.

Our system uses a mechanism similar to Henry Lieberman's Letizia [9]. The Letizia system tracks the user's browsing behavior, processes it and employs some heuristics. Then it displays the recommendations. As in the case of Letizia, we also use the history profile of the users. However, browsing in an online store is quite different than browsing on the Web. In an online store there is a tight connection between the links the user follows, while in Web browsing the connection between the visited pages is much less tight. Browsing on the Web can only provide a limited view of the user's intentions. This is because the user usually searches numerous sites, and most of them do not have a specific relationship among them. As opposed to this, browsing in a specific online store can be used to estimate the user's intention more quickly and accurately, since the focus is only on a certain limited domain. Thus, our algorithms can be more easily adjusted and fine-tuned to the specific domain.

3   The Online Store Guided Search System (OSGS)

We propose a general system for guided search in an online store (OSGS) that helps a customer attain a fast and successful search within the vast array of products available. OSGS assists the customer in the two most popular search techniques today: keyword and browse search. We tested OSGS using the domain of GM's auto-spare parts and we call this system GMSIM.

A product search can be implemented using a search tree. Each internal node of the tree is labeled by a category name, and the leaves are labeled by the name of the products. Each successor node is a sub-category of its predecessor node. The root node represents the initial problem situation. For example, in GM's "Auto Spare Parts" domain, the root node is labeled by "Auto Spare Parts," and a leaf can be labeled by "Relay Fan." When a customer searches for a product in OSGS a search tree is constructed in both the cases of keyword search and browse search. A product path is denoted $<v_0, v_1, ..., v_k>$, where v_0 is the root node, v_k is the leaf that is labeled by a product's name, there is an edge between v_i and v_{i+1}, $0 \le i \le k-1$, and v_{i+1} is a successor node of v_i. For example, in GM's "Auto Spare Parts" domain, one of the paths from the root node to the leaf node labeled by "Relay Fan" contains the nodes labeled: "Auto Spare Parts" → "2001" → "Cadillac" → "Catera" → "Relay Fan."

Fig. 1. An overview of OSGS

In a keyword search, the search tree is hidden from the customer, while in a browse search the search tree is presented incrementally to him. In addition, in a browse search the customer interactively influences how the search tree is developed by choosing which category to further explore. Efficiency of the search and the satisfaction of the customer depend on the size of the developed search tree and on the decision of which nodes to explore. It also depends on the order in which the nodes in a given level of the tree are presented to him.

We suggest personalizing the search for each customer using a combination of common techniques that are used today in recommendation systems. OSGS prunes the search tree according to the customer's profiles and the profiles of customers that are similar to him. Thus, for each category only a subset of its sub-categories is included in the search tree. In addition, in a browse search the order in which categories and the products are presented to the customer is personalized.

For the personalizing of the search, OSGS maintains two different profiles for each customer: (a) the customer's history profile and (b) the customer's demographics and preference profile. OSGS can choose which combination of the personalization techniques described above to use during each search, as summarized in Table 2 of Section 3.5. Figure 1 displays an overview of our proposed OSGS.

3.1   Customer History

The history is used for predicting the customer's needs, under the assumption that customers often buy similar products. A customer's search or browsing is included in his history by saving the path from the root of the search tree to the destination product. (Note that using either searching or browsing eventually gives us a path.)

A *historical event* h consists of a triplet $(<v_1, v_2, ..., v_k>, t, l)$, indicating that at time t the customer performed a search or browsed for a product whose path on the search tree consists of the vertices $<v_1, v_2, ..., v_k>$. v_k is labeled by a product the customer is interested in, v_i, $0 < i < k$, denotes a category in the product's path and l is the *likeability* parameter, which helps to distinguish between a successful search or browsing (a search or browsing which led to a purchase by the customer), and an unsuccessful search or browsing. Every time a customer is interested in a product, we add an historical event, which consists of that product, to the customer's history. A customer *is interested* in product j if one of the following two conditions holds: (a) the customer purchased the product, or (b) the customer visited the product path at least K times, where K is a predefined bound. The motivation behind entering into the history products the customer did not buy but only visited a certain number of times is our assumption that if the customer visited the product many times, even without buying the product online, he may be interested in some details about the product. Maybe he has not bought the product yet because he wants to compare it with other products or products from stores, maybe he is interested in a similar product, or maybe he purchased the product offline in a regular store or by phone. We define the *history H* of a customer to be the set of his most recent historical events.

3.2   Customer Demographics and Preference Profile

The demographics and preference profile captures general information and preferences about the customer and his domain-dependent information. For example, in GMSIM the profile consists of the following fields: name, gender, age range, occupation, and location. The fields of the domain dependent information are quality preference, price preference, warranty preference, expertise knowledge and car details (make, model, and year). The values of the demographic and preferences profile are given explicitly by the customer himself, and can be modified at any time. This as opposed to the history profile which is an implicit one, very dynamic and changes quite often.

3.3   Neighborhood Formation

The main goal of the neighborhood formation is to find for each customer x a set of n customers that are the most similar to him. The similarity is given by the similarity function *sim*. The neighbors are formed by applying proximity measures, such as the *Pearson correlation* [12, 13], or *cosine similarity* [6, 12] or *mean squared differences* [13], between two opinions or profiles of the customers. Given experiments done in other systems ([7], [13]), OSGS uses the mean squared differences proximity measure. We apply it to (a) the history of the customers and to (b) their demographics and preference profile in order to decide if *customer x* is a neighbor of *customer y*. This is done by applying a similarity function for each field of the profiles (see [10] for a detailed description). Different similarity functions are used for each field in order to normalize the fields' values to the range [0..1]. As stated above, the similarities of all the fields are combined using the mean squared differences proximity measure in order to obtain one weight for the profile [13].

For example, in GMSIM the similarity function for the gender, age, quality, price, domain expertise, and warranty fields is given by the following formula:

$$sim(P_{x_i}, P_{y_i}) = \frac{W(P_{x_i})}{1 + |P_{x_i} - P_{y_i}|},$$
(1)

where x_i and y_i represent field i in the profile for customers x and y, respectively, P_{x_i} and P_{y_i} represent the values of the fields, and $W(P_{x_i})$ represents the importance of the field. OSGS constructs two neighborhoods for each customer, as described above. The idea behind this is that when a customer is searching for a specific product, it might be useful to assist him in finding the desired product by using information derived from customers who have similar tastes, or similar characteristics.

Table 1. Summary of weights and notation used in OSGS

Customer's Weights	Notation
Preference weight	W_p
Keyword weight	W_k
Customer's x history weight	W_h^x
Neighbor weight according to history profile	W_{n_h}
Neighbor weight according to demographics and preference profile	W_{n_p}
Customer's x category weight	$W^x(category)$

3.4   Weight Functions

In order to prune the search tree effectively, each vertex in the search tree is assigned a weight that estimates the customer's interest in the category or product associated with the vertex. In this section we present a description of the four weight functions that are used in our algorithms. The weight functions are based on the customer's preferences, the keywords provided by the customer (in case of a keyword search), the customer's history and his neighbors (neighbors-by-history-profile and neighbors-by-demographics-and-preference-profile). Table 1 summarizes all the weight functions and their notations.

3.4.1   Customer's Preference Weight

In addition to constructing a neighborhood for a customer from his profile, we use the customer demographics and preference profile to give weight to products and categories in the search tree. Since each product is constituted of different attribute fields (such as price, quality, and so on), we give higher weights to products that correspond to the preferences indicated in the customer's profile. The demographics and preference profile also includes, for example, the car information of the customer, and this information is also used to give weight to different categories, since each category is associated with a different car. This weight is calculated using a proximity measure between the fields of the products that correspond to the profile's fields. We denote that weight as W_p. The customer's preference weight is static and only changes if the customer changes his profile or if a product or a category is updated or added.

3.4.2   Keyword Weight

When the customer searches using keywords, he supplies the keywords, which are then used in order to select the relevant products from the entire collection of products. The weight that captures the relevance of the product with respect to the keywords is denoted W_k and is calculated using the *IDF*TF* approach [4, 5], which is the one most commonly used in search engines. However, since this method can be used only with respect to a corpus of documents, in order to use this approach we needed to define what constitutes a document in OSGS. For each *product$_i$* we define *document$_i$* to be the collection of the following fields of the product: (a) description, (b) name, (c) category, (d) notes, and (e) keywords.

3.4.3 History Weight

We define the weight of each historical event (see Section 3.1) to be equal to the likeability value of the product to which the historical event belongs multiplied by $exp(\frac{t}{current\_time})$. The history weight of a product or category is defined to be the sum of total weight of the historical events in which it appears, divided by the number of historical events in which it appears. The history weight for customer x is denoted W_h^x.

3.4.4 Neighborhood Weight

The neighborhood weight is based on the proximity measure. For each neighbor N_i we compute the product of the category's history weight for that neighbor with the value of the neighbor's similarity to the customer:

$$W_h^{N_i}(category) \cdot sim(x, N_i). \tag{2}$$

The total neighbors' weight is an average of all the products above. We denote the neighbors' weight according to the customer's history profile as W_{n_h} and the one according to customer's demographics and preference profile by W_{n_p}.

3.5   Searching Using Keyword(s)

There are two techniques that are applicable when searching using keywords: (1) *bottom-up* search and (2) *top-down* search. The most common technique among online shops is bottom-up search (for example, as in Amazon: http://www.amazon.com). In top-down search the search begins with the categories themselves and ends with the products. This can be achieved if the domain's structure is hierarchical and if there is some sort of a link or relation between each category and its products.

As opposed to a top-down search, in a bottom-up search the search begins with the possible products and continues to the top-most category. In this approach the keywords and their weights are used to find products that are most likely wanted, and then OSGS tries to reconstruct the path back to the root category. Though the products have already been found, when deciding on which products to present to the customer OSGS uses the weight functions that take the paths into consideration. The reason behind this approach is to consider more than just the products found according to the keyword weight. Thus, in case of a failure in the search, the customer can see the categories that were related by OSGS to each product and choose from among them in order to find more appropriate products. This approach is also good when the customer does not really know what he is looking for, but has some idea as to the direction of the search. In particular, in bottom-up search OSGS first computes the keyword weight for all products, according to the customer's query. Afterwards, it computes the neighbors' weight, history weight, and preference weight for those products, in order to choose the products with the highest normalized weight.

Then, for *each* product with positive weight OSGS chooses at least one ancestor, using the normalized weight of the neighbors' (neighbors by history profile and neighbors by demographics and preference profile), history and customer's preferences, as described below. OSGS continues this process until for each chosen product it gets to the root, i.e., to the top-most category.

In top-down search OSGS does approximately the same thing, but in reverse. At each iteration it chooses sub nodes with the highest weights.

The total normalized weight for the category and customer x is given by:

$$W^x(category) = \alpha_1 W^x_{n_h}(category) + \alpha_2 W^x_{n_p}(category) +$$
$$\beta W^x_h(category) + \gamma W_k(category) + \eta W^x_p(category). \tag{3}$$

The parameters $\alpha_1, \alpha_2, \beta, \gamma, \eta$ are determined by the implementation of OSGS, using trial and error. Table 2 lists the different algorithm versions available in OSGS.

When considering the history and the historical events, using a top-down search gives more consideration to the path of the products, meaning that we will get to the final product using the most common path the customer uses. Using a bottom-up search gives more consideration to the weight of the product, with less consideration to the path of that product. Using a top-down search enables us to consider the number of keywords searched per category, i.e., giving more weight to categories in which the likelihood of finding a product that fits the keywords is higher. In a bottom-up search only the number of keywords searched per product is taken into consideration, thus possibly avoiding finding other solutions that might appeal more to the customer. The keywords impose constraints on the search domain. We would like to avoid conditions in which too many keywords cause over-constraint (not enough results) and too few keywords cause under-constraint (too many results). Thus we use the number of keywords in order to decide whether to use a bottom-up search or a top-down search. The formal justification of this intuition can be found in [10].

Table 2. Versions of algorithms in OSGS

Algorithm Version	Option	Formula
History-based algorithm	$\alpha_1 = \alpha_2 = 0$	$W^x(category) = \beta W^x_h(category) + \gamma W_k(category)$ $+ \eta W^x_p(category).$
Neighbors-by-history algorithm	$\alpha_2 = \beta = 0$	$W^x(category) = \alpha_1 W^x_{n_h}(category) + \gamma W_k(category)$ $+ \eta W^x_p(category).$
Neighbors-by-demographics-and-preference algorithm	$\alpha_1 = \beta = 0$	$W^x(category) = \alpha_2 W^x_{n_p}(category) + \gamma W_k(category)$ $+ \eta W^x_p(category).$
Search without algorithms	$\alpha_1 = \alpha_2 =$ $\beta = \eta = 0$	$W^x(category) = \gamma W_k(category).$

3.6   Searching Using Browsing

In browsing, the idea is to start with the categories and get to the final product. Unlike searching with keywords, there is little logic in allowing browsing to use the bottom-up method, so we focus only on the top-down method.

We use a similar normalized weight for a product or category as used in the keyword search (formula 3), but without the keyword weight. At each level the customer is presented with a list of categories, ordered according to the weights. The customer takes an active part in the search and decides on how the developed search tree is to be constructed. At any point the customer can also choose to backtrack and change or retry his selection. This can be easily done since the entire category tree is presented to him. Since the weights of the categories differ from one customer to another, the order in which the categories are displayed to each customer also differs. This is as opposed to a regular browse search, in which all customers see the same categories, in the same order.

4   Experiments

To test the applicability and efficiency of our approach, we conducted experiments on GMSIM. In those experiments, the subjects used (a) GMSIM with our suggested algorithms, (b) GMSIM without our algorithms, and (c) ACDelco system (http://www.acdelco.com). The ACDelco system provides services similar to those of GMSIM and allows the customer to use either a keyword or browse search, but not, to our knowledge, any special algorithm.

When analyzing the experiments' results we say that system A is better than system B if (a) the customer's satisfaction with the search process is higher when using system A than when using system B, and if (b) the customer's effort (the effort the customers exert to find what they are looking for, measured by search time and number of clicks) is lower when using system A than when using system B.

Our main hypothesis was that GMSIM is always better than ACDelco. In addition, we had the following three hypotheses:

(a) If customers, who have a similar history of purchases, tend to buy products similar to products their "soul-mates" (customers with a similar profile) have already purchased, then GMSIM with a neighborhood by history algorithm will be better than GMSIM without algorithms.
(b) If customers, who have a similar demographics and preference profile, tend to buy products similar to products their "soul-mates" have already purchased, then GMSIM with neighborhood by demographics and preference profile algorithm will be better than GMSIM without algorithms.
(c) If customers, who buy products and thus have a history of purchases, tend to buy products similar to products they have already purchased, then GMSIM with a customer's history-based algorithm will be better than GMSIM without algorithms.

Although a plain search with no algorithm can be best, or can at least generate the same results as any of the stated algorithms, in cases such as those in which the customer is looking for a "one-time product", there is no advantage from the algorithm when dealing with repeated and veteran customers. Thus, those customers might feel unsatisfied with the system and choose another system instead.

The reason we tested all three hypotheses, and not just one, and designed a system which uses algorithms that support this hypotheses, is that there are domains in which one algorithm might perform better than the other. For example, in the domain of drugstores, if the customer has a history of disease, an algorithm that supports the customer's history (hypothesis c) might be the best solution. On the other hand, in the domain of books, if the customer is a science-fiction fan, we might find the algorithm that supports neighborhood according to the customer's preferences (hypothesis b) more useful. In yet another option, in the domain of accessories, one might find the algorithm which supports neighbors according to the customer's history (hypothesis a) more useful, since it might be useful to use items other customers, with taste similar to that of the current customer, have bought. Using the algorithm that supports only the customer's history might even turn out to be futile.

Thus, if we have one system which supports all of those hypotheses, we can adjust and adapt it to many domains. We can also use trial and error in order to empirically test which algorithm performs better and even combine different algorithms.

4.1   Experiments Methodology

We divided our experiments into three sub-experiments. In each sub-experiment, when the subjects used the "GMSIM with our proposed algorithms" option they were provided with a different algorithm. The subjects themselves did not know which algorithm the system was using. In the first sub-experiment, the neighborhood-by-history-algorithm was used; in the second, the neighborhood-by-demographics-and-preference-profile based algorithm was used; and in the third sub-experiment the customer's history-based algorithm was used. Twenty people participated in each sub-experiment. Thus, a total of 60 people experimented with our system.

The algorithms were tested using the domain of GM's auto spare parts, which contains about 45,000 products (about 5,000 different catalog numbers).

Each subject participated in only one sub-experiment in which he or she was given a list of 25 short scenarios. Each scenario describes in a short paragraph the reason for the need to buy a car part (for example, due to a problem with the part). The subjects needed to use the scenarios in order to find each part, either using the keyword search or the browse search. When the subject had to use the keyword search, he had to extract the keywords from the scenario. When the subject had to search using the browse search, he had to associate the item in the scenario with its categories.

In order to enable the subjects to know whether or not they found the right part, a picture of the part or some other identification was attached to each scenario. The subjects were instructed to search for at least several minutes, in case they did not find the right part, before skipping to the next part.

Note that either using GMSIM with our proposed algorithms or using GMSIM without it or using ACDelco, eventually returns results to the subject. The question is how much time and effort it will take the subject until he finds the desired product from the results list, and thus how satisfied the subject will be with the search process.

For example, one of the scenarios was as follows: "Last night an officer stopped you since one of your taillight lamps wasn't working. You were instructed to have the problem fixed. You noticed that the problem was caused by a blown bulb." An image was attached to the scenario so the subject would know if he got to the right part. A keyword search for this item could consist of these keywords: "lamp," "taillight," "bulb." After obtaining the results the subject had to find the right item from the results list. If the subject had to use a browse search, he could have seen all categories from which he had to select the correct ones associated with the item. In this case, the subject had to choose the "Electrical" category and then "Lamp – Taillight" in order to get the items in the last category, which contains the item in the scenario.

Among the 25 different products of the scenario, 10 products were searched using a GMSIM browse search and a keyword search with our algorithms (the exact one depends on the part of the experiment), 10 products were searched without our algorithms, and 5 products were searched using ACDelco. A search using only ACDelco and our system without our algorithms allowed us to compare our system to ACDelco, in general, and to compare the efficiency of our algorithms in particular.

Note that in order not to bias results due to, perhaps, scenarios that are more "difficult" than others, the order of the scenarios for each subject was drawn from the uniform distribution (with limits [0-1]). Thus, some subjects had to search for certain scenarios, for example, by using a keyword search with our proposed algorithm, while other subjects had to search for the same scenarios by using a keyword search without an algorithm, or by doing a browse search. Also, the order in which the subjects searched, e.g., searching with an algorithm before searching without an algorithm, or vice versa, was also chosen using the uniform distribution. This was done in order not to bias the results as a result of the subjects becoming more familiar with the searches and the system, thereby yielding better results in their second search.

During the experiment we measured (a) the satisfaction of the subjects with the search process; (b) the overall satisfaction with GMSIM; (c) the time taken for each purchase; and (d) the number of times the customer clicked until he found the desired part. The time and overall satisfaction were acquired using questionnaires presented to each subject. An example of such questionnaire is presented in the Appendix.

After concluding each sub-experiment we performed *t-tests* for the time duration and the average number of clicks and *non-parametric test - Wilcoxon matched-pairs signed-ranks test* [14] for the answers in the questionnaires, comparing the rankings (1-7) and the general preferences.

In order to perform our experiments we had to create and maintain virtual customers, create profiles for our subjects, assign them a history, and compute their neighbors. To do this we created 3 different clusters of customers, each cluster containing 30 customers. For each cluster we randomly chose, using the uniform distribution, 100 products. In each cluster, the products were taken from the same car year and make. Then, for each customer in the cluster we randomly chose about 40 products out of the products associated with his cluster. Each customer derived from a certain cluster had values in the demographics and preference profile fields similar to those of other virtual customers in the same cluster. After creating all of the virtual customers, we calculated (a) the history weight, (b) the neighbors by history profile, and (c) the neighbors by demographics and preference profile for each customer. Each subject was associated with one of those profiles and the products of the scenarios were chosen randomly from the larger set of products associated with his cluster.

Table 3. Average results (*avg*) and standard deviation (*stdev*) of GMSIM's keyword search, GMSIM, and ACDelco in general. Satisfaction and flexibility varied between 1-7

	General Satisfaction		Time Satisfaction		Ease and Flexibility		Average Time Duration		Average No. of Clicks	
	avg	stdev	avg	Stdev	avg	stdev	avg	stdev	avg	stdev
Keyword Search with alg.	6.00	0.92	5.65	0.99	5.95	1.00	12.70	5.25	4.49	2.23
Keyword Search w/o algorithm	4.75	1.59	4.40	1.98	4.65	1.90	14.85	5.71	6.92	5.06
Keyword Search – general	5.60	0.75	5.45	1.00	5.45	1.00				
GMSIM – general	5.95	0.69	5.65	0.88	5.85	0.88				
ACDelco	4.80	1.70	4.65	1.79	4.45	1.88				

4.2   Experiments Summary

Due to space limitations we cannot present the results of all our experiments. Full details can be found in [10]. We first present some results of the third sub-experiment, and then we present the combined results of all sub-experiments.

Table 3 presents the average ratings the subjects gave to the general satisfaction, time satisfaction, and the ease and flexibility in both the keyword search with the history algorithm and without any algorithm, and to the keyword search in general. The table also presents the average time duration and the corresponding standard deviation in both searches, and the average number of clicks and its standard deviation. The third row in the table presents the average ratings the subjects gave to the keyword search in general. The results of the experiment supported our hypothesis (c) above. The general satisfaction of the keyword search with the history algorithm was significantly higher than with the keyword search without the algorithm ($z = -2.48, p < 0.006$). The ease and flexibility were also significantly better in the keyword search with the history algorithm, in comparison to the keyword search without the algorithm ($z = -2.91, p < 0.002$).

The time it took to perform a keyword search with the history algorithm was significantly lower than the time it took for the keyword search without the algorithm ($t(19) = 1.39, p < 0.1$). This also explains the fact that the time-frame satisfaction using a keyword search with the history algorithm was significantly lower than the level of satisfaction when using the keyword search without the algorithm ($z = -2.23, p < 0.01$). This is also supported by the fact that the average number of clicks was significantly lower in the keyword search with the history algorithm than in the keyword search without the algorithm ($t(19) = 1.8, p < 0.05$). At the end of the experiment, the subjects were explicitly asked which search technique they would prefer to use in the future: a keyword search with the history algorithm or a keyword search without the algorithm. Significantly more subjects (80% of the subjects) preferred the keyword search with the history algorithm, as compared to only 15%, who preferred the keyword search without the algorithm ($z = -2.62, p < 0.004$). The other 5% had no preference.

Table 3 also presents the results of the subjects' ratings for the GMSIM and ACDelco system in general after finishing the experiment with the history algorithm. The average general satisfaction is significantly higher in GMSIM than in ACDelco (z = -2.78, p < 0.002). The time-frame satisfaction was also significantly higher in GMSIM, in comparison to ACDelco (z = -2.29, p < 0.01). Finally, the ease and flexibility were also significantly higher in GMSIM, in comparison to ACDelco (z = -2.81, p < 0.002). We can conclude that these results support our hypothesis that, all in all, in the third sub-experiment the subjects prefer using GMSIM to ACDelco. Similar results were obtained in all the sub-experiments.

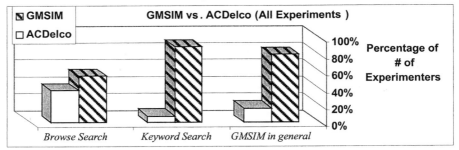

Fig. 2. Preference of all the subjects concerning GMSIM vs. ACDelco

We now discuss the combined results of all the sub-experiments. We compared our keyword search with any one of our algorithms to ACDelco. We asked the subjects which system they would prefer to use in the future, ACDelco or GMSIM? The results presented in Figure 2 show that significantly more subjects prefer using keyword search with algorithm in future searches (90% of the subjects) than using ACDelco in future searches (only 8% of the subjects) (z = -4.6, p < 0.001).

The results presented in Figure 2 also show that significantly more subjects in all of the experiments prefer to use a browse search with an algorithm in the future (55% of the subjects) and not ACDelco (only 38% of the subjects) (z = -1, p < 0.16). Although the results are significant, the difference in the percentages is not as high as in the keyword search. The reasons for that might include the lack of proficiency of the subjects with the auto-spare parts domain, or the general preference of most of our subjects for using a keyword search rather than a browse search. Also, the browse search requires more effort than a keyword search. The subject must constantly think of the product and try to relate it to the desired category.

The results presented in Figure 2 also show that significantly more subjects (80% of the subjects) would prefer to use GMSIM in the future (regardless of whether they use a keyword search or a browse search), as compared to only 17%, who prefer to use ACDelco (z = -4.34, p < 0.001). These results are also supported by the data in Table 4 that presents the average results and standard deviation of all the subject ratings for the GMSIM system in general and for ACDelco. The general satisfaction using GMSIM is significantly higher than using ACDelco (z = -3.07, p < 0.001). Also, the time-frame satisfaction in GMSIM is significantly higher than in ACDelco (z = -2.03, p < 0.02). Finally, we can see that the ease and flexibility of GMSIM are significantly better than in ACDelco (z = -4.38, p < 0.001). We can conclude that all of the ratings for GMSIM are markedly higher than the ratings for ACDelco.

Table 4. Average results (*avg*) and standard deviation (*stdev*) of GMSIM in general and ACDelco, for all the experiments. Satisfaction and flexibility varied between 1-7

	General Satisfaction		Time Satisfaction		Ease and Flexibility	
	avg	stdev	avg	stdev	avg	stdev
GMSIM	5.72	0.94	5.53	0.95	5.75	0.88
ACDelco	5.05	1.37	5.05	1.59	4.62	1.75

Together, the three sub-experiments supported all of our hypotheses and the main hypothesis that combining the algorithms would yield better satisfaction and less effort than using a simple search system.

5   Conclusions

In this paper we have proposed adding recommendation system logic and functionality to customer searches in online store systems. Thus, OSGS tries to bridge the gap between finding the right product the customer is looking for and the search time involved. We used algorithms from collaborative filtering and information retrieval to help customers in search for products, and have thus created a personalized online store, adapting itself to each customer in the system.

Providing such service and customer convenience seems to increase sales and benefits [11, 12], and time saving is a factor that is as significant as cost for on-line customers [1]. Thus, as long as the personalization is good enough and generates satisfactory results for the customer, the better the chances will be that the customer will visit the online store again and develop a long-term relationship with the retailer.

Our experiments demonstrate that OSGS outperforms other non-personalized search systems.

References

[1]   Bellman S., Lohse G. L., and Johnson E. J. Predictors of Online Buying: Findings from the Wharton Virtual Test Market. Communications of the ACM, 42(12): 32-38, 1999.

[2]   Brin S. and Page L. The Anatomy of a Large-Scale Hypertextual Web Search Engine. Proc. of WWW-7, 1998, pp. 107-117.

[3]   Charu C. Aggrawal, Wolf J. L, Wu K., and Yu P. S. Horting Hatches an Egg: A New Graph-Theoretic Approach to Collaborative Filtering. Proc. of ACM KDD'99 Conference, CA, 1999.

[4]   Chen L., and Sycara K. WebMate: A Personal Agent for Browsing and Searching. Proc. of ICMAS 1998, pp. 132-139.

[5]   Goffinet L. and Noirhomme-Fraiture M. Automatic Hypertext Link Generation based on Similarity Measures between Documents. Research Paper, RP-96-034, Institut d'Informatique, FUNDP, 1995.

[6]   Good N, Schafer J. B, Konstan J. A, Borchers A, Sarwar B, Herlocker J, Riedl J. Combining Collaborative Filtering with Personal Agents for Better Recommendations. Proc. of AAAI-99, pp. 439-446, 1999.

[7]   Herlocker J.L, Konstan J. A, Riedl J. Explaining Collaborative Filtering Recommendations. CSCW. ACM 2000 Conference on Computer Supported Cooperative Work, 2000, pp. 241-250.

[8]   Holte, R. C. and Drummond, C. A learning apprentice for browsing. In Working Notes of the AAAI Spring Symp. on Software Agents, CA, pp. 37-42, 1994.

[9]   Lieberman H.. Letizia: An Agent that Assists Web Browsing. Proc. of IJCAI-95, Montreal, CA, 1995.

[10]   Lin R. Attaining Fast and Successful Search in E-Commerce Environments. A Master's Thesis, Bar-Ilan University, June 2002.

[11]   Lohse G. L., and Spiller P. Electronic Shopping: The Effect of Customer Interfaces on Traffic and Sales. Communications of the ACM, 41(7): 81-87, 1998.

[12]   Sarwar B., Karypis G., Konstan J., and Riedl. J. Analysis of Recommendation Algorithms for E-Commerce. Proc. of ACM E-Commerce, 2000, pp. 158-167.

[13]   Shardanand U. and Maes P. Social Information Filtering: Algorithms for Automating "Word of Mouth". Proc. of CHI-95, ACM Press, New York, 1995, pp. 210-217.

[14]   Siegel, S. Nonparametric Statistics for the Behavioral Sciences. New York: McGraw-Hill, 1956, pp. 75-83.

Appendix: Performance Evaluation

After each search group (5 items) a questionnaire was given to the subjects. In it the subjects needed to rate three statements in the range of 1 to 7, where 1 indicates "I completely disagree with the statement", and 7 indicates "I completely agree with the statement". A sample questionnaire is presented below:

General Satisfaction with GMSIM							
General satisfaction with GMSIM.	1	2	3	4	5	6	7
Satisfaction with the time-frame for finding items.	1	2	3	4	5	6	7
Ease and flexibility of GMSIM.	1	2	3	4	5	6	7

Remarks: _____

Learning User Similarity and Rating Style for Collaborative Recommendation

Lily F. Tian and Kwok-Wai Cheung

Department of Computer Science
Hong Kong Baptist University, Kowloon Tong, Hong Kong
{ftian,william}@comp.hkbu.edu.hk

Abstract. Information filtering is an area getting more important as we have long been flooded with too much information. Product brokering in e-commerce is a typical example and systems which can recommend products to their users in a personalized manner have been studied rigorously in recent years. Collaborative filtering is one of the commonly used approaches where careful choices of the user similarity measure and the rating style representation are required, and yet there is no guarantee for their optimality. In this paper, we propose the use of machine learning techniques to learn the user similarity as well as the rating style. A criterion function measuring the prediction errors is used and several problem formulations are proposed together with their learning algorithms. We have evaluated our proposed methods using the EachMovie dataset and succeeded in obtaining significant improvement in recommendation accuracy when compared with the standard correlation method.

Keywords: Recommender systems, collaborative filtering, machine learning, user similarity, rating style

1 Introduction

Information filtering is an area which is getting more and more important as we can hardly escape from the *information overload* problem nowadays. One typical example is product brokering in on-line shopping. On one hand, there are a tremendous number of the on-line shops on the Web. Even within an on-line shop, the number of product items can be pretty large. People have well recognized [1] the need of personalization, which has gone beyond the capability of conventional keyword search engines. Rapid development of different personalization technologies has been observed in recent years. Recommender systems is one of them.

Recommender systems refer to systems which can filter out the uninterested items (or predict the interested ones) automatically on behalf of the users. To achieve that, there are basically two main approaches, namely *content-based* and *collaborative* approaches. Content-based systems predict the user preferences for product items by comparing the user profiles with the item characteristics. This

F. Sebastiani (Ed.): ECIR 2003, LNCS 2633, pp. 135–145, 2003.

approach is close to the traditional information retrieval techniques used in keyword search engines, except that we now have the user profiles for ranking items in a personalized manner. In order to achieve high recommendation accuracy, the set of features for the profile/product representation has to be carefully chosen [6]. Besides, it is well known that the content-based approach suffers from the *over-specialization* problem [2] To avoid the representation bias, another approach, commonly called *collaborative* recommendation (or collaborative filtering), predicts user preferences for product items in a word-of-mouth manner. That is, user preferences are predicted by considering the opinions of other "like-minded" users. In particular, one can define a similarity measure between a pair of user preference ratings to identify the like-minded users. The success of this collaborative approach relies on the availability of a sufficiently large set of users with sufficiently large set of preference ratings. In practice, it is hard to require the system users to provide you too many preference ratings, at least when they first register onto your system. So, when the available data is sparse, how to make the recommendation accurate is one of the main challenges for building recommender systems.

Techniques for building a collaborative recommender system can be divided into memory-based or model-based, as pointed out in [4]. It has been shown that memory-based methods works best when there are sufficient data and model-based methods have advantage when the data are sparse [5]. In this paper, we focus on memory-based methods only.

Memory-based methods compute the preference ratings of a user by considering directly the ratings of the user's "neighbors". These techniques are similar in spirit to the k-nearest neighbor (kNN) related methods. The kNN method has been applied to many different pattern recognition problems, where a a distance metric between a pair of feature vectors has to be defined. The commonly used ones include the Euclidean distance and the Mahalanobis distance [3]. However, in recommender systems, those distances are no longer useful as preference ratings are not objective measures but are provided subjectively. Even for the same range of preference ratings value, say [0,1], identical rating scores of two different users, e.g., one being critical and the other being generous, should carry quite different messages. In other words, different users have their own biases in providing preference ratings. To get rid of the individual biases, different statistics have been proposed, where Pearson correlation coefficient is probably the most commonly used one for comparing the "like-mindedness" between users. Although these statistics have shown to be quite effective in providing recommendations, they are not intrinsically designed to be "optimal" for prediction accuracy. The focus of this paper is to address the problem of learning an optimal similarity function between users for maximizing the system's generalization performance in prediction. Besides, we are interested to see whether the user rating styles can be captured with the use of some non-parametric regression models for transforming preference ratings.

The remaining of the paper is organized as follow. Section 2 gives an overview on memory-based collaborative recommendation. Section 3 describes the criterion function we propose for deriving the optimal similarity function as well as various ratings transformation models proposed for capturing user rating styles. Section 4 describes our experimental setup for performance comparison of the various proposed methods. Section 5 discusses our findings in the experiments. Section 6 contrasts our work with some related ones and Section 7 concludes the paper.

2   Memory-Based Collaborative Recommendation

As mentioned above, memory-based collaborative recommendation is to predict the preference of an active user for available product items based on a preference ratings database collected from a set of users. Let a denote the index of the active user and $p_{a,j}$ denote the predicted value of the preference ratings of the active user for the jth item. A commonly adopted prediction formulation for $p_{a,j}$ is a weighted average of all the user ratings on the jth item, given as

$$p_{a,j} = \overline{v}_a + k \sum_{i=1}^{N} w_{a,i} (v_{i,j} - \overline{v}_i), \tag{1}$$

where N is the total number of users, $\overline{v}_i$ is the mean ratings for the ith user, $v_{i,j}$ is the ith user's preference rating for item j, $w_{a,i}$ denotes the weight computed as some similarity between the ath user (i.e., the active user) and the ith user (i.e., other users of the system), and lastly k is a normalization factor computed as $\sum_{i=1}^{N} |w_{a,i}|$.

Formulations other than the weighted sum (e.g., taking the maximum instead of sum) can also be used. But in this paper, we focus on this weighted sum formulation. So, the remaining question becomes how to compute the similarity function $w_{a,i}$ with the objective to achieve the best prediction accuracy. Pearson correlation coefficient is one of the most popular measures proposed as the similarity function, given as

$$w_{a,i} = \frac{\sum_{j=1}^{N}(v_{a,j} - \overline{v}_a)(v_{i,j} - \overline{v}_i)}{\sqrt{\sum_{j=1}^{N} (v_{a,j} - \overline{v}_a)^2 \sum_{j=1}^{N} (v_{i,j} - \overline{v}_i)^2}}. \tag{2}$$

This formulation assumes that the biases of individual users equal the mean values of their preference ratings. Then, the deviations from the means are normalized by the ratings' standard deviations before computing the dot products. The goal is to remove the subjective components from the preference ratings before the comparison. Other similarity measures like vector similarity [4] and feature weighting [8] have also been proposed.

3   Learning User Similarity Function

Instead of proposing yet another similarity function for further improving the prediction accuracy, we propose to learn the "optimal" one given a set of training data. Referring to Eq.(1), our goal is to obtain the set of optimal values for $w_{a,i}$ such that the prediction errors can be minimized. To define the optimality criterion function, we divide the training data of each user into two parts: the *training* set $\mathbf{T}_i$ and the *validation* set $\mathbf{V}_i$. The training set $\mathbf{T}_i$ is mainly for computing the similarity of preference ratings between users, and in turn the predicted values of user ratings. $\mathbf{V}_i$ is for computing the prediction errors. So, the criterion function for measuring prediction errors given a set of weights $\mathbf{w} := \{w(a,i)\}$ becomes

$$J(\mathbf{w}) = \frac{1}{2} \sum_{a=1}^{N} \sum_{j \in \mathbf{V}_a} (p_{a,j} - d_{a,j})^2, \tag{3}$$

where

$$p_{a,j} = \bar{v}_a + k \sum_{i=1}^{N} w_{a,i} (v_{i,j} - \bar{v}_i) \tag{4}$$

which is computed only for $j \in \mathbf{V}_a$. The optimal set of weights can thus be computed as $\mathbf{w}^* = \arg\min_{\mathbf{w}} J(\mathbf{w})$. The simple gradient descend method is used here for obtaining w^* and the weights updating rule can be computed as:

$$\triangle w_{a,i} = -\eta^w \frac{\partial J}{\partial w_{a,i}}, \tag{5}$$

where η^w denotes the learning rate for $w_{a,i}$ which controls the step size for searching $\mathbf{w}^*$. There are possibilities that other minimization methods or criterion functions may give better results. Our contribution here is to investigate the feasibility of computing the optimal similarity function with better prediction performance.

Other than the value of $\mathbf{w}$, we could also relax the assumption of taking the mean rating score of a user as his/her bias, but to let the system to learn the bias instead. In general, we could assume each user to have a ratings transformation function which models the user's rating style. To do that, we modify Eq.(1) as

$$p_{a,j} = \bar{v}_a + k \sum_{i=1}^{N} w_{a,i} f_i(v_{i,j}; \bar{v}_i), \tag{6}$$

where $f_i(x; \mu)$ denotes the ratings transformation function of the ith user. Referring to the original prediction formula Eq.(1), $f_i(x; \mu) \equiv x - \mu$. As it is by the no means that the transformation function must be linear, some non-linear functions should also be the possible candidates. In the following sections, we first consider the formulations of some linear ratings transformations and then move on to non-linear transformations.

3.1   Linear Ratings Transformations

According to Eq.(5) and using Eq.(6) for computing the predicted ratings, the updating rule of $\mathbf{w}$ is given as,

LM1-W:

$$\triangle w_{a,i} \;=\; -\eta^w \sum_j k \; (p_{a,j} - d_{a,j})(v_{i,j} - \overline{v}_i). \qquad (7)$$

Based on this updating rule, $w_{a,i}$ decreases as (increases) when the predicted value of the preference rating $p_{a,j}$ is larger (smaller) than the desired one $d_{a,j}$ and the preference ratings of others are supporting that. After **w** is updated, the value of k for each user is updated according to its definition. The updating process iterates until it converges.

Other than the weighting function **w**, the similarity between two preference ratings, as mentioned above, is also affected by user biases. Normally, generous users tend to give higher rating scores for all the items while critical users like to give lower scores. By arguing that the mean value of a user's preference ratings may not be the optimal estimate of his bias, the formulation of Eq.(6) can further be relaxed to model also the user bias by replacing the $\overline{v}_i$ with a bias parameter b_i. The corresponding prediction formula becomes

$$p_{a,j} \;=\; b_a + k \sum_{i=1}^{N} w_{a,i} \; (v_{i,j} - b_i). \qquad (8)$$

Using the gradient descent method, the updating rule for $w_{a,i}$ should be modified as

LM2-W:

$$\triangle w_{a,i} \;=\; -\eta^w \sum_j k \; (p_{a,j} - d_{a,j})(v_{i,j} - b_i). \qquad (9)$$

and the updating rule of b_i is given as

LM2-B:

$$\triangle b_i \;=\; -\eta^b \frac{\partial J}{\partial b_i} \qquad (10)$$

$$\triangle b_i \;=\; \begin{cases} \eta^b \sum_a k w_{a,i}(p_{a,j} - d_{a,j}) & a = i \\ -\;\eta^b(p_{i,j} - d_{i,j}) \\ \eta^b \sum_a k w_{a,i}(p_{a,j} - d_{a,j}) & a \neq i \end{cases} \qquad (11)$$

According to Eq.(11), it is noted that the bias value of the ith user b_i decreases (increases) when the user has a positive (negative) support, i.e., positive (negative) value of $w_{a,j}$, to a user whose predicted rating scores are too large (small) when compared with the desired scores. For a given set of **w**, one can interpret this iterative process as finding the subjective neural rating scores of all the individual users for the overall benefit in a cooperative manner.

3.2   Nonlinear Ratings Transformation

Adopting a linear function for $f_i(x)$ in Eq.(6) implies that we assume that users follow linear scales in providing preference ratings. However, such "linearity" is in fact a subjective impression. It is extremely hard to say objectively that the degree of improvement for a rating score changing from 0.3 to 0.4 is the same as that for the rating score changing from, say 0.8 to 0.9. Using the linear ratings transformation function as described in the last section, we cannot model that. But, we can assume that the users are rational and give higher rating scores only when they find some items better than others. Then, we can replace the linear transformation function by a non-linear one which is monotonically increasing and with bounded output values. In this paper, we propose the use of *sigmoid function* as a non-linear candidate of $f_i(x; b_i)$, which is given as

$$f_i(x; b_i) = \frac{2 \times max\_score}{1 + e^{-(x-b_i)}} - max\_score \tag{12}$$

where max_score refers to the largest values of possible rating scores. Other than the fact that it fulfills the two aforementioned requirements, its functional form being differentiable is an additional advantage, making the subsequent parameter updating rules much easier to derive.

Using the gradient descend again but without modeling the bias, the updating rule of the weights is given as

NLM1-W:

$$\triangle w_{a,i} = -\eta^w k_a \sum_j (p_{a,j} - d_{a,j}) f(v_{i,j}; \ \overline{v}_i). \tag{13}$$

Adding back the bias b_i, the weights and the bias updating rules become

NLM2-W:

$$\triangle w_{a,i} = -\eta^w k_a \sum_j (p_{a,j} - d_{a,j}) f(v_{i,j}; \ b_i). \tag{14}$$

and

NLM2-B:

$$\triangle b_i = \begin{cases} -\eta^b \sum_a k w_{a,i}(p_{a,j} - d_{a,j}) \frac{\partial f(v_{i,j}; \ b_i)}{\partial b_i} & a = i \\ - \eta^b(p_{i,j} - d_{i,j}) & \\ -\eta^b \sum_a k w_{a,i}(p_{a,j} - d_{a,j}) \frac{\partial f(v_{i,j}; \ b_i)}{\partial b_i} & a \neq i \end{cases} \tag{15}$$

where the partial derivatives can be computed as

$$\frac{\partial f(x; \ b)}{\partial b} = \frac{-2 \times max\_score \ e^{-(x-b)}}{[1 + e^{-(x-b)}]^2}. \tag{16}$$

4   Experimental Setup

4.1   Dataset

To evaluate and compare the prediction performance of the recommender systems which adopt the proposed optimal similarity functions and various ratings transformation functions, we have performed a number of experiments based on the EachMovie dataset. The dataset was collected by Digital Equipment Research Center from 1995 through 1997 and contains ratings of **72916** users for **1628** movies. In our experiments, we chose the first 500 users who have more than 10 ratings over the **1628** movies to be our dataset. Among the 500 users, part of them are set aside as the training users and the others as the test users. The preference ratings of the training users are all used for training while those of the test users are divided into training set, validation set and test set as described in Section 3.

According to the format of the dataset, a user preference is quantified by two attributes, score and weight. Weight indicates whether the person rated a movie as zero to five stars (*weight* $= 1$) or as "sounds awful" (*weight* < 1). Since a movie either rated as zero or as "sounds awful" was still assigned with a zero score, we differentiate two cases by mapping the latter case to -2. For the scores associated with weight=1, they were mapped correspondingly to 1 to 6. So, the range of the rating scores in our experiments becomes $[-2, 6]$.

4.2   Protocols

Same as [4] and [8], we apply two protocols for our experiments, namely *AllBut1* and *GivenN*. In the first protocol, we randomly hide one rating score for each test user and try to predict its value given all the remaining scores from all the users. This protocol reflects the situation when each user has a relatively large amount of preference ratings. The second protocol, *GivenN*, randomly selects N preference ratings for each test user as given ratings for the prediction of others. The result of this protocol indicates the performance during the startup stage when the user is quite new to a particular recommender system. In our experiments, we employed three protocols — *AllBut1*, *Given10* and *Given5*. Also, in order to examine the performance of recommender systems under different system situations, we have evaluated our proposed systems under different *user divisions* as summarized in Table 1.

As noted before, the preference ratings of the training users are all used for training, while those of the test users are divided into three subsets, i.e., training set, validation set and test set. The test set consists of all the hidden ratings and thus its size is determined by the protocol used. There left however freedom to determine the size of the other two sets. In order to examine extensively the performance with different selection of training and validation sets, three

Table 1. User Division Setup

No. of training users	400	300	200
No. of test users	100	200	300
Denotation	U41	U32	U23

different *vote division* ratios of the number of votes for each user in training set to the number of votes for the same user in validation set are chosen as 1:1, 1:2 and 2:1.

4.3   Evaluation Criterion

We employ *Mean Absolute Error* (MAE) to evaluate the accuracy of prediction. MAE is the average difference between the actual rating value and the predicted one. This measure has widely been used in the literature of recommender systems [4, 8].

5   Experimental Results and Discussion

Based on the experiment protocols, we have compared six algorithms. Four of them are different variations of the proposed machine learning method denoted by LM1, LM2, NLM1, and NLM2. The initial values of the weights for learning the four recommender systems are random values between -1.0 and 1.0, and that for the biases are the mean values of individuals' ratings. The remaining two algorithms we have evaluated, mainly for comparison, are BP and PC. BP represents *Baseline Performance*, where we use the mean vote of a user in the test user set as the final prediction of his vote on any target movie. PC refers to *Pearson-correlation Coefficient*. Note that, we used the extended Pearson correlation coefficient with a default rating score, as suggested in [4]. Supported by our prestudy, we used each user's mean rating value as the default score instead of a general constant.

Table 2 to 4 show the empirical results using the various algorithms given different user divisions. For each protocol and user division, we have evaluated our four algorithms under different vote divisions. For brevity, only the result of vote division as 1:1 is presented. The best scores are shown in **bold** face.

Comparing the three tables with different settings of user division, it is observed that in general, the prediction error decreases as more training users are used. That agrees with the principle that a larger training set can result in better performance in parameter estimation.

Table 2. Performance Comparison using MAE under U41 Division

Algorithm	AllBut1	Given10	Given5
BP	0.852	0.934	0.984
PC	0.792	0.915	0.967
LM	0.775	0.911	0.962
LM-B	0.790	0.907	0.986
NLM	0.731	0.906	**0.954**
NLM-B	**0.730**	**0.900**	0.994

Table 3. Performance Comparison using MAE under U32 Division

Algorithm	AllBut1	Given10	Given5
BP	0.887	0.967	1.017
PC	0.834	0.948	1.002
LM1	0.821	0.943	0.992
LM2	0.828	0.942	1.017
NLM1	0.812	0.941	**0.988**
NLM2	**0.798**	**0.934**	1.006

Table 4. Performance Comparison using MAE under U23 Division

Algorithm	AllBut1	Given10	Given5
BP	0.915	0.984	0.989
PC	0.880	0.970	0.979
LM1	0.862	0.957	0.978
LM2	0.874	0.994	1.015
NLM1	0.845	**0.950**	**0.975**
NLM2	**0.825**	0.955	0.990

Also, when compared with BP and PC, almost all the machine learning-based methods can achieve better performance for all the user divisions and all the protocols (with the exception of LM2). Between linear and non-linear rating transformations, it is noted that the non-linear versions can achieve more significant performance gain than the linear versions. For example, in *AllBut1* experiments with the user division setting of U41 (Table 2), the MAE is reduced from 0.792 for PC to 0.775 for LM1. The reduction factor is only 2.1%. However, when comparing NLM1 with PC, the error is reduced further to 0.731, thus by a factor of 7.7%. Similar observations are also found in Table 3 and Table 4. We consider this to be an interesting finding in recommender systems. As the non-linear function we used is the sigmoid function (see Figure 1), it makes ratings transformation approximately linear (but with a bigger slope) around the bias but clamps the rating scores of extreme values to some constant (which is 8 and -8 for our case). This implies that in order to achieve better recommendation prediction, the rating scores with values in the neighbourhood of the bias (neutral rating score) should be taken more seriously in the way that their values should be enlarged before being taken into account in predicting the other users' preference ratings. On the other hand, for the rating scores with extreme values, they should be considered less seriously and their effect in the ratings prediction should be suppressed to some saturated values.

With regards to the two versions of non-linear rating transformation functions, NLM2 is the more sophisticated one which includes both the weights and the biases in the prediction formula. For AllBut1 and Given10, NLM2 gives the

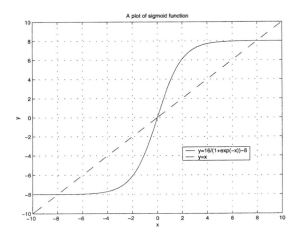

Fig. 1. A plot of sigmoid function

best performance among all the algorithms (see Table 2 and 3). However, for Given5, NLM1 outperforms the more complicated model NLM2 (see Table 4). This is mainly due to the fact that when the training data is insufficient, NLM2 turns out to be too flexible, and thus results in over-fitting.

6   Related Works

In the literature, there are not many related works on learning user similarity and rating style. The one closest in spirit to ours is the work done by Nakamura *et al.* [7]. They formulated the collaborative filtering problem as a many-valued relations estimation problem and used the algorithm known as the weighted majority prediction algorithm for the estimation. The estimation process involves a weight (user ratings similarity) updating step where the weight value grows or decays based on the discrepancy between the predicted ratings and the desired ratings. To contrast their formulation with ours, our updating rules are based on an optimization formulation and explicit transformation functions are used while it is not the case in Nakamura's work. Also, it is not clear whether different types of non-linear rating styles can be incorporated into Nakamura's work as their formulation is rather implicit. For our case, non-linear rating styles can readily be introduced and estimated.

7   Conclusion and Future Works

In this paper, we proposed the use of the machine learning approach to obtain the optimal user similarity function for memory-based collaborative recommender systems. Besides, we proposed several versions of rating transformation functions for modeling user rating styles together with their parameter estimation under the machine learning framework. Promising results when compared with the Pearson correlation coefficient have been obtained. It is to be noted that other than achieving a higher prediction accuracy for recommendation, there is a high potential that the estimated parameters, e.g., the user biases, can provide us further information for discovering different types of users (e.g., the most authoritative users, the most influential users, etc.) within such a virtual community of users simply linked together via their ratings.

References

[1] Url=http://www.personalization.org/pr050901.html, personalization Consortium News, may 9. 2001.
[2] M. Balabanović and Y. Shoham. Content-based, collaborative recommendation. *Communications of the ACM*, 40(3):66–72, March 1997.
[3] Allen L. Barker. *Selection of Distance Metrics and Feature Subsets for kNN Classifiers*. PhD thesis, Department of Computer Science, University of Virginia, 1997.
[4] J. S. Breese, D. Heckerman, and C. Kadie. Empirical analysis of predictive algorithms for collaborative filtering. In *Proceedings of the Fourteenth Conference on Uncertainty in Artificial Intelligence*, Madison, WI, July 1998.
[5] Kwok-Wai Cheung, Kwok-Ching Tsui, and Jiming Liu. Extended latent class models for collaborative recommendation. submitted, 2002.
[6] M. Dash and H. Liu. Feature selection for classification: A survey. *Intelligent Data Analysis*, 1(3), 1997.
[7] A. Nakamura and N. Abe. Collaborative filtering using weighted majority prediction algorithms. In *Proceedings of the Fifteenth International Conference on Machine Learning*, pages 395–403, July 1998.
[8] K Yu, X. Xu, M. Ester, and H.-P. Kriegel. Feature weighting and instance selection for collaborative filtering: An information-theoretic approach. *to appear in: Knowledge and Information Systems: An International Journal*, 2002.

Spoken Information Extraction from Italian Broadcast News

Vanessa Sandrini and Marcello Federico

ITC-irst – Centro per la Ricerca Scientifica e Tecnologica
38050, Povo, Trento, Italy
{sandrini,federico}@itc.it
http://munst.itc.it

Abstract. Current research on information extraction from spoken documents is mainly focused on the recognition of named entities, such as names of organizations, locations and persons, within transcripts automatically generated by a speech recognizer. In this work we present research carried out at ITC-irst on named entity recognition in Italian broadcast news. In particular, an original statistical named entity tagger is described which can be trained with relatively little language resources: a seed list of named entities and a large untagged text corpus. Moreover, the paper discusses and presents named entity recognition experiments with case sensitive automatic transcripts, generated by the ITC-irst speech recognizer, and by training the named entity model with seed lists of different size.

1   Introduction

Information Extraction (IE) is the task of extracting meaningful information from verbal information sources. Information to be searched for can range from named entities, to attributes, facts, or events entities have or participate in.

The difficulty of IE is related to the natural language processing required to recognize complex concepts, the intrinsic ambiguity of named entities, and finally, the steady evolution over time of language (e.g. new names steadily appear in the news).

For the aim of accessing spoken documents, information extraction permits to automatically select pieces of content which are of interest to the user. Moreover, by maintaining links between the extracted information and the original documents, context for each retrieved concept can be provided.

Recent research on IE from spoken documents has been carried out under the IE Entity Recognition and Automatic Content Extraction programs under DARPA. One of the considered tasks is the detection of Named Entities (NE) within transcripts of broadcast news (BN) automatically generated by a speech recognizer. NEs include names of locations, organizations, and people, temporal expressions, currency amounts, percentages. State-of-the-art performance were achieved as well by rule-based and statistical approaches [13].

F. Sebastiani (Ed.): ECIR 2003, LNCS 2633, pp. 146–160, 2003.

In previous work [6], we presented a NE tagger based on a statistical NE language model (LM). An interesting feature of the approach, is that the NE-LM can be estimated starting from a relatively short *seed* list of known NEs and a large untagged corpus of newspapers. An incremental training procedure can be applied which is statistically sound and makes use of intermediate models with less parameters than the original one. The NE tagger was developed on the Italian BN domain and provided performance comparable with those reported by state-of-the-art English NE systems trained on the same task.

In this work, we concentrate on two issues related to the development of a NE system: (i) the amount of supervision needed to bootstrap the system, and (ii) the use of capitalization in the automatic transcripts. The first issue is related to the development cost of a NE recognizer: producing supervised lists of NEs can be an expensive task. In this paper, we train a new system starting from a much larger seed list. The second issue tries to reduce the loss in performance due to the lack of capitalization in the automatic transcripts.

The paper is structured as follows. Section 2 presents the Named Entity recognition task and explains how a NE recognition system can be evaluated. Section 3 introduces the parametric structure of the NE LM, the statistical criterion used for NE recognition, and the incremental training procedure. Section 4 explains the development of the baseline model for Italian BN NE recognition on case sensitive automatic transcripts. Section 5 presents experiments done by using an augmented seed list of NEs. Section 6 investigates the use of case sensitive speech transcripts for NE recognition. Finally, Section 7 states some conclusions.

2   Named Entity Recognition and Its Evaluation

Named Entity recognition is the task of spotting and classifying proper names, temporal expression and quantities inside written or spoken documents. According to the guidelines in [3] and the recent BN evaluation sponsored by DARPA (e.g. Hub-4E IE-ER) seven classes have been defined: three classes for proper names (location, organization and person), two for temporal expressions (time and date) and two for numerical expressions (money and percent).

Though NE recognition seems straightforward in written documents because of the presence of contextual clues (e.g capitalization information and punctuation), there are several special cases. Many entities could be ambiguous (e.g. "Washington" could refer to a person or location) or could not correspond to NE (e.g. names of events, artifacts, nationalities).

In contrast with written documents, automatic transcripts present a harder challenge due to the lack of capitalization and punctuation and, more importantly, the presence of speech recognition errors.

As concerns with evaluation, this is based on automatic word alignment of a reference transcript and an hypothesis transcript. It is worth noticing that the reference transcript is manually generated and annotated with NEs. The hypothesis transcript can either be generated manually or automatically, while

Table 1. Examples of NE errors

TYPE	XTNT	CONT	REF_TYPE	HYP_TYPE	REF_CONT	HYP_CONT
cor	cor	cor	ORG	ORG	"Aprilia"	"Aprilia"
inc	cor	cor	PER	ORG	Jervolino	jervolino
cor	inc	cor	PER	PER	"Giuseppe Butera"	"giuseppe"
inc	inc	inc	LOC	PER	"Marche"	"d ' alema"
inc	cor	inc	LOC	PER	"Georgia"	"giorgio"

NEs are annotated automatically. Examples of reference transcript and automatic transcript are showed in Appendix.

NE recognition is evaluated by taking into account three different kinds of error: *type* error when a NE is tagged with a uncorrect class, *extent* error when a wrong number of words are tagged as NE, and *content* error when wrong words are identified as NE. Examples of aligned NEs and tagging errors are shown in Table 1. Excerpts of the corresponding reference and hypothesis transcripts are reported in Appendix. Error types are weighted equally on the overall error count. NE recognition performance can be calculated in terms of Precision (P) and Recall (R). For the sake of conciseness, results will be mainly reported in terms of F-score, the harmonic mean of Precision and Recall:

$$F - score = \frac{2PR}{P + R} \qquad (1)$$

3   NE Language Model

The proposed NE LM generalizes an ordinary trigram LM [8] as follows. Trigram probabilities are defined over a vocabulary $\mathcal{V}$ of roughly 64k-words, a set of NE categories $\mathcal{E} = \{loc, per, org, oth\}$, and a class oov (out-of-vocabulary) which allows to capture words not belonging to $\mathcal{V}$. NE categories correspond to classes *location*, *person*, and *organization* as defined in the DARPA 1999 IE-ER evaluation [3], plus a filler class for other types of proper nouns. In Figure 1 for the sake of clarity, the Probabilistic Finite State Network (PFSN) representing a bigram NE LM is shown.

Moreover, each NE class has associated a binary random variable which switches between a bag-of-word distribution of known-entries, for that class, and a distribution of generic NE templates. Figure 2 shows PFSNs corresponding to the switch variable (top) and to the known-entry distribution (bottom), for the class *loc*. NE templates model four special cases of the regular expression $\mathcal{T}$:

$$(< \texttt{prep} >? < \texttt{Word} >)+$$

where <Word> denotes any up-case word and <prep> any preposition that may occur before or between proper names. (A list of 38 preposition was defined for

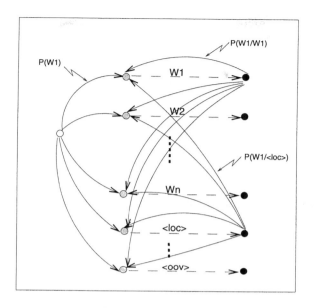

Fig. 1. Network of a bigram NE LM. Transitions with probabilities correspond-ing to parameters to be estimated are drawn with solid lines. Transitions with fixed probabilities are drawn with dashed lines. The *initial* state is in white colour, *final* states are in black colour, and other states are in gray colour. La-bels on transitions may either correspond to word strings or to names of other networks, e.g. <loc>

this purpose, see Appendix.) Figure 2 shows the PFSNs corresponding, respec-tively, to the template selection variable (top), and to each of the four templates, which essentially model proper names of different lengths and formats.

Formal Definition The NE LM is defined by a 4-tuple of parameters (Π, Λ, T, E), where:

- Π is the set of LM trigram probabilities $\pi(x, y, z) = \Pr(z \mid xy)$, $x, y, z \in \mathcal{V} \cup \mathcal{E}$;
- Λ is the set of template vs. list probabilities associated to each NE class, $\lambda(e) \in [0, 1]$, $e \in \mathcal{E}$;
- T is the set of probabilities which select the templates, $\tau_i \in [0, 1]$ $i = 1, 2, 3, 4$;
- E is the set of NE distributions of known-entries for each class, $\epsilon(t, e) = \Pr(t \mid e)$, $e \in \mathcal{E}$, $t \in \mathcal{T}$

Notice that by convention each NE class of the set $\mathcal{E}$ can only contain strings of $\mathcal{T}$. Moreover, the support set of each distribution in E is defined over a class and

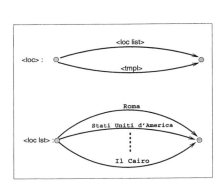

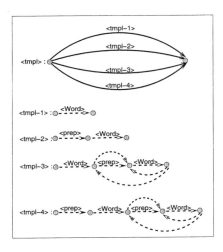

Fig. 2. Left: PFSNs of the switch variable (top) and of the bag-of-word distribution (bottom) for NE class *loc*. Right: PFSs of the template switch variable (top), and of the single template models (bottom)

model specific list of strings. Finally, probabilities in Λ, T, E are defined by discrete probability schemes, while those in Π are smoothed using an interpolation scheme coupled with an absolute discounting method [6, 8].

3.1   NE Recognition

Given a text W, its probability can be computed through the LM PFSN by taking into account all possible paths (sequence of states) that exactly span W, starting from the initial state, and ending in one final state. It is easy to see that if paths trace all the traversed sub-networks, they correspond to parse trees, which indicate, at the top level, eventually recognized NEs.

For the sake of NE recognition, the most probable parse tree T^* for W is considered, i.e.:

$$T^* = \arg\max_{T \in T(W)} \Pr(W, T) \qquad (2)$$

where $T(W)$ indicates the set of paths described in the begin of this section. It can be shown that the here represented NE LM is equivalent to a cascade of hidden Markov models (HMMs) [8] and that the most probable path for an input text can be efficiently computed through a Viterbi-like decoding algorithm [2]. In our implementation, the NE LM is compiled into a set of distinct PFSNs corresponding to the main trigram LM, the class related models, etc. Significant memory savings are achieved by exploiting a tree-based topology for the trigram and NE distribution models [1, 8].

3.2   NE LM Training

Given a sufficiently large tagged corpus, Maximum Likelihood (ML) estimation of the NE LM just requires collecting sufficient statistics for its parameter sets. If an untagged corpus is only available, training of the LM can be performed by the Expectation-Maximization algorithm [5] or, more easily, by the Viterbi training method as follows.

Viterbi Training Let $\tilde{M}$ be an available estimate of the NE LM and W an untagged text. A new estimate $\hat{M}$ can be obtained by searching for the best parse tree $\tilde{T}$, under $\tilde{M}$, and by computing, then, the ML estimate $\hat{M}$, under $\tilde{T}$. This corresponds to iterating the two following steps:

1. $\tilde{T} = \arg\max_{T} \log \Pr(T, W; \tilde{M})$
2. $\hat{M} = \arg\max_{M} \log \Pr(\tilde{T}, W; M)$

The effectiveness of the Viterbi training procedure depends on the initial guess of the parameters. For estimating statistical models with many parameters, the training method can be improved by estimating intermediate models, with less parameters, and by using them to initialize more complex models.

Incremental Training The NE LM described in Section 3 is bootstrapped by using a relatively small seed list of NEs and two intermediate models which are obtained by fixing some of the parameters in (Π, Λ, T, E). In particular, the parameters Λ are fixed either to inhibit the template part, indicated by $\Lambda = 0$, or the NE distributions, $\Lambda = 1$. The seed list contains frequent NEs discovered in a large training corpus. Entries of the list are manually classified into one or more NE classes of $\mathcal{E}$.

Initial Model M_0 A model $(\Pi, \Lambda = 0, E)$ is estimated starting from a corpus deterministically annotated with the seed list of NEs. The initialization of distributions in Π and E is based on a sub-corpus of sentences containing only tagged NEs. In particular, the part of sentences containing univocally tagged NEs is used to estimate the trigram probabilities Π, while all the sub-corpus is used to estimate NE distributions E. After just one Viterbi training step, the initial estimates of Π and E are significantly improved.

Intermediate Model M_1 A model $(\Pi = \Pi_0, \Lambda = 1, T)$ is initialized with the final probabilities Π of model M_0, which are also kept fixed, and with uniform probabilities in T. Because model M_1 just requires estimating three free parameters, a very small corpus can been used. Notice that model M_1 gives an indirect measure of the tagging accuracy achieved by the trigram LM component.

Written NE Model M_2 A full model ($\Pi = \Pi_0, \Lambda, T, E$) is initialized with the final estimates of model M_1. Trigram probabilities are again kept fixed. Each probability $\lambda(e)$ is initialized with the relative frequency of new entries of type e tagged by M_1. The model is trained on a corpus of contemporary data, with respect to the test set. At each Viterbi training iteration, new NE are possibly recognized in the corpus through step 1, by means of the templates. Step 2 updates the NE distributions of the model with NEs recognized at step 1. To just consider NEs with significative statistics, only those accuring at least twice are included in the NE lists.

Spoken NE Model M_3 As model M_2 exploits capitalization information in texts, for the template matching, it cannot be directly applied to case-insensitive automatic transcripts. Hence, the list model ($\Pi = \Pi_2, \Lambda = 0, E = E_2$) is derived directly from M_2, by inhibiting the template case and re-estimating trigram probabilities on the tagged corpus used to estimate M_0, after removal of punctuation and capitalization information. Finally, capitalization is also eliminated from the entries in E_2.

4   Baseline System

The incremental training procedure was applied on the Italian news domain. In the following, details are given about the used training and test texts, the NE seed list, and the achieved performance.

Training and Testing Data The training corpus is a 240M-word collection of Italian newspapers spanning the period 1992-1999. The test sets consists of two broadcast news shows, of November 1999, with a total duration of 40 minutes. Reference transcripts were manually produced and include punctuation and capitalization for a total of about 7,000 words and 322 tagged NEs. Automatic transcripts were generated with the ITC-irst broadcast news transcription system [1] which features continuous-density context-dependent HMMs, a 64K-word trigram LM, a beam-search Viterbi decoder, and MLLR adaptation. The average word error rate (WER) achieved on the test transcripts is 19.8%.

NE Seed List A list of about 2,700 most frequent proper names, matching template <tmpl-3>, were extracted from the training corpus and manually tagged according to the annotation guidelines in [3]. Among the collected strings, only 2,360 were actually tagged either as *location*, *organization*, *person*, or *other*, where the last category was used for names of events, products, etc. With respect to the degree of ambiguity of the 2,360 entries, 2,009 were assigned to one category, 315 to two categories and only 36 to three categories.

Experiments and Results NE recognition experiments were performed under different training and test. NE recognition performance was computed with the scoring software of the 1999 IE-ER DARPA evaluation[1]. Tests were performed on manual transcripts (man-case) providing capitalization and punctuation information, on case insensitive and punctuation free versions of the manual transcripts (man-nocase), and on automatic transcripts (auto-nocase). The intermediate transcripts man-nocase can be regarded as hypothetic error-free automatic transcripts.

In Table 2, experimental results are reported, in terms of F-score, for model M_0, model M_2 and model M_3. As model M_2 relies on capitalization information, is could only be applied to man-case transcripts.

Experiment on the manual case-sensitive transcripts (man-case) show a 23.3% relative improvement between the initial model M_0 and the final model M_2 i.e. F-score goes from 71.78 to 88.49. The foremost reason for this improvement is in the significant increase of the model NE lists i.e. the support set of the NE distributions. Their coverage, with respect to the test set, rises from 59.94% to 93.93%, see Table 3. In fact, the inhibition of the template model (model M_3) does not cause a consistent loss in performance: F-score slightly drops from 88.49 to 88.37 (about 0.1%). It is worth remarking that the NE distributions have been augmented by iterating model M_2 on a training data close to the test set period, i.e. newspapers between January and October 1999.

Results on the case insensitive transcripts man-nocase showed that the lack of punctuation and capitalization causes a 6.7% relative loss in performance, i.e. F-score drops from 88.37 to 82.40. This is mainly due to the increase in ambiguity caused by common words which may also occur as proper names. However, the incremental training procedure allowed for a significantly improvement over the initial model M_0, i.e. a 22% F-score relative improvement, from 67.42 to 82.40.

Finally, experiments on automatic transcripts (WER 19.8%) showed a further 11% relative loss (from F-score 82.40 to F-score 73.18) due to the presence of speech recognition errors. The deterioration on automatic transcripts is similar to that reported in other papers [13].

5   NE Seed List Expansion

Several NE recognition systems make use of manually supervised lists of proper names [9, 10]. However, such lists could be a bottleneck for a NE system because of their limited availability and the high cost of development and maintenance [4]. Moreover, the quality and size of such lists could also be important factors in developing a NE system [11]. For this reason, the impact of using a larger NE seed list was investigated in our system. An extended set of NEs was collected from meta-data available in the newspaper collection. In the Appendix, an excerpt of newspaper article and available meta-data are shown.

---

[1] http://www.nist.gov/speech/tests/.

Table 2. F-score for initial model M_0, written NE model M_2 and spoken NE model M_3, for different setting (e.g. hand-made transcripts (man-case), hand-made transcripts without capitalization (man-nocase) and automatic transcripts (auto-nocase) with 19.8% WER)

Model	man-case	man-nocase	auto-nocase
Initial NE Model M_0	71.78	67.42	62.95
Written NE Model M_2	88.49		
Spoken NE Model M_3	88.37	82.40	73.18
Word Error Rate			19.8%

Table 3. Size of the NE lists of model M_0 and M_2 and coverage statistics with respect to test data

	M_0		M_2	
	size	coverage	size	coverage
loc	662	75.42%	52,378	97.19%
org	608	62.66%	41,203	90.90%
per	1,132	44.19%	75,135	90.29%
all	2,122	59.94%	100,741	93.92%

Experiments and Results A new seed list of NEs was generated by taking the most frequent entries found in the meta-data of the whole (240M-word) newspaper corpus, with at least 50 occurrences. The resulting list of 5,545 entries was added to the original seed list of 2,360 entries, resulting in an extended seed list of 7,905 entries. The extended seed list was used to initialize the NE LM according to the incremental training procedure explained in Section 3.2.

In Table 4, F-scores achieved on the manual transcripts (man-case) are reported for models M_0, M_2 and M_3. Results show a high relative improvement, on average around 16%, for model M_0, with respect to results reported with the original seed list. The reason for this is the higher coverage of the extended seed list on test set. In particular, the extended seed list allows for a 28.8% relative improvement in coverage by the NE distributions of M_0, i.e. from 59.94% with the baseline seed list to 77.20% with the extended list, see Table 5.

However, after training, the F-score of the written NE model M_2 improves by only 0.3%, with respect to baseline, going from 88.49 to 88.82. This not significant change in performance is some way confirmed by the very comparable coverage shown by the NE distributions of the same model in the two training conditions, i.e. 93.92% vs 93.31% (see Table 4).

Table 4. F-score achieved on the manual case sensitive transcripts (`man-case`) by using models initialized with the baseline seed list (2,360) and expanded seed lists (7,905)

	baseline seed list	extended seed list
Initial model M_0	71.78	83.79
Written NE model M_2	88.49	88.82
Spoken NE model M_3	88.37	89.05

Table 5. Statistics about size and coverage of NE distributions of models M_0 and M_2 after initializing the NE LM with a baseline seed list of 2,360 NEs or with an extended list of 7,905 entries

	M_0		M_2	
	size	coverage	size	coverage
baseline seed list	2,122	59.94%	100,741	93.92%
extended seed list	7,905	77.20%	102,298	93.31%

Discussion The performed experiment indicates that little knowledge was gained by the NE LM after augmenting the seed list of known NEs. This result well supports the proposed unsupervised training procedure, which however relies very much on the availability of a large untagged training corpus.

6   Automatic Case Sensitive Transcriptions

Performance achieved by model M_3 on the case-insensitive automatic transcripts shows a 17.2% relative decreases with respect to the case-sensitive manual transcripts `man-nocase` (see Table 2). The reason is twofold: first, the lack of capitalization increases the ambiguity of proper names, which may also occur as common words; second, the presence of speech errors may corrupt NE tokens, hence not permitting the proper match with the NE lists, or their surrounding words, which can mislead the trigram LM from recognizing a NE. The impact of the first reason can be appreciated by looking at the degradation in precision and recall when moving from `man-case` to `man-nocase` transcripts, as reported in Table 7. In particular, we observe an absolute loss of about 11 points in recall, and about 1 point in precision. The gap increases even more if the corrupted `auto-nocase` transcripts are considered.

In order to cope with the performance degradation due to the loss of case-information, a case-sensitive version of the ITC-irst automatic transcription system was developed. In particular, the trigram LM of the recognizer was estimated on a case sensitive text corpus, in which words at the begin of sentences, i.e. occurring after a full stop, were eliminated. In this way, trigram statistics should also include the appropriate case information of proper names. The case sensitive transcripts (`auto-case`) produced by the new recognizer were evaluated in terms of word-error-rate in two ways. A case sensitive WER (WER-case) was computed by aligning the `auto-case` transcripts with the case sensitive reference `man-case`, by disregarding punctuation. For the purpose of direct comparison with the previously computed WER, a case insensitive WER was computed by aligning the `auto-case` transcripts with the case-insensitive reference `man-nocase`, by disregarding case information. The two WERs were respectively of 21.8% and 20.5%.

The higher WER figure is related to an important issue which has to be taken into account for NE recognition, namely the high variability in the use of case information on proper names, inside real texts. As a consequence, an automatic transcription system trained on real texts cannot provide case information perfectly consistent with a given predefined reference. However, as our goal is not that of producing and evaluating case-sensitive transcripts but to improve NE recognition, variability on case information was included in the NE recognizer. More specifically, entries included in the NE lists of the tagger were automatically extended to cover different case variants. Examples of variants for a couple of NEs are shown in Table 6.

Table 6. Examples of automatically induced variations inside the named entity lists estimated by the statistical NE LM

Reference	Permitted Variations
Commissione Europea	Commissione Europea
	Commissione europea
	commissione Europea
Guardia di Finanza	Guardia di Finanza
	Guardia di finanza
	guardia di Finanza

Table 7. Precision, Recall, and F-score achieved by the spoken NE Model on different types of transcripts

Spoken NE Model M_3	F-score	Precision	Recall	WER
`man-case`	88.37	85.71	91.19	
`man-nocase`	82.40	84.78	80.14	
`auto-nocase`	73.18	74.68	71.73	19.8%
`auto-case`	75.44	75.10	75.79	20.5%

Table 8. F-score achieved by the spoken NE Model on automatic transcripts using baseline list and extended seed lists

Spoken NE Model M_3	*baseline seed list*	*extended seed list*	*WER*
auto-nocase	73.18	73.81	19.8%
auto-case	75.44	75.87	20.5%

Experiments and Results Results on mixed-case automatic transcripts (auto-case), for the spoken NE Model M_3, are reported in Table 7. The achieved F-score was 75.44% which corresponds to a relative improvement of 3% over the F-score with auto-nocase transcripts. Interestingly, a significant increase in recall was achieved, 4% absolute, while precision improved by only 0.4% absolute. This reflects, on a different scale, the differences in precision and recall measured between the man-case and man-nocase transcripts.

By using both the extended seed list and capitalization information in the transcripts, the relative improvement over the baseline was of 0.5% on the auto-case transcripts (see Table 8).

Discussion Considering case-sensitive automatic transcripts seems promising for the sake of NE recognition. Probably there are several means to generate case information from spoken documents, e.g. by some post-processing; here, case information was simply added to the language model of the speech recognizer. As a matter of fact, case information permits a better selection of NEs from the NE lists, as the burden of discriminating proper nouns from common words is solved at a different stage.

7   Conclusion

In this paper a statistical approach to named entity recognition in Italian broadcast news was presented. A statistical model was defined based on words and NE classes. Training of NE LM model can be done, from scratch, through an iterative procedure by exploiting two relatively cheap resources: a large untagged corpus of Italian newspapers and a little seed list of manually annotated NEs. During training the model exploits the unsupervised data to discover new NEs which are added to the model parameters. The level of performance achieved by the baseline model results comparable to that reported for other systems [7, 12] developed on the corresponding English task.

Moreover, this work has investigated two issues: (i) the amount of supervised NE lists needed to bootstrap the system, and (ii) the use of capitalization information in the automatic transcripts.

With regard to the first issue, experiments showed that the amount of supervision needed to bootstrap the statistical model is not critical for performance, given that the initial seed list contains sufficiently frequent items. By training two models with seed lists including, respectively, 2,360 and 7,905 tagged NEs, chosen among the most frequent ones inside a large newspaper corpus, almost the same level of performance was achieved at the end.

Concerning the importance of capitalization inside transcripts, experiments indicated that the gap in precision and recall between transcripts with and without capitalization is mainly due to the increase in ambiguity of proper names which may also be common words. Results showed that the gap could be partially closed after introducing capitalization into the automatic transcripts, by suitably modifying the language model of the speech recognition system.

Acknowledgement

This work was carried out within the European project CORETEX (IST-1999-11876) and the project WebFAQ funded under the FDR-PAT program of the Province of Trento.

References

[1] N. Bertoldi, F. Brugnara, M. Cettolo, M. Federico, and D. Giuliani. From broadcast news to spontaneous dialogue transcription: portability issues. In *Proceedings of the IEEE International Conference on Acoustics, Speech and Signal Processing*, Salt Lake City, UT, 2001.

[2] F. Brugnara and M. Federico. Dynamic language models for interactive speech applications. In *Proceedings of the 5th European Conference on Speech Communication and Technology*, pages 2751–2754, Rhodes, Greece, 1997.

[3] N. Chinchor, E. Brown, L. Ferro, and P. Robinson. 1999 Named Entity Recognition Task definition. Technical Report Version 1.4, MITRE, Corp., August 1999. http://www.nist.gov/speech/tests/ie−er/er_99/ doc/ne99_taskdef_v1_4.ps.

[4] A. Cucchiarelli, D. Luzi, and P. Velandri. Automatic semantic tagging of unknown proper names. In *In Proceedings of COLING-ACL 1998*, Montreal, Canada, 1998.

[5] A. P. Dempster, N. M. Laird, and D. B. Rubin. Maximum-likelihood from incomplete data via the EM algorithm. *Journal of the Royal Statistical Society, B*, 39:1–38, 1977.

[6] M. Federico, N. Bertoldi, and V. Sandrini. Bootstrapping named entity recognition for Italian broadcast news. In *Proceedings of the 2002 Conference on Empirical Methods in Natural Language Processing (EMNLP)*, Philadelphia, PA, July 2002.

[7] Y. Gotoh and S. Renals. Information extraction from broadcast news. *Journal of the Royal Statistical Society, A*, pages 1295–1310, 2000.

[8] X. Huang, A. Acero, H.-W. Hon, and R. Reddy. *Spoken language processing: a guide to theory, algorithm and system development*. Prentice Hall, 2001.

[9] K. Humphreys, R. Gaizauskas, S. Azzam, C. Huyck, B. Mitchell, H. Cunningham, and Y. Wilks. University of Sheffield: description of the LASIE-II system as used for MUC-7. In *In Meggase Understanding Conference Proceedings: MUC-7*, 1998.

[10] G. Krupke and K. Hausman. Isoquest Inc: description of the NetOwl(TM) extractor system as used for MUC-7. In *In Meggase Understanding Conference Proceedings: MUC-7*, 1998.

[11] A. Mikheev, M. Moens, and C. Grover. Named entity recognition without gazetteers. In *In Proceedings. of 9th Conference of the European Chapter of the Association for Computatinal Linguistics*, Bergen, Norway, June 1999.

[12] D. Miller, R. Schwartz, R. Weischedel, and R. Stone. Named entity extraction from broadcast news. In *Proceedings of the DARPA Broadcast News Workshop*, Herndon, VA, February 1999.

[13] M. A. Przybocki, J. G. Fiscus, J. S. Garafolo, and D. S. Pallett. 1998 Hub-4 information extraction evaluation. In *Proceedings of the DARPA Broadcast News Workshop*, Herndon, VA, February 1999.

Appendix: Examples of NE Annotated Texts

Excerpts of reference and automatic transcripts tagged with NEs are shown below. In addition to NE identification errors, automatic transcripts include speech recognition errors as word substitutions, insertions and deletions.

Reference transcripts

1. allarme ecstasy . la <PER>Jervolino</PER>
2. il <PER>Papa</PER> in <LOC>Georgia</LOC> . ricorda il crollo del Muro di Berlino
3. ore e' ufficiale : divorziano <PER>Valentino Rossi</PER> e l' <ORG>Aprilia</ORG>
4. flagellato il litorale adriatico , dalla provincia di <LOC>Ravenna</LOC> , sino alle <LOC>Marche</LOC>
5. la vittima e' <PER>Giuseppe Butera</PER>
6. ci sono ancora nubi sulla <LOC>Georgia</LOC>

Automatic transcripts

1. allarme ecstasy la <ORG>jervolino</ORG>
2. il papa in <LOC>georgia</LOC> ricorda il crollo del muro di berlino
3. ore ufficiale di corsi hanno <PER>valentino rossi</PER> e l' <ORG>aprilia</ORG>
4. flagellato litorale adriatico dalla provincia in realta' sin <PER>d' alema</PER>
5. la vittima e' <PER>giuseppe</PER> votera'
6. ci sara' ancora non vi sono <PER>giorgio</PER>

Appendix: List of Prepositions

NE templates are modelled with regular expressions (see Section3) corresponding to sequences of capitalized words (<Word>) and prepositions (<prep>). Prepositions may occur before or between proper names, covering almost all possible ways to write proper names e.g. Massimo *D'* Alema, Yves Thibault *de* Silguy, Hans *van den* Broek, Robrecht *Van* Doorme, etc.

A small list of prepositions (both capitalized and uncapitalized) for different languages i.e. English, French, German, Italian, Spanish, etc. is defined as follows:

```
Di, Del, Dello, Dell', Della, Degli, Delle, Dei, De, D', Da, Dal,
Dallo, Dall', Dalla, Dagli, Dalle, Dai, di, del, dello, dell', della,
degli, delle, dei, de, d', da, dal, dallo, dall', dalla, dagli, dalle,
dai, El, Es, de Los, de Las, de Lo, e La, Des, Du, el, es, de los, de
las, de lo, de la, des, du, Von, Vvon den, Von der, Von dem, Van, Van
den, Van der, Van dem, von, von den, von der, von dem, van, van den,
van der, van dem, Of, of, Al, Am, Au, al, am, au,
```

Appendix: Example of Metadata

Example of Italian newspapers including metadata.

```
<LOCATION>KUALA LUMPUR</LOCATION>
<NAMES>CORDERO DI MONTEZEMOLO LUCA , SCHUMACHER MICHAEL , VESPA BRUNO ,
MAX BIAGI , EDDI IRVINE</NAMES>
<ORGANIZATION>FERRARI</ORGANIZATION>
<TEXT>
Tutta la Ferrari , guidata da Montezemolo , con Todt , i piloti
Schumacher e Irvine , i tecnici e anche alcuni meccanici partecipera'
martedi' sera alla trasmissione televisiva " Porta a~Porta " condotta
da Bruno Vespa su Raiuno dalle 20,50 . Molti gli ospiti d' eccezione
(...) Non  ci sara' Max Biaggi , impegnato nei  test motociclistici a
Kuala Lumpur dove la F1 arrivera' in autunno . (...)
</TEXT>
```

Taming Wild Phrases

Cornelis H. A. Koster and Mark Seutter

Dept. Comp. Sci., University of Nijmegen, The Netherlands
{kees,marcs}@cs.kun.nl

Abstract. In this paper the suitability of different document representations for automatic document classification is compared, investigating a whole range of representations between bag-of-words and bag-of-phrases. We look at some of their statistical properties, and determine for each representation the optimal choice of classification parameters and the effect of Term Selection.

Phrases are represented by an abstraction called Head/Modifier pairs. Rather than just throwing phrases and keywords together, we shall start with pure HM pairs and gradually add more keywords to the document representation. We use the classification on keywords as the baseline, which we compare with the contribution of the pure HM pairs to classification accuracy, and the incremental contributions from heads and modifiers. Finally, we measure the accuracy achieved with all words and all HM pairs combined, which turns out to be only marginally above the baseline.

We conclude that even the most careful term selection cannot overcome the differences in Document Frequency between phrases and words, and propose the use of term clustering to make phrases more cooperative.

Keywords: syntactic phrases, Head/Modifier pairs, term selection, text categorization.

1 Introduction

Anyhow, you've been warned and I will not be blamed
If your Wild Strawberry cannot be tamed..
– Shel Silverstein, "A Light in the Attic", Harper & Row, 1981

Over the last decades, many researchers in Information Retrieval have tried to combine keywords with phrases, extracted from documents by linguistic or statistical techniques, in order to raise the accuracy of Retrieval (for an overview see [Strzalkowski, 1999]). Little is known about the best way to combine phrases and words in one language model, but the common approach followed in query-based Information Retrieval is to *add* the phrases to the words rather than to *replace* the words by phrases.

Just adding phrases (or collocations) as terms besides keywords has led to disappointingly small improvements [Fagan, 1988][Lewis and Croft, 1990]. This

F. Sebastiani (Ed.): ECIR 2003, LNCS 2633, pp. 161–176, 2003.

is commonly attributed to the fact that phrases have a distribution over documents which is very different from that of (key)words. Moreover it is obvious that a (composed) phrase is statistically correlated with its components, which may violate assumptions of statistical independence. At any rate, the improvements gained by using more precise terms (phrases) may well be offset by a loss in recall.

In this paper, we compare the suitability of different document representations for automatic document classification, investigating a whole range of representations between bag-of-words and bag-of-phrases. Being aware of the fact that different representations may need different classification parameters, we shall first determine the optimal tuning and Term Selection parameters for each representation.

Text categorization is a wonderful area for performing experiments in Information Retrieval: given the availability of large labeled corpora and the high performance of modern classification engines, it is a simple matter to measure the way in which the Accuracy achieved depends on the parameter settings and the choice of document representation. In traditional query-based Information Retrieval, doing such controlled experiments is much harder and costlier.

1.1 HM Pairs

We are investigating the effect of using linguistically motivated terms (phrases) in Information Retrieval, particularly in Text Categorization. Following many earlier authors (e.g. [Fagan, 1988][Lewis and Croft, 1990][Strzalkowski, 1992] [Ruge, 1992][Evans and Lefferts, 1994][Lin, 1995]), these will be represented by *Head/Modifier pairs* (HM pairs) of the form

    [head, modifier]

where the head and the modifier are (possibly empty) strings of words, usually one word. A *pure HM pair* is one where head and modifier are not empty. There may also be HM pairs with an empty modifier (only a single head).

As an example, the phrase "new walking shoes" will first be transduced to the HM tree [[shoes, walking], new] and then unnested to one of the following:

- pure HM pairs

    [shoes,walking] [shoes,new]

- HM pairs including single heads

    [shoes] [shoes,walking] [shoes,new]

- idem plus single modifiers

    [shoes] [shoes,walking] [shoes,new] [walking] [new]

In distinction to many other researchers, we shall represent not only the Noun Phrase and its elements by HM pairs, but we shall also express the subject relation (as a Noun/Verb pair) and the object relation (a Verb/Noun pair). The effectiveness of these different representations will be compared in section 5.

1.2   The EP4IR Parser/Transducer

For generating the HM pairs, we made use of the EP4IR parser/transducer described in [Koster and Verbruggen, 2002], which is available under the GPL/LGPL license. It is generated from the EP4IR grammar and lexicon by means of the AGFL system[1].

Being especially directed towards IR applications, the EP4IR grammar does not set out to give a linguistically impeccable "account" of all English sentences, but it describes mainly the Noun Phrase (NP), including its adjuncts, and the various forms of the Verb Phrase (VP), consisting of the application of a certain verbal part to certain noun phrases (NP's) which occur as its complements. These phrases are transduced into HM pairs, in the process performing certain *syntactic and morphological normalizations*: elements of the phrase are selected, reordered and grouped. Furthermore, NP's not covered by a VP are also extracted.

The transformations are purely syntactic, i.e. they take no other information into account than the grammar, the lexicon and the input. In some cases this may result in linguistically suspect interpretations.

Precision and Recall of the EP4IR version used in the experiments are barely satisfactory, between .6 and .7 according to measurements. In interpreting the following experiments it should be kept in mind that the linguistic resources are not perfect – phrases are missed or mangled. But rather than waiting for perfect resources, we started experimenting with the available ones.

1.3   About the Classification Engine

The classification engine used in the experiments is the Linguistic Classification System LCS, developed for the PEKING project [2]. It implements two classification algorithms, Winnow [Dagan et al, 1997] and Rocchio [Rocchio, 1971], with a number of Term Selection algorithms and automatic Threshold Selection.

2   Statistics of Phrases

According to the literature, the improvement in precision and/or recall obtained by using phrases as terms in retrieval and classification has repeatedly been found disappointing. There is a common feeling that "the statistics of phrases are wrong". In this section we shall compare the statistics of words and HM pairs in various ways.

A moment's thought gives support to the idea that the statistical distribution of HM pairs (pairs of keywords) is definitely different from that of the keywords themselves: according to a well-known folklore law in corpus linguistics, in any sufficiently long text, the number of words occurring precisely once (*hapaxes*) is about 40%; therefore the expected percentage of random pairs of words occurring precisely once is $1 - (1 - 0.4)^2 = 64\%$.

---

[1] www.cs.kun.nl/agfl

[2] http://www.cs.kun.nl/peking

2.1   The Corpus

Our corpus, EPO1A, is a mono-classified corpus with 16 classes totalling 16 × 1000 abstracts of patent applications in English from the European Patent Office, see [Krier and Zaccà, 2001][Koster et al, 2001], with an average length of 143 words. From this corpus we used 4 subsets of 4000 documents each, chosen at random, in a four-fold cross-validation (training on each of the subsets while using the union of the other three as test set). The reasons for taking this unusual 25/75 split are:

- there is an abundance of labeled documents (1000/category) so that a 25% subset as train set is enough to reach stable classification
- 4-fold cross-validation is a reasonable compromise with efficiency
- testing is much faster than training and the large size of the test set reduces the variance.

The documents have been only lightly pre-processed: de-capitalization and elimination of certain characters from the keywords, but no lemmatization. For the HM pair representation they were completely parsed and the resulting trees unnested, also without lemmatization.

As a measure of the Accuracy, we take the micro-averaged F1-value (a harmonic average between Precision and Recall, combining the hits and misses of all categories before averaging). In the EPO1A corpus, all classes have the same size, so that the differences between macro- and micro-averaging are small.

2.2   Playing Zipf

Using the EP4IR parser/transducer, each of the EPO1A documents was parsed and transduced to a bag of unnested HM pairs. We omit the phrases with an empty modifier (i.e., consisting of only one word) to avoid all overlap with the bag of words. This provides us with bag of pairs representation of the same 16000 documents, with the following statistics:

corpus id	total terms	different terms	total size (bytes)
EPO1A words	2004011	21921	12069192
EPO1A pairs	921466	541642	20302454

It appears that the total number of HM pairs is about half the number of words, but there are 25 times as many *different* HM pairs. The average word frequency in EPO1A is about 9, the average HM pair frequency is about 2. The statistics of words and phrases are definitely different, which may well explain the bad experiences reported in literature. This also becomes clear from a comparison of the Zipf curves (frequency of words, pairs and, for comparison, squared frequency of pairs):

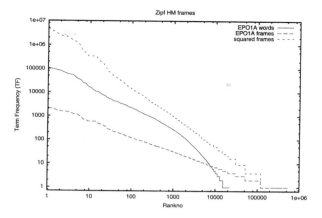

According to Zipf's law, on a log-log scale the relation between the frequency of a word in a corpus and its rank (ordering the words by frequency) looks like a straight line.

Compared to the graph for words, the graph for pairs is ramrod straight and much less steep. Representing a document by HM pairs gives an enormous number of low-frequency terms, among which the significant terms are cunningly hidden. Intuitively, some of the HM pairs must be much more indicative of a particular class than the keywords out of which they are composed. But the space of HM pairs is much larger than that of keywords, and therefore much more sparse.

2.3   The Trouble with Phrases

We first compare the effect of the two classification algorithms (Winnow and Rocchio) on phrases (represented as pure HM pairs) and keywords, using standard (default) parameters for the classification algorithms and without performing any term selection at all. We show three individual results (different 25% train sets) for each combination.

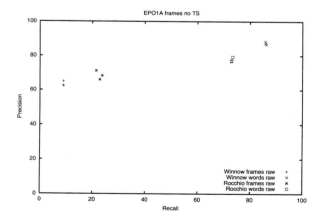

In comparison to the classification on phrases, words give not only a much higher Recall but even a higher precision. The naive use of phrases always leads to disappointing results. We must be doing something wrong.

3   Improving the Statistics

The classification algorithms are subject to noise, because their work is based on term statistics, including very many irrelevant terms, and because of the imperfect labeling of the documents. When eliminating irrelevant terms by Term Selection, we expect not only increased performance but also increased Accuracy (see [Yiming and Pedersen, 1997] [Peters and Koster, 2002]).

In order to get the best Accuracy out of different document representations, we may also have to adapt some classification parameters to the representation. On the basis of extensive experiments, we found three parameter settings to be crucial:

- the Rocchio parameters Beta and Gamma
- the Winnow parameters for the Thick Threshold heuristic
- the choice of Term Selection and in particular the number of terms per class.

We found that by an optimal choice of these parameters, the Accuracy is remarkably improved, even for the baseline (keyword representation). In the following section we shall do the same analysis for the other representations. It will turn out that the optimal values are in fact not strongly dependent on the representation, but that they differ quite a lot from their usual values in literature.

3.1   Winnow and Its Parameters

The Balanced Winnow algorithm [Grove et al, 2001][Dagan et al, 1997] is a child of the Perceptron. For every class c and for every term t two weights W_t^+ and W_t^- are kept. The score of a document d for a class c is computed as

$$SCORE(c,d) = \sum_{t \in d} (W_{t,c}^+ - W_{t,c}^-) \times s(t,d)$$

where $s(t,d)$ is the (ltc normalized) strength of the term t in d. A document d belongs to a class c if $SCORE(c,d) > \theta$, where the threshold θ is usually taken to be 1.

Winnow learns multiplicatively, driven by mistakes, one document at a time: When a train document belonging to some class c scores below θ, the weights of its terms t in W_t^+ are multiplied by a constant $\alpha > 1$ and those in W_t^- multiplied by $\beta < 1$; and conversely for documents *not* belonging to c which score above θ. The default values for the Winnow parameters are (following [Dagan et al, 1997]) $\alpha = 1.1$ and $\beta = 0.9$.

3.2   Rocchio and Its Parameters

The Rocchio algorithm [Rocchio, 1971][Cohen and Singer, 1999] computes for each class c a weight for each feature (another word for term) by

$$w(t, c) = max(0, \frac{\beta}{|D_c|} \sum_{d \in D_c} s(t, d) - \frac{\gamma}{|\overline{D}_c|} \sum_{d \in \overline{D}_c} s(t, d))$$

where [3]

- $s(t, d)$ is the normalized strength of the term t in the document d
- D_c is the set of documents classified as c and $\overline{D}_c$ the set of non-c documents.

The score of a document for a class is the inproduct of the weights of its features times their strength, and a document is assigned to class c if its score for c exceeds a class threshold which is computed from the train set (as is done for Winnow).

3.3   Tuning Rocchio

The Rocchio parameters β and γ control the relative contribution of the positive and negative examples to the weight vector; standard values in literature are $\beta = 16$ and $\gamma = 4$ [Cohen and Singer, 1999][Caropreso et al, 2000]. These values are rather puzzling, because only the *ratio* between β and γ is important for the outcome. We may fix one of the parameters arbitrarily at one without loosing generality.

In order to tune Rocchio to the base line (keywords), we determine experimentally its Accuracy as a function of the parameter β, keeping $\gamma = 1$ ($\beta = 4$ amounts to the traditional choice, [Arampatzis et al., 2000a] proposed $\beta = \gamma = 1$).

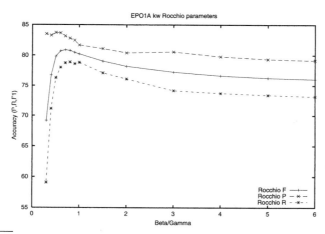

<hr>

[3] In the experiments we used a variant of Rocchio in which the maximazation to 0 is not performed, thus allowing negative term contributions. Recently we found that the version with maximization can be tuned to even higher Accuracy.

The graph shows that the optimum for $\gamma = 1$ is not at $\beta = 4$ but at $\beta = .7$, which means that negative contributions are favoured! Taking the optimal choice of β raises the F1-value from .76 to .81, which is an important improvement.

3.4   Tuning Winnow

Phrases do not reoccur as often as words, because there are more of them; that is our main problem. The appearance of a phrase in a document may indicate that it belongs to a certain class, but its absence does not say much. Somehow, we must reward its presence stronger than we deplore its absence.

In the Winnow algorithm, this can be achieved by means of the *thick threshold* heuristic. In training, we try to force the score of relevant documents up above $\theta^+ > 1.0$ (rather than just 1) and irrelevant documents below $\theta^- < 1.0$. This resembles the "query zoning" heuristic for Rocchio, in the sense that documents on the borderline between classes get extra attention.

According to [Dagan et al, 1997] the optimal values for these Thick Threshold parameters are 1.1 and 0.9, respectively (just like the Winnow α and β). The following graphs show the effect of the thickness of the threshold for (key)words, our baseline.

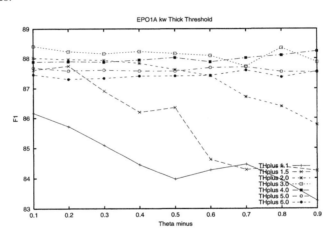

The F1-value fluctuates wildly, but by and by an increase of θ^+ improves the Accuracy, and [3.0,0.4] raises the F1-value over [1.1,0.9] by more than 2 points.

As was the case for Rocchio (see 3.3), it turns out that a non-traditional choice of parameters for Winnow may lead to a large improvement of the Accuracy. Obviously, the textbook values are far from optimal for every dataset!

3.5   Changing the Statistics by Term Selection

Term selection is based on certain statistics of the terms, in particular their distribution over (documents belonging to) the various classes. We expect the classification process to be more accurate when two kinds of terms are eliminated [Peters and Koster, 2002]:

1. stiff terms – terms distributed evenly across documents of all categories, therefore occurring frequently. The traditional stop list is an attempt to eliminate on linguistic grounds the most frequent stiff terms.
2. noisy terms – terms distributed unreliably within a category and between classes. These often have a small frequency, but there are very many of them, causing *dispersion* of the document scores.

A good Term Selection criterion will remove both.

At the optimal values for the Rocchio and Winnow parameters, we apply Simplified χ^2 (SX) as a local (i.e. category-dependent) Term Selection criterion in order to find the optimal number of terms per category (i.e. the number or rather range that maximizes Accuracy).

For our baseline, the keyword representation, term selection does not improve the Accuracy further, because the optimal choice of parameters apparently has the effect of removing most of the noisy terms. But for other representations we found that suitable term selection definitely raised the Accuracy (see later).

3.6   Summarizing the Baseline

Here we summarize the best results obtained in classifying EPO1A using keywords.

algorithm	method	max F1 value	parameter value
Winnow	raw	.83	$\theta^+ = 1.1, \theta^- = 0.9$
Winnow	tuned	.88	$\theta^+ = 3.0, \theta^- = 0.4$
Winnow	TSel	.88	1400-2000 terms/class
Rocchio	raw	.75	β=4, γ=1
Rocchio	tuned	.81	$\beta = .7, \gamma$=1
Rocchio	TSel	.81	100-1000 terms/class

At the optimal parameter values, Term Selection makes hardly any improvement to the Accuracy, but the number of terms per class can be quite low without losing Accuracy.

4   Adding Phrases to Words

All authorities (e.g. [Fagan, 1988][Lewis and Croft, 1990][Strzalkowski, 1999]) agree that phrases should be used *besides* keywords, not *instead of* keywords. This is based on experience made with some form of phrases in query-based retrieval, where adding more precise terms to a query may always be beneficial. In document classification, the classification engine has to choose a subset of the terms available, not only for reasons of efficiency but also to optimize the Accuracy of the classification. It has to choose from a plethora of possible terms the most discriminative ones. What happens when we add to the tens of thousands of keywords many hundred thousands of phrases, all clamouring for attention? Is the Term Selection mechanism capable of coping with this riot? Will we need many more terms per category? Or will the (low-frequency) phrases simply be ignored with respect to the much more frequent keywords?

After combining each document with the phrases extracted from it, we have repeated the experiment described above, and the results can be summarized as follows:

algorithm	method	max F1 value	parameter value
Winnow	raw	.82	$\theta^+ = 1.1, \theta^- = 0.9$
Winnow	tuned	.88	$\theta^+ = 3.0, \theta^- = 0.4$
Winnow	TSel	.88	1400+ terms/class
Rocchio	raw	.78	$\beta=4, \gamma=1$
Rocchio	tuned	.82	$\beta = .7, \gamma=1$
Rocchio	TSel	.83	100-1000 terms/class

Rocchio performs a little bit better than for keywords alone, but the optimal choice of β is the same. Winnow is not improved. Again, Term Selection makes no appreciable difference.

Inspection of the generated classifier shows that on the average only one HM pair is included among the top 40 terms, confirming our fear that the HM pairs are overwhelmed by the much more frequently occurring keywords.

5   Phrases Instead of Words

The easiest way to liberate the phrases from the aggressive keywords is to dispense with the keywords altogether and to use phrases instead of keywords. It also seems likely that only some well-chosen subset of the keywords should be used, in order to achieve optimal precision and recall.

In this section we shall compare the properties of a wide spectrum of text representations, ranging from pure HM pairs (bag-of-phrases representation) to all (key)words (bag-of-words representation).

The baseline which we want to exceed is remarkably high, due to the good statistical properties of the words in the text, even without lemmatization.

5.1   Pure HM Pairs

Starting at the extreme end, we investigate the effect of using only "pure" HM pairs, with a nonempty modifier, corresponding to the composed phrases and the traditional collocations.

Optimal Choice of Parameters As was the case with the keyword representation, we have first determined the optimal Winnow and Rocchio parameters.

At the traditional value of those parameters, the Accuracy was much lower than for the keyword representation. In particular, the Recall is much less than the Precision. Tuning the Winnow and Rocchio parameters in order to adapt them to this different representation greatly improves the Accuracy (see the table in 5.1), but the optimal parameters values are practically the same as for keywords.

Term Selection has no positive effect for Rocchio, but Winnow with SX manages to raise the Accuracy by another 7%.

Using all 16000 documents as the train set (so that all terms are included) for Winnow with optimal parameters and Term Selection (first eliminating the hapaxes (MinTF=2) and then selecting 3000 terms per category), the following results show the effect of term selection on the number of terms:

```
541537 different terms in train set
119773 global terms in train set
30289 final terms in train set
```

It is clear that about 421000 of the terms are hapaxes. Of the remaining HM pairs about 90000 are eliminated by term selection. Only 30289 terms (instead of 16×3000) remain, because there is much overlap in the terms selected for the 16 classes.

The following graph shows for a typical example the selected terms with their Document Frequencies (DF); both at the high end and at the low end terms have been eliminated.

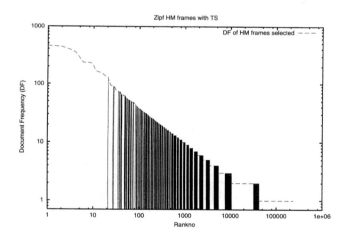

Summary HM Using only the "pure HM pairs, the Accuracy falls far short of the baseline, even with the best choice of parameters:

algorithm	method	max F1 value	parameter value
Winnow	raw	.37	$\theta^+ = 1.1, \theta^- = 0.9$
Winnow	tuned	.56	$\theta^+ = 3.0, \theta^- = 0.1$
Winnow	TSel	.63	3000-4000 terms/class
Rocchio	raw	.40	$\beta=4, \gamma=1$
Rocchio	tuned	.57	$\beta = .7, \gamma=1$
Rocchio	TSel	.57	no term selection

5.2   Phrases Plus Single Heads

Not all phrases are composed. A non-composed phrase will have an empty modifier, which excludes it from the pure HM pairs. In this section we therefore add the single heads taken from the HM pairs as terms.

[shoes] [shoes,walking] [shoes,new]

Due to the prominent semantical role of heads, they are very promising classification terms, but we expect them to be less precise than pure HM pairs (since the modifiers were added to them to increase precision), and to have higher Term and Document Frequencies so that they might overwhelm the pure HM pairs.

Again we optimize the parameters and determine the Accuracy as a function of the number of terms per category, selected with the SX criterion. The effect of Term Selection is small, the optimum number of terms per class is in a broad band at a high number of terms, much higher than for keywords. It appears that many infrequent terms have to be combined in order to achieve good Precision and Recall.

Training and testing on seen documents again, we now obtain:

```
573222 different terms in train set
137451 global terms in train set
26546 final terms in train set
```

There are 32000 more terms to begin with, of which 14000 are eliminated as hapaxes. At the bottom line, fewer terms are selected. Inspection of the generated classifiers shows that only 4 HM pairs are included among the top 40 terms.

Summary HM+H Adding the heads to the pure HM pairs greatly improves the Accuracy, provided the parameters are well-chosen. The additional effect of Term Selection is small.

algorithm	method	max F1 value	parameter value
Winnow	raw	.54	$\theta^+ = 1.1, \theta^- = 0.9$
Winnow	tuned	.77	$\theta^+ = 3.0, \theta^- = 0.4$
Winnow	TSel	.79	3000-7000 terms/class
Rocchio	raw	.55	$\beta=4, \gamma=1$
Rocchio	tuned	.715	$\beta = .7, \gamma=1$
Rocchio	TSel	.72	5000-7000 terms/class

5.3   Phrases Plus Heads and Modifiers

In the next representation, we include besides the pure HM pairs and their heads also their modifiers, which we also expect to be be important keywords.

Using this representation, the example tree [[shoes,walking],new] is now unnested to

[shoes] [shoes,walking] [shoes,new] [walking] [new]

We expect this addition to be a mixed blessing: again the number of different terms is increased, and the heads and modifiers are certainly not statistically independent from the HM pair from which they are derived.

The effect of Term Selection on the number of terms is:

633412 different terms in train set
162758 global terms in train set
24650 final terms in train set

The modifiers add about 60000 modifiers new terms, of which only 25000 are not eliminated as hapaxes. The number of terms after term selection is reduced by about 2000, mostly replacing a number of HM pairs by one word. Indeed, the top 40 terms now contain only one HM pair.

Summary HM+H+M The Accuracy is now much improved by tuning and Term selection, and nearly as good as for keywords alone ...

algorithm	method	max F1 value	parameter value
Winnow	raw	.59	$\theta^+ = 1.1, \theta^- = 0.9$
Winnow	tuned	.85	$\theta^+ = 3.0, \theta^- = 0.5$
Winnow	TSel	.855	3000-7000 terms/class
Rocchio	raw	.715	$\beta=4, \gamma=1$
Rocchio	tuned	.78	$\beta = .7, \gamma=1$
Rocchio	TSel	.79	2000-7000 terms/class

But what we have achieved looks more like a linguistic form of term selection than like the best way to use phrases as terms.

5.4   Conclusion

It is clear that we have not succeeded in domesticating the wild phrases. The experiments described here did not yield a document representation based on Head/Modifier pairs which gives better classification Accuracy than the traditional keywords, but it did give many surprises.

The first surprise is that the optimal setting of the Winnow and Rocchio parameters are so far from the values given in literature. Our main result is that the choice of parameters is crucial. By themselves the optimal parameter settings for Winnow and Rocchio differ little from one representation to another, at least for the EPO1A corpus, but the parameters value quoted in literature are far from optimal.

The use of an appropriate Term Selection (Simplified ChiSquare) adds some further Accuracy (7% in the case of pure HM pairs and 0-2% with keywords added), which shows that Term Selection is an important issue when using HM pairs.

The Winnow algorithm again clearly outperforms the Rocchio algorithm, although before tuning and Term Selection Rocchio behaves slightly better than Winnow.

Compared to the use of all keywords as a baseline, adding phrases helps very little, because their Document Frequencies are so low that they get very little weight. The various ways to use phrases *instead of* keywords all give less Accuracy than the baseline. Even with the best Term Selection, pure HM pairs give the lowest Accuracy. Adding the single heads improves it, and adding the modifiers even more, closely approaching the baseline but still below it (but with this last representation very few HM pairs are actually selected).

This may mean that at least some of the best classification terms are not heads or modifiers, as found by the syntax analysis. Maybe they are not verbs, nouns or adjectives and therefore do not appear in the HM pairs.

The quality of the linguistic resources is another concern: the limited Precision and Recall of the HM pair extraction (presently between 60 and 70%) causes the system to miss about one third of them. The free resources used here need more work.

Text Categorization is still an area where Statistics wins over Linguistics. It profits less from the use of phrases than traditional Query-based Retrieval, because the latter involves human formulation of queries.

5.5   Outlook

> *An expert is a man who has made all the mistakes, which can be made, in a very narrow field.*
>
> – Niels Henrik David Bohr (1885-1962).

In spite of this, we are convinced that the use of phrases in Text Categorization merits further research.

Intuitively, a document yields very many highly precise phrases with a very low Document Frequency. We can try to improve term conflation by lemmatization and syntactical or semantical normalizations. Furthermore, many of the phrases are statistically and linguistically related, or at least not independent, as is the case for two HM pairs with the same head. We may perform some form of Term Clustering [Lewis and Croft, 1990] or fuzzy matching [Koster et al., 1999] in order to conflate terms that are not independent.

But most urgently, new language models capturing some of the richness of phrase structure must be found. In the present experiment, we have used HM pairs as monolithic terms, disregarding their internal structure. There is additional information to be found in the co-occurrence of heads with different modifiers, in particular when generalizing from HM pairs to complete HM trees of varying depth.

References

[Arampatzis et al., 2000a] Avi Arampatzis, Jean Beney, C. H. A. Koster, Th.P. van der Weide, KUN on the TREC-9 Filtering Track: Incrementality, Decay, and Threshold Optimization for Adaptive Filtering Systems. The Ninth Text REtrieval Conference (TREC-9), Gaithersburg, Maryland, November 13-16, 2000.

[Caropreso et al, 2000] M. F. Caropreso, S. Matwin and F. Sebastiani (2001), A learner-independent evaluation of the usefulness of statistical phrases for automated text categorization, In: A. G. Chin (Ed.), *Text Databases and Document Management: Theory and Practice*, Idea Group Publishing, Hershey, US, pp. 78–102.

[Cohen and Singer, 1999] W. W. Cohen and Y. Singer (1999), Context-sensitive learning methods for text categorization. *ACM Transactions on Information Systems 13*, 1, 100-111.

[Dagan et al, 1997] I. Dagan, Y. Karov, D. Roth (1997), Mistake-Driven Learning in Text Categorization. In: *Proceedings of the Second Conference on Empirical Methods in NLP*, pp. 55-63.

[Evans and Lefferts, 1994] D. Evans and R. G. Lefferts (1994), Design and evaluation of the CLARIT-TREC-2 system. Proceedings TREC-2, NIST Special Publication 500-215, pp. 137-150.

[Fagan, 1988] J. L. Fagan (1988), *Experiments in automatic phrase indexing for document retrieval: a comparison of syntactic and non-syntactic methods*, PhD Thesis, Cornell University.

[Grove et al, 2001] A. Grove, N. Littlestone, and D. Schuurmans (2001), General convergence results for linear discriminant updates. Machine Learning 43(3), pp. 173-210.

[Koster et al., 1999] C. H. A. Koster, C. Derksen, D. van de Ende and J. Potjer, Normalization and matching in the DORO system. Proceedings of IRSG'99, 10pp.

[Koster et al, 2001] C. H. A. Koster, M. Seutter and J. Beney (2001), Classifying Patent Applications with Winnow, Proceedings Benelearn 2001, Antwerpen, 8pp.

[Koster and Verbruggen, 2002] C. H. A. Koster and E. Verbruggen (2002), The AGFL Grammar Work Lab, Proceedings FREENIX/Usenix 2002, pp 13-18.

[Krier and Zaccà, 2001] M. Krier and F. Zaccà (2001), Automatic Categorisation Applications at the European Patent Office, International CHemical Information Conference, Nimes, October 2001, 10 pp.

[Lewis and Croft, 1990] Term Clustering of Syntactic Phrases (1990), Proceedings SIGIR 90, pp. 385-404.

[Lin, 1995] D. Lin (1995), A dependency-based method for evaluating broad-coverage parsers. *Proceedings IJCAI-95*, pp. 1420-1425.

[Peters and Koster, 2002] C. Peters and C. H. A. Koster (2002), Uncertainty-based Noise Reduction and Term Selection, Proceedings ECIR 2002, Springer LNCS 2291, pp 248-267.

[Rocchio, 1971] J. J. Rocchio (1971), Relevance feedback in Information Retrieval, In: Salton, G. (ed.), *The Smart Retrieval system - experiments in automatic document processing*, Prentice - Hall, Englewood Cliffs, NJ, pp 313-323.

[Ruge, 1992] G. Ruge (1992), Experiments on Linguistically Based Term Associations, Information Processing & management, 28(3), pp. 317-332.

[Strzalkowski, 1992] T. Strzalkowski (1992), TTP: A Fast and Robust Parser for Natural Language, In: Proceedings COLING '92, pp 198-204.

[Strzalkowski, 1999] T. Strzalkowski, editor (1999), *Natural Language Information Retrieval*, Kluwer Academic Publishers, ISBN 0-7923-5685-3.

[Yiming and Pedersen, 1997] Y. Yiming and J. P. Pedersen (1997), A Comparative Study on Feature Selection in Text Categorization. In: ICML 97, pp. 412-420.

Stemming and Decompounding
for German Text Retrieval

Martin Braschler[1,2] and Bärbel Ripplinger[1]

[1] Eurospider Information Technology AG
Schaffhauserstrasse 18, CH-8006 Zürich, Switzerland
`martin.braschler@eurospider.com`
`bripplinger@web.de`
[2] Université de Neuchâtel, Institut Interfacultaire d'Informatique
Pierre-à-Mazel 7, CH-2001 Neuchâtel, Switzerland
`martin.braschler@unine.ch`

Abstract. The stemming problem, i.e. finding a common stem for different forms of a term, has been extensively studied for English, but considerably less is known for other languages. Previously, it has been claimed that stemming is essential for highly declensional languages. We report on our experiments on stemming for German, where an additional issue is the handling of compounds, which are formed by concatenating several words. Rarely do studies on stemming for any language cover more than one or two different approaches. This paper makes a major contribution that transcends its focus on German by investigating a complete spectrum of approaches, ranging from language-independent to elaborate linguistic methods. The main findings are that stemming is beneficial even when using a simple approach, and that carefully designed decompounding, the splitting of compound words, remarkably boosts performance. All findings are based on a thorough analysis using a large reliable test collection.

1   Introduction

Most modern information retrieval (IR) systems implement some sort of what is commonly known as "stemming". A system using stemming conflates derived word forms to a common stem, thereby both reducing the size of the search index and, more importantly, allowing to retrieve documents independent of the specific word form used in the query and documents.

The main reason for the use of stemming is the hope that through the increased number of matches between search terms and documents, the quality of search results is improved. In terms of the most popular measures for determining retrieval effectiveness, precision and recall, stemmed terms retrieve additional relevant documents that would have otherwise gone undetected (improved recall). There is

F. Sebastiani (Ed.): ECIR 2003, LNCS 2633, pp. 177–192, 2003.

also potential for improved precision, since additional term matches can contribute to a better weighting for a query/document pair.

Viewing stemming as a vehicle to enhance retrieval effectiveness necessitates an analysis of the produced stems with regard to overstemming or understemming. If a stemmer conflates terms too aggressively, many extraneous matches between the query and irrelevant documents are produced; and we talk of "overstemming". Even though the stems that are produced may be correct from a linguistic viewpoint, they are not helpful for retrieval. In contrast, if crucial relevant documents are missed because of a conservative stemming strategy, we speak of "understemming". A good stemmer has to find the right balance of conflation for effective retrieval.

Where most previous studies compare their stemming method only to no stemming or to simple affix stripping methods such as proposed by Lovins [15] and Porter [21], the experiments described here compare a complete spectrum of methods, ranging from language-independent to sophisticated linguistic analysis. We consider this an important step forward since only an exhaustive comparison can indicate the potential in using complex methods versus simpler approaches.

The paper deals with the German language, where, besides stemming, decompounding seems to be an additional issue in retrieval. In most Germanic languages (e.g. German, Dutch, Swedish), but also in some other languages (e.g. Finnish), it is possible to build compounds by concatenating several words. Performance, especially recall, may be negatively affected if this word formation process is not taken into account. If the user enters only parts of compound words or replaces the compound with a phrasal construction, relevant documents may not be found.

Similar to stemming, there are different approaches to analyze and split compounds ("decompounding"). We again concentrate on the usefulness of compound splitting for information retrieval, and not as a linguistic exercise. The splitting of some compounds words can cause a shift of meaning. This is e.g. often the case for complex technical terminology. Such compounds should be left intact ("conservative decompounding"). On the other hand, the productive nature of German compound formation, which allows for ad-hoc formation of new compounds, makes it impossible to correctly split all potential compound words. "Aggressive decompounding" attempts to produce a maximum number of splittings by using heuristics. In our experiments, we also investigated different approaches to decompounding, ranging from essentially surface-based to well-developed linguistic methods.

Most studies on stemmer and decompounding behavior have been conducted using small test collections. The size of the collection, especially the length of the retrieval items, is important, since short documents (e.g. only titles, or titles and abstracts) increase the likelihood for word mismatch if no stemming is used. It is therefore not immediately obvious if a performance improvement measured on small collections with short documents, such as widely used before 1990, translates into an improvement on larger collections with long documents. In our work we used a part of the German collection from the CLEF corpus to get appropriate statistical data.

The remainder of the paper is structured as follows: we will first give an overview of related work (section 2) and a summary of some relevant key characteristics of the German language (section 3), before detailing the experimental setup in section 4 (test collection), section 5 (stemming and decompounding approaches) and section 6 (retrieval system). The experiments themselves are then discussed, along with a careful statistical analysis and a query-by-query analysis (section 7 through section 9). The paper closes with conclusions and an outlook.

2   Related Work

The role of stemming is well explored for English, even though results are controversial. Where Harman [7] reported that stemming gives no benefit, Frakes [4] and Hull [9] claim at least a small benefit. Especially notable is the study by Hull [9], which describes a very careful analysis of different stemmers and provides one of the rare attempts to compare a wide range of different approaches to stemming. Furthermore, in this study, data from the popular TREC test collections [8] is used, which are much larger than earlier collections and contain lengthy documents. Because English has no productive compounding process, the effects of decompounding were never an issue in these studies.

In recent years, more studies on stemming behavior for languages other than English have been published. While simple stemmers are considered sufficient for languages such as English, it is claimed that rich declensional languages require more sophisticated stemming approaches. Studies exist on Slovene [20], Hebrew [2], Dutch [13], German [30], [19], Italian [26] French [23], and others. For most of these languages, significant benefits (from 10% to 130%) can be observed. Decompounding has been investigated, at least for German [19] and Dutch [12]. The improvements reported are about 17% to 54%.

Previous work on what could be termed as "German stemming" was mainly conducted in the context of studies comparing manual and automatic indexing in databases. The PADOK studies [30][14], conducted in the late eighties, compared several approaches to automatic indexing on patent data. The baseline system indexed every token in the original form as it appears in the document. However, queries could make use of string truncation and wildcards. This baseline system was compared to the two systems "PASSAT", comprising morphological analysis, including decompounding (used in PADOK I & PADOK II), and "CTX" which additionally applied a syntactical analysis (used in PADOK I only). In PADOK I [30], documents consisting of titles and abstracts only were used. It was found that PASSAT achieved higher recall and CTX achieved higher precision than the baseline system. In PADOK II [14], the full text of the documents was used. In this new setting, no significant gain from using the morphological analysis employed by PASSAT could be detected.

The later GIRT pretest used texts from the field of social sciences [5]. Two systems were compared: "freeWAISsf" and "Messenger". The two systems differ in more areas than just in the stemming approaches employed (freeWAISsf uses weak morphological analysis, Messenger apparently no stemming), making it hard to draw conclusions on the effectiveness of the stemming component based on the published results.

Recent work by Moulinier et al. [19] reported a performance gain of 20% using linguistic analysis (stemming plus compound analysis) for German. A gain of 89% in recall together with a loss of 24% in precision are the results obtained by Ripplinger [22] in a small experiment within a domain specific environment. The experiments by Monz and de Rijke [18] show a gain of 25% to 69% for German and Dutch respectively using blind relevance feedback in addition to a linguistic processing. Tomlinson [28] applied linguistic stemming including decompounding, and obtained a performance improvement of 43% for German, and 30% for Dutch. He also conducted experiments for English and Romance languages (French, Italian, and Spanish) with a performance gain of 5% to 18%.

Most of this recent work came in the context of the TREC CLIR task and the CLEF campaigns. The experiments are usually confined to a comparison between one particular stemming or decompounding approach and not using any form of stemming at all. It is therefore unclear how the findings can assist in the choice of a particular stemming approach or how to assess the absolute potential of stemming for performance improvement in the German language.

3   Characteristics of the German Language

German, in contrast to English, is a highly declensional language, a fact expressed by a rich system of inflections and cases. Depending on the word class, i.e. noun, verb, or adjective, there is a set of possible inflections for each particular word (e.g. 144 forms for verbs), which makes stemming more complicated compared to languages such as English. Furthermore, words can be formed by attaching multiple derivational inflections to a stem in order to build new forms. For instance, the lexeme "inform" is the stem for "informieren", "informiert", "informierte" "informierend", "Information", "Informant", "informative", "informatorisch", etc.

Additionally, in most Germanic languages (e.g. Dutch, Swedish) and also in some other languages (e.g. Finnish), it is possible in German to build compounds by concatenating several words, such as e.g., "Haustür" (house door) or "Frühstück" (breakfast). In almost all languages such compound formation occurs, such as "hairdresser", "speedboad" in English, and "portefeuille" (wallet), "bonhomme" (fellow) in French. However, in English and in Romance languages these words are lexicalised, i.e. they cannot be expressed by a nominal phrase the way compounds in Germanic languages could be ("Haustür" vs. "Tür des Hauses"). Because Germanic languages also know lexicalised compounds, the treatment of such words is quite complicated. The success of compound analysis depends more on linguistic knowledge than stemming does.

In principle, only words with certain types of part-of-speech can be coupled, for instance noun/noun, adjective/noun, or verb/noun. Some analyzers split only those compounds where the constituents have the same part-of-speech (noun/noun, adjective/adjective), and could be thus classified as "conservative". Others split the compounds into all possible word forms (often by means of a lexicon lookup). Because these methods do not consider the part of speech of the constituents, i.e. also splitting pronouns, prepositions or articles, this approach can be described as "aggressive". Linguistic compound analyzers lie in between, splitting compounds only into valid word forms, i.e. nouns, verbs, adjectives.

Table 1. Key characteristics of the test collection

Document source	Frankfurter Rundschau 1994, Der Spiegel 1994, 1995
Number of documents	153,694
Size (MByte)	383
Number of topics	85
Mean number of indexing terms per document (tokens minus stopwords)	156.09
Relevance Assessments	20,980
Total number of relevant documents	1,790

4   The Test Collection

Many of the studies on stemming behavior for languages other than English suffer from scarce availability of suitable test collections. Whereas for English there exist the well-known TREC collections, comparable test data became available only recently for important European and Asian languages (through the CLEF and NTCIR campaigns). For their 2001 evaluation campaign, the CLEF consortium distributed a multilingual document collection of roughly 1,000,000 documents written in one of six languages (Dutch, English, French, German, Italian and Spanish). For the German part of this data, CLEF 2000 used articles from the daily newspaper "Frankfurter Rundschau" and the weekly news magazine "Der Spiegel". CLEF 2001 used a superset of this, adding newswire articles taken from the "Schweizerische Depeschenagentur SDA". To go with this data, there is a total of 90 topics[1] (40 for 2000, 50 for 2001) with corresponding relevance assessments. By eliminating the SDA articles, we were able to form a unified German test collection, using the topics from both years. Of the 90 topics, 85 have matches in the German data that we used. This comparatively high number of topics (many studies use only 50 queries or less) facilitates the detection of significant differences in stemming an decompounding behavior (see also Table 1).

5   Stemming and Decompounding Approaches

One of the main objectives of this study is to compare approaches from a spectrum as wide as possible. This spectrum covers methods ranging from completely language-independent methods to components that use elaborate linguistic knowledge. Apart from using different stemming and decompounding methods, all other indexing parameters remain constant (tokenization, stopword list, etc.). The approaches used in this study are:

---

[1] Topics are "statements of user needs". They form the basis for the construction of queries, which are then run against the document collection. In all our experiments, we constructed the queries without manual intervention ("automatic experiments"), by indexing all or part of the topic text.

1. No stemming ("n" run)

As a baseline, we indexed all documents without using any form of stemming or decompounding.

2. Combination of word-based and n-gram based retrieval ("6" run)

The use of combined character n-gram and word-based indexing was reported as a successful approach to German text retrieval by Mayfield et al. [17] and Savoy [24]. Based on their findings, we chose to combine 6-grams and unstemmed words. The individual 6-grams, built on the unstemmed words, potentially span word boundaries. A main benefit of this approach is its complete language independence - no specific linguistic knowledge is needed to form the n-grams, and the word-based indexing is done without attempting conflation. On the other hand, the method is storage-intensive: the large number of different n-grams leads to a massively increased index size (roughly three times that of an unstemmed word-based index).

3. Linguistica: Automatic machine learning ("l" run)

Linguistica [6] performs a morphological segmentation based on unsupervised learning. The aim is to find the correct morphological splits for individual words, in a language-independent way. Possible categories of stems are identified using a set of suffixes that is detected solely based on surface forms. As an outcome Linguistica produces a lexicon comprising each word of the collection together with its possible affixes, for instance "machbar" (feasible), "machbar|en" (feasible), "machbar|es" (feasible), "machbar|keit" (feasibility). For our experiment we used these entries, which often do not really denote a proper stem from a linguistic viewpoint.

Decompounding occurs only by accident; i.e. if a word is frequently used as a compound constituent, the systems may incorrectly classify this word as an affix. Unfortunately, this means some compounds are conflated with only their modifier, i.e. "Datenbank" (data base) is conflated to "daten" (data), losing the constituent "bank".

4. NIST stemmer: Rule-based approach ("t" run, "T" run)

The NIST German rule-based stemmer has been constructed by analysis of the frequency of German suffixes in large wordlists. The stemmer is available as a part of the NIST ZPrise 2 retrieval system. Its approach is similar to the Porter English stemmer [21]. The rules were hand-crafted to produce as many valid conflations of high-frequency word forms as possible, while keeping the rate of incorrect conflations low. The stemmer attempts to iteratively strip suffixes from a word. For instance the word "glück|lich|er|weis|e" (luckily) is reduced to "gluck" (same stem as for "luck").

The stemmer can be combined with a corpus-based decompounding component based on co-occurrence analysis. After collecting a list of candidate nouns, the component tries to find valid splittings by looking for potential constituents that co-occur in the same documents. This purely corpus-based approach produces a number of errors, but is overall rather conservative in the number of splittings generated.

For our experiments, we used both the pure stemming approach ("t" NIST_s run) and the combination with decompounding ("T" NIST_d run). This study represents the first careful evaluation of the NIST German stemmer.

5. Spider stemmer: Commercially motivated (rule -based and lexicon) approach ("s" run, "S" run)

For our experiments we had access to the stemming component used in the commercial Eurospider retrieval system. The approach is based on a combination of a lexicon and a set of rules which are used for suffix stripping and unknown words [29].

This stemmer has been used for over five years in all commercial installations of the Eurospider system, and has therefore been constantly adapted according to customer feedback. Extensive performance figures for Spider stemmer are published publicly for the first time in this study.

The component includes optional decompounding, which can be applied in one of three modes, from conservative to aggressive splitting. For our runs we used the version without decompounding (run "s" Spider_NS) as well as the aggressive splitting (run "S" Spider_FS). For example, "Schiffskollision" (ship collision) is split and reduced to "schiff_kollid" and "Bevölkerung" (population) is reduced to "bevolk" (same stem as e.g. "to populate").

6. MPRO: Morpho-syntactic analysis ("m" run, "M" run)

MPRO, a development by the IAI [16], performs a morpho-syntactic analysis consisting of lemmatization, part-of-speech tagging, and, for German, a compound analysis. To lemmatize and tag words with their part-of-speech(s), MPRO uses general morphological rules in form of small subroutines which co-operate with a morphological dictionary. As result for each word a set of attribute-value pairs describing inflectional attributes (e.g. gender, number, tense, mood, etc.), word structure and semantics (lexical base form, derivational root form, compound constituents, semantic class, etc.) is produced. With this tool, the corpus has been analyzed and for each word, information about the lexical base form (lu), and the derivational root (ls) is used to generate lexical resources. For instance, the analysis of the word "Kollision" (collision) results in

{string=kollision,c=noun,lu=kollision,nb=sg,g=f,t=kollision,
ts=kollision, ds=kollidieren~ation,ls=kollidieren,s=ation,...}

and produces as a lexical unit "kollision" and as a root form "kollidieren" (collide); for the compound "Schiffskollision" (ship collision) MPRO generates a splitting based on lexical base forms, "schiff_kollision", and one based on derivational root forms of the compound constituents, "schiff#kollidieren". For our experiments, we used the lexical base forms and no decompounding information for the stemming only run, MPRO_LU ("m"), and the more aggressive splitting by considering derivational information for the decompounding run, MPRO_LS_d ("M").

6   The Retrieval System

For retrieval, the commercial *relevancy* system from Eurospider is used. Since the system uses a modular approach, the lexical resources generated from the individual approaches described above can easily be used for indexing. *relevancy* also offers the possibility of indexing n-grams. For weighting of both documents and queries, we chose the Lnu.ltn weighting scheme [25], with the "slope" parameter set to 0.15 (determined empirically to be the optimal value). There is no different weight for compound constituents as proposed by Hull et al. [11]. Lnu.ltn is widely used and has given competitive performance on the CLEF collection (see e.g. [2]). The scheme includes document length normalization, a factor influenced by stemming, and some caution may be appropriate when generalizing to very different weighting approaches.

7   Experiments

For each of the approaches described above, we produced several results sets ("runs"), using different sections of the topics. The topics are structured into title, description and narrative fields, which express a user's information need in different length. The title section ("T") typically consists of one to three keywords, the description section ("D") typically consists of one sentence, and the narrative section ("N") usually is several sentences long, giving detailed instructions on how to determine the relevance of retrieved documents. Using these fields, seven different combinations are possible (TDN, TD, TN, DN, N, D, T). In this paper, we report on the results obtained using the longest possible queries "TDN" and the shortest possible queries "T", two popular choices for retrieval experiments.

In Table 2, we give the mean average precision numbers for all runs. This is the most popular single-valued measure for TREC-style retrieval experiments, and is defined as non-interpolated average precision over all relevant documents. According to these numbers, methods that use decompounding (lower half of Table 2) perform better than methods that do not split compound words (upper half of Table 2). An exception is the combined 6-gram/word-based indexing run, which we treat as a "decompounding run", since the 6-grams allow matching of compound parts. This is the only run that for long queries (TDN) performs worse than the baseline of no stemming. The two top methods, "S" Spider_FS and "M" MPRO_LS_d, show almost identical performance, while "T" NIST_d performs slightly worse (see also Fig. 2 and Fig. 4). They obtain performance gains of between 33% and 60% depending on query length when compared to no stemming. The gap to the best method without decompounding ("t" NIST_s) is fairly large – "S" Spider_FS outperforms "t" NIST_s by 30.7% (T queries) and 21.4% (TDN queries), respectively.

Table 2. Retrieval results (mean average precision)

Mean Average Precision	T	TDN
"n" no stemming	0.2275	0.3321
"l" Linguistica	0.2302 (+1.2%)	0.3435 (+3.4%)
"m" MPRO_LU	0.2682 (+17.9%)	0.3461 (+4.2%)
"s" Spider_NS	0.2722 (+19.6%)	0.3616 (+8.9%)
"t" NIST_s	0.2792 (+22.7%)	0.3682 (+10.9%)
"6" 6-gram + Word	0.2757 (+21.2%)	0.3219 (-3.1%)
"T" NIST_d	0.3240 (+42.4%)	0.4022 (+21.1%)
"M" MPRO_LS_d	0.3547 (+55.9%)	0.4440 (+33.7%)
"S" Spider_FS	**0.3650 (+60.4%)**	**0.4471 (+34.6%)**

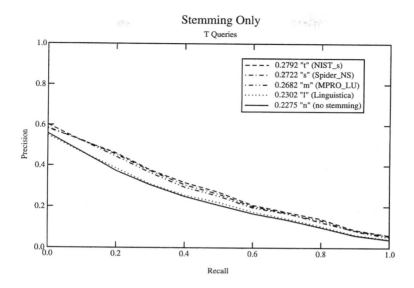

Fig. 1. Recall/precision curve for "stemming only" runs (short "T" queries). The top three methods show very similar performance

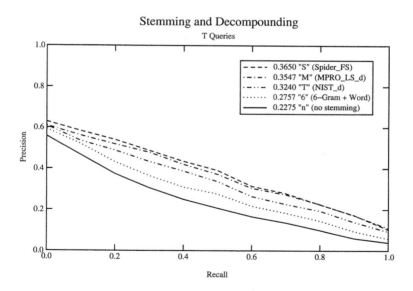

Fig. 2. Recall/precision curve for runs using stemming and decompounding (short "T" queries). The choice of decompounding method produces much larger performance differences than those observed for "stemming only" experiments

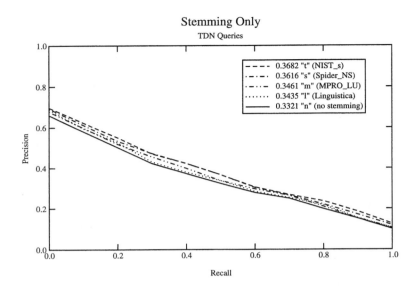

Fig. 3. Recall/precision curve for "stemming only" runs (long "TDN" queries). As for short queries, the performance of the top methods is very similar

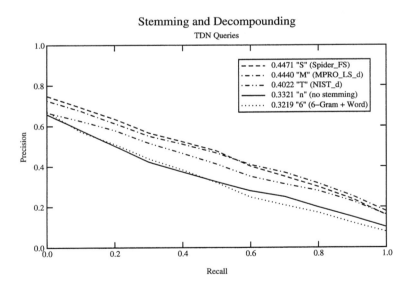

Fig. 4. Recall/precision curve for runs using stemming and decompounding (long "TDN" queries). As for short queries, the performance differences are more evident than for the "stemming only" experiments

Table 3. Number of relevant documents retrieved (total number of relevant documents: 1790)

# Relevant Docs Retrieved	T	TDN
"n" no stemming	1281	1535
"l" Linguistica	1300 (+1.5%)	1538 (+0.2%)
"t" NIST_s	1427 (+11.4%)	1584 (+3.2%)
"m" MPRO_LU	1433 (+11.9%)	1547 (+0.8%)
"s" Spider_NS	1434 (+11.9%)	1595 (+3.9%)
"6" 6-gram + Word	1551 (+21.1%)	1594 (+3.8%)
"T" NIST_d	1577 (+23.1%)	1632 (+6.3%)
"M" MPRO_LS_d	1625 (+26.9%)	1704 (+11.0%)
"S" Spider_FS	**1669 (+30.3%)**	**1690 (+10.1%)**

The top three non-decompounding methods, "t" NIST_s, "s" Spider_NS, and "m" MPRO_LU, have similar performance for both query lengths, as does the 6-gram/word-based run, but for T queries only (see also Fig. 1 and Fig. 3). The latter performs clearly worse for TDN queries.

Looking at the total number of relevant documents retrieved (Table 3), all methods outperform no stemming for both query lengths. Again, the three decompounding methods "S" Spider_FS, "M" MPRO_LS_d and "T" NIST_d (lower half of Table 3) perform best, with the first two methods being very close. In this statistic, the combined 6-gram/word-based run compares favorably to the stemming methods that do not use decompounding ("s" Spider_NS, "m" MPRO_LU, "t" NIST_s, "l" Linguistica; upper half of Table 3). Of the latter four methods, "s" Spider_NS performs best.

8   Statistical Analysis

We used the IR-STAT-PAK tool by Blustein [1] for a statistical analysis of the results in terms of average precision. This tool provides an Analysis of Variance (ANOVA) which is the parametric test of choice in such situations but requires to check some assumptions concerning the data. Hull [10] provides details of these; in particular, the scores in question should be approximately normally distributed and their variance has to be approximately the same for all runs. IR-STAT-PAK uses the Hartley test to verify the equality of variances, and in our case, indicates that the assumption is satisfied. The program also offers an arcsine transformation, $f(x) = \arcsin\left(\sqrt{x}\right)$, which Tague-Sutcliffe [27] suggests for use with Precision/Recall measures to better meet the demand for normally distributed data. We used both raw and transformed scores to assure the suitability of our data for an ANOVA test (see Table 4). For the short "T" queries, we obtained the following results for average precision (after Tukey T test grouping):

$$\{"S","M"\} \succ \{"t","6","s","m","l","n"\}, "T" \succ \{"m","l","n"\} \qquad \text{(raw data)}$$
$$\{"S","M"\} \succ \{"6","t","s","m","l","n"\}, "T" \succ \{"l","n"\} \qquad \text{(arcsine)}$$

when using the arcsine transformation. The " $\succ$ " symbol denotes a statistically significant difference between two runs with probability p=0.95.

The analysis thus indicates that the "S" Spider_FS and "M" MPRO_LS_d runs, two methods that use decompounding, significantly outperform all methods without decompounding. They also outperform "T" NIST_d, but that difference is not statistically significant.

For "TDN" queries, the findings remain constant. There is a slight shift in ranking of the individual methods, but essentially the same significant differences are found:

$$\{"S","M"\} \succ \{"t","s","m","l","n","6"\}, "T" \succ \{"l","n","6"\} \quad \text{(raw data)}$$
$$\{"M","S"\} \succ \{"t","s","m","l","n","6"\}, "T" \succ \{"m","l","n","6"\} \quad \text{(arcsine)}$$

Table 4. ANOVA of Average Precision. Critical values: 1.9522 (Runs)/1.2892 (Query)

Experiment		T raw		T arcsine		TDN raw		TDN arcsine	
Source	DF	Mean Sq	F	Mean Sq	F	Mean Sq	F	Mean Sq	F
Runs	8	0.208	15.828	0.382	15.780	0.185	12.730	0.344	13.855
Query	84	0.574	43.757	0.969	40.079	0.619	42.630	1.013	40.751
Error	672	0.013		0.024		0.015		0.025	

9   Query-by-Query Analysis

In addition to the overall analysis presented in sections 7 and 8, we also analyzed the performance of individual queries in more detail. A set of nine queries were selected for showing conspicuous behavior, either in terms of overall performance or because of outliers by individual methods. Various measures, such as mean average precision, high precision measures (mean precision at 5, 10, 15 documents retrieved, mean precision at 10, 20, 30 documents retrieved, and precision at 100 documents retrieved) and uniquely retrieved relevant documents, as well as their respective standard deviations, were used to identify a set of interesting queries. For each query in this set, we determined the most important keywords, and examined all methods with regard to the stems that they produce for them, and the constituents of the compounds as identified by the various decompounding approaches.

We found that stemming is in most cases beneficial independent of the method applied. Approaches conducting a balanced conflation, avoiding both understemming and overstemming as best as possible, seem to be superior.

However, there are some queries where no stemming outperforms most or all of the stemming methods. Examples include queries where the keywords are already present in their base forms (and occur rarely in inflected forms) and represent simple concepts (no compound nouns). Furthermore, queries consisting of proper names show such effects, especially in short queries. For long queries, in these cases, the noise introduced by stemming cancels out the benefits from matching additional word forms.

Not surprisingly, we found a number of queries where the key to successful retrieval is clearly the ability to split compound words, since the constituents are important to the respective topic statements, and the compound commonly is transcribed in phrasal form in the documents.

However, there are also cases where decompounding is counterproductive. It seems that splitting is not beneficial for some types of compounds: For example, pure lexical approaches split "Mitgliedschaft" (membership), which is not a real compound, into "Mitglied" (member) and "Schaft" (shaft), although "schaft" (-ship) is in this case a derivational inflection and not a proper word. Linguistic-based approaches avoid in most cases such incorrect splittings. They also prevent splitting of proper names. Furthermore, compounds for which the splitting causes a shift of meaning such as "Frühstück" (breakfast), composed of "Früh" (early) and "Stück" (piece), should be left intact. Also, decompounding of words which are rarely written in phrasal form e.g. "Waldbrand" (forest fire) may negatively impact weighting.

Lastly, we found some oddities, which were either due to the evaluation measure that was used (e.g. mean average precision in case that there are very few relevant documents for a query) or to some erroneous conflations, which turned out to produce good matches by chance.

10   Conclusions

In our experiments, we demonstrated that stemming is useful for German text retrieval in most cases. Compared to a system without stemming, we obtained performance gains measured in mean average precision of up to 23% for short (T) and up to 11% for long queries (TDN). For recall we observed improvements of 12% for T, and 4% for TDN. Exceptions where stemming is detrimental are queries comprising proper names or other invariant words (where no inflection exists, or the inflection is rarely used). The different stemming methods show only weak significant differences, mainly in the high recall range.

An important finding of this study is that decompounding contributes more to performance improvement than stemming, 16% to 34% for short and 9% to 28% for long queries. In contrast to stemming, we observed larger differences between individual methods implying that it is important to carefully choose the right degree of decompounding. There are two main goals with respect to decompounding: Firstly to produce as many extra matches for retrieval as possible, and secondly to avoid inappropriate splittings. The two best runs, "S" Spider_FS and "M" MPRO_LS_d, put different emphasis on these goals. "S" Spider_FS splits aggressively, and "M" MPRO_LS_d avoids linguistically incorrect splittings. However, they show almost the same performance.

This report makes a major contribution to the discussion on the benefits of stemming that transcends its focus on the German language by employing a complete spectrum of stemming and decompounding approaches on a large reliable corpus, which allowed us to conduct a thorough analysis of the results. One outcome is that stemming can be done using comparatively simple approaches such as the NIST German stemmer, which showed competitive performance. In contrast, decompounding requires a more sophisticated approach, either providing a sufficient lexical coverage or linguistic knowledge to achieve correct handling of compounds.

Furthermore, we found that for German as a morphological rich language, purely language independent methods do not give competitive performance. The exception is the 6-gram/word-based run, but only for short queries. Even so, the results are still significantly worse than for other methods using decompounding, and the increased index size from using n-grams is a substantial drawback.

Future work could validate these findings that we obtained for unrestricted text for settings where domain specific terminology is frequent. Such terminology can have properties which may necessitate adaptations especially related to decompounding (e.g. medical terms of Latin origin, or names of chemical substances).

Acknowledgements

We would like to thank IAI for the opportunity to use MPRO. Thanks go to John Goldsmith for providing the Linguistica software, and the CLEF consortium and its data providers for the construction of the test collection. Decompounding for the NIST stemmer is based joint work with Paul Over from NIST. Jacques Savoy and three anonymous referees provided detailed comments and suggestions that helped improve the paper.

References

[1]   Blustein, J.: IR STAT PAK. URL: http://www.csd.uwo.ca/~jamie/IRSP-overview.html (last visit 11/19/2002).

[2]   Braschler, M., and Schäuble, P.: Experiments with the Eurospider Retrieval System for CLEF 2000. In Peters C. (Ed.): Cross-Language Information Retrieval and Evaluation, Workshop of the Cross-Language Evaluation Forum, CLEF 2000, pp. 140-148, 2001.

[3]   Choueka, Y.: Responsa: An Operational Full-Text Retrieval System With Linguistic Components for Large Corpora. In: Computational Lexicology and Lexicography: a Volume in Honor of B. Quemada, 1992.

[4]   Frakes, W. B.: Stemming Algorithms. In: Frakes, W. B. and Baeza-Yates, R. (Eds.): Information Retrieval, Data Structures & Algorithms, pp. 131-160. Prentice Hall, Eaglewood Cliffs, NJ, USA, 1992.

[5]   Frisch, E., and Kluck, M.: Pretest zum Projekt German Indexing and Retrieval Testdatabase (GIRT) unter Anwendung der Retrievalsysteme Messenger und freeWAISsf. IZ Arbeitsbericht Nr. 10, GESIS IZ Soz., Bonn, Germany, 1997. [in German].

[6]   Goldsmith, J.: Unsupervised Learning of the Morphology of a Natural Language. In Computational Linguistics, 27(2), pp. 153-198, MIT Press. URL: http://humanities.uchicago.edu/faculty/goldsmith/Linguistica2000/ (last visit 11/19/2002).

[7]   Harman, D.: How Effective is Suffixing?. In Journal of the American Society for Information Science, 42(1), pp. 7-15, 1991.

[8]   Harman, D.: The TREC Conferences. In Sparck-Jones, K. and Willett, P. (Eds.): Readings in Information Retrieval, Morgan Kaufmann Publishers, San Francisco, CA, USA 1997.

[9]   Hull, D. A.: Stemming Algorithms - A Case Study for Detailed Evaluation. In Journal of the American Society for Information Science 47(1), pp. 70-84, 1986.

[10]   Hull, D. A: Using Statistical Testing in the Evaluation of Retrieval Experiments. In Proceedings of the 16th ACM SIGIR Conference, Pittsburg, USA, 1993.

[11]   Hull, D. A., G. Grefenstette, B. M. Schultze, E. Gaussier, H. Schütze, O. Pedersen: Xerox TREC-5 Site Report: Routing, Filtering, NLP and Spanish Tracks. In Proceedings of the Fifth Text Retrieval Conference (TREC 5), Gaithersburg, USA, 1996.

[12]   Kraaij, W. and Pohlmann, R.: Using Linguistic Knowledge in Information Retrieval. OTS Working Paper OTS-WP-CL-96-001, University of Utrecht, The Netherlands, 1996.

[13]   Kraaij, W. and Pohlmann, R.: Viewing Stemming as Recall Enhancement. In Proceedings of the 19th Annual International ACM SIGIR Conference on Research and Development in Information Retrieval, Zurich, Switzerland, 1996.

[14]   Krause, J., and Womser-Hacker, C.: Das Deutsche Patent-informationssystem. Entwicklungstendenzen, Retrievaltests und Bewertungen. Carl Heymanns, 1990. [in German].

[15]   Lovins, J. B.: Development of a Stemming Algorithm. In Mechanical Translation and Computational Linguistics, 11(1-2), pp. 22-31, 1968.

[16]   Maas, D.: MPRO – Ein System zur Analyse und Synthese deutscher Wörter. in R. Hauser (ed.): Linguistische Verifikation, Max Niemeyer Verlag, Tübingen, 1996. [in German].

[17]   Mayfield, J., McNamee, P. and Piatko, C.: The JHU/APL HAIRCUT System at TREC-8. In Proceedings of the Eighth Text REtrieval Conference (TREC-8), NIST Special Publication 500-246, pp. 445-451.

[18]   Monz, C., and de Rijke, M.: Shallow Morphological Analysis in Monolingual Information Retrieval for Dutch, German and Italian. In Peters, C., Braschler, M., Gonzalo, J. and Kluck, M. (Eds): Evaluation of Cross-Language Information Retrieval Systems. CLEF 2001, Lecture Notes in Computer Science, LNCS 2406, pp. 262-277, 2002.

[19]   Moulinier, I., McCulloh, J. A., Lund, E.: West Group at CLEF 2000: Non-English Monolingual Retrieval. In Peters C. (Ed.): Cross-Language Information Retrieval and Evaluation, Workshop of the Cross-Language Evaluation Forum, CLEF 2000, pp. 253-260, 2001.

[20]   Popovic, M., and Willet, P.: The effectiveness of stemming for natural-language access to Slovene textual data. In Journal of the American Society for Information Science, 3(5), pp. 384-390, 1992.

[21]   Porter, M. F.: An Algorithm for Suffix Stripping. In Program, 14(3), pages 130-137, 1980. Reprint in: Sparck Jones, K. and Willett, P. (Eds.): Readings in Information Retrieval, pp. 313-316. Morgan Kaufmann Publishers, San Francisco, CA, USA. 1997.

[22]   Ripplinger, B.: Linguistic Knowledge in Cross-Language Information Retrieval, PhD Thesis, , Herbert Utz Verlag, Munich, Germany, 2002.

[23]   Savoy, J.: A stemming procedure and stopword list for general French corpora. Journal of the American Society for Information Science, 50(10), pp. 944-952, 1999.

[24]   Savoy, J.: Cross-Language Information Retrieval: Experiments Based on CLEF 2000 Corpora. Information Processing & Management, to appear, 2002.

[25]   Singhal, A., C. Buckley, and M. Mitra: Pivoted Document Length Normalization. In Proceedings of of the 19th Annual International ACM SIGIR Conference on Research and Development in Information Retrieval, Zurich, Switzerland, 1996.

[26]   Sheridan, P., and Ballerini, J. P.: Experiments in Multilingual Information Retrieval using the SPIDER System. In Proceedings of the 19th Annual International ACM SIGIR Conference on Research and Development in Information Retrieval, Zurich, Switz., 1996.

[27]   Tague-Sutcliffe, J.: The Pragmatics of Information Retrieval Experimentation, Revisited. In Sparck-Jones, K. and Willett, P. (Eds.): Readings in Information Retrieval, Morgan Kaufmann Publishers, San Francisco, CA, USA, 1997.

[28]   Tomlinson, S.: Stemming Evaluated in 6 Languages by Hummingbird SearchServer[TM] at CLEF 2001. In Peters, C., Braschler, M., Gonzalo, J. and Kluck, M. (Eds): Evaluation of Cross-Language Information Retrieval Systems. CLEF 2001, Lecture Notes in Computer Science, LNCS 2406, pp. 278-287, 2002.

[29]   Wechsler, M., Sheridan, P., and Schäuble, P.: Multi-language text indexing for internet retrieval. In Proceedings of the 5th RIAO Conference, Computer-Assisted Information Searching on the Internet, Montreal, Canada, pp. 217--232, 1997.

[30]   Womser-Hacker, C.: Der PADOK-Retrievaltest. In "Sprache und Computer" Band 10, Georg Olms Verlag, 1989. [in German].

Question Answering System for Incomplete and Noisy Data
Methods and Measures for Its Evaluation

Lili Aunimo, Oskari Heinonen, Reeta Kuuskoski, Juha Makkonen, Renaud Petit, and Otso Virtanen

University of Helsinki, Department of Computer Science
P. O. Box 26 (Teollisuuskatu 23), FIN–00014 University of Helsinki, Finland
{lili.aunimo,oskari.heinonen,reeta.kuuskoski}@cs.helsinki.fi
{juha.makkonen,renaud.petit,otso.virtanen}@cs.helsinki.fi

Abstract. We present a question answering system that can handle noisy and incomplete natural language data, and methods and measures for the evaluation of question answering systems. Our question answering system is based on the vector space model and linguistic analysis of the natural language data. In the evaluation procedure, we test eight different preprocessing schemes for the data, and come to the conclusion that lemmatization combined with breaking compound words into their constituents gives significantly better results than the baseline. The evaluation process is based on stratified random sampling and bootstrapping. To measure the correctness of an answer, we use partial credits as well as full credits.

1 Introduction

Many organizations have to cope with an increasing amount of customer feedback. The fairly recent channels, such as email and SMS (Short Message Service[1]), amplify the volume of the incoming data and emphasize the need for prompt response. Typically, some questions are asked more often than others and a considerable portion of enquiries fall under the same reply. Responding to these questions manually is surely a tedious task, and hence the case for automatic answering tools or systems arises.

In this paper, we present a QA (question answering) system that can handle noisy natural language data, the kind of language typical of email and SMS messages. Typically, the questions are very short and incomplete. They consist of colloquial language, and they contain many spelling errors. Often the customer service has to do quite a lot of reasoning in order to answer the question. This reasoning uses information on the products of the company, the context of the user (such as time and location) and information in the customer database.

The system presented can handle this kind of noisy and incomplete questions based on a database of about 24,000 existing question-answer pairs. Our

---

[1] http://www.gsm.org/technology/sms/

F. Sebastiani (Ed.): ECIR 2003, LNCS 2633, pp. 193–206, 2003.

attention is focused on evaluation methods and measures used to assess the performance of the system in order to find the most effective preprocessing scheme.

The paper is organized as follows. In Sect. 2, we will briefly discuss some previous work regarding QA systems. Section 3 will present the QA system developed, and Sect. 4 the evaluation methods and measures used. Our experimental setup and corresponding results will be portrayed in Sect. 5. Results with several different types of linguistic preprocessing will be given. Finally, Sect. 6 is a short conclusion.

2   Related Work

The domain of question answering systems is by no means a novel territory. The last three Text Retrieval Conferences (TREC) have included a QA Track for open-domain question answering systems. The task is to find answers to well-formed, grammatically correct natural language questions from a large database of nearly one million documents. The systems should return an ordered list of five answers of limited size. The results are evaluated by human assessors, who decide whether the answers are correct or incorrect.

The basic idea behind the best-performing systems is the same. First, the document collection is processed to identify and mark named entities (e.g. location, date). Then, the question is parsed and the expected type of answer is resolved (e.g. person, numerical value). Thereafter, the query is formulated and information retrieval (IR) performed. Finally when the documents have been retrieved, the exact spot where the text snippet containing the answer is, has to be detected. Many systems have used WordNet[2] in query expansion and as the basis of the question type categorization.

The complexity of these phases varies. Some of the best and most complex systems were developed by a group of researchers led by Sanda Harabagiu. The systems, LASSO in TREC-8 [1], FALCON in TREC-9 [2] and QAS in TREC-10 [3], have constantly been among the best performing in the TREC conference. These systems use profound natural language processing and inferring when trying to resolve the correct answer.

The QA Track task differs from our system in a few ways. First, the data and the questions in the track are grammatically correct. One does not have to worry about the noise in the data. Secondly, the domain of the questions is not restricted. Our system is clearly focused on a specific area, since the data consists of feedback (mostly information requests about products and services) from the clients of a company. Thirdly, our current system is based on a collection of question-answer pairs, and therefore we do not have to concern ourselves with extracting the answer from a lengthy retrieved document. Finally, our system deals with questions in Finnish, a language fairly different from English.

A work more similar to ours is described by Busemann et al. [4]. Their QA system, called ICC-MAIL, is meant for call-center (i.e. helpdesk) personnel answering customer questions received via email. ICC-MAIL still differs from our

---

[2] http://www.cogsci.princeton.edu/ wn/

system since it relies on text categorization, whereas ours has its roots in traditional IR technology. Nevertheless, the basic setting is the same, and both systems attempt to

- increase the helpdesk agents' performance,
- improve the quality of the answers since the helpdesk agents will behave more homogeneously,
- reduce the training effort required since helpdesk agents don't have to know every possible solution for every possible problem [4].

3   QA System for Incomplete and Noisy Data

Our QA system was designed to respond to SMS text messages sent using mobile phones. These messages are typically rather short (at most 160 characters as dictated by the medium), share some characteristics with spoken language and thus often evade syntactic parsing. In addition, the questions are quite prone to typing errors. Only 15 percent of the questions in the collection could be parsed and analyzed without any problems by a parser[3] that was originally designed for standard language.

3.1   Description of the System

Our QA system TIPU relies on a simple and light architecture, based on client-server communication. Existing data is stored in a relational database accessible by the server. The data consists of SMS-message question-answer pairs, questions asked by customers, answers given by helpdesk agents.

The client side is composed of CGI scripts accessible through a WWW interface. A script retrieves a new question from an external source (e.g. a queue of incoming SMS messages). The client sends the question to the server, then waits for the result to be found and finally displays it. The result is a list of QA pairs in the database that the system identified as most likely answers to the question asked. The helpdesk agent can then select one of the provided answers to reply to the current question, edit its contents if necessary, or even write a new answer from scratch if no answer in the result was relevant enough, and send the answer to the customer.

Upon receiving a new question from the client, the server searches for the most similar existing questions in the database. A vector-based method is used to represent question strings, and their comparison relies on the cosine similarity measure [6]. The server dynamically generates a vector representing each incoming question. Vectors for existing questions in the database are calculated once, prior to starting the QA system, and stored and accessed on each request.

---

[3] The functional dependency grammar based parser [5] from Connexor Oy was used. See a demo of the parser at http://www.connexor.com/demos.html.

Table 1. Term space dimensions

Term Type	Dimension
Baseline	27,835
Lemma	13,130
Root	11,277

3.2   Vectors: Term Types and Weighting Methods

There are several ways to create vectors for the cosine comparison, depending on the way the question strings are parsed and how the identified terms are weighted. The goal of our experiments is to evaluate which type of vectors are the most effective to obtain accurate results to questions written in Finnish.

The baseline method, which is the simplest way to create a vector out of a string, considers every single word in the string as a term to include in the baseline vector.

A usual approach to identify terms in a sentence is to stem words, that is, to strip their inflectional suffixes. Unfortunately, when dealing with languages such as Finnish, dropping the case endings etc. may not be sufficient to identify a term. For example, stemming the word *käden* (of a hand) gives the stem *käde*. Stemming does not recognize *käden* as the genitive form of *käsi* and a separate term is generated instead. On the other hand, lemmatization recognizes *käden* as an inflected form of *käsi*. Using Connexor natural language parser, question strings are lemmatized into lemma vectors.

Another difficulty appears with compound words, which are rather frequent in Finnish. Since the nature of the messages is SMS, one cannot expect the compound words to be correctly written as one word, but rather as a series of separate words. Lemmatization of a mistyped word is more likely to fail. Thus, identifying the roots of compound words sounds promising. For example, root parsing of *matkapuhelinkaupassa* (in a/the mobile phone shop) identifies *matka* (mobile), *puhelin* (telephone) and *kauppa* (shop). Using the same natural language parser as for lemma vectors, a root vector is created out of the roots of terms identified in a question string.

The amount of recognized terms in our corpus differs from one method to another as Table 1 illustrates. The baseline approach takes into account every single word form and therefore its dimension is the highest. Lemmatizing reduces the dimension by a factor of two. Finally, the root method reduces the size of the term space even more by breaking compound words into their components and by lemmatizing all terms.

A simple solution to term weighting is to consider each term of a vector as important as any other one. All term weights are set to 1. A more sophisticated approach is to consider the grammatical function of terms, and to give a term more weight if it is, e.g., the subject or the object of the sentence. This weighting method, called syntax weighting, requires a syntactical analysis of the string, and is therefore only available for lemma and root type vectors. The last considered weighting method is standard tf.idf [6].

Combining described term types and term weighting methods, the following eight vector types become the candidates for evaluation.

- Baseline Unweighted
- Baseline tf.idf-weighted
- Lemma Unweighted
- Lemma Syntax-weighted
- Lemma tf.idf-weighted
- Root Unweighted
- Root Syntax-weighted
- Root tf.idf-weighted

This list is not exhaustive, and the system itself can handle any other types of vectors as well. The most tedious task is to find a vector type adapted to the characteristics of the language analyzed.

3.3   Evaluation Interface

Evaluation of the system consists of rating the correctness and preciseness of each resulting answer given by the QA server to each incoming question. Basically, the correct expected answer is the one that was actually submitted by the helpdesk agent. In the WWW interface, each resulting answer is attached to a set of choices (detailed in Sect. 4.3) corresponding to the decisions that a human evaluator can make concerning the validity of the answer with respect to the question.

During the evaluation process, queues of questions are created out of a sample of the database (see Sect. 4.1). Evaluation is realized by several evaluators at the same time, so that each of them is given a predefined queue of questions. Evaluators proceed through the same set of questions and evaluate the results once for each vector type.

Different vector types can lead the system to give the same answer to a question again and again during the evaluation process. As a matter of fact, a considerable amount of time and effort can be saved by recording the decisions made by evaluators in the first place, thus avoiding re-evaluation of the same question-answer pair. Moreover, this assists evaluators in acting consistently and coherently in their decision-making through time. From the system point of view, a CGI script sends the decisions of evaluators to a decision recording server that handles their storing and the calculation of the scores (see Sect. 4.3).

Some questions and answers appear frequently in the database, even with exactly the same wording. That is why decisions are extended to cover all possible combinations with exactly matching questions and answers (providing for variation in some named entities). For example, if an answer is evaluated as incorrect to a given question, any answer with the same text is automatically marked as incorrect to that specific question and all matching questions. Should any of these combinations ever come up in the evaluation process, there is no need to burden the evaluator with the decision again.

4   Methods and Measures for Evaluation

The evaluation of a QA system, like any other system, has to be designed and documented carefully in order to obtain comparable and reliable results. We focused our attention on both methods and measures. When choosing the appropriate evaluation methods, our goal was to minimize the number of QA pairs that the human evaluators had to go through, but still to get reliable results. This was achieved by using two methods, stratified random sampling and bootstrapping. When developing new measures for the evaluation, our goal was to create an intuitive system for human evaluators as well as a system that would describe the nature of the questions and answers in a suitable way. As the basis for measures, accuracy and reciprocal rank were used. On top of these, we defined a system that contains partial credits as well as full credits and where questions are classified as negative or non-negative.

4.1   Stratified Random Sampling

In order to create a sample that would be representative of the whole QA database, we used stratified sampling [7]. Stratified sampling is a random sampling technique where the records are first grouped into mutually exclusive subgroups, or strata, and then selected randomly from each stratum. This technique ensures that the sample contains proportionally as many records from each stratum as the original database does.

In our case, each record is a QA pair and the strata are groups of these pairs whose answers have the same number of similar answers. In other words, all QA pairs whose answer is not similar to any other answer form one group, those pairs whose answer is similar to one answer form another group, and so on. This grouping indicates the commonness of the QA pair type in the database. Thus, for example, QA pairs which are of an equally rare type belong to the same stratum even though they are about different subjects. In the same way, all QA pairs that are of an equally common type belong to the same stratum regardless of their subjects. To measure the similarity between answers and to form the strata we used TiPU. The similarity measure used was the cosine measure.

The distribution of pairs into different strata is very uneven. The largest stratum is the one that contains QA pairs of the rarest type, that is, those that do not have any similar answers. This stratum contains 17,291 records out of 23,929. The next stratum contains those records that have one similar answer, and it contains 599 QA pairs. The most common type of QA pair in the database has 872 similar answers, and there is one of those in the database.

The size of the representative sample can be kept quite small when using stratified random sampling instead of pure random sampling. Pure random sampling is a good choice when the size of the database and the application type make it impossible to use the computationally expensive similarity measurements across the whole database. The time complexity of the similarity measurement is squared with respect to the number of rows in the database. In our case, however, the database is relatively small because it contains only 23,929 records.

After removing the records with exactly the same answer, the number of records to be processed was only 18,241. Furthermore, as we use stratified sampling as part of the evaluation procedure, and not as part of an interactive application, the computational overhead is not a problem.

4.2   Bootstrapping

Bootstrapping is a computer-intensive statistical method that makes it possible to construct sampling distributions and confidence intervals for most statistics, without making any assumptions about the distribution of the data [8, 9]. We use bootstrapping to obtain the significance levels of our evaluation results for the different vector types because the distribution of the data is unknown.

The basic idea behind bootstrap sampling is the following [9].

- Repeat K times, $i := 1 \ldots K$:
  - Draw a bootstrap pseudosample S_i^* of size N by sampling with replacement as follows.
  - Repeat N times:
    - Select a member of the original sample S at random and add it to S_i^*.
  - Calculate and record the value of a pseudostatistic θ_i^* for S_i^*.

The number of pseudosamples formed was 1,000, and the size of the original sample as well as that of the pseudosamples, was 250. The pseudostatistics, which were the mean accuracy and the mean reciprocal rank, were calculated for each of the eight vector types. The distribution of each set of pseudosamples is roughly a normal distribution, and based on that distribution, the parameters (mean and variance) can be estimated.

We use the Baseline Unweighted type vectors as a baseline for evaluation of the performance of the other vectors. In addition to the exact figures on the performance of each vector type, the evaluation should tell us whether the difference in performance is statistically significant or not. Knowing the standard deviation of the baseline vector type it is straightforward to conduct the Z test for each of the vector type and for both measures used. The Z and p values and the significance levels of the results are reported in Table 4 in Sect. 5.

4.3   Measures

The basic measures used in the evaluation were mean accuracy and mean reciprocal rank. However, in order to better describe the attained level of performance, a system for giving partial credits was constructed. The need for incorporating a more fine-grained measure than a simple binary measure has been noted also in the TREC QA Track [10].

A special scoring system had to be constructed for negative questions, which are defined as those questions that do not belong to the scope of the system or are too complicated or incomprehensible without interactive communication between the agent and the customer. If the answer belongs to the scope of the helpdesk service, but the data collection does not happen to contain an answer to it, the question is not considered a negative question. In the evaluation performed, the correct answer to a negative question is no answer at all, or an answer that basically means "We only answer questions concerning our products and services" or "Please contact our customer service, the toll-free phone number is . . . ". Any other answer to a negative question would be a wrong answer. When evaluating negative questions, mostly binary relevance judgments were used. An empty answer, which denoted "no answer at all" was added to the end of the returned list of answers for all negative questions. An example of a negative question is given in Table 3.

Accuracy is a widely used measure in categorization. It is defined as the number of correctly classified items in the class divided by the total number of items classified into that class by the system. In the case of a QA system, accuracy is defined as the number of correct answers divided by the total number of answers retrieved for the question. To calculate the average performance of the system, we used macroaveraging. In macroaveraging, the average is the sum of the scores of each question divided by the number of questions. In microaveraging, the average is calculated by summing up all the scores of all the answers given by the system and then dividing it by the total number of answers [11]. Thus macroaveraging gives an equal importance to all questions, but microaveraging gives more importance to those questions that get a lot of answers. Typically, macroaveraging is used in evaluating information retrieval systems and microaveraging in evaluating categorization systems.

The mean reciprocal rank is calculated as follows. For each question, find the rank of the first correct answer from the set of answers returned by the system. The score of the question is the reciprocal of the rank. For example, if the correct answer is the first answer, the question is scored 1, if the correct answer is the second one, the score is $\frac{1}{2}$ and so on. If none of the returned answers is correct, the score is 0. To obtain the score of the system as a whole, the average of the scores of the questions is calculated. This measure is also used in the TREC QA Track [10].

Our system for giving partial credits to different answer types is described in the following. The answer types are classified into 13 categories, which include binary right, 1 (B1), and binary wrong, 0 (B2). The rest of the categories are given partial credit, which can be 0.5 or 0.25. If one option from specificity or number of questions is chosen, then the answer gets 0.5 credits. There are five categories that get the credit of 0.5. If one option from both sets is chosen, the credit is 0.25. There are six different ways to choose an option from both sets. The cases for partial credits are listed in Table 2 and three examples are given in Table 3.

The accuracy for each question is calculated as the average of the credits of all the answers to the question. For example, the accuracy of Q1 in the example of Table 3 would be 0.38. The accuracy of the negative question Q3 would be 0.5. The reciprocal rank ϱ for each question is calculated as follows.

$$\varrho = \max_{a \in A} \left\{ \frac{1}{n} \cdot \mathrm{credit}(a) \right\} \quad ,$$

Table 2. Partial credit types

Specificity	
S1	Specific question, generic answer.
S2	Generic question, specific answer.
Number	
N1	More than one question, one answer.
N2	One question, more than one answer.
N3	More than one question, more than one answer (but not all of them match).

Table 3. Partial credit and negative question examples

Q/A	Credit/Type	Text
Q1		Is the Elbonia City University closed during Christmas?
A1.1	0.5/S1	All the universities in Elbonia are closed during Christmas.
A1.2	0.25/S1,N2	All the universities in Elbonia are closed during Christmas and Midsummer.
Q2		What was the temperature outside last Wednesday and was it sunny?
A2.1	0.25/S1,N1	During the last 10 days, the temperature has been 5 degrees.
A2.2	0.5/N3	Last Wednesday, the temperature was 5 degrees and it was windy.
Q3	Neg.	How are you?
A3.1	0/B2	The temperature inside is 20 degrees.
A3.2	1/B1	(empty answer)

where A is the group of answers given to the question, $\text{credit}(a)$ is the credit (0, 0.25, 0.5 or 1) for $a \in A$, and n is the rank of the answer. For example, the reciprocal rank of Q1 would be calculated as

$$\varrho_{Q1} = \max\left\{\tfrac{1}{1} \cdot 0.5, \tfrac{1}{2} \cdot 0.25\right\} = \max\{0.5, 0.125\} = 0.5 \ .$$

5 Experiments and Results

In the experiments a sample of 250 questions out of 23,929 was chosen according to the stratified random sampling procedure presented in Sect. 4.1. There were altogether five evaluators with a set of 50 questions each. For all the questions, the results given by TIPU using each vector type of Sect. 3.2 had to be evaluated.

This lead to 400 questions for each evaluator. The evaluation interface described in Sect. 3.3 provided useful and time-saving support for the evaluation process.

TIPU is designed so that its performance can be modified to suit the needs of a specific situation by setting its parameters. Some of these parameters are the similarity threshold and the soft and hard limits for the number of answers returned. The soft limit can be exceeded if the list of answers cannot be cut off at the soft limit because the similarity of the answers is the same. Duplicate answers were always pruned, though. In the experiments described below, the similarity threshold was set to 0.5, the soft limit to 5 and the hard limit to 10.

It has been detected that several people working at a non-trivial classification task relatively seldom agree on the classifications (see, e.g., [12]). This applies to our evaluation process as well, since the task of the evaluators is basically a kind of a classification task. Therefore, we assumed that the evaluators probably would disagree on the evaluation judgments. We expected, however, each evaluator to assess consistently within his or her set of questions and with different vector types. In this way, we get results that are comparable across the different vector types (but not necessarily comparable with an evaluation performed on other QA systems).

To give an idea of some cases difficult to evaluate, a few examples follow. The principle in the evaluation was that the original answer given to the question was the correct answer. However, sometimes the original answer was clearly incorrect, incomplete or contained superfluous information, and the ones returned by the system were better. Another type of problem was that of classification of questions into negative or non-negative ones. Sometimes the questions were so vague that some of the helpdesk personnel had answered "We only answer questions concerning our products and services", some had answered "Please contact our customer service, the toll-free phone number is ...", and some had guessed what the question meant and answered it normally. In all these difficult cases, each evaluator paid special attention to evaluating all the vector types in a uniform way.

The results of the experiments are given in Table 4. In Fig. 1 and Fig. 2 we give box-and-whisker plots of the sampling distributions of the bootstrapped

Table 4. Experimental results

	Mean Accuracy				Mean Reciprocal Rank			
	value	p	Z	significancy	value	p	Z	significancy
Baseline Unweighted	0.414	n/a	n/a	n/a	0.464	n/a	n/a	n/a
Baseline tf.idf	0.365	0.097	−1.66	not significant	0.393	0.026	−2.22	almost significant
Lemma Unweighted	0.463	0.093	1.68	not significant	0.548	0.008	2.65	significant
Lemma Syntax	0.468	0.069	1.82	not significant	0.571	0.0006	3.39	very significant
Lemma tf.idf	0.492	0.008	2.64	significant	0.550	0.007	2.72	significant
Root Unweighted	0.500	0.004	2.91	significant	0.592	<0.0004	4.05	very significant
Root Syntax	0.501	0.003	2.96	significant	0.612	<0.0004	4.68	very significant
Root tf.idf	0.511	0.001	3.30	very significant	0.570	<0.0004	3.36	very significant

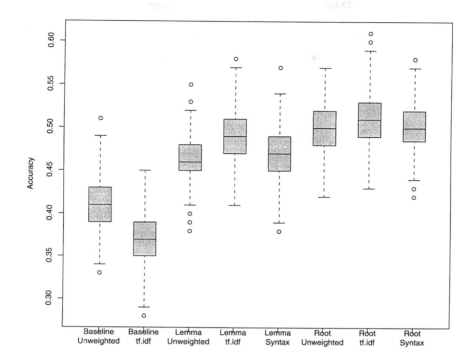

Fig. 1. Accuracy measures

mean accuracy and mean reciprocal rank measures. A box-and-whisker plot gives the upper and lower quartiles (the top and the bottom of the box), the median (the horizontal line within the box), and the values for minimum and maximum (the whiskers) [7]. The minimum and the maximum are the minimum and maximum observations that fall within $1.5 \cdot$ IQR below the lower quartile and above the upper quartile, respectively, where IQR (interquartile range) is the difference between the upper and lower quartiles. The circles represent outliers.

Among the 250 different questions to be assessed, the evaluators marked 21, which amounts to 8 percent, as negative questions. Since there were eight different vector types, the total number of questions evaluated was 2,000. Among the total number of answers assessed, which was 9,556, the evaluators judged 5,217 (54.6 %) with a positive binary judgment (B1), 3,303 (34.6 %) with a negative binary judgment (B2) and 1,036 (10.8 %) with partial credits.

The results indicate that the root vectors perform best, and that the difference to the baseline is statistically very significant. This is in line with the experiments previously performed in information retrieval on Finnish language [13].

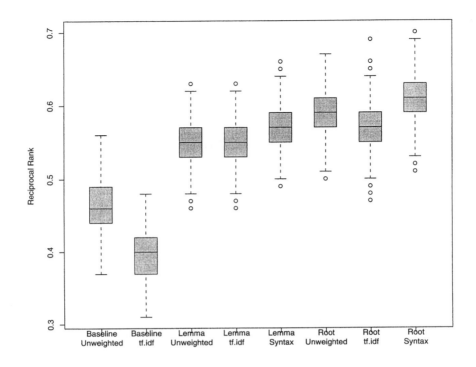

Fig. 2. Reciprocal rank measures

Both experiments conclude that lemmatization increases the performance of the systems. In our experiments combining lemmatization with breaking words into their components gives even better results, whereas Alkula states only that breaking words into their components does not harm the perfomance when combined with lemmatization. No inference can be drawn from the results as to which weighting scheme is the best, because the best weighting varies with the vector type and with the measures used. For two reasons it is not very surprising that the best results are obtained by using the root vectors. The first reason is that the root vectors make no difference between correctly written compound words and those compound words that are written as separate words as a result of a misspelling. Our data contained a lot of compound words that were misspelled in this way. The second reason is that the root vector space contains the smallest number of dimensions. This means that the root vectors are not as sparse as the other vectors and thus there is greater similarity between root vectors than between vectors of the two other types.

From the result table we can also read that the mean reciprocal rank gives better overall scores to TIPU than the mean accuracy. This can be interpreted so that the correct answers are mainly in the beginning part of the answer list returned by TIPU, but that there are some superfluous answers after the correct answer. In a future system, better accuracy might be obtained if the system could detect a sudden drop in similarity and as a result increase the similarity threshold for that specific question. This might omit the superfluous answers from the end of the list, and the soft and hard limits would no more be needed.

In general, the system works very well. It can be used to find correct answers to questions that are expressed in a language that contains misspellings and grammatical errors. This is not very surprising since the system is based on a database that contains about 24,000 questions, many of which are erroneous in a similar way. The system cannot answer any questions that are totally new, but it can be used to reduce or facilitate the work of the helpdesk agents by taking care of the most common ones.

6 Conclusion and Future Work

We have presented a question answering system that can rather effectively handle incomplete and noisy questions with errors typical of SMS messages. The system is based on the vector space model and utilizes natural language processing suitable to our material and target language. The focus in this paper was largely on the methods and measures for the evaluation of our system and QA systems in general. Methods based on stratified random sampling and bootstrapping were used in the evaluation process, as well as measures, namely mean reciprocal rank and accuracy, augmented with a partial crediting scheme.

An evaluation involving five human evaluators was conducted. Eight different preprocessing options for the data were evaluated. The conclusion is that lemmatization combined with breaking compound words into their constituents seems to work best and gives significantly better results than the simple baseline.

In the future, we are going to experiment with further preprocessing options including correction for typical errors of colloquial written Finnish. At the moment, the core of our QA system is purely statistical, but will be extended with question understanding and database lookup for generating answers to a limited number of domain-specific questions. This is likely to boost the performance of the already viable system when answering questions of a specific nature requiring specific answers.

References

[1] Moldovan, D., Harabagiu, S., Paşca, M., Mihalcea, R., Goodrum, R., Gîrju, R., Rus, V.: LASSO: A tool for surfing the answer net. In: Proceedings of the Text Retrieval Conference (TREC-8), Gaithersburg, Maryland, USA (1999)
[2] Harabagiu, S., Moldovan, D., Paşca, M., Mihalcea, R., Surdeanu, M., Bunescu, R., Gîrju, R., Rus, V., Morărescu, P.: FALCON: Boosting knowledge for answer engines. In: Proceedings of TREC-9, Gaithersburg, Maryland, USA (2000)

[3] Harabagiu, S., Moldovan, D., Paşca, M., Surdeanu, M., Mihalcea, R., Gîrju, R., Rus, V., Lăcătuşu, F., Morărescu, P., Bunescu, R.: Answering complex, list and context questions with LCC's question-answering server. In: Proceedings of TREC-10, Gaithersburg, Maryland, USA (2001)

[4] Busemann, S., Schmeier, S., Arens, R. G.: Message classification in the call center. In: Proceedings of 6th Applied Natural Language Processing Conference, Seattle, Washington, USA (2000)

[5] Tapanainen, P., Järvinen, T.: A non-projective dependency parser. In: Proceedings of the 5th Conference on Applied Natural Language Processing, Washington, D. C., USA, Association for Computational Linguistics (1997)

[6] Salton, G.: Automatic Text Processing: The Transformation, Analysis, and Retrieval of Information by Computer. Addison-Wesley (1989)

[7] Nolan, D., Speed, T.: Stat Labs Mathematical Statistics Through Applications. Springer-Verlag (2001)

[8] Efron, B.: The Jackknife, the Bootstrap and Other Resampling Plans. Society for Industrial and Applied Mathematics (1983)

[9] Cohen, P.: Empirical Methods for Artificial Intelligence. The MIT Press (1995)

[10] Voorhees, E. M.: Overview of the TREC-2001 question answering track. In Voorhees, E. M., Harman, D. K., eds.: Proceedings of TREC-10, Gaithersburg, Maryland, USA, Department of Commerce, National Institute of Standards and Technology (2001)

[11] van Rijsbergen, C. J.: Information Retrieval. 2nd edn. Butterworths (1980)

[12] Carletta, J.: Assessing agreement on classification tasks: The kappa statistic. Computational Linguistics **22** (1996) 249–254

[13] Alkula, R.: From plain character strings to meaningful words: Producing better full text databases for inflectional and compounding languages with morphological analysis software. Information Retrieval **4** (2001) 195–208

Term Proximity Scoring
for Keyword-Based Retrieval Systems

Yves Rasolofo and Jacques Savoy

Université de Neuchâtel, Neuchatel, Switzerland
{yves.rasolofo,jacques.savoy}@unine.ch

Abstract. This paper suggests the use of proximity measurement in combination with the Okapi probabilistic model. First, using the Okapi system, our investigation was carried out in a distributed retrieval framework to calculate the same relevance score as that achieved by a single centralized index. Second, by applying a term-proximity scoring heuristic to the top documents returned by a keyword-based system, our aim is to enhance retrieval performance. Our experiments were conducted using the TREC8, TREC9 and TREC10 test collections, and show that the suggested approach is stable and generally tends to improve retrieval effectiveness especially at the top documents retrieved.

1 Introduction

When Web users submit requests to search engines, they expect to retrieve highly relevant Web pages. This presents quite a challenge, especially when search engine queries are rather short. Studies by Spink *et al.* [16][27] have shown that the average query length is between two and three keywords. Moreover, these requests tend to cover a rather wide variety of information needs, and are often expressed with ambiguous terms. Their study [27] demonstrates also that users expect the system to retrieve relevant documents at the top of the result list. Indeed, more than 50% of Web users tend to consult only the first 2 result pages. Besides of looking for relevant pages, a great number of Web users search for online service location or homepages. As for the other types of queries, the page must to be in the top of the list. A new task handling these kinds of requests was introduced in TREC-10 (Text Retrieval Conference). This search mechanism allows users to submit a request such as "Quantas" in order to retrieve the Quantas Airlines homepage, not several other Web pages referring to this airline company. Previous efforts to resolve this approach based on content only were not really effective [6]. During TREC-10 and as reported in [14], systems performed best when, in addition to information taken from document content, URL texts and/or URL depths were used. Another recent study by Singhal & Kaszkiel [26] involving analogous query types came to similar conclusion. Indeed, as suggested in [7], if one is to improve retrieval effectiveness combining approaches now seems imperative.

F. Sebastiani (Ed.): ECIR 2003, LNCS 2633, pp. 207–218, 2003.
© Springer-Verlag Berlin Heidelberg 2003

We introduce in the first part of this study a simple approach to address the problem of distributed index. The advantage of this approach is its ability to provide retrieval status scores (RSV) as if documents were searched using a single centralized index. Nevertheless, the proposed approach requires that each index use the same scheme. It means that during the document indexing, the term weight is calculated based only on document statistics or local information (e.g. term frequency, document length, …). Collection statistics (e.g. document frequency) are computed only when user's request is submitted to the system. Thus our approach can be used in the digital library context within which various collections are indexed and searched using the same retrieval system. It is also possible to apply our approach locally to a particular commercial search engine, as it normally uses the same indexing and search model when dealing with various inverted files. However, the proposed approach does not apply when metasearching various search engines using different indexing and retrieval techniques [20].

In an effort to improve retrieval effectiveness at the top ranked items, in the second part of this work we propose an enhanced search strategy that can help to resolve both Web-page and online service location searches. We will thus focus on adding a word-pair scoring module to our implementation of the keyword-based Okapi system. This study is based on previous approaches where phrase, term proximity or term distance were used in information retrieval.

Various phrase-finding and indexing methods have been proposed in the past and generally, retrieval performance conclusions on the use of phrases as indexing units were inconsistent. Salton & McGill [23] suggested generating statistical phrases based on word co-occurrence and then incorporating them into document representation as additional index terms. Fagan [10][11] evaluated this method by combining words-based and phrase-based weighting. In his study [10], he considered syntactic phrase information, generated from considering syntactic relations or syntactic structures. This seemed to enhance retrieval performance marginally while statistical phrase discovery approaches seem to produce better results. More recently, leading groups including [1], [3], [9], [15] and [28], who have participated in TREC campaigns, used phrases as indexing units and were able to obtain some improvement. Mitra *et al.* [17] re-examined the use of statistical and syntactic phrases and came to the conclusion that "once a good basic ranking scheme is used, the use of phrases do not have a major effect on precision at high ranks." Finally, Arampatzis *et al.* [2] came up with some possible reasons for the lack of success when using Natural Language Processing (NLP) techniques in information retrieval, particularly when using syntactic phrases. They stated that "first, the currently available NLP techniques suffer from lack of accuracy and efficiency and second, there are doubts if syntactic structure is a good substitute for semantic content."

The work of Hawking & Thistlewaite [12] is more directly related to ours, and they explored the use of proximity scoring within the PADRE system. Their Z-mode method has the advantage of being totally independent of collection statistics and in distributed information retrieval it represents a good solution for merging result lists[1].

---

[1]   Result lists merging or collection merging is one of the critical issues of distributed information retrieval [19].

Clarke *et al.* [5] developed a similar technique and obtained results worthy of consideration. Papka & Allan [18] extracted multiword features from documents using certain proximity measures and obtained some retrieval performance success by using these multiword features for massive query expansions.

The rest of this paper presents our approach based on term proximity scoring. We will use the word-based Okapi system as a baseline for comparisons, and evaluate our approach using TREC-8, TREC-9 and TREC-10 test collections. The main objectives of our work in this paper are the following:

- to propose a framework manipulating the use of distributed indexes in order to cope with index size limitation,

- to determine whether or not simple term proximity scoring can improve retrieval effectiveness: we do not intend to compare existing term proximity approaches with ours. Our baseline will therefore be a word-based system using no proximity measures and we will measure to what extent our term proximity scoring can improve this system in terms of retrieval effectiveness.

In the next section, we will discuss the Okapi probabilistic model and examine its appropriateness within distributed index frameworks. Term pair scoring is presented in Section 3, and finally Section 4 describes our experiments and results.

2   OKAPI and Distributed Index Frameworks

Okapi is an enhanced probabilistic retrieval model based on the binary independence model proposed by Robertson & Spark Jones [21]. By incorporating term frequency and document length considerations, the Okapi model was able to demonstrate interesting retrieval performances during the last TREC campaigns [22]. In this paper, we will use a simplified Okapi weighting function, in which the weight w_i was assigned to a given term t_i in a document d and was computed according to the following formula:

$$w_i = (k_1 + 1) \cdot \frac{tf_i}{K + tf_i} \tag{1}$$

where:

$$K = k \cdot \left[(1-b) + b \cdot \frac{l}{avdl} \right]$$

l is the document length,
$avdl$ is the average of document length (set to 750),
b is a constant (set to 0.9),
k is a constant (set to 2),
k_1 is a constant (set to 1.2),
tf_i is the occurrence frequency of the term t_i in document d.

The following formula shows the weight given to the same term t_i within a query:

$$qw_i = \frac{qtf_i}{k_3 + qtf_i} \cdot \log\left(\frac{n - df_i}{df_i} \right) \tag{2}$$

where:

qtf_i is the frequency of term t_i in the query,
df_i is the number of documents in the collection containing the term t_i,
n is the number of documents included in the collection.
k_3 is a constant (set to 1000).

The retrieval status value is then calculated as follows:

$$RSV_{Okapi}(d,q) = \sum_i w_i \cdot qw_i$$

During the last three years, the TREC adhoc task (Web track) has been based on test collections containing more than 10 GB of Web pages. Since creating a single inverted file from a collection of this size might be impossible within a 32-bit system (e.g., Linux), we suggest that one way to resolving this problem would be the use of index pruning [4] or distributing inverted files [24]. In both cases there might be some risk of decreasing retrieval performance depending on how the index pruning or the index distributions are implemented. In this paper, our only interest is the second approach, and in this case, we could follow the approach suggested by [24], where result lists obtained from searching different collections are merged. This is achieved by using document scores computed by each collection (collections are searched using the same retrieval scheme). Dumais [8] mentioned however that various statistics are collection dependant (e.g., the idf values) and that these values may vary widely across collections. The resultant document scores might not therefore be directly comparable.

The Okapi weighting function imparts interesting characteristics within distributed collection frameworks. Equation 1 shows how document term weight is based on within-document term frequency and document length only, while the search keyword weight as depicted in Equation 2 uses collection dependant statistics (namely, the *idf* value). Those characteristics facilitate data exchange in a distributed information retrieval (DIR)[2] environment when collections are indexed and searched using the same retrieval scheme. Indeed, when the system indexes documents, it gives term weight independently of this term's collection frequency. Collection frequencies need only be exchanged during query processing. Thus Equation 2 becomes:

$$qw_i = \frac{qtf_i}{k_3 + qtf_i} \cdot \log\left(\frac{N - DF_i}{DF_i}\right) \tag{3}$$

where:
N is the sum of documents within all collections,

---

[2] In a distributed information retrieval environment, documents are distributed across various collections which may be searched using the same or different retrieval schemes.

DF_i is the number of documents containing the term t_i within all collections. Each collection sends the local collection frequency (df_i) to the broker[3] on request, qtf_i query term frequency.

As in [13], this process needs to exchange data between the broker and the collections involved. The amount of data exchanged during this process equals $Nt \cdot Nc$, for both the request of collection statistics and the response reception. In this formula, Nt denotes the number of query terms and Nc the number of collections. Therefore in order to perform the search within this proposed framework, the broker must weight query terms using Equation 3 and then send this information to the collections. Following this step, document scores returned by collections are directly comparable because they are based on the same collection statistics [8].

3   Term Proximity Weighting

Efficiency and effectiveness are critical concerns for users, for they expect the search engine to return only what they need and as quickly as possible. With our proposed approach, we expect improvement at the top ranks, in a computationally tractable manner. We thus decided to add the suggested extension to Okapi because we wanted to use an effective keyword-based search model and we hoped to improve its retrieval performance by using term proximity scoring.

Our approach is able to cope with multi-term queries and is based on the assumption that if a document contains sentences having at least two query terms within them, the probability that this document will be relevant must be greater. Moreover, the closer are the query terms, the higher is the relevance probability. Most of the time, search engine users submit a query which is a concept (e.g. "lung cancer"), a proper name (e.g. "Buck Danny"), a place name (e.g. "Pisa Tower") or other types of queries where terms are likely to be found in a narrow context or even adjacent within a relevant document. It is then important to assign more importance to those keywords having a short distance between their occurrences, under the assumption that if the distance increases, the underlying meaning may change.

To achieve this objective we will expand the request using keyword pairs extracted from the query's wording. We will assume that queries are short and that users will only write relevant terms. If stopwords appear in the request's formulation, then they will be automatically removed. Finally, the process described below is applied only for queries having more than one keyword.

First, we establish a set of all possible search keyword pairs. If the query wording consists of $q = (t_i, t_j, t_k)$, we obtain the following set S of term pairs: $\{(t_i, t_j), (t_i, t_k), (t_j, t_k)\}$, with the ordering of terms not being important. During the indexing process, we create an inverted file containing the occurrence positions of each term in each document. The term pair retrieval within a given document is performed by sequen-

---

[3]   A broker is an interface between the user and the collections. It is responsible for receiving the user's request, sending this query to various selected collections, merging the result lists provided by each selected collection and returning a single list to the user.

tially reading the query term positions, and for each instance the term pair (t_i, t_j) within a maximal distance of five (or having a maximal of four terms between the keyword pair), we compute a term pair instance (tpi) weight as follows:

$$tpi(t_i, t_j) = \frac{1.0}{d(t_i, t_j)^2}$$

where $d(t_i, t_j)$ is the distance expressed in number of words between search term t_i and t_j.

Our hypothesis is that the closer two search keywords appear together within a document, the higher is the weight attached to the occurrence of this term pair. Based on this formulation, the higher value is 1.0, corresponding to a distance of one (the terms are adjacent), and the lower value is 0.04 corresponding to a distance of 5. For example, based on the request "information retrieval", the resulting tpi of an occurrence of the same string "information retrieval" will be 1.0 while the tpi of "the retrieval of medical information" will be 1/9 or 0.11.

Of course, a given term pair may appear more than once in a document. Therefore, the weight attached to this given term pair (t_i, t_j) is evaluated by summing all the corresponding term pair instances tpi. In a manner similarly to Equation 1, we obtain:

$$w_d(t_i, t_j) = (k_1 + 1) \cdot \frac{\displaystyle\sum_{occ(t_i, t_j)} tpi(t_i, t_j)}{K + \displaystyle\sum_{occ(t_i, t_j)} tpi(t_i, t_j)}$$

Given a document d and a request q, we compute the contribution of all occurring term pairs in that document. This value, denoted $TPRSV$, and based on the set S of query term pairs included in the request q, is evaluated using the following formula:

$$TPRSV(d, q) = \sum_{(t_i, t_j) \in S} w_d(t_i, t_j) \cdot \min(qw_i, qw_j)$$

where qw_i and qw_j are the weights of the query terms t_i and t_j calculated according to eq. 3.

This $TPRSV$ is only calculated for the top 100 documents returned by the Okapi search model. This choice is motivated by efficiency needs and our main interest is to achieve improvement at top ranks. The final retrieval status value for a given document d, denoted $RSV_{NEW}(d,q)$, is computed as follows:

$$RSV_{NEW}(d, q) = RSV_{Okapi}(d, q) + TPRSV(d, q)$$

This formulation accounts for both the original Okapi score (RSV_{Okapi}) and our proximity scoring function ($TPSRSV$). During this process no new document is retrieved, as it is performed on the top 100 documents retrieved by Okapi. Instead, the scores and therefore the ranks of documents containing at least one query term pair are improved based on the following assumption: The presence of query terms within a document would not always imply a match related to the true meaning of the request, whereas account for search keyword pairs using some distance constraint may reduce this error. Using our approach and in response to the request "operating system", a document containing theses two terms close each other will be presented to the user before any other documents having these two terms within two different paragraphs.

4   Experiments

4.1   Test Collections

Experiments were conducted based on 150 topics used for the adhoc task for TREC-8, TREC-9 and TREC-10. The TREC-8 collection contains 528,155 documents (representing 1,904 MB) extracted from four different sources, namely *Financial Times* (FT, 210,158 documents), *Federal Register* (FR, 55,630 documents), *Foreign Broadcast Information Service* (FBIS, 130,471 documents) and *Los Angeles Times* (LA Times, 131,896 documents). An assessed set of 50 topics was provided, covering a rather broad range of subjects, including for example "Estonia, economy," "suicides," "airport security," "osteoporosis" and "cosmic events." We decided to split the TREC-8 document collection into four collections according to their sources (FT, FR, FBIS, LA Times), with the number of documents and the collection size varying from one collection to another.

The TREC-9 and TREC-10 test collections contain the same documents, corresponding to Web pages from various sites around the world (1,692,096 Web pages with a total size of 11,033 MB). Thus, their volume is roughly six times greater than TREC-8. Both the TREC-9 and TREC-10 test collections include 50 topics, representing various information needs, and they contain a larger number of spelling mistakes. Topics originate from various domains (e.g., "Parkinson's disease," "hunger," "how e-mail benefits businesses," "Mexican food culture," "Titanic went wrong" and "history of Cambodia"). In order to simulate a distributed environment, we divided this Web page collection into four separate collections, each having roughly the same number of pages and same size.

As our approach deals with search keyword pairs, we removed queries containing a single word. The evaluations were performed on 62 two-words queries, 55 with three search terms, 7 with four and 1 with five terms (see Table 1).

Table 1. Query length statistics after stopword removal

Collection	2 words	3 words	4 words	5 words	Average
TREC-8	25	22	0	0	2.47
TREC-9	18	15	3	0	2.58
TREC-10	19	18	4	1	2.69
Sum	62	55	7	1	2.58

4.2   Evaluations

Table 2 depicts various retrieval performances resulting from the use of our models. In the first column, we indicate the test collection ("TREC8", "TREC9", "TREC10" or "All" when considering the three collections as a whole) and the search model used ("Okapi", and "OkaTP"), with the "OkaTP" rows showing performances achieved by our term proximity scoring. In the second column, we compute the average precision using the TREC-EVAL software and in the following column lists precision levels achieved after retrieving 5 (P@5), 10 (P@10) and 20 (P@20) documents.

In terms of average precision (column two), differences between our enhanced model and Okapi scheme are fairly small. This can be explained as follows: our proximity algorithm takes accounts for each instance of a search keyword pair within a maximal distance of 5. This constraint limits the number of documents that will have their retrieval status value increased. At the same time, this constraint discards a large number of poor term pair candidates where the distance between the two search keywords is too great (under the assumption that in such cases, there is no semantic relationship between the two keywords). Moreover we processed only the top 100 documents, while for some queries it is possible that most relevant documents were located beyond the limit of top 100 documents.

Table 3 serves as a query-by-query average precision analysis, depicting the number of requests for which the OkaTP scheme was better (+), worse (-) or showed similar (=) performance levels as did Okapi. The last column of Table 3 lists the results of Sign tests, with a significance level $\alpha = 0.05$. When considering the TREC-8 corpus (first row), comparisons show that the model (OkaTP) revealed better performance for 29 requests, worse for 15 and identical performance for three queries.

Table 2. Average precision, precision after 5, 10 and 20 documents

Collection	AvPrec	Diff.	P@5	Diff	P@10	Diff.	P@20	Diff
TREC-8-Okapi	0.2465		0.4809		0.4489		0.3979	
TREC-8-OkaTP	0.2525	2.43%	0.5021	4.41%	0.4702	4.74%	0.4000	0.53%
TREC-9-Okapi	0.2399		0.3389		0.2750		0.2014	
TREC-9-OkaTP	0.2447	2.00%	0.3500	3.28%	0.2722	-1.02%	0.2069	2.73%
TREC-10-Okapi	0.1920		0.3333		0.3143		0.2607	
TREC-10-OkaTP	0.1869	-2.66%	0.3952	18.57%	0.3442	9.83%	0.2798	7.33%
All-Okapi	0.2263		0.3904		0.3536		0.2952	
All-OkaTP	0.2282	0.84%	0.4224	8.20%	0.3712	4.98%	0.3040	2.98%

Table 3. Query-by-query average precision analysis: OkaTP vs. Okapi

Collection	+	-	=	Sign test
TREC-8	29	15	3	Okapi < OkaTP
TREC-9	19	12	5	Okapi = OkaTP
TREC-10	23	16	3	Okapi = OkaTP
Sum	71	43	11	Okapi < OkaTP

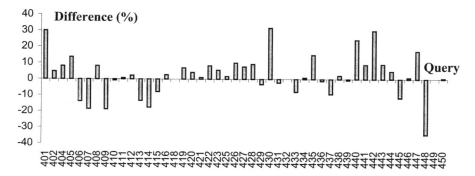

Fig. 1. TREC-8: Query-by-query differences in average precision (OkaTP-Okapi)

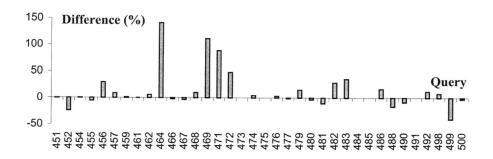

Fig. 2. TREC-9: Query-by-query average precision difference (OkaTP-Okapi)

The Sign test reports the OkaTP (Okapi + term pair scoring) significantly better than Okapi. Taken separately, the TREC-9 and TREC-10 collections do not show any statistically significant differences between the two retrieval models. But based on the last row we can conclude that we encountered significant differences when testing all three corpora, with the OkaTP tending to be better than the Okapi.

As the Sign test does not account for differences in magnitude, Figure 1, Figure 2 and Figure 3 show that for our three corpora, the enhancements in average precision are generally far greater than are the degradations.

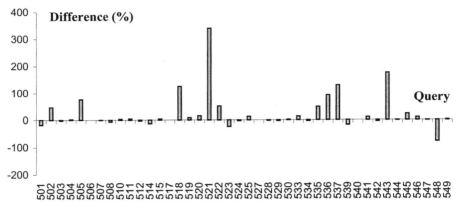

Fig. 3. TREC-10: Query-by-query differences in average precision (OkaTP-Okapi)

Our main concern however is to enhance search performances after retrieving only a few documents. To analyze this aspect, in Table 2 we reported the precision achieved by our two models after retrieving 5, 10 or 20 items. From looking at these evaluations, precision improvements obtained by the proximity measure are more noticeable after retrieving 5 documents, and in this case the overall improvement is around 8.20%. Such results would prove useful for those users looking at the top 5 or 10 documents returned [27]. Moreover, these results would also prove interesting when locating online services [14] or when examining question-answering systems [29] where most of the time, the expected answer is a single URL or a short sentence of only a few words extracted from a document.

5   Conclusion

In this paper we introduced a distributed information retrieval framework based on the Okapi probabilistic model, a framework capable of achieving the same levels of retrieval effectiveness as those achieved by a single centralized index system. Moreover, the impact of a new term proximity algorithm on retrieval effectiveness for a keyword-based system was examined. The approach we suggested seems to improve ranking for documents having query term pairs occurring within a given distance constraint. It seems the term proximity scoring approach that we proposed may potentially improve precision after retrieving a few documents and thus could prove useful for those users looking only at the top ranked items (e.g., when using search engines available on the Web) or in search systems that must provide users with a short and complete answer (e.g., homepage searching, question-answering systems).

Acknowledgement

This research was supported by the SNSF (Swiss National Science Foundation) under grant 21-58'813.99.

References

[1]   Allan, J., Ballesteros, L., Callan, J.P., Croft, W.B. and Lu, Z.: Recent experiments with INQUERY. In Proceedings of TREC-4, NIST Special Publication #500-236, 49-63, 1996.

[2]   Arampatzis, A., van der Weide, T., Koster, C. and van Bommel, P.: Linguistically motivated information retrieval. Encyclopedia of Library and Information Science, 39, 2000.

[3]   Buckley, C., Singhal, A., and Mitra, M.: Using query zoning and correlation within SMART: TREC-5. In Proceedings of TREC-5, NIST Special Publication #500-238, 105-118, 1997.

[4]   Carmel, D., Amitay, E., Herscovici, M., Maarek, Y., Petruschka, Y., and Soffer, A.: Juru at TREC-10: Experiments with index pruning. In Proceedings TREC-10, NIST Special Publication #500-250, 228-236, 2002.

[5]   Clarke, C.L.A., and Cormack, G.V. and Tudhope E. A.: Relevance Ranking for One to Three Term Queries. Information Processing and Management, 36(2):291-311, 2000.

[6]   Craswell, N., Hawking, D., and Robertson, S.E.: Effective site finding using link anchor information. In Proceedings SIGIR-2001, ACM Press, 250-257, 2001.

[7]   Croft, W.B.: Combining approaches to information retrieval. In W.B. Croft (Ed.), Advances in information retrieval, Kluwer Academic Publishers, 1-36, 2000.

[8]   Dumais, S.T.: Latent semantic indexing (LSI) and TREC-2. In Proceedings of TREC-2, NIST Special Publication, #500-215, 105-115, 1994.

[9]   Evans, D.A., Milic-Frayling, N., and Lefferts, R.G.: CLARIT TREC-4 experiments. In Proceedings of TREC-4, NIST Special Publication, #500-236, 305-321, 1996.

[10]   Fagan, J.: Experiments in automatic phrase indexing for document retrieval: A comparison of syntactic and non-syntactic methods. PhD thesis, Computer Science Department, Cornell University. 1987.

[11]   Fagan, J.: The effectiveness of a nonsytactic approach to automatic phrase indexing for document retrieval. Journal of the American Society for Information Science, 40(2), 115-132, 1989.

[12]   Hawkings, D. and Thistlewaite, P.: Proximity operators – So near and yet so far. In Proceedings of TREC-4, NIST Special Publication #500-236, 131-143, 1996.

[13]   Hawking, D., and Thistlewaite, P.: Methods for information server selection. ACM Transactions on Information Systems, 17(1), 40-76, 1999.

[14]   Hawking, D. and Craswell, N.: Overview of the TREC-2001 Web track. In Proceedings TREC-10, NIST Special Publication #500-250, 61-67, 2002.

[15]   Hull, D.A., Grefenstette, G., Schulze, B.M., Gaussier, E., Schutze, H. and Pedersen, J.O.: Xerox TREC-5 site report: Routing, filtering, NLP, and Spanish tracks. In Proceedings of TREC-5, NIST Special Publication #500-238, 167-180, 1997.

[16]   Jansen, B.J., Spink, A. and Saracevic, T.: Real life, real users and real needs: A study and analysis of user queries on the Web. Information Processing and Management, 36(2), 207-227, 2000.

[17]   Mitra, M., Buckley, C., Singhal, A., and Cardie, C.: An analysis of statistical and syntactic phrases. In Proceedings of RIAO-97, 1997.

[18]   Papka, R., and Allan, J.: Document classification using multiword features. In Proceedings of CIKM-98, ACM Press, 124-131. 1998.

[19]   Rasolofo, Y., Abbaci, F. and Savoy, J.: Approaches to collection selection and results merging for distributed information ietrieval. In Proceedings of CIKM-2001, ACM Press, 191-198, 2001.

[20]   Rasolofo, Y., Hawking, D., Savoy, J.: Result Merging Strategies for a Current News MetaSearcher. Information Processing & Management, 2003 (to appear).

[21]   Robertson, S.E., and Spark Jones, K.: Relevance weighting of search terms. Journal of the American Society for Information Science, 27(3), 129-146, 1976.

[22]   Robertson, S.E., Walker, S., and Beaulieu, M.: Experimentation as a way of life: Okapi at TREC. Information Processing & Management, 36(1), 95-108, 2000.

[23]   Salton G., and McGill, M.J.: Introduction to modern information retrieval. McGraw-Hill, 1983.

[24]   Savoy, J., and Rasolofo, Y.: Report on the TREC-10 experiment: Distributed collections and entrypage searching. In Proceedings TREC-10, NIST Special Publication #500-250, 586-595, 2002.

[25]   Silverstein, C., Henzinger, M., Marais, H. and Moricz, M.: Analysis of a very large Web search engine query log. ACM SIGIR Forum, 33(1), 6-12, 1999.

[26]   Singhal, A., and Kaszkiel, M.: A case study in Web search using TREC algorithms. In Proceedings of WWW'10, Elsevier, 708-716, 2001.

[27]   Spink, A. Wolfram, D., Jansen, B.J., and Saracevic, T.: Searching the Web: The public and their queries. Journal of the American Society for Information Science and Technology, 52(3), 226-234, 2001.

[28]   Strzalkowski, T., Guthrie, L., Karlgren, J., Leistensnider, J., Lin, F., Perez-Carballo, J., Straszheim, T., Wang, J., and Wilding, J.: Natural language information retrieval: TREC-5 report. In Proceedings TREC-5, NIST Special Publication #500-238, 291-313, 1997.

[29]   Voorhees, E.M.: Overview of the TREC 2001 question answering track. In Proceedings TREC-10, NIST Special Publication #500-250, 42-51, 2002.

Propositional Logic Representations for Documents and Queries: A Large-Scale Evaluation

David E. Losada[1] and Alvaro Barreiro[2]

[1] Intelligent Systems Group, Department of Electronics and Computer Science
University of Santiago de Compostela, SPAIN
dlosada@usc.es
[2] AIlab, Department of Computer Science
University of A Coruña, SPAIN
barreiro@dc.fi.udc.es

Abstract. Expressive power is a potential source of benefits for Information Retrieval. Indeed, a number of works have been traditionally devoting their efforts to defining models able to manage structured documents. Similarly, many researchers have looked at query formulation and proposed different methods to generate structured queries. Nevertheless few attempts have addressed the combination of both expressive documents and expressive queries and its effects on retrieval performance. This is mostly due to the lack of a coherent and expressive framework in which both documents and queries can be handled in an homogeneous and efficient way. In this work we aim at filling this gap. We test the impact of logical representations for documents and queries under a large-scale evaluation. The experiments show clearly that, under the same conditions, the use of logical representations for both documents and queries leads to significant improvements in retrieval performance. Moreover, the overall performance results make evident that logic-based approaches can be competitive in the field of Information Retrieval.

1 Introduction

Query structure has been extensively studied in the literature of Information Retrieval (IR). There is evidence that queries involving boolean operators are more effective than weaker query structures. Belkin and others combined manual boolean queries and found improvements in retrieval performance [1]. Hull investigated the impact of boolean structured queries in cross-language information retrieval and noticed that structured queries produce better performance [7]. Kekäläinen and Järvelin studied the effects of query structure in query expansion and found positive effects for expanded queries [8] .

The quest for methods for capturing the internal document structure has also been an active area of research in IR. For instance, a number of investigators proposed different approaches to divide documents into passages [6, 21, 24, 2]

F. Sebastiani (Ed.): ECIR 2003, LNCS 2633, pp. 219–234, 2003.

and there exists strong evidence that this additional information produces better retrieval performance results.

Although structured queries and structured documents have demonstrated their merits in the context of IR, their combination into the same retrieval model was not evaluated so far. More precisely, expressive document representations are usually matched against flat query expressions and, on the other hand, structured query formulations are often run against non-structured document representations. We claim that it is not sufficient to provide IR systems with powerful query languages if the representation of documents oversimplifies their information content. The reverse argument also holds. Both documents and queries should benefit from the full expressive power of the formalism involved. This was not addressed so far mainly because of the lack of an appropriate framework in which expressive documents and queries are homogeneously handled. This leads to unbalanced models, full of artificial ad-hoc elements, whose results can be hardly generalized.

One of the major advantages which stands on the foundations of logic-based approaches to IR [3] is precisely their ability to produce general and homogeneous retrieval models. In this work we adopt Propositional Logic as the underlying framework and show that better retrieval performance results are obtained when expressive representations are used for both documents and queries. There has been recurrent criticism against logical models of IR focused on complexity and evaluation issues. In this respect, we have taken great care of the actual applicability of the theoretical model. First, the efficiency of the logical approach followed here was recently assured [12, 13, 15]. Second, following the large-scale experimentation presented here, the model appears as a competitive retrieval model under realistic circumstances.

In most of the works on query structure, the formulation of queries was done either manually or assisted by external tools such as thesauri. In our work, we applied simplistic techniques to extract automatically expressive representations from both TREC topics and documents. The development of adequate and generic methods to build automatically expressive representations is indeed a great challenge for logical models of IR. Nevertheless, our simple automatic indexing method facilitates a large-scale evaluation on the impact of logical representations on retrieval performance.

The rest of this paper is organized as follows. In section 2 we briefly sketch the theoretical details of the underlying model. Section 3 reports the experiments conducted and section 4 discusses the evaluation results and other relevant issues. The paper ends with some conclusions.

2   Background

In this work we follow the logical approach for IR suggested by Losada and Barreiro [11, 15, 10]. This model is based on the combined use of Propositional Logic and Belief Revision. Along this paper, we will refer to this model as PLBR model. There are a number of reasons supporting this election. First, the PLBR model was efficiently implemented and polynomial-time algorithms were supplied to match documents and queries [13, 12, 15]. Second, the model was evaluated against four small test collections [16, 14] and the advantages of the use of an expressive formalism became apparent in those experiments. Nevertheless, those experiments could not test the combined effect of expressive documents and expressive queries because of the poor topic structure in those small collections.

Furthermore, the generality of the logical framework is appropriate for the objectives pursued here. Indeed, the PLBR model was successfully used in the past to model documents, queries, feedback information and retrieval situations in an homogeneous way [15]. More recently, the model was extended to include term similarity and inverse document frequency information [17].

2.1   The PLBR Model

This section depicts the basic foundations of the PLBR model. The review is intentionally brief because further details can be found elsewhere [15, 10].

Documents and queries are represented as Propositional Logic formulas. Given a document and a query represented by the propositional formulas d and q respectively, it is well known that the application of the notion of logical consequence to decide relevance, i.e. $d \models q$, is too strict [23]. The entailment $d \models q$ simply tests whether or not each logical interpretation that makes d true makes also q true (i.e. each model of d is also a model of q). This is not in accordance with what we expect from an IR measure of relevance. Let us illustrate it through an example. Imagine two documents represented as $d_1 = a \wedge b \wedge \neg c \wedge d$ and $d_2 = \neg a \wedge \neg b \wedge \neg c \wedge d$ and a query represented as $q = a \wedge b \wedge c$. Both documents fail to fulfill the entailment, i.e. $d_1 \not\models q$ and $d_2 \not\models q$. This is because there exist models of d_1 that map the query into false[1]. Similarly, there are also models of d_2 that map the query into false[2]. As a consequence, the application of the logical entailment to decide relevance would assign the same status to both d_1 and d_2 with respect to the query q. This is not appropriate for IR purposes because d_1 is likely more relevant than d_2 (d_1 fulfills partially the query).

In [11] a method to get a non-binary measure of the entailment $d \models q$ was proposed. To define a non-binary measure of relevance the distance from each model of d to the set of models of q is measured. In the field of Belief Revision (BR) measures of distance between logical interpretations are formally defined. The basic BR problem can be defined as follows. Let T be a logical theory and A a new formula to be included in the theory. BR methods define a way to include the new information in the theory. If there is no contradiction between T and A, the solution is trivial because the new theory, $T \circ A$ ($\circ$ stands for a revision operator), is just $T \wedge A$. However, if contradiction arises some old knowledge has to be removed in order to get a consistent new theory. Model-based approaches

---

[1] Note that any model m of d_1 maps the propositional letter c into false and, hence, m cannot be a model of q.

[2] Note that any model m of d_1 maps the propositional letters a, b, and c into false and, hence, m has to map q into false.

to BR work on the logical interpretations of T and A. Basically, a measure of closeness to the set of models of the theory T is defined and the models of A which are the closest to the models of T are chosen to be the models of the new theory. As a consequence, BR model-based approaches are suitable for measuring distances from documents to queries when both are represented as logical formulas. Next paragraph sketches the details of this formulation.

In [11] there was found an interesting connection between Dalal's BR operator [4], $\circ_D$, and IR matching functions. Let us regard a query q as a logical theory and a document d as a new information. In the revision process $q \circ_D d$ a measure from a given document interpretation to the set of models of the query is defined. An important circumstance is that the semantics of this measure is appropriate for IR. Given a model of the document, the measure represents the number of propositional letters (i.e. index terms) that should be changed in that model in order to satisfy the query. For instance, let us assume a complete document d (i.e. a document having a single model) represented as neural $\wedge$ science $\wedge$ ¬network and a query q represented as neural $\wedge$ network. The distance from the document to the query would be equal to one because we would need to change the truth value of one propositional letter in the document (network) in order to satisfy the query. For that hypothetical changed document d', $d' \models q$ would hold.

In the general case, a document representation may be partial and, hence, there might be several interpretations in which the document is satisfied (i.e. several document models). In order to get a non-binary measure of the entailment $d \models q$ we can compute the distance from each model of the document to the set of models of the query and, finally, calculate the average over document's models. This average over document's models is translated into a similarity measure, $BRsim$, in the interval $[0, 1]$.

Because $BRsim$ is model-based, a direct computation would require exponential time (the number of logical interpretations grows exponentially with the size of the alphabet). In [13, 12] efficient procedures to approximate the computation of $BRsim$ were proposed. A restriction in the syntactical form of the logical formulas involved allows to define polynomial-time algorithms to compute similarity. Specifically, the propositional formulas representing documents and queries have to be in disjunctive normal form (DNF). A DNF formula has the form: $c_1 \vee c_2 \vee \ldots$ where each c_j is a conjunction of literals (also called *conjunctive clause*): $l_1 \wedge l_2 \wedge \ldots$. A literal is a propositional letter or its negation. As a result, a document d and a query q can be efficiently matched as long as d and q are in DNF. This restriction is acceptable because the expressiveness of generic propositional formulas and DNF formulas is the same. Indexing procedures have to represent documents as DNF formulas. From the user perspective, the use of DNF formulas does not introduce additional penalties. A translation from a natural language information need into a DNF query can be done automatically (this will be shown in section 3) or, alternatively, users can be asked to write generic propositional formulas and a translation into DNF is automatically done[3].

Let us imagine a document d represented by a DNF formula $dc_1 \vee dc_2 \vee \ldots$ and a query q represented by a DNF formula $qc_1 \vee qc_2 \vee \ldots$, where each dc_i (qc_i) is a conjunctive clause. The distance from the document to the query is measured as the average distance from document clauses to the set of query clauses. The distance from an individual document clause dc_j to the set of query clauses is measured as the minimum distance from dc_j to query clauses. Intuitively, different query clauses represent different requirements in the information need and the distance from dc_j to the query is measured as the distance to the requirement(s) that dc_j best fulfills. The clause-to-clause distance depends on (1) the number of literals appearing as positive literals within one clause and as negative literals within the other clause and (2) the number of literals in the query clause whose propositional letter is not mentioned by the document clause. The clause-to-clause distance helps to determine how good is the document clause for satisfying the query clause. In this respect, a contradicting literal, case (1), produces an increment of 1 to the distance whereas a query literal not mentioned by the document, case (2), increases 0.5 the value of the distance. This is because we do not know whether or not the document clause actually deals with that term[4] (recall that document representations are partial: information about presence/absence is not available for all the terms in the alphabet). The example depicted in fig. 1 helps to clarify the measure of distance applied. Note that the final value of distance is 0 because each document clause completely satisfies one or more query clauses, i.e. any document view satisfies one query requirement[5]. Observe that dc_1 does not include information about the term e and, hence, its distance from qc_1, which asks for e, gets an increment of 0.5.

An extension of the PLBR model was defined to include idf and term similarity information [17]. New efficient algorithms were designed and the experiments against small collections revealed that the model can be competitive with the vector-space model with the tf/idf weighting scheme.

3   Experiments

In our experiments, we used a subset of the TIPSTER/TREC collection consisting in about 173.000 documents. Specifically, we considered all Wall Street Journal (WSJ) documents (years 87-92) in TIPSPER/TREC volumes 1&2.

---

[3] Although a translation from a propositional formula into DNF can take in the worse case exponential time, queries have usually few terms and, then, the translation time is acceptable.

[4] This decision is theoretically supported by the fact that half of the models of the document clause map the term into true and half of the models of the document clause map the term into false or, alternatively, half of the models of the document clause *agree* with the query clause and half of the models of the document *disagree* with the query clause.

[5] Since query requirements are combined through logical disjunctions the satisfaction of one single requirement is enough to satisfy the query.

```
𝒫 = {a, b, c, d, e}
d = (a ∧ b ∧ d) ∨ (a ∧ ¬b ∧ ¬d ∧ e), q = (a ∧ e) ∨ (a ∧ d)
            document d = dc₁ ∨ dc₂, dc₁ = (a ∧ b ∧ d), dc₂ = (a ∧ ¬b ∧ ¬d ∧ e)
            query q = qc₁ ∨ qc₂, qc₁ = (a ∧ e), qc₂ = (a ∧ d)
Distance from dc₁ to q
    Distance from dc₁ to qc₁
        #contradicting literals = 0
        #terms in q clause not mentioned by the doc clause = 1 (e)
        Distance(dc₁,qc₁)= 0 + 1/2 = 0.5
    Distance from dc₁ to qc₂
        #contradicting literals = 0
        #terms in q clause not mentioned by the doc clause = 0
        Distance(dc₁,qc₂)= 0 + 0/2 = 0
    Distance from dc₁ to q = 0
Distance from dc₂ to q
    Distance from dc₂ to qc₁
        #contradicting literals = 0
        #terms in q clause not mentioned by the doc clause = 0
        Distance(dc₂,qc₁)= 0 + 0/2 = 0
    Distance from dc₂ to qc₂
        #contradicting literals = 1 (d)
        #terms in q clause not mentioned by the doc clause = 0
        Distance(dc₂,qc₂)= 1 + 0/2 = 1
    Distance from dc₂ to q = 0
Distance from d to q = (0+0)/2 = 0
```

Fig. 1. Distance from a DNF document to a DNF query

In order to index this collection, we used GNU mifluz [18]. GNU mifluz provides a C++ library to build and query a full text inverted index. Mifluz was developed by Senga [22], which is a development group focused on IR software. The flexibility of mifluz routines allowed us to create an inverted file in which, for each term, we store both document and clause information. Recall that we store documents as DNF formulas and conventional inverted files were not designed to store clause information. Mifluz is very flexible and allows to define explicitly the structure of the inverted file. As a consequence, we could design and build an inverted file able to efficiently store documents as DNF formulas.

A total of 50 TREC topics were used in this experimentation. Topics #151 - #200 from TREC-3 adhoc retrieval task [5] were used to generate automatically DNF queries for representing user needs. We used a stoplist of 571 words and terms were stemmed using Porter's algorithm [19].

3.1 Evaluating the PLBR Model

Two main strategies were applied to define logical queries. First, a baseline with flat query structure is built as follows. All query terms are extracted and, after stopword and stemming, the query terms are collected into a single clause, i.e. a DNF formula with a single conjunctive clause is built. A second class of tests are based on expressing queries as DNF formulas having several clauses. Each query clause is formed from a subfield of the TREC topic. Figure 2 shows an example of both strategies for topic No. 160.

It is important to observe that, although simplistic, this approach is able to build automatically structured queries for TREC topics. Most of the works

<title> Topic: Vitamins - The Cure for or Cause of Human Ailments
<desc> Description:
Document will identify vitamins that have contributed to the cure for human diseases or ailments
or documents will identify vitamins that have caused health problems in humans.
<narr> Narrative:
A relevant document will provide information indicating that vitamins may help to prevent or cure
human ailments. Information indicating that vitamins may cause health problems in humans is also
relevant. A document that makes a general reference to vitamins such as "good for your health"
or "having nutritional value" is not relevant. Information about research being conducted without
results would not be relevant. References to derivatives of vitamins are to be treated as the vitamin.

Strategy 1: DNF with a single clause
vitamin ∧ cure ∧ caus ∧ human ∧ ailment ∧ document ∧ identifi ∧ contribut ∧ diseas ∧ health ∧
problem ∧ relevant ∧ provid ∧ inform ∧ indic ∧ prevent ∧ make ∧ gener ∧ refer ∧ good ∧ nutrit ∧
research ∧ conduct ∧ result ∧ deriv ∧ treat

Strategy 2: DNF with several clauses
(vitamin ∧ cure ∧ caus ∧ human ∧ ailment) ∨ (document ∧ identifi ∧ vitamin ∧ contribut ∧ cure ∧
human ∧ diseas ∧ ailment ∧ caus ∧ health ∧ problem) ∨ (relevant ∧ document ∧ provid ∧ inform
∧ indic ∧ vitamin ∧ prevent ∧ cure ∧ human ∧ ailment ∧ caus ∧ health ∧ problem ∧ make ∧ gener
∧ refer ∧ good ∧ nutrit ∧ research ∧ conduct ∧ result ∧ deriv ∧ treat)

Fig. 2. Representing a TREC topic

aforementioned [1, 7] are based on structured queries built manually. Kekäläinen
and Järvelin work on automatic queries but query structure produces only better
results after expansion [8]. The small-scale experiments of the PLBR model
reported in [14, 16] do not provide a detailed study of the effect of query structure
because of the poor variety of subfields in the topics.

The first aim of these experiments is to determine whether or not the separation of query information into several clauses is beneficial in terms of retrieval
performance. Note that, intuitively, each subfield represents a different view of
the information need and it seems sensible to think that a separate representation is adequate.

In order to isolate the effect of expressive queries from the effect of expressive documents, we first ran experiments on flat document representations with
varying *degree of expressiveness* for queries. Specifically, we first considered documents as conjunctions of terms (i.e. DNF formulas having a single conjunctive
clause) where all terms from different document subfields are represented into the
same document clause, i.e. no structure information is handled for documents.
In table 1 we present performance results for this first pool of experiments. Tests
with and without idf information were run. The use of expressive query representations leads to spectacular improvements in retrieval performance. Observe that
the test using structured queries with no idf is even better than the test using
idf on flat queries. This supports the idea that IR needs flexible query languages
able to express user information needs in a more adequate way. Recall that DNF
formulas having several clauses involve the use of both logical disjunctions and
logical conjunctions whereas DNF formulas with a single clause involve only the
use of logical conjunctions. Negations were not used in this evaluation. From the

Table 1. Effect of expressive queries on retrieval performance

Recall	no idf		idf	
	1 clause in docs 1 clause in qs	1 clause in docs several clauses in qs	1 clause in docs 1 clause in qs	1 clause in docs several clauses in qs
0.00	0.3235	0.4922	0.5260	0.5173
0.10	0.1535	0.2730	0.2792	0.3474
0.20	0.0896	0.2402	0.2010	0.3112
0.30	0.0485	0.1785	0.1407	0.2589
0.40	0.0304	0.1478	0.0978	0.2024
0.50	0.0169	0.1110	0.0692	0.1581
0.60	0.0087	0.0932	0.0454	0.1356
0.70	0.0020	0.0737	0.0269	0.1178
0.80	0.0006	0.0475	0.0162	0.0871
0.90	0.0001	0.0352	0.0055	0.0652
1.00	0.0001	0.0171	0.0042	0.0248
Avg.prec. (non-interpolated)	0.0451	0.1316	0.1055	0.1792
% change		+191.8%		+69.9%

evaluation results obtained, it appears that the variety of logical connectors to formulate queries is a good property of the query language.

In a second pool of experiments we considered documents as DNF formulas having several conjunctive clauses and queries as DNF formulas having a single conjunctive clause. As for queries, to get DNF representations for WSJ documents we used the subfield structure of the WSJ documents. In the experiments reported here, we considered the subfields HL, TEXT and LP which corresponds to headlines, main text and lead paragraphs, respectively. Terms from each subfield are collected into a conjunctive clause and the document representation is composed of the disjunction of all these clauses. We also considered an additional clause which is composed of all the terms from all the subfields. In this way, we have an additional view which represents the full document. This was inspired by some works on Passage Retrieval [21, 24] that use both local (document passages) and global (full document) information. Nevertheless, it has been traditionally difficult to decide which view is adequate for a particular retrieval. The logical formalism is flexible enough and can cope with alternative views of the documents and all of them are considered at retrieval time.

In table 2 performance results obtained from expressive document representations are presented. All these results were obtained using queries having a single conjunctive clause. The effect of expressive document representations is negative when no idf information is available and positive when idf information is considered. Unfortunately, following these results we cannot reach a clear conclusion about the effect of expressive document representations when flat query expressions are used. In table 3 we show the performance ratios obtained when both documents and queries are represented as DNF formulas having several clauses. We also show results for conjunctive representations for both documents and queries. The improvements found in retrieval performance from the use of generic DNF formulas for both documents and queries are huge. Clearly, expressive formulas appear as an important tool to improve retrieval performance. However, the effect of expressive document representations when flat queries are used is unclear. This experimentation provides no clear evidence about the adequacy of expressive document representations when the query language is poor. This might indicate that it is not sufficient to apply expressive document

Table 2. Effect of expressive documents on retrieval performance

	no idf		idf	
Recall	1 clause in qs 1 clause in docs	1 clause in qs several clauses in docs	1 clause in qs 1 clause in docs	1 clause in qs several clauses in docs
0.00	0.3235	0.3188	0.5260	0.4988
0.10	0.1535	0.1279	0.2792	0.2753
0.20	0.0896	0.0866	0.2010	0.2192
0.30	0.0485	0.0439	0.1407	0.1634
0.40	0.0304	0.0276	0.0978	0.1014
0.50	0.0169	0.0170	0.0692	0.0715
0.60	0.0087	0.0101	0.0454	0.0507
0.70	0.0020	0.0041	0.0269	0.0320
0.80	0.0006	0.0009	0.0162	0.0208
0.90	0.0001	0.0003	0.0055	0.0088
1.00	0.0001	0.0003	0.0042	0.0038
Avg.prec. (non-interpolated)	0.0451	0.0425	0.1055	0.1104
% change		-5.8%		+4.6%

Table 3. Effect of expressive documents and expressive queries on retrieval performance

	no idf		idf	
Recall	1 clause in docs & qs	several clauses in docs & qs	1 clause in docs & qs	several clauses in docs & qs
0.00	0.3235	0.6231	0.5260	0.6445
0.10	0.1535	0.4489	0.2792	0.5023
0.20	0.0896	0.3485	0.2010	0.4128
0.30	0.0485	0.2755	0.1407	0.3387
0.40	0.0304	0.2182	0.0978	0.2646
0.50	0.0169	0.1666	0.0692	0.2106
0.60	0.0087	0.1376	0.0454	0.1783
0.70	0.0020	0.0929	0.0269	0.1342
0.80	0.0006	0.0743	0.0162	0.1009
0.90	0.0001	0.0396	0.0055	0.0695
1.00	0.0001	0.0138	0.0042	0.0206
Avg.prec. (non-interpolated)	0.0451	0.1980	0.1055	0.2378
% change		+339.0%		+125.4%

representations if the representation of queries oversimplifies their information content. This idea is supported by the fact that the best performance of the logical model is obtained when the full expressive power is applied to both documents and queries. In the discussion section we provide an additional analysis about the effects of the logical approach on retrieval performance.

3.2 Comparison with the Vector-Space Model

In this section we compare the results obtained with the PLBR model against results obtained with the Vector-Space model. The latter results were obtained using the Lemur toolkit [9]. Lemur supports the construction of text retrieval systems using popular IR models such as Vector-Space and Okapi or newer ones such as Language Modeling approaches. It is designed to facilitate research in IR using large-scale databases. Lemur was developed by the Computer Science Department of the University of Massachusetts and the School of Computer Science at Carnegie Mellon University in the framework of the so-called Lemur Project. This does not pretend to be a strict comparison because the PLBR model can only deal with binary term frequency information and, on the other hand, the VSP model can not handle documents and queries divided into parts.

Table 4. PLBR model vs Vector-Space Model

Recall	no idf VSP bin tf	no idf VSP raw tf	no idf PLBR	idf VSP bin tf	idf VSP raw tf	idf PLBR
0.00	0.3386	0.4500	0.6231	0.6235	0.6699	0.6445
0.10	0.1473	0.2383	0.4489	0.3520	0.3988	0.5023
0.20	0.0863	0.1726	0.3485	0.2858	0.3460	0.4128
0.30	0.0465	0.1379	0.2755	0.2096	0.2967	0.3387
0.40	0.0303	0.1086	0.2182	0.1567	0.2563	0.2646
0.50	0.0156	0.0699	0.1666	0.1092	0.2001	0.2106
0.60	0.0085	0.0443	0.1376	0.0858	0.1565	0.1783
0.70	0.0021	0.0261	0.0929	0.0584	0.1115	0.1342
0.80	0.0006	0.0148	0.0743	0.0363	0.0741	0.1009
0.90	0.0001	0.0042	0.0396	0.0165	0.0330	0.0695
1.00	0.0001	0.0015	0.0138	0.0071	0.0118	0.0206
Avg.prec. (non-interpolated)	0.0450	0.0946	0.1980	0.1532	0.2104	0.2378
% change		+110.2%	+340.0%		+37.3%	+55.2%

However, it is interesting to see the absolute retrieval performance of the logical approach against the retrieval performance of a popular IR model.

The procedure to obtain VSP retrieval performance results was as follows. First, we ran Lemur routines to build a classical inverted file for the WSJ collection[6]. As in the experiments with the PLBR model, we indexed the HL, TEXT and LP subfields (headlines, full text and lead paragraph, respectively) and terms were stemmed using Porter's algorithm [19]. The stoplist was the same used in the tests of the PLBR model. Note that evaluation is done at the document level. Although documents have several clauses, there are not relevance assessments for particular clauses (only whole documents have their relevance assessment).

Table 4 depicts the results obtained for the WSJ collection using several weighting schemes[7] and figure 3 shows the corresponding precision vs recall graph. For comparison, we also show the performance results obtained with the PLBR model when both documents and queries are represented as DNF formulas having several clauses.

These experiments allow us to extract a number of conclusions. First, when no idf information is available, the PLBR model is always superior to the VSP[8]. Even though the VSP uses raw tf, the PLBR model keeps being better (19.8% average non-interpolated precision vs 9.46% average non-interpolated precision). Recall that the PLBR model can only deal with binary term frequency information. Nevertheless, the positive effect obtained from expressive representations is superior to the negative effect related to the lack of a non-binary term frequency notion. When idf information is available, the same tendency holds. If the notion of term frequency is binary the PLBR model performs better than the VSP (55.2% better in average non-interpolated precision). The raw tf/idf VSP experiment is slightly inferior to the PLBR model. However, it is well known that

---

[6] In this step, we introduced minor changes in Lemur source code to be able to select which document subfields were indexed.

[7] We also had to introduce minor additions in Lemur source code to handle some of the weighting schemes depicted in the table.

[8] Observe that neither the VSP model nor the PLBR model were tested using normalization. Indeed the incorporation of some kind of normalization (maybe clause-based) in the PLBR model is a future line of work.

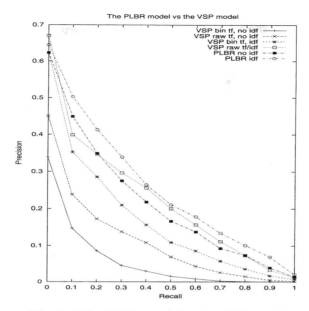

Fig. 3. The PLBR model vs the VSP model

important improvements can be obtained with the VSP if weighting schemes such as BM25 [20] are applied. This suggests that additional investigation is needed to determine whether or not the PLBR model can be competitive in terms of absolute ratios of retrieval performance. However, we still do not know the limits of the PLBR model because the full expressive power was not utilized. Negations were not considered in these experiments. As it was mentioned before, the quest to design techniques that obtain automatically better logical representations of texts is a major challenge for logical approaches to the IR problem. Furthermore, the PLBR model used so far does not apply any normalization factor. In order to ascertain the real limits of a logical approach such as ours, it is very important to investigate on formal ways to encompass non-binary term frequency information and methods to apply clause-based normalization. Anyway, the results of this experimentation are clear: IR models can obtain large benefits if structure is handled for both documents and queries. Under the same conditions, the structured version was always significantly better.

4 Discussion

In the experiments reported in this paper logic appears as a tool to enhance retrieval precision. In this section we look deeply into the characteristics of the matching process trying to find explanations for that good behaviour. Specifically, we look at query expressiveness, whose benefits in retrieval performance are especially large.

Consider documents as DNF formulas with a single clause and queries as DNF formulas having several clauses. In this case, the PLBR model behaves clearly better than the PLBR model with flat representations. If queries have a single conjunctive clause then all the terms appearing in the TREC topic (even in different subfields) are mixed up into that clause. This clause is used to match the document clause. On the other hand, if we can represent queries with several conjunctive clauses then we will be able to separate distinct parts of the information need into distinct conjunctive clauses. As argued in section 2, the distance from the document clause to the query is measured as the distance to the closest query clause(s). Let us imagine a topic whose title is "Dog maulings" and a relevant document d_r which mentions both terms. If all the query terms are collected into a single conjunctive clause the position in the rank of d_r will depend on how many query terms appear in the document. Alghough d_r mentions "dog" and "maulings", it might be the case that it receives a low retrieval score because most of the other query terms are not present in d_r (e.g. because the relevant document is short). Intuitively, if the query language forces us to store all the terms into the same flat structure then, the meaning of the information need is blurred. Think that, the longer the query is, the more chance to have generic terms which are not very important to decide relevance (and, hence, the more chance for long documents to match the query). If we represent the title into a single conjunctive clause and the rest of the topic is separated into distinct clauses, then the retrieval score of d_r will be maximum (because one query clause - the title query clause - fares 0 from the document), no matter how far the rest of the query clauses are. This means that the satisfaction of a single query clause is enough to assign a high rank to the document. Although a given document does not share many terms with a query, it can receive a good retrieval score because it fulfills completely one of the query views. As a consequence, the semantics of the distance that PLBR uses helps to move relevant documents towards higher positions in the rank.

One can reasonably argue that a similar behaviour might be obtained in the VSP model if we assign weights for query terms taking into account the subfield of the topic in which the terms are mentioned. This would allow to measure the relative importance of the query terms but, as structure is not handled, we could not recognize whether or not a part of the query is fully satisfied.

When documents are DNF formulas having several clauses the retrieval performance of the PLBR model gets further improvements. The separation of the document information into several parts helps to refine the matching process and, for each document clause, its closest query clause(s) is located. This means that an ellaborated matching is done that takes into account matches between portions of the document and portions of the query. The practical advantages in retrieval performance of this formulation are clear. On the other hand, if queries have a single clause, there is no evidence that the separation of documents into several parts is beneficial. More experimental work is needed to shed light on this issue. Anyway, the use of expressive representations for both documents and queries was always significantly better than any other approach and, thus, there is no doubt about the role of expressiveness for enhancing retrieval systems. On the contrary, that circumstance supports the idea that representational power should be fully provided to both documents and queries.

Observe that the logical approach followed in this work captures only a binary notion of term frequency (tf). The reader might wonder why the model does not include the tf factor. The idf factor and a measure of similarity between terms are *global* notions, i.e. they do not depend on a particular document but are characteristics of the whole collection (furthermore, the notion of term similarity is not collection-dependent because we can even get a measure of similarity between terms from a thesaurus, from other collections, etc.). These notions introduce additional information about the involved terms which is considered by the distance measured at retrieval time. However, our representational formalism keeps being the same: Propositional Logic. The tf factor, which is determined by the number of occurrences of a term within a document, is not a global notion but it is associated to a particular document. At matching time, we can use the idf factor and term similarity information for measuring the distance between two interpretations because they are global factors and, hence, we do not need to know which document/query is being handled. On the contrary, to apply the tf factor we would need to know which document/query corresponds to the interpretations being handled [15]. If we want to adhere to the theoretical formalism, this would not be possible because a given Propositional Logic interpretation can be a model of many documents and queries. Hence, the notion of interpretation would have to incorporate term frequencies giving rise to a totally different model. As a consequence, the PLBR model cannot consider term frequency information.

5   Conclusion

The most popular IR models have been traditionally driven by efficiency rather than expressiveness. This leads to IR systems which retrieve large amounts of documents very quickly but whose representational power is poor. As a result, generalization is hardly possible and the structure of documents and queries receives a marginal role. It is difficult to get increasingly better performance results based on such models. Research on weighting schemes, normalization, etc. has made a tremendous effort to enhance IR but they are limited by the characteristics of the underlying representational apparatus. We claim that IR systems should consider formalisms able to capture an enhanced notion of document and query. We are not sure about which the best framework is but we are pretty confident that the expressive power is a fundamental tool to improve retrieval performance.

The performance results obtained in this work support the intuitions reflected in the last paragraph. Huge benefits were found when documents and queries are represented as expressive formulas. Under the same conditions, the logical approach was always superior to the classical vector-space model. The combined use of split representations and a matching process driven by the closest query clause appear as adequate tools to model IR systems.

Previous experiments using the PLBR model against small collections [16, 14] anticipated its good behaviour but the full expressive power was not utilized. Following the evaluation reported here, we can say without doubt that the more expressive the model is, the better it does retrieval. This suggests that IR systems should allow to match expressive documents against expressive queries. Moreover, the size of the collection utilized here assures the good operation of the PLBR model under realistic circumstances.

Note also that significant improvements were obtained with coarse techniques for separating a document/query into several clauses. In the future we plan to apply more complex procedures to divide documents/queries into clauses. Moreover, in the experiments presented here we did not make use of negations. The incorporation of negated terms into queries in a relevance feedback loop was recently evaluated with very good performance results [14]. We believe that negations can play an important role as a precision-oriented mechanism.

Although the expressiveness of Propositional Logic is limited, further extensions of the PLBR model towards more expressive logics such as First Order Logic can be undertaken. As logical models are more general, newer models can inherit results obtained previously.

Acknowledgements

The work reported here was co-funded by "Ministerio de Ciencia y Tecnología" and FEDER funds under research project TIC2002-00947 (R&D program: "Tecnologías de la Información y las Comunicaciones"). The first author is supported in part by "Ministerio de Ciencia y Tecnología" and in part by FEDER funds through the "Ramón y Cajal" R&D program.

References

[1] N. J. Belkin, C. Cool, W. B. Croft, and J. P. Callan. The effect of multiple query representations on information retrieval system performance. In *Proc. of SIGIR-93, the 16th ACM Conference on Research and Development in Information Retrieval*, pages 339–346, Pittsburgh, PA, June 1993.

[2] J. P. Callan. Passage-level evidence in document retrieval. In *Proc. SIGIR-94, the 17th ACM Conference on Research and Development in Information Retrieval*, pages 302–310, Dublin, UK, July 1994.

[3] F. Crestani, M. Lalmas, and C. J. van Rijsbergen (editors). *Information Retrieval, Uncertainty and Logics: advanced models for the representation and retrieval of information*. Kluwer Academic, Norwell, MA., 1998.

[4] M. Dalal. Investigations into a theory of knowledge base revision:preliminary report. In *Proc. AAAI-88, the 7th National Conference on Artificial Intelligence*, pages 475–479, Saint Paul, USA, 1988.

[5] D. Harman. Overview of the third text retrieval conference. In *Proc. TREC-3, the 3rd text retrieval conference*, 1994.

[6] M. Hearst and C. Plaunt. Subtopic structuring for full-length document access. In *Proc. SIGIR-93, the 16th ACM Conference on Research and Development in Information Retrieval*, pages 59–68, Pittsburgh, USA, June 1993.

[7] D. A. Hull. Using structured queries for disambiguation in cross-language information retrieval. In *Proc. of AAAI spring symposium on cross-language text and speech retrieval*, Stanford, CA, March 1997.

[8] J. Kekäläinen and K. Järvelin. The impact of query structure and query expansion on retrieval performance. In *Proc. of SIGIR-98, the 21st ACM Conference on Research and Development in Information Retrieval*, pages 130–137, Melbourne, Australia, August 1998.

[9] The lemur toolkit. http://www.cs.cmu.edu/ lemur.

[10] D. E. Losada. *A logical model of information retrieval based on propositional logic and belief revision*. PhD thesis, University of A Corunna, 2001.

[11] D. E. Losada and A. Barreiro. Using a belief revision operator for document ranking in extended boolean models. In *Proc. SIGIR-99, the 22nd ACM Conference on Research and Development in Information Retrieval*, pages 66–73, Berkeley, USA, August 1999.

[12] D. E. Losada and A. Barreiro. Efficient algorithms for ranking documents represented as DNF formulas. In *Proc. SIGIR-2000 Workshop on Mathematical and Formal Methods in Information Retrieval*, pages 16–24, Athens, Greece, July 2000.

[13] D. E. Losada and A. Barreiro. Implementing document ranking within a logical framework. In *Proc. SPIRE-2000, the 7th Symposium on String Processing and Information Retrieval*, pages 188–198, A Coruña, Spain, September 2000.

[14] D. E. Losada and A. Barreiro. An homogeneous framework to model relevance feedback. In *Proc. of SIGIR-2001, the 24th ACM Conference on Research and Development in Information Retrieval (poster session)*, pages 422–423, New Orleans, USA, September 2001.

[15] D. E. Losada and A. Barreiro. A logical model for information retrieval based on propositional logic and belief revision. *The Computer Journal*, 44(5):410–424, 2001.

[16] D. E. Losada and A. Barreiro. Rating the impact of logical representations on retrieval performance. In *Proc. DEXA-2001 Workshop on Logical and Uncertainty Models for Information Systems, LUMIS-2001*, pages 247–253, Munich, Germany, September 2001.

[17] D. E. Losada and A. Barreiro. Embedding term similarity and inverse document frequency into a logical model of information retrieval. *Journal of the American Society for Information Science and Technology*, 2003 (to appear).

[18] GNU mifluz. http://www.gnu.org/software/mifluz.

[19] M. F. Porter. An algorithm for suffix stripping. In K.Sparck Jones and P.Willet, editors, *Readings in Information Retrieval*, pages 313–316. Morgan Kaufmann Publishers, 1997.

[20] S. E. Robertson, S. Walker, S. Jones, M. M. HancockBeaulieu, and M. Gatford. Okapi at TREC-3. In D.Harman, editor, *Proc. TREC-3, the 3rd Text Retrieval Conference*, pages 109–127. NIST, 1995.

[21] G. Salton, J. Allan, and C. Buckley. Approaches to passage retrieval in full text information systems. In *Proc. SIGIR-93, the 16th ACM Conference on Research and Development in Information Retrieval*, pages 49–58, Pittsburgh, USA, June 1993.

[22] Senga: Information retrieval software. http://www.senga.org.

[23] C. J. van Rijsbergen. A non-classical logic for information retrieval. *The Computer Journal*, 29:481–485, 1986.

[24] R. Wilkinson. Effective retrieval of structured documents. In *Proc. SIGIR-94, the 17th ACM Conference on Research and Development in Information Retrieval*, pages 311–317, Dublin, UK, July 1994.

From Uncertain Inference to Probability of Relevance for Advanced IR Applications

Henrik Nottelmann and Norbert Fuhr

Institute of Informatics and Interactive Systems
University of Duisburg-Essen
47048 Duisburg, Germany
{nottelmann,fuhr}@uni-duisburg.de

Abstract. Uncertain inference is a probabilistic generalisation of the logical view on databases, ranking documents according to their probabilities that they logically imply the query. For tasks other than ad-hoc retrieval, estimates of the actual probability of relevance are required. In this paper, we investigate mapping functions between these two types of probability. For this purpose, we consider linear and logistic functions. The former have been proposed before, whereas we give a new theoretic justification for the latter. In a series of upper-bound experiments, we compare the goodness of fit of the two models. A second series of experiments investigates the effect on the resulting retrieval quality in the fusion step of distributed retrieval. These experiments show that good estimates of the actual probability of relevance can be achieved, and the logistic model outperforms the linear one. However, retrieval quality for distributed retrieval (only merging, without resource selection) is only slightly improved by using the logistic function.

1 Introduction

Probabilistic models are widely used in information retrieval: Besides the fact that even classical 'non-probabilistic' models can be given a probabilistic interpretation [21], current language models extend classical probabilistic models by methods for considering specific representations of documents and queries. The key advantage of probabilistic models is their underlying theoretic justification, the Probability Ranking Principle (PRP) [16]. The PRP states that optimum retrieval (defined with respect to (w. r. t.) document representations) is given if the documents are ranked according to their probability $Pr(\text{rel}|d,q)$ that document d is relevant to a user query q ("probability of relevance").

For ad-hoc retrieval, probabilistic IR algorithms do not have to estimate these probabilities of relevance directly; instead it is sufficient to rank the documents according to the documents' retrieval status values (RSVs) if these are monotonically increasing with $Pr(\text{rel}|d,q)$ (where d denotes a document, q a query and rel stands for the event that this relationship is judged relevant by the user). For example the well-known binary independence retrieval model ranks documents

F. Sebastiani (Ed.): ECIR 2003, LNCS 2633, pp. 235–250, 2003.
© Springer-Verlag Berlin Heidelberg 2003

according to the RSVs $Pr(d|\text{rel}, q)/Pr(d|\neg\text{rel}, q)$. Computation of these RSVs is easier than estimating the exact probabilities of relevance.

Classical probabilistic IR models are relevance-oriented, i.e. they explicitly refer to the fact that a query-document relationship is judged relevant by a user. In contrast, Rijsbergen [19] introduced a new paradigm for probabilistic information retrieval, namely uncertain inference. This generalisation of the logical view on databases aims at computing the probability $Pr(q \leftarrow d)$ that document d logically implies a given query q ("probability of inference"). As the relationship between $Pr(q \leftarrow d)$ and $Pr(\text{rel}|q, d)$ is assumed to be monotonically increasing, it is sufficient to rank documents w.r.t. the probabilities of inference. As a consequence, little effort has been spent so far on approximating the relationship. Rijsbergen [20] proposed a linear function. In this paper we show that a logistic function yields better results. Logistic functions have been used in different application areas within IR for quite some time, e.g. for text categorisation [7] or retrieval functions [2, 8] (logistic variant of the model proposed in [6]).

Although estimating the probabilities of inference is sufficient for ad-hoc retrieval, the filtering task requires the probabilities of relevance, and thus a mapping function is necessary: Following the decision-theoretic justification of the PRP, let C_r ($\bar{C}_r$) denote the costs for retrieving a relevant (non-relevant) document; similarly, C_o ($\bar{C}_o$) is the cost for omitting a relevant (non-relevant) document from the retrieved set. Then the filtering task corresponds to the problem of determining the cut-off point for ranked retrieval: A document should only be presented to the user if the costs for retrieval are lower than those for omitting the document, i.e.

$$Pr(\text{rel}|q, d) \cdot C_r + [1 - Pr(\text{rel}|q, d)] \cdot \bar{C}_r < Pr(\text{rel}|q, d) \cdot C_o + [1 - Pr(\text{rel}|q, d)] \cdot \bar{C}_o. \quad (1)$$

Our current research focuses on distributed IR, where we also need estimates for the probability of relevance: The decision-theoretic framework [12, 5] for resource selection (the task to determine the best collections to be searched) aims at estimating the number of relevant documents;[1] for this, the probabilities of relevance of the top-ranked documents have to be approximated. The probabilities of relevance also play an important role in the fusion step of distributed retrieval, where the documents retrieved from the selected collections have to be merged in order to get a single ranked list; for this application, we describe experiments below.

This paper is organised as follows: Section 2 mapping function), and the drawbacks of this specific function. Section 3 proposes the logistic function as an alternative function for mapping the probabilities of inference onto probabilities of relevance. Section 4 reports on the results of our evaluation; we measured the overall quality of the estimates of the real probabilities as well as their impact on retrieval quality in the context of distributed IR. Finally, Sec. 5 contains concluding remarks and an outlook on future work.

---

[1] In contrast to resource-ranking algorithms like GlOSS [10, 9] or CORI [1] which only compute a matching score between collections and the given query.

2   Probabilistic Information Retrieval

In this section we describe uncertain inference, a probabilistic generalisation of the logical view on databases, and the standard way of mapping the probability of inference onto the probability of relevance. Finally, we present the drawbacks of this specific linear mapping function.

2.1   Probabilistic IR as Uncertain Inference

Risjbergen's [19] paradigm of IR as uncertain inference can be seen as a generalisation of the logical view on databases, where queries and document contents are treated as logical formulae. For a given query q, the database only returns those documents d which logically imply the query, i.e. it proves $q \leftarrow d$. In order to satisfy this formula, external knowledge like a thesaurus or an ontology can be included as well.

For considering the intrinsic uncertainty of information retrieval, Rijsbergen used probabilistic inference. Thus, probabilistic IR can be interpreted as estimating the probability $Pr(q \leftarrow d)$ that the document logically implies the query. Rijsbergen pointed out that this probability should not be considered in the traditional sense, i.e. $Pr(q \leftarrow d) \not\equiv Pr(\neg d \wedge q)$, but as the conditional probability $Pr(q|d)$.

In this paper, we assume that a query q is represented as a set of terms, where each term t has a query term weight $Pr(q \leftarrow t)$. Similar, a document d is represented as a set of terms with probabilistic indexing weights $Pr(t \leftarrow d)$ for each term t.

Assuming disjointness of query terms, the widely used linear retrieval function [18, 21] can be applied for computing the probability of inference:

$$Pr(q \leftarrow d) = \sum_{t \in q} Pr(q \leftarrow t) \cdot Pr(t \leftarrow d) \ . \tag{2}$$

2.2   Uncertain Inference and Probabilities of Relevance

So far, this model does not cope with the concept of relevance. If we assume a monotonically increasing function mapping the probability of inference onto the probability of relevance, it is sufficient to rank documents according to $Pr(q \leftarrow d)$. Thus, only little work has been done on determining a "good" mapping function.

One of the possible mappings from the probability of inference $Pr(q \leftarrow d)$ onto the probability of relevance $Pr(\text{rel}|q, d)$ is given in [20] based on the total probability theorem:

$$Pr(\text{rel}|q, d) = Pr(\text{rel}|q \leftarrow d) \cdot Pr(q \leftarrow d) + Pr(\text{rel}|\neg(q \leftarrow d)) \cdot Pr(\neg(q \leftarrow d)) \ . \tag{3}$$

This equation can be transformed into:

$$Pr(\text{rel}|q, d) = Pr(\text{rel}|q \leftarrow d) \cdot Pr(q \leftarrow d) + Pr(\text{rel}|\neg(q \leftarrow d)) \cdot Pr(\neg(q \leftarrow d)) \quad (4)$$
$$= Pr(\text{rel}|q \leftarrow d) \cdot Pr(q \leftarrow d) + Pr(\text{rel}|\neg(q \leftarrow d)) \cdot [1 - Pr(q \leftarrow d)] \quad (5)$$
$$= Pr(\text{rel}|\neg(q \leftarrow d)) + [Pr(\text{rel}|q \leftarrow d) - Pr(\text{rel}|\neg(q \leftarrow d))] \cdot Pr(q \leftarrow d) \quad (6)$$
$$= f(Pr(q \leftarrow d)) \ . \quad (7)$$

Thus, we have an affine linear mapping function:

$$f(x) := Pr(\text{rel}|\neg(q \leftarrow d)) + [Pr(\text{rel}|q \leftarrow d) - Pr(\text{rel}|\neg(q \leftarrow d))] \cdot x = c_0 + c_1 \cdot x \ . \quad (8)$$

This mapping function is query-specific. As the parameters $Pr(\text{rel}|q \leftarrow d)$ and $Pr(\text{rel}|\neg(q \leftarrow d))$ are unknown as long as no relevance judgements are available, query-independent constants are used instead.

Function (8) can be further simplified if we assume $Pr(\text{rel}|\neg(q \leftarrow d)) \approx 0$ [20]. Then, we obtain

$$f(x) := Pr(\text{rel}|q \leftarrow d) \cdot x = c_1 \cdot x \ . \quad (9)$$

This linear mapping function is used in the original version of the decision-theoretic framework [12, 5] for resource selection.

2.3   Drawbacks of the Linear Model

The linear model described above has several drawbacks.

First, it does not ensure that the results are between 0 and 1 in the general case of $c_0, c_1 \in \mathbb{R}$. In other words, the result cannot necessarily be regarded as a probability.

Furthermore, experiments show that the relationship between the probability of inference and the probability of relevance is not a linear one (see Sec. 4.2).

Finally, the linear function $c_1 \cdot x$ has the additional disadvantage that the probability of relevance cannot be larger than the probability of inference (interpreting the linear factor c_1 as the conditional probability $Pr(\text{rel}|q \leftarrow d) \leq 1$). If we allow for an affine linear function and/or any real values $c_0, c_1 \in \mathbb{R}$, this problem can be solved. Anyway, as we show in the next two sections, even these more general functions are inappropriate for modelling the shape of the actual mapping function.

3   Logistic Functions

In this section, we propose an alternative to the linear mapping functions described above.

For this, we take a closer look on the ideal situation. Here, exactly the documents in the ranks $1, \ldots, l$ are relevant, and the documents in the remaining

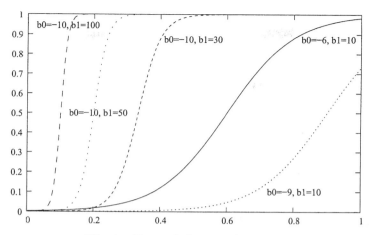

Fig. 1. Example logistic functions

ranks $l + 1, \ldots$ are irrelevant. Let a be the probability of inference of the documents in rank l (i.e., the lowest probability of inference of any relevant documents). Then, the relationship function should be a step function

$$f(x) := \begin{cases} 1 & , \quad x >= a, \\ 0 & , \quad x < a \end{cases} . \tag{10}$$

Obviously, no information retrieval system can ensure this requirement. Thus, in general some of the top-ranked documents are irrelevant, and some of the lower-ranked documents are relevant. But, less documents with lower probabilities of inference should be relevant than documents with higher probabilities. In other words, the probability that any arbitrary document is relevant should decrease with decreasing probability of inference.

For modelling this characteristics, we want a continuous function f which approximates the discrete step function (10). Obviously, the pure and affine linear functions (8,9) are not appropriate.

Instead, one good candidate is the logistic function [3, 4]

$$f : [0, 1] \to [0, 1], \ f(x) := \frac{\exp(b_0 + b_1 \cdot x)}{1 + \exp(b_0 + b_1 \cdot x)} \tag{11}$$

with the two parameters b_0 and b_1. Figure 1 depicts some logistic functions with different parameters. One of the nice properties of logistic functions is that the result is always in $[0, 1]$. In addition, a large variety of curves can be obtained by varying b_0 and b_1. The curve can be moved along the x axis by varying b_0; the slope can be adjusted by varying b_1.

The plots in Fig. 2 (in Sec. 4.2) indicate that the logistic function outperforms the linear function. A more detailed analysis is given later in this paper.

The parameters b_0 and b_1 of the logistic function are query-specific (similar to the parameters c_0 and c_1 of the linear function).

For learning the parameters b_0 and b_1, a learning sample is required. This sample contains the tuples (document, query, probability of inference, relevance judgement). Optimum parameters can then be computed by means of regression methods. Possible optimisation criteria are maximum likelihood [7] or least-square polynomials [13]. In both cases extrema of a function (the likelihood function or the square error) have to be determined, i.e. the points where the first derivative equals zero. The resulting equation cannot be solved directly; instead, an iterative method (e.g. Newton-Raphson) has to be applied.

Usually the parameters are unknown before retrieval, and relevance feedback data is not available. Therefore, global parameters (learned with a sample based on several queries) have to be used.

4   Evaluation

This section presents the experiments we conducted. For a fair comparison, we used the affine linear variant as it has the same number of degrees of freedom as the logistic function.

In the following, we first describe the test-bed, including the documents, the queries, the relevance judgements and the learning algorithms.

Our first evaluation step is to prove our hypothesis that probabilities of inference $Pr(q \leftarrow d)$ can be mapped onto probabilities of relevance $Pr(\text{rel}|q, d)$ using a logistic function. For this, we investigate the approximation errors of the probabilities of relevance with logistic and linear functions. This is an upper bound experiment, since we use complete relevance judgements.

The second series of experiments focuses on the effect of the choice of the mapping function on the resulting retrieval quality. For this purpose, we investigate the case of distributed retrieval, where documents are merged according to the estimates of $Pr(\text{rel}|q, d)$. In this case, training and test samples are disjoint, so the outcome is representative for this type of retrieval task.

4.1   Experimental Setup

We used the TREC-123 test bed with the CMU 100 collection split [1]. The collections are of roughly the same size (about 33 megabytes), but vary in the number of documents they contain. The documents inside a collection are from the same source and the same time-frame. Table 1 depicts the summarised statistics for this 100 library test-bed.

The document index only contains the <text> sections of the documents. Terms are indexed employing a modified BM25 weighting scheme [17]:

$$P(t \leftarrow d) := \frac{tf(t, d)}{tf(t, d) + 0.5 + 1.5 \cdot \frac{dl(d)}{avgdl}} \cdot \frac{\log \frac{|DL|}{df(t)}}{\log |DL|} \ . \tag{12}$$

Here, $tf(t, d)$ is the term frequency (number of times term t occurs in document d), $dl(d)$ denotes the document length (number of terms in document d),

Table 1. Summarised statistics for the 100 collection test-bed

Collection	Minimum	Average	Maximum
Documents	752	10,782	33,723
Bytes	28,070,646	33,365,514	41,796,822

avgdl the average document length, $|DL|$ the collection size (number of documents), and $df(t)$ the document frequency (number of documents containing term t).

We modified the standard BM25 formula by the normalisation component $1/\log|DL|$ to ensure that indexing weights are always in the closed interval $[0, 1]$, and can thus be regarded as a probability.

The resulting indexing weights are rather small; but this can be compensated by the linear components of both the linear and the logistic mapping function (see also below).

Queries are based on TREC topics 51–100 and 101–150 [11], respectively. We use three different sets of queries:

1. Short queries, where we only used the `<title>` field. Short queries contain between 1 and 7 terms (average 3.3), and are similar to those submitted to a WWW search engine.
2. Mid-length queries, where we only used the `<description>` field. Here, queries typically contain between 4 and 19 terms (average 9.9), and may be used by advanced searchers.
3. Long queries, where we used all fields. These queries contain 39–185 terms (average 87.5) and are common in TREC-based evaluations.

Normalised tf values are used as query term weights:

$$P(q \leftarrow t) := \frac{tf(t, q)}{ql(q)} \ . \tag{13}$$

Here, $tf(t, q)$ denotes the term frequency (number of times a term t occurs in query q), and $ql(q) := \sum_{t \in q} tf(t, q)$ is the query length (number of terms in query q).

For both documents and queries, terms are stemmed (using the Porter stemmer [14]), and stop words (the TREC "common words") are removed.

The relevance judgements are the standard TREC relevance judgements [11], documents with no judgement are treated as irrelevant.

In our experiments, we use the Gnuplot[2] implementation of the nonlinear least-squares (NLLS) Marquardt-Levenberg algorithm [15] for learning the parameters c_0, c_1 of the linear function and b_0, b_1 of the logistic function. NLLS

---

[2] http://www.ucc.ie/gnuplot/gnuplot.html

does not ensure further properties of the learned parameters, i.e. we obtain optimum parameters $c_0, c_1 \in \mathbb{R}$. These parameters do not match the underlying theory

$$Pr(\mathrm{rel}|q \leftarrow d) = c_0 + c_1 \qquad Pr(\mathrm{rel}|\neg(q \leftarrow d)) = c_0 \qquad (14)$$

as in general $Pr(\mathrm{rel}|q \leftarrow d)$ and $Pr(\mathrm{rel}|\neg(q \leftarrow d))$ cannot be regarded as probabilities. However, as we learn optimum parameters, this can only lead to an increased approximation quality for the linear model (w. r. t. parameters derived from the underlying theory), and so it does not favor our new model (the logistic function).

4.2   Approximation Errors of the Mapping Functions

In our first set of experiments we evaluated our hypothesis that the mapping between probabilities of inferences $Pr(q \leftarrow d)$ and probabilities relevance $Pr(\mathrm{rel}|q, d)$ can be approximated by a logistic function. For this purpose, we performed an upper-bound experiment where we have complete relevance judgements, and then measured the goodness of fit of the two models.

We randomly chose 10 out of the 100 TREC-123 collections. The characteristics of these 10 collections are rather different but representative for the whole 100 collection test-bed; the collection sizes are depicted in Tab. 1.

For each of the TREC topics 51–100 we learned query-specific parameters b_0, b_1 and c_0, c_1, respectively, and used these parameters for evaluating the same query (optimal parameters). In the result plots in Fig. 2, the x-axis denotes the probabilities of inference and the y-axis the probabilities of relevance. The three curves represent the actual relevance judgements (where probabilities of inference and the corresponding relevance judgements of the documents in ranks 1–5, 6–10, 11–15 … are averaged), the logistic function and the affine linear function.

Where our retrieval algorithm performs well (Fig. 2a, 2b, 2c), the logistic function obviously is a better approximation than the linear functions. For other queries (here, Fig. 2d), the retrieval algorithm performs badly (i.e., the top-ranked documents are irrelevant), and the logistic function does not improve approximation quality in comparison to the linear ones.

Plots can only give a brief overview of the resulting quality. Thus, we also computed the mean square approximation error of the relevance judgement for all of the 10 selected collections for short, mid-length and long queries (pure linear, affine linear and logistic mapping function). The results are listed in Tab. 2.

Using a logistic function instead of a pure or affine linear one always reduces the mean square error; for the affine linear function, the improvement ranges between 4.1% (collection ziff3_9, mid-length queries) to 34.8% (collection ap89_5, long queries). The improvement is higher for long queries than for short and mid-length queries; the same is true for the approximation error (this seems due to the fact that the retrieval algorithms performs better for long queries, i.e. more relevant documents are top-ranked). Obviously, the difference is significant (assuming a simple sign test over the ten subcollections).

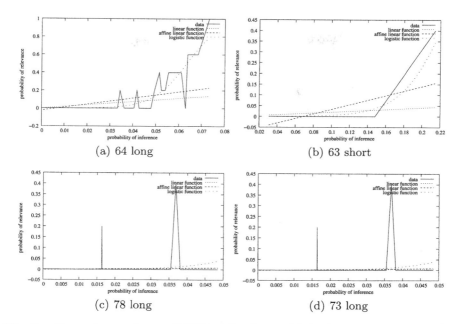

Fig. 2. Example queries on TREC collection ap88_6, showing average probability of relevance, logistic and linear fit

The reported differences between the pure/affine linear and logistic mapping functions are slightly biased in favor of the linear function, as we map results of the linear function outside $[0, 1]$ onto the corresponding margin (as we learned parameters $c_0, c_1 \in \mathbb{R}$ for the linear mapping function, thus the range is not restricted to $[0, 1]$). Without this mapping, the quality is slightly worse.

As a consequence, the bad quality of the linear approximation of the relationship between the probability of inference and the probability of relevance cannot be blamed on the fact that the results of the linear function are not always in $[0, 1]$.

In addition, Fig. 3 shows the mean square error when retrieving $1, \ldots, 100$ documents (as we are more interested in the top-ranked documents). The average is computed over all 10 selected collections and topics 51–100; computation is done separately for short, mid-length and long queries.

One can see that the logistic function performs much better for the top-ranked documents (which are typically the most interesting documents in retrieval). The difference between the two approximation errors decreases for the low-ranked documents; here the two linear functions and the logistic function are very close to zero, and most of the documents are irrelevant (yielding a very low square error for the lower ranks).

These results show a significant improvement for the logistic function, especially for the most interesting ranks.

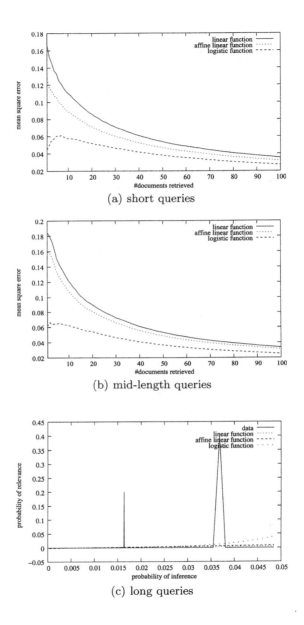

(a) short queries

(b) mid-length queries

(c) long queries

Fig. 3. Mean square approximation error when retrieving $1, \dots, 100$ documents

Table 2. Evaluation results: mean square approximation error (in 10^{-3}) and improvement (in %)

(a) Affine linear function $c_0 + c_1 \cdot x$

Collection	size	short queries			mid-length queries			long queries		
		alin.	log.	Δ	alin.	log.	Δ	alin.	log.	Δ
ap88_6	9210	307	270	+11.9	135	121	+11.0	079	058	+26.2
ap89_5	10542	339	291	+14.1	153	127	+17.4	087	057	+34.8
ap90_4	9955	581	518	+10.7	261	229	+12.4	155	121	+21.8
ap90_6	8934	461	418	+9.4	208	188	+10.0	127	099	+21.9
ap90_7	9794	524	487	+7.1	235	218	+7.2	136	108	+21.0
patn3_5	1021	158	137	+13.2	078	072	+7.1	054	049	+10.4
wsj88_3	13602	355	318	+10.4	138	120	+12.9	074	055	+26.6
wsj90_2	10560	370	342	+7.4	158	144	+8.9	094	079	+16.3
ziff1_2	8847	207	189	+8.7	082	076	+7.1	049	042	+13.9
ziff3_9	9670	233	224	+4.1	086	083	+4.2	053	050	+6.1

(b) Linear function $c_1 \cdot x$

Collection	size	short queries			mid-length queries			long queries		
		lin.	log.	Δ	lin.	log.	Δ	alin.	log.	Δ
ap88_6	9210	330	270	+18.0	140	121	+14.0	084	058	+30.2
ap89_5	10542	381	291	+23.7	159	127	+20.5	093	057	+39.3
ap90_4	9955	635	518	+18.5	277	229	+17.5	166	121	+26.9
ap90_6	8934	501	418	+16.6	217	188	+13.4	133	099	+25.4
ap90_7	9794	554	487	+12.1	240	218	+9.4	143	108	+24.7
patn3_5	1021	165	137	+16.7	079	072	+8.7	056	049	+13.1
wsj88_3	13602	379	318	+16.0	142	120	+15.8	078	055	+30.1
wsj90_2	10560	388	342	+11.6	163	144	+11.5	097	079	+18.8
ziff1_2	8847	213	189	+11.1	083	076	+8.5	050	042	+15.8
ziff3_9	9670	242	224	+7.8	089	083	+6.4	055	050	+9.1

4.3 Retrieval Quality in Distributed IR

In our second set of experiments, we want to test whether a logistic relationship function improves quality for distributed IR.

All 100 TREC-123 collections are used for this experiment. For every collection, we learned the mapping functions (i.e., their parameters b_0, b_1 and c_o, c_1, respectively) with TREC topics 51–100 (only the first 30 documents per query) and evaluated them with topics 101–150 and vice versa (cross evaluation). In this experiment, we are not interested in the influence of resource selection, thus retrieval is performed always on all collections (without resource selection), the top 30 documents of each collection are retrieved, and the resulting 3,000 documents are merged according to the approximations of $Pr(\mathrm{rel}|q, d)$ (with collection-specific parameters).

Table 3. Average precision at given ranks and improvement (in %)

(a) Affine linear function $c_0 + c_1 \cdot x$

Rank	short queries			mid-length queries			long queries		
	alin.	log.	Δ	alin.	log.	Δ	alin.	log.	Δ
5	0.4000	0.3860	-3.5	0.4200	0.4240	+1.0	0.5940	0.5660	-4.7
10	0.3850	0.3800	-1.3	0.3940	0.4050	+2.8	0.5670	0.5560	-1.9
15	0.3840	0.3787	-1.4	0.3820	0.3967	+3.8	0.5467	0.5473	+0.1
20	0.3835	0.3745	-2.3	0.3790	0.3910	+3.2	0.5375	0.5460	+1.6
30	0.3703	0.3567	-3.7	0.3693	0.3687	-0.2	0.5177	0.5320	+2.8

(b) Linear function $c_1 \cdot x$

Rank	short queries			mid-length queries			long queries		
	lin.	log.	Δ	lin.	log.	Δ	lin.	log.	Δ
5	0.3620	0.3860	+6.6	0.3580	0.4240	+18.4	0.5300	0.5660	+6.8
10	0.3730	0.3800	+1.9	0.3350	0.4050	+20.9	0.5030	0.5560	+10.5
15	0.3587	0.3787	+5.6	0.3127	0.3967	+26.9	0.4787	0.5473	+14.3
20	0.3495	0.3745	+7.2	0.3080	0.3910	+26.9	0.4755	0.5460	+14.8
30	0.3297	0.3567	+8.2	0.2930	0.3687	+25.8	0.4563	0.5320	+16.6

Average precision at ranks 5, 10, 15, 20 and 30 is given in Tab. 3. Table 3(a) contains the results for the affine linear function $c_0 + c_1 \cdot x$; Table 3(b) contains the results for the linear function $c_1 \cdot x$.

The results show a significant improvement when an affine linear function is used instead of a pure linear one (particularly for mid-length and long query). This is interesting as it contrasts the assumption that the conditional probability $Pr(\text{rel}|\neg(q \leftarrow d))$ can be neglected.

Precision in the top ranks can also be increased by using a logistic mapping function instead of an affine linear one, although this improvement is quite small (and in a few cases precision also decreases).

In addition, recall/precision graphs for the linear, the affine linear as well as the logistic mapping function are given in Fig. 4.

Here the recall-precision graphs of the affine linear function are much better than the graphs for the pure linear one (especially for the mid-length and long queries). The difference between the graphs for the affine linear function and the logistic function is rather small, however on average we obtained slight improvements by using the logistic function.

5 Conclusion

In this paper, we have investigated the relationship between the probability of inference $Pr(q \leftarrow d)$ and the probability of relevance $Pr(\text{rel}|q, d)$. In the past, little effort has beeen spent on estimating the latter, since the most popular retrieval task—ad-hoc retrieval—needs only a monotonic function of this probability in order to yield a ranking according to the probability ranking principle.

However, advanced IR applications are based on estimates of the actual probabilities of relevance, e.g. for approximating the number of relevant documents in the result set for resource selection (decision-theoretic framework [12, 5]) or for merging the documents retrieved from the selected collections into a single ranked list.

Rijsbergen proposed a linear mapping function for modelling the relationship between the probability of inference and the probability of relevance. Here we showed that this approach has only a moderate approximation quality, in particular in the top-ranked documents.

In this paper we prososed the use of a logistic function. The logistic function can be justified from a theoretical point of view, as it is a continuous approximation of the discrete step function (the ideal relationship). Our experiments showed a significant approximation improvement compared to a linear function. Quality for distributed retrieval (without resource selection) can be significantly improved using an affine linear instead of a linear function, and the results for the logistic function are slightly better than those for the affine linear one (in addition to the nice properties of the logistic function, e.g. the fact that the resulting values are always between zeo and one).

In future, we will investigate in more detail how many documents per query and how many queries are required for obtaining good parameters.

Furthermore, we will extend the decision-theoretic framework [5] so that it can use a logistic mapping function [12] and evaluate the quality compared to the linear function and other resource selection methods. The experiments we conducted for distributed retrieval did not include any resource selection, but this is not realistic. Thus we will investigate whether we can improve retrieval quality when using a logistic function for resource selection.

Acknowledgements

This work is supported by the EU commission under grant IST-2000-26061 (project MIND).

A major part of this work was performed while both authors where affiliated at the University of Dortmund.

References

[1] Jamie Callan and Margaret Connell. Query-based sampling of text databases. *ACM Transactions on Information Systems*, 19(2):97–130, 2001.

[2] W. S. Cooper, F. C. Gey, and D. P. Dabney. Probabilistic retrieval based on staged logistic regression. In N. Belkin, P. Ingwersen, and M. Pejtersen, editors, *Proceedings of the Fifteenth Annual International ACM SIGIR Conference on Research and Development in Information Retrieval*, pages 198–210, New York, 1992. ACM.

[3] S. Fienberg. *The Analysis of Cross-Classified Categorial Data*. MIT Press, Cambridge, Mass., 2. edition, 1980.

[4] D. H. Freeman. *Applied Categorial Data Analysis*. Dekker, New York, 1987.

[5] N. Fuhr. A decision-theoretic approach to database selection in networked IR. *ACM Transactions on Information Systems*, 17(3):229–249, 1999.

[6] N. Fuhr and C. Buckley. A probabilistic learning approach for document indexing. *ACM Transactions on Information Systems*, 9(3):223–248, 1991.

[7] N. Fuhr and U. Pfeifer. Combining model-oriented and description-oriented approaches for probabilistic indexing. In A. Bookstein, Y. Chiaramella, G. Salton, and V. V. Raghavan, editors, *Proceedings of the Fourteenth Annual International ACM SIGIR Conference on Research and Development in Information Retrieval*, pages 46–56, New York, 1991. ACM.

[8] F. C. Gey. Inferring probability of relevance using the method of logistic regression. In Bruce W. Croft and C. J. van Rijsbergen, editors, *Proceedings of the Seventeenth Annual International ACM SIGIR Conference on Research and Development in Information Retrieval*, pages 222–231, London, et al., 1994. Springer-Verlag.

[9] L. Gravano and H. Garcia-Molina. Generalizing GlOSS to vector-space databases and broker hierarchies. In U. Dayal, P. M. D. Gray, and S. Nishio, editors, *VLDB'95, Proceedings of 21th International Conference on Very Large Data Bases*, pages 78–89, Los Altos, California, 1995. Morgan Kaufman.

[10] L. Gravano, H. Garcia-Molina, and A. Tomasic. The effectiveness of GlOSS for the text database discovery problem. In R. T. Snodgrass and M. Winslett, editors, *Proceedings of the 1994 ACM SIGMOD. International Conference on Management of Data.*, pages 126–137, New York, 1994. ACM.

[11] D. Harman, editor. *The Second Text REtrieval Conference (TREC-2)*, Gaithersburg, Md. 20899, 1994. National Institute of Standards and Technology.

[12] Henrik Nottelmann and Norbert Fuhr. MIND resource selection framework and methods. Technical report, Universität Dortmund, February 2002. http://ls6-www.cs.uni-dortmund.de/ir/projects/mind/d31.pdf.

[13] Michael Pollmann. Entwicklung und untersuchung von verbesserten probabilistischen indexierungsfunktionen für freitext-indexierung. Diploma thesis, Universität Dortmund, Fachbereich Informatik, 1993.

[14] M. F. Porter. An algorithm for suffix stripping. *Program*, 14:130–137, July 1980.

[15] William H. Press, Saul A. Teukolsky, William T. Vetterling, and Brian P. Flannery, editors. *Nested Relations and Complex Objects in Databases*. Cambridge University Press, 1992.

[16] S. E. Robertson. The probability ranking principle in IR. *Journal of Documentation*, 33:294–304, 1977.

[17] Stephen E. Robertson, Steve Walker, Micheline Hancock-Beaulieu, Aarron Gull, and Marianna Lau. Okapi at TREC. In *Text REtrieval Conference*, pages 21–30, 1992.

[18] H. R. Turtle and W. B. Croft. Efficient probabilistic inference for text retrieval. In *Proceedings RIAO 91*, pages 644–661, Paris, France, 1991. Centre de Hautes Etudes Internationales d'Informatique Documentaire (CID).

[19] C. J. van Rijsbergen. A non-classical logic for information retrieval. *The Computer Journal*, 29(6):481–485, 1986.

[20] C. J. van Rijsbergen. Probabilistic retrieval revisited. *The Computer Journal*, 35(3):291–298, 1992.

[21] S. K. M. Wong and Y. Y. Yao. On modeling information retrieval with probabilistic inference. *ACM Transactions on Information Systems*, 13(1):38–68, 1995.

Topic Detection and Tracking
with Spatio-Temporal Evidence

Juha Makkonen, Helena Ahonen-Myka, and Marko Salmenkivi

Department of Computer Science, University of Helsinki, Finland
{jamakkon,hahonen,salmenki}@cs.helsinki.fi
http://www.cs.helsinki.fi/group/doremi

Abstract. Topic Detection and Tracking is an event-based information organization task where online news streams are monitored in order to spot new unreported events and link documents with previously detected events. The detection has proven to perform rather poorly with traditional information retrieval approaches. We present an approach that formalizes temporal expressions and augments spatial terms with ontological information and uses this data in the detection. In addition, instead using a single term vector as a document representation, we split the terms into four semantic classes and process and weigh the classes separately. The approach is motivated by experiments.

1 Introduction

Topic Detection and Tracking (TDT) is fairly recent area of information retrieval. It aims to monitor the online news stream in order to automatically spot new unreported news events (*first story detection*) and assigning documents to previously detected events (*topic tracking, cluster detection*)(see e.g. [1, 2, 3]). For example, think of an information worker or a specialist who has to deal with several incoming news-streams that report various things taking place in the world. The information worker might want to follow the course of events regarding bush fires in Australia, the development of the presidential elections in France, or just be informed if anything new takes place in Portugal or in the metal industry, for example. Given a news story, a TDT system would have to be able to attach it to any previous discussions about the event portrayed in the story – else the story would be regarded as new. The process of detecting new events has been considered difficult and the existing information retrieval methodology has had difficulties in this kind of event-based information organization [4].

We present an approach for TDT that exploits *semantic classes*, i.e., classes consisting terms that have similar meaning: locations, proper names, temporal expressions and general terms. Instead of the traditional document vector, our representation has four vectors that reside in disparate spaces. In addition, we formalize temporal expressions and provide them an interpretation on a global time-line and we evaluate the relevance of two spatial references with respect to an ontology. We outline a simple approach utilizing this kind of complex representations and compare it with single-vector methods.

F. Sebastiani (Ed.): ECIR 2003, LNCS 2633, pp. 251–265, 2003.

This paper is organized as follows: Section 2 gives a short introduction to the previous results in TDT. The event vectors are presented in Section 3 and Section 4 deals with the comparing these vectors. Section 5 illustrates our experiments. Section 6 is a conclusion.

2   Previous Work

TDT related research begun in 1996 with DARPA funded pilot study [1]. The researchers set out to experiment the feasibility of TDT systems using existing technology. Quite soon the traditional methods for information retrieval were found more or less inadequate for online detection purposes. First story detection was characterized *queryless information retrieval* as we do not know what we are looking for, i.e., we want to detect the unexpected, *new*. Thus, query-based retrieval methods seemed insufficient [2]. The tracking task is similar to information filtering but with very few examples to work with. Since the tasks are interrelated, the poor performance in detection results in poor tracking performance. Allan, Lavrenko and Jin reduced the topic detection to topic tracking, and showed that the performance of tracking is unacceptably low for efficient first story detection. They concluded that *"effective first story detection is either impossible or requires substantially different approaches"* [4].

Furthermore, the concept of event is problematic: though it appears to be intuitively quite clear, it is difficult to establish a solid definition. Usually, it is understood as *"something happening in a certain place at a certain time"* [5]. Soon after the launching of TDT program, the scope was confined to *event detection and tracking* (e.g. [6]), but recently the focus has returned to spotting dynamic *topics* that center around a seminal events [3, 7]. However, the definition one adopts has an impact on the performance of the system [8].

The methods applied in TDT cover a good portion of the prevailing IR methods: the majority of the approaches in TDT have relied on some sort of clustering: Single-Pass Clustering [1, 2, 8] or hierarchical Group-Average Clustering [2]. Also, Hidden Markov Models [9], Rocchio [10], k-Nearest Neighbours [10], naive Bayes [11], probabilistic Expectation-Maximization models [12] and Kullback–Leibler divergence [7] have been used.

In these approaches, the documents are represented as vectors while the events are either centroids, i.e., compilations of the vectors assigned to the event, or a set of document vectors without generalization, as is the case with kNN. The terms have been weighted with tf-idf variants [4, 10], surprisingness [6], and Time Decay [1], for instance. Allan *et al.* investigated the use of named entities (NE) in the vector model [13]. Similarly, Yang *et al.* [14] extracted locations, names of individuals and organizations, time and date references, and sums of money and percentages for NE-weighting.

3   Event Vector

Making the distinction between two different air disasters or train accidents has not been easy. The terms of two documents discussing the same *kind* of event tend to converge and therefore a term vector is not able to represent the delicate distinction between documents regarding similar but not the same event [1]. However, Allan, Lavrenko and Papka suspect that only a small number of terms is adequate to make the distinction between different news events [6]. Intuitively, it would be temporal expressions, locations and names that would vary more than other terms.

A news document regarding an event reports at the barest *what* happened, *where* it happened, *when* it happened, and *who* was involved. Previous detection and tracking approaches have tried to encapsulate these facts in a single vector. In order to attain the delicate distinctions mentioned above, to avoid the problems with the term-space maintenance and still maintain robustness, we assign each of the questions a *semantic class* [8], i.e., the words that have meaning of the same type. The semantic class of LOCATIONS contains all the places mentioned in the document, and thus gives an idea, where the event took place. Similarly, TEMPORALS, i.e., the temporal expressions name a logical object, that is, a point of on a global time-line, and bind the document onto the time-axis. NAMES are proper names and tell who was involved. What happened is represented by 'normal' words which we call TERMS. These comprise nouns, adjectives and verbs.

The representation of the document using semantic classes is illustrated in Figure 1. This *event vector* comprises four sub-vectors that reside in distinct spaces due to the semantical dissimilarity. If two documents coincide in temporal expressions and locations, for example, it would suggest that they are discussing the same event. Obviously, news events are reported quite promptly, and thus the temporal similarity would be quite high for the news published on the same day. Likewise, the spatial similarity based solely on large areas, such as continents, is of course weaker than similarity based on more specific locations.

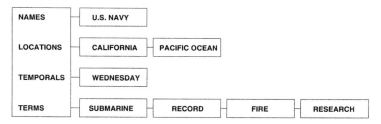

Fig. 1. An example of event vector. *"The U.S. Navy diesel research submarine that holds the world's deep-diving record caught fire in the Pacific Ocean off California on Wednesday and all 43 people aboard were rescued, the Navy said."* *(Washington Post, May 22, 2002)*

4   Measuring Similarity

The use of semantic classes enables us to perform the similarity comparisons class-wise, i.e., examining the corresponding sub-vectors of two event vectors at a time. This results in slight difference in the ways of determining the similarity. First, we present a general term weighting approach, which is elaborated from our previous work [8]. Then, we outline comparison of temporal and spatial references, and finally our detection and tracking algorithm.

4.1   General Term Weight

Typically, the short online news differ from detective stories in that they give away story in the first few sentences. We aim to exploit this structural feature in term weighting. Thus, we use the *ranking* of each occurrence of the term, i.e., the ordinal of the sentence in which the term takes place in measuring the importance of the term. The *rank-score* of a term t occurring m times is

$$rs(t) = \sum_{k=1}^{m} \frac{1}{2^{\ln t_k}},\tag{1}$$

where t_k is the ranking of the kth instance of term t. With rank-scoring, the instances of terms in the first sentence (or title) are assigned weight $\frac{1}{2^{\ln 1}} = \frac{1}{1} = 1$. The rank-score decays as the ranking of the sentence grows, but the (natural) logarithm is there to modify the difference between two consecutive rankings: instances in the eighth and ninth sentences have a difference only of $0.019\ (= 0.237 - 0.218)$.

In order to determine the weight of the intersection of two documents, we calculate the ratio between the rank-score of the intersection and the rank-scores of the documents. Naturally, the informativeness of the terms themselves varies as well. Thus, loyal to the traditions of IR, we multiply the rank-scores with inverted document frequency, IDF. For example, let X and Y be sets of terms. Then their ranking-weighted similarity (RWS) equals to

$$RWS(X,Y) = \frac{\sum_{k=1}^{|X \cap Y|} rs(t_k) * IDF(t_k)}{\sum_{j=1}^{|X|} rs(t_j) + \sum_{l=1}^{|Y|} rs(t_l)}\tag{2}$$

The intersection $|X \cap Y|$ contains all the occurrences of terms common to both documents. Thus, if word 'airport' occurs twice in X and once in Y, there are three occurrences in the intersection. Therefore, the weight of the intersection equals to 1, if the two documents are identical, and 0 if the documents have no common terms.

4.2   Temporal Similarity

Temporal expressions often convey their information implicitly. This means that by examining the surface forms is seldom of any avail. For example, finding the expression 'last Monday' in two documents tells little of their similarity, since the

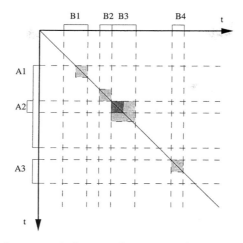

Fig. 2. A cross-tabulation of two sets of intervals A and B

referent of the expression changes with respect to the moment of utterance. We construct automata for temporal expression pattern recognition similarly to [15]. The found patterns do not make sense without augmented information, and thus we *canonize* the expressions with a formalized *calendar* [16] and a set of *shift* and *span* operations [17]. As a result, we provide each recognized expression with a semantical interpretation as an interval on a global time-line $\mathcal{T}$ with respect to the publication date-stamp.

In our approach, the temporal similarity of two documents is a result of a pair-wise comparison of the expressions: each start-end pair of one document is compared to each of the start-end pairs of the other. Krippendorff has conducted various investigations with intervals [18] and motivated by his work we propose a cross-tabulation illustrated in Figure 2. It shows intervals of two sets $A = \{A_1, A_2, A_3\}$ and $B = \{B_1, B_2, B_3, B_4\}$ on time-axis t. The diagonal represents the synchronous points between the two time-axis. The shaded areas correspond to the overlapping intervals. For example, A_3 and B_4 have matching starting point on the time-axis, but mismatching end points. Thus, B_4 covers A_3 only partially.

If the two sets contain the same intervals, they cover each other completely. In such case, all of the intervals would be shaded completely along the diagonal in Figure 2. In case there are disparate intervals, the larger intervals provide weaker coverage than shorter ones. As an example, consider comparing a day and a year versus a day and a weekend.

Galton lists 13 possible relations for two intervals [19]. In Table 4.2, we are not concerned, whether A is **before** B or vice versa, and hence the number of relations is decreased down to seven. We want to take these relations into account while comparing the temporal evidence of two documents. The more the intervals overlap each other with respect to their lengths, the higher the

Table 1. The possible relations of two intervals. Note that the first six relations also have the converse

$[t_i, t_j]$ is **before** $[t_k, t_l]$	if $t_j < t_k$
$[t_i, t_j]$ **meets** $[t_k, t_l]$	if $t_j = t_k$
$[t_i, t_j]$ **overlaps** $[t_k, t_l]$	if $t_i < t_k < t_j < t_l$
$[t_i, t_j]$ **begins** $[t_k, t_l]$	if $t_i = t_k \wedge t_j < t_l$
$[t_i, t_j]$ **falls within** $[t_k, t_l]$	if $t_i < t_k \wedge t_j < t_l$
$[t_i, t_j]$ **finishes** $[t_k, t_l]$	if $t_i < t_k \wedge t_j = t_l$
$[t_i, t_j]$ **equals** $[t_k, t_l]$	if $t_i = t_k \wedge t_j = t_l$

similarity. We employ a simple weight function $\mu_t : \mathcal{T} \times \mathcal{T} \to \mathbb{R}$ such that

$$\mu_t([t_i, t_j], [t_k, t_l]) = \frac{2\,\Delta([t_i, t_j] \cap [t_k, t_l])}{\Delta(t_i, t_j) + \Delta(t_k, t_l)}, \tag{3}$$

where $\Delta : \mathcal{T} \times \mathcal{T} \to \mathbb{R}$, $\Delta(t_i, t_i) = 1$ is the duration (in days) of the given interval. The weight function results in 1 if the expressions are an exact match and 0 if the expressions are distinct. All of the relations presented above are contained within the μ_t-function, since they can be represented in terms of the intersection.

In Figure 2, the intersections $A_3 \cap B_4$ and $A_2 \cap B_3$ would result in higher μ_t-value than the any of the intersections $A_1 \cap B_1$, $A_1 \cap B_3$, and $A_1 \cap B_2$, because the sizes of $A_3 \cap B_4$ and $A_2 \cap B_3$ are closer to the sizes of the union of the intervals, i.e., $|A_3 \cup B_4|$ and $|A_2 \cup B_3|$, and thus there is less uncovered area.

In practice, the pair-wise μ_t-weights are calculated in what we call a *cover matrix* illustrated in Table 2. The coverage of an interval $T_{i,j}$ is calculated by choosing the maximum $v_{i,j}$ of the weights for that term. If an interval $T_{1,i}$ is covered with an interval $T_{2,j}$ of equal weight, the maximum value is $v_{1,i} = 1$. On the contrary, if it is not covered at all, the maximum value yields $v_{1,j} = 0$. In cases of partial or weak cover the value varies in $(0, 1)$ depending on the sizes of the intervals.

Table 2. A cover matrix. The maximum coverage for the interval $T_{1,1}$ would yield $v_{1,1} = \max_{j \leq m}(\mu_t(T_{1,1}, T_{2,j}))$

	$T_{2,1}$	$\cdots$	$T_{2,m}$	max
$T_{1,1}$	$\mu_t(T_{1,1}, T_{2,1})$	$\cdots$	$\mu_t(T_{1,1}, T_{2,m})$	$v_{1,1}$
$\vdots$	$\vdots$		$\vdots$	$\vdots$
$T_{1,n}$	$\mu_t(T_{1,n}, T_{2,1})$	$\cdots$	$\mu_t(T_{1,n}, T_{2,m})$	$v_{1,n}$
max	$v_{2,1}$		$v_{2,m}$	

The total *coverage* of the two sets of intervals is the sum of all the maximum values $v_{i,j}$ divided by the number of intervals. Let T_1 and T_2 be sets of intervals such that T_1 contains n intervals and T_2 contains m intervals. The coverage of the intervals is

$$cover_t(T_1, T_2) = \frac{\sum_{i=1}^n v_{1,i} + \sum_{j=1}^m v_{2,j}}{n + m}. \tag{4}$$

Because $\mu_t = 1$ stands for the perfect match, $v_{i,j} \in [0,1]$ and, since $cover_t(T_1, T_2)$ is really an average of the maximums, also $cover_t(T_1, T_2) \in [0,1]$

We want to weight the temporal expressions with respect to the their ranking-weighted similarity of Equation 2, but without the IDF-weight. Thus the temporal similarity of documents X and Y yields

$$sim_t(X, Y) = cover_t(X_t, Y_t) * RWS'(X_t, Y_t) \tag{5}$$

where X_t and Y_t are the temporal expressions in X and Y, respectively, and $RWS'(X_t, Y_t)$ is the ranking score without the IDF-value.

4.3   Spatial Similarity

The introduction of a geographical ontology enables measuring similarity of the spatial references on a finer scale than just binary decision match–mismatch. For example, when reporting floods in Siberia, the terms such as Russia, Lena, Vilyuy, Lensk and Yakutsk have nothing in common in the surface forms, but their geographical proximity and relevance can be understood by the virtue of an ontology. In other words, we tie each spatial expression to a global structure and thus provide it with a meaning that relates to other spatial expressions.

We employ a 5-level hierarchy in our knowledge of the world as portrayed in Table 3. The levels involved depend on the type of the location. As to land, the levels are continent, region, country, administrative region (e.g., province, state, commune, municipality, municipio, gemeente, kommun), and city. In addition to administrative region, level 4 can also be mountains, seas, lakes and (larger) rivers that include or connect to mountain peaks and (smaller) rivers.

Figure 3 shows a simplified taxonomy containing a number of places. Each node in the tree stands for a location. In case we want to measure the similarity of two such locations, we compare the length of the common path to the sum of the lengths of the paths to the elements, and hence the spatial similarity μ_s of two spatial terms l_1 and l_2 yields

$$\mu_s(l_1, l_2) = \frac{(level(l_1 \cap l_2))}{(level(l_1) + level(l_2))} \tag{6}$$

In case of identity, we assign $\mu_s(l_1, l_1) = 1$. Now, comparing France and Germany would result in $1/(2 + 2) = 1/4$ since the length of the common path (Europe) is 1 and the length of path to both France and Germany equals to 2. Similarly, comparing China and Paris would result in $0/(2+3) = 0$. Paris and France have similarity of $2/(2 + 3) = 2/5$.

Table 3. An example of ontology

Location	Type	Level 1	Level 2	Level 3	Level 4	Level 5
Delft	city	Europe	W.Europe	Netherlands	Zuid-Holland	Delft
Europe	continent	Europe	–	–	–	–
Haag	city	Europe	W.Europe	Netherlands	Zuid-Holland	Haag
Main	river	Europe	W.Europe	Germany	Rhine	Main
Netherlands	country	Europe	W.Europe	Netherlands	–	–
North Sea	sea	Atlantic	North Sea	–	–	–
Rhine	river	Europe	W.Europe	Switzerland, Germany, France, Netherlands	North Sea	Rhine

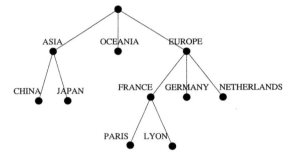

Fig. 3. A simplified ontological taxonomy

Since all the spatial references of one document are to be compared with all of the spatial references of another, we employ the cover matrix presented in Section 4.2. For each term we choose only the maximum similarity, and let the average of maximums stand for the spatial similarity of two documents analogously to temporal coverage. Let L_1 and L_2 be sets of spatial terms such that L_1 contains n terms and L_2 contains m terms, respectively. The spatial coverage is defined as follows

$$cover_s(L_1, L_2) = \frac{\sum_{i=1}^{n} v_{1,i} + \sum_{j=1}^{m} v_{2,j}}{n+m}. \tag{7}$$

Analogously to Equation 5, although here we employ IDF, the spatial similarity of documents X and Y is

$$sim_s(X, Y) = cover_s(X_s, Y_s) * RWS(X_s, Y_s) \tag{8}$$

where X_s and Y_s are the spatial references in X and Y.

4.4 TDT Algorithm

As stated in Section 2, the detection of first stories relies on the tracking. In other words, if a document is not found sufficiently similar to any of the previously detected ones, it is considered a first story. This kind of method is called *single-pass clustering* [20], as the cluster of a new data point is resolved in a single run. We employ two kinds of approaches: one using Kullback-Leibler divergence and another of heuristic kind.

Skew Divergence Kullback-Leibler divergence measures the distance between two probability mass functions. It has been used with relevance models in TDT with some success [7]. We adopt it in a different manner: in order to determine the relative significance of the evidence of each semantic class, we build a model for similarity, m_{yes}, and a model for dissimilarity, m_{no}. The models are average distributions of pair-wise comparisons in the training material. The underlying assumption is that the model for similarity m_{yes} has higher values in each of the semantic classes than those of the model of dissimilarity m_{no}. Therefore, when comparing two documents that discuss the same event, the distribution of the class-wise comparison should be closer to the model m_{yes} than to the model m_{no}

We utilize the Kullback-Leibler divergence to measure the distance to both of the models to see whether the output of the comparison is closer to the average distribution between two documents on the same or different event. Thus, we write

$$D(m||r) = \sum_c m(c)(\log m(c) - \log r(c)) \qquad (9)$$

where c is a semantic class, m is the model, and r is the distribution of the similarity per semantic class. Since the results of the semantic class comparisons do not necessarily yield a probability distribution, we need to tackle the zero values. Instead of smoothing, we adopt the Skew Divergence [21],

$$s_\alpha(r, m) = D(m||\alpha r + (1 - \alpha)m) \qquad (10)$$

where $\alpha \in [0, 1]$. Now, the algorithm described in Figure 4 uses the ratio of the Skew Divergence with the similarity and dissimilarity models, i.e.,

$$\frac{s_\alpha(r, m_{yes})}{s_\alpha(r, m_{no})}, \qquad (11)$$

in determining to which the comparison result r is closer to. The suitable threshold value θ is obtained by empirical experiments with the training data.

The algorithm proceeds as follows: Initially, the set of events is empty as we start processing the incoming documents one by one. The document vector v has a sub-vector v_c for each semantic class c. The document vector is then compared to each of the found events, and the results from the class-wise comparisons are stored in distribution *dist*. If the maximum of Equation 11 exceeds the threshold θ, the vector of the resulting event is updated (line 16). Otherwise, the document is considered a first story and is added to the found events.

```
1          found ← ();
2          for each new document d
3              v ← buildVector(d);
4              max ← 0; event ← ();
5              for each found e
6                  dist ← ();
7                  for each semantic class c
8                      add(sim_c(v_c, e_c), dist);
9                  end;
10                 if ( s_α(dist,m_yes)/ s_α(dist,m_no) > max )
11                     then max ← s_α(dist,m_yes)/ s_α(dist,m_no));
12                         event ← e;
13                 fi;
14             end;
15             if ( max > θ )
16                 then update(event, v);
17                 else add(v, found);
18             fi;
19         end;
```

Fig. 4. A single-pass clustering algorithm using Skew Divergence

Heuristic Thresholding Another approach is to assign heuristically found weights to semantic classes. The difference to the algorithm of Figure 4 is that on lines 10 and 11 there is a sum of the similarity scores of the semantic classes,

$$\sum_{c \in C} \beta_c * sim_c(v_c, e_c), \tag{12}$$

instead of Equation 11. The β_c reflects the importance of semantic class c with respect to the others, for we do not consider semantic classes equally important. That is, we multiply the similarity of the LOCATIONS, NAMES, TERMS and TEMPORAL with $\beta_{locations} = 2.0, \beta_{names} = 2.0, \beta_{terms} = 0.8$ and $\beta_{temporal} = 1.0$, respectively. TEMPORAL evidence is the least important since it tends to be high for the documents published on the same day. On the average, TERMS co-occur more frequently than NAMES and LOCATIONS, and hence the latter two have higher weights. A proper optimization would be an obvious improvement. However, the optimization criteria would be rather tricky, because the evaluation of a TDT is system is not straight-forward.

We also reward for having positive values in any three of the classes NAMES, LOCATIONS, TEMPORAL and TERMS, and especially if there non-zero values in all of them. On the contrary, we do not want to determine two documents similar based only on LOCATIONS, TEMPORALS or NAMES, and therefore we punish for the absence of evidence of TERMS. In practice, rewarding means multiplying with 1.5 and punishing by 0.5.

Table 4. Test c orpus statistics: $Exp(X)$ is the expectation, $Var(X)$ the variance and $Std(X)$ the standard deviation of the size X of the given semantic class

semantic class	$Exp(X)$	$Var(X)$	$Std(X)$
LOCATIONS	4.460	16.698	4.086
NAMES	6.541	37.629	6.134
TERMS	56.363	576.363	24.008
TEMPORALS	2.669	5.013	2.239
total words	105.578	1773.370	42.285

5   Experiments

5.1   Corpus

Our corpus consists of 10384 Finnish online news documents from April 1st 2001 to December 31st, 2001. We have manually assigned 5807 documents to events. The training material consisting of 1918 documents yields 79 events and the testing material comprises 3909 documents with 85 events. The events in the testing set vary from the Siberian floods and the prolonged doctors' strike in Finland to the first space tourist, the presidential elections in Peru and the riots of June 2001 in Gothenburg, Sweden.

We employ Connexor's [1] functional dependency grammar based parser in extracting TERMS, i.e., nouns, adjectives and verbs. The details of our approach to recognizing and resolving temporal expressions are reported in [17]. In extracting LOCATIONS and NAMES we rely on Connexor's Named Entity recognizer. Table 4 describes the average document in the corpus. There are less than 5 instances of LOCATIONS and over 6 instances of NAMES in each document on the average. The portion of TERMS is considerably larger than that of any of the other classes.

In addition, we have manually classified the testing documents to 17 categories that form the first level of the International Press and Telecommunications Council (IPTC) taxonomy [2]. The distribution of the classes is illustrated in Figure 5. On the average, a document is assigned to 1.46 categories. The largest classes are number 4, *economy, business and finance*, and number 11, *politics*.

This classification has been done in order to decrease the number of pairwise comparisons. Although our corpus at present does not encourage to build a classifier, the reported performance of automatic text categorization, however, makes the use of the classes highly feasible. There are four documents in the test set that are classified outside of the class of the first story, and they cannot be correctly tracked. In other words, these four documents do not have mutual categories with the rest of the documents dealing with the same events.

The contents of our ontology is listed in Table 5. The data is based on material provided by Statistics Finland [3]. Since the corpus contains a good number of

---

[1] http://www.connexor.com
[2] http://www.iptc.org
[3] http://www.stat.fi

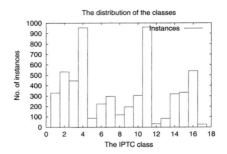

Fig. 5. The distribution of IPTC classes in the test corpus

domestic events, we have added another ontology from the same source in addition to the global one. The domestic locations contain all the counties, provinces and communes of Finland.

5.2   Detection and Tracking Results

We have made the following assumptions: The documents that do not have an event assigned to them in the corpus do not count as first stories. In addition, if two documents that are not assigned to any event are found to discuss the same event, it does not affect the results. These unlabeled documents interfere with the tracking, if they are assigned to some event or if some labeled document is found similar to them.

The methods were evaluated with precision, recall, and their combination F1-measure. The evaluation measures comply with the following formulas:

$$\text{Precision} = P = \frac{relevants\ found}{all\ found}$$
$$\text{Recall} = R = \frac{relevants\ found}{all\ relevant}$$
$$\text{F1-measure} = F1 = \frac{2PR}{P+R}$$

An event is represented by a centroid, or actually the average of the first and the last document assigned to an event.

Table 5. Ontology statistics

type		type	
continents	6	mountain peaks	269
regions	23	mountains	116
countries	270	rivers	369
administrative districts	1422	domestic locations	576
cities	4116	oceans/seas	77
deserts	35	lakes	276

Table 6. The results of detection and tracking

method	Detection			Tracking			$\frac{F1_D+F1_T}{2}$
	P	R	$F1_D$	P	R	$F1_T$	
Cosine	0.473	0.237	0.315	0.214	0.766	0.334	0.325
Cosine (SC)	0.531	0.294	0.379	0.286	0.500	0.363	0.371
Skew Divergence	0.400	0.190	0.258	0.207	0.545	0.300	0.279
Heuristic	0.551	0.905	0.685	0.688	0.450	0.544	0.620

We ran experiments with Skew Divergence and Heuristic Thresholding. In addition, in order to provide a baseline, we ran test also with Cosine coefficient [20], with and without the semantic classes. Table 6 shows the results of the experiments. In order to compare the methods, we combined the F1-measures to indicate overall efficiency of each method. The average is listed on the right. The overall F1-measure was maximized to obtain the results. Each row is produced by one threshold value, i.e., the same threshold is used in both the tracking and the detection. The considerable difference between precision and recall shows the difficulty of optimizing both tasks at the same time. Because the tasks are so interrelated, it is hard to come up with a good optimization criteria.

Secondly, the performance of Skew Divergence seems very poor. Either there is something wrong with the model, or four variables is not enough for measuring divergence. Presumably, this kind of modeling requires larger masses of data and variables. However, the result does not contradict those reported in [22]: Kullback-Leibler, though applied in different way, performed consistently worse precision and recall than Cosine.

Another striking observation is the high performance of the heuristic approach. Simple rules based on intuition and observations outperform all of the other methods by far. The high recall in detection is probably due to the lower precision: since there are more documents considered first stories, there are more correct ones. A decent precision in tracking also helps.

Uniformly through out the results, there seems to be a connection between the detection precision and the tracking recall as well as between the detection recall and the tracking precision. A high value in one results in a high value in the other.

In all, the results, though modest, are at least not considerably worse than those reported by Papka [5], for example. They are still less than what Allan *et al.* would call acceptable.

6 Conclusions

We have presented a topic detection and tracking approach that employs semantic classes in event representation. We identified four classes, places, names, temporal expressions and general terms, and ran the comparisons of two documents class-wise. The approach relies on heavy use of NLP techniques.

We have also presented a method to compare temporal and spatial information in the context of TDT. The method enables the comparison of two relevant terms that differ in the surface forms.

We used a divergence of models and heuristic approach in the detection, and provided results of plain and simple cosine coefficient as a baseline.

In the future, we will obviously concentrate on developing the models more accurate, that is, finding ways in which to represent the yes- and no-distributions with less noise. We will also make efforts to build the heuristic approach a solid theoretical background. Also, we will run the experiments on the Linguistic Data Consortium's TDT data in order to have results that are fully comparable with the previous work.

References

[1] Allan, J., Carbonell, J., Doddington, G., Yamron, J., Yang, Y.: Topic detection and tracking pilot study final report. In: Proc. DARPA Broadcast News Transcription and Understanding Workshop. (1998)

[2] Yang, Y., Carbonell, J., Brown, R., Pierce, T., Archibald, B. T., Liu, X.: Learning approaches for detecting and tracking news events. IEEE Intelligent Systems Special Issue on Applications of Intelligent Information Retrieval 14 (1999) 32 – 43

[3] Allan, J., ed.: Topic Detection and Tracking – Event-based Information Organization. Kluwer Academic Publishers (2002)

[4] Allan, J., Lavrenko, V., Jin, H.: First story detection in TDT is hard. In: Proc. 9th Conference on Information Knowledge Management CIKM, McClean, VA USA (2000) 374–381

[5] Papka, R., Allan, J.: On-line new event detection using single-pass clustering. Technical Report IR–123, Department of Computer Science, University of Massachusetts (1998)

[6] Allan, J., Lavrenko, V., Papka, R.: Event tracking. Technical Report IR – 128, Department of Computer Science, University of Massachusetts (1998)

[7] Lavrenko, V., Allan, J., DeGuzman, E., LaFlamme, D., Pollard, V., Thomas, S.: Relevance models for topic detection and tracking. In: Proc. Human Language Technology Conference (HLT). (2002)

[8] Makkonen, J., Ahonen-Myka, H., Salmenkivi, M.: Applying semantic classes in event detection and tracking. In: Proc. International Conference on Natural Language Processing (ICON'02), Mumbai, India (2002)

[9] van Mulbregt, P., Carp, I., Gillick, L., Lowe, S., Yamron, J.: Text segmentation and topic tracking on broadcast news via a hidden markov model approach. In: Proc. 5th Intl. Conference on Spoken Language Processing (ICSLP'98). (1998)

[10] Yang, Y., Ault, T., Pierce, T., Lattimer, C.: Improving text categorization methods for event detection. In: Proc. ACM SIGIR. (2000) 65–72

[11] Seymore, K., Rosenfeld, R.: Large-scale topic detection and language model adaptation. Technical report, School of Computer Science, Carnegie Mellon University (1997)

[12] Baker, L. D., Hofmann, T., McCallum, A., Yang, Y.: A hierarchical probabilistic model for novelty detection in text. unpublished manuscript (1999)

[13] Allan, J., Jin, H., Rajman, M., Wayne, C., Gildea, D., Lavrenko, V., Hoberman, R., Caputo, D.: Topic-based novelty detection. Technical Report Summer Workshop Final Report, Center for Language and Speech Processing, Johns Hopkins University (1999)

[14] Yang, Y., Zhang, J., Carbonell, J., Jin, C.: Topic-conditioned novelty detection. In: Proc. ACM SIGKDD (to appear), Edmonton, Canada (2002)

[15] Schilder, F., Habel, C.: From temporal expressions to temporal information: Semantic tagging of news messages. In: Proc. ACL-2001 Workshop on Temporal and Spatial Information Processing. (2001) 65–72

[16] Goralwalla, I. A., Leontiev, Y., Özsu, M. T., Szafron, D., Combi, C.: Temporal granularity: Completing the puzzle. Journal of Intelligent Information Systems **16** (2001) 41–63

[17] Makkonen, J., Ahonen-Myka, H.: Extraction and comparison of temporal evidence in identifying news events. Unpublished manuscript

[18] Krippendorff, K.: On the reliability of unitizing continuous data. In Marsden, P. V., ed.: Sociological Methodology. Blackwell (1995) 47–76

[19] Galton, A.: Time and change for AI. In Gabbay, M., Hogger, C. J., Robinson, J. A., eds.: Handbook of Logic in Artificial Intelligence and Logic Programming, Volume 4, Epistemic and Temporal Reasoning. Oxford University Press (1995) 175–240

[20] van Rijsbergen, C. J.: Information Retrieval. 2nd edn. Butterworths (1980)

[21] Lee, L.: On the effectiveness of the skew divergence for statistical language analysis. In: Arficial Intelligence and Statistics. (2001) 65–72

[22] Allan, J., Lavrenko, V., Swan, R.: Explorations within topic tracking and detection. In Allan, J., ed.: Topic Detection and Tracking – Event-based Information Organization. Kluwer Academic Publisher (2002) 197–224

Clustering and Visualization in a Multi-lingual Multi-document Summarization System

Hsin-Hsi Chen, June-Jei Kuo, and Tsei-Chun Su

Department of Computer Science and Information Engineering,
National Taiwan University, Taipei, Taiwan
hh_chen@csie.ntu.edu.tw
{jjkuo,tcsu}@nlg.csie.ntu.edu.tw

Abstract. To measure the similarity of words, sentences, and documents is one of the major issues in multi-lingual multi-document summarization. This paper presents five strategies to compute the multilingual sentence similarity. The experimental results show that sentence alignment without considering the word position or order in a sentence obtains the best performance. Besides, two strategies are proposed for multilingual document clustering. The two-phase strategy (translation after clustering) is better than one-phase strategy (translation before clustering). Translation deferred to sentence clustering, which reduces the propagation of translation errors, is most promising. Moreover, three strategies are proposed to tackle the sentence clustering. Complete link within a cluster has the best performance, however, the subsumption-based clustering has the advantage of lower computation complexity and similar performance. Finally, two visualization models (i.e., focusing and browsing), which consider the users' language preference, are proposed.

1   Introduction

In a basic multi-document summarization system (Chen and Huang, 1999; Mckeown, Klavans, Hatzivassiloglou, Barzilay and Eskin, 1999; Goldstein, Mittal, Carbonell and Callan, 2000; Hatzivassiloglou, Klavans, Holcombe, Barzilay, Kan and Mckeown 2001), how to decide which documents deal with the same topic, and which sentences touch on the same event are indispensable. Because a document is composed of sentences and a sentence consists of words, how to measure the similarity on different levels (i.e., words, sentences and documents), is one of the major issues in multi-document summarization (Barzilay and Elhadad, 1997; Mani and Bloedorn, 1999; Goldstein, Mittal, Carbonell and Callan, 2000; Radev, Jing and Budzikowska, 2000). In multi-lingual multi-document summarization, we have to face one more issue, i.e., the multilinguality problem (Chen and Lin, 2000). However, most of the previous works did not touch this issue. The same concepts, themes and topics may be in terms

F. Sebastiani (Ed.): ECIR 2003, LNCS 2633, pp. 266–280, 2003.

of different languages. Translation among words (sentences, documents) in different languages, idiosyncrasy among languages, implicit information in documents, and user preference should be tackled.

Clustering puts together those words/sentences/documents that denote the same concepts/themes/topics. The granuality of clustering units and the features used in the clustering should be considered. Because sentences contain less information than documents, i.e., fewer features can be employed in sentence clustering, similarity computation among sentences is more challenging than that among documents. In multilingual clustering, three possible ways may be adopted. That is, (1) merge the documents from different language sources, do the document and sentence clustering; (2) do the document clustering for each language source, merge the documents clusters denoting the same topic in different languages, and do the sentence clustering; (3) do the document and sentence clustering for each language source, and merge the sentence clusters denoting the same event in different languages.

This paper presents methods for event clustering on different levels, and show how to summarize the results from event clusters. Section 2 depicts the basic architecture of a multi-lingual multi-document summarization system. Section 3 touches on similarity measurement. Section 4 proposes clustering models for multi-lingual documents. Section 5 deals with multi-lingual sentence clustering. After linking the sentences denoting the same event, Section 6 addresses the visualization issue, e.g., which sentence in which language will be selected, and the preference. Section 7 concludes the remarks.

2   Basic Architecture

Figure 1 shows a multi-lingual multi-document summarization system. We receive documents from multi-lingual sources and send them for document pre-processing. Different languages have their own specific features. Document pre-processing module deals with idiosyncrasy among languages. For example, a Chinese sentence is composed of characters without word boundary. Word segmentation is indispensable for Chinese. Document clustering partitions documents into event clusters. Document content analysis module analyzes document in each event cluster, and links together those sentences denoting the same themes. Finally, summaries are generated.

The major issues behind such a system are how to represent documents in different languages; how to measure the similarity among document representations of different languages; the granularity of similarity computation; and visualization of summaries. The following sections will discuss each issue in detail.

3   Similarity Measurement

3.1   Methods

Word exact matching cannot resolve paraphrase problem. Relaxation with WordNet-like resources (Fellbaum, 1998) postulates that words in the same synset are similar.

EuroWordNet (Vossen, 1998) and Chinese-English WordNet (Chen, Lin and Lin, 2002) facilitate the inexact matching among different languages.

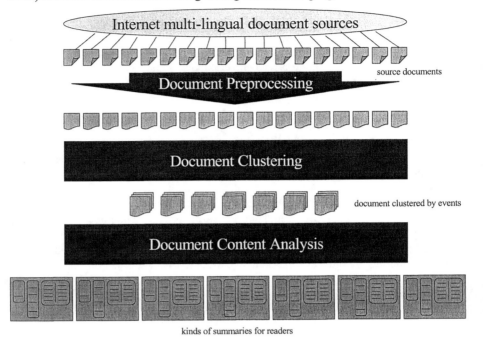

Fig. 1. A Multi-lingual Multi-document Summarization System

Predicate and the surrounding arguments form the basic skeleton in a sentence, so that verbs and nouns are considered as the basic features for similarity measurement. The similarity of two monolingual sentences is defined as follows.

$$SIM(S_i, S_j) = \frac{|S_i \cap S_j|}{\sqrt{|S_i|}\sqrt{|S_j|}} \tag{1}$$

where S_i and S_j are two sets denoting two sentences, $S_i \cap S_j$ denotes the common occurrences of two sentences by inexact matching, and $|S_i|$, $|S_j|$ and $|S_i \cap S_j|$ denote the number of elements in the sets S_i, S_j, and $S_i \cap S_j$, respectively.

For computing the similarity of two sentences in different languages, the ambiguity problem floats up. That is, a word may have more than one translation equivalent in a bilingual dictionary. Five strategies are proposed.

1. position-free

   This strategy is similar to the above method. For each word in S_i, find its translation equivalents by a bilingual dictionary. Then, merge all the equivalents. Let the set be S_i'. Formula 1 is modified as follows.

$$SIM(S_i, S_j) = \frac{\left|S_i' \cap S_j\right|}{\sqrt{\left|S_i\right|}\sqrt{\left|S_j\right|}} \qquad (2)$$

2. first-match-first-occupy
    Compare the translation of each word in S_i with the words in S_j. When a word in S_j is matched, it is removed from S_j and the similarity score (SC) is added by 1. In other words, the word is occupied, and will not be considered in the later comparison. Formula (3) shows the revision.

$$SIM(S_i, S_j) = \frac{SC}{\sqrt{\left|S_i\right|}\sqrt{\left|S_j\right|}} \qquad (3)$$

3. first-match-first-occupy and position-dependent within a window
    This method is similar to Strategy (2) except that the latter comparison is restricted by the results of the previous matching. The range of comparison is limited within a window size of the previous matching. Figure 2 shows an example. Assume C2 has been matched by E1 and the window size is 3. The candidates for E2 in the later comparisons are C1 and C3.

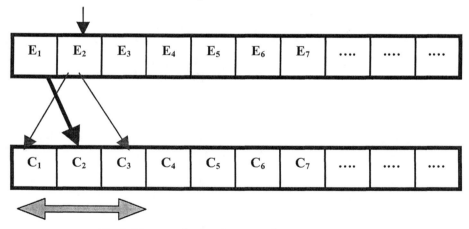

Fig. 2. First-Match-First-Occupy and Position-Dependent

4. unambiguous-word-first and position-dependent within a window
    This strategy links those pairs without ambiguity first, and then performs the similar operation as strategy (3).

5. unambiguous-word-first and position-dependent within a range
    This strategy does not set the window size beforehand. The range for matching
    is restricted by the decided pairs.

We adopt the same five strategies to compute the document similarity except that
the window size is changed. Formula (4) defines the document similarity.

$$SIM(D_i, D_j) = \frac{|D_i \cap D_j|}{\sqrt{|D_i|}\sqrt{|D_j|}} \qquad (4)$$

Here, D_i and D_j are two sets denoting two documents.

3.2   Experiments

We selected 81 pairs of English and Chinese news stories from the web site of United
Daily News in Taiwan. Another 80 unrelated news stories, i.e., 40 English ones and
40 Chinese ones, were added and mixed together. For each English news story, we try
to find the best matching from the remaining 241 candidates. Besides, from the above
81 pairs of English and Chinese news stories we extracted 43 pairs of English and
Chinese sentences at random and regarded them as an answer set to evaluate the performance of sentence similarity computation. For each English news sentences, we try
to find the best matching from the remaining 85 candidates. Correct rate is defined as
follows.

$$CorrectRate = \frac{CorrectPairsSystemFind}{TotalCorrectPairs} \qquad (5)$$

Table 1. Performance of Document Alignment

	Strategy 1	Strategy 2	Strategy 3	Strategy 4	Strategy 5
Best 1	0.951	0.839	0.506	0.320	0.320
Best 2	0.987	0.925	0.604	0.432	0.444
Best 3	1.000	0.925	0.666	0.469	0.469
Best 4	1.000	0.950	0.740	0.518	0.518
Best 5	1.000	0.975	0.740	0.530	0.530

Table 2. Performance of Sentence Alignment

	Strategy 1	Strategy 2	Strategy 3	Strategy 4	Strategy 5
Best 1	0.883	0.767	0.441	0.255	0.255

Best 2	0.930	0.813	0.674	0.279	0.279
Best 3	0.976	0.860	0.697	0.325	0.325
Best 4	1.000	0.930	0.790	0.372	0.372
Best 5	1.000	0.930	0.790	0.372	0.372

Tables 1 and 2 summarize the experimental results for document and sentence alignments, respectively. Best n means n documents should be proposed to cover the correct matching. The experimental results show that Strategies 1 and 2 are better than the other three strategies. Moreover, Strategy 1 is also superior to Strategy 2. The position-dependent seems not to be useful in both first-match-first-occupy and unambiguous-word-first models. This is due to the difference of word order between Chinese and English sentences, e.g., the arguments in relative clause may be extra-posed to different positions in Chinese and in English. To fix the non-ambiguous word first does not have a clear effect in the experiments. After analyzing the results, we find that there are 172,734 lexical items in our bilingual dictionary. Of these, 111,120 lexical items have only one translation. The average number of translation equivalents per lexical item is 2.17. However, only 841 of 9,636 words in the test corpus are unambiguous. On the average, each lexical item has 10.84 translation equivalents. The experimental results also reveal that the performance of document alignment is better than that of sentence alignment. The amount of information affects the similarity computation.

4   Event Clustering

4.1   Clustering Models

Translation is indispensable for multi-lingual multi-document clustering. Three possi-ble models are proposed as follows. They deal with when translation is performed.

1. translation BEFORE document clustering
    This model clusters the multi-lingual multi-documents directly. Figure 3 shows this model, which is a one-phase model. The similarity computation among documents in Section 3 belongs to this type.
2. translation AFTER document clustering
    This model clusters documents in each language separately, and merges the clustering results. Figure 4 shows this model, which is a two-phase model.
3. translation DEFERRED to sentence clustering
    In this model, multilingual problem is dealt with on the sentence level. Figure 5 shows this model which will be discussed further in Section 5.

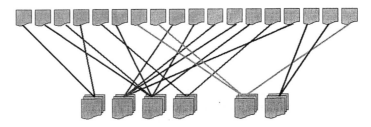

Fig. 3. Translation before Document Clustering

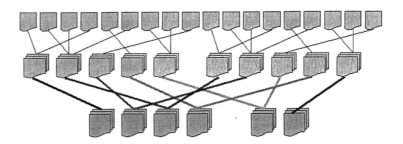

Fig. 4. Translation after Document Clustering

4.2   Experiments

We collected English and Chinese news articles reported on May 8, 2001 from the following news sites in Taiwan. There are 460 news articles in the test corpus.

1.   English: Central News Agency, China Post, China Times and United Daily
      News
2.   Chinese: Central News Agency, Central Daily News, China Times and United
      Daily News

First, we cluster those news articles manually and the result is shown as in Table 3. Tables 4 and 5 show the experimental results of one-phase model (i.e., translation before clustering) and two-phase model (i.e., translation after clustering), respectively. In the one-phase scheme, only one threshold is used. Table 4 lists three sets of results under three different threshold assignments. Comparatively, due to the different document features, e.g. document numbers, three different thresholds are used in the two-phase scheme (see Table 5), including one for Chinese document clustering (i.e., 0.3), one for English document clustering (i.e., 0.5), and one for the final cluster merging (i.e., 0.2). The performance of two-phase scheme is better than that of one-phase scheme. The major reason is translation is performed after monolingual clustering. That reduces not only the translation errors, but also the computation complexity. This concept leads to the Model 3 (translation deferred to sentence cluster-ing).

Table 3. Manual Clustering Result

	Article Number	Cluster Number	Cluster Number = 1	Cluster Number > 1
Chinese	360	265	230	35
English	91	75	65	10
CE	460	318	276	42

Table 4. Experimental Result Using One-Phase Model

Threshold	Number of Articles in a Cluster			Exact Match	Precision	Recall
	1	1<N<5	>5			
0.1	156	37	50	154	0.633	0.484
0.2	250	16	36	223	0.738	0.701
0.4	430	0	1	264	0.612	0.830

Table 5. Experimental Results Using Two-Phase Model

	Threshold	Number of Articles in a Cluster			Exact Match	Precision	Recall
		1	1<N<5	>5			
C	0.3	240	33	21	253	0.860	0.954
E	0.5	52	13	6	60	0.845	0.800
CE	0.2	281	29	44	296	0.841	0.931

5   Sentence Clustering

5.1   Clustering Models

Figure 5 shows that after monolingual document clustering, those documents in a cluster denote the same event in a specific language. To generate the extract summary of an event, we must cluster the similar sentences among documents and then choose a representative sentence from each cluster. Position-free strategy proposed in Section 2 has the best performance, thus it is employed to compute the similarity between two bilingual sentences.

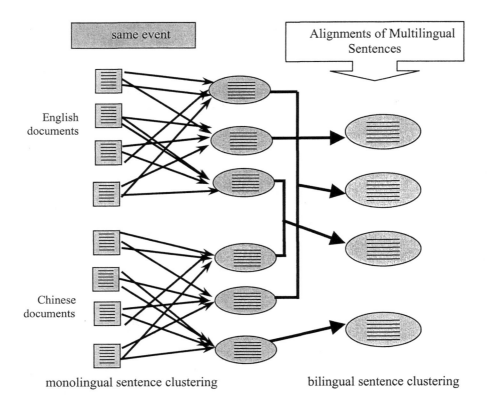

Fig. 5. Translation Deferred to Sentence Clustering

There are three alternatives shown as follows for sentence clustering.

1. complete link using all sentence
    We compute the similarity between any two sentences in the same event cluster, and employ complete link strategy to cluster the sentences.
2. complete link within a cluster
    To tackle the computational issue, we read each sentence in the same event cluster in sequence. The first sentence s_1 is assigned to a cluster c_1. Assume there already are k clusters when a new sentence s_i is considered. The sentence s_i may belong to one of k clusters, or it may form a new cluster c_{k+1}. The determination depends on the similarity between s_i and all the sentences in each cluster. If all the sentence similarities in a specific cluster are greater than the threshold, it is added into that cluster. If there is no such a cluster, s_i becomes a new cluster.
3. subsumption-based clustering
    The basic idea is similar to Model 2 except that in this model a centroid is determined for each cluster and a subsumption test is used to tell if a sentence be-

longs to a specific cluster. The following formula (6) defines an information score of a sentence in a cluster. Total 25 words of higher document frequency in a cluster are considered as topic words of this cluster.

$$\inf(S) = \left(|S_n| + |S_v| + |S_t| \right) \tag{6}$$

where S denotes a sentence,
$|S_n|$ is the number of nouns in S,
$|S_v|$ is the number of verbs in S, and
$|S_t|$ is the number of topic words in S.

The sentence of the highest information score in a cluster is selected as the centroid of this cluster. We only compute sentence similarity between a sentence and a centroid, and the sentence similarity is in terms of a subsumption score shown as follows.

$$SIM\ (S_i, S_j) = \frac{|S_i \cap S_j|}{\min \left(|S_i|, |S_j| \right)} \tag{7}$$

where S_i and S_j are two sets representing two sentences,
$S_i \cap S_j$ denotes the common occurrences[1] of two sentences, and $|\ S_i\ |$, $|\ S_j\ |$ and $|\ S_i \cap S_j\ |$ denotes the number of elements in the sets S_i, S_j, and $S_i \cap S_j$, respectively.
The larger the score is, the more the subsumption is.

5.2   Experiments

We used the same materials specified in Section 4.2. After manual clustering, we selected five events shown below and the related numbers of English and Chinese articles are listed in Table 5.

1.   Investment for bioinformatics
2.   The relation between President Chen and Vice President Lu
3.   Mr. Hsiao Wuan-Chang visited mainland China
4.   Can the management of Kaoshong harbor return to city government?
5.   The court rejected the application from the Journalist Magazin

Besides, we also cluster the related sentences munually for each event. There are 662 correct links. The following shows sample of answer keys used in evaluation. Each sentence is denoted by NewsAgencyType_DocumentID_Sentence_ID. For example, ChinaEng_022_001 is an English sentence (ID : 001) in a news (ID : 022) published by China Times. This sentence is related to CnaEng_021_001, UdnBI_e_003_001, and UdnBI_c_003_001.

Sentence	Link1	Link2	Link3
ChinaEng_022_001	CnaEng_021_001	UdnBI_e_003_001	UdnBI_c_003_01
ChinaEng_022_007	CnaEng_021_007		
UdnBI_e_007_001	ChinaEng_002_001	CpostEng_004_017	
UdnBI_e_007_002	CpostEng_004_003		

---

[1] The synonym matching and position-free method specified in Section 2 are adopted.

Tables 7-9 list experimental results using the three sentence clustering methods.

Table 6. Test Data for Sentence Clustering

	Total Chinese Documents	Total English Documents	Total Chinese Sentences	Total English Sentences
Event 1	4	3	69	25
Event 2	5	2	87	39
Event 3	5	3	92	40
Event 4	5	2	82	16
Event 5	2	3	23	46

Table 7. Performance of Complete Link Using All Sentences

Threshold	Total Links Proposed	Number of Correct Links	Precision	Recall
0.20	852	436	0.511	0.658
0.25	702	408	0.581	0.616
0.30	668	384	0.574	0.580

Table 8. Performance of Complete Link within a Cluster

Threshold	Total Links Proposed	Number of Correct Links	Precision	Recall
0.50	892	478	0.536	0.722
0.55	718	420	0.585	0.634
0.60	622	376	0.604	0.567

Table 9. Performance Using Subsumption-based Links

Threshold	Total Links Proposed	Number of Correct Links	Precision	Recall
0.50	874	462	0.529	0.698
0.55	708	418	0.590	0.631
0.60	602	358	0.595	0.540

By observing Tables 7 and 8, the performance of Strategy 2 is better than that of Strategy 1. Although the performance of Strategy 3 is a little worse than that of Strategy 2, its time complexity is decreased very much. If the score function can be further improved to obtain the more representative sentence, this strategy is competible.

6   Visualization

In multi-lingual multi-document summarization, how to display the results to readers is an important issue. Two models, i.e., focusing model and browsing model, are proposed. The readers' preference is also taken into consideration. For example, a Chinese reader prefers to read more Chinese summarization than English one.

6.1   Focusing Model

A summarization is presented by voting from reporters. For each event, reporter records a news story from his own viewpoint. Recall that a news story is composed of several sentences. Those sentences that are similar in a specific event are common focus of different reporters. In other words, they are worthy of reading. For each set of similar sentences, only the longest sentence is displayed. The display order of the extracted sentences is determined by the related position in the original news articles. The following formula defines a position score function.

$$PositionScore = \frac{position(S,D)}{sizeof(D)} \tag{8}$$

where $position(S,D)$ denotes the position of sentence S in document D,
         $sizeof(D)$ is the size of document D.

The extracted sentences are sorted in the ascending order of position scores. When users' language preference is considered, the sentences are selected by languages and voting of reporters, and displayed by position scores. That is, they are grouped by languages. Figure 6 sketches the concepts of focusing model. Chinese i-j means the j-th sentence in i-th Chinese news article.

6.2   Browsing Model

The news articles are listed by information decay and chronological order. The first article is shown to the user in its whole content. In the latter news articles, those sentences, that have higher similarity scores with the sentences in former news articles, are shadowed (or eliminated), so that the reader can only focus on the novel information. We also consider the readers' preference in multi-lingual multi-document summarization. The news articles in the preferred language are shown before those in other languages. Figure 7 sketches the concepts of browsing mode with Chinese preference. Chinese news article 1 is the first article, so the whole content is shown to the reader. However, due to the high similarity with sentences in Chinese news article 1, sentences 3, 4 and 5 in English news article 1 are shadowed (underlined). Similarly, sentence 3 in Chinese news article 3 has high similarity score with some sentences in Chinese news article 1, 2 or English news article 1, 2.

Chinese 1-1	English 2-1
Chinese 1-2	English 1-2
Chinese 2-2	English 1-3
Chinese 3-3	English 5-3
Chinese 3-4	English 6-4
Chinese 2-5	English 2-5
Chinese 1-6	Chinese 1-2
English 2-1	Chinese 3-3
English 1-2	Chinese 3-4
English 1-3	Chinese 1-6

Prefer Chinese   Prefer English

Fig. 6. Visualization in Focusing Model

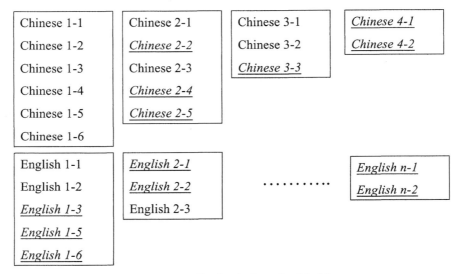

Fig. 7. Visualization in Browsing Model

7   Concluding Remarks

This paper presents a multi-lingual multi-document summarization system.   Five strategies are proposed to measure the similarities between two bilingual sentences. The position-free strategy is better than the position-dependent strategy. Besides, two strategies are proposed for multi-lingual document clustering. The two-phase strategy (translation after clustering) is better than one-phase strategy (translation before clustering). Translation deferred to sentence clustering, which reduces the propagation of translation errors, is most promising. Moreover, three strategies are proposed to tackle the sentence clustering. Complete link within a cluster has the best performance, however, the subsumption-based clustering has the advantage of lower computation complexity and similar performance. Finally, two visualization models (i.e., focusing and browsing), which considers the users' language preference, are proposed.

Acknowledgements

Part of the research results of this paper was supported by National Science Council, Taiwan, under the contract NSC90-2213-E-002-045.

References

[1]   Barzilay, Regina and Elhadad, Michael (1997) "Using Lexical Chains for Text Summarization," *Proceedings of ACL/EACL 1997 Workshop on The Intelligent Scalable Text Summarization*, pp. 10-16.

[2]   Chen, Hsin-Hsi and Huang, Sheng-Jie (1999) "A Summarization System for Chinese News from Multiple Sources," *Proceedings of the 4th International Workshop on Information Retrieval with Asian Languages*, Taipei, Taiwan, pp. 1-7.

[3]   Chen, Hsin-Hsi and Lin, Chuan-Jie (2000) "A Multilingual News Summarizer," Proceedings of 18th International Conference on Computational Linguistics, pp. 159-165.

[4]   Chen, Hsin-Hsi, Lin, Chi-Ching and Lin, Wen-Cheng (2002) "Building a Chinese-English WordNet for Translingual Applications," *ACM Transactions on Asian Language Information Processing*, 1(2), pp. 103-122.

[5]   Fellbaum, Christinae., Ed. (1998) WordNet: An Electronic Lexical Database. MIT Press, Cambridge, MA.

[6]   Goldstein, Jade, Mittal, Vibhu, Carbonell, Jaime and Callan, Jamie (2000) "Creating and Evaluating Multi-Document Sentence Extract Summaries," *Proceedings of the 2000 ACM International Conference on Information and Knowledge Management*, pp. 165-172.

[7]   Hatzivassiloglou, Vasileios, Klavans, Judith L., Holcombe, Melissa L. Barzilay, Regina, Kan, Min-Yen and Mckeown, Kathleen R. (2001) "SIMFINDER: A Flexible Clustering Tool for Summarization," *Proceedings of NAACL2001 Workshop on Automation Summarization*, pp. 41-49.

[8]   Mani, Inderjeet and Bloedorn, Eric (1999) "Summarizing Similarities and Difference among Related Documents," *Information Retrieval*, 1(1-2), pp. 35-67.

[9]   Mckeown, Kathleen, Klavans, Judith L., Hatzivassiloglou, Vasileios, Barzilay, Regina and Eskin, Eleazar (1999) "Towards Multi-document Summarization by Reformulation," *Proceedings of AAAI-99*, pp. 453-460.

[10] Radev, Dragomir.R., Jing, Hongyan and Budzikowska, Malgorzata (2000) "Centroid-based Summarization of Multiple Documents: Sentence Extraction, Utility-based Evaluation, and User Studies," *Proceedings of Workshop on Summarization*, ANLP/NAACL, 2000.

[11] Vossen, Piek (1998) "EuroWordNet: Building a Multilingual Database with Wordnets for European languages," *The ELRA Newsletter*, 3(1), 7-10.

A Hybrid Relevance-Feedback Approach
to Text Retrieval

Zhao Xu[1], Xiaowei Xu[2], Kai Yu[3], and Volker Tresp[4]

[1] Tsinghua University, Beijing, P.R. China
`xuzhao00@mails.tsinghua.edu.cn`
[2] University of Arkansas at Little Rock, Little Rock, USA
`xwxu@ualr.edu`
[3] University of Munich, Munich, Germany
`yu_k@dbs.informatik.uni-muenchen.de`
[4] Siemens AG, Corporate Technology, Munich, Germany
`volker.tresp@mchp.siemens.de`

Abstract. Relevance feedback (RF) has been an effective query modification approach to improving the performance of information retrieval (IR) by interactively asking a user whether a set of documents are relevant or not to a given query concept. The conventional RF algorithms either converge slowly or cost a user's additional efforts in reading irrelevant documents. This paper surveys several RF algorithms and introduces a novel hybrid RF approach using a support vector machine (HRFSVM), which actively selects the uncertain documents as well as the most relevant ones on which to ask users for feedback. It can efficiently rank documents in a natural way for user browsing. We conduct experiments on Reuters-21578 dataset and track the precision as a function of feedback iterations. Experimental results have shown that HRFSVM significantly outperforms two other RF algorithms.

1   Introduction

The World Wide Web continues to grow at an amazing speed, as does the number of text and hypertext documents in organizational intranets. These documents represent the accumulated knowledge that becomes more and more important for an organization's success in today's information society. Search Engines (SE) became important tools in order for people to use the information on the Internet or intranets. But generally, they return a small number of relevant web pages with a large number of irrelevant web pages. Therefore, much effort has been aimed at improving the precision of SE–a challenging task due to the web's huge size, high dynamics, and large diversity.

In using a SE, users usually enter keywords that are often ambiguous and that may have different meanings in different contexts. For instance, the term "java" means "a kind of programming language" for some users, while for others it may mean "an island in Indonesia." Therefore, users may find it difficult to formalize their query concepts clearly by just using simple key words. Furthermore, because of the often long lists of results, users, who want to spend as little

F. Sebastiani (Ed.): ECIR 2003, LNCS 2633, pp. 281–293, 2003.
© Springer-Verlag Berlin Heidelberg 2003

time possible, may browse only the first dozen or so results. Hence, they expect powerful retrieval technology.

Traditionally an iterative and interactive process, relevance feedback (RF) improves the quality of the information retrieval [9, 10, 5]. After the initial user query, the system returns a set of ranked documents from the text base. Although the system may retrieve many documents, it only presents one screen of documents at a time. Search engines usually use screens of 10-20 documents. We assume that the abstracts of returned documents on the initial screen have enough information for the user to gauge whether a document is relevant. The user gives relevance feedback to the results on the screen. Users can give their relevance feedback by either explicitly voting or implicitly clicking documents. This way, the system learns a query concept model from the feedback and generates another list of ranked documents. This interactive process continues until the user terminates it.

The conventional RF algorithms converge slowly because users are led to label only the most relevant documents, which is usually not informative enough for systems to improve the learned query concept model. Recently, active learning algorithms have been proposed to speed up the convergence of the learning procedure [11, 12]. In active learning, the system has access to a pool of unlabelled data and can request the user's label for a certain number of instances in the pool. However, the cost of this improvement is that users must label documents when the relevance is unclear or uncertain for the system. These "uncertain documents" are also proven to be very informative for the system to improve the learned query concept model quickly.

From a machine learning point of view, both RF and active learning are two extreme instance selection schemas: the RF selects the most probably relevant instances (documents), while active learning selects the most uncertain yet informative ones. The conventional RF algorithms converge slowly, while active learning costs a user's additional efforts in reading "uncertain documents". Therefore, both methods are far from being optimal in information retrieval.

In this paper, we compare several relevance feedback algorithms for document retrieval and summarize their strengths as well as weaknesses; secondly, we introduce a novel Hybrid Relevance Feedback approach using Support Vector Machines (HRFSVM), which takes a heuristic strategy to overcome weaknesses and achieve optimal performance.

2   Relevance Feedback Algorithms for Document Retrieval

In the past 30 years, relevance feedback (RF) has become an effective way of modifying and expanding user queries for improving the quality of retrieval systems. Various approaches were proposed and investigated. In this section we give a survey on representative approaches. By analyzing their strengths and weaknesses, we show the reasons of why to propose a new approach.

2.1   The Rocchio Algorithm

One of the earliest RF algorithms was proposed by J.J. Rocchio [9]. The feedback iteration using Rocchio's algorithm expands the query in the following way:

$$Q_j = \alpha Q_{j-1} + \frac{\beta}{N_r} \sum_{i=1}^{N_r} R_i - \frac{\gamma}{N_s} \sum_{i=1}^{N_s} S_i \qquad (1)$$

where, α, β, γ are three constants, Q_j is the vector for the j-th updated query, R_i is the vector for relevant document i, S_i is the vector for irrelevant document i, N_r is the number of labelled relevant documents, and N_s is the number of labelled irrelevant documents.

Here Q, R, and S are all represented as vectors of terms within the framework of a vector space model. All negative components of the resulting optimal query are assigned a zero weight. Once the new query Q_j is obtained, we compute its inner product with each unlabelled document and form a ranking of them. The higher inner product indicates a higher relevance. The intuitive idea of Rocchio's algorithm is to iteratively increase the weights of those terms contained in labelled relevant documents while penalizing the terms in irrelevant documents. In practice, how to determine the optimal values of three constants, as in Equation (1), is always a problem.

Later, many extensions or modifications of Rocchio's RF algorithm were proposed, like Ide Regular algorithm and Ide dec-hi algorithm [10, 5]. The basic operational procedure in these methods is the merging of labeled relevant document vectors and original query vectors. Queries are automatically expanded by adding the terms not in the original query but in the labeled relevant documents. On the other hand, the term weights are increased or decreased based on whether the terms are coming from relevant or irrelevant documents. Rocchio's RF algorithm and its extensions perform well when a user gives enough feedback. No optimizing mechanism exists in them to guarantee an optimal retrieval quality in different situations, especially when few relevant or irrelevant documents are obtained from user feedback. A recent study [3] revealed that Rocchio's algorithm has a poor performance when the proportion of relevant documents in the whole corpus is quite low.

2.2   The SVM Relevance Feedback Algorithm (SVMRF)

In general, any classification algorithm can be applied for RF. The retrieval system iteratively obtains positive (relevant) and negative (irrelevant) instances (documents) from a user and trains a classifier at each iteration; it then uses the classifier to predict any unlabelled document as relevant or not. Due to its strong mathematic foundations and excellent empirical successes, support vector machines (SVM) [13] recently gained wide attention in the research communities of machine learning and information retrieval. Drucker, Shahraray, and Gibbon [3] applied a SVM classifier in RF and reported a much better retrieval performance, especially when just a few relevant feedbacks were obtained at the beginning iterations.

In simplest form, SVMs are hyperplanes that separate the training data by a maximal margin (see Fig. 1). All vectors lying on one side of the hyperplane are labelled as "cross" (e.g. positive), and all vectors lying on the other side are labelled as "circle". The training instances that are closest to the hyperplane are called "support" vectors. Generally, SVMs allow one to project the original training data in space X to a higher dimensional feature space F via an operator K. In other terms, we consider the set of classifiers of the form:

$$f(x) = (\sum_{i=1}^{n} \alpha K(x_i, x)) \tag{2}$$

When K satisfies Mercer's condition [1], we can write:

$$K(u, v) = \Phi(u) \bullet \Phi(v) \tag{3}$$

where $\Phi : X \to F$. We can rewrite f as:

$$f(x) = w \bullet \Phi(x) \tag{4}$$

where $w = \sum_{i=1}^{n} \alpha_i \Phi(x_i)$.

By choosing different kernel functions, we can implicitly project the training data from X into spaces F for which hyperplanes in F correspond to more complex decision boundaries in the original space X. Commonly used kernel functions include linear kernel, polynomial kernel, and radials basis function kernel.

It has been reported that SVMs achieved notable success in the task of text classification [6, 4]. Furthermore, by calculating distances of document vectors to the trained hyperplane, SVMs give a straightforward ranking of documents, which is more desired in document retrieval than a hard class decision. A reasonable intuition is that those remote documents far away from the decision boundary can be judged relevant or irrelevant with a high confidence. Drucker et al. [3] applied this idea to document retrieval and proposed a SVM relevance feedback scheme. SVMRF proceeds in the following iterative way:

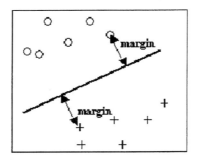

Fig. 1. A support vector machine with its corresponding margin and two support vectors

1. Users label some of documents in the top ranked list to be relevant or irrelevant according to their query concepts.
2. The system trains a new SVM model using the relevance-feedback data gathered so far.
3. The system presents a ranking of documents to users, according to the documents' distances to the newly trained hyperplane. The remotest one on the positive side is ranked at the top of the list, while the remotest one on the negative side is ranked at the bottom.
4. If the user is satisfied with current ranking, the system ends this section; otherwise, it goes to Step 1.

SVMRF was found much more effective than the Rocchio algorithm, especially in the case of searching the least frequently occurring topics [3]. This excellent performance is mainly due to the maximum margin optimization of hyperplane, which promises good generalization ability even when observed training data are quite limited. SVMRF can be viewed as an approach of passively obtaining information from a user and then learning the user's query concept (represented by a SVM model). Normally, a user gives relevance feedback in the order of ranking, e.g. rating the documents in the first screen, and thus, the system obtains feedback on those documents that are likely to be truly relevant. Normally, a learning system gets little information from the data familiar to the system, i.e. the correctly classified data. Our concern regarding this method is mainly the low learning rate, since relevance feedback on the most certainly relevant documents are not actually informative to the system for improving the model. In a machine learning community, it has been revealed that a learning system can always gain maximum information by learning from the most uncertain instances [2, 7, 12]. For the purpose of document retrieval, there should be a more effective way to actively obtain information from a user and thereby speed up the learning process. We emphasize that improving the learning rate is an essential issue in document retrieval, since people are always impatient.

2.3   SVM Active Learning for Relevance Feedback (ActiveSVMRF)

The idea of active learning has been widely studied in a machine learning community. Pool-based active learning was introduced by Lewis and Gate [7]. They applied a Naïve Bayesian classifier combined with logistic regression to choose the instance (a document) in which the class is most uncertain for the current classifier.

Later, two other studies [11, 12] independently investigated a similar idea of uncertainty sampling using SVM, and both applied it for document classification. In particular, Tong and Koller [12] theoretically analyzed the learning process of SVM in the framework of shrinking version space [8], and this led to three interesting and important active learning schemes: *Simple Margin*, *MaxMin Margin* and *Ratio Margin*. These methods all substantially outperform standard passive learning (e.g. random sampling) in text classification tasks. In the following, we will briefly introduce the *Simple Margin* since it has good performance and is the simplest scheme in terms of computational cost and mathematical complexity. It was also independently proposed [7, 11]. For simplicity, we will skip the theoretical details of *Simple Margin* and give only the algorithm and intuitive explanation. (Fig. 2 presents an illustration of this algorithm.)

The key idea of *Simple Margin* is that the unlabelled vector closest to current decision boundary in F is the most uncertain one and should be queried for labels, e.g. positive or negative. Under some simplifying assumptions [12], this approach leads to minimizing the version space [8]. A version space of SVM can be viewed as a space of hyperplanes that can perfectly classify labelled training instances. Imagine that in the version space there is one SVM classifier that is the target of our learning task; shrinkage of such a space means reducing our uncertainty of knowledge regarding the target classifier.

The unlabelled vector that is closest to the current boundary is the most uncertain one for classification. Intuitively, a sensible learning method should actively learn knowledge from the instances that the learning system is currently not familiar with.

In document classification tasks, a model is to be built for classifying documents in a digital library. It is always expensive for human experts to label a large number of example documents. Active learning provides a principled way to reduce the cost. However, this idea is not suitable for the tasks of document retrieval where users search documents that are relevant to their query concepts. Our considerations are mainly based on two reasons:

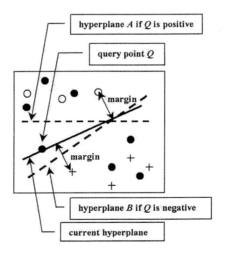

Fig. 2. SVM active learning algorithm - *Simple Margin* (The hollow points are negative-labelled vectors; cross points are positive vectors; and solid points, unlabelled vectors. The unlabelled vector Q is the selected query vector which is the one closest to the current hyperplane. If Q is positive, then the next trained SVM hyperplane is A, otherwise B.)

1. It is unnatural to require users to rate a certain number of uncertain documents, e.g. the system has to supply one window to browse and another one to ask questions. Furthermore, most documents are likely to be irrelevant ones (see the experimental section of this paper). Users may lose patience if they read many uncertain or irrelevant documents in browsing initial screens. A classification system can explicitly require some experts to label a number of documents and then train a model. However, a retrieval system should present many relevant results to users and meanwhile gather information for further improving the ranking of unlabelled documents.

2. ActiveSVMRF, like *Simple Margin*, is actually a "myopic" algorithm. The idea is to select the only one optimal vector to label. There is no clear way to address the question of how to select the best n vectors. But in practice, a document retrieval system typically presents a screen of documents to users. In many studies, researchers simply extend the conclusions of single-point optimization to multi-point optimization. For example, *Simple Margin* algorithm has been extended to select the five vectors closest to the boundary as query points [12]. In our study, we found that this extension was not effective.

3   A Hybrid SVM RF Approach to Document Retrieval (HRFSVM)

The following is a review of the two analyzed algorithms:

1. SVMRF: It is a natural way for getting user feedback and presents many relevant documents when gathering information from the user. However, its learning rate is not optimal since it does not select the most informative documents to label.

2. ActiveSVMRF: It is suitable for document classification rather than document retrieval. It has a fast learning rate but requires users to read many irrelevant or uncertain documents (or their abstracts). Also, it has no substantial justification on how to present several query documents.

As mentioned above, SVMRF and ActiveSVMRF each have their own strengths and weaknesses. Combinations of these may overcome their drawbacks and achieve an optimal performance for document retrieval. Therefore, we propose a hybrid approach, which presents both the most likely relevant documents and the most uncertain documents on one screen and obtains feedback about them from the user. In detail, the proposed relevance feedback approach proceeds in the following way:

1. The system learns a SVM model from a user's initial query.
2. The system then presents a screen of M (e.g. 10) documents consisting of K $(K \leq M)$ with the remotest ones on the positive side of the SVM hyperplane and $M - K$ closest ones to the hyperplane.
3. The user returns relevance feedback to the system.

4. The system trains a new SVM model using all the obtained training data and goes to Step 2 until the user feels satisfied.

HRFSVM has a faster learning rate than SVMRF, since it integrates the mechanism of active learning into the relevance feedback process. On the other hand, compared with ActiveSVMRF, HRFSVM presents more relevant documents to users by retaining the advantages of SVMRF. While HRFSVM is going on, the trained SVM hyperplane is getting more precise to model the user's query concept; we accordingly reduce the proportion of uncertain documents on the presented screen. The reason is that at the beginning, when the SVM model is not precise enough to return many really relevant documents, we take the opportunity to gain more information about the query concept by including more uncertain documents on the screen. We found that this idea resulted in a better performance than the constant proportion of uncertain documents across iterations (see experimental section below).

4 Experiments

4.1 Experiment Description

To enable an objective evaluation of system performance and simulate the behavior of users, we assume that a query concept is a document topic. The goal of a system is to learn a given query concept through an interactive process. We assume that at each step the system returns $M = 10$ documents to a user and the user evaluates them by labelling them as "relevant" or "irrelevant," according to the query concept. Then, the system uses the total, cumulated, labelled documents so far to rebuild a new model (a SVM hyperplane), which is then used to predict all of the unlabelled documents in which the top-K most relevant documents as well as the top-$(M - K)$ most uncertain documents are returned to the user. As mentioned in Section 3, we decrease the number of returned uncertain documents while iteration is going on. In our work, we empirically set $K = 6$ in the first 4 iterations and 10 in later iterations.

HRFSVM is compared with SVMRF and ActiveSVMRF. We did not consider Rocchio's RF as a competitive method since it has been demonstrated that SVMRF impressively outperforms it [3].

4.2 Performance Metrics

There are many ways to measure the effectiveness of the feedback process. We use *precision* since it not only indicates the accuracy of ranking but also reflects the user's satisfaction [3]. In particular, we investigate $P50$ and $P100$, the precision of the top 50 and 100 documents respectively, which are defined in the following way:

$$PN_i = \begin{cases} \frac{n_{R_i}}{N}, & n_{R_i} \leq N \\ 1, & \text{otherwise} \end{cases} \tag{5}$$

where n_{R_i} is the total number of relevant documents in the first N (50 or 100) documents at iteration i. n_{R_i} consists of two parts: one includes the $n^1_{R_i}$ user-labelled relevant documents, and the other includes the relevant documents in the top $N - n^1_{R_i}$ unlabelled ones ranked by the system. Therefore, the adopted $P50$ and $P100$ not only show the accuracy of the predicting-model but also demonstrate how many relevant documents a user has browsed during the interactions. Furthermore, more detailed distribution of relevant documents in top 100 ones can be discovered through combining $P50$ and $P100$ together. For example, if $P50$ is larger than $P100$, it means there is more fraction of relevant documents in the first 50 ones than the later 50 ones.

4.3   Experimental Data Set

For evaluating the performance of the proposed approach (HRFSVM) as opposed to SVMRF and ActiveSVMRF, a test data set needs to be a set of documents labeled with topics. Therefore, we use the Reuters-21578 database (http://www.daviddlewis.com/resources/testcollections/reuters21578/), a collection of news documents that have been assigned a single topic, multiple topics, or no topic. By eliminating documents without topics, titles, or texts, we finally retain 10369 documents.

As in Drucker et al. [3], we use the visibility to indicate the percentage of a topic in the corpus:

$$visibility = \frac{n_R}{N} \qquad (6)$$

where N is the total number of documents in Reuters database; n_R is the number of documents having the given topic.

As shown in Table 1, we select 5 topics for experiments. We will track PN as a function of iteration in cases of different visibility. Since in real situations it is common that the percentage of documents meeting query concept is rather low in the documents retrieved by a search engine, we mainly investigate the low-visibility topics. Note that searching for the low-visibility topics is a more challenging task.

Table 1. Topics selected for experiments

Topic	Number	Visibility (%)
Earn	3775	36.4
Gnp	153	1.5
Soybean	111	1.1
Iron-steel	65	0.6
Palm-oil	42	0.4

As with Drucker et al. [3], the number of returned relevant documents in the initial search is restricted to one. We assume that the system starts with one relevant document having been labelled by a user. A user has to go to subsequent screens to find a relevant document. The number of screens one has to search will depend on the sophistication of the preliminary query.

We ran 30 trials for each topic and reported the averaged precisions. Each run of the 30 experiments started with a set of random preliminary documents.

4.4   Experiment Results

In Fig. 3, each curve presents the averaged test results over the 5 topics, including 150 trials. We evaluate 3 methods in terms of $P50$ and $P100$. It has been shown that our method significantly outperforms SVMRF and ActiveSVMRF. In particular, a more impressive performance of HRFSVM is observed in initial iterations. For example, at the third iteration, HRFSVM, SVMRF, and ActiveSVMRF respectively achieve 77.6%, 71.8%, and 50.1% in the case of $P50$. It has also been observed that their differences are getting smaller, which shows all three methods get sufficient training data. We emphasize that a good performance at the early stage of relevance feedback is highly preferred by users. As shown in Fig. 3, the increase of ActiveSVMRF is slow at the beginning because a user labels few relevant documents.

For the topics with high visibility such as *earn* with visibility 36.4% (Fig. 4), all three methods have good performance. However, our approach still outperforms the other two. After the first iteration, the $P50$ of HRFSVM reaches 100% three steps earlier than SVMRF.

In the case of topics with small visibility such as *soybean* with visibility 1.1% (Fig. 5), our method demonstrates many advantages over SVMRF and ActiveSVMRF. After 6 iterations, proposed work reaches 98.6% with $P50$ and

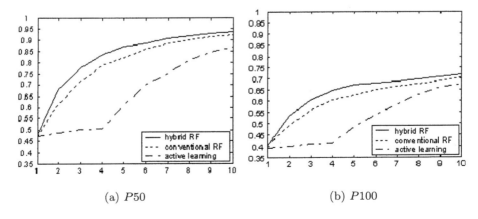

(a) $P50$ (b) $P100$

Fig. 3. Average value of five different visibilities versus number of iterations

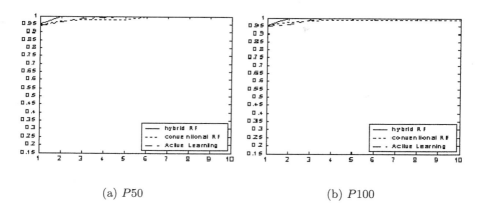

(a) *P*50   (b) *P*100

Fig. 4. Average value of 30 experiments versus number of iterations for 36.4% visibility

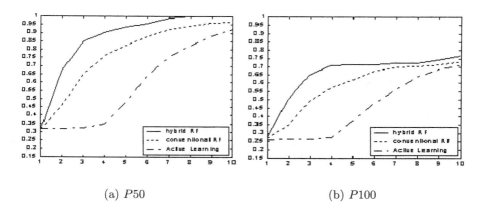

(a) *P*50   (b) *P*100

Fig. 5. Average value of 30 experiments versus number of iterations for 1.1% visibility

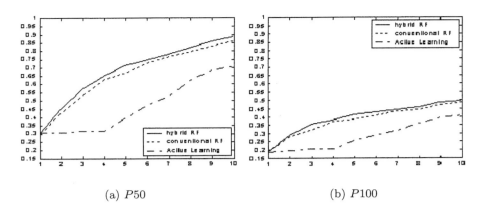

(a) $P50$ (b) $P100$

Fig. 6. Average value of 30 experiments versus number of iterations for 0.6% visibility

72.1% with $P100$, while SVMRF does 87.8% and 67.4% and ActiveSVMRF does 64.2% and 48.3%.

For the topics with extremely low visibility such as *iron-steel* with visibility 0.6% (Fig. 6), our methods also have better performance compared with the other two methods. The $P50$ of the proposed method reached 70% at 5th iteration, while ActiveSVMRF only does 30%. The $P100$ of HRFSVM finally reaches 49.6%. In fact, as this topic just has 65 documents, 77% of relevant documents have been found.

5   Conclusion

We analyzed performance of SVM-based hybrid Relevance Feedback (RF), conventional RF, and active learning. The initial relevant documents retrieved are one in every ten. We tested 5 different visibilities from 36.4% to 0.4%. The experimental results reveal that the hybrid RF outperforms the other two methods regardless of visibilities. Our method efficiently satisfies a user in a natural browsing way by mixing the most uncertain documents and the most relevant ones together to ask for user labelling. Currently the method is a heuristic and we will improve it with optimization technology in the future.

References

[1] C. Burges. A tutorial on support vector machines for pattern recognition. *Data Mining and Knowledge Discovery*, (2):121–167, 1998.
[2] D. Cohn and Z. Ghahramani. Active learning with statistical models. *Journal of Artificial Intelligence Research*, (4):129–145, 1996.

[3] H. Drucker, B. Shahraray, and D. Gibbon. Relevance feedback using support vector machines. In *Proceedings of the 18th International Conference on Machine Learning*, pages 122–129, 2001.

[4] S. Dumais, J. Platt, D. Heckerman, and M. Sahami. Inductive learning algorithms and representations for text categorization. In *Proceedings of the Seventh International Conference on Information and Knowledge Management*. ACM Press, 1998.

[5] D. Harman. Relevance feedback revisited. In *Proceedings of the Fifth International SIGIR Conference on Research and Development in Information Retrieval*, pages 1–10, 1992.

[6] T. Joachims. Text categorization with support vector machines. In *Proceedings of the European Conference on Machine Learning*. Springer Verlag, 1998.

[7] D. Lewis and W. Gale. A sequential algorithm for training text classifiers. In *Proceedings of the Eleventh International Conference on Machine Learning*, pages 148–156. Morgan Kaufmann, 1994.

[8] T. Mitchell. Generalization as search. *Artificial Intelligence*, (28):203–226, 1982.

[9] J. J. Rocchio. Relevance feedback in information retrieval. In *The SMART Retrieval System: Experiments in Automatic Document Processing*, pages 313–323. Prentice Hall, 1971.

[10] G. Salton and C. Buckley. Improving retrieval performance by relevance feedback. *Journal of the American Society of Information Science*, 41:288–297, 1990.

[11] G. Schohn and D. Cohn. Less is more: Active learning with support vector machines. In *Proceedings of the Seventeenth International Conference on Machine Learning*, 2000.

[12] S. Tong and D. Koller. Support vector machine active learning with applications to text classification. *Journal of Machine Learning Research*, (2):45–66, 2001.

[13] V. Vapnik. *Estimation of Dependences Based on Empirical Data*. Springer Verlag, 1982.

Experiments with Document Archive Size Detection

Shengli Wu, Forbes Gibb, and Fabio Crestani

Department of Computer and Information Sciences
University of Strathclyde, Glasgow, Scotland, UK
{S.Wu,F.Gibb,F.Crestani}@cis.strath.ac.uk

Abstract. The size of a document archive is a very important parameter for resource selection in distributed information retrieval systems. In this paper, we present a method for automatically detecting the size (i.e. number of documents) of a document archive, in case the archive itself does not provided such information. In addition, a method for detecting the incremental change of the archive size is also presented, which can be useful for deciding if a resource description has become obsolete and needs to be regenerated. An experimental evaluation of these methods shows that they provide quite accurate information.

1 Introduction

When a huge number of document archives or document resources are available via the Internet or large corporate networks, using a broker to select a subset of available resource servers to satisfy the user's information need becomes an important research issue. Many algorithms (see below) have been proposed which can automatically rank a set of document resources, according to the degree of their match with the given query.

Content-based resource selection algorithms need information about what each resource contains. This information is called resource description. In some situations a resource description can be obtained from a cooperative resource. However, in multi-party environments such as the Internet or large corporate networks, this information may not be available. As discussed in [3], this can be caused by several reasons: older database systems may be unable to cooperate; some services will refuse to cooperate because they have no incentive or are allied with competitors; and some services may misrepresent their contents, for example, to lure people to the site. Callan, Lu and Croft concluded that all of these characteristics can be found today on the Internet; some of them also occur in large corporate networks.

The size of a document resource is one of the most important pieces of information needed for resource selection. It is used in many resource selection methods such as GlOSS/gGlOSS [5], CVV [10], decision-theoretic approach [4], multi-objective model [9], and so on. CORI [3] does not depend on this information, but considers that it is desirable and that discovering the size of a document resource by sampling is an open problem.

F. Sebastiani (Ed.): ECIR 2003, LNCS 2633, pp. 294–304, 2003.
© Springer-Verlag Berlin Heidelberg 2003

A number of researches and surveys (e.g. [1, 6]) have been conducted with respect to the WWW for estimating various statistical characteristics, such as the total number of web pages, web sites, institutions having web sites, web pages indexed by major search engines, and so on. Very recently, Liu, Yu, and Meng [7] proposed a method for estimating the number of documents indexed by a search engine. They randomly chose a group of sample documents n (without overlap), then randomly chose another group of documents m (with possible overlap). A formula $Total = n \times \frac{m}{o}$ is used for estimating the total number of documents, where o is the number of overlaps between these two groups. The method may be useful, but the discussion is very brief and many aspects remains unknown.

In this paper we present a method for detecting the size of document resources automatically where such information cannot be accessed from the resource server directly; or, if it is provided by the resource server, its accuracy is questionable and confirmation is required.

The paper is organised as follows: In Section 2 we present an algorithm for detecting the size of a document resource. Section 3 gives the setting and results of experiments for the algorithm introduced in Section 2. In Section 4 we discuss a method for detecting the incremental change in the resource size, provided that a thorough analysis has been done before. Section 5 concludes the paper.

2 Detecting the Size of a Document Resource

We use the following algorithm to detect the size of a document resource:

1. Use query-based sampling to obtain the language model of that resource.
2. Delete the words which have the highest frequency in the language model.
3. Use the remaining words in the language model to generate a group of queries.
4. Send the queries to the document resource and collect the top N documents returned by the resource for all those queries.
5. Count the number of different documents that have been retrieved.

A number of specific choices could be taken for some of these steps. For example, how many queries should be used for query-based sampling in step 1, or how to generate queries in step 3. In the following section, we will explain some of these choices, others of which have been discussed in Section 3.

2.1 Acquiring the Language Model by Sampling

The query-based sampling method was proposed by Callan, Connell and Du in [2] to create the language model (a group of words with their frequencies) of a document resource. This language model can be used for various activities, e.g., resource selection, summarising resource contents, query expansion, and so on. Callan, Connell and Du found that about 400 documents taken from the results of 100 queries can usually produce quite an accurate language model, even though the words included in the language model are much less than those in the resource. A similar method has been used in our approach to create the language model. However, for our purpose, it is better to discover a larger set of words which appear in the resource than that used for resource selection. The reason for this is that in Steps 3 and 4 of the above algorithm, if there are more different words in the queries this should result in more documents and less document overlaps.

2.2   Query Formation

After we have obtained the language model of the resource, another issue is how to use those words in the language model to form queries. This mainly depends on the information retrieval system which may use a particular form of query interface. Here we assume that a query is composed of a group of words. This is the normal method used in many retrieval systems including Lemur [8], with which we carried out the experiments.

A simple method has been used for generating queries from those words. After deciding on the number of words which should be used in each query, words were randomly selected from the available word collection. Once a word was chosen, it was removed from the word collection so that it would not be used for any other queries.

From the language model, we can estimate the frequency of each word that appears in the resource. Through careful selection, e.g., by generating queries with words with diversified frequencies, and by avoiding using only low (or high) frequency words in a single query, we could have a better chance that the resource would return a similar number of documents for each query. Otherwise, some queries may only retrieve very few documents, while some others may retrieve a lot more. However, in our experiments we still used the simple random selection method, as we found that when a query is composed of more than 10 words, either carefully or randomly selected, the difference between the two approaches is negligible.

After a group of queries was generated, we specified a maximum number of documents which needed to be retrieved for every query. This is a simple approach. A more complicated approach would have been to assign to each query a different number of retrieved documents. However, we consider that that is more complicated and the effect is dubious since there is not much evidence for us to make sensible decisions. In the following, we have not considered this option.

If we have s queries, and specify that each query retrieves up to m documents, then we can get $n = s \times m$ documents in all. The ideal situation is that all the retrieved documents from different queries are different; that is to say, we can get n different documents in all. However, that is not likely and we need to find solutions to reduce document overlaps after retrieving a certain number of documents.

One issue that needs addressing is: how many words should we use for each query? We answer this question in Section 3 as a result of experiments.

Table 1. Resources used in the experimentation

Resource	Size	N. of documents
FT (1991-94)	564 MB	210,158
WSJ (1988-90, 1992-94)	518 MB	173,252
TREC-123	3.2 GB	1,078,166

3   Experiments and Results

Three full-text resources were used for the experiments. They were the Financial Times (FT), the Wall Street Journal (WSJ) and the first three CDROMs of the TREC Collection (TREC-123). The characteristics of these resources are presented in Table 3. The Lemur information retrieval system, developed at Carnegie Mellon University, was used [8]. Lemur provides three options as the retrieval model: vector space, okapi, and language model. Users can select one of the models for his/her retrieval task.

The first experiment focused on testing the relationship between the number of sampling documents and the number of different words appearing in them. Figure 1 presents the results, in which the horizontal axis indicates the percentage of documents that were randomly selected with respect to the total documents in the resource, while the vertical axis indicates the percentage of words that were obtained from selected documents with respect to the total words used in the resource. At first, the number of words increased very fast, slowing down as about 5% of all documents were retrieved. However, the curves continued to increase when we obtained more and more documents. With 5% of the documents, we retrieved about 30% to 40% of the words; With 50% of the documents, we retrieved about 80% of the words for each of the three resources. Probably among the three resources, TREC-123 is the biggest of the three resources and the most heterogeneous, and its rate of increase was the lowest. On the contrary, WSJ is the smallest and the most homogeneous, and its rate of increase was the highest. However, the difference between the three cases is not large.

As we will see later, experiments showed that using 5% to 15% of all words in the queries is enough for our purpose. Therefore, using 0.5% to 1% of all documents is reasonable for document sampling, as about 10% to 20% of the words could be identified. In practice, as we do not know the exact size of the resource, several options can be used:

- If we have some knowledge of the resource, we can make a guess of the resource size, then decide how many document samples we need.
- Take a certain number (say, 40,000) as the threshold, and try to identify that number of words in the resource.
- Specify a threshold t. Each time take a certain number of new documents. Check how many new words that these new documents introduce. If it is less than t, we stop the sampling process; otherwise, continue.

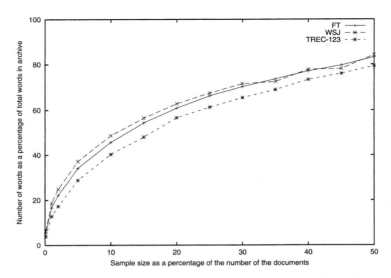

Fig. 1. The relationship between documents and words

The second experiment was carried out to find an appropriate way of generating queries by checking the results of different queries. We generated queries with different numbers of words, from 2 to 100, then saw which one would produce the best result. We report the results from using two resources: FT and TREC-123. For FT, 2500 randomly selected documents (1.2%) were used for the sampling. Over 25,000 different words (Porter stems) were identified, which is about 11% of the total words in the resource. For TREC-123, 3200 documents (0.3%) were used for the sampling. Over 56,000 different words (Porter stems) were identified (about 5%). Then only a few (100-300) top frequency words were removed from the word collection in each case. As we only used a small percentage of all documents, low frequency words may not be really rare in the resource and therefore we did not remove any of them. Using the remaining words, we generated queries by randomly selecting a certain number of words from the collection. Each word could only be included in one query and every query had the same number of words. We submitted those queries to Lemur with a specified number of retrieved documents. The same number applied to all queries. Since the number of words was fixed, the less words in each query the more queries were generated. Tables 2 to 3 present the experimental results from resources FT and TREC-123, using the vector and okapi models in Lemur.

Each data item in Tables 2 to 3 represents the percentage (p) of different documents in the resource, which is achieved by all queries with n words and $p \times |D|$ documents retrieved, where $|D|$ is the size of the resource. n is given in the first column, and p is given in the first row for that data item. The general tendency is that when we retrieved more and more documents, we obtained more and more different documents, while the percentage of overlaps increased as well.

Table 2. Percentage of different documents retrieved from the resource compared to the total number of documents in the resource (vector space model, FT collection)

Number of words in query	Percentage of retrieved documents compared to total documents in resource							
	50%	100%	150%	200%	250%	300%	350%	400%
2	29.2	49.6	61.6	70.6	76.3	81.2	84.5	87.5
4	30.8	50.4	62.5	71.2	78.3	83.4	86.2	89.0
6	31.2	51.4	64.0	71.5	79.7	84.2	87.6	90.2
8	31.7	51.9	65.1	71.8	80.1	84.7	87.8	90.3
10	31.9	52.0	65.4	72.1	80.4	84.9	88.2	90.7
14	32.3	52.1	65.6	72.6	80.5	85.1	88.4	90.9
16	32.4	51.8	65.4	72.8	80.4	85.3	88.7	91.2
20	32.6	52.0	65.6	73.1	80.8	85.8	89.0	91.6
25	33.5	52.8	65.9	73.5	81.3	86.0	89.4	92.1
30	32.8	52.1	65.7	73.2	80.9	85.7	89.0	91.7
40	32.2	51.3	64.3	72.4	79.9	84.9	88.6	90.6
60	30.3	50.5	63.2	71.5	78.7	82.5	85.6	89.9
80	30.0	50.1	62.5	71.3	77.0	81.2	84.4	88.8
100	29.3	49.8	62.1	71.0	76.5	81.0	83.5	88.1

However, it seems that the percentage of overlapping documents was quite stable once a certain percentage of documents were retrieved. For example, when the number of retrieved documents by all queries was equal to the size of resource (100%), the number of different documents we obtained was around 50% of the total documents.

The experiment also shows that using between 10 and 40 words for each query produce better results. When the number of documents retrieved is 4 times the size of the resource, we obtain over 90% of different documents in most cases. The experiment also indicates differences between the two retrieval models (vector or okapi).

In addition to the experiment above, we used more sample documents and more words to generate queries. The experimental results do not show significant improvement over the above results. This suggests that using about 10% of the total words in the resource is enough for generating queries.

Also, in Figure 2, we present more detailed results for four specific situations. Each of these is composed of queries with 30 words, the number of retrieved documents ranging from 50% to 800% of resource size. Two resources TREC-123 and FT were used, as were the vector and okapi models from Lemur. These showed that in every case, when we retrieved more documents, we obtained more different documents. Over 99% of the documents could be detected when we retrieved a total of 650% of resource documents using the okapi model and FT resource; the same level was obtained for the other three cases: 800%, okapi model and TREC-123; 900%, vector model and FT; 1000%, vector model and TREC-123.

Table 3. Percentage of different documents retrieved from the resource compared to the total number of documents in the resource (okapi model, FT collection)

Number of words in query	Percentage of retrieved documents compared to total documents in resource							
	50%	100%	150%	200%	250%	300%	350%	400%
2	34.5	54.8	68.0	76.8	83.5	87.7	90.7	93.0
4	34.6	55.9	69.2	77.9	84.3	88.4	91.3	93.7
6	35.7	57.5	70.5	79.3	85.2	89.1	92.1	94.2
8	36.2	57.8	71.0	79.8	85.4	89.4	92.3	94.3
10	36.7	58.3	71.6	80.1	85.8	89.6	92.5	94.5
16	36.7	58.5	71.9	80.6	86.4	90.4	93.0	95.0
18	36.7	58.6	72.0	80.9	86.5	90.5	93.2	95.1
20	36.6	58.6	72.2	81.1	86.8	90.7	93.4	95.2
25	36.7	58.8	72.4	81.5	87.2	91.0	93.7	95.4
30	36.3	58.3	72.3	81.2	87.1	91.1	93.8	95.5
40	35.8	57.6	71.6	80.7	86.6	90.7	93.4	95.3
60	34.9	55.9	69.7	79.2	85.4	89.5	92.5	94.6
80	34.2	54.8	67.9	77.0	83.4	87.9	91.2	93.4
100	33.2	52.9	66.1	75.2	81.7	86.3	89.6	92.0

4 Detecting the Incremental Change

Most document resources change their contents over time, and hence their sizes. As the above detection algorithm may require considerable time and resources, it would be desirable if we had a more efficient algorithm for detecting changes. In the following, we discuss an algorithm for detecting incremental change in resource size supposing we have already estimated the size of the resource before by using the algorithm in Section 2, and that a log, which records the queries and results returned from the resource, is available. The algorithm is as follows:

1. Randomly select a subset of queries S from all queries in the log.
2. Send out those S queries to the resource and collect the results.
3. For each query that has been selected, compare its old and new result list in reverse order (from the end to the beginning), identify the overlapping documents which appear in both lists. For each pair of overlapping documents, calculate the ratio of its position in the new list to that in the old list. Average all these ratios.
4. Average all the values obtained in Step 3 and take the final value as the ratio of the size change. If we multiply it by the previously detected resource size, we obtain the estimated size of the present resource.

One experiment was carried out with 2 resources: WSJ 1 (WSJ 87-90), and WSJ 2 (WSJ 87-92). These have 120,437 and 173,252 documents, respectively and the former is a subset of the latter resource. 10 queries containing 25 words were used in each test. 100 groups of tests were conducted. On average, the

Table 4. Percentage of different documents retrieved from the resource compared to the total number of documents in the resource (okapi model, TREC-123 collection)

Number of words in query	Percentage of retrieved documents compared to total documents in resource							
	50%	100%	150%	200%	250%	300%	350%	400%
2	28.9	49.0	62.0	71.7	78.3	83.4	86.9	89.7
6	35.1	56.9	70.5	79.1	84.9	88.9	91.6	93.5
10	36.9	58.8	72.3	80.9	86.4	90.0	92.5	94.3
14	37.4	59.4	72.7	81.2	89.8	90.2	92.6	94.3
16	37.7	59.6	73.1	81.4	86.8	90.3	82.7	94.4
20	37.8	59.9	73.2	81.5	86.8	90.4	92.8	94.4
25	37.9	60.0	73.4	81.8	87.1	90.6	92.9	94.5
30	37.3	59.2	72.7	81.2	86.8	90.5	93.0	94.7
40	38.1	60.1	73.4	81.7	87.0	90.5	92.8	94.4
50	36.6	58.2	71.6	80.3	86.1	90.0	92.6	94.4
60	36.5	57.8	71.2	79.9	85.7	89.6	92.3	94.1
70	36.3	57.6	70.8	79.4	85.1	89.1	91.8	93.7
80	36.2	57.1	70.3	78.9	84.6	88.6	91.4	93.4
90	35.9	56.7	69.7	78.3	84.1	88.1	90.9	93.0
100	35.6	56.3	69.2	77.7	83.5	87.5	90.5	92.5

error rate $r = abs(|D_e| - |D_r|)/D_r$ was 2.8%, where $|D_e|$ is the estimated size of resource D, and $|D_r|$ is the real size of resource D.

Another experiment was carried out with 2 resources WSJ 3 (WSJ 87, 89, 91) and WSJ 4 (WSJ 88-92). This time, each of the two resources included some documents that the other did not have. This was designed to simulate the situations where some new documents may be added to the initial resource, and at the same time, some documents may be removed from the resource as well. 10 queries with 20 words were used for each test and 100 tests were carried out. On average, the error rate was 3.2%.

In the above experiments, change in document content was not considered. If many documents have had their contents changed, then the above algorithm may not work as effectively. We can use the following method to check if that is the case.

Once we have the two lists of overlapping documents from the above algorithm, we can compare their rankings by either Kendall Tau or Spearman correlation coefficients. Here only relative rankings of overlapping documents are considered. For example, if we have two lists l_1 and l_2 for a given query. $l_1 = (d_1, d_2, d_3, d_4, d_5, d_6)$, and $l_2 = (d_2, d_4, d_6, d_8, d_{10}, d_{12})$, then we consider the overlapping parts of l_1 and l_2. That is, $l_{1'} = (d_2, d_4, d_6)$, and $l_{2'} = (d_2, d_4, d_6)$, and the two lists correlate perfectly. If the two rankings correlate quite positively, that suggests we can use the algorithm to estimate the incremental change; otherwise, the algorithm for detecting incremental change may not work properly. The reason could be any one or a combination of the following three reasons.

Table 5. Percentage of different documents retrieved from the resource compared to the total number of documents in the resource (vector space model, TREC-123 collection)

Number of words in query	Percentage of retrieved documents compared to total documents in resource							
	50%	100%	150%	200%	250%	300%	350%	400%
2	27.7	46.6	57.7	66.4	72.5	77.3	80.9	83.8
4	31.8	50.3	62.2	70.4	76.2	80.5	83.8	86.4
6	33.1	52.1	64.1	72.1	77.8	82.0	85.1	87.5
8	33.8	52.7	64.5	72.5	78.1	82.1	85.2	87.6
10	34.2	53.2	65.0	72.8	78.3	82.3	85.3	87.6
15	34.9	53.8	65.5	73.3	78.7	82.5	85.5	87.8
20	34.9	53.8	65.4	73.1	78.5	82.4	85.2	87.4
25	34.9	53.6	65.2	72.9	78.2	82.1	85.1	87.3
30	33.8	52.5	64.4	72.2	77.8	81.8	84.9	87.1
40	32.9	52.1	63.1	71.4	76.4	80.9	84.1	86.9
50	32.0	50.2	61.9	70.0	75.7	80.0	83.3	85.8
60	31.7	49.6	61.1	69.2	75.0	79.3	82.6	85.2
70	31.3	49.0	60.5	68.5	74.3	78.6	82.0	84.6
80	30.9	48.2	59.6	67.6	73.4	77.9	81.3	84.0
90	30.5	47.6	58.9	66.9	72.7	77.1	80.6	83.4
100	30.1	47.0	58.2	66.2	72.1	76.5	80.0	82.8

1. Either or both of the two documents has been changed in content;
2. The information retrieval model has been changed/updated;
3. The information retrieval model does not rank documents or does not use a deterministic algorithm to rank documents for a query.

Item 3 is beyond our consideration. Content change in documents may happen more often than changes or upgrades to the information retrieval model. However, for our purpose, it is not necessary to identify which situation has happened. When we find that the two rankings do not correlate very positively, it is an indication that the resource size should be estimated by the thorough estimation process discussed in Section 2.

5   Conclusion

In this paper, we have discussed a method of automatically detecting the size of a document resource. It is a two-phase process, including sampling documents to find a certain percentage of words used in the resource, and querying the information retrieval system with those words to detect its resource size. Also, an algorithm for detecting incremental change to a resource is proposed. Experiments have been carried out to test the effectiveness of the algorithm.

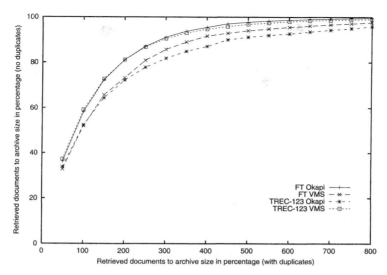

Fig. 2. Performance of four groups of queries, each with 30 words

From those experiments with TREC data, we have the following observations:

- Sampling 1% of total documents randomly discovers over 10% of words used in a resource.
- Usually, using 5% to 10% of all words in the resource is adequate for making queries. Using more words does not bring better results.
- Each query should contains between 10 and 40 randomly selected words.
- In many cases, when the overlap rate from the results aggregated from all the queries reaches 75%, we retrieve over 90% of the total documents in the resource.

Acknowledgements

This work was supported by the European Commission under the IST Project MIND (IST-2000-26061). More information about MIND can be found at http://www.mind-project.net/.

References

[1] K. Bharat and A. Z. Broder. A Technique for Measuring the Relative Size and Overlap of Public Web Search Engines. In *Proceedings of 7th WWW Conference*, Brisbane, Australia, April 1998.

[2] J. K. Callan, M. Connell, and A. Du. Automatic Discovery of Language Models for Text Databases. In *Proceedings of ACM SIGMOD International Conference*, pages 479–490, Philadelphia, USA, May 1999.

[3] J. K. Callan, Z. Lu, and W. Croft. Searching Distributed Collections with Inference Networks. In *Proceedings of the 18th Annual International ACM SIGIR Conference*, pages 21–28, Seattle, USA, June 1995.

[4] Norbert Fuhr. A Decision-Theoretic Approach to Database Selection in Networked IR. *ACM Transaction on Information Systems*, 17(3):229–249, 1999.

[5] L. Gravano and H. García-Molina. Generalizing GlOSS to Vector-Space Database and Broker Hierarchies. In *Proceedings of 21st VLDB International Conference*, pages 78–89, Zürich, Switzerland, 1995.

[6] S. Lawrence and C. L. Giles. Searching the World Wide Web. *Science*, 280(3):98–100, April 1998.

[7] K. Liu, C. Yu, and W. Meng. Discovering the Representative of a Search Engine. In *Proceedings of the ACM CIKM International Conference*, pages 652–654, Mclean, Virginia, USA, November 2002.

[8] P. Ogilvie and J. Callan. Experiments using the Lemur Toolkit. In *Proceedings of the 2001 Text Retrieval Conference (TREC)*, pages 103–108, Gaithersburg, Maryland, USA, November 2001.

[9] S. Wu and F. Crestani. Multi-objective Resource Selection in Distributed Information Retrieval. In *Proceedings of IPMU02, International Conference on Information Processing and Management of Uncertainty in Knowledge-Based Systems*, pages 1171–1178, Annecy, France, July 2002.

[10] B. Yuwono and D. Lee. Server Ranking for Distributed Test Retrieval Systems on the Internet. In *Proceedings of the Fifth International Conference on Database Systems for Advanced Application*, pages 41–50, Melbourne, Australia, April 1997.

Using Kullback-Leibler Distance
for Text Categorization

Brigitte Bigi

CLIPS-IMAG Laboratory, UMR CNRS 5524
B.P. 53, 38041 Grenoble cedex 9, FRANCE
brigitte.bigi@imag.fr

Abstract. A system that performs text categorization aims to assign appropriate categories from a predefined classification scheme to incoming documents. These assignments might be used for varied purposes such as filtering, or retrieval. This paper introduces a new effective model for text categorization with great corpus (more or less 1 million documents). Text categorization is performed using the Kullback-Leibler distance between the probability distribution of the document to classify and the probability distribution of each category. Using the same representation of categories, experiments show a significant improvement when the above mentioned method is used. KLD method achieve substantial improvements over the *tfidf* performing method.

1 Introduction

Text Categorization is an important component of many large Information Retrieval or Machine Learning system. It is often defined as the content-based assignment of one or more predefined categories to texts. It is commonly conjectured that it is infeasible to manually classify all of the new documents that are added to a system in a timely manner. Therefore, automatic methods of document classification are needed.

Information processing needs have increased with the rapid growth of textual information sources, such as news media and the World Wide Web. Text retrieval systems find or route texts in response to arbitrary user queries or interest profiles. Text categorization can be used to support Information Retrieval or to perform information extraction, document filtering and routing to topic-specific processing mechanisms.

Recent research has been concerned with scaling-up (e.g. data mining). Text categorization is a domain where large data sets are available and which provides an application field to Machine Learning. Indeed, manual categorization is known to be an expensive and time-consuming task. Machine Learning approaches to classification (text categorization is a classification task) suggest the construction of categorization means using induction over pre-classified samples. They have been rather successfully applied in various studies.

F. Sebastiani (Ed.): ECIR 2003, LNCS 2633, pp. 305–319, 2003.
© Springer-Verlag Berlin Heidelberg 2003

A growing number of statistical classification and machine learning techniques have been applied to text categorization [1], including nearest neighbor classifiers [2], probabilistic bayesian models [3], neural networks [4], etc. Term-frequency/inverse-document-frequency ($tfidf$) [5] is the common term weighting method and a cosine similarity is used for the categorization. In the paper [6], the author presents an analysis of the word weighting scheme based on $tfidf$ and the similarity metric. The empirical results suggest that a probabilistically founded modelling is preferable to the heuristic $tfidf$ modelling. Moreover, the author says that the probabilistic methods are preferable from a theoretical viewpoint because they are more well founded. The paper [7] presents a controlled study with significance analyses on five text categorization methods: the Support Vector Machine (SVMs), a k-Nearest Neighbor (kNN) classifier, a neural network (NNet) approach, the Linear Least-squares Fit (LLSF) mapping and a Naive Bayes (NB) classifier. It suggests that SVMs and kNN significantly outperform the other classifiers. In the paper [8], the author explores the use of SVMs for learning text classifiers, and this method achieve substantial improvements over others compared methods, including Rocchio algorithm. Moreover, in the paper [9] authors compare the effectiveness of five different automatic learning algorithms for text categorization and observe that SVMs are particularly promising. It is commonly conjectured that SVMs is the best categorization method for small corpus (around 10,000 documents). In [10], SVMs are applied on a corpus made of about 42,000 documents. Nevertheless, the problem that we put forward in the literature is the small size of the corpus. Especially as with the rapid growth of online information: text categorization has become one of the key techniques for handling and organizing numerous data. As an example, one year of the Reuters corpus is composed about 807,000 news stories. We do not know how the SVMs can be applied in this case because the literature do not explore these conditions.

The method proposed in this paper is based on the symmetric Kullback-Leibler divergence, also called Kullback-Leibler distance measure, well known in Information Theory [11]. We propose to perform text categorization using this distance between the probability distribution of the document to classify and the probability distribution of each category. In information retrieval, the Kullback-Leibler divergence is used for query expansion in [12]. The approach is simple and very efficient (tests are made on TREC 7 and 8). Authors introduce a new term-scoring function that is based on the differences between the distribution of terms in relevant documents and the distribution of terms in all documents.

This paper explores and identifies the benefits of Kullback-Leibler distance for text categorization. The size of textual data is itself a challenge: a real-size corpus, composed of several hundred of thousand texts, may include several thousand of words. The organization of the paper is as follows. Section 2 presents the classical $tfidf$ classifier. Section 3 is devoted to the KLD-based method we propose. In the last section, performance on a corpus derived from the Reuters is summarized and analyzed. The resulting categorization rates compare favorably for our method with those of the standard method.

2   The Reference Model Based on tfidf

2.1   The TfIdf Term Weighting

One of the most common weighting used is referred to as term-frequency/inverse-document-frequency ($tfidf$) [5]. Documents are represented by term vectors of the form $d = (t_i, t_j, ..., t_p)$ where each t_k identifies a *content term* assigned to some sample document d as is done in the popular vector representation for information retrieval [5]. Typically, each jth document d is represented as a vector of *weights* $\vec{d_j} = (w_{1j}, w_{2j}, ..., w_{|V|j})$ of the content terms selected, where V is the set of terms that occur at least once in at least one document, and w_{kj} represents how much term t_k contributes to the semantics of document d_j. Each element w_{kj} is calculated as a combination of the statistics $tf(t_k, d_j)$ and $idf(t_k)$ [13]. This weighting scheme starts with the frequency of a term in a given document $tf(t_k, d_j)$, and multiplies this by the "inverse document frequency" $idf(t_k)$ of the term in the corpus. The idf of a term is lower the more documents appears in. The idea is that the more documents a word apprears in, the less likely it is to be a good measure for distinguishing one document from another. The $tfidf$ formula for a term t_k is as follows:

$$w_{kj} = tf(t_k, d_j) \times idf(t_k)$$

where $tf(t_k, d_j)$ is equal to 0 when term t_k is not assigned to document d_j, and equal to $\#(t_k, d_j)$ for the assigned terms. The idf term is calculated as follows:

$$idf(t_k) = \log\left(\frac{|T_r|}{df(t_k)}\right)$$

where T_r is the set of training documents ($|T_r|$ is the total number of documents in the training) and $df(t_k)$ is the document frequency for the term t_k.

The $tfidf$ word weighting heuristic says that a term t_k is an important indexing term for document d_j if it occurs frequently in it (the term frequency is high). On the other hand, terms which occur in many documents are rated less important indexing terms due to their low inverse document frequency. However, in many cases, the added "information" contained in the idf is not needed for a particular algorithm, just the term frequency tf can be used for a weighting scheme. Moreover, calculating the idf of a term requires a count across all documents in a corpus.

2.2   The Classifier

The construction of a text categorization classifier for category $c_i \in C$ usually consists in the definition of a function that, given a document d_j returns a categorization status value for it. There are various policies for determining this measure, and the most common is defined in [5] as a cosine similarity, which represents the cosine of the angle that separates the two vectors $\vec{c_i}$ and $\vec{d_j}$:

$$similarity(\vec{c_i}, \vec{d_j}) = \frac{\sum_{k=1}^{|V|}(w_{ki} \times w_{kj})}{\sqrt{\sum_{k=1}^{|V|}(w_{ki})^2 \times \sum_{k=1}^{|V|}(w_{kj})^2}} \tag{1}$$

where $w_{kj} = tf(t_k, d_j) \times idf(t_k, d_j)$ and $w_{ki} = tf(t_k, c_i) \times idf(c_i)$. All the comparisons between the document and the category vectors provides ranked category output in decreasing order of the computed similarity between $\vec{c_i}$ and $\vec{d_j}$. The document is assigned to the category with which its document vector has the highest cosine:

$$H_{tfidf}(d_j) = \arg\max_{c_i \in C} similarity(\vec{c_i}, \vec{d_j})$$

To compute w_{kj}, $tf(t_k, d_j)$ represents the number of times t_k apprears in $d_j \in T_r$. To compute w_{ki}, a category learning model, as defined previously for documents, is needed. For the vector $\vec{c_i}$, it is possible to use the *category frequency*. This problem will be discussed in section 4, because unlike in text retrieval, in text categorization the high dimensionality of the term space (i.e. the large value of $|V|$) may be problematic.

3   The KLD Classifier

This model makes use of term sets automatically selected for each category c_i. Let $|C|$ be the number of categories and V the vocabulary made of the union of all terms for all categories. For each topic category, a statistical distribution $P(t_k \mid c_i)$ *made only of the selected terms* is obtained from a training corpus. Such a distribution is compared with the distribution of the content of the document to classify. A word is considered in the document if and only if it belongs to any category-terms list. The document content, which is limited to terms, is compared with each category term probability distribution. The comparison is performed introducing a symmetric Kullback-Leibler (KL) divergence. As the document may contain only a limited number of terms in comparison to categories, the frequency of many terms in the document is zero. This causes problems in the KL distance computation when probabilities are estimated by frequencies of occurrence. In order to avoid them, a special type of back-off scheme is introduced in this paper.

3.1   Kullback-Leibler Distance

Kullback and Leiber in 1951 [14] studied a measure of information from statistical aspects of view, involving two probability distributions associated with the same experiment, calling discrimination function, later different authors named as cross entropy, relative information, etc. The Kullback-Leibler divergence - also known as the relative entropy, is a measure of how different two probability distributions (over the same event space) are. The KL divergence of probability distributions P, Q on a finite set χ is defined as:

$$D(P||Q) = \sum_{x \in \chi} P(x) log \frac{P(x)}{Q(x)} \tag{2}$$

The KL divergence between P and Q can also be seen as the average number of bits that are wasted by encoding events from a distribution P with a code based on a not-quite-right distribution Q. This KL divergence is a non-symmetric information theoretic measure of distance of P from Q. The smaller the relative entropy, the more similar the distribution of the two variables, and conversely.

It has to be noted that the measure is asymmetrical. During the past years, various measures have been introduced in the literature generalizing this measure. Since the expression of equation 2 is not symmetric, it is not strictly a distance metric. We therefore use the symmetric Kullback-Leibler divergence i.e. the Kullback-Leibler Distance (KLD) metric as:

$$D(P||Q) = \sum_{x \in \chi} \left((P(x) - Q(x)) \log \frac{P(x)}{Q(x)} \right) \qquad (3)$$

KL or KLD have been used in many natural language applications as for query expansion [12]. They have also been used, for example, in natural language and speech processing applications based on statistical language modeling [15], and in information retrieval, for topic identification [16], for choosing among distributed collections [17]. Here, the idea is that categories to be considered for document are those which mostly contribute to the distance defined in the equation 3.

The text categorization model proposed in this paper shares with other commonly used models the assumpion that a document is properly represented by a vector of weights. Each weight corresponds to a word called term and belonging to a vocabulary V. In this model, a document is represented by a term vector of probabilities $\vec{d_j}$ while a category is represented by a term vector of probabilities $\vec{c_i}$. The distance measure should be that which maximizes the KLD (the symmetric Kullbach-Leibler divergence defined in Information Theory as equation 3) between the document represented in $\vec{d_j}$ and the category $\vec{c_i}$.

3.2   The Probability Distributions

As mentionned above, the term probability distribution of a document is compared with each category probability distribution. A *back-off model* is proposed in which term frequencies appearing in the document are discounted and all the terms which are not in the document are given an epsilon probability equal to the probability of unknow words. The reason is that in practice, often not all the terms in V appear the documented represented in d_j. Let $V(d_j) \subset V$ be the vocabulary of the terms which do appear in the documents represented in d_j. For the terms not in $V(d_j)$, it is useful to introduce a back-off probability for $P(t_k, d_j)$ when t_k does not occur in $V(d_j)$, otherwise the distance measure will be infinite. The use of a back-off probability to overcome the data sparseness problem has been extensively studied in statistical language modelling (see, for example, [18]).

The resulting definition of document probability $P(t_k, d_j)$ is:

$$P(t_k, d_j) = \begin{cases} \beta P(t_k \mid d_j) & if\ t_k\ occurs\ in\ the\ document\ d_j \\ \varepsilon & else \end{cases} \qquad (4)$$

with:

$$P(t_k \mid d_j) = \frac{tf(t_k, d_j)}{\sum_{x \in d_j} tf(t_x, d_j)}$$

where:

- $P(t_k \mid d_j)$ is the probability of the term t_k in the document d_j with $\sum_{x \in d_j} tf(t_x, d_j) = 1$;
- β is a normalisation coefficient which varies according to the size of the document;
- ε is a threshold probability for all the terms not in d_j.

The probability of a term t_k in a category c_i is expressed as:

$$P(t_k, c_i) = \begin{cases} \gamma.P(t_k \mid c_i) & if\ t_k\ occurs\ in\ the\ category\ c_i \\ \varepsilon & else \end{cases} \tag{5}$$

with:

$$P(t_k \mid c_i) = \frac{tf(t_k, c_i)}{\sum_{x \in c_i} tf(t_x, c_i)}$$

where:

- $P(t_k \mid c_i)$ is a category unigram probability of t_k in c_i with $\sum_{x \in c_i} tf(t_x, c_i) = 1$;
- γ is a normalisation coefficient;
- ε is the same probability in equation (5) as in equation (4) for all the terms not in c_i.

3.3   Constraints on the Coefficients

β, γ and the ε value have to be chosen in order that the corresponding probabilities sum to 1.

The γ Estimation Equation (5) must respect the following constraint:

$$\sum_{k \in c_i} \gamma.P(t_k \mid c_i) + \sum_{k \notin c_i, k \in V} \varepsilon = 1$$

The γ can be easily estimated as follows:

$$\gamma = 1 - \sum_{k \notin c_i, k \in V} \varepsilon$$

Constraints on ε ε is a threshold probability given to terms not in the document in equation (4), or given to terms not in the category in equation (5). Thus, this probability must be smaller than the minimum probability of a term in the document, and must be smaller than the minimum probability of a term in a category (i.e. smaller than $P(t_k \mid c_i)$ for each possible term t_k in c_i). Consequently, this value is obtained experimentaly.

The β Estimation Equation (4) must respect the following property:

$$\sum_{k \in d_j} \beta.P(t_k \mid d_j) + \sum_{k \notin d_j, k \in V} \varepsilon = 1$$

β can be easily estimated for a document with the following computation:

$$\beta = 1 - \sum_{k \notin d, k \in V} \varepsilon$$

3.4 Using KLD for Text Categorization

The categorization method based on the Kullback-Leibler distance computes the distance as follows:

$$KLD(c_i, d_j) = \sum_{k \in V} \left\{ (P(t_k, c_i) - P(t_k, d_j)) \times log\left(\frac{P(t_k, c_i)}{P(t_k, d_j)}\right) \right\} \qquad (6)$$

This computation involves four cases:

1. $(t_k \in d_j) \wedge (t_k \in c_i)$, i.e. the term t_k appears in the document d_j and in the category c_i;
2. $(t_k \in d_j) \wedge (t_k \notin c_i)$, i.e. the term t_k appears in the document d_j but not in the category c_i;
3. $(t_k \notin d_j) \wedge (t_k \in c_i)$, i.e. the term t_k appears in the category c_i but not in the document d_j;
4. $(t_k \notin d_j) \wedge (t_k \notin c_i)$, i.e. the term t_k does not appears in the document d_j and in the category c_i.

As mentionned above, any term which is not a category-term, has a probability assigned to ε in $P(t_k, c_i)$ and the same probability in $P(t_k, d_j)$ (case 4) ; thus, its contribution to the KL distance is null. That is the reason why these terms do not need to be represented in the document. It is the case for all unknown terms regarding to V.

For each category, it is necessary to normalize the distance because the categories are very differents. Consequently, we use the following Kullback-Leibler normalized:

$$KLD^\star(c_i, d_j) = \frac{KLD(c_i, d_j)}{KLD(c_i, 0)}$$

where $KLD(c_i, 0)$ represents the distance of equation (6) between a category c_i and an empty document. The distribution probability of an empty document is an ε probability for all words of the vocabulary.

The document d_j is assigned to the category with which its document has the smallest $KLD^\star$ measure:

$$H_{KLD^\star}(d_j) = \arg \min_{c_i \in C} KLD^\star(c_i, d_j)$$

4   Experimental Results

This paper describes the results of experiments run on print news stories to test the categorization method based on the Kullback-Leibler distance. Our primary aim is to apply the KLD method to text categorization and estimate its capability and not to study the category learning. It is the reason why our results are not optimal. In future works, the results will be improved by a rigorously study of the category learning problem.

4.1   Corpus

We carried out our experiments on the Reuters dataset of newswire stories from exactly one year over 1996-1997. A description and some statistics about this corpus are available on the web (http://about.reuters.com/researchandstandards/corpus/statistics/index.asp). The corpus consists of 806,791 XML files in NewsML format (approximatively 3.7 Gb of uncompressed data). We divide this corpus in a learning set, a development set (not used in experiments described in this paper) and a test set as shown in figure 1.

Each strory is manually indexed by zero to several topics. In figure 2 we report some statistics about this topic indexing distributed by Reuters. These charts are available at the following addresses:

http://about.reuters.com/researchandstandards/corpus/statistics/topic_count.gif
http://about.reuters.com/researchandstandards/corpus/statistics/topics.gif

We work on the set of 126 topics/categories that were provided with the formatted version of the corpus. All the performances were assessed by measuring the ability of the methods to reproduce manual assignments on a given dataset.

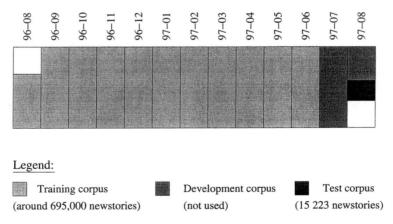

Legend:

☐ Training corpus   ☐ Development corpus   ■ Test corpus
(around 695,000 newstories)   (not used)   (15 223 newstories)

Fig. 1. The Reuters Corpus used in experiments

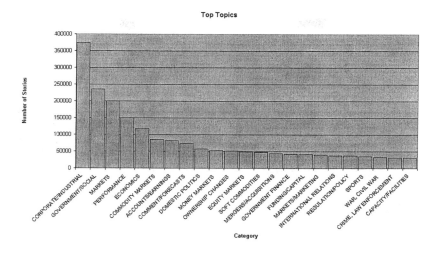

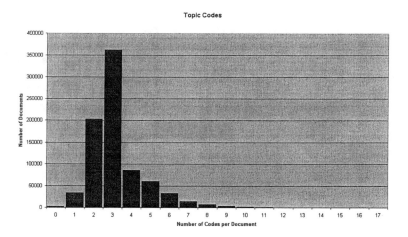

Fig. 2. Top topics and Topic Codes of the Reuters Corpus

4.2   Category Learning

In order to make a category decision, a representation of categories must be chosen. As it is commonly made, we introduce one or more intermediate steps between the input representation of documents and the output category representation. The first step is to transform documents, which typically are strings of characters, into a representation suitable for the learning algorithm and the classification task. All data (training and test) are filtered to extract only the body of newstories (the title, etc. are ignored). In our experiments, we use words

An example of document dj   Partial representation of tf for dj

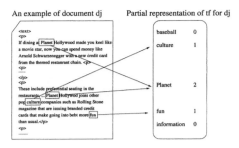

Fig. 3. Representation of document term frequencies in the training

without more complicated representation as it is recommended in [9]. Indeed, authors found that the simplest document representation (using individual words delimited by white spaces with no stemming) was at least as good as representations involving more complicated syntactic and morphological analysis. And, representing documents as binary vectors of words, chosen using a mutual information criterion for each category, was as good as finer-grained coding. Stemming can be avoided as shown in [19]. Consequently, the case of characters has only been lowered. Several techniques are possible to select category-dependent terms. We have chosen to ranking the training corpus words and selecting the first K words of this ordered list. For this purpose, words like numbers or determinants are not good candidates. These words have been identified and placed into a stop-list (318 stop-words for the examples described in this paper). For each category, the ranked words according to their frequency in a training corpus are selected only if they are not in the stop-list. Thus, the text categorization methods make use of sets of K words automatically selected by frequency order. The category parameters are then estimated as:

$$\vec{c_i} = \sum_{\vec{d_j} \in C_i} \vec{d_j}$$

where $\vec{d_j} = (tf(w_1, d_j), tf(w_2, d_j), ..., tf(w_N, d_j))$ and w_n are words of training documents, as described in the figure 3. When a category is too small (i.e. less than K words), it is ignored in the evaluation (but these categories can appear in the test corpus).

Our aim is to apply the KLD method (using probabilities term weighting) to a text categorization task and to compare the results obtained using the well-known similarity based method (using $tfidf$ term weighting). To do so, we conducted a set of 3 experiments resulting from 3 different term selections:

1. In the first experiment, we use all words of the documents not in the stop-list, not numbers or punctuations.
2. The second experiment uses the same as the previous one and adds a lexicon to select words. This lexicon is composed of 86,000 entries.

3. The third experiment use the same filter as the first one and add a term
   selection at the document-level. We select a maximum of 50 words by document with the mutual information measure [20]. These measures allow to
   compute the association degree between a word in the document d_j compared to this word in the corpus and then to make up lists of the most
   important words for this document. This average mutual information (MI)
   measure between A and B can be evaluated as:

$$MI(A:B) = \sum_{a,b} P(a,b) log \frac{P(a,b)}{P(a).P(b)}$$

A value of MI is computed for each word of a document. These values are
then ranked, and the 50 best MI are selected as terms for the document.
These features are used as input to learn categories, with a term frequency
of 1 for each word by document.

In these 3 experiments, the KLD method uses probabilities from the learned
categories as defined previously in Section 3. The $tfidf$ method assigns w_{kj} for
a term t_k in a category c_i as defined in Section 2, i.e. as follows:

$$w_{kj} = tf(t_k, c_j) \times log \left(\frac{|c_i|}{df(t_k, c_i)} \right)$$

4.3   Evaluation Criteria

For each category, the categorization goal is viewed as a binary classification
problem. Given a category, the categorization methods decide whether each document is in or not in this category. With a single category as the focus, let:

- MA be the number of documents assigned to the category both manually
  and automatically,
- A be the number of documents assigned to the category automatically but
  not manually,
- M be the number of documents assigned to the category manually but not
  automatically.

Then the two common measures of Recall (R) and Precision (P) can be defined
as:

$$R = \frac{MA}{MA+M}$$
$$P = \frac{MA}{MA+A}$$

Now, theses measures are adapted to the categorization decisions. Given
a document and a category, a categorization decision is made to determine
whether or not to assign this category to the document. When automatic categorization is conducted, a number of these decisions are made. Out of these
decisions, some may match with the manual ones, while others may not. We
want to compare the various automated decisions with the manual ones. An
"assignment" is defined as the positive decision to assign a category to a document. Let:

- c be the number of correct assignments made automatically,
- a be the number of assignments made automatically,
- m be the number of assignments made manually.

Then, we can define the recall (r) and precision (p) measures as follows:

$$r = \frac{c}{m}$$
$$p = \frac{c}{a}$$

Recall r is the proportion of correctly predicted YESes by the system among the true YESes for all the document category pairs given a dataset. Precision p is the proportion of correctly YESes among all the system predicted YESes. These values consider that the model give a single solution and the notion of precision can be extanded. The precision-at-N is the proportion of correctly YESes in the N first solutions of the model among all the system predicted YESes.

4.4   Overall Performance

Table 1 summarizes our results obtained for the test set. The vocabulary selection of terms for each category is a subset of $K = 2,000$ terms of the category vocabulary. We have not rigorously explore the optimum number of terms for this problem, but this number provided goog results. As we said above, the vocabulary V is the union of all terms of all categories. With this size by category we obtain a vocabulary size $|V|$ of 101,276 in the first experiment, 11,281 in the second experiment and 22,056 in the third experiment.

We can see in table 1 that KLD method performs best among the conventional method. Compared to the $tfidf$ method, all KLD results perform best independently of the choice of category selection features. It is well known that the feature selection is an important goal, and we observe the same in these experiments: the third experiment is significantly better than the first and the second one.

Finally, only for comparison, we carried out some experiments on the well-known Reuters-21578 corpus. We do not detail these experiments in this paper

Table 1. Results of text categorization for the $tfidf$ and KLD methods

$tfidf$	Recall	Precision-at-1	Precision-at-5	Precision-at-10
First experiment	0.449	0.145	0.475	0.606
Second experiment	0.480	0.155	0.552	0.726
Third experiment	0.613	0.198	0.635	0.783

KLD	Recall	Precision-at-1	Precision-at-5	Precision-at-10
First experiment	0.624	0.221	0.535	0.601
Second experiment	0.649	0.210	0.630	0.790
Third experiment	0.731	0.236	0.734	0.874

Table 2. Preliminary results on Reuters-21578

tfidf	Recall	Precision	K
First experiment	0.731	0.545	200
Third experiment	0.755	0.564	200
Third experiment	0.723	0.538	50

KLD	Recall	Precision	K
First experiment	0.785	0.585	200
Third experiment	0.799	0.597	200
Third experiment	0.749	0.557	50

because this work is still in hand. Some results are also available. The corpus consists of a set of 21,578 Reuters newswire stories from 1987 which have been indexed manually using 135 financial topics to support document routing and retrieval for Reuters customers. We divided this corpus into a training set containing 16,300 stories and a test set containing all the other 5,278 stories. Several thousand documents in the data set have no topic assignments and we have chosen to ignore them as we cannot possibly learn from them. The resulting test set is composed of 2,475 stories. The results presented in table 2 refer to experiments made in the same conditions as the previous ones excepted for the K value because the categories are too small. The results remain favorable to KLD.

At last, comparing time of the two methods, the training time is the same for the two methods since we used the same category learning! The time to estimate the appropriate categories for a document is around 20% to 400% faster for KLD.

5   Conclusion and Future Works

This paper introduces a new effective method to perform text categorization. It provides that KLD based method is well suited for this task even in the following conditions: high number of documents and high dimentional feature space. The experimental results show that KLD consistently achieve good performance on text categorization task, outperforming the reference method substantially and significantly. All this makes KLD a very promising and easy-to-use method for text categorization.

We think that our research directions are experimental ones. We want to continue to validate the KLD method. We will initially test other solutions issued from the literature to learn categories. We will investigate the role of document length in this step, looking for correspondence between variations in document length and the comparative performances of KLD and tfidf. An other solution we want to experiment is proposed in [21] ; learning is achieved by combining document vectors into a prototype vector $\vec{c_i}$ for each category. As described in [6], the vector is calculated as a weighted difference between the normalized document vectors of the positive examples for a category and the normalized document vectors of the negative examples, as follow:

$$\overrightarrow{c_i} = \alpha \frac{1}{|c_i|} \sum_{\overrightarrow{d} \in c_i} \frac{\overrightarrow{d}}{\left\| \overrightarrow{d} \right\|} - \beta \frac{1}{|T_r - c_i|} \sum_{\overrightarrow{d} \in (T_r - c_i)} \frac{\overrightarrow{d}}{\left\| \overrightarrow{d} \right\|}$$

where $|c_i|$ is the number of documents assigned to c_i ; $\left\| \overrightarrow{d} \right\|$ denotes the Euclidian length of a vector $\overrightarrow{d}$; α and β are parameters that adjust the relative impact of positive and negative training examples. Because we think it is difficult to use SVMs on our large corpus, after these experiments we will validate the KLD method with the Reuters-21578 dataset even if our method was imagined for larger corpora. Finally, we are motivated to attempt to build a better "meta-classifier" (as for example in [22]) resulting from the combination of KLD and SVMs because they are qualitatively different.

We also plan experiments with varying amounts of training data because we hypothesize that the optimal vocabulary size may change with the size of the training set.

References

[1] Sebastiani, F.: Machine learning in automated text categorization. ACM Computing Surveys **34** (2002) 1–47
[2] Yang, Y.: Expert network: Effective and efficient learning from human decisions in text categorization and retrieval. In: Proceedings of the 17th Annual International ACM SIGIR Conference on Research and Development in Information Retrieval. (1994) 13–22
[3] Lewis, D., Ringuette, M.: A comparison of two learning algorithms for text categorization. In: Proceedings of the Third Annual Symposium on Document Analsysis and Information Retrieval. (1994) 81–93
[4] Wiener, E., Pedersen, J., Weigend, A.: A neural network approach to topic spotting. In: Proceedings of the Fourth Annual Symposium on Document Analsysis and Information Retrieval. (1995)
[5] Salton, G., McGill, M.: The smart and sire experimental retrieval systems, McGraw-Hill, New York (1983) 118–155
[6] Joachims, T.: A probabilistic analysis of the Rocchio algorithm with TFIDF for text categorization. In Fisher, D. H., ed.: Proceedings of ICML-97, 14th International Conference on Machine Learning, Nashville, US, Morgan Kaufmann Publishers, San Francisco, US (1997) 143–151
[7] Yang, Y., Liu, X.: A re-examination of text categorization methods. In: Proceedings of ACM Conference on Research and Development in Information Retrieval. (1999) 42–49
[8] Joachims, T.: Text categorization with support vector machines: Learning with many relevant features. In: Proceedings of the European Conference on Machine Learning, Springer (1998)
[9] Dumais, S., Platt, J., Heckerman, D., Sahami, M.: Inductive learning algorithms and representations for text categorization. In: Proceedings of ACM-CIKM98. (1998) 148–155

[10] Kindermann, J., Paass, G., Leopold, E.: Error correcting codes with optimized kullback-leibler distances for text categorization. In Raedt, L., ed.: Principles of data mining and knowledge discovery. (2001) 133–137

[11] Cover, T., Thomas, J.: Elements of Information Theory. Wiley (1991)

[12] Carpineto, C., De Mori, R., Romano, G., Bigi, B.: An information theoretic approach to automatic query expansion. ACM Transactions On Information Systems **19** (2001) 1–27

[13] Salton, G.: Developments in automatic text retrieval. Science **253** (1991) 974–980

[14] Kullback, S., Leibler, R.: On information and sufficiency. **22** (1951) 79–86

[15] Dagan, I., Lee, L., Pereira, F.: Similarity-based models of word cooccurrence probabilities. Machine Learning **34** (1999) 43–69

[16] Bigi, B., De Mori, R., El-Bèze, M., Spriet, T.: A fuzzy decision strategy for topic identification and dynamic selection of language models. Special Issue on Fuzzy Logic in Signal Processing, Signal Processing Journal **80** (2000)

[17] Xu, J., Croft, B.: Cluster-based language models for distributed retrieval. In: Proceedings of the 22nd Annual International ACM SIGIR Conference on Research and Development in Information Retrieval, Berkeley, CA (1999) 254–261

[18] De Mori, R.: SPOKEN DIALOGUES WITH COMPUTERS. Academic Press (1998)

[19] Leopold, E., Kindermann, J.: Text categorization with support vector machines: How to represent texts in input spaces? Machine Learning **46** (2002) 423–444

[20] Rosenfeld, R.: A maximum entropy approach to adaptive statistical language modeling. Computer, Speech and Language **10** (1996) 187–228

[21] Buckley, C., Salton, G., Allan, J.: The effect of adding relevance information in a relevance feedback environment. In: Proceedings of the seventeenth annual international ACM-SIGIR conference on research and development in information retrieval, Springer-Verlag (1994)

[22] Bennett, P., Dumais, S., Horvitz, E.: Probabilistic combination of text classifiers using reliability indicators: Models and results. In: Proceedings of ACM International Conference on Research and Development in Information Retrieval. (2002) 207–214

Discretizing Continuous Attributes in AdaBoost for Text Categorization

Pio Nardiello[1], Fabrizio Sebastiani[2], and Alessandro Sperduti[3]

[1] MercurioWeb SNC, Via Appia
85054 Muro Lucano (PZ), Italy
pionardiello@mercurioweb.net
[2] Istituto di Scienza e Tecnologie dell'Informazione
Consiglio Nazionale delle Ricerche
56124 Pisa, Italy
fabrizio@iei.pi.cnr.it
[3] Dipartimento di Matematica Pura ed Applicata
Università di Padova
35131 Padova, Italy
sperduti@math.unipd.it

Abstract. We focus on two recently proposed algorithms in the family of "boosting"-based learners for automated text classification, AD-ABOOST.MH and ADABOOST.MH^{KR}. While the former is a realization of the well-known ADABOOST algorithm specifically aimed at multi-label text categorization, the latter is a generalization of the former based on the idea of learning a committee of classifier sub-committees. Both algorithms have been among the best performers in text categorization experiments so far.

A problem in the use of both algorithms is that they require documents to be represented by binary vectors, indicating presence or absence of the terms in the document. As a consequence, these algorithms cannot take full advantage of the "weighted" representations (consisting of vectors of continuous attributes) that are customary in information retrieval tasks, and that provide a much more significant rendition of the document's content than binary representations.

In this paper we address the problem of exploiting the potential of weighted representations in the context of ADABOOST-like algorithms by discretizing the continuous attributes through the application of entropy-based discretization methods. We present experimental results on the Reuters-21578 text categorization collection, showing that for both algorithms the version with discretized continuous attributes outperforms the version with traditional binary representations.

1 Introduction

In the last ten years an impressive array of learning techniques have been used in text categorization (TC) research, including probabilistic methods, regression methods, decision tree and decision rule learners, neural networks, batch and

F. Sebastiani (Ed.): ECIR 2003, LNCS 2633, pp. 320–334, 2003.

incremental learners of linear classifiers, example-based methods, genetic algorithms, hidden Markov models, support vector machines, and classifier committees (see [16] for a review). Among these, the two classes of methods that most seem to have caught the attention of TC researchers are boosting (a subclass of the classifier committees class) and support vector machines. The reasons for this attention are twofold, in the sense that both classes exhibit strong justifications in terms of computational learning theory and superior effectiveness once tested on TC benchmarks of realistic size and difficulty. It is on the former class of methods that this paper focuses.

Classifier *committees* (aka *ensembles*) are based on the idea that, given a task that requires expert knowledge to perform, k experts may be better than one if their individual judgments are appropriately combined. In TC, this means applying k different classifiers $\Phi_1, \ldots, \Phi_k$ to the same task of deciding whether a document d_j belongs or not to category c_i, and then combining their outcome appropriately. Boosting is a method for generating a highly accurate classifier (also called *final hypothesis*) by combining a set of moderately accurate classifiers (also called *weak hypotheses*). In this paper we will make use of two algorithms, called ADABOOST.MH [15] and ADABOOST.MH^{KR} [17], which are based on the notion of *adaptive boosting*, a version of boosting in which members of the committee can be sequentially generated after learning from the classification mistakes of previously generated members of the same committee. ADABOOST.MH [15] is a realization of the well-known ADABOOST algorithm, which is specifically aimed at multi-label TC[1], and which uses *decision stumps* (i.e. decisions trees composed of a root and two leaves only) as weak hypotheses. ADABOOST.MH^{KR} [17] is instead a generalization of ADABOOST.MH based on the idea of learning a committee of classifier sub-committees; in other words, ADABOOST.MH^{KR} weak hypotheses are themselves committees of decision stumps. So far, both algorithms have been among the best performers in text categorization experiments run on standard benchmarks.

A problem in the use of both algorithms is that they require documents to be represented by binary vectors, indicating presence or absence of the terms in the document. As a consequence, these algorithms cannot take full advantage of the "weighted" representations (consisting of vectors of continuous attributes) that are customary in information retrieval tasks, and that provide a much more significant rendition of the document's content than binary representations.

In this paper we address the problem of exploiting the potential of weighted representations in the context of ADABOOST-like algorithms by discretizing the continuous attributes through the application of entropy-based discretization methods. These algorithms attempt to *optimally* split the interval on which these attributes range into a sequence of disjoint subintervals. This split engenders a new vector (binary) representation for documents, in which a binary term indicates that the original non-binary weight belongs or does not belong to a given sub-interval. We present experimental results on the Reuters-21578

---

[1] Given a set of categories $\mathcal{C} = \{c_1, \ldots, c_{|\mathcal{C}|}\}$, *multilabel text categorization* is the task in which any number $0 \leq n_j \leq |\mathcal{C}|$ of categories may be assigned to each $d_j \in \mathcal{D}$.

text categorization collection, showing that for both algorithms the version with discretized continuous attributes outperforms the version with traditional binary representations.

The paper is organized as follows. In Section 2 we briefly introduce AD-ABOOST.MH and ADABOOST.MH^{KR}, while in Section 3 we describe the modified, improved version of ADABOOST.MH^{KR} that we have used in all the experiments described in this paper. In Section 4 we introduce the issue of discretizing continuous attributes, and we propose two discretization algorithms based on information-theoretic intuitions. In Section 5 we describe the experimental results we have obtained by applying both discretization algorithms to both ADABOOST.MH and ADABOOST.MH^{KR}; the benchmark used is **Reuters-21578**, the standard benchmark of text categorization research. In Section 6 we give our concluding remarks.

2   Boosting Algorithms for Text Categorization

In the following we briefly recall ADABOOST.MH and ADABOOST.MH^{KR}, two boosting algorithms that have been specially developed for text categorization applications[2]. For more details on both algorithms, see [17].

2.1   AdaBoost.MH

ADABOOST.MH is a boosting algorithm proposed by Schapire and Singer [15] for multilabel text categorization applications and derived from ADABOOST, Freund and Schapire's general purpose boosting algorithm [3]. The input to the algorithm is a training set $Tr = \{\langle d_1, C_1 \rangle, \ldots, \langle d_{|Tr|}, C_{|Tr|} \rangle\}$, where $C_j \subseteq C$ is the set of categories to each of which d_j belongs.

ADABOOST.MH works by iteratively calling a *weak learner* to generate a sequence $\Phi_1, \ldots, \Phi_S$ of weak hypotheses; at the end of the iteration the final hypothesis Φ is obtained by a summation

$$\Phi(d_j, c_i) = \sum_{s=1}^{S} \Phi_s(d_j, c_i) \tag{1}$$

of these weak hypotheses. A weak hypothesis is a function $\Phi_s : \mathcal{D} \times C \rightarrow \mathbb{R}$, where $\mathcal{D}$ is the set of all possible documents. We interpret the sign of $\Phi_s(d_j, c_i)$ as the decision of Φ_s on whether d_j belongs to c_i (i.e. $\Phi_s(d_j, c_i) > 0$ means that d_j is believed to belong to c_i while $\Phi_s(d_j, c_i) < 0$ means it is believed not

---

[2] In this paper we concentrate on ADABOOST.MH *with real-valued predictions*, one of three variants of ADABOOST.MH discussed in [15], since it is the one that, in the experiments of [15], has been experimented most thoroughly and has given the best results, and since it is the one used in the ADABOOST.MH^{KR} system of [17]. The methods that we discuss in Section 4 straightforwardly apply also to the other two variants.

to belong to c_i), and the absolute value of $\Phi_s(d_j, c_i)$ (indicated by $|\Phi_s(d_j, c_i)|$) as the strength of this belief.

At each iteration s ADABOOST.MH applies the newly generated weak hypothesis Φ_s to the training set and uses the results to update a distribution D_s of weights on the training pairs $\langle d_j, c_i \rangle$. The weight $D_{s+1}(d_j, c_i)$ is meant to capture how effective $\Phi_1, \ldots, \Phi_s$ were in correctly deciding whether the training document d_j belongs to category c_i or not. By passing (together with the training set Tr) this distribution to the weak learner, ADABOOST.MH forces this latter to generate a new weak hypothesis Φ_{s+1} that concentrates on the pairs with the highest weight, i.e. those that had proven harder to classify for the previous weak hypotheses.

The initial distribution D_1 is uniform. At each iteration s all the weights $D_s(d_j, c_i)$ are updated to $D_{s+1}(d_j, c_i)$ according to the rule

$$D_{s+1}(d_j, c_i) = \frac{D_s(d_j, c_i) \exp(-C_j[c_i] \cdot \Phi_s(d_j, c_i))}{Z_s} \tag{2}$$

where $C_j[c_i]$ is defined to be 1 if $c_i \in C_j$ and -1 otherwise, and

$$Z_s = \sum_{i=1}^{|C|} \sum_{j=1}^{|Tr|} D_s(d_j, c_i) \exp(-C_j[c_i] \cdot \Phi_s(d_j, c_i)) \tag{3}$$

is a normalization factor.

Each document d_j is represented by a vector $\langle w_{1j}, \ldots, w_{|T|j} \rangle$ of $|T|$ binary weights, where $T = \{t_1, \ldots, t_{|T|}\}$ is the set of terms. The weak hypotheses ADABOOST.MH uses are *real-valued decision stumps*, i.e. functions of the form

$$\Phi_s(d_j, c_i) = \begin{cases} a_{0i} \text{ if } w_{kj} = 0 \\ a_{1i} \text{ if } w_{kj} = 1 \end{cases} \tag{4}$$

where $t_k \in T$, a_{0i} and a_{1i} are real-valued constants. The choices for t_k, a_{0i} and a_{1i} are in general different for each iteration, and are made according to a policy that attempts to minimize Z_s, since this is known to be an error-minimization policy (although not an optimal one) [14].

ADABOOST.MH^R chooses weak hypotheses of the form described in Equation 4 by a two step-process:

1. For each term $t_k \in T$ it pre-selects, among all weak hypotheses that have t_k as the "pivot term", the one (indicated by Φ_{best}^k) for which Z_s is minimum. From a computational point of view this is the easier step, since Schapire and Singer [14] provide the provably optimal values for Φ_{best}^k as a function of $D_t(d_j, c_i)$, w_{kj} and $C_j[c_i]$.
2. Among all the hypotheses $\Phi_{best}^1, \ldots, \Phi_{best}^{|T|}$ pre-selected for the $|T|$ different terms, it selects the one (indicated by Φ_s) for which Z_s is minimum. From a computational point of view this is the harder step, since this is $O(|T|)$, which in text categorization applications is typically in the tens of thousands.

2.2 AdaBoost.MH^{KR}

In [17] a variant of ADABOOST.MH^R, called ADABOOST.MH^{KR} (for ADABOOST.MH *with K-fold real-valued predictions*), has been proposed. This algorithm differs from ADABOOST.MH^R in the policy according to which weak hypotheses are chosen, since it is based on the construction, at each iteration s of the boosting process, of a *complex weak hypothesis* (CWH) consisting of a sub-committee of *simple weak hypotheses* (SWHs) $\Phi_s^1, \dots, \Phi_s^{K(s)}$, each of which has the form described in Equation 4. These are generated by means of the same process described in Section 2.1, but for the fact that at iteration s, instead of selecting and using only the best term t_k (i.e. the one which brings about the smallest Z_s), it selects the best $K(s)$ terms and use them in order to generate $K(s)$ SWHs $\Phi_s^1, \dots, \Phi_s^{K(s)}$. The CWH is then produced by grouping $\Phi_s^1, \dots, \Phi_s^{K(s)}$ into a sub-committee

$$\Phi_s(d_j, c_i) = \frac{1}{K(s)} \sum_{q=1}^{K(s)} \Phi_s^q(d_j, c_i) \tag{5}$$

that uses the simple arithmetic mean as the combination rule. For updating the distribution it still applies Equations 2 and 3, where Φ_s is now defined by Equation 5. The final hypothesis is computed by plugging Equation 5 into Equation 1, thus obtaining

$$\Phi(d_j, c_i) = \sum_{s=1}^{S} \alpha_s \frac{1}{K(s)} \sum_{q=1}^{K(s)} \Phi_s^q(d_j, c_i) \tag{6}$$

The number $K(s)$ of SWHs to include in the sub-committee is obtained using a simple heuristics which adds a constant C to K every N iterations, using a fixed value for N and using a value of 1 for $K(1)$, i.e. $K(s) = 1 + C\lfloor \frac{s-1}{N} \rfloor$.

3   An Improved Version of AdaBoost.MH^{KR}

In this work we have implemented and experimented a new version of ADABOOST.MH^{KR} in which each SWH in a sub-committee is weighted by a value which is inversely proportional to its score. This means replacing Equation 5 with

$$\Phi_s(d_j, c_i) = \frac{1}{K(s)} \sum_{q=1}^{K(s)} \frac{Z_q^{-1}}{\sum_{j=1}^{K(s)} Z_j^{-1}} \cdot \Phi_s^q(d_j, c_i) \tag{7}$$

The rationale of this choice is that the weight associated to a SWH that contributes more to maximizing effectiveness should be higher. This is especially important in the first iterations since, as noted in [17], it is here that the variance of the Z_s values of members of the same sub-committee is higher.

In experiments that we do not report for reasons of space we have observed that this new version consistently improves the performance of the basic version of ADABOOST.MH^{KR} of more than 1%. From now on when referring to ADABOOST.MH^{KR} we thus mean this improved version.

4   Term Discretization

The aim of this section is to define a *discretization* procedure that allows to exploit the rich information conveyed by the non-binary term weights produced by traditional IR weighting techniques (such as $tf * idf$ or others) while at the same time allowing the use of algorithms derived by the original BOOST-EXTER algorithm [15](such as ADABOOST.MH and ADABOOST.MH^{KR}) that requires discrete (in this case: binary) input. An alternative way to directly exploit non-binary term weights would have been to use the traditional ADABOOST algorithm in conjunction with weak hypotheses able to deal with continuous features. We preferred to avoid this more direct solution since it would have been computationally more onerous.

In machine learning, the basic idea that underlies a discretization procedure is that of segmenting the continuous interval $[\alpha, \beta]$ on which an attribute (in our case: a term) t_k ranges on, into an ordered sequence $I = \langle [\alpha = \gamma_0, \gamma_1], (\gamma_1, \gamma_2], \ldots, (\gamma_{|I|-1}, \gamma_{|I|} = \beta] \rangle$ of disjoint sub-intervals such that

- in the vector representation term t_k is replaced by $|I|$ different terms $\{t_{k1}, t_{k2}, \ldots, t_{k|I|}\}$, where w_{krj} (the weight that term t_{kr} has in document d_j) is computed as

$$w_{krj} = \begin{cases} 1 \text{ if } w_{kj} \in (\gamma_{r-1}, \gamma_r] \\ 0 \text{ otherwise} \end{cases} \tag{8}$$

- among all the possible replacements, the one chosen maximizes effectiveness.

Different techniques for discretizing a continuous attribute have been proposed in the field of machine learning. These include 1R [5], ChiMerge and Chi2 [6], plus several entropy-based algorithms [1, 2, 7, 10, 11, 12]. In this paper, we adopt a very simple discretization algorithm based on *(multiclass) information gain*, which is defined in terms of the well-known *(multiclass) entropy* measure [9]; for reasons discussed later in this section, we take $|I|$ to be equal to 2. This approach is based on the following rationale. Given a term t_k which can take values from a continuous interval $[\alpha, \beta]$, we look for a value γ^k (which we call the *split value*, or simply *split*) that partitions $[\alpha, \beta]$ into two sub-intervals $[\alpha, \gamma^k]$ and $(\gamma^k, \beta]$ such that the dichotomy induced on the training set (i.e. the dichotomy between the examples for which $t_k \in [\alpha, \gamma^k]$ and the examples for which $t_k \in (\gamma^k, \beta]$) generates two training subsets which are expected to be globally easier to classify (and thus lead to better classifiers) by just using the membership of t_k in the two subintervals as discriminant. Specifically, information gain is a measure that quantifies how easier it is to classify the examples when using the split γ^k (i.e. how well the two newly generated terms separate the positive from the negative examples), and selecting the split that maximizes information gain thus means selecting the split that maximizes separability.

4.1   Algorithm A

Let us fix some notation: if t_k is the term under consideration,

- Let $\alpha > 0$ and β be the upper and lower bounds of the range of values (except 0) that all the terms in T can take (which we assume to be equal for all terms), and let γ^k be a split.
- Let Tr_{in} be the set of training examples d_j for which $w_{kj} \in [\alpha, \beta]$.
- Let Tr_{in}^c be the set of training examples belonging to category c for which $w_{kj} \in [\alpha, \beta]$.
- Let $Tr_{in1}(\gamma^k)$ and $Tr_{in2}(\gamma^k)$ be the sets of training examples d_j for which $w_{kj} \in [\alpha, \gamma^k]$ and $w_{kj} \in (\gamma^k, \beta]$, respectively.

Definition 1. *The (multiclass) entropy of Tr with respect to an interval $[\alpha, \beta]$ is defined as*

$$H(Tr, \alpha, \beta) = - \sum_{c \in C} \frac{|Tr_{in}^c|}{|Tr_{in}|} log_2 \frac{|Tr_{in}^c|}{|Tr_{in}|} \tag{9}$$

The (multiclass) information gain of a value with respect to Tr is defined as

$$IG(Tr, \alpha, \beta, \gamma^k) = H(Tr, \alpha, \beta) - \tag{10}$$
$$\frac{|Tr_{in1}(\gamma^k)|}{|Tr|} H(Tr, \alpha, \gamma^k) - \frac{|Tr_{in2}(\gamma^k)|}{|Tr|} H(Tr, \gamma^k, \beta)$$

$\square$

The basic idea of our discretization process is to find, for each term t_k and among all possible splits γ^k, the split $\hat{\gamma}^k$ that maximizes the information gain. On the basis of this split, a term t_k is replaced by two new terms t_{k0} and t_{k1}, and the weights they have in the training documents are computed according to Equation 8. The fact that these weights are binary will allow us to work with both ADABOOST.MH and ADABOOST.MH^{KR} while at the same time exploiting the rich information present in the non-binary weights of the term t_k which has originated the (binary-weighted) terms t_{k0} and t_{k1}. It should be stressed that, because of $\alpha > 0$, if term t_k is not present in a document, both t_{k0} and t_{k1} will assume zero value.

In general, the application of this discretization strategy to all the terms will double the number of terms. This may not be advisable if the ratio $\frac{|Tr|}{|T|}$ between the number $|Tr|$ of training documents and the number $|T|$ of terms used to represent the documents is not high enough. In fact, it is well known that a low such ratio will in general give rise to overfitting, since in the classifier each term corresponds to a free parameter of the learning problem, and this parameter is set by the training algorithm based on the training examples available, which correspond to constraints on the problem. Therefore, if the $\frac{|Tr|}{|T|}$ ratio is low the learning problem is underconstrained, and the probability that an overspecialized classifier is learnt is high. This is the reason why we have limited the number of intervals into which a term is discretized to two.

Input: $Tr = \{\langle d_1, C_1 \rangle, \ldots, \langle d_{|Tr|}, C_{|Tr|} \rangle\}$, the training set of documents
$T = \{t_1, \ldots, t_{|T|}\}$, the set of terms
$\mathcal{C} = \{c_1, \ldots, c_{|\mathcal{C}|}\}$, the set of categories p, the percentage of computed splits to be actually selected

Body: 1. $Optimal\_splits \leftarrow \emptyset$

2. For each $t_k \in T$ do

- Sort the values that term t_k actually takes in Tr into an ordered sequence $\langle v_1, v_2, \ldots \rangle$ and compute the set of possible splits (see [2])

$$Splits_k = \{\gamma_r^k | \gamma_r^k = \frac{v_r + v_{r+1}}{2}\}$$

- Let

$$\hat{\gamma}^k = \arg \max_{\gamma_q^k \in Splits_k} IG(Tr, \alpha, \beta, \gamma_q^k)$$

- $Optimal\_splits \leftarrow Optimal\_splits \cup \{(t_k, \hat{\gamma}^k)\}$

Output: Return the $p\%$ splits $(t_k, \hat{\gamma}^k)$ in $Optimal\_splits$ with highest $IG(Tr, \alpha, \beta, \hat{\gamma}^k)$

Fig. 1. Algorithm A

For pretty much the same reason, we also introduce a selection procedure on the terms to be discretized: among all the pairs $(t_k, \hat{\gamma}^k)$ generated by our algorithm, we select for discretization only the $p\%$ with the highest information gain. Thus, after this selection, terms which have not been selected will not be discretized and, for input to our learners, will be considered as binary-valued (i.e. only presence/absence of the term in the document will be considered). Each selected term will instead be replaced by two new terms, as previously described.

A full description of this algorithm, that in the following we will refer to as Algorithm A, is given in Figure 1.

4.2   Algorithm B

Given a term t_k, a variant of Algorithm A can instead be obtained by first of all computing the best split with respect to a single category c_i. This is done by computing the information gain over a training set in which a document belonging to c_i is considered positive, otherwise it is considered negative. Then, again, we select the $p\%$ splits with highest information gain.

A full description of the algorithm, that in the following we will refer to as Algorithm B, is given in Figure 2.

Input:	$Tr = \{\langle d_1, C_1 \rangle, \ldots, \langle d_{|Tr|}, C_{|Tr|} \rangle\}$, the training set of documents

Input: $Tr = \{\langle d_1, C_1 \rangle, \ldots, \langle d_{|Tr|}, C_{|Tr|} \rangle\}$, the training set of documents
$T = \{t_1, \ldots, t_{|T|}\}$, the set of terms
C, the set of categories
p, the percentage of computed splits to be actually selected

Body:
1. For each $c_i \in C$ define a training set Tr_i in which documents belonging to category c_i are positive examples and documents not belonging to category c_i are negative examples
2. $Optimal\_splits \leftarrow \emptyset$
3. For each $t_k \in T$ do
   - Sort the values that term t_k actually takes in Tr into an ordered sequence $\langle v_1, v_2, \ldots \rangle$ and compute the set of possible splits (see [2])

$$Splits_k = \{\gamma_r^k | \gamma_r^k = \frac{v_r + v_{r+1}}{2}\}$$

   - $Candidate\_splits_k \leftarrow \emptyset$
   - For each category $c_i \in C$ that has at least one positive training example d_j such that $w_{kj} > 0$ do
     - compute

$$\hat{\gamma}_i^k = \arg \max_{\gamma_q^k \in Splits_k} IG(Tr_i, \alpha, \beta, \gamma_q^k)$$

     - $Candidate\_splits_k \leftarrow Candidate\_splits_k \cup \{(t_k, \hat{\gamma}_i^k)\}$
   - Let $(t_k, \hat{\gamma}^k) \in Candidate\_splits_k$ be the split with highest IG for t_k
   - $Optimal\_splits \leftarrow Optimal\_splits \cup \{(t_k, \hat{\gamma}^k)\}$
4. For each $(t_k, \hat{\gamma}_k) \in Optimal\_splits$ compute $IG(Tr, \alpha, \beta, \hat{\gamma}^k)$

Output: Return the best $p\%$ splits $(t_k, \hat{\gamma}^k)$ in $Optimal\_splits$

Fig. 2. Algorithm B

5   Experimental Results

5.1   Experimental Setting

We have conducted a number of experiments to test the validity of the two algorithms proposed in Section 4. For these experiments we have used the well-known "Reuters-21578, Distribution 1.0" corpus[3], which consists of a set of 12,902 news stories, partitioned (according to the "ModApté" split we have adopted) into a training set of 9,603 documents and a test set of 3,299 documents. The documents have an average length of 211 words (that become 117 after stop word removal). We have run our experiments on the set of 115 categories that

---

[3] The Reuters-21578 corpus is freely available for experimentation purposes from http://www.daviddlewis.com/resources/testcollections/~reuters21578/

have at least 1 positive training example; the average number of categories per document is 1.08, ranging from a minimum of 0 to a maximum of 16. The number of positive training examples per category ranges from a minimum of 1 to a maximum of 3964.

As the set of terms T we use the set of words occurring at least once in the training set. This set is identified by previously removing punctuation and then removing stop words. Neither stemming nor explicit number removal have been performed. As a result, the number of different terms is 17,439. Starting from this set of terms, *term space reduction* has been applied using χ^2_{max} as term selection function and a reduction factor of 90%, since this proved one among the best choices in the thorough experiments of [18].

Classification effectiveness has been measured in terms of the classic IR notions of precision (π) and recall (ρ) adapted to the case of text categorization. In our experiments we have evaluated both the "microaveraged" and the "macroaveraged" versions of π and ρ. As a measure of effectiveness that combines the contributions of both π and ρ, we have used the well-known F_1 function [8], in both the microaveraged and the macroaveraged versions.

5.2   The Experiments

We have tested our discretization algorithms on the implementations of both ADABOOST.MH and ADABOOST.MH^{KR} described in [17], running them in the same experimental conditions in experiments with or without discretization. An alternative method might have been to just run the experiments with discretization and compare the results with the ones of the experiments without discretization published in [15] and [17]. We decided to avoid this latter method because of a number of reasons that would have made this comparison difficult:

- [15] uses an older version of the REUTERS benchmark, called REUTERS-22173. This benchmark is known to suffer from a number of problems that make its results difficult to interpret, and the research community universally prefers the better version Reuters-21578. No experiments using both collections have been reported in the literature, so there is no indication as to how results obtained on these two different collections might be compared.
- Apart from single words, [15] uses also bigrams (i.e. statistical phrases of length 2) as terms, while we use unigrams (i.e. single words) only.
- The experiments presented in [17] were run with a suboptimal version of the text preprocessing algorithm[4], which would make the comparison unfair towards [17].
- The experiments presented here use the optimized version of ADABOOST. MH^{KR} described in Section 3, and not the original one described in [17].

---

[4] Among other things, that version of the text preprocessing algorithm mistakenly did not make use of the TITLE field and of part of the BODY field of Reuters-21578 articles, which means that information important for the categorization task went unused.

Our experiments were conducted by applying both ADABOOST.MH and ADABOOST.MH^{KR} to the data:

- **data1**: original binary representations, i.e. obtained without discretization by just checking the presence/absence of a term in the document;
- **data2**: binary representations obtained by discretizing previously obtained non-binary representations by means Algorithm A;
- **data3**: same as **data2**, but with Algorithm B in place of Algorithm A.

The non-binary representations used in **data2** and **data3** were obtained by means of the $tfidf$ function in its standard "ltc" variant [13], i.e.

$$tfidf(t_k, d_j) = tf(t_k, d_j) \cdot \log \frac{|Tr|}{\#_{Tr}(t_k)} \tag{11}$$

where $\#_{Tr}(t_k)$ denotes the number of documents in Tr in which t_k occurs at least once and

$$tf(t_k, d_j) = \begin{cases} 1 + \log \#(t_k, d_j) & \text{if } \#(t_k, d_j) > 0 \\ 0 & \text{otherwise} \end{cases}$$

where $\#(t_k, d_j)$ denotes the number of times t_k occurs in d_j. Weights obtained by Equation 11 are normalized by cosine normalization to yield the final weights, i.e.

$$w_{kj} = \frac{tfidf(t_k, d_j)}{\sqrt{\sum_{s=1}^{|T|} tfidf(t_s, d_j)^2}} \tag{12}$$

In all the experiments with ADABOOST.MH^{KR} we have used the parameter settings $C = 1$ and $N = 20$, since in [17] these choices had been empirically found to give the best results.

Preliminary experiments involving the application of both ADABOOST.MH and ADABOOST.MH^{KR} to data preprocessed by methods **data2** and **data3** with different values for the p parameter had shown that, for both learners, the best performance is obtained for $p = 20$ [5].

In Figure 3 we have thus reported both the microaveraged F_1 (top) and the macroaveraged F_1 (bottom) curves obtained by ADABOOST.MH when applied for 5,000 iterations to **data1**, **data2**, and **data3** (with $p = 20$ used for obtaining **data2** and **data3**). From the results it is clear that

- The use of discretization algorithms (either A or B) brings about an improvement in both microaveraged and macroaveraged F_1 with respect to the application of ADABOOST.MH without discretization. This is relevant, since ADABOOST.MH has been shown to be one of the top performers in text categorization experiments so far.

---

[5] The values we have tested for parameter p are 10, 20, 35, 50, 75, 100. For values of p higher than 20 we observed overfitting, while the performance obtained for $p = 10$ was intermediate between the one obtained without discretization and the one obtained for $p = 20$.

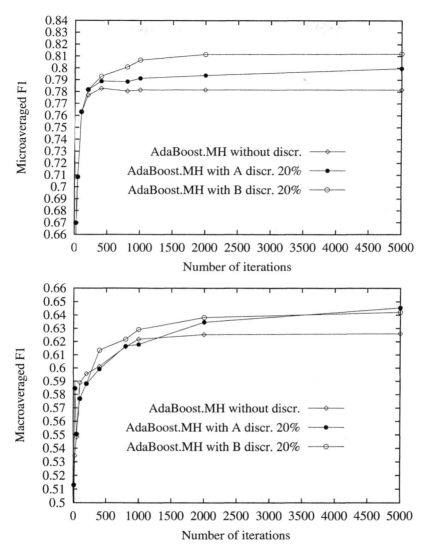

Fig. 3. F_1 curves for ADABOOST.MH applied to data without discretization and with $p = 20\%$ discretization (by both Algorithm A and Algorithm B)

- The improvement obtained by Algorithm B is more significant than that of Algorithm A on microaveraged F_1, while on macroaveraged F_1 the performances of the two algorithms are comparable. This indicates that Algorithm A performs well also on scarcely populated categories, while Algorithm B is more at home with densely populated ones.

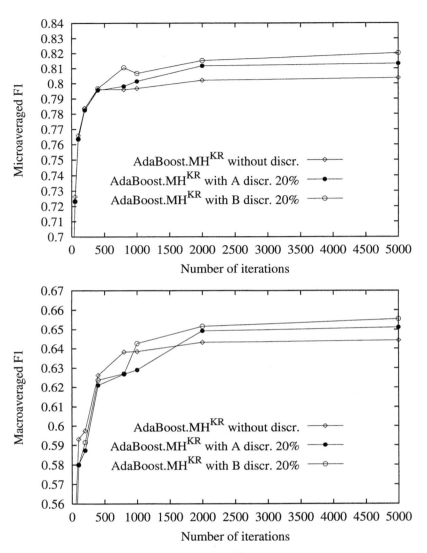

Fig. 4. F_1 curves for ADABOOST.MH^{KR} applied to data without discretization and with $p = 20\%$ discretization (by both Algorithm A and Algorithm B)

The results of analogous experiments for the ADABOOST.MH^{KR} learner are shown in Figure 4. Even in this case we may observe that the representations obtained by the discretization algorithms (either Algorithm A or B) consistently outperform the original binary representations. This time, however, Algorithm B is superior to Algorithm A both in terms of microaveraged and macroaveraged F_1, but the differential between the two is smaller than with ADABOOST.MH.

Finally, we note that ADABOOST.MH^{KR} proves superior to ADABOOST.MH also with representations obtained by discretization (either Algorithm A or B), and for both microaveraged and macroaveraged F_1, thus confirming the results obtained in [17] in which the two learners had been experimentally compared on binary representations obtained without any discretization.

6   Conclusion

We have presented two algorithms for the discretization of non-binary term weights, a task that addresses the problem of exploiting the rich information contained in the non-binary weights produced by standard statistical or probabilistic term weighting techniques, in the context of high performance learners requiring binary input. Although these algorithms can also be used in connection with learners not belonging to the "boosting" family, we have focused on experimenting them with two boosting-based learners, ADABOOST.MH and ADABOOST.MH^{KR}, since these had delivered top-notch performance in previous text categorization experiments.

These experiments have shown that binary representations obtained by discretizing previously obtained non-binary $(tf * idf)$ representations by means of any of our two algorithms, outperform the original binary representations. This improvement is especially significant in the case of microaveraged F_1, for which an improvement of more than 3% was observed for ADABOOST.MH. This is significant, since ADABOOST.MH is in the restricted lot of the peak text categorization performers nowadays, a lot where the margins for performance improvement are slimmer and slimmer.

Acknowledgements

We thank Luigi Galavotti for making available his REALCAT text classification software environment [4], which greatly simplified our experimental work. We also thank Marco Danelutto for giving us access to the BACKUS cluster of PCs.

References

[1] J. Dougherty, R. Kohavi, and M. Sahami. Supervised and unsupervised discretization of continuous features. In *Proceeding of ICML-95, 12th International Conference on Machine Learning*, pages 194–202, Lake Tahoe, US, 1995.

[2] U. Fayyad and K. Irani. Multi-interval discretization of continuous-valued attributes for classification learning. In *Proceedings of IJCAI-93, 13th International Joint Conference on Artificial Intelligence*, pages 1022–1027, Sidney, AU, 1993.

[3] Y. Freund and R. E. Schapire. A decision-theoretic generalization of on-line learning and an application to boosting. *Journal of Computer and System Sciences*, 55(1):119–139, 1997.

[4] L. Galavotti, F. Sebastiani, and M. Simi. Experiments on the use of feature selection and negative evidence in automated text categorization. In J. L. Borbinha and T. Baker, editors, *Proceedings of ECDL-00, 4th European Conference on Research and Advanced Technology for Digital Libraries*, pages 59–68, Lisbon, PT, 2000.

[5] R. C. Holte. Very simple classification rules perform well on most commonly used datasets. *Machine Learning*, 11(1):63–90, 1993.

[6] R. Kerber. Chimerge: Discretization of numeric attributes. In *Proceedings of AAAI-92, 10th Conference of the American Association for Artificial Intelligence*, pages 123–128, San Jose, US, 1998.

[7] R. Kohavi and M. Sahami. Error-based and entropy-based discretization of continuous features. In *Proceedings of KDD-96, 2nd International Conference on Knowledge Discovery and Data Mining*, pages 114–119, Portland, US, 1996.

[8] D. D. Lewis. Evaluating and optimizing autonomous text classification systems. In E. A. Fox, P. Ingwersen, and R. Fidel, editors, *Proceedings of SIGIR-95, 18th ACM International Conference on Research and Development in Information Retrieval*, pages 246–254, Seattle, US, 1995.

[9] T. M. Mitchell. *Machine learning*. McGraw Hill, New York, US, 1996.

[10] L. C. Molina Félix, S. Oliveira Rezende, M. C. Monard, and C. Wellington Caulkins. Some experiences with the discretization process: from regression to classification. In *Proceedings of ASAI-99, 1st Argentinian Symposium on Artificial Intelligence*, pages 155–166, Buenos Aires, AR, 1999.

[11] B. Pfahringer. Compression-based discretization of continuous attributes. In *Proceeding of ICML-95, 12th International Conference on Machine Learning*, pages 339–350, Lake Tahoe, US, 1995.

[12] J. R. Quinlan. Improved use of continuous attributes in C4.5. *Journal of Artificial Intelligence Research*, 4:77–90, 1996.

[13] G. Salton and C. Buckley. Term-weighting approaches in automatic text retrieval. *Information Processing and Management*, 24(5):513–523, 1988.

[14] R. E. Schapire and Y. Singer. Improved boosting algorithms using confidence-rated predictions. *Machine Learning*, 37(3):297–336, 1999.

[15] R. E. Schapire and Y. Singer. BOOSTEXTER: a boosting-based system for text categorization. *Machine Learning*, 39(2/3):135–168, 2000.

[16] F. Sebastiani. Machine learning in automated text categorization. *ACM Computing Surveys*, 34(1):1–47, 2002.

[17] F. Sebastiani, A. Sperduti, and N. Valdambrini. An improved boosting algorithm and its application to automated text categorization. In A. Agah, J. Callan, and E. Rundensteiner, editors, *Proceedings of CIKM-00, 9th ACM International Conference on Information and Knowledge Management*, pages 78–85, McLean, US, 2000.

[18] Y. Yang and J. O. Pedersen. A comparative study on feature selection in text categorization. In D. H. Fisher, editor, *Proceedings of ICML-97, 14th International Conference on Machine Learning*, pages 412–420, Nashville, US, 1997.

Combining Naive Bayes and n-Gram Language Models for Text Classification

Fuchun Peng and Dale Schuurmans

School of Computer Science, University of Waterloo
200 University Avenue West, Waterloo, Ontario, Canada, N2L 3G1
{f3peng,dale}@cs.uwaterloo.ca

Abstract. We augment the naive Bayes model with an n-gram language model to address two shortcomings of naive Bayes text classifiers. The *chain augmented* naive Bayes classifiers we propose have two advantages over standard naive Bayes classifiers. First, a chain augmented naive Bayes model relaxes some of the independence assumptions of naive Bayes—allowing a local Markov chain dependence in the observed variables—while still permitting efficient inference and learning. Second, smoothing techniques from statistical language modeling can be used to recover better estimates than the Laplace smoothing techniques usually used in naive Bayes classification. Our experimental results on three real world data sets show that we achieve substantial improvements over standard naive Bayes classification, while also achieving state of the art performance that competes with the best known methods in these cases.

1 Introduction

Naive Bayes classifiers have been proven successful in many domains, especially in text classification [12, 14, 20], despite the simplicity of the model and the restrictiveness of the independence assumptions it makes. Domingos and Pazzanni [4] point out that naive Bayes classifiers can obtain near optimal misclassification error even when the independence assumption is strongly violated. Nevertheless, it is commonly thought that relaxing the independence assumption of naive Bayes ought to allow for superior text classification [12], and it has been shown in practice that functionally dependent attributes can indeed improve classification accuracy in some cases [7, 19].

A significant amount of research has been conducted on relaxing the naive Bayes independence assumption in machine learning research. A popular extension is the **T**ree **A**ugmented **N**aive Bayes classifier (TAN) [7] which allows for a tree-structured dependence among observed variables in addition to the traditional dependence on the hidden "root" variable. However, learning tree structured Bayesian network is not trivial [10], and this model has rarely been used in text classification applications. In this paper we investigate a convenient alternative that lies between pure naive Bayes and TAN Bayes models in the strength of its assumptions; namely, the **C**hain **A**ugmented **N**aive *Bayes* (CAN)

F. Sebastiani (Ed.): ECIR 2003, LNCS 2633, pp. 335–350, 2003.

model. A CAN Bayes model simplifies the TAN model by restricting dependencies among observed variables to form a Markov chain instead of a tree. Interestingly, it turns out that the model that results is closely related to the n-gram language models that have been widely studied in statistical natural language modeling and speech recognition. In this paper, we augment the naive Bayes text classifier by including attribute dependencies that form a Markov chain, and use techniques from statistical n-gram language modeling to learn and apply these models. The result is a combination of naive Bayes and statistical n-gram methods that yields simple yet surprisingly effective classifiers.

In addition to proposing the CAN model, we also investigate the use of advanced smoothing techniques from statistical language modeling to obtain better parameter estimates. In the standard naive Bayes approach, Laplace smoothing is commonly used to avoid zero probability estimates. However, Laplace smoothing is usually less effective than smoothing techniques from statistical language modeling. We consider four more advanced smoothing techniques that have been commonly used in n-gram language modeling to improve naive Bayes classifier.

Below we first describe the naive Bayes classifier (Section 2) and then present the basic n-gram language model (Section 3). These two models form the basis of the chain augmented naive Bayes classifier we propose in Section 4. We then experimentally evaluate the proposed classifier on three real world data sets in Section 5, and conclude with a brief discussion in Section 6.

2   The Naive Bayes Text Classifier

Text classification is the problem of assigning a document D to one of a set of $|C|$ pre-defined categories $C = \{c_1, c_2, ..., c_{|C|}\}$. Normally a supervised learning framework is used to train a text classifier, where a learning algorithm is provided a set of N labeled training examples $\{(d_i, c_i) : i = 1, ..., N\}$ from which it must produce a classification function $F : D \rightarrow C$ that maps documents to categories. Here d_i denotes the ith training document and c_i is the corresponding category label of d_i. We use the random variables D and C to denote the document and category values respectively. A popular learning algorithm for text classification[1] is based on a simple application of *Bayes' rule* [5, chapter 10]:

$$P(C = c | D = d) = \frac{P(C = c) \times P(D = d | C = c)}{P(D = d)} \tag{1}$$

To simplify the presentation, we re-write Eq. (1) as

$$P(c|d) = \frac{P(c) \times P(d|c)}{P(d)} \tag{2}$$

---

[1] Other popular learning algorithms for text classification include decision tree learning, support vector machines, regression methods, neural network, rule learning methods, and on-line learning [22].

Bayes' rule decomposes the computation of a posterior probability into the computation of a likelihood and a prior probability. In text classification, a document d is normally represented by a vector of K attributes[2] $d = (v_1, v_2, ...v_K)$. Computing $p(d|c)$ in this case is not generally trivial, since the space of possible documents $d = (v_1, v_2, ...v_K)$ is vast. To simplify this computation, the naive Bayes model introduces an additional assumption that all of the attribute values, v_j, are independent given the category label, c. That is, for $i \neq j$, v_i and v_j are conditionally independent given c. This assumption greatly simplifies the computation by reducing Eq. (2) to

$$P(c|d) = P(c) \times \frac{\prod_{j=1}^{K} P(v_j|c)}{P(d)} \tag{3}$$

Based on Eq. (3), maximum a posterior (MAP) classifier can be constructed by seeking the optimal category which maximizes the posterior $P(c|d)$:

$$c^* = \arg\max_{c \in C} \{P(c|d)\} \tag{4}$$

$$= \arg\max_{c \in C} \left\{ P(c) \times \frac{\prod_{j=1}^{K} P(v_j|c)}{P(d)} \right\} \tag{5}$$

$$= \arg\max_{c \in C} \left\{ P(c) \times \prod_{j=1}^{K} P(v_j|c) \right\} \tag{6}$$

Note that going from Eq. (5) to Eq. (6) is valid because $P(d)$ is a constant for every category c. A MAP classifier (Eq. (4)) is optimal in the sense of minimizing *zero-one* loss (misclassification error). If the independence assumption holds, then a classifier based on Eq. (6) is also optimal [5].

The prior distribution $P(c)$ can also be used to incorporate additional assumptions. Two commonly used prior distributions are Dirichlet distribution and uniform distribution. When uniform distribution is used as the prior, the MAP classifier becomes equivalent to the maximum likelihood (ML) classifier.

$$c^* = \arg\max_{c \in C} \left\{ \prod_{j=1}^{K} P(v_j|c) \right\} \tag{7}$$

Eq. (7) is called the *maximum likelihood* naive Bayes classifier. There are several variants of naive Bayes classifiers, including the binary independence model, the multinomial model, the Poisson model, and the negative binary independence model [6]. It has been shown that for text categorization applications, the multinomial model is most often the best choice [6, 14], therefore we will only consider the multinomial naive Bayes model in this paper. Fig. 1 gives a graphical representation of the multinomial naive Bayes model, showing that each attribute node is independent of the other attributes given the class label C.

---

[2] Attributes are also called features in many papers. Feature selection is an important procedure in many classifiers [21].

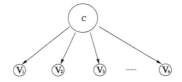

Fig. 1. Graphical model of a naive Bayes classifier

The parameters of a multinomial naive Bayes classifier are given by $\Theta = \{\theta_j^c = P(v_j|c) : j = 1, ..., K; c = 1, ..., |C|\}$. The likelihood of a given set of documents D^c for a given category c is given by

$$P(D^c|\Theta) = \frac{N^c!}{\prod_j N_j^c!} \prod_j (\theta_j^c)^{N_j^c} \qquad (8)$$

where N_j^c is the frequency of attribute j occurring in D^c and $N^c = \sum_j N_j^c$. A maximum likelihood estimate yields the parameter estimates

$$\theta_j^c = \frac{N_j^c}{N^c} \qquad (9)$$

Note that Eq. (9) puts zero probability on attribute values that do not actually occur in D^c (i.e., $N_j^c = 0$). Unfortunately, a zero estimate can create significant problems when we classify a new document, for example, when we encounter a new attribute value that has not been observed in the training corpus D^c. To overcome this problem, Laplace smoothing is usually used to avoid zero probability estimates in practice:

$$\theta_j^c = \frac{N_j^c + a_j}{N^c + a} \qquad (10)$$

where $a = \sum_j a_j$. A special case of Laplace smoothing is *add one* smoothing [13, chapter 6] obtained by setting $a_j = 1$. However, Laplace smoothing is not as effective in language modeling as some other smoothing techniques [2]. We will show that more advanced smoothing techniques can be used to improve naive Bayes classifiers, and therefore play an important role in developing effective text classifiers using naive Bayes models.

Going back to Equ. (7), we can see that a naive Bayes classifier only considers the selected K attributes while ignoring all other attributes (OOV attributes). Although infrequent attributes contribute less information than common attributes individually, their cumulative effect of can still have an important effect on classification accuracy. Our language modeling based classifier alleviates this problem by implicitly consider all possible attributes. We will experimentally show that considering OOV attributes has notable effects on classification performance.

We now describe the next main component of our models—statistical n-gram language models—which we will use to later augment naive Bayes classifiers.

3   Markov n-Gram Language Modeling

Although the dominant motivation for language modeling has come from speech recognition, statistical language models have recently become more widely used in many other application areas, including information retrieval [9, 17].

The goal of language modeling is to predict the probability of natural word sequences; or more simply, to put high probability on word sequences that actually occur (and low probability on word sequences that never occur). Given a word sequence $w_1 w_2 ... w_T$ to be used as a test corpus, the quality of a language model can be measured by the empirical perplexity (or entropy) on this corpus

$$Perplexity = \sqrt[T]{\prod_{i=1}^{T} \frac{1}{P(w_i|w_1...w_{i-1})}} \tag{11}$$

$$Entropy = \log_2 \, Perplexity \tag{12}$$

The goal of language modeling is to obtain a small perplexity. The simplest and most successful basis for language modeling is the n-gram model: Note that by the chain rule of probability we can write the probability of any sequence as

$$P(w_1 w_2 ... w_T) = \prod_{i=1}^{T} P(w_i|w_1...w_{i-1}) \tag{13}$$

An n-gram model approximates this probability by assuming that the only words relevant to predicting $P(w_i|w_1...w_{i-1})$ are the previous $n - 1$ words; that is, it assumes the Markov n-gram independence assumption

$$P(w_i|w_1...w_{i-1}) = P(w_i|w_{i-n+1}...w_{i-1})$$

A straightforward maximum likelihood estimate of n-gram probabilities from a corpus is given by the observed frequency

$$P(w_i|w_{i-n+1}...w_{i-1}) = \frac{\#(w_{i-n+1}...w_i)}{\#(w_{i-n+1}...w_{i-1})} \tag{14}$$

where $\#(.)$ is the number of occurrences of a specified gram in the training corpus. Unfortunately, using grams of length up to n entails estimating the probability of W^n events, where W is the size of the word vocabulary. This quickly overwhelms modern computational and data resources for even modest choices of n (beyond 3 to 6). Also, because of the heavy tailed nature of language (i.e. Zipf's law) one is likely to encounter novel n-grams that were never witnessed during training. Therefore, some mechanism for assigning non-zero probability to novel n-grams is a central and unavoidable issue. One standard approach to smoothing probability estimates to cope with sparse data problems (and to cope with potentially missing n-grams) is to use some sort of back-off estimator

$$P(w_i|w_{i-n+1}...w_{i-1}) = \begin{cases} \hat{P}(w_i|w_{i-n+1}...w_{i-1}), \\ \qquad \text{if } \#(w_{i-n+1}...w_i) > 0 \\ \beta(w_{i-n+1}...w_{i-1}) \times P(w_i|w_{i-n+2}...w_{i-1}), \\ \qquad \text{otherwise} \end{cases} \qquad (15)$$

where

$$\hat{P}(w_i|w_{i-n+1}...w_{i-1}) = \frac{discount \, \#(w_{i-n+1}...w_i)}{\#(w_{i-n+1}...w_{i-1})} \qquad (16)$$

is the discounted probability, and $\beta(w_{i-n+1}...w_{i-1})$ is a normalization constant calculated to be

$$\beta(w_{i-n+1}...w_{i-1}) = \frac{1 - \displaystyle\sum_{x \in (w_{i-n+1}...w_{i-1}x)} \hat{P}(x|w_{i-n+1}...w_{i-1})}{1 - \displaystyle\sum_{x \in (w_{i-n+1}...w_{i-1}x)} \hat{P}(x|w_{i-n+2}...w_{i-1})} \qquad (17)$$

The discounted probability (16) can be computed using different smoothing approaches including linear smoothing, absolute smoothing, Good-Turing smoothing and Witten-Bell smoothing [2].

Note that the basic unit used in the language models described above is the word. However, we can also consider text as a concatenated sequence of *characters* instead of words. The formulation of a character based language model is the same as above, except that the size of the vocabulary is much smaller, which greatly reduces the sparse data problem. Character level models also avoid the word segmentation problems that occur in many Asian languages such as Chinese and Japanese.

To allow a comparison to Laplace smoothing (Eq. (10)), we briefly describe the standard smoothing techniques used in n-gram language modeling.

Absolute Smoothing   Here, the frequency of a word is subtracted by a constant b, so the discounted probability (Eq. 16) is calculated as

$$\hat{P}(w_i|w_{i-n+1}...w_{i-1}) = \frac{\#(w_{i-n+1}...w_i) - b}{\#(w_{i-n+1}...w_{i-1})}$$

where b is often defined as the upper bound $b = \frac{n_1}{n_1 + 2n_2}$, and n_i is the number of events which occur *exactly* i times in training data [15]. This notation also applies to other smoothing techniques.

Linear Smoothing   Here, the discounted probability is calculated as

$$\hat{P}(w_i|w_{i-n+1}...w_{i-1}) = (1 - \frac{n_1}{Z}) \times \frac{\#(w_{i-n+1}...w_i)}{\#(w_{i-n+1}...w_{i-1})}$$

where Z is the number of uni-grams, which corresponds to the number of words in the training data [15].

Good-Turing Smoothing Good-Turing smoothing discounts the frequency of r by $GT_r = (r+1)\frac{n_{r+1}}{n_r}$ where the discounted probability is calculated as

$$\hat{P}(w_i|w_{i-n+1}...w_{i-1}) = \frac{GT_{\#(w_{i-n+1}...w_i)}}{\#(w_{i-n+1}...w_{i-1})}$$

Witten-Bell Smoothing Witten-Bell smoothing [3] is very similar to Laplace smoothing, except it reserves probability mass for OOV values, whereas Laplace smoothing does not. Here the discounted probability is calculated as

$$\hat{P}(w_i|w_{i-n+1}...w_{i-1}) = \frac{\#(w_{i-n+1}...w_i)}{\#(w_{i-n+1}...w_{i-1}) + W}$$

where W is the number of distinct words that can follow $w_{i-n+1}...w_{i-1}$ in the training data. In the uni-gram model, this corresponds to the size of vocabulary.

We now show how naive Bayes models and statistical n-gram models can be combined to form a chain augmented naive Bayes classifier.

4 Using n-Gram Language Models as Text Classifiers

Text classifiers attempt to identify attributes which distinguish documents in different categories. Such attributes may include vocabulary terms, word average length, local n-grams, or global syntactic and semantic properties. Language models also attempt capture such regularities, and hence provide another natural avenue to constructing text classifiers. An n-gram language model can be applied to text classification in a similar manner to a naive Bayes model. In this case

$$c^* = \arg\max_{c \in C} \{P(c|d)\} = \arg\max_{c \in C} \{P(d|c)P(c)\} \tag{18}$$

$$= \arg\max_{c \in C} \{P(d|c)\} \tag{19}$$

$$= \arg\max_{c \in C} \left\{ \prod_{i=1}^{T} P_c(w_i|w_{i-n+1}...w_{i-1}) \right\} \tag{20}$$

where the step from Eq. (18) to Eq. (19) assumes a uniform prior over categories, and the step from Eq. 19 to Eq. (20) uses the Markov n-gram independence assumption. Likelihood is related to perplexity and entropy by Eq. (11) and Eq. (12). The principle for using an n-gram language model as a text classifier is to determine the category that makes a given document *most likely* to have been generated by the category model (Eq. (20)). Thus, we train a separate language model for each category, and classify a new document by evaluating its likelihood under each category, choosing the category according to Eq. (20). The parameters in the model are $\Theta = \{\theta_i^c = P_c(w_i|w_{i-n+1}...w_{i-1}) : i = 1, ..., |T|; c = 1, ..., |C|\}$.

---

[3] Witten-Bell smoothing is a misnomer since it was actually invented by Alistair Moffat, and is called method C in PPM text compression.

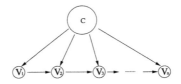

Fig. 2. Graphical model of a bi-gram chain augmented naive Bayes classifier

Different from naive Bayes classifier (Equ. (7)), Equ. (20) considers all the words during testing although some may be out of vocabulary. This is one difference between naive Bayes text classifier and language modeling based text classifier. Later we will see that this difference actually makes noticeable improvements.

In a naive Bayes text classifier, attributes (words) are considered independent of each other given the category. However, in a language modeling based approach, this is enhanced by considering a Markov dependence between adjacent words. Due to this similarity, we refer the n-gram augmented naive Bayes classifier as a **C**hain **A**ugmented **N**aive Bayes classifier (CAN). A graphical model of a bi-gram augmented naive Bayes text classifier is given in Fig. 2, where each leaf node is a word sequentially occurring in a document.

We now experimentally evaluate the performance of chain augmented naive Bayes classifier on three real word data sets.

5   Empirical Evaluation

We present experimental results on different text classification problems in three different languages. First, we consider a Greek authorship attribution problem, where Greek documents must be classified as being written by one of 10 modern Greek authors. Then we consider an English newsgroup topic detection problem, where documents must be classified as belonging to one of 20 newsgroups. Finally, we consider a Chinese TREC topic detection problem, where Chinese documents must be classified into one of 6 topics.

5.1   Data Sets and Performance Measure

The Greek authorship attribution data we used has been previously investigated in [23], and can be downloaded from the WWW site of the Modern Greek weekly newspaper "TO BHMA". The corpus consists of two document collections containing 20 works from 10 different authors (totaling 200 documents) each. In our experiments, we divided the collections into 10 training and 10 testing documents from each author. (The authors used in the data sets are shown in Table 1.) We also considered any concatenated character string delimited by white-space to be a word, which introduces some noise since many character strings are concatenated with punctuation marks. Nevertheless, we did not perform any extra

Table 1. Authors in the Greek data set

code	Author Name	code	Author Name
0	S. Alaxiotis	5	D. Maronitis
1	G. Babiniotis	6	M. Ploritis
2	G. Dertilis	7	T. Tasios
3	C. Kiosse	8	K. Tsoukalas
4	A. Liakos	9	G. Vokos

Table 2. Topics in the Chinese TREC data set

code	Topic
0	Politics, Law and Society
1	Literature and Arts
2	Education, Science and Culture
3	Sports
4	Theory and Academy
5	Economics

pre-processing to remove this noise. The number of unique words observed in the training corpus is 31,502. From these, we select the most frequent 30,000 words to form the vocabulary, which comprises 98.7% of the total word occurrences.

The English 20 Newsgroup data[4] we used has been investigated in research on text categorization [6, 14, 18]. It contains 19,974 non-empty documents evenly distributed across 20 newsgroups, which form our categories. We randomly select 80% of the documents to be used for training and leave the remaining 20% for testing. In our experiments, we selected the 70,000 most frequent words to form the vocabulary, which comprises 92.3% of total word occurrences. As with the Greek data set, the selected words have some noise which we did not remove.

Finally, the Chinese data set we used has been previously investigated in [8]. The corpus is a subset of the TREC-5 *People's Daily news corpus* published by the Linguistic Data Consortium (LDC) in 1995. The entire TREC-5 data set contains 77,733 documents on a variety of topics, including international and domestic news, sports, and culture. The corpus was originally intended for research on information retrieval. To make the data set suitable for text categorization, He et al. [8] first clustered documents into 101 groups that shared the same headline (as indicated by an SGML tag). The six most frequent groups were selected to make a Chinese text categorization data set, as shown in Table 2. In each group, 500 documents were randomly selected for training and 100 documents were reserved for testing. In our experiments, we selected the most frequent 2,000 Chinese characters to serve as the vocabulary, which comprised over 99% of the total character occurrences in the training corpus.

---

[4] Available at http://www.ai.mit.edu/~jrennie/20Newsgroups/

Table 3. Results on Greek authorship attribution

	Considering OOV words								
n	Adding One		Absolute		Good-Turing		Linear		Witten-Bell	
	Acc.	F-Mac	Acc.	F-Mac	Acc.	F-Mac	Acc.	F-Mac	Acc.	F-Mac
1	0.7600	0.7298	**0.9600**	0.9593	0.9300	0.9262	**0.9600**	0.9580	0.6100	0.5731
2	0.6000	0.5681	**0.9600**	0.9580	0.9500	0.9479	0.9500	0.9483	0.8300	0.7847
3	0.5400	0.5111	**0.9600**	0.9585	0.9500	0.9479	0.9500	0.9483	0.8300	0.7838
4	0.5600	0.5365	**0.9600**	0.9585	0.9500	0.9479	0.9500	0.9483	0.8400	0.8049
	Not considering OOV words : 0.2277 OOV rate									
1	0.6900	0.6769	0.9400	0.9337	0.9300	0.9239	0.9100	0.9015	0.5500	0.5178
2	0.5000	0.4674	0.9300	0.9233	0.9300	0.9235	0.8900	0.8751	0.8200	0.7760
3	0.4500	0.4050	0.9500	0.9464	0.9300	0.9235	0.8900	0.8751	0.8300	0.7847
4	0.4900	0.4557	0.9500	0.9464	0.9300	0.9235	0.8900	0.8751	0.8300	0.7847

For the sake of consistency with previous research [18, 23], we measure categorization performance by the *overall accuracy*, which is the number of correctly identified texts divided by the total number of texts considered. We also measure the performance with *Macro F-measure*, which is the average of the F-measures across all categories. F-measure is a combination of precision and recall [26].

5.2 Experimental Results

The results of Greek authorship attribution are shown in Table 3. The upper half shows the results when considering out of vocabulary (OOV) words, and the lower half shows the results without considering OOV words. The OOV rate is the average rate of words that are out of vocabulary on all testing documents. The first column is the order of n-gram model, and each other column represents a different smoothing technique.

The results of topic detection on the English 20 Newsgroup data set are shown in Table 4.

Chinese topic detection is more difficult because words are not white-space delimited, as they are in English and Greek. Normally, a word segmenter is required for Chinese text classification [8]. However, we avoid the need for explicit segmentation by using a *character level* CAN Bayes classifier. Table 5 shows our experimental results on Chinese topic detection.

For Greek and English, we can also apply character level CAN Bayes classifiers. The results of character level models on Greek and English are shown in Table 6 and Table 7 respectively. The size of the character vocabulary is 150 for Greek and 100 for English.

5.3 Discussion

The performance of a language model based text classifier depends on several factors, including order n of n-gram models, smoothing techniques, whether or

Table 4. Topic detection results on the English 20 Newsgroup data with word models

n	Considering OOV words									
	Adding One		Absolute		Good-Turing		Linear		Witten-Bell	
	Acc.	F-Mac	Acc.	F-Mac	Acc.	F-Mac	Acc.	F-Mac	Acc.	F-Mac
1	0.8505	0.8442	0.8664	0.8628	0.8595	0.8559	0.8720	0.8691	0.8449	0.8386
2	0.4751	0.4768	0.8796	0.8754	0.8778	0.8741	0.8796	0.8759	0.8749	0.8712
3	0.3287	0.3339	0.8751	0.8718	0.8741	0.8708	0.8733	0.8700	0.8693	0.8659
4	0.3152	0.3198	0.8757	0.8726	0.8727	0.8697	0.8743	0.8713	0.8706	0.8674
	Not considering OOV words : 0.1121 OOV rate									
1	0.8431	0.8344	0.8717	0.8673	0.8611	0.8562	0.8727	0.8686	0.8375	0.8287
2	0.4751	0.4752	**0.8804**	0.8760	0.8791	0.8748	0.8794	0.8755	0.8733	0.8690
3	0.3348	0.3388	0.8757	0.8718	0.8746	0.8707	0.8765	0.8728	0.8704	0.8663
4	0.3213	0.3251	0.8780	0.8742	0.8757	0.8718	0.8770	0.8735	0.8704	0.8665

Table 5. Topic detection results on Chinese TREC data with character models

n	Considering OOV words									
	Adding One		Absolute		Good-Turing		Linear		Witten-Bell	
	Acc.	F-Mac	Acc.	F-Mac	Acc.	F-Mac	Acc.	F-Mac	Acc.	F-Mac
1	0.7650	0.7704	0.7667	0.7713	0.7600	0.7665	0.7567	0.7630	0.7667	0.7720
2	0.7217	0.7085	0.8050	0.8041	0.8050	0.8050	0.7950	0.7922	0.8017	0.7997
3	0.7033	0.6919	0.8017	0.7989	0.8133	0.8101	0.8000	0.7978	0.8000	0.7952
4	0.6967	0.6842	0.8017	0.7989	0.8117	0.8085	0.8067	0.8049	0.8000	0.7956
	Not considering OOV words : 0.0514 OOV rate									
1	0.7750	0.7769	0.7783	0.7799	0.7783	0.7799	0.7783	0.7799	0.7783	0.7799
2	0.6633	0.6431	0.7967	0.7950	0.7933	0.7914	0.7850	0.7811	0.7933	0.7901
3	0.6500	0.6288	0.7883	0.7843	0.7933	0.7890	0.7883	0.7845	0.7883	0.7832
4	0.6500	0.6274	0.7783	0.7722	0.7917	0.7875	0.7883	0.7851	0.7833	0.7777

Table 6. Results on Greek authorship attribution with character models (only 0.12% OOV characters encountered)

n	Laplace		Absolute		Good-Turing		Linear		Witten-Bell	
	Acc.	F-Mac	Acc.	F-Mac	Acc.	F-Mac	Acc.	F-Mac	Acc.	F-Mac
1	0.5600	0.5051	0.5700	0.5318	0.5500	0.4944	0.5500	0.4944	0.5500	0.4944
2	0.8200	0.7900	0.8500	0.8395	0.8000	0.7536	0.8400	0.8339	0.8400	0.8187
3	0.7000	0.6348	**0.9000**	0.8902	0.7900	0.7453	0.8900	0.8801	0.8900	0.8742
4	0.4700	0.3878	0.8700	0.8507	0.7900	0.7221	0.8500	0.8235	0.8800	0.8613
5	0.3500	0.2869	0.8600	0.8307	0.7900	0.7240	0.8700	0.8524	0.8600	0.8309
6	0.1600	0.1001	0.8600	0.8326	0.7900	0.7250	0.8700	0.8534	0.8600	0.8329

Table 7. Topic detection results on English 20 Newsgroup data with character models (no OOV characters)

n	Laplace		Absolute		Good-Turing		Linear		Witten-Bell	
	Acc.	F-Mac	Acc.	F-Mac	Acc.	F-Mac	Acc.	F-Mac	Acc.	F-Mac
1	0.2216	0.2126	0.2214	0.2123	0.2211	0.2120	0.2211	0.2120	0.2211	0.2120
2	0.6718	0.6531	0.6760	0.6580	0.6861	0.6675	0.6837	0.6650	0.6686	0.6503
3	0.8417	0.8344	0.8645	0.8602	0.8600	0.8554	0.8584	0.8548	0.8629	0.8578
4	0.8266	0.8173	0.8831	0.8795	0.8757	0.8725	0.8746	0.8719	0.8865	0.8828
5	0.7359	0.7246	0.8863	0.8832	0.8717	0.8684	0.8823	0.8801	0.8897	0.8865
6	0.6471	0.6393	0.8863	0.8830	0.8791	0.8751	0.8794	0.8773	**0.8908**	0.8874
7	0.5740	0.5691	0.8855	0.8822	0.8783	0.8746	0.8844	0.8824	0.8900	0.8864
8	0.5178	0.5088	0.8828	0.8796	0.8730	0.8709	0.8818	0.8798	0.8892	0.8855
9	0.4616	0.4521	0.8796	0.8767	0.8743	0.8715	0.8823	0.8807	0.8897	0.8861

not considering OOV words, using character level model or word level model. We will discuss the influence of these factors below.

Effects of Order n of n-Gram Models Relaxing the naive Bayes independence assumption to consider local context dependencies is one of the main motivations of the CAN Bayes model. From Table 6 and Table 7, we can obviously see the increase of classification accuracy with longer context. However, the increase stops at some point. This is due to the sparseness of data when larger n is used. That is, the additional information provided by longer context becomes compromised by data sparseness. Data sparseness also explains why the context information does not help in the Chinese data beyond 2-grams. The performance increase 3-4% from 1-gram to 2-gram, but does not increase any more. There are 3573 most commonly used characters in Chinese compared to 100 (upper case, lower case, and punctuation) in English. Data sparseness is much more serious in Chinese than in English. Also, most Chinese words consist of 1-2 characters. Bi-grams have been found very effective in Chinese IR [11]. Longer context information does not help improve classification accuracies in Greek and English at the word level (except for Witten-Bell smoothing, which may be due to its poor performance on uni-gram models), because the sparse data problem at the word level is more much serious than at the character level. Overall, relaxing independence assumptions can help in cases where there is sufficient training data to reduce the sparse data problem, such as with character level models. However, when one does not have sufficient training data, it becomes important to use short context models that avoid sparse data problems. These results may offer another explanation of why the naive Bayes classifier is preferred in practice, because normally one can not get sufficient labeled training data to train a large-context model.

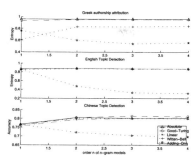

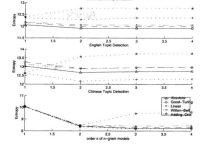

Fig. 3. Classification performance curves

Fig. 4. Entropy curves

Effect of Smoothing Technique To make the results more comprehensible, we illustrate the upper parts of Table 3, 4 and 5 in Figure 3. We also illustrate the corresponding entropy curves in Figure 4. The entropy is averaged across all testing documents. One obvious phenomena is that the different smoothing techniques behave quite differently in our experiments. Add-one smoothing performs much worse than other smoothing techniques (except uni-gram model on Greek dataset). A interesting consequence of add-one smoothing is that it overfits much earlier than other smoothing. Absolute smoothing and linear smoothing generally perform well. Witten-Bell smoothing (Moffat smoothing) does not perform as well on the word level model, despite the fact that it performs best in character level models (Table 7). Overall, absolute and linear smoothing performed best, and Laplace smoothing performed worst in our experiments.

Effect of Considering OOV Words As mentioned in the introduction, discarding OOV words forgoes some information provided by these values. This weakness is revealed in our experiments. By comparing the upper parts with the lower parts of the tables, one can see that when the OOV rate is low (for example, Table 4 and 5), the performance obtained when ignoring OOV words is roughly the same as when considering OOV words (performance within 2%). However, when the OOV rate is high (for example as in Table 3, where the Greek data set has 22.77% OOV words), ignoring OOV words can noticeably damage performance of most smoothing techniques (up to a 7% reduction). This implies that considering OOV words is better than ignoring them when the sparse data problem is serious.

Character Level versus Word Level For many Asian languages such as Chinese and Japanese, where word segmentation is a hard, our character level CAN Bayes model is well suited for text classification because it avoids the need for word segmentation. For Western languages such as Greek and English, we can work at both the word and character levels. In our experiments, we actually found that the character level models worked slightly better than the word level models in the English 20 Newsgroup data set (89% vs. 88%). It appears that the character level models are capturing some regularity that the word level models are missing in this case. By relaxing the context, character level models can also capture regularities at the word level, and even phrase level regularities. However, in our experiments on the Greek data, we found that the character level models performed worse than the word level models (90% vs. 96%). So far, it remains inconclusive which level is the best to use for text classification with Western languages. This suggests that perhaps combining the two levels would result in more robust and better results.

Overall Performance Compared to State-of-the-Art The results we have reported here are comparable to (or much better than) the start-of-the-art results on the same data sets. Our 96% accuracy on the Greek authorship attribution is much better than 72% reported in [23] which is based on a much more complicated analysis. Our 89.08% accuracy on the 20 Newsgroups data set is better than the best results 87.5% reported in [18] which is based on a combination of SVM and error correcting output coding (ECOC). Our 81.33% accuracy on the Chinese TREC data is at the same level as the results reported in [8] which is based on SVM, word segmentation, and feature selection. Overall, the chain augmented naive Bayes classifier works very well, even though it is a much simpler technique than these other methods and it is not specialized to any particular data set.

5.4   Relationship to Other Work

Using n-gram language models for text categorization has been considered in [3]. However, this work used n-grams as features for a traditional feature selection process, and then deployed classifiers based on calculating feature vector similarities. In our CAN Bayes models, we do not perform explicit feature selection at all (although of course we have to choose a few factors, such as the order n, smoothing technique and vocabulary size). Thus, in our case, all n-grams remain in the model, and their importance is implicitly considered by their contribution to perplexity.

Using language modeling techniques for text categorization is a relatively new research area in IR, although some work has already been done. Harper [24] used a PPM compression method [1] for text categorization where they seek a model that obtains the best compression on a new document. The PPM compression model deals with OOV words with an escape method which essentially is a weighted linear interpolation of several different n-gram models. Also, the use of n-gram models is related to the phrase weighting in IR [25]. An n-gram could be considered as a phrase and its weight is calculated by smoothed frequency counting.

Relaxing the independence assumption of the Naive Bayes model is a much researched idea in machine learning, and other researchers have considered learning tree augmented naive Bayes classifiers from data [7, 10]. However, learning the hidden tree structure is problematic, and our chain augmented naive Bayes model, being a special case of TAN Bayes, better preserves the simplicity of the naive Bayes classifier while introducing some of the additional dependencies of TAN Bayes.

6 Conclusions

We have presented a chain augmented naive Bayes classifier (CAN) based on statistical n-gram language modeling. Our CAN Bayes model captures dependence between adjacent attributes as a Markov chain. By using better smoothing techniques than Laplace smoothing we obtain further performance improvements. Our CAN Bayes modeling approach is able to work at either the character level or the word level, which provides language independent abilities to handle Eastern languages like Chinese and Japanese just as easily as Western languages like English or Greek. Our experimental results support the utility of our approach. We are currently investigating other data sets such as Reuters-21578 data set.

Acknowledgments

We thank E. Stamatatos for supplying us with the Greek authorship attribution data, Ji He for the Chinese topic detection data, the four anonymous reviewers for their constructive comments, and William Teahan for his clarification of Witten-Bell smoothing. Research supported by Bell University Labs and MITACS.

References

[1] T. Bell, J. Cleary and I. Witten. (1990). *Text Compression*. Prentice Hall.
[2] S. Chen and J. Goodman. (1998). An Empirical Study of Smoothing Techniques for Language Modeling. *Technical report*, TR-10-98, Harvard University.
[3] W. Cavnar, J. Trenkle. (1994). N-Gram-Based Text Categorization. In Proceedings of SDAIR-94.
[4] P. Domingos and M. Pazzani. (1997). Beyond Independence: Conditions for the Optimality of the Simple Bayesian Classifier. *Machine Learning*, 29, 103-130
[5] R. Duda and P. Hart. (1973). *Pattern Classification and Scene Analysis*. Wiley, NY.
[6] S. Eyheramendy, D. Lewis and D. Madigan. (2003). On the Naive Bayes Model for Text Categorization. To appear in *Artificial Intelligence & Statistics 2003*.
[7] N. Friedman, D. Geiger, and M. Goldszmidt. (1997). Bayesian Network Classifiers. In *Machine Learning* 29:131–163.
[8] J. He, A. Tan, and C. Tan. (2000). A Comparative Study on Chinese Text Categorization Methods. In *Proceedings of PRICAI'2000 International Workshop on Text and Web Mining*, p24-35.
[9] D. Hiemstra. (2001). Using Language Models for Information Retrieval. Ph.D. Thesis, Centre for Telematics and Information Technology, University of Twente.

[10] E. Keogh and M. Pazzanni. (1999). Learning Augmented Bayesian Classifiers: A Comparison of Distribution-based and Classification-based Approaches. In *Artificial Intelligence & Statistics 1999*

[11] K. Kwok. (1999). Employing Multiple Representations for Chinese Information Retrieval, *JASIS*, 50(8), 709-723.

[12] D. Lewis. (1998). Naive (Bayes) at Forty: The Independence Assumption in Information Retrieval. In *Proceedings ECML-98*.

[13] C. Manning, and H. Schütze. (1999). *Foundations of Statistical Natural Language Processing*, MIT Press, Cambridge, Massachusetts.

[14] A. McCallum and K. Nigam. (1998). A Comparison of Event Models for Naive Bayes Text Classification. In *Proceedings of AAAI-98 Workshop on "Learning for Text Categorization"*, AAAI Presss.

[15] H. Ney, U. Essen, and R. Kneser. (1994). On Structuring Probabilistic Dependencies in Stochastic Language Modeling. In *Comput. Speech and Lang.*, 8(1), 1-28.

[16] M. Pazzani and D. Billsus. (1997). Learning and Revising User Profiles: The identification of interesting web sites. *Machine Learning*, 27, 313-331.

[17] J. Ponte, W. Croft. (1998). A Language Modeling Approach to Information Retrieval. In *Proceedings of SIGIR1998*, 275-281.

[18] J. Rennie. (2001). Improving Multi-class Text Classification with Naive Bayes. *Master's Thesis*. M. I. T. AI Technical Report AITR-2001-004. 2001.

[19] I. Rish. (2001). An Empirical Study of the Naive Bayes Classifier. In *Proceedings of IJCAI-01 Workshop on Empirical Methods in Artificial Intelligence*.

[20] S. Robertson and K. Sparck Jones. (1976). Relevance Weighting of Search Terms. *JASIS*, 27, 129-146.

[21] S. Scott and S. Matwin. (1999). Feature Engineering for Text Classification. In *Proceedings of ICML' 99*, pp. 379-388.

[22] F. Sebastiani. (2002). Machine Learning in Automated Text Categorization. *ACM Computing Surveys*, 34(1):1-47, 2002.

[23] E. Stamatatos, N. Fakotakis and G. Kokkinakis. (2000). Automatic Text Categorization in Terms of Genre and Author. *Comput. Ling.*, 26(4), pp.471-495.

[24] W. Teahan and D. Harper. (2001). Using Compression-Based Language Models for Text Categorization. In *Proceedings of Workshop on LMIR*.

[25] A. Turpin and A. Moffat. (1999). Statistical Phrases for Vector-Space Information Retrieval. *Proceedings of SIGIR 1999*, pp. 309-310.

[26] Y. Yang. (1999). An Evaluation of Statistical Approaches to Text Categorization. *Information Retrieval*, Vol. 1, No. 1/2, pp. 67–88.

WebDocBall: A Graphical Visualization Tool for Web Search Results

Jesús Vegas[1], Pablo de la Fuente[1], and Fabio Crestani[2]

[1] Dpto. Informática, Universidad de Valladolid
Valladolid, Spain
{jvegas,pfuente}@infor.uva.es
[2] Dept. Computer and Information Sciences, University of Strathclyde
Glasgow, Scotland, UK
F.Crestani@cis.strath.ac.uk

Abstract. In the Web search process people often think that the hardest work is done by the search engines or by the directories which are entrusted with finding the Web pages. While this is partially true, a not less important part of the work is done by the user, who has to decide which page is relevant from the huge set of retrieved pages. In this paper we present a graphical visualisation tool aimed at helping users to determine the relevance of a Web page with respect to its structure. Such tool can help the user in the often tedious task of deciding which page is relevant enough to deserve a visit.

1 Introduction

Searching the Web is one of the most frequent tasks nowadays. Unfortunately, it is often also one of the most frustrating tasks. The user gets little help from a Web search engines or a Web directories. The former lacks precision, while the scope of the latter is often too small. The only tool the user has to initiate the search is usually just a small set of query terms and, after the query process, the user is left with a huge amount of information to process manually. While much work has been devoted to design and develop algorithms to improve the query process, little has been done to help the users to find the needle in this *"document stack"*. In the remainder of this paper we will use the terms We page and document interchangeably.

According to Shneiderman, the search process can be divided in four phases [15]:

1. formulation: the information need is expressed in the query.
2. search: the query is submitted to the search engine and is processed.
3. reviewing of the results: the retrieved document set obtained is reviewed by the user.
4. refinement: the query is reformulated in a manual or semi-automatic way to try to improve the retrieval results.

F. Sebastiani (Ed.): ECIR 2003, LNCS 2633, pp. 351–362, 2003.

The third phase is where *information visualisation* can help the user improve the effectiveness of the manual task of browsing the results set. In this phase, the user has to identify a relevance relation between the query he formulated and the results obtained. Usually, the user sees a list of URLs and titles of documents with little more information about them, so this task is hard and tedious and, frequently, the user has to wait several seconds to see that a page is not interesting. It is clear that this is the phase where the user needs assistance to identify potentially relevant documents and discard those that are not useful. This phase is very important, since it has a major impact on the user satisfaction with a system.

The areas of interest in this phase are three [12]: set level, site level and document level.

At the set level the objective is to represent the entire set of results. Several techniques has been developed, such as, for example, scatter-plots and star-fields [1], maps or landscapes metaphors [5], wall metaphor [11], or cone trees [13].

The Web site level tries to locate the retrieved documents in the Web site structure, since the user could be interested in Web sites, not just Web pages. It also tries to tackle the "lost in hyperspace" problem [10].

At the document level, the objective is to help the user to decide if one page is relevant to his/her information need or not. Our work is directed at this level. For this task, we propose a graphical tool to assist the user in the review phase. The visualisation tool displays to the user the structure of the HTML document and the estimated relevance of its parts with respect the query. The tool is based on two assumptions: pages have a hierarchical structure, and the result set can be post-processed. Both assumptions can be easily satisfied.

The paper is structured as follows. In Section 2 we review related work, concentrating on visualisation tools used at document level. In Section 3 we introduce a new tool for the visualisation of retrieved documents in Web searches. In addition, we compare our proposal with related work. A description of a Web search engine that incorporated the visualisation tool is reported in Section 4. Finally, Section 5 reports our initial conclusions and provides an outline of future work.

2   Information Visualisation Tools at the Document Level

The document level is the one in which the user analyse the answers obtained from a Web search engine. Here, a large number of pages (the actual number can vary from one to thousands) are presented to the user, who has the hard task of identifying those relevant to his/her information need. Usually, the user is provided with little help for this task. The most important tools designed for this tasks are Tilebars [9], relevance curves [14] and the thumbnail view [4].

Before we present and compare about these three tools, we need a framework for comparison. In order to build it, we need to answer the following question: what does the user need when he is browsing at the document level a result set obtained from a Web query? An established answer, to which we fully subscribe,

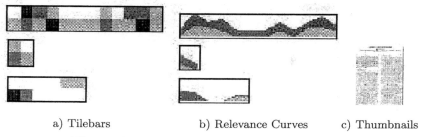

a) Tilebars   b) Relevance Curves   c) Thumbnails

Fig. 1. Tilebars, Relevance Curves and Thumbnails

is that the user not only needs to know about the relevance of a document, but also "where" the document is relevant.

The vast majority of documents that are available on the Web have some hierarchical structure [2], which can either be explicit, like in XML documents, or implicit, like in HTML documents. We argue that the user could get very quickly an idea of the actual relevance of a document by looking at the way the parts estimated to be relevant are distributed in it. In addition, the user can be interested not only about the concentration of relevant parts, but in what are the hierarchical relations among them. Another important information about the retrieved document is its type. This can be inferred from the structure of the document. The user could be more interested in a document with a very flat structure, than in one with a more deep structured. Another important aspect of the retrieved documents is its size. A short letter and an extend technical report are clearly not the same.

So, there are three aspects that can help the user analyse the results of a Web search at document level: the relevance the document and how this is distributed on the document parts, the structure of the document, and the size of the document.

Figure 1 shows document representations using Tilebars, relevance curves and thumbnail. The first two representations show the relevance of each passage or segment of the text, using a row for each query term. The size of the documents is represented by the Tilebars or the relevance curve size. The passages can correspond to paragraphs or sections, or units of fixed arbitrary length. Both Tilebars and relevance curves show whether and where the document is relevant. However, the use of the structure is only done in a linear way, being it impossible to appreciate the hierarchical relations between the structure elements found in the document. The third document representation is the thumbnail. In this case no information about the size or the structure of the document is provided. The only information represented is related to the appearance of the document. Therefore, a thumbnail representation can complement the two first representations and it is useful when the user works frequently with the same document set and can recognise a document by its thumbnail view. The only information about the structure that the user can obtain from this representation is the information that can be inferred from the appearance of the different elements in the document, and this is not enough, since the user also needs information about the relevance of the different parts of the document.

3 The Webdocball

In this paper we present a visual metaphor that can explain the user why a Web document was retrieved by a Web search engine, by showing where in the structure of the document estimated relevance lies. We call this metaphor *Webdocball*, in analogy to the Docball metaphor presented in [16], of which it is an extension in the Web domain. This visualisation element is included in a prototype system that works on top of a Web search engine by post-processing the results obtained from the search engine to allow the user to browse the result set using different representations of the documents. Figure 2 shows the Webdocball representation of a Web document.

In the Webdocball, each ring represents a level of the hierarchical structure of the document, where the centre represents the entire document. In a ring, the regions represent the structural elements in that level. Inside a ring elements are presented in a clockwise order.

Each region in the Webdocball is coloured with regard to its estimated relevance: a hotter colour indicates more relevance, a colder colour represents less relevance. White regions have been estimated to be not relevant.

Regions are "clickable", so that the Webdocball can be used as a navigation tool of the Web document.

The Webdocball representation can be considered as the representation of a tree structure, which depends on two parameters: the number of elements in the deeper structural level (the number of leaves) and the number of structural levels in the document (the height of the tree).

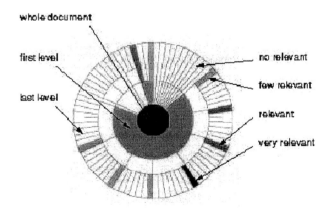

Fig. 2. The Webdocball metaphor

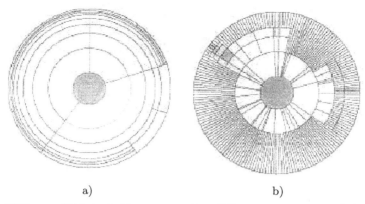

a)   b)

Fig. 3. Different Webdocballs representing different structures of Web documents

A Web document with a large number of elements will have very narrow regions in the corresponding rings. The regions corresponding to leaves are represented from their level ring to the exterior ring. In addition, in order to enable a clear representation of Web documents with many levels, the height of the rings decreases the deeper the structural level it represents. This feature was not present in the Docball representation. Such feature can be seen in Figure 3, where different Webdocball are shown with respect to the number of leaves and structural levels of the document represented. The Webdocball (a) represents a Web document with a deep structural hierarchy, whereas the document represented by the Webdocball (b) is more flat with respect the its structure, but has a larger number of leaves.

3.1 Comparing Webdocball and Tilebars Representations

In this section, we compare the Webdocball and the Tilebars representations. We do not consider relevance curves because they can be considered just a version of Tilebars. Also, we do not consider Thumbnails because they do not represent structural information.

A Webdocball exploits the structure of the documents to show the estimated relevance of the documents, in a similar way to Tilebars, but it goes one step beyond Tilebars. In Tilebars the structure is represented in a linear way, and it is impossible to extract the hierarchical relations between the structural elements as it can be done in the Webdocball representation. So, a Webdocball allows to visualise the structural complexity of the retrieved documents. However, it should be recognised that Tilebars enable the representation of the length of the document, something that is not possible in the Webdocball representation.

Another difference is that in Tilebars, the relevance of each single query term is displayed, whereas a Webdocball represents the relevance of all the query

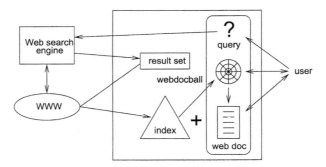

Fig. 4. Architecture of the Webdocball system

terms. In the case of few query terms Tilebars can be better that Webdocballs. However, in the case of many query terms, Webdocballs are clearly better. In fact, Tilebars cannot manage query expansion by relevance feedback process, where many query terms are often added to the query. In such case, Webdocballs are more useful, since the relevance representation is independent of the number of query terms.

4   A Description of the Webdocball System

The Webdocball visualisation tool is part of a prototype Web search engine we have developed on top of an existing search engine. The prototype is written in Java and the Webdocball visualisation tool has been developed using the SVG (*Scalable Vector Graphics*) standard [6]. The Web search engine is built on top of Google using the Google Web APIs[1]. Google uses the SOAP (*Simple Object Access Protocol*) [8] and the WSDL (*Web Services Description Language*) [7] standards, enabling us to use Java for the prototype development.

Since a Webdocball represents the estimated relevance of a Web document at each structural level, we need to be able to determine the structure of the Web document, and to estimate the relevance of each structural element with respect to the query. To achieve this, we need to post-process the results set obtained from Google to obtain the information needed to draw the Webdocball. All of this can be seen in the diagrammatic system architecture shown in Figure 4.

The query process is the usual one: the system enables the user to submit a natural language query, which is processed by Google. The search results are presented to the user as a list of Web documents with associated Webdocball representations. An example of result list is presented in Figure 5.

In the result list each document is presented with its KWIC (*Key Word in Context*), the link to the site where is the document, and the correspondent Webdocball. The Webdocball is connected with a post-processed form of the

---

[1] Google Web APIs are a free beta service and are available for non-commercial use only at |http://www.google.com/apis—

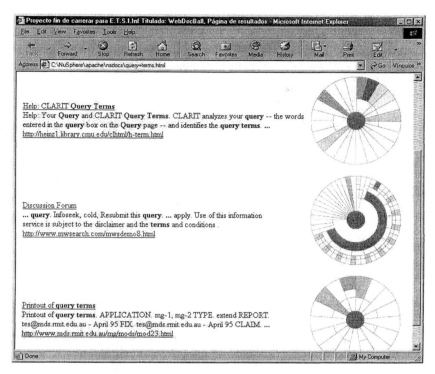

Fig. 5. Results in the Webdocball system

original Web document which is stored in a local cache. The Webdocball is then a simplified version of the Web document that shows to the user information related to the document structure, which is coloured in relation to the estimated relevance degree of each element. From this post-processed document, the user can visit the original one, either by accessing the system cache or by going to the real Web page following the link.

In the next sections, we are going to explain the two most interesting phases of the process of construction of a Webdocball representation: the document structure extraction and estimation of relevance of each structural element of the document.

4.1 Extracting the Structure of a Web Document

Documents on the Web are of many different types, but mostly they are HTML documents [2], although XML, PDF and other types of documents can also be found. As explained in the previous section, in order to construct a Webdocball we need to determine the structure of Web documents. To obtain this from XML documents is very easy, since the document structure is expressed explicitly. Unfortunately, the number of XML documents available on the Web is very limited, and most documents are in HTML, so we have to extract structural information from HTML labels. We found several problems in this process, the main two being that HTML labels are used with no discipline by the Web documents authors, and that the HTML labels express structural information in an implicit way. Therefore we need to answer these two questions: which are the most common HTML labels in the Web and what are their structural significance.

To answer these questions we build a random URL generator using the Google search engine. We retrieved via Google, using a random set of words, 30,000 distinct HTML pages, comprising 13,124,339 HTML (labels). From an analysis of the results we found that the most often used labels were, in decreasing order: content, p-implied, td, br, tr, img, p, comment, table, span, li, script, div. meta, input, title, center, hr, ul, body, html, head, form, link, select, frame, object, and ol.

In addition, we obtained some important information about the structure of HTML documents:

- The average number of structural levels in HTML documents is 10.66.
- Tables are widely used, with an average of 10 tables per page.
- The paragraph label (p) is used 13 times per page on average.
- The number of frames, forms and links per page is very low, less than 2, on average.

From the previous label set, we have chosen to consider those labels that have structural meaning, that is, labels used in Web documents to express hierarchical relations. These were the following:

- tables: table, tr, and td.
- lists: ul, ol, and li
- paragraphs: p, and br.

We do not use the main structural level labels html, body and head because there is only one of each per page and they do not add structural information that could be used to discriminate between the retrieved documents.

To understand how a Web document is represented using a Webdocball metaphor, let us consider the Web document shown in Figure 6, as it can be viewed using the Netscape We page editor (the boxed labels represent the HTML labels). This is a page of an introduction course in IR. The document is composed by four tables (title, navigational tool, content, and foot). The tables are used to organise the content in the Web page. The most interesting table is the content one, because its left column is used to index the content in the right column. In this right column, there are several HTML elements (paragraphs and lists, mainly) with structural meaning. This structural information can be seen in the Webdocball depicted in Figure 7.

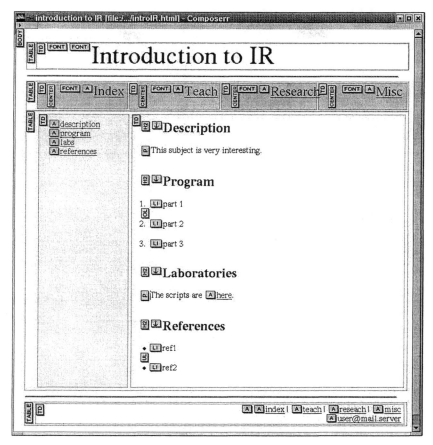

Fig. 6. Example of Web document

4.2 Determining the Relevance of a Structural Element

In order to colour the Webdocball we need to estimate the relevance of each structural element of the Web document with respect to the query. To do this we use a modified version of the Vector Space Model (VSM). The original VSM is not suitable to index Web documents, because it does not consider important aspects of the Web like the hyperlinks and other information useful to index the Web documents with success (see [3] for more information about indexing the Web). However, it can still be very useful for our very specific purpose.

The model we propose considers a Web document as the collection of items to index, where the elements of the document are the items to index. In a Web document there are two types of elements, content (text) and structural elements (labels). We can transform a Web document in a collection of items to index in a two phase process: first each content element is indexed using the VSM, then the indexing weight of the content elements are spread to the top of the

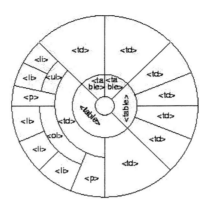

Fig. 7. The Webdocball of the Web document in the Figure 6

structural hierarchy (i.e. towards the centre of the Webdocball) as indicated by the structural elements. This process is more formally explained in the following.

Let us assume that a Web documents d is composed of a hierarchy S of m structural elements s, and can be viewed as $d=\{s_1, s_2, \ldots, s_m\}$. Two structural elements are related by an inclusion relation, $s_i \subset s_j$ when s_i is included in s_j according to the hierarchy S. The inclusion relation is called directed, denoted by $\subset'$, if $\not\exists s_k \ / \ s_i \subset s_k \subset s_j$. A structural element will be a leaf element when there is no element included in it.

A structural element s_j in a document will have a weight $w_{i,j} \geq 0$ with respect to the index term k_i calculated as follows:

$$
w_{i,j} = \begin{cases} \frac{freq_{i,j}}{max_l frec_{l,j}} \times \log \frac{m}{m_i} & \text{if } s_j \text{ is a leaf} \\ \\ \sum_{\forall s_l \subset' s_j} w_{i,l} & \text{if } s_j \text{ is not a leaf} \end{cases}
\tag{1}
$$

Therefore, as in the VSM, the weight vector of a structural element s_j in the document d is represented by $s_j = \{w_{1,j}, w_{2,j}, \ldots, w_{t,j}\}$.

The similarity between the query vector and the structural elements vector can be calculated using cosine correlation, as it is done in the standard VSM.

5   Conclusions and Future Work

We have presented a graphical tool for the visualisation of Web documents retrieved by a Web search. The proposed tool uses the structure of the Web documents to show the user where estimated relevance is located inside the document. In addition, we have developed a prototype system, based on Google, that retrieves documents from the Web and uses a modified version of the Vector Space Model to estimate the relevance of each structural element of Web documents to a user query.

Currently, we are carrying out an evaluation of the visualisation tool. Preliminary tests have been satisfactory with respect the appearance and utility of the visual metaphor, as it was already found for the Docball metaphor [16]. The most serious drawback, at this stage, is the answer time of the system, which it is very high due to the amount of post-processing work needed to calculate and to draw the Webdocball representation. We are currently working to reduce the time necessary to do that.

The work presented in this paper is part of a wider work aimed at the design, implementation, and evaluation of a complete system for Web retrieval. The next step in this project will be to answer the question of where retrieved documents are located in a Web site. We plan to use the same visual metaphor to represent the search results at the set, site and document level, to help the user in the Web searching process.

Acknowledgements

Large part of the implementation of the GUI has been carried out by Javier López González, student at the University of Valladolid.

This work was partially supported by the Spanish CICYT program (project TEL99-0335-C04).

References

[1] C. Ahlberg and B. Shneiderman. Visual Information Seeking: Tight Coupling of Dynamic Query Filters with Starfield Displays. In *Human Factors in Computing Systems. Conference Proceedings CHI'94*, pages 313–317, 1994.

[2] R. Baeza-Yates and B. Ribeiro-Neto. *Modern Information Retrieval*. Addison-Wesley, 1999.

[3] S. Brin and L. Page. The Anatomy of a Large-Scale Hypertextual Web Search Engine. *Computer Networks and ISDN Systems*, 30(1–7):107–117, 1998.

[4] S. K. Card, G. G. Robertson, and W. York. The Webbook and the Web Forager: an Information Workspace for the World Wide Web. In *Proceedings of the Conference on Human Factors in Computing Systems CHI'96*, 1996.

[5] M. Chalmers. Using a Landscape to Represent a Corpus of Documents. In *COSIT'93*, 1993.

[6] SVG Working Group. *Scalable Vector Graphics (SVG) 1.1 Specification. Candidate Recommendation*, 2002. http://www.w3.org/TR/2002/CR-SVG11-20020430/.

[7] Web Services Description Working Group. *Web Services Description Language (WSDL) Version 1.2. Working Draft.* http://www.w3.org/TR/2002/WD-wsdl12-20020709/.

[8] XML Protocol Working Group. *SOAP Version 1.2 Part 0: Primer. Working Draft.* http://www.w3.org/TR/2002/WD-soap12-part0-20020626/.

[9] M. A. Hearst. Visualization of Term Distribution Information in Full Text Information Access. In *ACM SIGCHI Conference on Human Factors in Computing Systems (CHI)*, 1995.

[10] J. Lamping and R. Rao. Laying out and Visualizing Large Trees using a Hyperbolic Space. In *ACM Symposium on User Interface Software and Technology*, pages 13–14, 1994.

[11] J. D. Mackinlay, G. G. Robertson, and S. K. Card. The Perspective Wall: Detail and Context Smoothly Integrated. In *CHI'91*, pages 173–179, 1991.

[12] T. M. Mann. Visualization of WWW Search Results. In *DEXA Workshop*, pages 264–268, 1999.

[13] G. Robertson, J. Mackinlay, and S. Card. Cone trees: Animated 3d Visualizations of Hierarchical Information. In *Conference on Human Factors in Computing Systems CHI'91*, pages 189–194, 1991.

[14] Arisem S. A. http://www.arisem.com.

[15] B. Shneiderman. *Designing the User Interface. Strategies for Effective Human-Computer Interaction*. Addison-Wesley, 1992.

[16] J. Vegas, P. de la Fuente, and F. Crestani. A Graphical User Interface for Structured Document Retrieval. In *ECIR 02, BCS-IRSG European Colloquium in Information Retrieval Research*, pages 268–283, March 2002.

Relevance feedback for content-based image retrieval: what can three mouse clicks achieve?

Daniel C Heesch and Stefan Rüger

Department of Computing
South Kensington Campus, Imperial College London
London SW7 2AZ, England
{dh500,s.rueger}@imperial.ac.uk

Abstract. We introduce a novel relevance feedback method for content-based image retrieval and demonstrate its effectiveness using a subset of the Corel Gallery photograph collection and five low-level colour descriptors. Relevance information is translated into updated, analytically computed descriptor weights and a new query representation, and thus the system combines movement in both query and weight space. To assess the effectiveness of relevance feedback, we first determine the weight set that is optimal on average for a range of possible queries. The resulting multiple-descriptor retrieval model yields significant performance gains over all the single-descriptor models and provides the benchmark against which we measure the additional improvement through relevance feedback. We model a number of scenarios of user-system interaction that differ with respect to the precise type and the extent of relevance feedback. In all scenarios, relevance feedback leads to a significant improvement of retrieval performance suggesting that feedback-induced performance gain is a robust phenomenon. Based on a comparison of the different scenarios, we identify optimal interaction models that yield high performance gains at a low operational cost for the user. To support the proposed relevant feedback technique we developed a novel presentation paradigm that allows relevance to be treated as a continuous variable.

1 Introduction

The efficient retrieval of images based on automatically extracted image data has become of great interest with a number of application areas ranging from remote sensing to medical diagnosis. Although the number of commercial and research systems addressing content-based image retrieval (CBIR) is growing rapidly, the area is still far from reaching maturity. Further progress is currently impeded by two fundamental problems. The first problem arises from the difficulty of inferring image meaning from primitive image features such as texture, colour and shape. It seems that a high-level representation of the image that speaks the same language as the user cannot be built from intrinsic image data alone but that a significant amount of world knowledge is essential. This problem which is commonly referred to as the semantic gap is quite distinct from, although

F. Sebastiani (Ed.): ECIR 2003, LNCS 2633, pp. 363-376, 2003.

sometimes confused with, the second problem which results from the semantic ambiguity inherent in images. Even if it were possible to derive image meaning from primitive features, and thus to bridge the semantic gap, the problem of polysemy would persist for it would still not be clear *a priori* which of the many high-level representations a user has in mind when querying a database with an example image.

User-system interaction is a promising step towards tackling the above challenges for it can furnish the system with more information than is contained in the image itself. In the earlier days of CBIR, interaction was limited to the user specifying various system settings such as the particular features to be employed for retrieval. This type of interaction binds the user to a primitive level that becomes very obscure once more sophisticated image descriptors are used. While most of the commercial systems are still limited to this type of interaction, a number of ideas have been developed with the aim of eliciting additional information from the user. The mechanisms that have emerged include *inter alia* supervised learning prior to retrieval [9], interactive region segmentation [4], and interactive image database annotation [12]. The mechanism which holds most promise of improving the efficiency of image retrieval systems is relevance feedback, which has long been applied successfully in the domain of traditional information retrieval [19]. In the context of CBIR, relevance feedback typically involves labelling a subset of retrieved images according to their perceived relevance. Unlike with text documents, looking at images and deciding whether they are relevant to a query constitutes a relatively small mental load. A number of different techniques have been used for relevance feedback. They broadly fall into one of two categories [1], namely (i) query point moving and (ii) weight update. The first comprises all those methods that alter the query representation [11]. The idea is to find not the best aggregation of image features but a representation of the query that renders it more similar to objects the user has marked out as relevant or, likewise, more dissimilar to non-relevant objects (e.g. [7,14,8]). Given a set of features, the similarity values derived for individual features are aggregated to yield an overall measure of similarity. Aggregation is often achieved by computing a weighted average of individual similarity values. Weight update techniques exploit relevance feedback to infer which features (and which representations thereof) best capture the user's perception of similarity. Examples include cluster analysis of the images using Kohonen's Learning Vector Quantization [23], non-parametric density estimation [11], the use of inverted files for feature selection [21], Bayesian Networks [3, 11], a statistical analysis of the feature distributions of relevant images [2], variance analysis [18] and analytic global optimisation [17].

In our system, we combine the idea of query point moving with weight update. Retrieved images are placed on the screen such that their distances to the centre represent their dissimilarities to the query image (see Figure 1). By moving an image closer to the centre or further away, the user indicates to what extent the image matches his information need. Because this match is given in terms of the chosen distance from the centre and is thus effectively continuous, this method of relevance feedback is likely to provide a more accurate representation of the user's idea of similarity. With the similarity function being a simple convex weight combination of basic feature similarity functions, new weight coefficients can be computed in such a way that the user's perception of similarity with respect to the query is as close as possible to the similarities computed by the system. The similarity model chosen allows us to compute the new weights analytically using a least squared error approach.

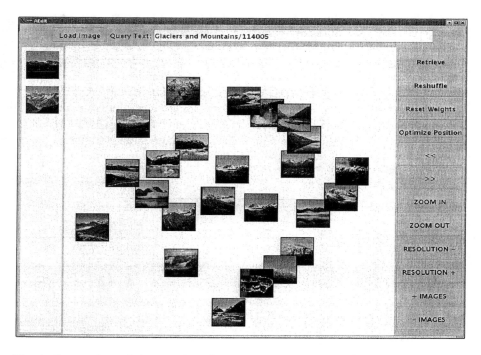

Fig. 1. Screen shot of the user interface. The query consists two images of snow-peaked mountains, depicted at the top of the leftmost canvas. The display shows the 30 top-ranked images. The distance of a retrieved image from the centre is proportional to its dissimilarity to the query as computed by the system. Subject to this distance constraint, images are arranged such that overlap is minimized.

Operationally, the relevance feedback approach of the present study is similar to [20], where the interface consists in a projection of the image objects in feature space onto the two dimensional plane using a distance metric derived from the user's interaction with the display. Instead of querying a database with an example, the user is invited to explore the database by changing the projection operator. This is done by marking out relevant and non-relevant images as well as by moving images closer to or further away from other images. In our system, rather than browsing the database, the user queries the database with an example image with the semantics of the interaction being kept deliberately simple.

While in [20] the arrangement of images on the screen is such that distances inform about respective dissimilarities, we consider and display dissimilarity of an image with respect to a query. This also differentiates our visualization from [15], which uses multi-dimensional scaling to arrange similar images close to one another without reference to a query.

A challenge pertaining to relevance feedback techniques lies in striking a balance between simplicity and efficiency. Ideally, feedback results in a significant gain in retrieval performance after a few iterations with a minimum of user operations. With this in mind, we have modelled different scenarios of relevance feedback that vary in the quantity and quality of the interaction. It turns out that the efficiency of relevance feedback is a general outcome across a broad range of interaction scenarios and, more importantly, that it is possible to define conditions under which the system rewards even the most partial feedback.

In summary, the contributions of this papers to CBIR are essentially twofold. Firstly, we describe a relevance feedback technique that is based on merging query expansion with analytical weight update. The novelty lies in the utilisation of continuous relevance feedback and the use of a squared error score function for weight update. To support this relevance feedback technique, we develop a simple yet highly expressive way of presenting the user with the retrieved images. Secondly, we model different scenarios of user-system interaction in order to formally quantify the improvement in retrieval performance that can be achieved through relevance feedback and to identify interaction models that are both user-friendly and efficient.

The paper is divided into four sections. Section 2 describes the five colour descriptors and introduces the relevance feedback technique along with the different interaction models used for evaluation. The results are presented in Section 3 and discussed in Section 4.

2   Methods

2.1   Colour descriptors

Descriptors for colour representation were chosen with the new MPEG-7 standard in mind. Both the colour structure descriptor (defined in the HMMD colour space) and the colour cluster descriptor (defined in the YCbCr colour space) are part of the MPEG-7 specification. It was also desirable to keep the set of descriptors sufficiently distinct from one another with the aim of representing different aspects of the image colour. Choosing descriptors from different colour spaces and allowing for different spatial emphasis appeared to be sensible ways to reduce representational overlap and motivated the addition of the standard HSV colour histogram and a local variant thereof.

HSV colour histogram We use a uniform quantization of the HSV colour space using 8 bins for each dimension. Two different descriptors are defined. One is a global histogram consisting of $8 \times 8 \times 8$ colour bins with loss of spatial information, while the other consists of an array of five local histograms each of size $8 \times 8 \times 8$, with the first four covering non-overlapping quarters of the image and the fifth covering the central 25% of the image. This second descriptor allows central emphasis and partial preservation of local colour information.

HMMD colour histogram The new HMMD (Hue, Min, Max, Diff) colour space, which is supported by MPEG-7, derives from the HSV and RGB spaces. The Hue component is as in the HSV space, and Max and Min denote the maximum and minimum among the R, G, and B values, respectively. The Diff component is defined as the difference between Max and Min. Three components suffice to uniquely locate a point in the colour space and thus the space is effectively three-dimensional. Following the MPEG-7 standard, we quantize the HMMD non-uniformly into 184 bins with the three dimensions being Hue, Sum and Diff (Sum being defined as (Max+Min)/2). For details about quantization see [10]. Two descriptors are defined with respect to the HMMD colour space. The first is a standard global histogram, the second, CSD or colour structure descriptor, is described in more detail below.

Colour Structure Descriptor This descriptor lends itself well for capturing local colour structure in an image. A 8×8 structuring window is used to slide over the image. Each of the 184 bins of the HMMD histogram contains the number of window positions for which there is at least one pixel falling into the bin under consideration. This descriptor is capable of discriminating between images that have the same global colour distribution but different local colour structures. Although the number of samples in the 8×8 structuring window is kept constant (64), the spatial extent of the window differs depending on the size of the image. Thus, for larger images appropriate sub-sampling is employed to keep the total number of samples per image roughly constant. The bin values are normalized by dividing by the number of locations of the structuring window and fall in the range $[0.0, 1.0]$. (see [10] for details)

Colour Cluster Descriptor The colour cluster descriptor is similar to the dominant colour descriptor defined as part of the MPEG-7 standard [10]. It exploits the fact that for most images across a wide range of applications, a small set of colours are sufficient to represent the global colour content. The colour space chosen is the perceptually uniform YCbCr colour space where

$$
\begin{aligned}
Y &= 0.299\ R + 0.587\ G + 0.114\ B \\
Cb &= -0.169\ R - 0.331\ G + 0.500\ B \\
Cr &= 0.500\ R - 0.419\ G - 0.081\ B
\end{aligned}
$$

With the issue of extraction efficiency in mind, the representative colours are determined by first computing a traditional colour histogram and then successively merging those non-empty bins which are closest in the colour space. An alternative with greater complexity consists in performing agglomerative clustering starting at the level of individual pixels [5].

2.2   Combination of image descriptors

Descriptors are integrated such that the overall similarity between two images Q and T is given by a convex combination

$$S(Q,T) = \sum_d w_d \sigma_d(Q,T)$$

of the similarity values calculated for each descriptor. Here $\sigma_d(Q,T)$ denotes the similarity for feature d of images Q and T using a possibly feature-specific similarity function and weighted by a factor $w_d \in [0,1]$ with $0 \le w_d \le 1$ and $\sum_d w_d = 1$. For all but the colour cluster descriptor we use as a similarity metric the l_1 norm which has successfully been employed in the past for histogram comparisons.

$$||h_1 - h_2||_1 = \sum_{i=0}^{N-1} |h_1(i) - h_2(i)|$$

where h_1 and h_2 are the two histograms being compared. For comparing two sets of colour clusters we compute the earth mover's distance as used in [16].

We allow the user to add more objects to the original query. With $Q = \{Q_1, Q_2, \ldots Q_n\}$ defining the set of images in a query, we define the similarity between a query and a database object as

$$S(Q,T) = \sum_d w_d \frac{1}{n} \sum_i \sigma_d(Q_i, T)$$

2.3   Evaluation

It needs little emphasis that claims regarding improved retrieval performance can only be validated using formal evaluation methods. Although evaluation is arguably more problematic in image retrieval as a result of semantic ambiguity, evaluation techniques from information retrieval may still be used profitably when applied with care. For the present study we deploy the two measures *recall* and *precision* to measure retrieval performance for *category searches* [11, 3]. The image collection used for testing and training is derived from the Corel Gallery 380,000 package, which contains some 30,000 photographs, sorted into 450 categories. From the set of categories that contain more than 40 images, we randomly selected 47 categories and for each category 40 images leaving us with a total of 1880 images. This image corpus is then split into two non-overlapping training and test sets. Each of these sets contains 20 images of each of the 47 categories. To find an initial weight set for the relevance feedback runs, we use each object in the training set as a query and measure retrieval performance when retrieving from the remaining set of training images. We then average performance over all queries and repeat the procedure for different weight sets. The weight set for which the average performance is maximal is then chosen as the initial weight set. The relevance feedback runs are carried out with all objects of the test set used as a query. Retrieval is from the remaining set of test images. For each query, we determine the baseline performance using the initial weight set determined on the training set and then measure the gain (or loss) in retrieval performance after repeatedly providing relevance feedback. Performance is measured by first determining the precision-against-recall values as described in [22] and then deriving from these the *mean average precision* as a more concise performance measure.

2.4   Relevance feedback

The mean average precision value for the multiple-descriptor model is derived by averaging over all queries of the training set. It appears reasonable to assume that the optimum weight set for *any particular* query is different from the weight set derived in 3.1 and this difference between *query* optimum and *query set* optimum should be greater for heterogeneous image collections (e.g. Corel Gallery). In the context of sketch retrieval, previous experiments in which we established the optimum weight sets for a number of smaller subsets of a sketch database confirm that the optimum does vary substantially between queries [6]. It is hoped that relevance feedback allows us to move from the *query set* optimum to each individual *query* optimum within a few iterations.

With five descriptor weights and the convexity assumption, our system has effectively four degrees of freedom that can be exploited through relevance feedback. Our retrieval system plots thumbnails of retrieved images $T_1, T_2, \ldots$ such that their respective distance from the centre of the screen is proportional to the dissimilarity $1 - S(Q, T_i)$ of thumbnail T_i to the query Q. Using this semantics of thumbnail location, the user can provide relevance feedback by moving thumbnails closer to the centre (indicating greater relevance than the system predicted) or further away (indicating less relevance). As a shortcut, clicking once on a thumbnail marks the image as highly relevant and places it in the centre, while double-clicking marks it as highly non-relevant and places it in the periphery. Effectively, the user provides a real-valued vector of distances $D_u(Q, T_i)$ which, in general, differ from the distances

$$D_s(Q, T_i) = 1 - \sum_d w_d \sigma_d(Q, T_i) \qquad (1)$$

which the system computes using the set of weights w_d. The sum of squared errors

$$\mathrm{SSE}(w) = \sum_{i=1}^{N} [D_s(Q, T_i) - D_u(Q, T_i)]^2$$

$$= \sum_{i=1}^{N} \left[1 - \sum_d w_d \sigma_d(Q, T_i) - D_u(Q, T_i) \right]^2 \qquad (2)$$

gives rise to an optimisation problem for the weights w_d such that (2) is minimized under the constraint of convexity. Using one Lagrangian multiplier we arrive at an analytical solution w' for the weight set which changes the similarity function. We get a different ranking of images in the database and, with (1), a new layout for the new set of top-retrieved images on the screen.

2.5   Modelling user-system interaction

We can envisage an "ideal" user who provides maximum feedback by interacting with each of the displayed images. This is a plausible scenario when the number of displayed images is small but is of little practical interest as the number of images is increasing. Rather, we shall assume that the user will want to limit her or his feedback to a subset of images. To evaluate the effect of relevance feedback on retrieval performance and, more specifically, to identify efficient ways of providing feedback, we model four different interaction scenarios. All four scenarios are based on the assumption that the similarity judgment of the user is fixed. In particular, an image is relevant if it is in the same category as the query and it is not relevant otherwise. Each scenario now defines a different set S of images with which the user interacts as follows:

W±   : Indifferent selection, the user interacts with a random subset of displayed images
W−   : Negative selection, the user only interacts with a random subset of irrelevant displayed images
W+   : Positive selection, the user only interacts with a random subset of relevant displayed images
QW+ : Same as Scenario W+, except that in addition to changing the distances between relevant objects and the query, the relevant objects are included in the query

For all scenarios we display the top 30 images as seen in Figure 1. The four models differ in the quality of user feedback. To model the extent to which feedback is given, we vary the maximum number (s) of images the user may interact with. Note that in Scenarios W−, W+ and QW+, it is $|S| \leq s$ since there might not be enough relevant or irrelevant images on display, while in Scenario W± it is $|S| = s$.

3   Results

3.1   Tuning the system for optimal *on average* performance

We evaluated retrieval performance for each of the five descriptors individually and used a genetic algorithm to find the best combination of descriptors (i.e. the weights set that maximizes *on average* performance on the training set as detailed in section 2.3). The precision-against-recall graphs for all five single-descriptor models and the best multiple-descriptor model are depicted in Figure 2. Performance of the best multiple-descriptor model improved significantly over that of the best single-descriptor model (paired t-test, $p < 0.05$) with the optimized weights being as follows: 0.526 (HSVN = global HSV histogram), 0.364 (HSVF = local HSV histogram), 0.032 (CSD = Colour Structure Descriptor), 0.076 (HMMD Descriptor) and 0.002 (Colour Cluster Descriptor). This weight set is used to define the baseline for subsequent relevance feedback experiments.

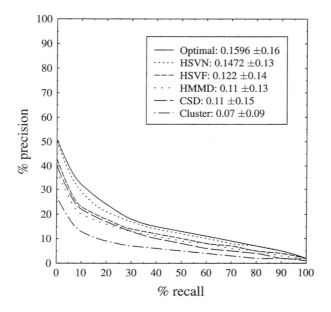

Fig. 2. Precision-against-recall graphs for the five single descriptor models and the optimal multiple-descriptor model. The box shows for each model its mean average precision ± one standard deviation.

3.2   Evaluation of relevance feedback

Our principal interest lies in investigating the possibility of using relevance feedback to increase retrieval performance beyond the level of the multiple-descriptor model. We here show the results for the four scenarios introduced in 2.5. The results are given in terms of relative percentage differences. A value of, say, 20%, implies an increase of mean average precision by 20% relative to the baseline performance.

Figure 3 summarizes the results for scenario W±, in which relevance feedback is given on both relevant and non-relevant images with the maximum number of images on which relevance feedback is given varying between 3 and 10. As is evident from the graphs, gains are higher when relevance feedback is more exhaustive. The difference becomes smaller after a few iterations, with all gain curves levelling off after around four iterations.

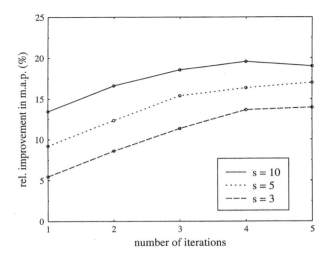

Fig. 3. Increase in mean average precision under Scenario W± with varying *s*

Scenarios W− and W+ are designed to investigate the impact of negative and positive feedback, respectively, on retrieval performance. Intuitively, the gain should be considerably lower under Scenario W− than under either scenario Scenario W± or Scenario W+ for it appears very difficult to infer what an object *is* from information about what it is not. This is precisely what Figure 4 tells us. Relevance feedback does improve performance but this improvement, at least over the first few iterations, is marginal. As before, the efficiency of relevance feedback increases with the extent of the interaction (*s*) and at least for the first iteration this relationship is nearly linear. Note that Scenario W± only differs from Scenario W− by allowing positive feedback and, thus, the difference between the results from Scenario W± and Scenario W− may in some sense be attributed to the additional effect of positive feedback. Comparison of the two scenarios already suggests, therefore, that positive feedback alone may be superior to either alternatives.

Figure 5 now shows the result for positive feedback. Already after one iteration, gains lie between 15% and 22% depending on the extent of the interaction. Unlike in the previous two scenarios, continued feedback does not provide further improvements which, lacking additional data, may suggest that the system has found the optimal weight set after one or two iteration. Note also that the results do not vary greatly with *s*. This is likely to result from the fact that quite often the number of relevant images displayed is low (typically below 10) and thus the *effective* extent of the interaction may often be the same no matter whether *s* is 5 or 10.

Given our shortcut for positive feedback (one mouse click per image), three mouse clicks under Scenario W+ achieve a considerable performance boost beyond the level of the globally optimized multiple-descriptor model.

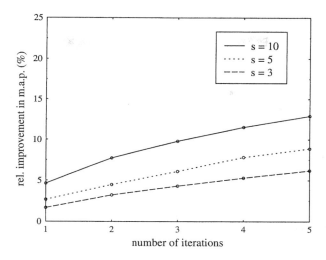

Fig. 4. Increase in mean average precision under Scenario W− with varying s

Let us finally turn to Scenario QW+ in which the original query is expanded by those images marked as relevant (Figure 6). After only one iteration, performance has improved by between $60 - 70\%$. As has already been observed for Scenario W+ and for the same reason, the performance gain does not greatly depend on s. Unlike in Scenario W+ however, continuous feedback results in additional improvement which may suggest that the addition of new images to the query allows the system to widen its "catchment area". Scenario QW+ thus achieves a substantial *and* instantaneous performance boost which is unmatched by any other scenario considered. The results after *one* iteration of relevance feedback are summarized in Table 1.

Scenario \ clicks	10	5	3
W−	4.7	2.5	1.7
W±	13.7	9.3	5.6
W+	21.8	19.8	15.3
QW+	70.0	65.1	58.4

Table 1. The relative gains in mean average precision for the four different scenarios, a constant display size of 30 and varying s (= number of mouse clicks). By far the highest values are achieved under Scenario QW+.

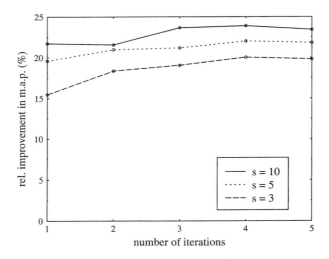

Fig. 5. Increase in mean average precision under Scenario W+ with varying s

4 Discussion

We have described and evaluated a novel relevance feedback method for CBIR that combines analytical weight update with query expansion. Evaluation was done automatically by modelling a number of user-system interaction scenarios. Our results show that feedback-induced performance gains over an already optimized multiple-descriptor model occur under a wide range of interaction scenarios. They also make very clear that some scenarios are decidedly better than others. Specifically, the data support the view that, for any level of interaction (i.e. the number of images on which feedback is given), positive feedback results in greater and more immediate improvement than either negative or mixed feedback. We show that through query expansion, the effect of positive feedback gets multiplied considerably and that this combination allows substantial gains in retrieval performance after only one iteration with a minimum of user-interaction (three mouse clicks).

As argued in the introduction, semantic ambiguity constitutes a challenge for CBIR which may be overcome through techniques such as relevance feedback. In this paper, by deciding *a priori* whether or not an image is relevant to a given query, it appears, however, as if we effectively ignore the issue of image polysemy. It is certainly true that we do enforce a particular "reading" of an image by assigning it to one particular category. The image of a yellow flower may happen to be in the category "Yellow" but not in the category "Flower" and would therefore be considered irrelevant with respect to any query image from the latter category. A user who deems it relevant to such a query is effectively not accommodated by our particular model. It is important to note, however, that the user we *do* model is essentially arbitrary. The categorization of images (and thus the fixation of image meaning) has not been performed with an eye on the strengths

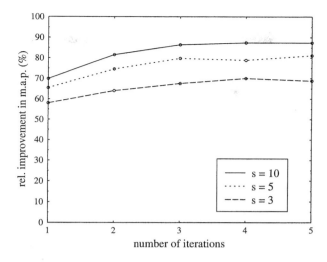

Fig. 6. Increase in mean average precision under Scenario QW+ with varying s

and weaknesses of the retrieval system (as it sometimes happens, whether deliberately or not [13]). Our categories are chosen at random from the total number of categories and comprise highly abstract categories that one may not expect a system that operates on low-level features to retrieve successfully. This suggests that the efficiency of relevance feedback as demonstrated here is relatively independent of the user. Meta-experiments with different categorizations would provide a way of assessing more precisely the degree of user-independence. Additional evidence for our claim that the results presented here are of a generic nature derive from similar experiments we performed on a sketch database using a variety of shape descriptors (results unpublished).

In its early years CBIR has been largely concerned with identifying better ways to represent particular image features. Our results strongly support the view that further progress can be made by addressing the question of how to integrate evidence from multiple of these generally low-level feature representations, and more importantly, how to elicit and utilize user-specific relevance information.

References

1. Y-S Choi, D Kim, and R Krishnapuram. Relevance feedback for content-based retrieval using the Choquet integral. In *Proc of the IEEE International Conference on Multimedia and Expo (II)*, 2000.
2. G Ciocca and R Schettini. A relevance feedback mechanism for content-based image retrieval. *Information Processing and Management*, 35(5):605–632, 1999.
3. I J Cox, M L Miller, T P Minka, T V Papathomas, and P N Yianilos. The Bayesian image retrieval system, pichunter. *IEEE Transactions on Image Processing*, 9(1):20–38, 2000.

4. D Daneels, D Campenhout, W Niblack, W Equitz, R Barber, E Bellon, and F Fierens. Interactive outlining: an improved approach using active contours. In *Proc. SPIE Storage and Retrieval for Image and Video Databases*, 1993.
5. Y Deng and B S Manjunath. An efficient color representation for image retrieval. *IEEE Transactions on Image Processing*, 10:140–147, 2001.
6. D Heesch and S Rüger. Combining features for content-based sketch retrieval — a comparative evaluation of retrieval performance. In *Proceedings of the European Colloquium on IR Research 2002*, Berlin, 2002. LNCS, Springer.
7. Y Ishikawa, R Subramanya, and C Faloutsos. MindReader: Querying databases through multiple examples. In *Proc. 24th Int. Conf. Very Large Data Bases, VLDB*, pages 218–227, 24–27 1998.
8. A Lelescu, O Wolfson, and B Xu. Approximate retrieval from multimedia databases using relevance feedback. In *SPIRE/CRIWG*, pages 215–223, 1999.
9. W Y Ma and B S Manjunath. Texture features and learning similarity. In *Proc. IEEE Conf. Computer Vision and Pattern Recognition*, pages 425–430, 1996.
10. B S Manjunath and J-R Ohm. Color and texture descriptors. *IEEE Transactions on circuits and systems for video technology*, 11:703–715, 2001.
11. C Meilhac and C Nastar. Relevance feedback and category search in image databases. In *Proc. IEEE Int. Conf. Multimedia Comp. and Syst.*, pages 512–517, 1999.
12. T P Minka and R W Picard. Interactive learning using a society of models. In *Proc. IEEE Computer Vision and Pattern Recognition*, pages 447–452, 1996.
13. H Mueller, S Marchand-Maillet, and T Pun. The truth about Corel - evaluation in image retrieval. In *Proceedings of CIVR*, pages 38–49, 2002.
14. K Porkaew, M Ortega, and S Mehrotra. Query reformulation for content based multimedia retrieval in MARS. In *ICMCS, Vol. 2*, pages 747–751, 1999.
15. K Rodden, W Basalaj, D Sinclair, and K Wood. Evaluating a visualization of image similarity. In *Proceedings of SIGIR'99, ACM*, pages 275–276, 1999.
16. Y Rubner and L J Guibas. The earth mover's distance, multi-dimensional scaling and color-based image retrieval. In *Proceedings of the APRA Image Understanding Workshop*, pages 661–668, 1997.
17. Y Rui and T S Huang. A novel relevance feedback technique in image retrieval. In *ACM Multimedia (2)*, pages 67–70, 1999.
18. Y Rui, T S Huang, and S Mehrotra. Relevance feedback techniques in interactive content-based image retrieval. In *Storage and Retrieval for Image and Video Databases (SPIE)*, pages 25–36, 1998.
19. G Salton and M J Gill. *Introduction to Modern Information Retrieval*. McGraw-Hill Book Co., 1983.
20. S Santini, A Gupta, and R Jain. Emergent semantics through interaction in image databases. *IEEE transactions on knowledge and data engineering*, 13(3):337–351, 2001.
21. D McG Squire, W Müller, H Müller, and T Pun. Content-based query of image databases: inspirations from text retrieval. *Pattern Recognition Letters*, 21(13–14):1193–1198, 2000.
22. E M Voorhees and D Harman. Overview of the eigth Text REtrieval Conference (TREC-8). In *Proc. TREC*, pages 1–33 and A.17 – A.18, 1999.
23. M E J Wood, N W Campbell, and B T Thomas. Iterative refinement by relevance feedback in content-based digital image retrieval. In *ACM Multimedia 98*, pages 13–20, Bristol, UK, 1998. ACM.

Acknowledgements: This work was partially supported by the EPSRC, UK.

Query-Based Document Skimming:
A User-Centred Evaluation of Relevance Profiling

David J. Harper, Ivan Koychev, and Yixing Sun

Smart Web Technologies Centre, School of Computing
The Robert Gordon University
St Andrew Street, Aberdeen AB25 1HG, UK
{djh,ik,sy}@comp.rgu.ac.uk

Abstract. We present a user-centred, task-oriented, comparative evaluation of two query-based document skimming tools. ProfileSkim bases within-document retrieval on computing a relevance profile for a document and query; FindSkim provides similar functionality to the web browser Find-command. A novel simulated work task was devised, where experiment participants are asked to identify (index) relevant pages of an electronic book, given subjects from the existing book index. This subject index provides the ground truth, against which the indexing results can be compared. Our major hypothesis was confirmed, namely ProfileSkim proved significantly more efficient than Find-Skim, as measured by time for task. Moreover, indexing task effectiveness, measured by typical IR measures, demonstrated that ProfileSkim was better than FindSkim in identifying relevant pages, although not significantly so. The experiments confirm the potential of relevance profiling to improve query-based document skimming, which should prove highly beneficial for users trying to identify relevant information within long documents.

1 Introduction

A user faced with finding textual information on the Web, or within a digital library, is faced with three challenges. First, the user must identify relevant repositories of digital text, usually in the form of document collections. In the context of the Web, this might be by identifying appropriate content portals, or by selecting appropriate search engine(s). Second, the user must find potentially relevant documents within the repository, usually through a combination of searching, navigating inter-document links, and browsing. Third, the user must locate relevant information *within* these documents. This paper is concerned with the latter challenge, which is becoming increasingly important as longer documents are published, and distributed, using Web and other technologies. Various approaches have been proposed for within-document retrieval, including passage retrieval [1], and user interfaces supporting content-based browsing of documents [2]. We have proposed a tool for within-document retrieval

F. Sebastiani (Ed.): ECIR 2003, LNCS 2633, pp. 377-392, 2003.
© Springer-Verlag Berlin Heidelberg 2003

based on the concept of relevance profiling [3], and in this paper we report on a user-centred, comparative evaluation of this tool.

We have been working on the design, development and implementation of a tool called ProfileSkim, whose function is to enable users to identify, efficiently and effectively, *relevant passages* of text within *long* documents. The tool integrates passage retrieval and content-based document browsing. The key concept underpinning the tool is relevance profiling, in which a profile of retrieval status values is computed across a document in response to a query. Within the user interface, an interactive bar graph provides an overview of this profile, and through interaction with the graph the user can select and browse *in situ* potentially relevant passages within the document.

The evaluation study reported herein was devised to test key assumptions underlying the design of the ProfileSkim tool, namely:

- That relevance profiling, as implemented and presented by the tool, is *effective* in assisting users in identifying relevant passages of a document;
- That by using the tool, users will be able to select and browse relevant passages more *efficiently*, because only the best matching passages need be explored;
- That users will find the tool satisfying to use for within-document retrieval, because of the overview provided by relevance profiling.

We only report experimental results in support of the first two assumptions, which are based on quantitative data collected in the user study. In pursuit of evidence to test these two assumptions, we have conducted a comparative evaluation of two within-document retrieval tools, namely ProfileSkim, and FindSkim which provides similar functionality to the well-known Find-command delivered with most text processing and browsing applications. We investigate the tools within a simulated work task situation [4], in which the participants in the study are asked to compile (part of) a subject index for a book. Within this task setting, we evaluate the comparative effectiveness and efficiency of the within-document retrieval tools, where the task itself requires content-based skimming of a digital version of a book.

This evaluation study is based on an evaluation approach that is beginning to emerge through the efforts of the those involved in the 'interactive track' of TREC [5], through end user experiments in the Information Retrieval community [4, 6, 7], and through the effort of groups such as the EC Working Group on the evaluation of Multimedia Information Retrieval Applications (Mira) [8]. Major elements of the approach are:

- The observation of 'real' users engaged in the performance of 'real-life' tasks (or, at least, convincing simulations of such tasks);
- A range of performance criteria are used, pertaining both to quantitative aspects of task performance (efficiency and effectiveness), and qualitative aspects of the user experience;
- A range of methods for acquiring and analysis of data are used, which can be quantitative in nature (e.g. time for task), and qualitative in nature (e.g. attitudes and reactions to the system, the task, etc.).

The paper is structured as follows. In Section 2, we provide an overview of relevance profiling, and describe how language modelling can be used as a basis for this.

An overview is provided in Section 3 of the salient features of the two within-document retrieval tools used in the study. The research questions are presented in section 4, and the experimental methods in section 5. In Section 6, we present the results of the experimental study, and these are discussed in Section 7. Finally, we offer some concluding remarks concerning the efficacy of relevance profiling as a basis for within-document retrieval, and we highlight the advantages of our particular approach for evaluating this type of retrieval tool.

2   Overview of Relevance Profiling Based on Language Modelling

Relevance profiling using language modelling was introduced in [3], and we provide a brief overview here. Based on a query, we want to compute a relevance profile across the document, and presented this profile to the user in the form of a bar graph. By interacting with this bar graph, the user can identify, and navigate to, relevant sections of a document. Effectively, a retrieval status value (RSV) is computed for each word position in the document. This RSV will be based on a *text window* (fixed number of consecutive words) associated with each word position. Language modelling is used to construct a statistical model for a text window, and based on this model we compute the window RSV as the probability of generating a query.

We employ the language modelling approach proposed for document retrieval in [9, 10], and adapt it for relevance profiling. We model the distribution of terms (actually stemmed words) over a text window, as a mixture of the text window and document term distributions as follows:

$$P(query \mid window) = \prod_{t_i \in query} p_{mix}(t_i \mid win) \tag{1}$$

where: $p_{mix}(t_i \mid win) = w_{win} * p_{win}(t_i \mid win) + (1 - w_{win}) * p_{doc}(t_i \mid doc)$

Thus, the probability of generating words is determined in part by the text window, and in part by the document in which the window is located. The estimates are smoothed by the document word statistics using the mixing parameter, w_{win}. The best value for this parameter needs to be determined empirically, and we have used 0.8 in our system. The individual word probabilities are estimated in the obvious way using maximum likelihood estimators:

$$p_{win}(t_i \mid win) = n_{iW}/n_W \quad p_{doc}(t_i \mid doc) = n_{iD}/n_D \tag{2}$$

where n_{iW} (n_{iD}) and n_W (n_D), are the number of word occurrences of word i in the window (document), and total word occurrences in the window (document) respectively.

The relevance profile is given by the retrieval status value at each word position i:

$$RSV_{window}(i) = P(query \mid window_i) \tag{3}$$

where text window i is the sequence of words $[w_i..w_i+L_W-1]$, and L_W is the fixed length of each text window.

In order to provide a plot of the relevance profile, and to support direct navigation to relevant parts of a document, retrieval status values are aggregated over fixed size, non-overlapping sections of text we call **text tiles**. We assume that the document text is divided into fixed length, non-overlapping text tiles. Let us assume that each tile is L_T words long. The aggregate RSV for a given tile j is given by:

$$RSV_{tile}(j) = agg\text{-}fun(\{RSV_{window}(i), i = (j\text{-}1)*L_T+1 .. j*L_T\}) \qquad (4)$$

Examples of aggregate functions (agg-fun) include average, minimum and maximum, and we opt for the maximum as this corresponds to the best text window starting within the tile. Note that some text windows will extend beyond the end of a tile.

Text windows and text tiles, although related, serve two different purposes. A text window is used to compute an RSV at each word position in the document. The fixed size of a text window is set to the "typical" size of a meaningful chunk of text, such as the average size of a paragraph (or possibly section). The average size of a paragraph can be determined empirically, and in our system we have set it to 200 words. A text tile is used to aggregate or combine the RSVs of **all** text windows that **start** within the given tile, and tiles are used for summarizing (and thence displaying) relevance profiles. The size of a fixed tile is computed based on the length of the document, and depends on the number of tiles, and hence bars, we wish to display in the relevance profile meter. The heights of the bars in the profile meter are proportional to the tile RSV, and are based on logarithm of the tile RSV (see [3] for reasons).

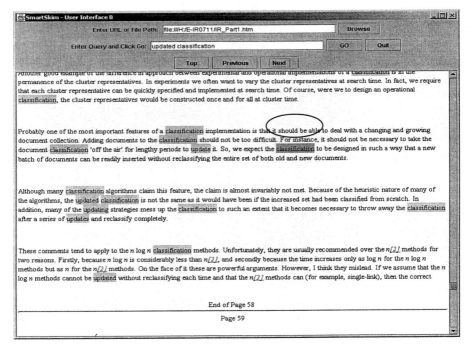

Fig. 1. Screen shot for FindSkim Tool

3   The Document Skimming Tools

Two within-document retrieval tools are used in the comparative user evaluation. One, ProfileSkim, is based on relevance profiling, and the other, FindSkim, is based on the ubiquitous Find-Command provided within most word processing and web browser applications. FindSkim will be described first, as much of its functionality is common to both tools. Then, ProfileSkim is described.

3.1   The FindSkim Tool

The FindSkim tool is based on the Find-command, although in many respects it provides additional functionality. A screenshot of the tool is illustrated in **Fig. 1**.

A user selects a file to skim, using the file chooser, and the file is displayed in a scrollable panel. Given a query, the tool highlights all query word variants that appear in the document in cyan. The document is positioned in the display panel at the first word occurrence, which becomes the *current word*. The current word is always highlighted in yellow (circled in **Fig. 1.**). The user can navigate from the current word to the next (or previous) query word occurrence in the document using the Next/Find buttons. Query words which are not present in the document are flagged as possible misspellings, and the user may choose to edit the query, if appropriate.

Note, that the query is treated as a "bag of words". Hence, no phrase matching is performed based on query word order.

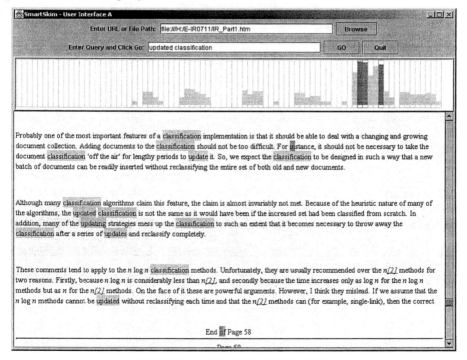

Fig. 2. Screen shot for ProfileSkim Tool

3.2   The ProfileSkim Tool

The ProfileSkim tool is based on relevance profiling, and displays an interactive analogue of the relevance profile for a given query, in the form on a bar graph. A screenshot of the tool is illustrated in **Fig. 2**.

File selection and query input are identical to the FindSkim tool. Query term variants are also highlighted in cyan, and the document is displayed in a scrollable panel.

Based on a query input by the user, a relevance profile is computed over the document (see Section 2), and presented in the form of an interactive bar graph. Each bar corresponds to a fixed length section (tile) in the text of the document, with the leftmost bar corresponding to the start of the document, and the rightmost bar to the end of the document. The height of a bar corresponds to the computed retrieval status value of the corresponding tile. By clicking on a bar, the corresponding tile within the document is centred in the document viewer. Effectively, the bars of the relevance profile meter act as "hypertext links" into the body of the document.

To assist the user in browsing the document using the relevance profile meter, feedback is provided as to which bars (and corresponding tiles) had been visited. Colour coding of the bars indicates which bar/tile has: yet to be visited (cyan), currently being visited (magenta) and visited (green). This colour-coding scheme reinforces the view that the bars acts as hypertext links, and the colours used correspond broadly to those used typically when browsing web pages. The currently visited tile is also indicated with yellow/magenta and magenta/yellow "brackets" on the document display.

A critique of the ProfileSkim interface using the Cognitive Dimensions Framework [11] is provided in [3].

3.3   Choice of Skimming Tools

In setting up the comparative user evaluation of ProfileSkim, we gave careful thought to the choice of the other skimming tool.

We opted for a tool based on the Find-command for three reasons. First, the Find-command is the *de facto* standard for document skimming, albeit in a number of guises in word processing applications and web browsers. Relevance profiling is a possible alternative to the Find-function, and it is therefore useful to provide comparative performance data. Second, we wanted to measure the relative performance of ProfileSkim against FindSkim to provide a benchmark for future developments of ProfileSkim itself. Third, developing our own Find-command variation might suggest ways of improving the Find-command itself.

We accept that the functionality of the tools is different, and in particular that additional information is made available to the users through the relevance profiling tool. However, we thought is best to establish the comparative performance of ProfileSkim against a *de facto* standard in the first instance, and investigate possible variants of relevance profiling tools at a later stage.

4   Research Questions and Hypotheses

In general terms, we wanted investigate whether within-document retrieval based on relevance profiling was more efficient in user time, and more effective in identifying relevant sections of long documents, than the competing tool based in functionality similar to the Find-command. Specifically, the user experiment was designed to test both user efficiency, and user effectiveness in performing the book indexing task. The effectiveness measures we use are described in Section 6.4.

More formally, a number of hypotheses were formulated, based on the expected performance of ProfileSkim and FindSkim. These are, with justifications:

Hypothesis HT: *That 'time to complete' the indexing task would be less using Pro-fileSkim compared with FindSkim (one-tailed).*

We expected that the relevance profile meter would enable the user to readily identify relevant sections of the text, and importantly not spend time browsing less relevant sections.

Hypothesis HP: *ProfileSkim is more effective than FindSkim as measured by Preci-sion (one tailed).*

Hypothesis HP is based on the observation that ProfileSkim encourages a user to explore the highest peaks of the relevance profile (potential relevance hotspots), and thus we might expect a user to achieve higher precision when using ProfileSkim.

Hypothesis HR: *FindSkim is more effective than ProfileSkim as measured by Recall (one tailed).*

Hypothesis HR is based on the observation that FindSkim encourages a user to visit all query word occurrences in the text and thus we might expect a user to achieve higher recall, and this possibly at the expense of precision. However, it is possible that ProfileSkim might achieve comparable levels of recall, depending on the extent to which a user is prepared to explore comprehensively the relevance profile.

Conjecture CF: *Supposing that hypotheses **HP** and **HR** hold, then we conjecture that effectiveness, as measured by the combined F-measure, will be comparable.*

This conjecture is simply a consequence of the fact that the F-measure "trades off" precision against recall.

5   Methods

In this evaluation of within-document retrieval using relevance profiling, and specifically the comparative evaluation of ProfileSkim and FindSkim, we wanted to address the following issues:

- the participants in the experiment should be placed in a simulated work task situation [4], such that document skimming is central in performing the task;

- the focus of the task should be document skimming, and not document retrieval;
- the documents used in the study should be long, in order to provide a realistic assessment of the tools being studied;
- the tasks should be realistic, understandable to the participants, and able to be completed in a reasonable time; and
- task performance can be measured against some ground truth established for the task.

A novel work task situation was devised that satisfied our requirements, namely creating a subject index for an electronic book.

5.1   Participants

The participants for the study were all graduate students drawn from various places in our University. We would have preferred to select from a homogeneous group, but this was not possible given that the experiment was performed with 24 participants (plus 6 additional participants for the pilot). Instead, we selected from a number of programmes, namely students in: MSc Information and Library Studies (10), MSc Knowledge Management (7), MSc Electronic Information Management (2), PhD in Business Studies (1) and PhD in Computing (4). Based on the entry questionnaire, the participants were mostly unfamiliar with the field of information retrieval, and hence the (electronic) book used in the study. They had on average of 3.8 years of experience in using computers for reading/browsing electronic text.

5.2   Instruments

Collection. An electronic version of van Rijsbergen's classic information retrieval text was obtained, and we added page numbers which are necessary in creating a subject index. The book was divided into four sections, two sections for training and two for the main experiment (see **Table 1**).

Topics. Eight topics[1] were selected at random from the subject index provided with the original textbook (see **Table 2**). The selected topics met the following criteria:

- between 4 and 7 pages indexed for the topic;
- at least two distinct ranges of page numbers;
- two or more words for the topic;
- (preferably) indexed pages present in both Part 1 and Part 2 of the text; and
- (as far as possible) minimize overlap between the pages for the different topics.

These criteria ensured that the corresponding indexing tasks could be performed in a reasonable time, and that the participants would be required to browse comprehensively both parts of the book. We opted for multi-word topics for two reasons. First, we were interested in assessing the benefits of relevance profiling in a more general setting, e.g. skimming documents retrieved by search engines, and multi-word queries

---

[1] Although we normally refer to 'subject indexing' and 'subjects' for books, we will adopt the standard IR terminology of 'topic indexing' and 'topic' in this paper.

are more typical in this setting. Second, relevance profiling is not particularly interesting for one word queries, as it equates to a simple count of word occurrences. The final criterion was included to try and minimize the learning effect of viewing many times the same, albeit, long document.

Table 1. Collection Details

Filename	Content	No of Pages	Word Count
Training1	Chapter 4	29	9526
Training2	Chapter 7	40	13181
Part1	Chapter 2, 3	52	18087
Part2	Chapter 5, 6	49	17296

5.3   Procedures

Scenario for Simulated Work Task. The experiment participants were asked to imagine they were graduate students, who had been asked by their tutor to assist him/her in creating a subject index for a book he/she has written. For a given topic they were asked to locate pages that should appear under that topic, using one of the skimming tools. The criteria for including a page, i.e. assessing the page relevant for the topic, were:

- the page must be topically relevant, i.e. about the subject;
- the page must be substantially relevant, i.e. the page would add to a potential reader's understanding of the topic;
- all pages in a set of contiguous relevant pages should be included; and
- pages in the bibliographies at the ends of chapter were not to be indexed.

These instructions accorded in general with the way the book was originally indexed by the author (Private communication from C. J. van Rijsbergen).

Tasks and Task Groups. Each topic was the basis for an indexing task, and to assist the participants, a short definition was provided for each topic. This provided some context for evaluating the relevance of page to a topic, and plays a similar role to the extended topic descriptions in TREC-1 [13]. The topics were divided into two groups for the experimental design, and we refer to these as Task Groups (see **Table 2**). Within each task group, the first task was used as a training task, and the other three tasks were arranged in increasing order of difficulty. This ordering was established based on a pilot study we performed.

Experiment Design. The design is summarised in **Table 3**.

Experiment Procedure. The procedure is summarised in **Fig. 3**.

The participants were asked to complete the indexing tasks as quickly as possible, while at the same time achieving good levels of indexing specificity and exhaustivity. The pilot study established that most tasks could be completed in 6-10 minutes, and thus we allocated 40 minutes for each task group. However, the participants were asked to complete all tasks in a group, even if they over-ran the allocated time. The majority of participants completed each task group within the 40 minutes.

Table 2. Indexing task groups

Task group	Order	Topic/Subject	File to Skim	Indexed Pages
1	Training	Expected Search Length	Training1	
			Training2	160-163
	First	Loss (or Cost) Function	Part1	29
			Part2	116-117, 126
	Second	Boolean Search	Part1	
			Part2	95-97, 109
	Third	Information Measure	Part1	41-42, 57
			Part2	123, 136, 138
2	Training	Relational Data Model	Training1	67, 90
			Training2	
	First	Maximum Spanning Tree (MST)	Part1	56, 57
			Part2	123, 132, 139
	Second	Relevance Feedback	Part1	
			Part2	105-108, 112
	Third	Cluster based Retrieval	Part1	47, 56
			Part2	103-105

Table 3. Experiment Design

Participant Group	First Task Set (System/Task Group)	Second Task Set (System / Task Group)
1	A / TG1	B / TG2
2	A / TG2	B / TG1
3	B / TG1	A / TG2
4	B / TG2	A / TG1

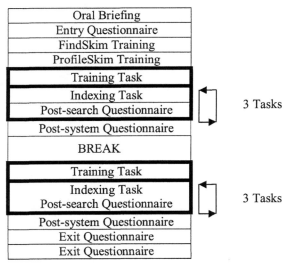

Fig. 3. Procedure for Experiment

A few observations are necessary regarding this procedure. We would have preferred to run the experiment with each participant individually. This was not possible due to timetabling and resource constraints. However, we minimised as far as possible interaction between the participants. We would have preferred to do the system training just prior to use of each system. This was not possible given the experiment was performed with participants from all participant groups (see **Table 3**). In mitigation, the training was mostly concerned with task training, as the systems were relatively easy to learn and use. Moreover, prior to using each system, there was a specific training task.

5.4   Measures

For each indexing task, allocated one at a time, the user was asked to record the page numbers of relevant pages they would include in the topic (subject) index. Using this information, we were able to assess the specificity and exhaustivity of the indexing, using traditional precision and recall measures (see below). The time for each task was recorded in minutes and seconds. Using this information, we were able to assess the user efficiency of the indexing process.

Precision, recall and the F-measure were computed as follows. The original subject index of the book provides the ground truth for the indexing tasks. That is, the pages indexed originally by the author of the book, are effectively the pages deemed relevant. Hence for a given subject, if A is the set of pages indexed by the author and B is the set of pages indexed by a participant in the study, then precision and recall can be computed in the obvious way:

$$P = |A \cap B|/|B| \qquad R = |A \cap B|/|A| \qquad (5)$$

The F-measure, which is a single measure of performance, is simply the harmonic mean of precision and recall, namely:

$$F = 2 * P * R/(P + R) \qquad (6)$$

This measure effectively "values" precision and recall equally, and thus it enables us to trade off precision and recall.

6   Experimental Results

In this paper, we will focus on presenting and analysing the quantitative data, as this data is the focus of the major hypotheses of the experimental study. Thus, we concentrate on presenting and analysing data relating to task efficiency, as measured by time for task, and task effectiveness, as measured by precision, recall, and F-measure.

In **Table 4**, the average time for task completion is given for each system. The average time for ProfileSkim and FindSkim is 5.76 and 7.74 minutes respectively, and this result is statistically significant at the level of p<0.001. The average effectiveness measures are presented for ProfileSkim and FindSkim. On average, precision, recall and F-measure are all higher for ProfileSkim compared with FindSkim. However, in no instance are these results significant at the level of *p<0.05*.

The boxplots in **Fig. 4** show the spread of the measures for 'time for task', precision, recall and F-Measure, for the ProfileSkim tool (System A) and the FindSkim tool (System B). These plots show that ProfileSkim is better than FindSkim with respect of 'time for task completion'. The task effectiveness, as measured by precision, recall and F-measure, are also better for ProfileSkim, although less markedly so than for the 'time for task'.

Table 4. Summary of experimental results analysis *(DF=23; t Critical one-tail$_{(0.05)}$ = 1.7139)*

	Mean (Variance)		T-statistic	P(T<=t) one-tail
	ProfileSkim	*FindSkim*		
Time	5.8076 (2.4553)	7.7435 (3.7676)	3.5688	0.0008
Precision	0.6224 (0.0237)	0.5503 (0.0126)	1.6962	0.0517
Recall	0.7394 (0.0288)	0.6869 (0.0538)	0.8417	0.2043
F	0.6354 (0.0178)	0.5819 (0.0225)	1.0863	0.1443

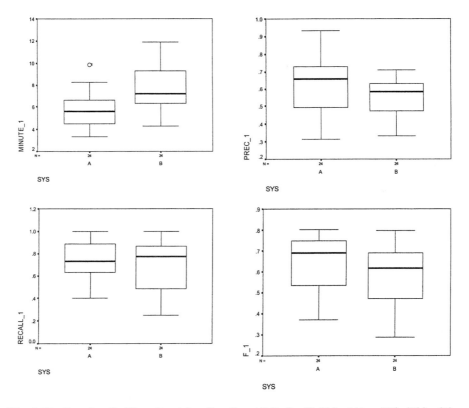

Fig. 4. The Boxplots for Time, Precision, Recall and F for ProfileSkim (A) and FindSkim (B)

7   Discussion of Results

In this experiment, we investigated within-document retrieval tools when used in a simulated subject indexing of a book task. Our results provide evidence that relevance profiling, as presented and implemented in ProfileSkim, is more efficient than the FindSkim for the book indexing task. The average time for ProfileSkim and FindSkim is 5.76 and 7.74 minutes respectively, and this result is statistically significant [$p<0.001$]. Hence, we fail to accept the null hypothesis corresponding to HT, and our results provide very strong evidence:

That 'time to complete' the indexing task is less using ProfileSkim
compared with FindSkim.

In respect of task effectiveness, the general trend suggests that ProfileSkim (PS) is more effective than FindSkim (FS) when measured by Precision (PS: 0.6224, FS: 0.5503), Recall (PS: 0.7394, FS: 0.6869) and the F-measure (PS: 0.6354, FS: 0.5819). However, in no case are the differences statistically significant at the level $p<0.05$. And, we fail to accept the hypotheses **HP** and **HR**, namely:

ProfileSkim is more effective than FindSkim as measured by Precision and
FindSkim is more effective than ProfileSkim as measured by Recall.

But, while the difference in Precision is not significant at the level $p<0.05$, it is significant at the slightly higher level of $p<0.06$. There is therefore weaker evidence that ProfileSkim is more effective that FindSkim as measured by Precision and one might tentatively conclude that relevance profiling is a precision-oriented device.

The F-measure results provide evidence for our conjecture, namely that overall effectiveness of ProfileSkim and FindSkim is comparable when used for the book indexing task. In summary, our results indicate that relevance profiling, as realised in ProfileSkim, is more efficient that FindSkim, and moreover this efficiency is achieved with no significant difference is indexing effectiveness, as measured by the F-measure. Furthermore, the absolute level of performance is pleasingly high, especially given that the indexing task was perceived by the users to be difficult as assessed through the questionnaires.

Given these results, what can we conclude about the efficiency and effectiveness of ProfileSkim, and by implication relevance profiling, for more general within-document retrieval tasks. That is, to what extent will these results carry over into other task settings and situations? The experiment task required the participants to locate relevant sections of long documents using the tools. In particular, given the efficiency of ProfileSkim for the task, we can conclude that it is likely to be equally efficient in more general document browsing settings. Relevance profiling could be usefully provided within word processing applications and document reading/browsing tools as a replacement for the commonly provided "Find" functionality.

The performance of ProfileSkim for the book indexing task, as measured by precision, was better than that of FindSkim, albeit at the slightly higher level $p<0.06$ than is usually accepted ($p<0.05$). This provides some evidence that relevance profiling is a precision-enhancing device. Thus, relevance profiling may be valuable in within-document retrieval tasks that require high precision, tasks such as question-answering. ProfileSkim is able to accurately pinpoint relevant sections of large text documents, and to do so using relatively short queries. These are characteristic of many question-answering tasks.

The simulated work task situation we used in our experiment, namely the book indexing task, proved highly successful in many respects. Preliminary analysis of the task questionnaire data shows that the scenario and task were understood by the participants, although admittedly the participants were all postgraduates. The participants were able to perform the tasks both efficiently and effectively, as evidenced by the performance analysis. Importantly, the experiment clearly explored within-document retrieval, as this was central to the indexing task.

The book indexing task provides a ready-made ground truth, namely the original subject index. Certainly, it would not always be straightforward to ascertain the original indexing policy, and incorporate this within the experiment setting. Nevertheless, the book index provides a useful starting point.

Our experience provides strong evidence that the book indexing task is highly suited to evaluating within-document retrieval. The subject matter of the book is critical, and we were fortunate that our participants were able to comprehend the relatively technical material we used. The provision of both the subject (topic) and a longer definition proved important is enabling these participants to make the necessary relevance assessments. It may be that using more assessable materials, such as general-interest reference books, e.g. an encyclopaedia, would make the task simpler for participants drawn from a wider population.

8   Conclusions and Future Work

In this paper, we have reported the results of a user-centred evaluation of within-document retrieval tools, in the simulated task of providing (part of) the subject index of an electronic book. Two tools were compared, one based on relevance profiling (ProfileSkim), and one based on a sequential search (FindSkim).

The major findings of our investigation are that, for the book indexing task:

- The 'time to complete' the task is significantly less with ProfileSkim than with FindSkim;
- While the results were not statistically significant, the general trend is that indexing effectiveness, as measured by traditional information retrieval measures, is on average better when using ProfileSkim compared with FindSkim; and
- The indexing effectiveness, as measured by precision is better for ProfileSkim than FindSkim, at the reduced standard of $p<0.06$.

Thus, a within-document retrieval tool based on relevance profiling is both efficient and effective for the book indexing task. We argued that there is ample justification for believing that these findings will hold in more general task settings, in which document skimming may be useful. Further, relevance profiling should prove a worthy replacement for the familiar Find-Command implemented in most text processing and/or browsing applications.

The book indexing task proved highly satisfactory for evaluating the comparative performance of within-document retrieval tools, and based on our experiences, we would advocate its use for this kind of study. Arguably, an experimenter might need to choose the subject matter of the books carefully, depending on the background of the study participants, and indeed the indexing task may prove too taxing for some.

Relevance profiling on ProfileSkim is based on a relatively simple mixture language model. This model favours term frequency over term discrimination. We would like to investigate other possible formulations of relevance profiling, based on more advanced divergence models, which we believe would allow term frequency to be combined with term discrimination c.f. tf*idf weighting. We would expect to evaluate alternative relevance profiling approaches using the book indexing data, albeit in a batch environment, i.e. without user involvement, at least initially.

Acknowledgements

We would like to thank C. J. "Keith" van Rijsbergen for permission to use the electronic version of his textbook "Information Retrieval" in our experiment. We are indebted to the following people for advice on experimental design and analysis: Diane Kelly, Alex Wilson, Anna Conniff, Stuart Watt, Ayse Goker, and Peter Lowit. We would also like to thank Robert Newton and Alan Maclennan for volunteering their MSc students for the study. Finally, we would like to offer our heartfelt gratitude to the 30 participants who gave freely of their time, and strived so hard to find "relevance feedback" in Part 1 of the book! Finally, we would like to thank the anonymous referees for these helpful comments.

References

1. Kaszkiel, M., Zobel, J.: Passage Retrieval Revisited. In: Proceedings of the Twentieth International ACM-SIGIR Conference on Research and Development in Information Retrieval. Philadelphia. ACM Press (1997) 178-185
2. Hearst, M.A.: TileBars: Visualization of Term Distribution Information in Full Text Information Access. In: Proceedings of the ACM SIGCHI Conference on Human Factors in Computing Systems (CHI), Denver, CO, (1995)
3. Harper, D.J., Coulthard, S., Sun, Y.: A Language Modelling Approach to Relevance Profiling for Document Browsing. In: Proceedings of the Joint Conference on Digital Libraries. Oregon, USA (2002) 76-83,
4. Borlund, P., Ingwersen, P.: The Development of a Method for the Evaluation of Interactive Information Retrieval Systems. Journal of Documentation. 53(3) (1997) 225-250
5. Beaulieu, M., Robertson, S.E. and Rasmussen, E.: Evaluating interactive systems in TREC. Journal of the American Society for Information Science. 47(1) (1996) 85-94
6. Hersh, W., Pentecost, J., Hickam, D.: A Task-Oriented Approach to Information Retrieval Evaluation. Journal of the American Society for Information Science 47(1) (1996) 50-56
7. Jose, J., Furner, J., Harper, D.J.: Spatial Querying for Image Retrieval: A User-Oriented Evaluation. In: Proceedings of the Twenty First International ACM-SIGIR Conference on Research and Development in Information Retrieval, ACM Press (1998) 232-240

8. Dunlop, M. (ed):. Proceedings of the Second Mira Workshop, Technical Report TR-1997-2. Department of Computing Science, University of Glasgow, Glasgow (1996). Available online at URL: http://wu.dcs.gla.ac.uk/mira/workshops /padua_procs/.
9. Ponte, J., Croft, W.B.: A Language Modeling Approach to Information Retrieval. In: Proceedings of the ACM SIGIR Conference on Research and Development in Information Retrieval. ACM Press (1998) 275-281
10. Song, F., Croft, W.B.: A General Language Model for Information Retrieval. In: Proceedings of the ACM SIGIR Conference on Research and Development in Information Retrieval. ACM Press (1999) 279-280
11. Green, T.R.G.: Describing Information Artifacts with Cognitive Dimensions and Structure Maps. In: Diaper, D., Hammond, N.V. (eds.): Proceedings of the HCI'91 Conference on People and Computers VI. Cambridge University Press, Cambridge (1991)
12. Hersh, W.R., Over, P.: TREC 2001 Interactive Track Structure, Proceedings of the Text Retrieval Conference (TREC) 2001, Gaithersburg, MD, (2001) 38-41
13. Harman, D.: Overview of the First Text REtrieval Conference (TREC-1), National Institute of Standards and Technology, Gaithersburg, Maryland (1992) 309-318

Representative Sampling for Text Classification Using Support Vector Machines

Zhao Xu[1], Kai Yu[2], Volker Tresp[3], Xiaowei Xu[4], and Jizhi Wang[1]

[1] Tsinghua University, Beijing, China
xuzhao00@mails.tsinghua.edu.cn
wjz-dci@tsinghua.edu.cn
[2] Institute for Computer Science, University of Munich, Germany
yu_k@dbs.informatik.uni-muenchen.de
[3] Corporate Technology, Siemens AG, Munich, Germany
volker.tresp@mchp.siemens.de
[4] University of Arkansas at Little Rock, Little Rock, USA
xwxu@ualr.edu

Abstract. In order to reduce human efforts, there has been increasing interest in applying active learning for training text classifiers. This paper describes a straightforward active learning heuristic, representative sampling, which explores the clustering structure of 'uncertain' documents and identifies the representative samples to query the user opinions, for the purpose of speeding up the convergence of Support Vector Machine (SVM) classifiers. Compared with other active learning algorithms, the proposed representative sampling explicitly addresses the problem of selecting more than one unlabeled documents. In an empirical study we compared representative sampling both with random sampling and with SVM active learning. The results demonstrated that representative sampling offers excellent learning performance with fewer labeled documents and thus can reduce human efforts in text classification tasks.

1 Introduction

Nowadays an enormous amount of text information is available in electronic form, like email, web pages or online news. Automatic text classification has become a key way to process text information. Typically, human experts have to set up the categories and assign labels to each text document. A supervised machine learning algorithm will then be applied to train a model based on the labeled documents so that future unlabeled documents can be automatically categorized. Since there are typically tens thousands of documents in a normal sized corpus, the required human labeling effort can be very tedious and time consuming.

Since in many cases a majority of unlabeled data are available, there have been many studies employing unlabeled documents in classification, like transductive

F. Sebastiani (Ed.): ECIR 2003, LNCS 2633, pp. 393–407, 2003.
© Springer-Verlag Berlin Heidelberg 2003

learning [Joachims, 1998], co-training [Blum & Mitchell, 1998], and active learning [Lewis and Gate, 1994 ; Schohn and Cohn, 2000; Tong and Koller, 2000]. This paper describes a heuristic *active learning* approach to sample the unlabeled data and thus to reduce the human efforts in text classification tasks.

In an active learning setting, a learner has access to a pool of unlabeled data and trains a classifier based on current observed labeled data. Then based on the current state of the classifier(s) one selects some of the "most informative" data so that knowing labels of the selected data can greatly improve the classification accuracy of the classifier(s). It provides a principled way to reduce the number of instances required to be labeled. In order to select the "most informative" data, typical active learning methods employ the idea of 'uncertainty sampling', in which the uncertain documents whose category labels are unclear based on current classifier(s) are presented to experts for labeling. For a linear classifier, e.g. a linear support vector machine (SVM), the most uncertain document is the one closest to the classification hyperplane. Two previous studies [Schohn and Cohn, 2000; Tong and Koller, 2000] independently proposed a similar idea of uncertainty sampling using SVM and both applied it to text classification.

Active learning with SVM uncertainty sampling (for simplicity, we call it SVM active learning in the rest of this paper.) is however a 'myopic' optimization algorithm, since it greedily selects the next optimal one document and is not suitable for selecting multiple documents at a time. The algorithm simply selects the one closest to the decision boundary and does not consider the underlying distribution of unlabeled documents. Although there are debates about the role of unlabeled data in supervised learning, we believe that information about document distribution, e.g. clustering structure, could bring useful knowledge to our training process. This paper attempts to examine this point and propose a heuristic algorithm to improve the active learning approach in terms of classification accuracy with fewer labeled training documents. The proposed representative sampling algorithm using SVM as the fundamental classifier can be viewed as an extension of SVM active learning described in [Schohn and Cohn, 2000; Tong and Koller, 2000], and achieves optimal performance for active learning. Summing up, the contributions of this work include: (1) it makes an attempt to involve the information of the distribution of unlabeled data in supervised learning, and (2) also proposes a novel active learning method for applications to text classification.

The remaining parts of this paper are organized in the following way. In Section 2 we briefly review active learning and a general topic of involving unlabeled data in supervised learning. The discussion provides a key motivation for this paper. In Section 3, we describe our proposed representative sampling algorithm and discuss the reasons behind it. Empirical results are presented in Section 4. We finally end this paper by conclusions and a discussion of future work.

2   Background

In this section we briefly introduce related work including active learning, supervised learning with unlabeled data, and support vector machines (SVMs). Giving a comprehensive review covering all the aspects and drawing very general conclusions are beyond the scope of this paper. Instead, by concentrating on a small number of representative work, we focus on issues involving motivation and necessary background of our work.

2.1   Active Learning

The query by committee algorithm [Seung et al., 1992] is one of the earliest algorithms with active learning. It uses a prior distribution over hypotheses. The method samples a set of classifiers from this distribution and queries an example based upon the degree of disagreement between the committee of these classifiers. This general algorithm has been used in domains with different classifiers. It has been used in probabilistic models and specifically in context with with the naïve Bayes model for text classification in a Bayes learning setting [McCallum & Nigam, 1998]. Lewis and Catlett (1994) initially applied active learning in text classification. They used a naïve Bayesian classifier combined with logistic regression to identify the most uncertain unlabeled examples and used them to train a C4.5 decision tree. Recently, several methods for active learning with SVM have been developed by [Schohn & Cohn, 2000;Tong and Koller, 2001]. These methods normally pick up the unlabeled examples lying closest to the decision boundary. Although similar algorithms were proposed, Schohn & Cohn (2000) mainly did their work from a heuristic perspective, while Tong and Koller (2001) demonstrated that active learning can be realized by minimizing the version space. We will examine the details of this work in Section 3. Summing up, the general idea of active learning is to explore the most uncertain examples according to the current classifier(s), while ignoring the distribution or generative models of the input domain.

2.2   The Role of Unlabeled Data in Supervised Learning

Due to the large amount of unlabeled data in applications like text classification, an interesting question is that whether unlabeled data can be used in supervised learning. As indicated in [Zhang and Oles, 2000], there are two existing approaches to this problem. The first approach is active learning. In the second approach, one trains a classifier(s) based on both the labeled data and the unlabeled data. Typically, the label of an unlabeled data point is imputed by certain means based on the current state of the classifier(s). The now augmented "labeled" data is then used to retrain the classifier(s). Examples of this approach include co-training with Gaussian mixture model (GMM) [Blum and Mitchell, 1998] and transductive SVM classifier [Joachims, 1999]. One point regarding the second approach is that it generally takes advantages of knowledge from the distribution of unlabeled data to boost the supervised learning. Given training data in the form of input-label pairs (x, y), Zhang and Oles (2000) examined two parametric probabilistic models:

Joint density models: $p(x, y|\alpha) = p(x|\alpha)p(y|x, \alpha)$, where both $p(x|\alpha)$ and $p(y|x, \alpha)$ have known functional forms. $p(x|\alpha)$ has a non-trivial dependency on parameter α. Typical examples are generative models like GMM.

Conditional density models: $p(x, y|\alpha) = p(x)p(y|x, \alpha)$, where the margin distribution $p(x)$ is independent of parameter α. Typical examples are discriminative classifiers like the SVM.

They concluded that for joint density models, e.g. GMM, it would be helpful to consider the distribution of unlabeled data, while for conditional density models, like SVM, it is not helpful to take into account the underlying distribution of unlabeled data. As also indicated by Zhang and Oles, this conclusion conflicts with the work of transductive SVM [Joachims, 1999]. This paper, although not intended to clarify the debate, makes an attempt to examine the value of the distribution of unlabeled data in SVM active learning. Our analysis as well as our empirical study challenge Zhang and Oles's conclusion.

2.3   Supports Vector Machines

Due to its strong mathematical foundations and excellent empirical successes, support vector machines (SVM) [Vapnik, 1982] recently gained wide attention. In particular the linear SVM represents a *state-of-the-art* method for text classification [Joachims, 1998]. Given a set of labeled data $D=\{(x_1, y_1), (x_2, y_2),\ldots, (x_m, y_m)\}$, where $x_i \in X$ and $y_i \in \{-1, +1\}$, a SVM is represented by a hyperplane:

$$f(x) = (\sum_{i=1}^{m} \alpha_i K(x_i, x)) + b = 0 \tag{2.3.1}$$

where $K(u, v)$ is a kernel function satisfying Mercer's condition [Burges, 1998]. The hyperplane defined above can be interpreted as a decision boundary and thus the sign of $f(x)$ gives the predicted label of input x. For a linear SVM, $K(u, v)$ is defined as the inner product between u and v. We can rewrite $f(x)$ as:

$$f(x) = w \cdot x + b, \text{ where } w = \sum_{i=1}^{m} \alpha_i x_i \tag{2.3.2}$$

where the Lagrange multipliers α_i are found such that $f(x)=0$ represents the optimal hyperplane with maximum margin in the following way:

$$\max_{w,b}\left\{\min_{x_i}\left\{\|x - x_i\| : x \in X, w \cdot x + b = 0\right\}\right\} \tag{2.3.3}$$

where *margin* is defined as the minimum distance of training instance x_i to the optimal hyperplane. For details of the optimization algorithm, please refer to [Burges, 1998]. In Eq.(2.3.2), the x_i for which α_i are non-zero are called support vectors. They are the training examples which fall *on* the margin and thus limit the position of the decision hyperplane. Those training examples with zero α_i are the ones lying outside of the margin and are farther away from the hyperplane than the support vectors.

For the following discussion it is important to note examples far away from the decision boundary can be classified with a high confidence while the correct classes for examples close to the hyperplane or within the margin are uncertain.

3   Representative Sampling Using SVMs

In this section we will describe the details of the proposed *representative sampling* algorithm for active learning with SVMs. We also discuss the heuristics behind the described algorithm. The discussion does not stick to rigorous mathematics but focuses on principled and intuitive explanations.

3.1   Representative Sampling: A Heuristic Algorithm for Active Learning

To examine whether it benefits the SVM if the distribution of the input domain $\mathcal{X}$ has been taken into account, we concentrate on the *clustering structure* of $\mathcal{X}$ in SVM active learning. The proposed representative sampling follows the idea that the learner should focus on the *important informative* vectors x_i whose labels are yet unknown and quite uncertain according to the current SVM. The algorithm proceeds as follows:

1. Train a linear SVM model based on all the labeled documents gathered so far.
2. Let U be the set of the unlabeled documents that lie in the margin of newly trained SVM.
3. Cluster document set U into k groups by k-means clustering and identify the k medoid documents. The inner product is applied as similarity measure.
4. Present the k selected documents to human experts for labeling.
5. Return to the first step.

The above iteration continues until some stopping criterion is satisfied. The algorithm differs from the SVM active learning algorithm in that it analyzes the distribution of the unlabeled documents within the margin where the classification of the SVM is with low confidence; in comparison, SVM active learning only simply picks up the unlabeled data closest to the current SVM hyperplane. In the following subsections, we will discuss the reasons of representative sampling from several aspects.

3.2   Density Distribution Preserving

Clustering methods normally provide a principled way to pick a subset of samples which preserve the *density distribution* information of the whole set[1]. A common assumption of many *supervised learning* methods is that the training data D, $\{x_i, y_i\}$, $i=1, \ldots, m$, are generated from the real distribution $\mathcal{D}$ with a joint probability density $p(x, y ; \mathcal{D})$. The goal of supervised learning tasks is to determine the parameter α of a probabilistic classifier[2] by maximizing the expected log likelihood log $p(y \mid x, \alpha)$ over the density distribution $\mathcal{D}$:

---

[1] Vector quantization (VQ) widely applied in speech compression is such an example, which selects the center of clusters to form a codebook representing the distribution of speech signal [Gray, 1984].

[2] In this section we slightly abuse the probabilistic framework. Although originally SVM is not a probabilistic classifier, it is very desirable for us to analyze it in this way. As it did for other

$$\alpha_{opt} = \arg \max_{\alpha} E_{\mathcal{D}}[\log p(y \mid x, \alpha)]$$

$$= \arg \max_{\alpha} \int p(x, y; \mathcal{D}) \log p(y \mid x, \alpha) dx dy$$

(3.2.1)

where $E_{\mathcal{D}}[\cdot]$ denotes the expectation over $p(x, y ; \mathcal{D})$. Assuming that each $\{x_i, y_i\}$ in training set D is drawn randomly from the density distribution $p(x, y ; \mathcal{D})$, we can approximate the expected log likelihood by Monto-Carlo Integration [Fishman, 1996]:

$$E_{\mathcal{D}}[\log p(y \mid x, \alpha)] \approx \frac{1}{m} \sum_{i=1}^{m} \log p(y_i \mid x_i, \alpha) \sim p(\mathbf{Y} \mid \mathbf{X}, \alpha)$$

(3.2.2)

Thus the log-likelihood maximization over the whole distribution can be approximated by *empirical* log-likelihood maximization over the observed training samples D:

$$\alpha_{opt}^* \approx \arg \max_{\alpha} p(\mathbf{Y} \mid \mathbf{X}, \alpha) = \arg \max_{\alpha} p(\mathbf{Y} \mid \mathbf{X}, \alpha) p(\mathbf{X})$$

$$= \arg \max_{\alpha} p(\mathbf{D} \mid \alpha)$$

(3.2.3)

where $p(X)=p(X \mid \alpha)$. Approximation (3.2.3) gives the *maximum likelihood estimate* (MLE) which is normally applied to determine the model parameter based on observations D^3.

Since $p(x, y; \mathcal{D}) = p(x; \mathcal{D}) p(y \mid x; \mathcal{D})$, we can imagine the following data generation process for text classification: the learner first picks up a document x_i according to $p(x; \mathcal{D})$ and then human experts assign labels y_i according to $p(y \mid x; \mathcal{D})$. The process is repeated m times and finally a training set D is obtained. Therefore, for deriving the approximations (3.2.2) and (3.2.3), it is crucial that an active learning algorithm should *preserve* the underlying distribution $\mathcal{D}$ by selecting the unlabeled documents according to the real distribution of documents $p(x; \mathcal{D})$.

For defining the value of data for active learning it is important to take into account two issues: First, data points are relevant which define the class boundary best, i.e. data points close to the separating hyperplane. The second issue is concerned with the input data distribution. In general the prediction of statistical models will be best in regions of the input space, where a sufficient number of training data points were available: one would assume best generalization performance if the input data distribution of test set and training set coincide. In conclusion, both input data distribution and closeness to the (expected) separating hyperplane should be taken into account in active learning.

---

learning methods, probabilistic framework gives a principled way to understand SVM and the conclusions drawn can then be applied to SVM. Also, some recent studies introduced probabilistic SVM models by using logistic regression, e.g. [Platt, 1999].

[3] In practice, the MLE formulation is always ill-conditioned, *regularization* is thus imposed to serve as a prior and avoid over-fitting the observations.

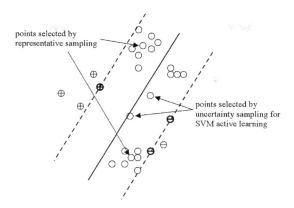

points selected by
representative sampling

points selected by
uncertainty sampling for
SVM active learning

Fig. 1. An illustration representative sampling vs. uncertainty sampling for active learning— Unlabeled points selected by representative sampling are the centers of *document clusters* and preserve the distribution of the pool of data. While uncertainty sampling selects the points, which are *the closest to the decision boundary* and not relevant to the distribution of documents. (Note: Bold points are support vectors. Dashed lines indicate the Margin. And the solid line is the decision boundary.)

The SVM active learning approach selects unlabeled documents closest to the classification hyperplane. Although this approach experimentally demonstrated attractive properties, this approach manipulates the distribution of the labeled training documents and might degrade the generalization performance in classifying future unlabeled documents.

It is yet unclear that how this manipulation will influence the learning process. However, given a large pool of unlabeled documents, it should be desirable to preserve the density distribution of the 'pool' in the learning. Our representative sampling algorithm pursues this idea. It focuses on the uncertain unlabeled documents (e.g. the ones lying within the margin) as other active learning algorithms do and selects representative ones (e.g. cluster centers). As shown in Fig. 1, it guides the learner to concentrate on the *most important uncertain* data instead of *the most uncertain* data.

3.3   Orthogonal Subspace Spanning

SVMs have demonstrated state of the art performance in high dimensional domains such as text classification, where the dimensionality may be an order magnitude larger than the number of examples. As indicated by Eq.(2.3.2), the decision boundary is constructed by a subset of the training examples. Typically the subspace spanned by a given set of training examples will cover only a fraction of the available dimensions. One heuristic active learning approach would be to search for examples that are as orthogonal to each other as possible such that a large dimensionality of document space can be explored. The proposed representative sampling provides such a method. Intuitively, the k-means clustering algorithm detects the subspaces of documents and picks the cluster centers as representatives of the subspaces. Therefore the representative sampling algorithm chooses the uncertain unlabeled examples which also gain most in covered dimensions.

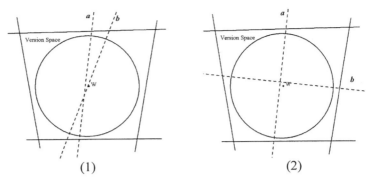

Fig. 2. Two examples *a* and *b* respectively halve the version space. In the case (1), *a* and *b* are two analog examples close to the hyperplane *w*; while in the case (2), *a* and *b* are two orthogonal examples close to the hyperplane *w* and the combination of them almost quarters the version space. (Note: the center of the inscribed circle is the maximum margin hyperplane.)

3.4   Version Space Shrinkage

Given a set of labeled training data, there is a set of hyperplanes that correctly separate the data. This set of consistent hypotheses is called the *version space* [Michell,1982]. Learning problems could be generally viewed as searching the version space to find the in some sense best hypothesis. A reasonable approach is to shrink the version space by eliminating hypotheses that are inconsistent with the training data. Tong and Koller (2001) analyzed the SVM active learning by focussing on the shrinking of the version space and obtained the same algorithm described in [Schohn and Cohn, 2000]. Their discussion is built on the assumption that the data is linearly separable, which, as many experiments have shown is the case for text classification.

Let's visit Eq. (2.3.2) again. There exists a *duality* between the input feature pace X and the hyperplane parameter space W : points in X correspond to hyperplanes in W and vice versa. By having this duality, the version space is a region in the parameter space W restricted by support vectors which are hyperphanes in W (see Fig.2). And the decision boundary is the point *w* within this region (as shown in Fig. 2). Then the maximum margin is interpreted as the maximum distance from the point *w* to restricting boundaries in W, which correspond support vectors in X. If a new labeled example $a = (x_a, +1)$ is observed, then the region $w \cdot x + b < 0$ will be eliminated so that a smaller version space is obtained. Therefore adding more labeled instances can be imagined as using more hyperplanes in W to 'cut' and thus decease the version space.

In [Tong and Koller, 2001], Lemma 4.3, it was shown that the *maximum expected size of the version space* over all conditional distributions of *y* given *x* can be minimized by halving the version space. It should be noticed that the theory just answered the question of how to select the optimal *one* unlabeled instance. In [Schohn and

Cohn, 2000; Tong and Koller, 2001], the authors implicitly generalized this conclusion to the cases of selecting multi examples without providing a clear justification. It turns out that the issue is more subtle. As illustrated in Fig. 2, two analog examples might lead to non-optimal version space shrinkage, although they both halve the version space. A reasonable heuristic optimization is to divide the version space as equally as possible (as shown in Fig. (2)). This approach is in the same spirit as previous work on SVM active learning and further address the problem of selecting multi unlabeled examples. It can be viewed as a generalization of previous work in [Schohn and Cohn, 2000; Tong and Koller, 2001].

Clustering is a useful approach to identify the optimal clusters such that the inter similarities are minimized and meanwhile the intra similarities are maximized. We use the inner product as the similarity measure, which is exactly the cosine of angle between two x vectors if they have already been normalized to unit length. When the angles between cluster centers (respresented by medoids) are maximized, it is reasonable to believe that the medoid examples evenly divide the version space at the most. Thus our proposed representative sampling provides a straightforward heuristic to optimally choose multi unlabeled examples for active learning.

4   Empirical Study

4.1   Experimental Data Set

To evaluate the performance of the proposed representative sampling algorithm we compared it with random sampling and with SVM active learning using uncertainty sampling. We used the Reuters-21578 database, a collection of news documents that have been assigned with one topic, multiple topics or no topic. By eliminating documents without topics, titles or texts, finally 10369 documents are obtained. Then from these documents, 1000 documents are randomly selected as training set, and another 2000 documents are randomly selected as test set. No overlap exists in the two sets. For text preprocessing, we use the well-known *vector space model* under the 'bag of words' assumption [Salton and McGill, 1983]. The space of the model has one dimension for each word in the corpus dictionary. Finally each document is represented as a stemmed, TFIDF weighted word frequency vector.

We use the visibility v to indicate the occurring frequency of a topic in the corpus [Drucker et al., 2001].

Table 1. Topics selected for experiments

topic	Document number	Visibility (%)
earn	3775	36.4
acq	2210	21.3
Money-fx	682	6.6
grain	573	5.5
crude	564	5.3

$$v = \frac{n_R}{N} \qquad (4.1.1)$$

where N is the total number of documents in Reuters database; n_R is the number of documents with the given topic. As shown in Table 1, we follow the way of [Schohn & Cohn, 2000; Tong and Koller, 2001] and choose 5 most frequently occurring topics for the experiments. We will track the classification performance in cases of different topics.

4.2   Experiment Description and Performance Metrics

The purpose of a learner is to train a model (the SVM hyperplane in this work) to identify documents about the desired topic (labeled as "positive") from the rest documents (labeled as "negative"). To measure the performance of a learner we use a metric of classification accuracy r, which is defined as:

$$r = \frac{n_{correct}}{N} \qquad (4.2.1)$$

where $n_{correct}$ is the number of documents that are classified correctly in test set. N is the total number of documents in test set. We will track the classifier accuracy as a function of labeled training data size for each of the five topics. The proposed representative sampling algorithm will be compared with active learning and random sampling.

The experiments of the representative sampling method proceed as the following steps. First, m instances ($m/2$ positive instances and $m/2$ negative instances) are randomly selected as "seeds" to train an initial SVM model. At the second step, the instances inside the margin (determined by the SVM model) are clustered into m clusters with the k-means clustering algorithm. Then the instances nearest to each cluster center will be labeled according to their true topic. The learner uses the total cumulated labeled documents so far to rebuild a new model, which is then tested on the independent test set. The same operation is performed in the later iterations. In our experiments the number of iterations is 11, and different value of parameter m (4 and 10) are tested.

We will run 30 trials for each topic and report the averaged results. Each run of the thirty experiments starts with a set of randomly selected documents.

4.3   Experiment Results and Analysis

Figure 3 shows the average value of the test results over five topics (totally 30*5 trails). It shows the classification accuracy r as a function of the total labeled training data size when $m=4$ and 10. Both the active learning algorithm and the representative sampling algorithms have better performance than the random sampling method, which proves the effectiveness of the active learning strategy using representative sampling and uncertainty sampling.

It is observed in Figure 3 that representative sampling significantly outperforms the other two methods in the beginning stages. After a certain number of steps the increase of accuracy of representative sampling is getting slower while the SVM active learning's accuracy is increasing in a relatively stable manner and finally outperforms representative sampling. The observed results partially conflict with our former expectation and indicate that SVM classifier benefit from clustering only in the initial phase.

Figure 4, 5 and 6 show the experimental results for the topics *earn*, *acq* and *grain,* respectively. For the topic *earn*, the proposed representative sampling shows a very satisfying performance, which is much better than SVM active learning and random sampling. Figure 5 and 6 demonstrate a somewhat similar phenomenon as Figure 3: representative sampling first outperforms SVM active learning but eventually the latter one wins.

To clarify this unexpected behavior, we investigate the number of unlabeled instances within the margin. As shown in Figure 7, the number of unlabeled examples within the margin decreases with the representative sampling iterations. If we carefully compare Figure 4, 5, 6 and 7, it is apparent that there exists a strong connection between the accuracy performance of representative sampling and the curves shown in Figure 7. Consider as an example the topic *earn*: The number of unlabeled instances within the margin decreases consistently and its accuracy also consistently outperforms other two methods. For the example of topic *arc* or *grain*, one the other hand, the size of unlabeled data within the margin decreases quickly at the beginning but later decreases only slowly.

In comparison, accuracy increases quickly at first but then increases only slowly. The observed phenomenon might be interpreted as follows. If SVM learning progresses well, then the number of unlabeled data within the margin drops quickly. Thus the size of unlabeled data within the margin is a good indicator for the performance of the SVM. In particular, representative sampling performs badly if there is no clear cluster structure in those data. A good hybrid approach might be to start with representative sampling and to switch to normal active learning at an appropriate instance. This instance can be defined experimentally by observing the change in the number of unlabeled data within the margin. Figure 8 shows the initial result of such a *hybrid* algorithm applied to the topic *acq*. As shown, the strategy switches from representative sampling to active learning at the correct instance.

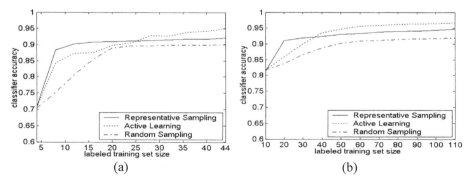

Fig. 3. Average classification accuracy r of five topics versus the number of labeled training instances, (a) m=4 (b) m=10

Finally we would like to emphasize that achieving a good performance in initial stages is an important feature for *text classification* since experts always expect the quality of a classification system by the initial interaction.

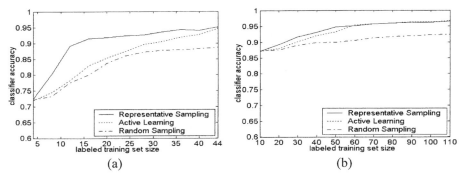

Fig. 4. Average classification accuracy r for topic earn versus the number of labeled training instances, (a) m=4 (b) m=10

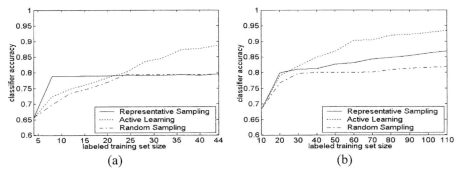

Fig. 5. Average classification accuracy r for topic acq versus the number of labeled training instances, (a) m=4 (b) m=10

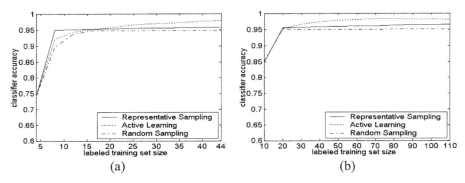

Fig. 6. Average classification accuracy r for topic grain versus the number of labeled training instances, (a) m=4 (b) m=10

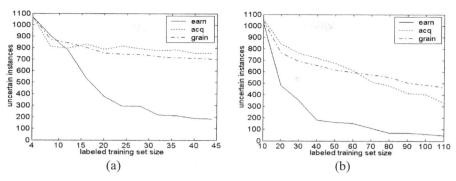

Fig. 7. Average number of the uncertain instances in the margin for three topics versus the number of labeled training instances, (a) m=4 (b) m=10

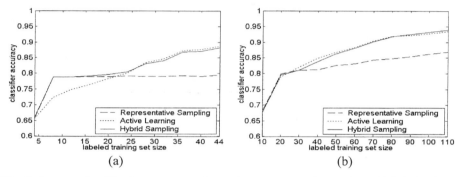

Fig. 8. Average classification accuracy r for topic *earn* versus the number of labeled training instances, with the hybrid method (a) $m=4$ (b) $m=10$

5   Conclusions

This paper made the attempt to investigate the value of the unlabeled data distribution, e.g. clustering structure, in SVM active learning and proposed a novel active learning heuristic for text classification. In addition, a novel hybrid strategy was presented. The analysis about optimal multi-instance selection for version space shrinkage provides a novel extension to previous work. The experiments demonstrated that in the beginning stages of active learning, the proposed representative sampling approach significantly outperformed SVM active learning and random sampling. This is a favorable property for the applications to text retrieval. However, in some cases SVM, active learning after a number of active learning iterations outperformed the representative sample. We initially analyzed the reasons for this phenomenon and found that the number of unlabeled instances within the SVM margin is a good indicator for the performance of our approach. The poor performance of representative sampling in some cases might be due to the poor clustering structure and high complexity of unlabeled data within the margin. This observed problem attracts us to further study the relation between data distribution within the margin and the performance of SVM in text classification tasks. Also, the work we described here is somewhat heuristic, but might provide a good starting point for further refinement towards a solid learning approach in future work.

References

1. Blum, A., Mitchell, T.: Combining Labeled and Unlabeled Data with Co-training. In Proceedings of the Eleventh Annual Conference on Computational Learning Theory, (1998) 92-100
2. Burges, C.J.: A tutorial on support vector machines for pattern recognition. Data Mining and Knowledge Discovery 2, (1998) 121-167
3. [Drucker et al., 2001] H. Drucker, B. Shahrary and D.C. Gibbon, Relevance feedback using support vector machines. Proc. 18th International Conf. On Machine Learning, 122-129, 2001.
4. Fishman, G.: Monte Carlo. Concepts, Algorithms and Applications. Springer Verlag, 1996
5. Gray, R.M., Vector Quantization, IEEE ASSP Magazine, (1984) 4--29.
6. Joachims, T.: Text Categorization with Support Vector Machines: Learning with Many Relevant Features. In European Conference on Machine Learning, ECML-98, (1998), 137-142
7. Joachims, T.: Transductive Inference for Text Classification using Support Vector Machines. In Proceedings of International Conference on Machine Learning, (1999)
8. Lewis, D., Gale, W.: A Sequential Algorithm for Training Text Classifiers. Proc. of the Eleventh International Conference on Machine Learning. Morgan Kaufmann, (1994) 148-156
9. McCallum, A., Nigam, K.: Employing EM in pool-based active learning for text classification. In Proceedingsof the fifteenth international conference of machine learning (ICML 98), (1998) 350-358
10. Mitchell, T.: Generalization as search. Artificial Intelligence 28 (1982) 203-226
11. Platt, J.: Probabilistics for SV Machines. In Advances in Large Margin Classifiers. A.Smola, P. Bartlett, Bscholkopf, D. Shuurmans eds., MIT Press (1999) 61-74
12. Schohn, G., Cohn, D.: Less is More: Active Learning with Support Vector Machines. Proc. of the Seventeenth International Conference on Machine Learning (2000)
13. Seung, H.S., Opper, M., Sompolinsky, H.: Query by committee. In Proceedings of the fifth annual ACM workshop on Computational Leanring Theory, (1992), 287-294
14. Tong, S., Koller, D.: Support Vector Machine Active Learning with Applications to Text Classification. Journal of Machine Learning Research. Volume 2, (2001) 45-66

15. Vapnik, V.: Estimation of Dependences Based on Empirical Data. Springer Verlag. 1982.
16. Zhang, T., Oles, F.: A probabilistic analysis on the value of unlabeled data for classification problems. International Conference on Machine Learning (2000)

Chinese Text Categorization
Based on the Binary Weighting Model
with Non-binary Smoothing

Xue Dejun and Sun Maosong

State Key Laboratory of Intelligent Technology and Systems
Department of Computer Science and Technology, Tsinghua University
Beijing, China 100084
xdj00@mails.tsinghua.edu.cn
lkc-dcs@mail.tsinghua.edu.cn

Abstract. In Text Categorization (TC) based on the vector space model, feature weighting is vital for the categorization effectiveness. Various non-binary weighting schemes are widely used for this purpose. By emphasizing the category discrimination capability of features, the paper firstly puts forward a new weighting scheme TF*IDF*IG. Upon the fact that refined statistics may have more chance to meet sparse data problem, we re-evaluate the role of the Binary Weighting Model (BWM) in TC for further consideration. As a consequence, a novel approach named the Binary Weighting Model with Non-Binary Smoothing (BWM-NBS) is then proposed so as to overcome the drawback of BWM. A TC system for Chinese texts using words as features is implemented. Experiments on a large-scale Chinese document collection with 71,674 texts show that the F1 metric of categorization performance of BWM-NBS gets to 94.9% in the best case, which is 26.4% higher than that of TF*IDF, 19.1% higher than that of TF*IDF*IG, and 5.8% higher than that of BWM under the same condition. Moreover, BWM-NBS exhibits the strong stability in categorization performance.

1 Introduction

The task of Text Categorization (TC) is to automatically assign natural language texts with thematic categories from a predefined category set [1]. With the popularization of Internet and electronic publications, TC has been studied extensively in the last decade, and a growing number of statistical classification methods and machine learning techniques have been explored to handle this challenging task, including Bayesian classifier [4, 5, 6], neural network classifier [7], the nearest neighbor classifier [8], decision rule classifier [9], centroid-based classifier [10], Rocchio classifier [11], support vector machine (SVM) [12], classifier committees [13, 14], hierarchical classification [15], etc. These efforts mainly aimed at English language.

F. Sebastiani (Ed.): ECIR 2003, LNCS 2633, pp. 408–419, 2003.

In recent years, some work of TC for Chinese texts has been reported as well [21, 22, 23, 24, 25].

In TC, Vector Space Model (VSM) is widely adopted to index texts [2]. In the model, a text is abstracted as a weighted feature vector. All potential features form a feature space with high dimensions in which a text (vector) can be seen as a point. Three basic issues arise consequently: (1) what should be regarded as features, (2) how to evaluate the weight of a feature in a feature vector, and (3) how to reduce the high dimension of the feature space.

A typical solution for the first issue is to take words occurring in texts as features. It is reported that complex features may yield worse categorization effectiveness [1].

Binary weighting and numeric weighting (non-binary weighting) are two common approaches to the second issue. In the binary weighting scheme, which is likely used in probabilistic model classifiers and decision rule classifiers, the weight of a feature is either 1 or 0, corresponding to whether the feature appearing in the text or not [4, 6, 9, 21]. The non-binary weighting scheme is more popular in TC, in which the weight of a feature ranges between 0 and 1 due to the contribution of the feature to representation of the text. The classical TF*IDF function from Information Retrieval (IR) and a variety of its variations are widely exploited [1, 2, 16, 20].

As for the third issue, a process called feature selection is often carried out by selecting the top significant features from the original feature set. Yang et al. [16] compared five kinds of statistics in dimension reduction, including Document Frequency (DF), Information Gain (IG), Chi-square (CHI), Mutual Information (MI), and Term Strength (TS). The experiments on Reuters-22173 (13,272 documents) and OHSUMED (3,981 documents) showed that CHI and IG are most effective. Galavotti et al. [18] came up with the Simplified Chi-square (SCHI). Their experiments on Reuters-21578 (12,902 documents) demonstrated that SCHI is superior to CHI in case of high level of reduction (above 95%), in other cases however, the result is reverse. Peters et al. [26] introduced an uncertainty-based method for feature selection which would be quite stable across data sets and algorithms.

Now we zoom in Chinese. One of the distinguishing characteristics of Chinese is that there is no explicit word boundary, like spacing in English, in texts. N-gram Chinese character string is therefore considered as an alternative of indexing unit in TC. Nie et al. [20] found through experiments that in Chinese IR using Chinese character bigrams as features performs slightly better than using Chinese words (the longest-word-matching algorithm). But they believed that larger room of improvement may exist for word-based IR. In addition, the dimension of the original feature space obtained by using words as features is much smaller than that of using character bigrams.

In the paper, we at first present a new non-binary weighting scheme, TF*IDF*IG, by incorporating IG into the standard TF*IDF, then recall the binary weighting model (BWM for short) accounting for the data sparseness problem produced by the huge feature space in TC. As a consequence, we propose a novel model for TC, named 'the Binary Weighting Model with Non-Binary Smoothing' (BWM-NBS for short), in which the binary weighting model will play the major role whereas the non-binary weighting only play the supplementary one. An automated TC system for Chinese texts using words as features and the centroid-based classifier for decision-making is also designed and implemented. Experimental results on a large-scale Chinese corpus

(71,674 documents) show that BWM-NBS improves the categorization effectiveness very significantly.

The remainder of this paper is organized as follows. The idea of our approach is explained in Section 2. In Section 3, we outline the experimental design. The experimental results and the related analyses are given in Section 4. The last section is with some conclusions and our future work.

2   The Idea

2.1   The TF*IDF*IG Weighting Scheme

Among the variations of the standard TF*IDF weighting function, we adopt formula 1, which has exhibited good performance in our experiments, to estimate the weight of a feature t_k regarding a category c_j:

$$w(t_k, c_j) = TF(t_k, c_j) \times IDF(t_k) = \log(tf_{kj} + 1.0) \times \log(N / df_k). \tag{1}$$

where tf_{kj} stands for the frequency of feature t_k with category c_j, df_k the document frequency of t_k, and N the total number of documents in the training set. All the non-binary feature weights are to be normalized throughout our experiments, but we omit this step in the paper for the purpose of simplicity.

According to IDF of formula 1, a feature which occurs in few documents would get a high weight, even if the feature evenly distribute in the category space. It is obvious that formula 1 somehow emphasizes the capability of features to distinguish documents rather than to distinguish categories. We thus introduce IG into formula 1 to enhance the capability of category discrimination, resulting in a new weighting scheme named TF*IDF*IG, as shown in formulae 2 and 3:

$$w(t_k, c_j) = TF(t_k, c_j) \times IDF(t_k) \times IG(t_k). \tag{2}$$

$$IG(t_k) = -\sum_{j=1}^{M} P(c_j) \log P(c_j) + P(t_k) \sum_{j=1}^{M} P(c_j | t_k) \log P(c_j | t_k)$$
$$+ P(\overline{t_k}) \sum_{j=1}^{M} P(c_j | \overline{t_k}) \log P(c_j | \overline{t_k}). \tag{3}$$

where $P(c_j)$ is the probability of category c_j, $P(t_k)$ the probability of documents containing t_k on document space (i.e., the number of documents containing t_k over the total number of documents in the training set), $P(c_j | t_k)$ the conditional probability that given t_k, for a random document x, feature t_k occurs in x and x belongs to category c_j (i.e., the number of documents containing t_k and belonging to c_j over the total number of documents containing t_k in the training set), and M the number of predefined categories.

2.2   The Binary Weighting Model

The shift from formula 1 to formula 2 reflects to some extent a strong tendency in TC that the refined statistics are likely to be used in describing the category discrimination capability of features. However, the higher the degree of the refined statistics used, the more the requirement of TC to the size of training set. The number of features in TC is usually at the magnitude of $10^3 \sim 10^4$, so even if the training set is composed of hundreds of thousands of documents, the problem of data sparseness still comes[3]. We would suffer from all disadvantages generated from data sparseness, such as over-fitting in modeling, and unreliability of derived statistics in which the noise might be seriously propagated and the distinction between categorization capabilities of features distorted [26].

Observe a typical case in TC. We randomly select a category 'archaeology', which contains 4,437 features in a specific feature set with 10,000 items, as target. The TF*IDF weights of the top 10 features and the last 10 features are listed in Table 1. Column 5 gives the result of the weight of the top 1 feature over the weights of the last 10 features respectively. As can be seen, the values are quite large, implying that the contributions of low ranked features to categorization could be easily submerged by the high ranked ones.

We believe that the effect of the refined statistics is two-fold: on the one hand, they might be beneficial to TC, as being desired, by amplifying important features and oppressing less-important features, on the other hand, they might also produce losses in TC because of improper treatment of amplification and oppression. In fact, unlike other machine learning tasks such as regression or density estimation that require the estimated function to match the real function as exactly as possible, the performance of TC would be guaranteed as long as the ranking of the calculated category scores still corresponds to the real order of document-to-category similarities, even if the semantics of a document fails to be understood [5].

Table 1. The Comparison of TF*IDF Weights Among the Top 10 Features and the Last 10 Features in the Category of Archaeology

Rank	TF*IDF: wt(rank)	Rank	TF*IDF: wl(rank)	wt(1) /wl(rank)
1	0.039095	4428	0.004160	9.40
2	0.039011	4429	0.004122	9.48
3	0.038988	4430	0.004042	9.67
4	0.038780	4431	0.003977	9.83
5	0.038244	4432	0.003818	10.24
6	0.038112	4433	0.003470	11.27
7	0.037558	4434	0.002114	18.50
8	0.037407	4435	0.002014	19.41
9	0.037190	4436	0.001642	23.81
10	0.037069	4437	0.000878	44.51

Based on the above considerations, we recall the binary weighting model (BWM) here, as given in formula 4, and re-evaluate the behavior of this simplest model of feature weighting in the context of large-size feature set.

$$w_b(t_k, c_j) = \begin{cases} 1 & \text{if } t_k \text{ occurs in category } c_j \\ 0 & \text{if } t_k \text{ does not occur in category } c_j \end{cases}. \tag{4}$$

2.3   The Binary Weighting Model with Non-binary Smoothing

In BWM, if all of the features in a document belong to more than one category, a non-definite assignment will happen. This case occurs frequently in particular when the feature set over all categories is not large enough and the document to be classified is small. We further incorporate the non-binary weighting information into BWM so as to overcome the drawback:

$$w(t_k, c_j) = w_b(t_k, c_j) + w_n(t_k, c_j). \tag{5}$$

where $w_b(t_k, c_j)$ stands for the binary weight of feature t_k in category c_j (refer to formula 4), $w_n(t_k, c_j)$ a normalized non-binary weight, such as formula 1 or formula 2, with value far less than 1. Apparently, $w_b(t_k, c_j)$ is a dominant factor in formula 5 and $w_n(t_k, c_j)$ is a supplementary one. The effect of the latter becomes significant only when values of the former for some categories are identical. In this sense, we view $w_n(t_k, c_j)$ as a smoothing of $w_b(t_k, c_j)$.

3   Experiment Design

In order to validate our idea, we design a TC system for Chinese texts, and experiment on a large-scale document collection.

3.1   Training Set and Test Set

We adopt the categorization system of Encyclopedia of China, which comprises 55 categories, as predefined category set. According to this categorization system, we build up a document collection consisting of 71,674 texts with about 74 million Chinese characters. Each text is manually assigned a category label out of the category set. The number of documents in the categories is quite different, ranging from 399 (Solid Earth Physics Category) to 3,374 (Biology Category). The average number of documents per category is 1303. The average length of documents is 921 Chinese characters. We randomly divide the document collection into two parts: 64,533 texts for training and 7,141 texts for testing in proportion of 9:1.

The longest-word-matching algorithm is used to segment texts into word strings with a dictionary of 87,189 entries. An original feature set involving 49,397 distinct Chinese words is obtained after removing words with *tf* under 10 from the segmented training set.

3.2   Dimension Reduction

In the experiments, we exploit CHI to further select features from the original feature set with 49,397 distinct words. Yang et al. [16] gave two versions of CHI. According to their report, we select the version that performs better (formulae 6 and 7).

$$w(t_k, c_j) = \frac{N[P(t_k, c_j) \times P(\overline{t_k}, \overline{c_j}) - P(t_k, \overline{c_j}) \times P(\overline{t_k}, c_j)]^2}{P(t_k) \times P(c_j) \times P(\overline{t_k}) \times P(\overline{c_j})} . \tag{6}$$

$$w(t_k) = \max_{j=1}^{M} \{w(t_k, c_j)\}. \tag{7}$$

where $w(t_k, c_j)$ is the weight of feature t_k regarding category c_j, $w(t_k)$ the weight of feature t_k regarding the training set, N the total number of documents in the training set, and $P(t_k, c_j)$ the probability of a random document containing feature t_k and belonging to category c_j (other probabilities involved in formula 6 are defined in a similar way).

The retained features after global feature selection under certain condition form the feature set with regard to that condition accordingly (see also section 4).

3.3   The Centroid-Based Classifier

In our TC system, we make use of the centroid-based classifier, a sort of profile-based classifier, because of its simplicity and efficiency. After word segmentation and dimension reduction, we build *tf* vectors for documents, and sum up *tf* vectors in each category to get the *tf* vector of the category, then weight the features based on the summed *tf* vectors of categories with a criterion as formulae 1, 2, 4 or 5 to create weighted feature vectors for categories. The resulting feature vectors are considered as the centroids of the categories:

$$V_j = (w_{1j}, w_{2j}, ..., w_{sj}) . \tag{8}$$

where w_{kj}, the weight of feature t_k regarding category j ($j=1, ..., M$), equals 0 or 1 in binary weighting, or a real number ranging between 0 and 1 in non-binary weighting.

Then, classifier f can be set up:

$$f = \arg\max_{j=1}^{M} (V_j \bullet d) . \tag{9}$$

where d is the relevant weighted feature vector of an input document.

In the experiments, the classification performance for each category is measured by Precision (Pr) and Recall (Re), and that for the whole category set, by the F1 metric with micro-averaging of individual Pr and Re.

4   Experimental Results

4.1   Experiment on TF*IDF*IG

As can be seen in Fig.1, TF*IDF*IG outperforms TF*IDF (The process of dimension reduction in section 3.2 is used to control the horizontal axis in all figures in section 4). In the best case (the original feature set with 49,397 distinct words), the F1 metric of TF*IDF*IG (79.7%) is 6.1% higher than that of TF*IDF (75.1%), indicating that IG can contribute a lot to the improvement of categorization performance. Note that the degree of improvement decreases as the number of selected features declines.

We further calculate the correlation coefficients among TF, IDF and IG, as given in Table 2. We can see that TF is negatively correlated with the other two statistics, and IDF and IG are correlated with a high positive coefficient 0.91 (this is consistent with the fact that a feature with a low *df* usually distributes in a few categories). It is assumed that the difference between IDF and IG, though not large enough, is still meaningful in promoting the categorization performance.

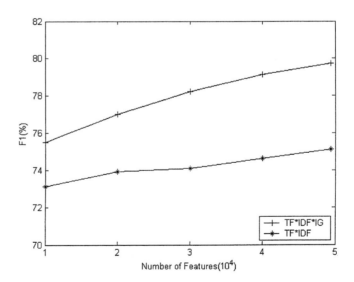

Fig. 1. The Categorization Performances of TF*IDF and TF*IDF*IG

Table 2. Correlation Coefficients between TF, IDF and IG

	TF	IDF	IG
TF	1		
IDF	-0.97	1	
IG	-0.86	0.91	1

4.2   Experiment on BWM

Fig. 2 illustrates the performances of BWM, TF*IDF and TF*IDF*IG. The curve of BWM is very steep compared to the curves of TF*IDF and TF*IDF*IG with comparatively flat shapes. It is amazing that as the number of selected features is above 30,000, BWM outperforms TF*IDF*IG and TF*IDF remarkably. In the best case (again, the original feature set with 49,397 distinct words), the F1 metric of BWM gets to 89.7%, which is 19.4% higher than that of TF*IDF, and 12.5% higher than that of TF*IDF*IG. This convinces our hypothesis in section 2.2 that the refined statistics may amplify noises while amplifying some 'important' features, and provides an evidence for Peter's points of view on feature uncertainty as well [26]. Note that as the number of selected features is below 20,000, the performance of BWM becomes very poor. The reason is obvious: binary weighting is too rough to profile the categories with a small-size feature set. Possessing enough features is a necessity for BWM to be powerful.

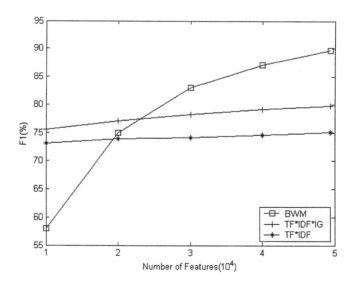

Fig. 2. The Categorization Performance of BWM

4.3   Experiment on BWM-NBS

Fig. 3 shows the performances of BWM-NBS, BWM, TF*IDF*IG, and TF*IDF. We can see that BWM-NBS outperforms all the other statistics in all cases. In the best case (still the original feature set with 49,397 distinct words), the F1 metric of BWM-NBS is up to 94.9%, which is 5.8% higher than that of BWM. With the help of smoothing, BWM-NBS is able to conquer the weakness of BWM to the maximum extent, as evidenced by the fact that the categorization performance increases considerably in cases of small-size feature sets, for instance, from 58.0% (BWM) to 83.9% (BWM-NBS) while the size of the feature set is 10,000. And, BWM-NBS becomes much more stable than its predecessor BWM.

Another interesting fact is that though TF*IDF*IG outperforms TF*IDF rather well if running alone, such an advantage almost disappears in the framework of BWM-NBS. It can be seen in Fig.3 that the curves of BWM-NBS+TF*IDF and BWM-NBS+TF*IDF*IG are merged together in all cases. The simpler one, i.e., BWM-NBS+TF*IDF, would therefore be recommended as the best solution for TC among all solutions discussed here.

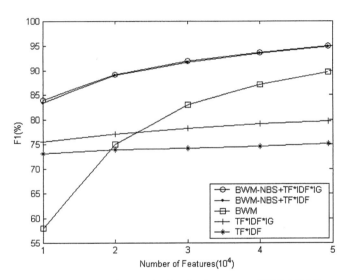

Fig. 3. The Categorization Performance of BWM-NBS

5   Conclusions

Feature weighting is vital to the categorization effectiveness in TC. Various non-binary weighting schemes are widely used for this purpose. By emphasizing the category discrimination capability of features, the paper firstly puts forward a new weighting scheme TF*IDF*IG, which seems superior to TF*IDF with a considerable enhancement. Upon the fact that refined statistics may have more chance to meet sparse data problem, we re-evaluate the role of the Binary Weighting Model (BWM) in TC for further consideration. What is surprising is that BWM, the simplest feature weighting scheme, performs much better than TF*IDF*IG if the feature set is large enough. A novel approach named the Binary Weighting Model with Non-Binary Smoothing (BWM-NBS) is then proposed consequently so as to overcome the drawback of BWM. A TC system for Chinese texts using words as features is implemented. Experiments on a large-scale Chinese document collection with 71,674 texts show that the F1 metric of categorization performance of BWM-NBS gets to 94.9% in the best case, which is 26.4% higher than that of TF*IDF, 19.1% higher than that of TF*IDF*IG, and 5.8% higher than that of BWM under the same condition. Moreover, BWM-NBS exhibits the strong stability in performance of categorization.

Future work includes: (1) some open topics inspired by the interesting phenomena observed from experimental results of this paper need to be studied in depth, for example, it seems that both the complex feature weighting scheme and the simple feature weighting approach are capable of increasing the performance of TC (TF*IDF*IG is better than TF*IDF, meanwhile BWM is better than TF*IDF*IG), but these two paths, one from TF*IDF to TF*IDF*IG (a procedure of complication) and the other one from TF*IDF to BWM (a procedure of simplification), are in fact reverse each other; and (2) the proposed model here is language-independent in nature, so we are planning to extend it to document collections of other languages such as Reuters-21578 or OHSUMED for further validation.

Acknowledgements

This research is supported by the National Plan for the Development of Basic Research of China under grant No. G1998030507.

References

1. Sebastiani, F.: Machine Learning in Automated Text Categorization. ACM Computing Surveys, Vol. 34(1). ACM Press New York (2002) 1-47.
2. Salton, G., McGill, M.: Introduction to Modern Information Retrieval. McGraw-Hill Book Company, New York (1983).
3. Vapnik, V. N.: The Nature of Statistical Learning Theory. Springer-Verlag New York, Inc. (1995).
4. Lewis, D.D.: Naïve Bayes at Forty: The Independence Assumption in Information Retrieval. In Proceedings of 10th European Conference on Machine Learning (1998) 4-15.
5. Domingos, P., Pazzani, M.: Beyond Independence: Conditions for the Optimality of the Simple Bayesian Classifier. In Proceedings of 13 rd International Conference on Machine Learning (1996) 105-112.
6. McCallum, A., Nigam, K.: A Comparison of Event Models for Naïve Bayes Text Classification. In AAAI-98 Workshop on Learning for Text Categorization (1998) 41-48.

7. Wiener, E., Pedersen, J.O., Weigend, A.S.: A Neural Network Approach to Topic Spotting. In Proceedings of 4th Annual Symposium on Document Analysis and Information Retrieval (1995) 317-332.
8. Yang, Y.M.: Expert Network: Effective and Efficient Learning from Human Decisions in Text Categorization and Retrieval. In Proceedings of 17th Annual International ACM SIGIR Conference on Research and Development in Information Retrieval (1994) 11-21.
9. Apte, C., Damerau, F., Weiss, S.M.: Automated Learning of Decision Rules for Text Categorization. ACM Transactions on Information Retrieval, Vol. 12(3). ACM Press New York (1994) 233-251.
10. Theeramunkong T., Lertnattee V.: Improving Centroid-Based Text Classification Using Term-Distribution-Based Weighting System and Clustering. In Proceedings of International Symposium on Communications and Information Technology (2001) 33-36.
11. Joachims, T.: A Probabilistic Analysis of the Rocchio Algorithm with TFIDF for Text Categorization. In Proceedings of 14th of International Conference on Machine Learning (1997) 143-151.
12. Joachims, T: Text Categorization with Support Vector Machines: Learnging with Many Relevant Features. In Proceedings of 10th European Conference on Machine Learning (1998) 137-142.
13. Quinlan, J.: Bagging, Boosting, and C4.5. In Proceedings of 13th National Conference on Artificial Intelligence, AAAI Press/ MIT Press (1996) 163-175.
14. Schapire, R.E., Singer, Y.: BoosTexter: A Boosting-Based System for Text Categorization. Machine Learning, Vol. 39(2/3), (2000) 135-168.
15. Theeramunkong, T., Lertnattee, V.: Multi-dimensional Text Classification. In Proceedings of 19th International Conference on Computational Linguistics (2002) 1002-1008.
16. Yang Y.M., Pedersen, P.O.: A Comparative Study on Feature Selection in Text Categorization. In Proceedings of 14th International Conference on Machine Learning (1997) 412-420.
17. Ng, H.T., Goh, W.B., Low, K.L.: Feature Selection, Perceptron Learning, and a Usability Case Study for Text Categorization. In Proceedings of 20th Annual International ACM SIGIR Conference on Research and Development in Information Retrieval (1997) 67-73.
18. Galavotti, L., Sebastiani, F., Simi, S.: Experiments on the Use of Feature Selection and Negative Evidence in Automated Text Categorization. In Proceedings of 4th European Conference on Research and Advanced Technology for Digital Libraries (2000) 59-68.
19. Nie, J.Y., Brisebois, M., Ren, X.B.: On Chinese Word Segmentation and Word-Based Text Retrieval. In Proceedings of International Conference on Chinese Computing (1996) 405-412.
20. Nie, J.Y., Ren, F.J.: Chinese Information Retrieval: Using Characters or Words? Information Processing and Management Vol. 35, (1999) 443-462.
21. Xue, D.J., Sun, M.S.: An Automated Text Categorization System for Chinese Based on the Multinomial Bayesian Model. In Proceedings of Digital Library – IT Opportunities and Challenges in the New Millennium (2002) 131-140.

22. Xie, C.F., Li, X.: A Sequence-Based Automatic Text Classification Algorithm. Journal of Software, Vol. 13(4), (2002) 783-789.
23. Huang, X.J., Wu, L.D., Hiroyuki, I., Xu, G.W.: Language Independent Text Categorization. Journal of Chinese Information Processing, Vol. 14(6), (2000) 1-7.
24. Gong, X.J., Liu, S.H., Shi, Z.Z.: An Incremental Bayes Classification Model. Chinese J. Computers, Vol. 25(6), (2002) 645-650.
25. Zhou, S.G., Guan, J.H.: Chinese Documents Classification Based on N-grams. In Proceedings of 3rd Annual Conference on Intelligent Text Processing and Computational Linguistics (2002) 405-414.
26. Peters, C., Koster, C.H.A.: Uncertainty-Based Noise Reduction and Term Selection in Text Categorization. In Proceedings of 24th BCS-IRSG European Colloquium on IR Research (2002) 248-267.

A Study on Optimal Parameter Tuning for Rocchio Text Classifier

Alessandro Moschitti

University of Rome *Tor Vergata*
Department of Computer Science Systems and Production
00133 Rome (Italy)
`moschitti@info.uniroma2.it`

Abstract. Current trend in operational text categorization is the designing of fast classification tools. Several studies on improving accuracy of *fast* but less accurate classifiers have been recently carried out. In particular, enhanced versions of the Rocchio text classifier, characterized by high performance, have been proposed. However, even in these extended formulations the problem of tuning its parameters is still neglected.
In this paper, a study on parameters of the Rocchio text classifier has been carried out to achieve its maximal accuracy. The result is a model for the automatic selection of parameters. Its main feature is to bind the searching space so that optimal parameters can be selected quickly. The space has been bound by giving a feature selection interpretation of the Rocchio parameters. The benefit of the approach has been assessed via extensive cross evaluation over three corpora in two languages. Comparative analysis shows that the performances achieved are relatively close to the best TC models (e.g. Support Vector Machines).

1 Introduction

Machine learning techniques applied to text categorization (TC) problems have produced very accurate although computationally complex models. In contrast, systems of real scenario such as Web applications and large-scale information management necessitate fast classification tools. Accordingly, several studies (e.g. [4, 6, 7]) on improving accuracy of low complexity classifiers have been carried out. They are related to the designing of efficient TC models in Web scenarios: feature space reduction, probabilistic interpretation of k-Nearest Neighbor and hierarchical classifiers are different approaches for optimizing speed and accuracy.

In this perspective, there is a renewed interest in the Rocchio formula. Models based on it are characterized by a low time complexity for both training and operative phases. The Rocchio weakness in TC application is that accuracy is often much lower than other more computationally complex text classifiers [19, 9]. Cohen and Singer [5] have suggested that a suitable tuning of parameters can improve the Rocchio text classifier accuracy. However, they did not propose

F. Sebastiani (Ed.): ECIR 2003, LNCS 2633, pp. 420–435, 2003.

a procedure for their estimation, as the parameters chosen to optimize the classification accuracy over the training documents were, in general, different from those optimizing the *test-set* classification. A possible explanation is that the searching in parameter space was made at random: a bunch of values for parameters was tried without applying a specific methodology.

Another attempt to enhance the Rocchio classifier is described in [14]. There, Schapire et al. show that Rocchio standard classifier can achieve the state-of-the art performances, although its efficiency is penalized. Improvements in accuracy are achieved by using more effective weighting schemes and *query zoning* methods, but a methodology for estimating Rocchio parameters was not considered.

Thus, the literature confirms the need of designing a methodology that automatically derives optimal parameters. Such a procedure should search parameters in the set of all feasible values. As no analytical procedure is available for deriving optimal Rocchio parameters, some heuristics are needed to limit the searching space. Our idea to reduce the searching space is to consider the feature selection property of the Rocchio formula. We will show that:

1. The setting of Rocchio parameters can be reduced to the setting of the rate among parameters.
2. Different values for the rate induce the selection of feature subsets ranked by relevance.
3. Only the features in the selected subset affect the accuracy of Rocchio classifier parameterized with the target parameter rate.
4. The parameter rate is inverse-proportional to the cardinality of the feature subset.

Therefore, increasing the parameter rate produces a subset collection of decreasing cardinality. Rocchio classifier, trained with these subsets, outcomes different accuracies. The parameter rate seems affect accuracy in the same way a standard feature selector [11] would do. From this perspective, the problem of finding optimal parameter rate can be reduced to the feature selection problem for TC and solved as proposed in [20].

Section 2 defines the Text Categorization problem and its accuracy measurements. The parameter setting algorithm and the underlying idea is presented in Section 3. The resulting system has been experimented via cross-validation over three different collections in two different languages (Italian and English) in Section 4. Finally, conclusions are derived in Section 5.

2   Profile-Based Text Classification

The classification problem is the derivation of a decision function f that maps documents $(d \in D)$ into one or more classes, i.e. $f : D \rightarrow 2^C$, once a set of classes $C = \{C_1, ..., C_n\}$, i.e. topics labels (e.g. *Politics* and *Economics*), is given. The function f is usually built according to an extensive collection of examples classified into C_i, called *training-set*.

Profile-based text classifiers are characterized by a function f based on a similarity measure between the synthetic representation of each class C_i and the incoming document d. Both representations are vectors, and similarity is traditionally estimated as the cosine angle between the two. The description C_i of each target class C_i is usually called *profile*, that is, a vector summarizing all training documents d such as $d \in C_i$. Vector components are called *features* and refer to independent dimensions in the similarity space. Traditional techniques (e.g. [13]) employ words or stems as basic features. The i-th component of a vector representing a given document d is a numerical value. It is the weight that the i-th feature of the *training-set* assumes in d (usually evaluated as $TF \cdot IDF$ product [13]). Similarly, profiles are derived from the grouping of positive and negative instances d for the target category C_i. A newly incoming document is considered a member for a given class *iff* the similarity estimation overcomes established thresholds. The latter are parameters that adjust the trade-off between *precision* and *recall*. In the next section, the performance measures to derive text classifier accuracy are shown.

2.1   Accuracy Measurements

We have adopted the following performance measurements:

$$recall = \frac{\texttt{categ. found and correct}}{\texttt{total categ. correct}} = \frac{\texttt{cfc}}{\texttt{tcc}} \tag{1}$$

$$precision = \frac{\texttt{categ. found and correct}}{\texttt{total categ. found}} = \frac{\texttt{cfc}}{\texttt{tcf}} \tag{2}$$

To maintain a single performance measurement, the interpolated *Breakeven point* (BEP) could be adopted. This is the point in which the *recall* is equal to the *precision*. It can be evaluated starting the threshold from 0 and increasing it until the *precision* is equal to the *recall*. The mean is applied to interpolates the BEP if it does not exist. However, this may provide artificial results [15] when *precision* is not *close* enough to *recall*. The f_1-measure improves the BEP definition by using the harmonic mean between *precision* and *recall*, i.e. $f_1 = \frac{2 \cdot precision \cdot recall}{precision + recall}$.

In our experiments we have evaluated the thresholds associated with the maximal BEP on a *validation-set*[1]. Then, the performances have been derived from the *test-set* by adopting the previous thresholds. Finally, as global measures of a set of classifiers, we apply the *microaverage* to the target performance measures (i.e. *precision*, *recall*, BEP and f_1) over all categories. In this case, the correct and found categories of Eq. 1 and 2 are summed[2] before the microaverage computation of the *recall* and *precision* for a pool of k binary classifiers[3]. These measures are then used for evaluating the *microaverage* of BEP and f_1 (MicroAvg-f_1).

---

[1] A separate portion of the *training-set* used for parameterization purposes.

[2] The microaverage *recall* R and the microaverage *precision* P are respectively $\sum_{i=1}^{k} \texttt{cfc}_i / \sum_{i=1}^{k} \texttt{tcc}_i$ and $\sum_{i=1}^{k} \texttt{cfc}_i / \sum_{i=1}^{k} \texttt{tcf}_i$. The *MicroAvg-$f_1$* is then evaluate as $\frac{2P \cdot R}{P+R}$.

[3] A binary classifier is a decision function that assigns or not a document to a single category.

3   Study on the Rocchio Parameter Spaces

The Rocchio's formula has been successfully used for building profiles in text classification [8] as follows. Given the set of training documents R classified under the topic C, the set $\bar{R}$ of training documents not classified in C, a document d and a feature f, the weight Ω_f assumed by f in the profile of C is:

$$\Omega_f = \max\left\{0, \frac{\beta}{|R|}\sum_{d \in R}\omega_f^d - \frac{\gamma}{|\bar{R}|}\sum_{d \in \bar{R}}\omega_f^d\right\} \tag{3}$$

where ω_f^d represents the weights[4] of features f in documents d. In Eq. 3, the parameters β and γ control the relative impact of positive and negative examples and determine the weight of f in the target profile. In [8], Eq. 3 has been used with values $\beta = 16$ and $\gamma = 4$ for the categorization task of low quality images. The success of these values possibly led to a wrong reuse of them in the TC task (e.g. [19]). In fact, as it has been pointed out in [5], these parameters greatly depend on the training corpus and different settings produce a significant variation in performances. Recently, some researchers [17] have found that $\gamma = \beta$ is a good setting for the document space, however, systematic methodologies for parameter setting were not definitively proposed.

3.1   Searching Space of Rocchio Parameters

As claimed in the previous section, to improve the accuracy of the Rocchio text classifier, parameter tuning is needed. The exhaustive search of optimal values for β and γ parameters is not a feasible approach as it requires the evaluation of Rocchio accuracy for all the pairs in the $\Re^2$ space.

To reduce the searching space, we observe that not both γ and β parameters are needed. In the following we show how to bind the parameter β to the threshold parameter. The classifier accepts a document d in a category C if the scalar product between their representing vectors is greater than a threshold s, i.e. $C \cdot d > s$. Substituting C with the original Rocchio's formula we get:

$$\left(\frac{\beta}{|R|}\sum_{d \in R}\omega_f^d - \frac{\gamma}{|\bar{R}|}\sum_{d \in \bar{R}}\omega_f^d\right) \cdot d > s$$

and dividing by β,

$$\left(\frac{1}{|R|}\sum_{d \in R}\omega_f^d - \frac{\gamma}{\beta|\bar{R}|}\sum_{d \in \bar{R}}\omega_f^d\right) \cdot d > \frac{s}{\beta} \Rightarrow \left(\frac{1}{|R|}\sum_{d \in R}\omega_f^d - \frac{\rho}{|\bar{R}|}\sum_{d \in \bar{R}}\omega_f^d\right) \cdot d > s'.$$

Once ρ has been set, the threshold s' can be automatically assigned by the algorithm that evaluates the BEP. Note that, to estimate the threshold from a *validation-set*, the evaluation of BEP is always needed even if we maintain both parameters. The new Rocchio formula is:

---

[4] Several methods are used to assign weights to a feature, as widely discussed in [13].

$$\Omega_f = \max\left\{0, \frac{1}{|R|} \sum_{d \in R} \omega_f^d - \frac{\rho}{|\bar{R}|} \sum_{d \in \bar{R}} \omega_f^d\right\} \qquad (4)$$

where ρ represents the *rate* between the original Rocchio parameters, i.e. $\frac{\gamma}{\beta}$.

Our hypothesis for finding *good* ρ value is that it deeply depends on the differences among classes in term of document contents. This enables the existence of different optimal ρ for different categories. If a correlation function between the category similarity and ρ is derived, we can bound the searching space.

We observe that in Equation 4, features with negative difference between positive and negative weights are set to 0. This aspect is crucial since the 0-valued features do not contribute in the similarity estimation (i.e. they give a null contribution to the scalar product). Thus, the Rocchio model does not use them. Moreover, as ρ is increased *smoothly*, only the features having a *high* weight in the negative documents will be eliminated (they will be set to 0 value). These features are natural candidates to be irrelevant for the Rocchio classifier. On one hand, in [11, 20] it has been pointed out that classifier accuracy can improve if irrelevant features are removed from the feature set. On the other hand, the accuracy naturally decreases if relevant and some weak relevant features are excluded from the learning [11]. Thus, by increasing ρ, irrelevant features are removed until performance improves to a maximal point, then weak relevant and relevant features start to be eliminated, causing Rocchio accuracy to decrease. From the above hypothesis, we argue that:

The best setting for ρ can be derived by increasing it until Rocchio accuracy reaches a maximum point.

In Section 4.2, experiments show that the Rocchio accuracy has the above behavior. In particular, the ρ/accuracy relationship approximates a convex curve with a single max point.

An explanation of linguistic nature could be that a target class C has its own specific set of terms (i.e. features). We define *specific-terms* as the set of words typical of one domain (i.e. very frequents) and at the same time they occur infrequently in other domains. For example, *byte* occurs more frequently in a *Computer Science* category than a *Political* one, so it is a *specific-term* for *Computer Science* (with respect to the *Politic* category).

The Rocchio formula selects *specific-terms* in C also by *looking* at their weights in the other categories C_x. If negative information is emphasized enough the *non specific-terms* in C (e.g., terms that occur frequently even in C_x) are removed. Note that these *non specific-terms* are misleading for the categorization. The term *byte* in political documents is not useful for characterizing the political domain. Thus, until the *non specific-terms* are removed, the accuracy increases since noise is greatly reduced. On the other hand, if negative information is too much emphasized, some *specific-terms* tend to be eliminated and accuracy starts to decrease. For example, *memory* can be considered *specific-terms* in *Computer Science*, nevertheless it can appears in *Political* documents; by emphasizing its negative weight, it will be finally removed, even from the Computer Science profile. This suggests that the specificity of terms in C depends on C_x and it can be captured by the ρ parameter.

In the next section a procedure for parameter estimation of ρ over the *training-set* is presented.

3.2   Procedure for Parameter Estimation

We propose an approach that takes a set of training documents for profile building and a second subset, the *estimation-set*, to find the ρ value that optimizes the Breakeven Point. This technique allows parameter estimation over data independent of the *test-set* (TS), and the obvious bias due to the training material is avoided as widely discussed in [11]. The initial corpus is divided into a first subset of training documents, called *learning-set LS*, and a second subset of documents used to evaluate the performance, i.e. TS.

Given the target category, estimation of its optimal ρ parameter can be carried out according to the following *held-out* procedure:

1. A subset of LS, called *estimation set ES* is defined.
2. Set $i = 1$ and $\rho_i =$ Init_value.
3. Build the category profile by using ρ_i in the Eq. 4 and the *learning-set $LS - ES$*.
4. Evaluate the BEP_i for the target classifier (as described in Section 2.1) over the set ES.
5. Optionally: if $i > 1$ and $BEP_{i-1} \geq BEP_i$ go to point 8.
6. if $\rho_i >$ Max_limit go to point 8.
7. Set $\rho_{i+1} = \rho_i + \Sigma$, $i = i + 1$ and go to point 3.
8. Output ρ_k, where $k = argmax_i(BEP_i)$.

The minimal value for ρ (i.e. the Init_value) is 0 as a negative rate makes no sense in the feature selection interpretation. The maximal value can be derived considering that: (a) for each ρ, a different subset of features is used in the Rocchio classifier and (b) the size of the subset decrease by increasing ρ. Experimentally, we have found that $\rho = 30$ corresponds to a subset of 100 features out of 33,791 initial ones for the *Acquisition* category of Reuters corpus. The above feature reduction is rather aggressive as pointed out in [20] so, we chose 30 as our maximal limit for ρ.

However, in the feature selection interpretation of ρ setting, an objective maximal limit exists: it is the value that assigns a null weight to all features that are also present in the negative examples. This is an important result as it enables the automatic evaluation of the maximum ρ limit on training corpus in a linear time. It can be obtained by evaluating the rate between the negative and the positive contributions in Eq. 4 for each feature f and by taking the maximum value. For example we have found a value of 184.90 for the *Acquisition* category.

The values for Σ also (i.e. the increment for ρ) can be derived by referring to the feature selection paradigm. In [20, 19, 9] the subsets derived in their feature selection experiments have a decreasing cardinality. They start from the total number of unique features n and then select $n - i \cdot k$ features in the i-th subset; k varies between 500 and 5,000. When $\Sigma = 1$ is used in our estimation algorithm, subsets of similar sizes are generated. Moreover, some preliminary experiments have suggested that smaller values for Σ do not select better ρ (i.e., they do not produce better Rocchio accuracy).

A more reliable estimation of ρ can be applied if steps 2-8 are carried out according to different, randomly generated splits ES_k and $LS - ES_k$. Several values $\rho(ES_k)$ can thus be derived at step k. A resulting $\bar{\rho}$ can be obtained by averaging the $\rho(ES_k)$. Hereafter we will refer to the Eq. 4 parameterized with estimated ρ values as the *Parameterized Rocchio Classifier* (*PRC*).

3.3   *PRC* Complexity

The evaluation of Rocchio classifier time complexity can be divided in to three steps: *pre-processing*, *learning* and *classification*. The *pre-processing* includes the document formatting and the extraction of features. We will neglect this extra time as it is common in almost all text classifiers.

The learning complexity for original Rocchio relates to the evaluation of weights in all documents and profiles. Their evaluation is carried out in three important steps:

1. The IDF is evaluated by counting for each feature the number of documents in which it appears. This requires the ordering of the pair set <*document, feature*> by feature. The number of pairs is bounded by $m \cdot M$, where m is the maximum number of features in a documents and M is the number of training documents. Thus, the processing time is $O(m \cdot M \cdot log(m \cdot M))$.
2. The weight for each feature in each document is evaluated in $O(m \cdot M)$ time.
3. The profile building technique, i.e. Rocchio formula, is applied. Again, the tuple set <*document, feature, weight*> is ordered by feature in $O(m \cdot M \cdot log(m \cdot M))$ time.
4. All weights that a feature f assumes in positive (negative) examples are summed. This is done by scanning sequentially the <*document, feature, weight*> tuples in $O(M \cdot m)$ time. As result, the overall learning complexity is $O(m \cdot M \cdot log(m \cdot M))$.

The classification complexity of a document d depends on the retrieval of weights for each feature in d. Let n be the total number of unique features; it is an upperbound of the number of features in a profile. Consequently, the classification step takes $O(m \cdot log(n))$.

In the *PRC* algorithm, an additional phase is carried out. The accuracy produced by ρ setting has to be evaluated on a *validation-set V*. This requires the re-evaluation of profile weights and the classification of V for each chosen ρ. The re-evaluation of profile weights is carried out by scanning all <*document, feature, weight*> tuples. Note that the tuples need to be ordered only one time. Consequently, the evaluation of one value for ρ takes $O(m \cdot M) + O(|V|m \cdot log(n))$. The number of values for ρ, as described in the previous section, is $k = Max\_limit/\Sigma$. The complexity to measure k values is $O(mM \cdot log(mM)) + k(O(m \cdot M) + |V| \cdot O(m \cdot log(n)))$. The cardinality of the *validation-set* $|V|$ as well as k can be considered constants. In our interpretation, k is an intrinsic property of the target categories. It depends on feature distribution and not on the number of documents or features. Moreover, n is never greater than the product $M \cdot m$. Therefore, the final PRC learning complexity is $O(mM \cdot log(mM)) + k \cdot O(mM) + k|V| \cdot O(m \cdot log(mM)) = O(mM \cdot log(mM))$, i.e. the complexity of the original Rocchio learning.

The document classification phase of PRC does not introduce additional steps with respect to the original Rocchio algorithm, so it is characterized by a very efficient time complexity, i.e. $O(m \cdot log(n))$.

3.4 Related Work

The idea of parameter tuning in the Rocchio formula is not completely new. In [5] it has been pointed out that these parameters greatly depend on the training corpus and different settings of their values produce a significant variation in performances. However, a procedure for their estimation was not proposed as the parameters chosen to optimize the classification accuracy over the training documents were, in general, different from those optimizing the *test-set* classification. A possible explanation is that the searching in parameter space was made at random: a group of values for parameters was tried without applying a specific methodology. Section 4.3 shows that, when a systematic parameter estimation procedure is applied (averaging over a sufficient number of randomly generated samples), a reliable setting can be obtained.

Another attempt to improve Rocchio classifier has been provided via probabilistic analysis in [10]. A specific parameterization of the Rocchio formula based on the $TF \cdot IDF$ weighting scheme is proposed. Moreover, a theoretical explanation within a vector space model is provided. The equivalence between the probability of a document d in a category C (i.e. $P(C|d)$) and the scalar product $C \cdot d$ is shown to hold. This equivalence implies that the following setting for the Rocchio parameters: $\gamma = 0$ and $\beta = \frac{|C|}{|D|}$, where $|D|$ is the number of corpus documents. It is worth noting that the main assumption, at the basis of the above characterization, is $P(d|w, C) = P(d|w)$ (for words w descriptors of d). This ensures that $P(C|d)$ is approximated by the expectation of $\sum_{w \in d} P(C|w)P(w|d)$. The above assumption is critical as it assumes that the information brought by w subsumes the information brought by the pair $<w, C>$. This cannot be considered generally true. Since the large scale empirical investigation, carried out in Section 4.2, proves that the relevance of negative examples (controlled by the γ parameter) is very high, the approach in [10] (i.e., $\gamma = 0$) cannot be assumed generally valid.

In [17, 16] an enhanced version of the Rocchio algorithm has been designed for the problem of document routing. This task is a different instance of TC. The concept of category refers to the important document for a specific query. In that use of the Rocchio's formula, β parameter cannot be eliminated as it has been in Section 3.1. Moreover, an additional parameter α is needed. It controls the impact of the query in routing the relevant documents. The presence of three parameters makes difficult an estimation of a good parameter set. The approach used in [17] is to try a number of values without a systematic exploration of the space. The major drawback is that the selected values could be only the local max of some document sets. Moreover, no study was done about the parameter variability. A set of values that maximize Rocchio accuracy on a *test-set* could minimize the performance over other document sets.

In [14] an enhanced version of Rocchio text classifier has been designed. The Rocchio improvement is based on better *weighting schemes* [1], on *Dynamic Feedback Optimization* [3] and on the introduction of *Query Zoning* [17]. The integration of the above three techniques has shown that Rocchio can be competitive with state-of-the art filtering approaches such as *Adaboost*. However, the problem of parameter tuning has been neglected. The simple setting $\beta = \gamma$ is adopted for every category. The justification given for such choice is that the setting has produced good results in [17]. The same reason and parameterization has been found even in [2] for the task of document filtering in TREC-9.

In summary, literature shows that improvements can be derived by setting the Rocchio parameters. However, this claim is neither proven with a systematic empirical study nor is a methodology to derive the good setting given. On the contrary, we have proposed a methodology for estimating parameters in a bound searching space. Moreover, in the next section we will show that our approach and the underlying hypotheses are supported by the experimental data.

4   Extensive Evaluation of *PRC*

The experiments are organized in three steps. First, in Section 4.2 the relationship between the ρ setting and the performances of Rocchio classifier has been evaluated. Second, *PRC* as well as original Rocchio performances are evaluated over the Reuters (fixed) *test-set* in Section 4.3. These results can be compared to other literature outcomes, e.g., [9, 19, 18, 5].

Additionally, experiments of Section 4.4 over different splits as well as different corpora in two languages definitely assess the viability of the *PRC* and the related estimation proposed in this paper. Finally, an evaluation of *SVM* on Ohsumed and Reuters corpora is given. This enables a direct comparison between *PRC* and one state-of-the art text classification model.

4.1   The Experimental Set-Up

Three different collections have been considered: The Reuters-21578[5] collection Apté split. It includes 12,902 documents for 90 classes, with a fixed splitting between *test-set* (here after RTS) and learning data LS (3,299 vs. 9,603); the Ohsumed collection[6], including 50,216 medical abstracts. The first 20,000 documents, categorized under the 23 *MeSH diseases* categories, have been used in

---

[5] Once available at http://www.research.att.com/~lewis and now available at http://kdd.ics.uci.edu/databases/reuters21578/reuters21578.html.

[6] It has been compiled by William Hersh and it is currently available at ftp://medir.ohsu.edu/pub/ohsumed.

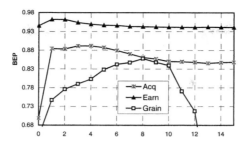

Fig. 1. Break-even point performances of the Rocchio classifier according to different ρ values for *Acq*, *Earn* and *Grain* classes of Reuters Corpus

all our experiments. The ANSA collection, which includes 16,000 news items in Italian from the ANSA news agency. It makes reference to 8 target categories (2,000 documents each). ANSA categories relate to typical newspaper contents (e.g. Politics, Sport and Economics).

Performance scores are expressed by means of *breakeven point* and f_1 (see Section 2.1). The global performance of systems is always obtained by *microaveraging* the target measure over all categories of the target corpus. The sets of features used in these experiments are all tokens that do not appear in the *SMART* [13] stop list[7]. They are 33,791 for Reuters, 42,234 for Ohsumed and 55,123 for ANSA. No feature selection has been applied. The feature weight in a document is the usual product between the logarithm of the feature frequency (inside the document) and the associated inverse document frequency (i.e. the SMART *ltc* weighting scheme [13]).

4.2 Relationship between Accuracy and ρ Values

In this experiments we adopted the fixed split of the Reuters corpus as our *test-set* (*RTS*). The aim here is simply to study as ρ influences the Rocchio accuracy. This latter has been measured by systematically setting different values of $\rho \in \{0, 1, 2, ..., 15\}$ and evaluating the BEP for each value.

Figures 1 and 2 shows the BEP curve on some classes of Reuters corpus with respect to ρ value. For *Earn*, *Acq* and *Grain* there is available a large number of training documents (i.e. from 2,200 to 500). For them, the BEP increases according to ρ until a max point is reached, then it begins to decrease for higher values of the parameter. Our hypothesis is that after BEP reaches the max point, further increase of ρ produces relevant or weakly relevant features to be removed. In this perspective, the optimal ρ setting would correspond to a quasi-optimal feature selection.

The *Trade*, *Interest* and *Money Supply* categories have a smaller number of documents available for training and testing (i.e. from 500 to 100). This reflects less regularity in ρ/BEP relationship. Nevertheless, it is still possible to identify

---

[7] No stop list was applied for Italian corpus.

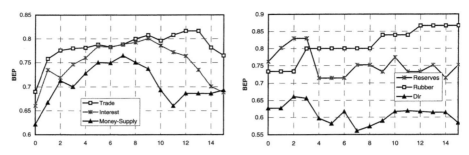

Fig. 2. Break-even point performances of the Rocchio classifier according to different ρ values for *Trade*, *Interest*, *Money Supply*, *Reserves*, *Rubber* and *Dlr* classes of Reuters corpus

convex curves in their plots. This is important as it allows us to infer that the absolute max is into the interval $[0, 15]$. The very small categories (i.e. less than 50 training documents) *Reserves*, *Rubber* and *Dlr* show a more chaotic relationship, and it is difficult to establish if the absolute maximum is in the target interval.

It is worth noting that the optimal accuracy is reached for $\rho > 1$. In contrast, is a common belief that for a classifier the positive information should be more relevant than negative information. This suggests that (a) in Rocchio classifier, the contribute of the feature weights in negative examples has to be emphasized and (b) the γ of Eq. 3 should not be interpreted as negative information control but as a simple parameter.

4.3 Performance Evaluation on Reuters Fixed *Test-Set*

In this experiment the performance of PRC model over the fixed Reuters *test-set* (RTS) has been measured. The aim is to provide direct comparison with other literature results (e.g. [19, 9, 5, 12]).

Twenty estimation sets $ES_1, ..., ES_{20}$ have been used to estimate the optimal rate as described in Section 3.2. Once $\bar{\rho}$ is available for the target category, its profile can be built and the performance can be measured. The PRC accuracy on RTS is a MicroAvg-f_1 of 82.83%. This score outperforms all literature evaluations of the original Rocchio classifier: 78% obtained in [5, 12], 75% in [19] and 79.9% in [9]. It is worth noting that this latter result has been obtained optimizing the parameters on RTS as the aim was to prove the SVM superiority independently on the parameters chosen (e.g. γ, β and thresholds) for Rocchio.

To investigate the previous aspect we have measured directly the original Rocchio parameterized as in literature: $\gamma = 4$ and $\beta = 16$ ($\rho = .25$) and with $\gamma = \beta$ ($\rho = 1$). The results are shown in columns 2 and 3 of Table 1. When $\rho = 1$ is used, the global performance (78.79%) replicates the results in [5, 12] while for $\rho = .25$, it is substantially lower (72.61%). The explanation is the high number of features used in our experiments without applying any feature selection algorithm. A low rate ρ cannot filter an adequate number of irrelevant features and, consequently, the performances are low. As ρ increases, a high number of noised features is removed and the performances improve. PRC, by determining the best parameter ρ for each category, improves the Rocchio performance at least by 5 percent points.

To confirm the generality of the above results, cross validation experiments on Reuters and other corpora are presented in next section.

4.4   Cross Evaluation of Parameterized Rocchio Classifier

With the aim to assess the general performances of the PRC and of the original Rocchio classifier, wider empirical evidences are needed on different collections and languages. Moreover, to estimate the best TC accuracies achievable on the target corpora, we have also evaluated the Support Vector Machine (SVM) classifier [9].

Performance figures are derived for each category via a cross validation technique applied as follows:

1. Generate $n = 20$ random splits of the corpus: about 70% for training (LS^σ) and 30% for testing (TS^σ).
2. For each split σ
   (a) Extract 20 sample[8] $ES^\sigma{}_1...ES^\sigma{}_{20}$ from LS^σ.
   (b) Learn the classifiers on $LS^\sigma - ES^\sigma{}_k$ and for each $ES^\sigma{}_k$ evaluate: (i) the thresholds associated to the BEP and (ii) the optimal parameters ρ.
   (c) Learn the classifiers Rocchio, SVM and PRC on LS^σ: in case of PRC use the estimated $\bar\rho$.
   (d) Use TS_σ and the estimated thresholds to evaluate f_1 for the category and to account data for the final processing of the global MicroAvg-f_1.
3. For each classifier evaluate the mean and the Standard Deviation for f_1 and MicroAvg-f_1 over the TS_σ sets.

It is worth noting that the fixed *test-set* (RTS) and the *learning-set* of Reuters corpus have been merged in these experiments to build the new random splits.

Again, original Rocchio classifier has been evaluated on two different parameter settings selected from the literature (i.e. $\gamma = \beta$ and $\gamma = 4$ and $\beta = 16$). Table 1 reports the MicroAvg-f_1 over 90 categories and the f_1 (see Section 2.1) for the top 10 most populated categories. Original Rocchio accuracy is shown in columns 2, 3, 4 and 5. Columns 6 and 7 refer to PRC while columns 8 and 9 report SVM accuracy. The RTS label indicates that only the Reuters fixed *test-set* has been used to evaluate the results. In contrast, the TS^σ label means that the measurements have been derived averaging the results on 20 splits.

The symbol $\pm$ precedes the Std. Dev. associated to the mean. It indicates the variability of data and it can be used to build the confidence limits. We observe that our SVM evaluation on Reuters RTS (85.42%) is in line with the literature (84.2 %) [9]. The slight difference in [9] is due to the application of a stemming algorithm, a different weighting scheme, and a feature selection (only 10,000

---

[8] Each ES_k includes about 30-40% of training documents.

Table 1. Rocchio, SVM and PRC performance comparisons via f_1 and the MicroAvg-f_1 on the Reuters corpus. RTS is the Reuters fixed *test-set* while TS^σ indicates the evaluation over 20 random samples

Category	Rocchio				PRC		SVM	
	RTS		TS^σ		RTS	TS^σ	RTS	TS^σ
	$\rho=.25$	$\rho=1$	$\rho=.25$	$\rho=1$				
earn	95.69	95.61	92.57±0.51	93.71±0.42	95.31	94.01±0.33	98.29	97.70±0.31
acq	59.85	82.71	60.02±1.22	77.69±1.15	85.95	83.92±1.01	95.10	94.14±0.57
money-fx	53.74	57.76	67.38±2.84	71.60±2.78	62.31	77.65±2.72	75.96	84.68±2.42
grain	73.64	80.69	70.76±2.05	77.54±1.61	89.12	91.46±1.26	92.47	93.43±1.38
crude	73.58	80.45	75.91±2.54	81.56±1.97	81.54	81.18±2.20	87.09	86.77±1.65
trade	53.00	69.26	61.41±3.21	71.76±2.73	80.33	79.61±2.28	80.18	80.57±1.90
interest	51.02	58.25	59.12±3.44	64.05±3.81	70.22	69.02±3.40	71.82	75.74±2.27
ship	69.86	84.04	65.93±4.69	75.33±4.41	86.77	81.86±2.95	84.15	85.97±2.83
wheat	70.23	74.48	76.13±3.53	78.93±3.00	84.29	89.19±1.98	84.44	87.61±2.39
corn	64.81	66.12	66.04±4.80	68.21±4.82	89.91	88.32±2.39	89.53	85.73±3.79
MicroAvg. (90 cat.)	72.61	78.79	73.87±0.51	78.92±0.47	82.83	83.51±0.44	85.42	87.64±0.55

features were used there). It is worth noting that the global PRC and SVM outcomes obtained via cross validation are higher than those evaluated on the RTS (83.51% vs. 82.83% for PRC and 87.64% vs. 85.42% for SVM). This is due to the non-perfectly random nature of the fixed split that prevents a good generalization for both learning algorithms.

The cross validation experiments confirm the results obtained for the fixed Reuters split. PRC improves about 5 point (i.e. 83.51% vs. 78.92%) over Rocchio parameterized with $\rho = 1$ with respect to all the 90 categories (MicroAvg-f_1 measurement). Note that $\rho = 1$ (i.e. $\gamma = \beta$) is the best literature parameterization. When a more general parameter setting [5] is used, i.e. $\rho = .25$, PRC outperforms Rocchio by ~ 10 percent points. Table 1 shows a high improvement even for the single categories, e.g. 91.46% vs. 77.54% for the *grain* category. The last two columns in Table 1 reports the results for the linear version of SVM[9].

Tables 2 and 3 report the results on other two corpora, respectively Ohsumed and ANSA. The new data on these tables is the BEP evaluated directly on the TS^σ. This means that the estimation of thresholds is not carried out and the resulting outcomes are upperbounds of the real accuracies. We have used these measurements to compare the f_1 values scored by PRC against the Rocchio upperbounds. This provides a strong indication of the superiority of PRC as both tables show that Rocchio BEP is always 4 to 5 percent points under f_1 of PRC. Finally, we observe that PRC outcome is close to SVM especially for the Ohsumed corpus (65.8% vs. 68.37%).

---

[9] We have tried to set different polynomial degrees (1,2,3,4 and 5). As the linear version has shown the best performance we have adopted it for the cross validation experiments.

Table 2. Performance Comparisons among Rocchio, SVM and PRC on Ohsumed corpus

Category	Rocchio (BEP) $\rho = .25$	Rocchio (BEP) $\rho = 1$	PRC BEP	PRC f_1	SVM f_1
Pathology	37.57	47.06	48.78	50.58	48.5
Cardiovasc.	71.71	75.92	77.61	77.82	80.7
Immunolog.	60.38	63.10	73.57	73.92	72.8
Neoplasms	71.34	76.85	79.48	79.71	80.1
Dig.Syst.	59.24	70.23	71.50	71.49	71.1
MicroAvg. (23 cat.)	54.4±.5	61.8±.5	66.1±.4	65.8±.4	68.37±.5

Table 3. Performance comparisons between Rocchio and PRC on ANSA corpus

Category	Rocchio (BEP) $\rho = 0.25$	Rocchio (BEP) $\rho = 1$	PRC BEP	PRC f_1
News	50.35	61.06	69.80	68.99
Economics	53.22	61.33	75.95	76.03
Foreign Economics	67.01	65.09	67.08	66.72
Foreign Politics	61.00	67.23	75.80	75.59
Economic Politics	72.54	78.66	80.52	78.95
Politics	60.19	60.07	67.49	66.58
Entertainment	75.91	77.64	78.14	77.63
Sport	67.80	78.98	80.00	80.14
MicroAvg	61.76±.5	67.23±.5	72.36±.4	71.00±.4

5   Conclusions

The high efficiency of Rocchio classifier has produced a renewed interest in its application to operational scenarios. In this paper, a study on Rocchio text classifier parameters aimed to improve performances and to keep the same efficiency of the original version has been carried out. The result is a methodology for reducing the searching space of parameters: first, in TC only one parameter is needed, i.e., the rate ρ between γ and β. Secondly, ρ can be interpreted as a feature selector. This has allowed us to bind the searching space for the rate values since the ρ maximal value corresponds to the selection of 0 features. Moreover, empirical studies have shown that the ρ/BEP relationship can be described by a convex curve. This suggests a simple and fast estimation procedure for deriving the optimal parameter (see Section 3.1).

The Parameterized Rocchio Classifier (PRC) has been validated via cross validation, using three collections in two languages (Italian and English). In particular, a comparison with the original Rocchio model and the SVM text classifiers has been carried out. This has been done in two ways: (a) on the Reuters fixed split that allows PRC to be compared with literature results on TC and (b) by directly deriving the performance of Rocchio and SVM on the same data used for PRC. Results allow us to draw the following conclusions:

- First, *PRC* systematically improves original Rocchio parameterized with the best literature setting by at least 5 percent points, and it improves the general setting by 10 percent points. Comparisons with *SVM* show the performances to be relatively close (-4% on Reuters and -2.5% on Ohsumed).
- Second, the high performance, (i.e., 82.83%) on the Reuters fixed *test-set* collocates *PRC* as one of the most accurate classifiers on the Reuters corpus (see [15]).
- Third, the low time complexity for both training and classification phase makes the *PRC* model very appealing for real (i.e. operational) applications in Information Filtering and Knowledge Management.

Finally, the feature selection interpretation of parameters suggests a methodology to discover the *specific-term* of a category with respect to the other ones. A short-term future research may be the application of our methodology to estimate parameters in the enhanced Rocchio proposed in [14].

Acknowledgments

I would like to tank the AI-NLP group at *Tor Vergata* University of Rome and in especial way Roberto Basili for the fruitful discussions and suggestions. Thanks to the reviewers of ECIR for their punctual and careful reviews. Many thanks to the Technical Communication Lecturers, Kathy Lingo and Margaret Falersweany, that helped me to revise the English syntax of this article.

References

[1] Pivoted document length normalization. Technical Report TR95-1560, Cornell University, Computer Science, 1995.
[2] Avi Arampatzis, Jean Beney, C. H. A. Koster, and T. P. van der Weide. Incrementality, half-life, and threshold optimization for adaptive document filtering. In *the Nineth Text REtrieval Conference (TREC-9),Gaithersburg, Maryland*, 2000.
[3] Christopher Buckley and Gerald Salton. Optimization of relevance feedback weights. In *Proceedings of SIGIR-95*, pages 351–357, Seattle, US, 1995.
[4] Wesley T. Chuang, Asok Tiyyagura, Jihoon Yang, and Giovanni Giuffrida. A fast algorithm for hierarchical text classification. In *Proceedings of DaWaK-00*, 2000.
[5] William W. Cohen and Yoram Singer. Context-sensitive learning methods for text categorization. *ACM Transactions on Information Systems*, 17(2):141–173, 1999.
[6] Harris Drucker, Vladimir Vapnik, and Dongui Wu. Automatic text categorization and its applications to text retrieval. *IEEE Transactions on Neural Networks*, 10(5), 1999.
[7] Norbert Gövert, Mounia Lalmas, and Norbert Fuhr. A probabilistic description-oriented approach for categorising Web documents. In *Proceedings of CIKM-99*.
[8] David J. Ittner, David D. Lewis, and David D. Ahn. Text categorization of low quality images. In *Proceedings of SDAIR-95*, pages 301–315, Las Vegas, US, 1995.
[9] T. Joachims. Text categorization with support vector machines: Learning with many relevant features. In *In Proceedings of ECML-98*, pages 137–142, 1998.

[10] Thorsten Joachims. A probabilistic analysis of the rocchio algorithm with tfidf for text categorization. In *Proceedings of ICML97 Conference*. Morgan Kaufmann, 1997.

[11] Ron Kohavi and George H. John. Wrappers for feature subset selection. *Artificial Intelligence*, 97(1-2):273–324, 1997.

[12] Wai Lam and Chao Y. Ho. Using a generalized instance set for automatic text categorization. In *Proceedings of SIGIR-98*, 1998.

[13] G: Salton and C. Buckley. Term-weighting approaches in automatic text retrieval. *Information Processing and Management*, 24(5):513–523, 1988.

[14] Robert E. Schapire, Yoram Singer, and Amit Singhal. Boosting and Rocchio applied to text filtering. In W. Bruce Croft, A. Moffat, C. J. van Rijsbergen, R. Wilkinson, and J. Zobel, editors, *Proceedings of SIGIR-98*, pages 215–223, Melbourne, AU, 1998. ACM Press, New York, US.

[15] Fabrizio Sebastiani. Machine learning in automated text categorization. *ACM Computing Surveys*, 34(1):1–47, 2002.

[16] Amit Singhal, John Choi, Donald Hindle, and Fernando C. N. Pereira. ATT at TREC-6: SDR track. In *Text REtrieval Conference*, pages 227–232, 1997.

[17] Amit Singhal, Mandar Mitra, and Christopher Buckley. Learning routing queries in a query zone. In *Proceedings of SIGIR-97*, pages 25–32, Philadelphia, US, 1997.

[18] K. Tzeras and S. Artman. Automatic indexing based on bayesian inference networks. In *SIGIR 93*, pages 22–34, 1993.

[19] Y. Yang. An evaluation of statistical approaches to text categorization. *Information Retrieval Journal*, 1999.

[20] Yiming Yang and Jan O. Pedersen. A comparative study on feature selection in text categorization. In *Proceedings of ICML-97*, pages 412–420, Nashville, US, 1997.

Optimization of Restricted Searches in Web Directories Using Hybrid Data Structures

Fidel Cacheda, Victor Carneiro, Carmen Guerrero, and Angel Viña

Department of Information and Communications Technologies
Facultad de Informática, Campus de Elviña s/n, 15.071, A Coruña, Spain
{fidel,viccar,clopez,avc}@udc.es

Abstract. The need of efficient tools in order to manage, retrieve and filter the information in the WWW is clear. Web directories are taxonomies for the classification of Web documents. These kind of information retrieval systems present a specific type of search where the document collection is restricted to one area of the category graph. This paper introduces a specific data architecture for Web directories that improves the performance of restricted searches. That architecture is based on a hybrid data structure composed of an inverted file with multiple embedded signature files. Two variants are presented: hybrid architecture with total information and with partial information. This architecture has been analyzed by means of developing both variants to be compared with a basic model. The performance of the restricted queries was clearly improved, especially the hybrid model with partial information, which yielded a positive response under any load of the search system.[1]

1   Introduction

The first information retrieval systems specifically designed for the Web appeared a few years after the World Wide Web was born. This was due to the huge growth suffered by the Web since its origins, which affected both the number of servers with published information and the number of users. In fact, the estimated number of pages in 1999 was 800 million, generating 6 terabytes of text information [1], without taking into account other multimedia contents.

Information retrieval systems appear in the Web with the purpose of managing, retrieving and filtering the information available in the WWW. There are three basic ways to locate information in the Web: search engines, Web directories and meta-searchers [2]. Search engines index, ideally, the whole documents available in the Web, placing quantity above quality of contents. Web directories are an ontology of the Web. The most relevant documents are classified according to topic, placing quality above quantity of documents. Finally, meta-searchers just resend queries to other search systems, and later they reorder the results.

---

[1] This work has been partially sponsored by the Spanish CICYT (TIC2001-0547).

F. Sebastiani (Ed.): ECIR 2003, LNCS 2633, pp. 436–451, 2003.

Search engines and meta-searchers are simply based on the search process in order to locate information. On the other hand, Web directories allow information retrieval by means of standard searches, through a process of navigation and through a mixed one. This navigation process consists of browsing the category structure browsing the available documents. This structure is defined as a directed acyclic category graph, since one node may present several parents. Equally, one document may be catalogued in different categories. This provides Web directories with a great power and cataloguing flexibility. However, Web directories have the added value of a search process combined with the navigation one, which improves the quality of the obtained results. In this case, the search is restricted to those documents linked to an area of the ontology specified by the root node to which the user has navigated.

The search process is based on an inverted file structure, which relates keywords to their associated documents, while the navigation process is based on an inverted file, which associates each category to its Web documents. On the contrary, the search process restricted to one area of the category graph must combine the results of both lists in an efficient way.

This paper examines in detail the restricted searches characteristic of Web directories, from the point of view of the data structures used and the performance obtained. Performance is improved by using a hybrid data model composed of an inverted file and dynamic signature files.

2   Goals

This paper focuses on data structures associated to Web directories with the purpose of analyzing and defining a data structure, which provides an adequate performance for queries restricted to one graph area. The detailed goals are the following:

- Analyzing the data structures associated to a basic model of Web directory and its repercussion on the search process restricted to one area in the category graph.
- Determining possible performance problems in the search process restricted to one area in the category graph.
- Defining a data architecture model which permits improving the performance of the restricted search, without a negative repercussion on the rest of information retrieval processes.
- Implementing the proposed model for analyzing the flexibility of the system, together with the required storage space restrictions.
- Evaluating the performance provided by the proposed system compared to a basic model with regard to restricted searches. Following the steps established at [17], several aspects should be evaluated, although we shall focus on the measured response times for different system load situations.
- Explaining the main conclusions based on the results obtained from the response times, storage space, and flexibility of the system.

3   Basic Model

This section describes the specific data structures for the components of a Web directory, establishing a basic model for determining fundamental design aspects for this type of information retrieval systems.

Generally speaking, the number of descriptive articles related to IR on the Web is very small, especially with regard to Web directories. Although this architecture is based on similar models, such as those described in [3, 11, 12] and [10].

A Web directory consists of three basic components that represent the information stored in it and the various interrelations (see Fig. 1). On the one hand, the vocabulary stands for the keywords indexed both in the documents and in the directory categories. There is a structure that represents the hierarchy of categories existing in the directory, typically composed of a directed acyclic graph. A small document file is required with the basic information about each of them (URL, title and description).

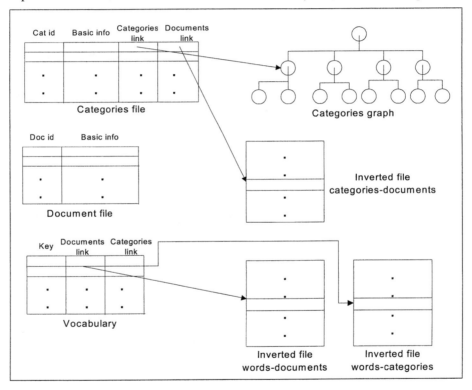

Fig. 1. Data structure of the basic model for a Web directory

With regard to the information that corresponds to the categories, each of them is identified by a single identifier. Thus, the basic information (name, brief description, etc.) shall be stored in a category file. Independently, a pointer-based structure based on the category identifiers shall represent the directed acyclic graph, which constitutes the ontology.

With regard to the keywords derived from the index process and from the associated documents, the inverted file structure constitutes at present the indexing technique that has the best performance for huge data volumes [2]. Thus, keywords are stored in the vocabulary, using the best structure: ordered arrays, B trees, PAT structures, etc., together with the corresponding inverted lists [9] [6] [8].

Inverted lists may present different orders that directly influence the performance of the standard search process, and, in consequence, the restricted searches. An order according to the document identifier facilitates the combination of several lists, while an order according to the criterion of document relevance makes simple searches trivial. There are also mixed alternatives, such as the one defined at [3], used in Goggle.

Furthermore, for Web directories, categories present keywords or descriptions according to which they are indexed. As in the previous case, the inverted file structure constitutes the most efficient option, creating a common vocabulary. However, a set of occurrences or inverted lists independent from the document one must be created, for reasons of efficiency and system complexity.

As was said before, an inverted file structure relates keywords to documents. However, a structure that relates each category to the associated documents is also necessary. This is intensely used during the navigation process. In this case, the inverted file structure also constitutes the most efficient option, so that the category file constitutes the vocabulary, while an inverted list of document identifiers is associated to each category. This list is preferably ordered according to the relevance or importance of each document.

3.1   Restricted Searches

The data model explained permits solving both the normal search process and the navigation process in an efficient way, using an inverted file structure as a basis in both cases.

The use of this technique for the standard search process is undoubted, being widely used in different traditional commercial systems and in the Web [2].

During the navigation process only the category is located (based on the identifier) and its list of associated documents is accessed, without any kind of combination operation, with an optimal performance if the list has been previously ordered according to a relevance criterion.

On the contrary, the restricted search process in a category graph area requires a more elaborated access to that information. On the one hand, a standard search is carried out by means of accessing the inverted word file and combining the inverted document lists in the usual way. Once the list of results is calculated, the key step consists of determining which resulting documents belonged to the specified graph area. From this basic data model, two alternatives are defined for the filtering process.

The first alternative consists of obtaining the list of documents associated to the specified graph area. Later on, this inverted list is combined with the list of results. Obtaining the list of documents included in a specific graph area is a hard process divided into three steps:

- Initially, the graph has to be explored until every leaf node is reached, starting from the root node of the restriction area.
- A list of associated documents must be obtained for each node.
- Each and every one of the lists obtained in the previous step has to be combined.

The result obtained is a list of all the documents associated to the restricted graph area, ordered by identifier. The next step is to intersect this list with the results one in order to obtain only the resulting documents related to the restricted graph area.

The inverted files technique has a disadvantage that directly influences the performance of this solution: the combination (intersection or union) of two or more inverted lists worsens performance [14]. Assuming that the lists have been previously ordered according to the document identifier, performance is inversely proportional to the number of combined lists and to the number of elements they have.

The second alternative consists of obtaining the category list from the restriction area (an easier process than obtaining the document list), and checking the results list sequentially, that is, which documents are located at the nodes of the category list.

Obtaining the category list (ordered by identifier) simply requires exploring part of the graph, storing the identifiers in an ordered list. The sequential exploration of the list of results does not require any previous order but may be especially hard if the list is extensive. Besides, an auxiliary structure indicating the categories associated to each document is required. This entails an inverted file relating each document to the categories it belongs to (reciprocal index structure relating categories to documents, already defined).

Generally speaking, the first method is adequately adapted to those queries where the restricted graph area is reduced (inferior graph levels), given that the number of involved categories (and, therefore, of documents to be combined) is inferior. On the other hand, the second alternative is efficient when the number of results obtained in the search is reduced (regardless of the amplitude of the restriction area), since both the sequential reading and the index access will be moderate.

However, none of the two solutions solves efficiently the searches which obtain a great number of results and which have been restricted to a wide graph area (the study explained at [4] shows that most searches are restricted to categories in the first three levels).

As a consequence, it is necessary to create a new data model that allows solving this type of queries in an efficient way. This aspect is reviewed in the next section.

4   Hybrid Architecture

From a descriptive point of view, the problem of restricted searches lies in obtaining an inverted list of results that undergoes a filtering process based on the value of an attribute (associated categories). The disadvantage is that the attribute has a complex hierarchical structure, which makes filtering difficult.

A model of data structures is proposed, based on the second alternative of the basic model described, with the purpose of solving this type of queries in an efficient manner when the number of results to be examined is too high.

The idea that lies under the proposed data model is based on the application of an inexact filter, which allows the elimination of most of the results that are non-associated to the restricted categories. Thus, the exact filtering only examines the rest of the documents, whose number will have been considerably reduced.

The signature files technique adapts well to these features. Signature files are an inexact filtering technique (measured through the false drop probability) based on sequential access to data, which constitutes its main disadvantage, producing a poor performance. However, in this case, that is no inconvenient, since the sequential filtering is only carried out with the search results, never with the whole set of documents in the collection.

In the proposed model each document must have a signature, which represents each and every one of the categories it belongs to, directly or indirectly. Nevertheless, this does not imply the existence of a global signature file for every document. On the contrary, signature files will be incorporated into inverted files, creating a hybrid scheme of inverted and signature file. Thus, in the proposed hybrid data structure, in order to guarantee an efficient access, the signature file is embedded into the inverted one, so that each inverted list is in turn a signature file. Therefore, the functioning scheme for the restricted searches is the following:

- Firstly, the list of results is obtained from the standard search process, with no restrictions on their order (normally, according to a relevance order).
- Secondly, the inexact filtering is carried out for the category to which the search is restricted from the signature file associated to the list of results.
- Thirdly, the exact filtering of the rest of results is carried out, according to the second alternative previously described.

The fact should be underlined that the third step is optional. In the case that the inexact filtering is of great purity, the exact filtering might be inefficient.

This constitutes the hybrid model proposed from a general perspective. However, certain aspects, such as the joint storing of both structures, the validity of signature files and the superimposing codes have to be defined in order to represent the categories associated to a document. These aspects are dealt with in detail in the following sections.

4.1   Signature Files Embedded into an Inverted File

The inclusion of signature files in the inverted lists is due to the possibility of dynamically generating the signature files associated to each query. Thus, when the combination operations of the inverted lists are carried out (intersections, unions or any other operation) the associated signature file will be automatically obtained.

That is the reason why a composed document identifier has been defined. This identifier is composed of the superimposed signature of every category to which the document is associated and of a local document identifier. Thus, those documents that belong to the same categories will have the same signature (obtained from the same superimposing) and will be distinguished by means of the local identifier. Fig. 2 shows the use of composed identifiers in a hybrid structure of inverted file and signature files.

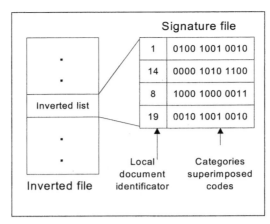

Fig. 2. Hybrid data structure of inverted file and signature files with composed document identifiers

By means of this scheme, documents are univocally identified and every combination operation carried out with the use of document identifiers is simultaneously and automatically performed on the associated signatures. So when the final list of identifiers is obtained, the associated signature file is indirectly available, regardless of the number and type of combination operation previously carried out.

The main disadvantage of this method lies in the space required by the composed identifier. The number of bytes required is a design parameter of the system that has to be fixed for every document in the collection. The signature assignment to categories (and consequently to documents) is analyzed in the next section, while the local document identifier follows a consecutive numbering of the documents associated to this signature.

4.2   Signature Files and Superimposing Codes Applied to Hierarchical Information

A key aspect of the development of the proposed architecture consists of using the signature file technique and the subsequent superimposing codes for representing the categories associated to each document. At the introductory level, the signature file technique is based on the superimposing codes initially developed by Mooers at [13], and later expanded by Roberts at [15]. In this technique, each document is divided into blocks that contain a constant number of different words. A signature is linked to each word, and the block signature is obtained by means of the bit to bit logic OR of its words' signatures. The search is carried out from the signature of the searched word, just by making a logic AND between the word's and the document's signatures, checking whether it coincides with the word's original signature.

The following design parameters are associated to this technique:

- D: the constant number of different words which integrate each block.
- b: number of bits integrating each signature.
- w: number of "1" bits in each signature.

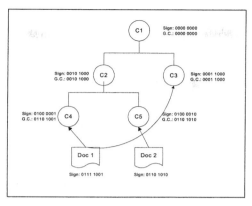

Fig. 3. Superimposing codes applied to a directed acyclic graph

An important concept in the signature file technique is that of the false drop probability (represented as F_d), which is defined as the probability for a block's signature to seem right, despite the fact that the block is wrong [7]. Stiassny in [16] estimates the optimal value of w for a specific value of b and D, together with the optimal value of F_d:

$$w = \frac{b \cdot \ln 2}{D} \quad \Rightarrow \quad F_d = 2^{-w}. \tag{1}$$

Based on this technique, several optimizations have been defined which are based on compression, horizontal or vertical storing techniques that are described in detail in [7].

The signature file technique applied to the directed acyclic graph of a Web directory consists of associating a different signature to each category (each node in the graph), and each document shall generate its signature by means of superimposing the category signatures to which it is directly or indirectly associated. The use of superimposing codes for representing hierarchical information is described in detail in [5], although the most relevant aspects are examined from this point onwards.

Fig. 3 shows a simple example of a Web directory. The image shows how document 1 belongs directly or indirectly to categories 4, 3, 2, and 1. Thus, in a restricted search in any of those categories, document 1 would be one of the possible results.

Following the example, each category has a unique signature, and the document signature is the result of superimposing the signatures of its categories. In the example, the signatures of categories 4, 3, 2, and 1 are, respectively, ($b=8$ bits and $w=2$ bits are assumed): 0100 0001, 0001 1000, 0010 1000 y 0000 0000 (the root category does not require a signature, since every document belongs to this category). Therefore, document one signature is: 0111 1001.

In the search process restricted to one area in the graph, the root category for that area is indicated. The genetic code has been defined associated to each category (represented as GC in Fig. 3), consisting of superimposing the codes of the category and all of its ancestors. The search in the signature file is carried out based on that genetic code, increasing the information contained in the signature. For instance, if we consider a search restricted to category 4, whose genetic code is 0110 1001, document 1 would be classified due to the signature's coincidence.

This example illustrates the main differences in the proposed method with regard to the traditional signature superimposing. First of all, in traditional signature files, the value of D guaranteed a constant number of superimposing operations. However, in this case, each document may belong to several categories, and, in turn, one category may present several parents. This implies that the number of superimposing operations in the document signatures is not constant.

The second difference lies in the values of D, b, and w. It is assumed that in traditional systems D takes a high value, and that the signature size (b) is of several hundreds of bits, while w takes only a few bits. In the proposed model, the value of D is directly related to the graph's depth, so it will never take too high values and we will try to take reduced values for b, since it affects the required storing space.

Consequently, these differences imply that the formulas expressed in (1) are not accurate anymore, so it is necessary to carry out a detailed analysis of the false drop probability in this model, together with the influential model parameters. This analysis is detailed in [5] and the main conclusions obtained are detailed from this point onwards.

First of all, it should be noted that the use of genetic codes instead of signatures for the verification of the fact of belonging to one category reduces F_d one magnitude order per each level dropped, since the information included in the code is bigger.

Secondly, different signature generation techniques have been analyzed for the categories according to their similitude to the parent node and/or siblings. Results show that it is possible to reduce the false drop probability by generating signatures which are somewhat similar to the parent nodes, and as different as possible from the sibling nodes, although this is just the first step, opening a future research line [5].

A key aspect is the determination of the system parameters that directly influence the performance of the signature file, i. e. the false drop probability. Only the percentage of documents associated to several categories and the percentage of categories with several parent nodes have a negative repercussion on F_d. Besides, these parameters have the feature of remaining stable throughout the life of a Web directory.

On the contrary, parameters such as the number of documents and categories of the search system that tend to increase with time do not affect the false drop probability.

To sum up, the superimposing codes used in the signature file technique adapt perfectly well to a Web directory and its category graph environment. Thus, the false drop probability remains stable in the dynamic context of these systems.

5   Implementation of the Hybrid Architecture

The main aspects of the hybrid data architecture of an inverted file and signature files have already been defined. Two variants based on that architecture have been established. They are called hybrid model with total information and hybrid model with partial information.

The next sections describe the two variants defined, with the corresponding implementation details. Finally, a comparison is drawn between the performance obtained by each variant and a basic model, underlining the improvements obtained.

The implementations that have been carried out consist of developing a Web directory prototype based on a real environment. That prototype consists of a category graph integrated by approximately 1,000 categories distributed into 7 depth levels, in which more than 51,000 Web directories have been classified. Obviously, there are categories that present several parents and documents associated to multiple categories in the same percentages as in a real environment (16% and 27% respectively). The development environment has been an Ultra Enterprise 250 machine with a processor at 300 MHz, 768 MB memory and 18 GB storage space.

5.1   Hybrid Model with Total Information

The hybrid architecture model with total information corresponds to the direct application of the superimposing codes technique to the category graph. In this case, each and every one of the categories have an associated signature (regardless of the level of depth), and therefore, they provide some information to their genetic code.

The first step in the design and implementation of this hybrid model of inverted file and signature files is the calculation of the parameters corresponding to the superimposing codes, obtaining a suitable false drop probability for this system (estimated at less than 1%).

The prototype has been implemented based on these data, generating and assigning the various codes to the categories and later calculating the composed identifier for each document. Thus, the changes of storage space requirements have been identified.

Fig. 4 shows with a dotted line the new data structures or those whose size has been increased. As a matter of fact, the increase in size is due to the signatures associated to the categories, especially to the new format of the document identifiers.

The incorporation of the signature into the information retrieval system only influences the category file (see Fig. 4 (a)), causing an estimated increase of 10KB. On the contrary, the increase in the size of document identifiers causes a generalized increase in the size of several data structures. Taking an initial size of 32 bits, now composed identifiers require 64 bits each. This implies an increase of 200 KB in the document file itself (see Fig. 4 (b)), while the indexes that relate categories to documents (see Fig. 4 (c)) and keywords to documents (see Fig. 4 (d)) are duplicated. Obviously, this increase in size is more obvious in the inverted index which associates keywords to documents, due to its great size (estimated in this instance at 12 MB, as opposed to the 6 MB of the basic model), and due to the fact of being used intensely in the standard search process, which may degrade performance since reading times increase. This aspect will be determined at the performance evaluation.

Finally, according to the proposed model, a new structure is required which allows obtaining, starting from a document, the categories to which it is directly associated. This index (see Fig. 4 (e)), which is not present in the basic model, requires a reduced size (around 275 KB), which means that there is an acceptable system overload.

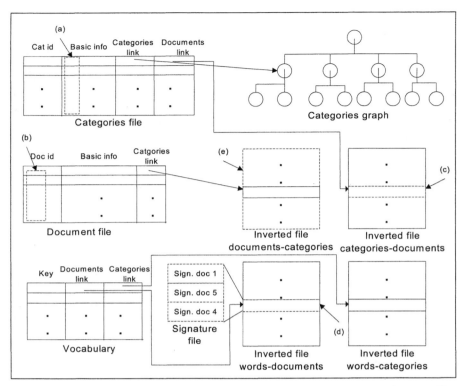

Fig. 4. Data structure of the hybrid architecture with inverted file and dynamic signature files

An important point is the maximum number of categories and documents supported by the system. The number of categories is limited to 22100, perfectly supporting the existing categories and the possible future increases. With regard to the number of documents, the system supports more than 90 million Web documents, which is two magnitude orders bigger than the estimated number of documents in Yahoo! [11].

5.2   Hybrid Model with Partial Information

This section describes a variant of the proposed hybrid architecture which aims at reducing the size of the signatures and document identifiers, and therefore, at reducing the storage space.

For this purpose, the superimposing codes will be applied only to the first levels categories, whereas the remaining categories will inherit the signatures of the higher levels. In this way, the size of the signatures and so, the documents identifiers is reduced, whereas the false drop probability is stable for the first levels. On the other hand, this variation implies an increase of the false drop probability at the lower levels, which should always be monitored with the purpose of avoiding a decrease in the system's performance.

However, this disadvantage is lessened by two factors. The statistical analysis of restricted queries carried out showed that more than 80% of queries are restricted to categories in the first three levels (based on the study developed in [4]). And, the typical values of the false drop probability for the lower levels are three to four magnitude orders smaller, while the increase is not significant, so the values of false drop probability are homogeneous for all levels.

Therefore, this variant was implemented applying the superimposing codes to the categories of the first three levels of the categories graph.

With regard to the increase in the required storage space, this is significantly smaller. Increases take place at the same structures that were described in the previous section, with an approximate reduction of 50% in the required space. It should be noted that the index of keywords and documents requires a 65% less storage space, decreasing up to 8.25 MB.

Besides, the hybrid variant with partial information is particularly flexible with regard to the number of categories it supports. A maximum of 4960 different categories can be assigned to the first three levels; however, there is no limitation for the lower levels, as opposed to what is true for the previous model. With regard to the number of documents, the size of the local identifier has been pondered in order to have a similar limitation to the previous case (approximately, a maximum of 80 million documents).

5.3   Performance Evaluation

Firstly the response times of the various models in normal searches have been analyzed, confirming that the three models behave in the same way.

On the other hand, this section's goal is to contrast the response times obtained in the two variants proposed, as opposed to a basic model based on the structure defined in Fig. 1.

The methodology used for the performance evaluation adapts to the environment of the information retrieval systems in the Web, which are characterized by supporting variable load levels through time. Five load situations shall be considered for evaluation: void, low, medium, high and saturation. The determination of the various load points has been made by determining the saturation point of the prototypes that were developed. The results were 5 searches per minute for low load, 12 searches for medium load, 19 searches for high load, and 23 for saturation, with the corresponding accesses to categories and documents.

The load generation is made using a simulation tool especially designed for that purpose. This tool sends requests (searches, access to categories and document visits) to the search system simulating the behavior of Internet users. The queries used in the tests are real queries obtained from our previous statistical work described in [4], which have been restricted to different categories in order to test all the relevant factors in our models. The analysis of the response times obtained is based on an ANOVA test, considering three factors: number of results, number of documents associated to the category and model.

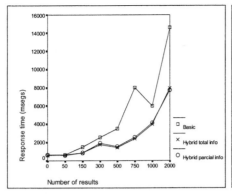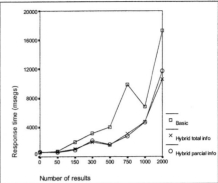

Fig. 5. Estimated response times according to the number of results (void load)

Fig. 6. Estimated response times according to the number of results (low load)

Very similar results were obtained for the void, low and medium loads. Fig. 5, 6 and 7 show the average response times for each model, according to the number of search results. As may be seen in the three figures, hybrid models clearly improve performance in approximately 50% with regard to the times yielded by the basic model. This improvement takes place when the number of results obtained in the ordinary search is high (over 500 results), since the performance of the basic model falls dramatically. Besides, the ANOVA test considers the type of system as an influent parameter with 99.9% of probabilities. The main difference in the three cases lies in a generalized increase in response times when the system load increases.

On the contrary, under a high load situation, the behavior of hybrid models varies considerably, as may be seen in Fig. 8. The performance of the hybrid model with total information worsens significantly, nearing that of the basic model. An ANOVA test was carried out only with the results of hybrid models. While in the previous cases both behave similarly, in a high load situation the hybrid model with partial information is still better than the basic model and the total information variant.

The worse performance of the total information model is due to the excessive size of the index of keywords and documents. A high load situation implies a high number of searches reaching the index, therefore, the disk undergoes more reading operations.

In the proposed architecture, the inexact filtering application allows a reduction of the response times. However, in the total information variant, the time required by the search process minimizes the positive effect of the inexact filtering. On the contrary, in the hybrid model with partial information, the search time is inferior (since it requires less access to the disk), adding to the benefits of the inexact filtering, which allows an improvement in response timing of up to 50% with regard to the basic model.

The experiments made at saturation situations do not produce conclusive results, due to the fact that the response times yielded by the system are very degraded and vary dramatically according to various parameters that are out of control.

The hybrid model with partial information has a better performance up to this point, however, as was described in the implementation details, since no signatures are assigned to the lower graph levels, it might be penalizing the searches restricted to these levels.

That is the reason why the searches have been studied up to a five depth level under different system loads. The associated graphs are not shown due to lack of space, although the results are conclusive, showing that the behavior of the hybrid model with partial information does not increase the response times for those queries restricted to the levels without signatures. This is due to the fact that the probability ratios of false drop have been stable at all the levels, without a dramatic worsening.

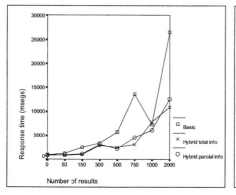
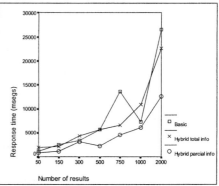

Fig. 7. Estimated response times according to the number of results (medium load)

Fig. 8. Estimated response times according to the number of results (high load)

6   Conclusions

This paper describes a hybrid data architecture composed of an inverted file and signature files, especially designed to improve the performance with searches restricted to one area in the category graph.

It should be noted that the superimposing codes adapt well to the directed acyclic graph of categories of Web directories, and also the definition of the composed document identifier for obtaining signature files dynamically with queries.

Two variants of the architecture are defined: the hybrid model with total information and the hybrid model with partial information. The second variant improves performance up to 50% with respect to the basic model under very high load situation of the system.

On the contrary, the hybrid model with total information, due to the bigger storage space required, suffers a dramatic decline of performance under high load situations, similarly to the basic model.

On the other hand, the implementations carried out have proved to be flexible enough with regard to the number of documents that the system can support, and also with regard to the number of categories in the directory.

Future research lines could be devoted to deepening the use of the superimposing codes for directed acyclic graphs. Besides, we could tackle the study for adapting the hybrid model, which was proposed and developed for this particular environment, to other search systems. These search systems would require a filtering of inverted lists sets, where the technique of combining inverted lists of inverted files is not adequate.

References

1. M. Agosti, M. Melucci. "Information Retrieval on the Web", in: M. Agosti, F. Crestani, G. Pasi (Eds). Lectures on Information Retrieval: Third European Summer-School, ESSIR 2000. Revised Lectures, Springer-Verlag, Berlin Heidelberg, 2001, 242-285.
2. R. Baeza-Yates, B. Ribeiro-Neto, "Searching the Web". In R. Baeza-Yates, B. Ribeiro-Neto, "Modern Information Retrieval", chapter 13, pps: 367-395. Addison Wesley.
3. S. Brin, L. Page, "The anatomy of a large-scale hypertextual web search engine". The 7th International World Wide Web Conference, Abril 1998.
4. F. Cacheda, A. Viña, "Experiencies retrieving information in the World Wide Web". 6th IEEE Symposium on Computers and Communications, pp 72-79, 2001.
5. F. Cacheda, A. Viña, "Superimposing Codes Representing Hierarchical Information in Web directories". 3rd International Workshop on Web Information and Data management (WIDM'01), in ACM CIKM 2001.
6. D. Cutting, J. Pedersen, "Optimizations for dynamic inverted index maintenance". 13th International Conference on Research and Development in Information Retrieval, 1990.
7. C. Faloutsos, S. Christodoulakis, "Description and performance analysis of signature file methods". ACM TOOIS, 5 (3), 237-257.
8. G. Gonnet, "Unstructured data bases or very efficient text searching". ACM PODS, volumen 2, 117-124, Atlanta, USA.
9. D. K. Harman, E. Fox, R. Baeza-Yates, W. Lee, "Inverted files". In W. Frakes y R. Baeza-Yates, "Information Retrieval: Data structures and algorithms, chapter 3, pps: 28-43. Prentice-Hall, 1992.
10. G. Jacobson, B. Krishnamurthy, D. Srivastava, D. Suciu, "Focusing Search in Hierarchical Structures with Directory Sets". Seventh International Conference on Information and Knowledge Management (CIKM), 1998.
11. Y. Labrou, T. Finin, "Yahoo! as an ontology – Using Yahoo! categories to describe documents". Eighth International Conference on Information Knowledge Management, pp. 180-187, 1999.
12. W. Lam, M. Ruiz, P. Srinivasan, "Automatic Text Categorization and Its Application to Text Retrieval". IEEE Transactions on Knowledge and Data Engineering, Volume 116, pp. 865-879, 1999.
13. C. Mooers, "Application of Random Codes to the Gathering of Statistical Information". Bulletin 31, Zator Co., Cambridge, USA.
14. G. Navarro, "Indexing and Searching". In R. Baeza-Yates, B. Ribeiro-Neto, "Modern Information Retrieval", chapter 8, pp 191-228. Addison Wesley.
15. C. S. Roberts, "Partial-match retrieval via the method of superimposed codes". Proceedings of the IEEE, 67:12, 1624-1642.

16. S. Stiassny, "Mathematical analysis of various superimposed coding methods". American Documentation, 11 (2), 155-169.

17. J. Zobel, A. Moffat, K. Ramamohanarao, "Guidelines for Presentation and Comparison of Indexing Techniques". SIGMOD Record, 25(3):10-15, October 1996.

18. J. Zobel, A. Moffat, K. Ramamohanarao, "Inverted files versus signature files for text indexing". Transactions on Database Systems, 23(4), December 1998, pp.453-490.

Similarity Join in Metric Spaces

Vlastislav Dohnal[1], Claudio Gennaro[2], Pasquale Savino[2], and Pavel Zezula[1]

[1] Masaryk University
Brno, Czech Republic
{xdohnal,zezula}@fi.muni.cz
[2] ISTI-CNR, Pisa, Italy
{gennaro,savino}@isti.pi.cnr.it

Abstract. Similarity join in distance spaces constrained by the metric postulates is the necessary complement of more famous similarity range and the nearest neighbors search primitives. However, the quadratic computational complexity of similarity joins prevents from applications on large data collections. We first study the underlying principles of such joins and suggest three categories of implementation strategies based on filtering, partitioning, or similarity range searching. Then we study an application of the D-index to implement the most promising alternative of range searching. Though also this approach is not able to eliminate the intrinsic quadratic complexity of similarity joins, significant performance improvements are confirmed by experiments.

1 Introduction

Contrary to the traditional database approach, the Information Retrieval community has always considered search results as a ranked list of objects. Given a query, some objects are more relevant to the query specification than the others and users are typically interested in the most relevant objects, that is the objects with the highest ranks. This search paradigm has recently been generalized into a model in which a set of objects can only be pair-wise compared through a distance measure satisfying the *metric space* properties.

For illustration, consider the text data as the most common data type used in information retrieval. Since text is typically represented as a character string, pairs of strings can be compared and the *exact match* decided. However, the longer the strings are the less significant the exact match is: the text strings can contain errors of any kind and even the correct strings may have small differences. According to [9], text typically contain about 2% of typing and spelling errors. This gives a motivation to a search allowing errors, or *approximate search*, which requires a definition of the concept of *similarity*, as well as a specification of algorithms to evaluate it.

Consider a database of sentences for which translations to other languages are known. When a sentence is to be translated, such a database can suggest a possible translation provided the sentence or its close approximation already exists in the database. For two strings of length n and m available in main

F. Sebastiani (Ed.): ECIR 2003, LNCS 2633, pp. 452–467, 2003.

memory, there are several dynamic programming algorithms to compute the *edit distance* of the strings in $O(nm)$ time. Refer to [10] for an excellent overview of the work and additional references.

Though the way how objects are compared is very important to guarantee the search effectiveness, indexing structures are needed to achieve efficiency of searching large data collections. Extensive research in this area, see [1], have produced a large number of index structures which support two similarity search conditions, the range query and the k-nearest neighbor query. Given a reference (or query) object, the *range queries* retrieve objects with distances not larger than a user defined threshold, while the *k-nearest neighbors* queries provide k objects with the shortest distances to the reference.

In order to complete the set of similarity search operations, *similarity joins* are needed. For example, consider a document collection of books and a collection of compact disc documents. A possible search request can require to find *all pairs of books and compact discs which have similar titles*. But the similarity joins are not only useful for text. Given a collection of time series of stocks, a relevant query can be *report all pairs of stocks that are within distance ϵ from each other*. Though the similarity join has always been considered as the basic similarity search operation, there are only few indexing techniques, most of them concentrating on vector spaces. In this paper, we consider the problem from much broader perspective and assume distance measures as metric functions. Such the view extends the range of possible data types to the multimedia dimension, which is typical for modern information retrieval systems.

The development of Internet services often requires an integration of heterogeneous sources of data. Such sources are typically unstructured whereas the intended services often require structured data. Once again, the main challenge is to provide consistent and error-free data, which implies the *data cleaning*, typically implemented by a sort of *similarity join*. In order to perform such tasks, similarity rules are specified to decide whether specific pieces of data may actually be the same things or not. A similar approach can also be applied to the *copy detection*. However, when the database is large, the data cleaning can take a long time, so the processing time (or the performance) is the most critical factor that can only be reduced by means of convenient similarity search indexes.

The problem of approximate string processing has recently been studied in [5] in the context of data cleaning, that is removing inconsistencies and errors from large data sets such as those occurring in *data warehouses*. A technique for building approximate string join capabilities on top of commercial databases has been proposed in [7]. The core idea of these approaches is to transform the difficult problem of approximate string matching into other search problems for which some more efficient solutions exist.

In this article, we systematically study the difficult problem of similarity join implementation. In Section 2, we define the problem, specify its search complexity, and define three categories of implementation strategies. In Section present results of a simplified performance evaluation. Finally in Section 4, we study an implementation of the most promising strategy, which is based on the similarity range search.

2   Similarity Join

A convenient way to assess similarity between two objects is to apply metric functions to decide the closeness of objects as a distance, that is the objects' dis-similarity. A *metric space* $\mathcal{M} = (\mathcal{D}, d)$ is defined by a domain of objects (elements, points) $\mathcal{D}$ and a total (distance) function d – a *non negative* $(d(x, y) \geq 0$ with $d(x, y) = 0$ iff $x = y)$ and *symmetric* $(d(x, y) = d(y, x))$ function, which satisfies the *triangle inequality* $(d(x, y) \leq d(x, z) + d(z, y), \forall x, y, z \in \mathcal{D})$.

In general, the problem of indexing in metric spaces can be defined as follows:

> *given a set $X \subseteq \mathcal{D}$ in the metric space $\mathcal{M}$, preprocess or structure the elements of X so that similarity queries can be answered efficiently.*

Without any loss of generality, we assume that the maximum distance never exceeds the distance d^+. For a query object $q \in \mathcal{D}$, two fundamental similarity queries can be defined. A *range query* retrieves all elements within distance r to q, that is the set $\{x \in X, d(q, x) \leq r\}$. A *k-nearest neighbor* query retrieves the k closest elements to q, that is a set $R \subseteq X$ such that $|R| = k$ and $\forall x \in R, y \in X - R, d(q, x) \leq d(q, y)$.

2.1   Similarity Join: Problem Definition

The *similarity join* is a search primitive which combines objects of two subsets of $\mathcal{D}$ into one set such that a similarity condition is satisfied. The similarity condition between two objects is defined according to the metric distance d. Formally, the similarity join $X \stackrel{sim}{\bowtie} Y$ between two finite sets $X = \{x_1, ..., x_N\}$ and $Y = \{y_1, ..., y_M\}$ $(X \subseteq \mathcal{D}$ and $Y \subseteq \mathcal{D})$ is defined as the set of pairs

$$X \stackrel{sim}{\bowtie} Y = \{(x_i, y_j) \mid d(x_i, y_j) \leq \epsilon\}, \tag{1}$$

where ϵ is a real number such that $0 \leq \epsilon \leq d^+$. If the sets X and Y coincide, we talk about the *similarity self join*.

2.2   Complexity

In the paper, we measure the computational complexity through the number of distance evaluations. The similarity join can be evaluated by a simple algorithm which computes $|X| \cdot |Y|$ distances between all pairs of objects. We call this approach the *Nested Loop* (NL). For simplicity and without loss of generality we assume $N = |X| = |Y|$. Therefore, the complexity of the NL algorithm is N^2. For the similarity self join $(X \equiv Y)$, we have to ignore the evaluation of an object with itself so that the number of computed distances is reduced by N. Moreover, due to the symmetric property of metric functions, it is not necessary to evaluate the pair (x_j, x_i) if we have already examined the pair (x_i, x_j). That means the number of distance evaluations is $N(N-1)/2$ for the similarity self join.

As a preliminary analysis of the expected performance, we specify three general approaches for solving the problem of the similarity join in the next section. The performance index used to compare these approaches is the *speedup* (s) with respect to the trivial NL algorithm. Generally, if an algorithm requires n distance evaluations to compute the similarity join, the speedup is defined as follows:

$$s = \frac{N^2}{n}.$$

In case of similarity self join, the speedup is given by

$$s = \frac{N(N-1)/2}{n} = \frac{N(N-1)}{2n}.$$

In the following, we present three categories of algorithms which are able to reduce the computational complexity:

1. The *Filter Based algorithms* (FB), which try to reduce the number of expensive distance computations by applying simplified distance functions,
2. the *Partition Based algorithms* (PB), which partition the data set into smaller subsets where the similarity join can be computed with a smaller cost,
3. and the *Range Query algorithms* (RQ), which for each object of one data set execute a range query in the other data set.

2.3   Filter Based Algorithms

The Filter Based algorithms eliminate all pairs (x, y) that do not satisfy the similarity join condition of Equation 1 by using the lower-bound and the upper-bound distances, $d_l(x, y)$ and $d_u(x, y)$, having the following property:

$$d_l(x, y) \leq d(x, y) \leq d_u(x, y).$$

Algorithm 2.1 *Generic Filter Based Algorithm*

```
for i = 1 to N
    for j = 1 to M
        if d_l(x_i, y_j) ≤ ε then
            if d_u(x_i, y_j) ≤ ε then
                add (x_i, y_j) to the result
            else if d(x_i, y_j) ≤ ε then
                add (x_i, y_j) to the result
            end if
        end if
    end for
end for
```

The assumption is that the computation of d_l and d_u is much less expensive than the computation of d. Given a generic pair of objects (x_i, y_j), the algorithm first evaluates the distance $d_l(x_i, y_j)$. If $d_l(x_i, y_j) > \epsilon$ then $d(x_i, y_j) > \epsilon$ and the pair can be discarded. On the contrary, if $d_u(x_i, y_j) \leq \epsilon$ then the pair qualifies. If $d_l(x_i, y_j) \leq \epsilon$ and $d_u(x_i, y_j) > \epsilon$, it is necessary to compute $d(x_i, y_j)$. In the following, we present a sketch of the algorithm.

Let us suppose that p_u is the probability that $d_u(x_i, y_i) \leq \epsilon$ and p_l is the probability that $d_l(x_i, y_i) \leq \epsilon$. Moreover, let T_u, T_l, and T be the average computation time of d_u, d_l and d, respectively. The total computation time T_{tot} of the FB algorithm is

$$T_{tot} = T_l N^2 + p_l(T_u N^2 + (1 - p_u)TN^2),$$

and therefore

$$s = \frac{TN^2}{T_{tot}} = \frac{1}{\alpha_l + p_l(\alpha_u + (1 - p_u))}, \tag{2}$$

where $\alpha_u = \frac{T_u}{T}$ and $\alpha_l = \frac{T_l}{T}$. Notice that we have implicitly assumed that the events associated with p_u and p_l are independent, which is not too far from the reality. From this equation, it is possible to see that changing the order of evaluation of d_u and d_l, we can get different performance.

2.4   Partition Based Algorithms

This technique divides each of the data sets X and Y into h subsets with non-null intersections. Usually, the subsets are generated by using a set of regions of the whole domain $\mathcal{D}$. Let $\mathcal{D}_1, \mathcal{D}_2, \ldots, \mathcal{D}_h$ be the regions of partitioning, we define the subsets as $X_i = \{x \in X | x \in \mathcal{D}_i\}$ and $Y_i = \{y \in Y | y \in \mathcal{D}_i\}$, where $X = \bigcup_{i=1}^h X_i$ and $Y = \bigcup_{i=1}^h Y_i$. The idea is that neighboring regions overlap, so that by computing the similarity join in each local region no pair of objects is lost. Therefore, the algorithm proceeds by evaluating the similarity join for each pair of subsets X_i, Y_i for $1 \leq i \leq h$. The algorithm can be designed in a way that it is able to recognize whether a pair has already been evaluated in another partition or not, therefore, the number of distance evaluations in a local region can be smaller than $|X_i| \cdot |Y_i|$. Let $n_i = |X_i|$ and $m_i = |Y_i|$; in the worst case the speedup is given by

$$s = \frac{N^2}{\sum_{i=1}^h n_i m_i}.$$

In case of similarity self join, the speedup is

$$s = \frac{N^2}{\sum_{i=1}^h n_i^2}.$$

The ideal case where objects are uniformly distributed among partitions is expressed by

$$s = \frac{N^2}{\sum_{i=1}^h (N/h)^2} = \frac{N^2}{h(N/h)^2} = h. \tag{3}$$

2.5   Range Query Algorithms

Algorithms based on RQ strategy use an access structure supporting the similarity range search in order to retrieve qualified pairs of objects. The idea is to perform N range queries for all objects in the database with radius $r = \epsilon$. Given the average performance of a range query, for a specific access structure, it is easy to estimate the performance of the RQ algorithm. Therefore, if we have on average n_r distance computations for a range query, the speedup is given by

$$s = \frac{N^2}{Nn_r} = \frac{N}{n_r}, \tag{4}$$

and

$$s = \frac{N(N-1)/2}{(Nn_r/2)} = \frac{N-1}{n_r}, \tag{5}$$

for the similarity self join.

3   Implementation and Performance Evaluation

In this section, we provide examples of implementations of the techniques described in the previous section, specifically, the Sliding Window algorithm for the PB approach and the Pivot Based Filtering for the FB approach. The implementation of RQ approach is provided in Section 4. We also present a simplified performance evaluation.

3.1   Sliding Window Algorithm

The Sliding Window algorithm belongs to the Partition Based category. In the following, we describe the variant of this algorithm specialized to execute the similarity self join. The idea is straightforward (see Figure 1). We order the objects of the data set X with respect to an arbitrary reference object $x_r \in \mathcal{D}$, and we partition the objects in n_w overlapping "windows" each one having the width of 2ϵ. The algorithm starts from the first window (partition), with extremes $[0, 2\epsilon]$ and centered in ϵ, collecting all the pairs of objects (x_i, x_j) such that $d(x_i, x_j) \leq \epsilon$. The NL algorithm is used for each window. The algorithm proceeds with the next window, with extremes $[\epsilon, 3\epsilon]$ and centered in 2ϵ; the distance evaluation of a pair of objects which are both in the overlap with the previous window is avoided. The algorithm continues until the last window is reached. The detailed description of the algorithm requires the following definitions:

- Reference object: an object x_r from $\mathcal{D}$
- Maximum distance with respect to x_r: $d_r^+ = max_{i \in X}[d(x_r, x_i)]$
- The number of windows used: $n_w = \left\lceil \frac{d_r^+}{\epsilon} \right\rceil$
- The set of objects contained in the window m:

$$W_m = \{x_i \in X \mid (m-1)\epsilon < d(x_r, x_i) \leq (m+1)\epsilon\}$$

- The number of objects in W_m: $w_m = |W_m|$

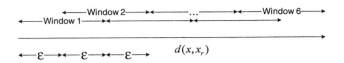

Fig. 1. Illustration of the Sliding Algorithm

The Algorithm Without loss of generality we study the algorithm for the case of similarity self join.

Algorithm 3.1 *Sliding Window*

> **for** $i = 1$ **to** n_w
>   **for** $j = 1$ **to** w_i
>   **for** $k = j + 1$ **to** w_i
>   **if** $i > 1$
>   **if** $d(x_j, x_r) > i\epsilon$ **or** $d(x_k, x_r) > i\epsilon$
>   **if** $d(x_j, x_k) \leq \epsilon$
>   *add* (x_j, x_k) *to the result*
>   **end if**
>   **end if**
>   **else**
>   **if** $d(x_j, x_k) \leq \epsilon$
>   *add* (x_j, x_k) *to the result*
>   **end if**
>   **end if**
>   **end for**
>   **end for**
> **end for**

Notice that the computation of distances $d(x_j, x_r)$ and $d(x_k, x_r)$ is done during the phase of ordering of objects with respect to x_r; they do not need to be computed again during the execution of the algorithm.

3.2 Pivot Based Filtering

Pivoting algorithms can be seen as a particular case of the FB category. In Figure 2, the basic principle of the pivoting technique is illustrated, where x is one object of a pair and p_i is a preselected object, called a pivot. Provided that the distance between any object and p_i is known, the gray area represents the region of objects y, that do not form a qualifying pair with x. This can easily be decided without actually computing the distance between x and y, by using the triangle inequalities $d(p_i, y) + d(x, y) \geq d(p_i, x)$ and $d(p_i, x) + d(p_i, y) \geq d(x, y)$ we have that $d(p_i, x) - d(p_i, y) \leq d(x, y) \leq d(p_i, y) + d(p_i, x)$, where $d(p_i, x)$ and $d(p_i, y)$ are pre-computed. It is obvious that, by using more pivots we can improve the probability of excluding an object y without actually computing its distance to x.

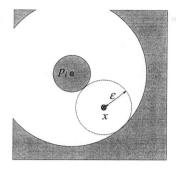

Fig. 2. Example of pivots behavior

Dynamic Pivots Since the evaluation of distances between pivots and all objects of the sets X and Y is very expensive, it is possible to generate the precomputed distances during the join elaboration. The idea is that each object of the data set X is promoted to a pivot during the elaboration of the join algorithm. For instance, when for all pairs (x_1, y_j) $(1 \leq j \leq M)$ distances $d(x_1, y_j)$ are computed, the object $x_1 \in X$ becomes a pivot.

Given K pivots $\{p_1, p_2, \ldots, p_K\}$, we can define a new lower-bound distance d_l as $d_l(x, y) = \max_{k=1..K}(d_l^k(x, y)) = \max_{k=1..K}(|d(p_k, y) - d(p_k, x)|)$, which is always less than or equal to $d(x, y)$. Naturally, this particular lower bound distance can be defined for every type of metric space; what we need is just a set of pivots with associated pre-computed distances to objects of the sets X and Y. If we define p_l as the probability that $\forall k = 1..K, d_l^k(x, y) \leq \epsilon$, and we neglect the evaluation of d_l^k (which involves only subtraction operations), we have

$$s = \frac{1}{p_l}.$$

3.3   Comparison

In order to compare the proposed approaches, we evaluate their speedups by using two simple data sets composed of vectors; the distances are measured by the Euclidean distance. The first set contains uniformly distributed vectors of dimension 10, while the vectors in the second data set are clustered and the dimension of each vector is 20. The experiments were conducted for different values of ϵ ranging from 0.20 up to 1.00. Figure 3 shows the results of experiments, on the left, there are speedups for the Pivot Based Filtering, on the right, the results for the Sliding Window are presented.

The problem with all the algorithms for the similarity join is that their complexity is $O(N^2)$ or, in other words, that their speedups are constant with respect to N. Unfortunately, even if the speedup is high, when the number of objects grows the number of distance computations grows quadratically. For the FB algorithm (see Equation 2), the speedup depends on the costs of distances d_l

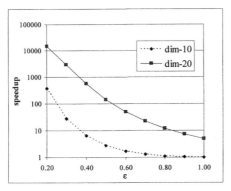 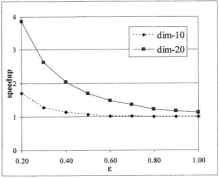

Fig. 3. Performance of the algorithms on the 10 and 20 dimensional data sets – Pivot Based Filtering (left), Sliding Window (right)

and d_u, i.e. α_l and α_u, which do not depend on N. Moreover, the probabilities p_u and p_l depend on an adopted distance functions and on distribution of objects in a metric space. We can conclude that FB has the constant speedup. As for the PB algorithm, from Equation 3 it is clear that the speedup cannot be greater than h. The only promising algorithm could be the RQ. In fact, as Equation 4 shows, in principle the speedup grows linearly if n_r is constant. Unfortunately, in the access structures in the literature, n_r increases linearly with N and therefore the speedup is constant also in the RQ case.

In the next section, we describe results of experiments obtained for the RQ algorithm. Particularly, we use the D-Index [4] access structure for the execution of range queries. We show that the D-Index executes range queries very efficiently, especially when applied on small query radii, which is the standard situation for similarity joins. Moreover, the D-Index also uses pivoting strategies, which, as shown in Figure 3, exhibit good performance, especially for small ϵ.

4   Experimenting the Range Query Algorithm

This section is dedicated to a detailed experimental evaluation of the RQ algorithm. The D-Index access structure is used to support the execution of range queries. We first summarize the basic idea of the D-Index and evaluate its performance for range queries with small radii. Next, we provide a detailed experimental evaluation of the similarity self join.

4.1   D-Index

The D-Index is a multi-level metric structure, consisting of *search-separable* buckets at each level. The structure supports easy insertion and bounded search costs because at most one bucket needs to be accessed at each level for range queries up

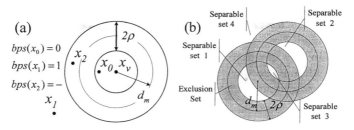

Fig. 4. The *bps* split function (a) and the combination of two *bps* functions (b)

to a predefined value of search radius ρ. At the same time, the applied *pivot-based strategy* significantly reduces the number of distance computations in accessed buckets. In the following, we provide a brief overview of the D-Index, more details can be found in [6] and the full specification, as well as performance evaluations, are available in [4].

The partitioning principles of the D-Index are based on a multiple definition of a mapping function, called the ρ-split function. Figure 4a shows a possible implementation of a ρ-split function, called the *ball partitioning split (bps)*, originally proposed in [11]. This function uses one reference object x_v and the *medium distance* d_m to partition a data set into three subsets. The result of the following *bps* function gives a unique identification of the set to which the object x belongs:

$$bps(x) = \begin{cases} 0 & \text{if } d(x, x_v) \leq d_m - \rho \\ 1 & \text{if } d(x, x_v) > d_m + \rho \\ - & \text{otherwise} \end{cases}$$

The subset of objects characterized by the symbol '$-$' is called the *exclusion set*, while the subsets of objects characterized by the symbols 0 and 1 are the *separable sets*, because any range query with radius not larger than ρ cannot find qualifying objects in both the subsets.

More separable sets can be obtained as a combination of *bps* functions, where the resulting exclusion set is the union of the exclusion sets of the original split functions. Furthermore, the new separable sets are obtained as the intersection of all possible pairs of the separable sets of original functions. Figure 4b gives an illustration of this idea for the case of two split functions. The separable sets and the exclusion set form the separable buckets and the exclusion bucket of one level of the D-index structure, respectively.

Naturally, the more separable buckets we have, the larger the exclusion bucket is. For the large exclusion bucket, the D-index allows an additional level of splitting by applying a new set of split functions on the exclusion bucket of the previous level. The exclusion bucket of the last level forms the exclusion bucket of the whole structure. The ρ-split functions of individual levels should be different but they must use the same ρ. Moreover, by using a different number of split functions (generally decreasing with the level), the D-Index structure can have different number of buckets at individual levels. In order to deal with overflow problems and growing files, buckets are implemented as *elastic buckets* and consist of the necessary number of fixed-size blocks (pages) – basic disk access units.

Due to the mathematical properties of split functions, precisely defined in [4], the range queries up to radius ρ are solved by accessing at most one bucket per level, plus the exclusion bucket of the whole structure. This can intuitively be comprehended by the fact that an arbitrary object belonging to a separable bucket is at distance at least 2ρ from any object of other separable bucket of the same level. With additional computational effort, the D-Index executes range queries of radii greater than ρ. The D-index also supports the nearest neighbor(s) queries.

4.2   Performance Evaluation

The experimental evaluation has been conducted on a real application environment. It was composed of 300.000 sentences from the Czech language corpus, with sentence similarity measured by the edit distance. The most frequent distance was around 100 and the longest distance was 500, equal to the length of the longest sentence.

The *edit distance*, also known as the *Levenshtein distance*, is a distance function which measures similarity between two text strings. In fact, it computes the minimum number of atomic edit operations needed to transform one string into the other. The atomic operations are *insertion*, *deletion* and *replacement* of one character.

For illustration, consider the following examples:

* d('lenght','length')=2 – two replacements of the two last letters, $h \rightarrow t$ and $t \rightarrow h$,
* d('sting','string')=1 – one insertion of r,
* d('application','applet')=6 – one replacement of the 5th letter, $i \rightarrow e$, two deletions of the 6th and 7th letters and three deletions of the three last letters (i, o, n).

The time complexity of algorithms implementing the edit distance function $d_{edit}(x, y)$ is $O(len(x) \times len(y))$, that is evaluations of the edit distance function are high CPU consuming operations. For more details, see the recent survey [10].

In all experiments, the search costs are measured in terms of the number of distance computations. The basic structure of D-index was fixed for all tests and consisted of 9 levels and 39 buckets. However, due to the elastic implementation of buckets with a variable number of blocks, we could easily manage data files of different sizes. In the following, we report results of our experiments separately for the similarity range queries and the similarity self join operations.

Range Search All presented cost values are averages obtained by execution of 50 queries with different query objects (sentences) and a constant search radius.

The objective of the first group of experiments was to study the relationship between the search radius (or the selectivity) and the search costs considering a data set of constant size. In the second group, we concentrated on small query radii and by significantly changing the cardinality of data sets, we studied the scalability of the query execution.

Selectivity-cost ratio. In order to test the basic properties of the D-index to search text data, we have considered a set of 50,000 sentences. Though we have tested all possible query radii, we have mainly focused on small radii. That corresponds to the semantically most relevant query specifications – objects that are very close to a given reference object can be interesting. Recall that a range query returns all objects whose distances from the query object are within the given query radius r.

Moreover, searching for typing errors or duplicates results in range queries with small radii and the D-index solves these types of queries very efficiently. Figure 5 shows the average number of distance computations needed by the D-index structure to evaluate queries of small radii. The number of distance computations is shown as percentage with respect to the sequential scan which always needs 50,000 distances. Due to the pivot-based strategy applied to the D-index, only some objects of accessed pages have to be examined and distances to them computed, this technique saves a lot of distance computations.

Searching for objects within the distance 1 to a query object takes less than 3 page reads and 29 distance computations – such queries are solved in terms of milliseconds. A range query with radius $r = 4$ is solved using 411 distance computations, which is less than 1% of the sequential scan, and 30 page reads, which is about 2.5% of all pages – all objects are stored in 1192 pages. But even queries with radii 4 take about 0.125 seconds at average. This is in a sharp contrast with 16 seconds of the sequential access.

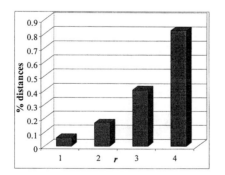

Fig. 5. Percentage of distance computations for range queries with r from 1 to 4

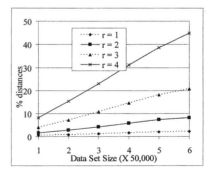

Fig. 6. Range search scalability

However, due to the computational complexity of the edit distance, the page reads are not so significant because one page is read from a disk in terms of milliseconds while the distance computations between a query object and objects in only one page can take tens of milliseconds.

Scalability. To analyze the range search scalability of D-index, we have considered collections of sentences ranging from 50,000 to 300,000 elements. We have conducted tests to see how the costs for range queries (from $r = 1$ to $r = 4$) grow with the size of the data set. The obtained results are reported in graphs in Figure 6, where individual curves correspond to different query radii.

From the figure we can see that the search costs scale up with slightly sublinear trends. This is a very desirable feature that guarantees the applicability of the D-index not only on small data sets but also on large collections of data.

Similarity Self Join To analyze basic properties of the D-index to process similarity self joins, we have conducted our experiments on a set of 50,000 sentences. Though this approach can be applied to any threshold ϵ, we have mainly concentrated on small ϵ, which are used in the data cleaning area. Figure 7 shows the speedup of the RQ algorithm based on the use of D-Index, for similarity self-join queries with different ϵ. As expected, since the number of distance computations (or the processing costs in general) increases quite fast with growing ϵ, the speedup s decreases quickly. However, the NL algorithm is much more expensive. For $\epsilon = 4$, the NL algorithm is 148 times slower, and for $\epsilon = 1$, the NL algorithm uses even 5700 times more distance computations. In this respect, the performance of our approach is quite comparable to the approximate string join algorithm proposed in [7]. This approach is based on segmenting strings into q-grams and introduces an additional overhead for building lists of q-grams. However, the reported search speedup with respect to NL, is practically the same.

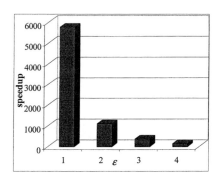
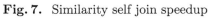

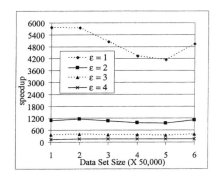

Fig. 7. Similarity self join speedup

Fig. 8. Join queries scalability: speedup

Another recent paper [5] proposes the *neighborhood join* algorithm (NJ), which uses the difference of lengths of compared strings $(abs(|x| - |y|))$ as the simplified distance function for the pre-filtering rule. The authors of [5] have tested NJ algorithm on bibliographic strings with ϵ equal to 15% of the maximum distance. The NJ has saved from 33% to 72% of distance computations with respect to the NL algorithm, depending on the distance distribution. In order to contrast such approach with our technique, we have also set ϵ to the 15% of the maximum distance of our data set, specifically $\epsilon = 35$. For this case, our algorithm saved 74% of distance computations.

Note that the experiments in [7] and [5] were conducted on data sets of comparable sizes, but quite shorter strings, which makes the problem of similarity joins easier. We can conclude that the implementation of the self-join through the general index structure, D-index, is very competitive to the specialized algorithms for strings.

Scalability. Considering the web-based dimension of data, scalability is probably the most important issue to investigate. In the elementary case, it is necessary to investigate what happens with the performance when the size of data grows. We have experimentally investigated the behavior of the D-index on data sets with sizes from 50,000 to 300,000 objects (sentences). Figure 8 presents speedup results for $\epsilon = 1, 2, 3$ and 4. The trends of speedups for individual values of ϵ are constant while the size of data set is enlarged 6 times (from 50,000 to 300,000 objects). The speedup for growing values of ϵ deteriorates, but even for $\epsilon = 4$, the performance of the RQ algorithm with the D-index is still 150 times faster than the NL algorithm. In [5], the authors have also studied the scale up and conducted experiments on a data set of two different sizes and the performance of their NJ specialized algorithm was deteriorating with the growing data set size. Specifically, the speedup for the five times larger data set was only 64% of the speedup for the original data set. This is in a sharp contrast with the constant speedup of our RQ algorithm.

In summary, the figure demonstrates that the speedup is very high and constant for different values of ϵ with respect to the data set size. This implies that the similarity self join with the D-index is suitable for much larger data sets than all the other algorithms can manage, even though the intrinsic quadratic complexity still remains. The same trends have been observed when the speedup was measured in terms of page reads instead of distance computations. But as explained before, the page reads are not so important compared to the distance computations.

5   Conclusions

Similarity search is an important concept of information retrieval. However, the computational costs of similarity (dis-similarity or distance) functions are typically high – consider the edit distance with the quadratic computational complexity. We have observed by experiments that a sequential similarity range search on 50,000 sentences takes about 16 seconds. But to perform the NL similarity self-join algorithm on the same data would take 25,000 times more, which is about 4 days and 15 hours. In order to reduce the computational costs, indexing techniques must be applied.

Though a lot of research results on indexing techniques to support the similarity range and nearest neighbors queries have been published, there are only few recent studies on indexing of similarity joins. In this article, we have analyzed several implementation strategies for similarity join indexes among which an application of the similarity range approach appears to be the most promising.

Accordingly, we have applied the D-index, a metric index structure, and we have performed numerous experiments to analyze its search properties and suitability for the similarity join implementation. Whenever possible, we have also contrasted our results with recent specialized proposals for approximate string processing. In general, we can conclude that the application of the D-index is never worse in performance than the specialized techniques. The D-index is strictly sub-linear for all meaningful search requests, that is search queries retrieving relatively small subsets of the searched data sets. The D-index is extremely efficient for small query radii where on-line response times are guaranteed. The important feature is that the D-index scales up well to processing large files and experiments reveal even slightly sub-linear scale up for similarity range queries. Though the scale up of the similarity self join processing is constant, it is still better than the scale up reported for the specialized techniques.

In principle, any metric index structure can be used to implement our algorithm of the similarity join. Our choice of the D-index is based on an earlier comparison of index structures summarized in [4]. Besides the D-index, the authors also studied the performance of the M-Tree [3] and a sequential organization – according to [1], other metric index structures do not consider disk storage and keep objects only in the main memory. Presented experiments reveal that for small range query radii, typical for similarity join operations, the D-index performs at least 6 times faster than the M-Tree, and it is much faster than the sequential scan. We plan to systematically investigate the impact of this issue on the similarity join evaluation in the near future.

We have conducted some of our experiments on vectors and a deep evaluation was performed on sentences. However, it is easy to imagine that also text units of different granularity, such as individual words or paragraphs with words as string symbols, can easily be handled by analogy. However, the main advantage of the D-index is that it can also perform similar operations on other metric data. As suggested in [8], where the problem of similarity join on XML structures is investigated, metric indexes could be applied for approximate matching of tree structures. We consider this challenge as our second major future research direction.

References

[1] E. Chavez, G. Navarro, R. Baeza-Yates, and J. Marroquin: Searching in Metric Spaces. *ACM Computing Surveys*, 33(3):273-321, 2001.

[2] T. Bozkaya and Ozsoyoglu. Indexing Large Metric Spaces for Similarity Search Queries. *ACM TODS*, 24(3):361-404, 1999.

[3] P. Ciaccia, M. Patella, and P. Zezula: M-tree: An Efficient Access Method for Similarity Search in Metric Spaces. *Proceedings of the 23rd VLDB Conference*, pp. 426-435, 1997.

[4] V. Dohnal, C. Gennaro, P. Savino, P. Zezula: D-Index: Distance Searching Index for Metric Data Sets. To appear in *Multimedia Tools and Applications*, Kluwer, 2002.

[5] H. Galhardas, D. Florescu,D. Shasha, E. Simon, and C. A. Saita: Declarative Data Cleaning: Language, Model, and Algorithms. Proceedings of *the 27th VLDB Conference*, Rome, Italy, 2001, pp. 371-380.

[6] C. Gennaro, P. Savino, and P. Zezula: Similarity Search in Metric Databases through Hashing. Proceedings of *ACM Multimedia 2001 Workshops*, October 2001, Ottawa, Canada, pp. 1-5.

[7] L. Gravano, P. G. Ipeirotis, H. V. Jagadish, N. Koudas, S. Muthukrishnan, and D. Srivastava: Approximate String Joins in a Database (Almost) for Free. Proceedings of *the 27th VLDB Conference*, Rome, Italy, 2001, pp. 491-500.

[8] S. Guha, H. V. Jagadish, N. Koudas, D. Srivastava, and T. Yu: Approximate XML Joins. Proceedings of *ACM SIGMOD 2002*, Madison, Wisconsin, June 3-6, 2002

[9] K. Kukich: Techniques for automatically correcting words in text. *ACM Computing Surveys*, 1992, 24(4):377-439.

[10] G. Navarro: A guided tour to approximate string matching. *ACM Computing Surveys*, 2001, 33(1):31-88.

[11] P. N. Yianilos. Excluded Middle Vantage Point Forests for Nearest Neighbor Search. Tech. rep., NEC Research Institute, 1999, Presented at Sixth DIMACS Implementation Challenge: Nearest Neighbor Searches workshop, January 15, 1999.

An Efficient Compression Code
for Text Databases*

Nieves R. Brisaboa[1], Eva L. Iglesias[2], Gonzalo Navarro[3], and José R. Paramá[1]

[1] Database Lab., Univ. da Coruña, Facultade de Informática
Campus de Elviña s/n, 15071 A Coruña, Spain
{brisaboa,parama}@udc.es
[2] Computer Science Dept., Univ. de Vigo
Escola Superior de Enxeñería Informática
Campus As Lagoas s/n, 32001, Ourense, Spain
eva@uvigo.es
[3] Dept. of Computer Science, Univ. de Chile
Blanco Encalada 2120, Santiago, Chile
gnavarro@dcc.uchile.cl

Abstract. We present a new compression format for natural language texts, allowing both exact and approximate search without decompression. This new code –called End-Tagged Dense Code– has some advantages with respect to other compression techniques with similar features such as the Tagged Huffman Code of [Moura et al., ACM TOIS 2000]. Our compression method obtains (*i*) better compression ratios, (*ii*) a simpler vocabulary representation, and (*iii*) a simpler and faster encoding. At the same time, it retains the most interesting features of the method based on the Tagged Huffman Code, i.e., exact search for words and phrases directly on the compressed text using any known sequential pattern matching algorithm, efficient word-based approximate and extended searches without any decoding, and efficient decompression of arbitrary portions of the text. As a side effect, our analytical results give new upper and lower bounds for the redundancy of d-ary Huffman codes.

Keywords: Text compression, D-ary Huffman coding, text databases.

1   Introduction

Text compression techniques are based on exploiting redundancies in the text to represent it using less space [3]. The amount of text collections has grown in recent years mainly due to the widespread use of digital libraries, documental databases, office automation systems and the Web. Current text databases contain hundreds of gigabytes and the Web is measured in terabytes. Although the capacity of new devices to store data grows fast, while the associated costs decrease, the size of the text collections increases also rapidly. Moreover, CPU

---

* This work is partially supported by CICYT grant (#TEL99-0335-C04), CYTED VII.19 RIBIDI Project, and (for the third author) Fondecyt Grant 1-020831.

F. Sebastiani (Ed.): ECIR 2003, LNCS 2633, pp. 468–481, 2003.

speed grows much faster than that of secondary memory devices and networks, so storing data in compressed form reduces I/O time, which is more and more convenient even in exchange for some extra CPU time.

Therefore, compression techniques have become attractive methods to save space and transmission time. However, if the compression scheme does not allow to search for words directly on the compressed text, the retrieval will be less efficient due to the necessity of decompression before the search.

Classic compression techniques, as the well-known algorithms of Ziv and Lempel [16, 17] or the character oriented code of Huffman [4], are not suitable for large textual databases. One important disadvantage of these techniques is the inefficiency of searching for words directly on the compressed text. Compression schemes based on Huffman codes are not often used on natural language because of the poor compression ratios achieved. On the other hand, Ziv and Lempel algorithms obtain better compression ratios, but the search for a word on the compressed text is inefficient. Empirical results [11] showed that searching on a Ziv-Lempel compressed text can take half the time of decompressing that text and then searching it. However, the compressed search is twice as slow as just searching the uncompressed version of the text.

In [13], Moura et al. present a compression scheme that uses a semi-static word-based model and a Huffman code where the coding alphabet is byte-oriented. This compression scheme allows the search for a word on the compressed text without decompressing it in such a way that the search can be up to eight times faster for certain queries. The key idea of this work (and others like that of Moffat and Turpin [8]) is the consideration of the text words as the symbols that compose the text (and therefore the symbols that should be compressed). Since in Information Retrieval (IR) text words are the atoms of the search, these compression schemes are particularly suitable for IR. This idea has been carried on further up to a full integration between inverted indexes and word-based compression schemes, opening the door to a brand new family of low-overhead indexing methods for natural language texts [14, 9, 18].

The role played by direct text searching in the above systems is as follows. In order to reduce index space, the index does not point to exact word positions but to text blocks (which can be documents or logical blocks independent of documents). A space-time tradeoff is obtained by varying the block size. The price is that searches in the index may have to be complemented with sequential scanning. For example, in a phrase query the index can point to blocks where all the words appear, but a only sequential search can tell whether the phrase actually appears. If blocks do not match documents, even single word searches have to be complemented with sequential scanning of the candidate blocks. Under this scenario, it is essential to be able of keeping the text blocks in compressed form and searching them without decompressing.

Two basic search methods are proposed in [13]. One handles plain Huffman code (over words) and explores one byte of the compressed text at a time. This is quite efficient, but not as much as the second choice, which compresses the pattern and uses any classical string matching strategy, such as Boyer-Moore [10].

For this second, faster, choice to be of use, one has to ensure that no spurious occurrences are found. The problem is that a text occurrence of the code of a word may correspond to the concatenation of other codes instead of to the occurrence of the word. Although Plain Huffman Code is a prefix code (that is, no code is a prefix of the other), it does not ensure that the above problem cannot occur. Hence Moura et al. propose a so-called Tagged Huffman Code, where a bit of each byte in the codes is reserved to signal the beginning of a code. The price is an increase of approximately 11% in the size of the compressed file.

In this paper we show that, although Plain Huffman Code gives the shortest possible output when a source symbol is always substituted by the same code, Tagged Huffman Code largely underutilizes the representation. We show that, by signaling the end instead of the beginning of a code, the rest of the bits can be used in all their combinations and the code is still a prefix code. The resulting code, which we call End-Tagged Dense Code, becomes much closer to the compression obtained by the Plain Huffman Code. Not only this code retains the ability of being searchable with any string matching algorithm, but also it is extremely simple to build (it is not based on Huffman at all) and permits a more compact vocabulary representation. So the advantages over Tagged Huffman Code are (*i*) better compression ratios, (*ii*) same searching possibilities, (*iii*) simpler vocabulary representation, (*iv*) simpler and faster coding.

2   Related Work

Huffman is a well-known coding method [4]. The idea of Huffman coding is to compress the text by assigning shorter codes to more frequent symbols. It has been proven that Huffman algorithm obtains an optimal (i.e., shortest total length) *prefix code* for a given text.

A code is called a *prefix code* (or instantaneous code) if no codeword is a prefix of any other codeword. A prefix code can be decoded without reference to future codewords, since the end of a codeword is immediately recognizable.

2.1   Word-Based Huffman Compression

The traditional implementations of the Huffman code are character based, i.e., they adopt the characters as the symbols of the alphabet. A brilliant idea [7] uses the words in the text as the symbols to be compressed. This idea joins the requirements of compression algorithms and of IR systems, as words are the basic atoms for most IR systems. The basic point is that a text is much more compressible when regarded as a sequence of words rather than characters.

In [13, 18], a compression scheme is presented that uses this strategy combined with a Huffman code. From a compression viewpoint, character-based Huffman methods are able to reduce English texts to approximately 60% of their original size, while word-based Huffman methods are able to reduce them to 25% of their original size, because the distribution of words is much more biased than the distribution of characters.

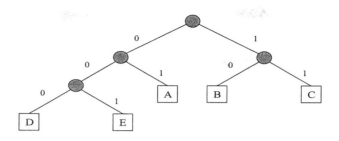

Fig. 1. Huffman tree

The compression schemes presented in [13, 18] use a semi-static model, that is, the encoder makes a first pass over the text to obtain the frequency of all the words in the text and then the text is coded in the second pass. During the coding phase, original symbols (words) are replaced by codewords. For each word in the text there is a unique codeword, whose length varies depending on the frequency of the word in the text. Using the Huffman algorithm, shorter codewords are assigned to more frequent words.

The set of codewords used to compress a text are arranged as a tree with edges labeled by bits, such that each path from the root to a leaf spells out a different code. Since this is a prefix code, no code is represented by an internal tree node. On the other hand, each tree leaf corresponds to a codeword that represents a different word of the text. For decompression purposes, the corresponding original text word is attached to each leaf, and the whole tree is seen as a representation of the vocabulary of the text. Hence, the compressed file is formed by the compressed text plus this vocabulary representation. The Huffman algorithm gives the tree that minimizes the length of the compressed file. See [4, 3] for a detailed description.

Example 1. Consider a text with vocabulary *A, B, C, D, E* where the corresponding frequencies are 0.25, 0.25, 0.20, 0.15, 0.15. A possible Huffman tree, given by the Huffman algorithm, is shown in Figure 1. Observe that *A* is coded with 01, *B* with 10, *C* with 11, *D* with 000 and *E* with 001.

□

2.2   Byte-Oriented Huffman Coding

The basic method proposed by Huffman is mostly used as a binary code, that is, each word in the original text is coded as a sequence of bits. Moura et al. [13] modify the code assignment such that a sequence of whole bytes is associated with each word in the text.

Experimental results have shown that, on natural language, there is no significant degradation in the compression ratio by using bytes instead of bits. In addition, decompression and searching are faster with byte-oriented Huffman code because no bit manipulations are necessary.

In [13] two codes following this approach are presented. In that article, they call *Plain Huffman Code* the one we have already described, that is, a word-based byte-oriented Huffman code.

The second code proposed is called Tagged Huffman Code. This is just like the previous one differing only in that the first bit of each byte is reserved to flag whether or not the byte is the first byte of a codeword. Hence, only 7 bits of each byte are used for the Huffman code. Note that the use of a Huffman code over the remaining 7 bits is mandatory, as the flag is not useful by itself to make the code a prefix code.

Tagged Huffman Code has a price in terms of compression performance: we store full bytes but use only 7 bits for coding. Hence the compressed file grows approximately by 11%.

Example 2. We show the differences among the codes generated by the Plain Huffman Code and Tagged Huffman Code. In our example we assume that the text vocabulary has 16 words, with uniform distribution in Table 1 and with exponential distribution ($p_i = 1/2^i$) in Table 2.

For the sake of simplicity, from this example on, we will consider that our "bytes" are formed by only two bits. Hence, Tagged Huffman Code uses one bit for the flag and one for the code (this makes it look worse than it is). We underline the flag bits.   □

Table 1. Codes for a uniform distribution

Word	Probab.	Plain Huffman	Tagged Huffman
A	1/16	00 00	10 00 00 00
B	1/16	00 01	10 00 00 01
C	1/16	00 10	10 00 01 00
D	1/16	00 11	10 00 01 01
E	1/16	01 00	10 01 00 00
F	1/16	01 01	10 01 00 01
G	1/16	01 10	10 01 01 00
H	1/16	01 11	10 01 01 01
I	1/16	10 00	11 00 00 00
J	1/16	10 01	11 00 00 01
K	1/16	10 10	11 00 01 00
L	1/16	10 11	11 00 01 01
M	1/16	11 00	11 01 00 00
N	1/16	11 01	11 01 00 01
O	1/16	11 10	11 01 01 00
P	1/16	11 11	11 01 01 01

Table 2. Codes for an exponential distribution

Word Probab.	Plain Huffman	Tagged Huffman
A 1/2	00	11
B 1/4	01	10 01
C 1/8	10	10 00 01
D 1/16	11 00	10 00 00 01
E 1/32	11 01	10 00 00 00 01
F 1/64	11 10	10 00 00 00 00 01
G 1/128	11 11 00	10 00 00 00 00 00 01
H 1/256	11 11 01	10 00 00 00 00 00 00 01
I 1/512	11 11 10	10 00 00 00 00 00 00 00 01
J 1/1024	11 11 11 00	10 00 00 00 00 00 00 00 00 01
K 1/2048	11 11 11 01	10 00 00 00 00 00 00 00 00 00 01
L 1/4096	11 11 11 10	10 00 00 00 00 00 00 00 00 00 00 01
M 1/8192	11 11 11 11 00	10 00 00 00 00 00 00 00 00 00 00 00 01
N 1/16384	11 11 11 11 01	10 00 00 00 00 00 00 00 00 00 00 00 00 01
O 1/32768	11 11 11 11 10	10 00 00 00 00 00 00 00 00 00 00 00 00 00 01
P 1/32768	11 11 11 11 11	10 00 00 00 00 00 00 00 00 00 00 00 00 00 00 01

The addition of a tag bit in the Tagged Huffman Code permits direct searching on the compressed text with any string matching algorithm, by simply compressing the pattern and then resorting to classical string matching.

On Plain Huffman this does not work, as the pattern could occur in the text and yet not correspond to our codeword. The problem is that the concatenation of parts of two codewords may form the codeword of another vocabulary word.

This cannot happen in the Tagged Huffman Code due to the use of one bit in each byte to determine if the byte is the first byte of a codeword or not.

For this reason, searching with Plain Huffman requires inspecting all the bytes of the compressed text from the beginning, while Boyer-Moore type searching (that is, skipping bytes) is possible over Tagged Huffman Code.

Example 3. Let us suppose that we have to compress a text with a vocabulary formed by the words *A, B, C, D* and assume that the Huffman algorithm assigns the following codewords to the original words:

A	00
B	01
C	10
D	11 00

Let us consider the following portion of a compressed text using the code shown above, for the sequence *ABAD*:

$$\dots 00\ 01\ 00\ 11\ 00 \dots$$

Finally, let us suppose that we search for word A. If we resort to plain pattern matching, we find two occurrences in the text. However, the second does not really represent an occurrence of A in the text, but it is part of D. The program should have a postprocessing phase where each potential occurrence is verified, which ruins the simplicity and performance of the algorithm.   □

The algorithm to search for a single word under Tagged Huffman Code starts by finding the word in the vocabulary to obtain the codeword that represents it in the compressed text. Then the obtained codeword is searched for in the compressed text using any classical string matching algorithm with no modifications. They call this technique *direct searching* [13, 18].

Today's IR systems require also flexibility in the search patterns. There is a range of complex patterns that are interesting in IR systems, including regular expressions and "approximate" searching (also known as "search allowing errors"). See [13, 18] for more details.

3   A New Compression Scheme: End-Tagged Dense Codes

We start with a seemingly dull change to Tagged Huffman Code. Instead of using the flag bit to signal the *beginning* of a codeword, we use it to signal the *end* of a codeword. That is, the flag bit will be 1 for the last byte of each codeword.

This change has surprising consequences. Now the flag bit is enough to ensure that the code is a prefix code, no matter what we do with the other 7 bits. To see this, notice that, given two codewords X and Y, where $|X| < |Y|$, X cannot be a prefix of Y because the last byte of X has its flag bit in 1, while the $|X|$-th byte of Y has its flag bit in 0.

At this point, there is no need at all to use Huffman coding over the remaining 7 bits. We can just use *all* the possible combinations of 7 bits in all the bytes, as long as we reserve the flag bit to signal the end of the codeword.

Once we are not bound to use a Huffman code, we have the problem of finding the optimal code assignment, that is, the one minimizing the length of the output. It is still true that we want to assign shorter codewords to more frequent words. Indeed, the optimal assignment is obtained with the following procedure.

1. The words in the vocabulary are ordered by their frequency, more frequent first.
2. Codewords from $\underline{1}0000000$ to $\underline{1}1111111$ are assigned sequentially to the first 128 words of the vocabulary, using the 2^7 possibilities.
3. Words at positions $128 + 1$ to $128 + 128^2$ are encoded using two bytes, by exploiting the 2^{14} combinations from $\underline{0}0000000{:}\underline{1}0000000$ to $\underline{0}1111111{:}\underline{1}1111111$.
4. Words at positions $128 + 128^2 + 1$ to $128 + 128^2 + 128^3$ are encoded using three bytes, by exploiting the 2^{21} combinations from $\underline{0}0000000{:}\underline{0}0000000{:}\underline{1}0000000$ to $\underline{0}1111111{:}\underline{0}1111111{:}\underline{1}1111111$. And so on.

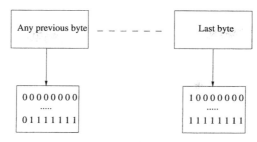

Fig. 2. End-Tagged Dense Codewords

The assignment is done in a completely sequential fashion, that is, the 130-th word is encoded as $\underline{0}0000000{:}\underline{1}0000001$, the 131-th as $\underline{0}0000000{:}\underline{1}0000010$, and so on, just as if we had a 14-bit number. As it can be seen, the computation of codes is extremely simple: It is only necessary to order the vocabulary words by frequency and then sequentially assign the codewords. Hence the coding phase will be faster because obtaining the codes is simpler.

In fact, we do not even need to physically store the results of these computations: With a few operations we can obtain on the fly, given a word rank i, its ℓ-byte codeword, in $O(\ell) = O(\log i)$ time.

What is perhaps less obvious is that *the code depends on the rank of the words, not on their actual frequency*. That is, if we have four words A, B, C, D with frequencies 0.27, 0.26, 0.25 and 0.23, respectively, the code will be the same as if their frequencies were 0.9, 0.09, 0.009 and 0.001.

Hence, we do not need to store the codewords (in any form such as a tree) nor the frequencies in the compressed file. It is enough to store the plain words sorted by frequency. Therefore, the vocabulary will be smaller than in the case of the Huffman code, where either the frequencies or the codewords or the tree must be stored with the vocabulary. (The difference in size, however, is minimal if one uses a canonical Huffman tree.)

In order to obtain the codewords of a compressed text, the decoder can run a simple computation to obtain, from the codeword, the rank of the word, and then obtain the word from the vocabulary sorted by frequency. An ℓ-byte code n can be decoded in $O(\ell) = O(\log n)$ time.

Table 3 shows the codewords obtained by the End-Tagged Dense Code for the examples in Tables 1 and 2 (remember that we are using bytes of two bits). Note that, independently of the distribution, exponential or uniform, the codification is the same.

It is interesting to point out how our codes look like on a Huffman tree. Basically, our codes can be regarded as a tree of arity 128 (like that of Tagged Huffman), but in this case we can use also the *internal* nodes of the tree, while Tagged Huffman is restricted to use only the leaves. Precisely, the use of the internal nodes is what makes it more efficient than Huffman in all cases. On the

Table 3. Example of End-Tagged Dense Code

Word	Rank	Codeword
A	1	10
B	2	11
C	3	00 10
D	4	00 11
E	5	01 10
F	6	01 11
G	7	00 00 10
H	8	00 00 11
I	9	00 01 10
J	10	00 01 11
K	11	01 00 10
L	12	01 00 11
M	13	01 01 10
N	14	01 01 11
O	15	00 00 00 10
P	16	00 00 00 11

other hand, note that dense coding always produces a tree that is as balanced as possible, independently of the vocabulary frequencies.

4   Analytical Results

We try to analyze the compression performance of our new scheme. Let us assume a word distribution $\{p_i\}_{i=1...N}$, where p_i is the probability of the i-th most frequent word and N is the vocabulary size. Let us assume that we use symbols of b bits to represent the codewords, so that each codeword is a sequence of b-bit symbols. In practice we use bytes, so $b = 8$.

It is well known [3] that Plain Huffman coding produces an average symbol length which is at most one extra symbol over the zero-order entropy. That is, if we call

$$E_b \;=\; \sum_{i=1}^{N} p_i \log_{2^b}(1/p_i) \;=\; \frac{1}{b} \sum_{i=1}^{N} p_i \log_2(1/p_i)$$

the zero-order entropy in base b of the text, then the average number of symbols to code a word using Plain Huffman is

$$E_b \;\leq\; H_b \;\leq\; E_b + 1$$

Tagged Huffman code is also easy to analyze. It is a Huffman code over $b-1$ bits, but using b bits per symbol, hence

$$E_{b-1} \;\leq\; T_b \;\leq\; E_{b-1} + 1$$

Let us now consider our new method, with average number of symbols per word D_b. It is clear that $H_b \leq D_b \leq T_b$, because ours is a prefix code and

Huffman is the best prefix code, and because we use all the $b-1$ remaining bit combinations and Tagged Huffman does not. We try now to obtain a more precise comparison. Let us call $B = 2^{b-1}$. Since B^i different words will be coded using i symbols, let us define

$$s_i \;=\; \sum_{j=1}^{i} B^j \;=\; \frac{B}{B-1}\,(B^i - 1)$$

(where $s_0 = 0$) the number of words that can be coded with up to i symbols. Let us also call

$$f_i \;=\; \sum_{j=s_{i-1}+1}^{s_i} p_j$$

the overall probability of words coded with i symbols.

Then, the average length of a codeword under our new method is

$$D_b \;=\; \sum_{i=1}^{S} i f_i$$

where $S = \log_B\left(\frac{B-1}{B}N + 1\right)$.

The most interesting particular case is a distribution typical of natural language texts. It is well known [3] that, in natural language texts, the vocabulary distribution closely follows a generalized Zipf's law [15], that is, $p_i = A/i^\theta$ and $N = \infty$, for suitable constants A and θ. In practice θ is between 1.4 and 1.8 and depends on the text [1, 2], while

$$A \;=\; \frac{1}{\sum_{i\geq 1} 1/i^\theta} \;=\; \frac{1}{\zeta(\theta)}$$

makes sure that the distribution adds up 1[1]. Under this distribution the entropy is

$$E_b \;=\; \frac{1}{b}\sum_{i\geq 1} p_i \log_2 \frac{1}{p_i} \;=\; \frac{A\theta}{b}\sum_{i\geq 1}\left(\frac{\log_2 i}{i^\theta} - \log_2 A\right) \;=\; \frac{-\theta\zeta'(\theta)/\zeta(\theta) + \ln\zeta(\theta)}{b\ln 2}$$

On the other hand, we have

$$D_b \;=\; A\sum_{i\geq 1} i \sum_{j=s_{i-1}+1}^{s_i} 1/j^\theta \;=\; 1 + A\sum_{i\geq 1} i \sum_{j=s_i+1}^{s_{i+1}} 1/j^\theta \;=\; 1 + A\sum_{i\geq 1}\sum_{j\geq s_i+1} 1/j^\theta$$

At this point we resort to integration to get lower and upper bounds. Since $1/j^\theta$ decreases with j, we have that the above summation is upper bounded as follows

$$D_b \leq 1 + A\sum_{i\geq 1}\int_{s_i}^{\infty} 1/x^\theta dx \;=\; 1 + \frac{A(B-1)^{\theta-1}}{(\theta-1)B^{\theta-1}}\sum_{i\geq 1}\frac{1}{(B^i-1)^{\theta-1}}$$

$$\leq 1 + \frac{A(B-1)^{\theta-1}}{(\theta-1)B^{\theta-1}}\frac{B^{1-\theta}}{1-B^{1-\theta}}(1 - 1/B)^{1-\theta} \;=\; 1 + \frac{1}{(\theta-1)\zeta(\theta)(B^{\theta-1}-1)}$$

---

[1] We are using the Zeta function $\zeta(x) = \sum_{i>0} 1/i^x$. We will also use $\zeta'(x) = \partial\zeta(x)/\partial x$.

A lower bound can be obtained similarly, as follows

$$
\begin{aligned}
D_b &\geq 1 + A \sum_{i \geq 1} \int_{s_i+1}^{\infty} 1/x^\theta dx &=& \quad 1 + \frac{A(B-1)^{\theta-1}}{\theta-1} \sum_{i \geq 1} \frac{1}{(B^{i+1}-1)^{\theta-1}} \\
&\geq 1 + \frac{A(B-1)^{\theta-1}}{(\theta-1)} \frac{B^{2(1-\theta)}}{1-B^{1-\theta}} &=& \quad 1 + \frac{(1-1/B)^{\theta-1}}{(\theta-1)\zeta(\theta)(B^{\theta-1}-1)}
\end{aligned}
$$

This gives us the length of the code with a precision factor of $(1-1/B)^{\theta-1}$, which in our case ($B = 128$, $\theta = 1.4$ to 1.8) is around 0.5%. This shows that the new code is also simpler to analyze than Huffman, as the existing bounds for Huffman are much looser.

In fact, the lower bound E_b for the performance of Huffman is quite useless for our case: For $b = 8$ bits, $E_b < 1$ for $\theta > 1.3$, where 1 symbol is an obvious lower bound. The same happens when using E_{b-1} to bound Tagged Huffman. We have considered tighter estimates [6, 12] but none was useful for this case.

In order to compare our results with Plain Huffman and Tagged Huffman, we resort to our own analysis. If we take $b = 9$ bits, then $B = 256$ and we obtain the length of a dense code where all the 8 bits are used in the optimal form. This is necessarily better than Huffman (on 8 bits), as not all the 8-bit combinations are legal for Huffman. On the other hand, consider $b = 7$. In this case our new code is a 7-bit prefix code, necessarily inferior to Tagged Huffman (over 8 bits). Hence we have the following inequalities

$$
D_{b+1} \quad \leq \quad H_b \quad \leq \quad D_b \quad \leq \quad T_b \quad \leq \quad D_{b-1}
$$

These results give us usable bounds to compare our performance. Incidentally, the analysis of our new code turns out to give new upper and lower bounds for the redundancy of d-ary Huffman codes. Figure 3 illustrates our analytical estimates as a function of θ. Our lower and upper bounds are rather close. Plain Huffman must lie between its lower bound and our upper bound. Tagged Huffman must lie between our lower bound and its upper bound.

5   Experimental Results

We show some experimental results now. We have used some large text collections from TREC-4 (AP-Newswire 1988, Ziff Data 1989–1990, Congressional Record 1993, and Financial Times 1991 to 1994). We have compressed them using Plain Huffman Code, Tagged Huffman Code, and our End-Tagged Dense Code. Separators (maximal strings between two consecutive words) were treated as words as well, all forming a single vocabulary. We used the *spaceless words* method [13], where the single space is taken as the default separator and omitted.

We have included the size of the vocabulary in the results. The size of this vocabulary is almost the same for our representation (where no Huffman tree is necessary, just the sorted list of words) and for the Huffman-based methods, as we use canonical Huffman codes to represent the Huffman trees in negligible

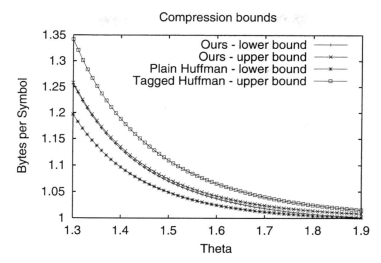

Fig. 3. Analytical bounds on the average code length for byte-oriented Plain Huffman, Tagged Huffman, and our new method. We assume a Zipf distribution with parameter θ (which is the x axis)

Table 4. Compression ratios for Plain Huffman, End-Tagged Dense and Tagged Huffman coding, using the *spaceless words* model and including the compressed vocabulary

Corpus	Original Size	Plain	Dense	Tagged
AP Newswire 1988	250,994,525	31.71%	32.53%	35.10%
Ziff Data 1989–1990	185,417,980	32.34%	33.24%	35.76%
Congress Record 1993	51,085,545	28.45%	29.27%	31.45%
Financial Times 1991	14,749,355	33.05%	33.92%	36.30%
Financial Times 1992	175,449,248	31.52%	32.33%	34.90%
Financial Times 1993	197,586,334	31.53%	32.42%	35.04%
Financial Times 1994	203,783,923	31.50%	32.39%	35.01%

space. Vocabulary tables were in turn compressed using the classical Huffman algorithm oriented to bits and using characters as symbols. On the large text collection we tested, the extra space they posed was rather small.

Table 4 shows the results. It can be seen that, in all cases, our End-Tagged Dense Codes are superior to Tagged Huffman Codes by about 8%, and worse than the optimal Plain Huffman by less than 3%.

Compression results usually worsen with smaller text collections. This is a common feature of all approaches where words are taken as symbols, and is due to the overhead of storing the vocabulary table. In an IR environment, however,

Table 5. Average symbol length (in bytes) for the different methods using the *spaceless words* model

Corpus	Tot. Words Tot. Sep.	Voc. Words Voc. Sep.	Plain Huffman	End-Tagged Dense	Tagged Huffman	Theta
AP Newswire 1988	52,960,212	241,315	1.477827	1.516603	1.638228	1.852045
Ziff Data 1989–1990	40,548,114	221,443	1.449977	1.490903	1.606416	1.744346
Congress Record 1993	9,445,990	114,174	1.475534	1.520167	1.638070	1.634076
Financial Times 1991	3,059,634	75,597	1.455481	1.497421	1.612230	1.449878
Financial Times 1992	36,518,075	284,904	1.465063	1.504248	1.627545	1.630996
Financial Times 1993	41,772,135	291,322	1.447384	1.489149	1.613115	1.647456
Financial Times 1994	43,039,879	295,023	1.447626	1.489669	1.613737	1.649428

the goal is to deal with very large collections, and for these the extra space of the vocabulary becomes negligible.

With respect to the analytical predictions based on Zipf's Law, Table 5 shows the average symbol length in bytes obtained for the three methods (vocabulary excluded). It can be seen that our analytical predictions are rather optimistic. This shows that Zipf's model is not precise enough and that we should resort to a more complex one, e.g. Mandelbrot's [5].

6   Conclusions

We have presented a new compression code useful for text databases. The code inherits from previous work, where byte-oriented word-based Huffman codes were shown to be an excellent choice. To permit fast searching over that code, Tagged Huffman codes were introduced, which in exchange produced an output about 11% larger.

In this paper we have introduced End-Tagged Dense Codes, which is a prefix code retaining all the searchability properties of Tagged Huffman code while improving it on several aspects: (*i*) codes are shorter: 8% shorter than Tagged Huffman and just less than 3% over Huffman; (*ii*) coding is much simpler and faster; (*iii*) the vocabulary representation is simpler.

We have shown analytically and experimentally the advantages of End-Tagged Dense Codes in terms of output size. An Information Retrieval system based on this new technique should also benefit from the other advantages. For example, (*iii*) means that we just need to store the vocabulary sorted by frequency, without any additional information, which simplifies integration to the IR system; (*ii*) means that we do not have to build Huffman code, but can just encode and decode on the fly with a program of a few lines.

As a side effect, our analysis has given new upper and lower bounds on the average code length when using *d*-ary Huffman coding. These bounds are of different nature from those we are aware of, and they could be better on some distribution. This was the case on Zipf's distributions. On the other hand, our experiments have shown that natural language does not fit so well a Zipf distribution. Indeed, sometimes better compression is achieved with a smaller θ value. We plan to try more sophisticated models of word frequencies, e.g. Mandelbrot's [5].

References

[1] M. D. Araújo, G. Navarro, and N. Ziviani. Large text searching allowing errors. In R. Baeza-Yates, editor, *Proc. 4th South American Workshop on String Processing (WSP'97)*, pages 2–20. Carleton University Press, 1997.

[2] R. Baeza-Yates and B. Ribeiro-Neto. *Modern Information Retrieval*. Addison-Wesley, 1999.

[3] T. C. Bell, J. G. Cleary, and I. H. Witten. *Text Compression*. Prentice Hall, 1990.

[4] D. A. Huffman. A method for the construction of minimum-redundancy codes. *Proc. Inst. Radio Eng.*, 40(9):1098–1101, September 1952.

[5] B. Mandelbrot. An informational theory of the statistical structure of language. In *Proc. Symp. on Applications of Communication Theory*, pages 486–500, 1952.

[6] D. Manstetten. Tight bounds on the redundancy of Huffman codes. *IEEE Trans. on Information Theory*, 38(1):144–151, January 1992.

[7] A. Moffat. Word-based text compression. *Software - Practice and Experience*, 19(2):185–198, 1989.

[8] A. Moffat and A. Turpin. On the implementation of minimum-redundancy prefix codes. In *Proc. Data Compression Conference*, pages 170–179, 1996.

[9] G. Navarro, E. Silva de Moura, M. Neubert, N. Ziviani, and R. Baeza-Yates. Adding compression to block addressing inverted indexes. *Information Retrieval*, 3(1):49–77, 2000.

[10] G. Navarro and M. Raffinot. *Flexible Pattern Matching in Strings – Practical on-line search algorithms for texts and biological sequences*. Cambridge University Press, 2002.

[11] G. Navarro and J. Tarhio. Boyer-moore string matching over ziv-lempel compressed text. In *Proc. 11th Annual Symposium on Combinatorial Pattern Matching (CPM'2000)*, LNCS 1848, pages 166–180, 2000.

[12] R. De Prisco and A. De Santis. On lower bounds for the redundancy of optimal codes. *Designs, Codes and Cryptography*, 15(1):29–45, 1998.

[13] E. Silva de Moura, G. Navarro, N. Ziviani, and R. Baeza-Yates. Fast and flexible word searching on compressed text. *ACM Transactions on Information Systems*, 18(2):113–139, April 2000.

[14] I. Witten, A. Moffat, and T. Bell. *Managing Gigabytes*. Morgan Kaufmann Publishers, second edition, 1999.

[15] G. Zipf. *Human Behaviour and the Principle of Least Effort*. Addison-Wesley, 1949.

[16] J. Ziv and A. Lempel. A universal algorithm for sequential data compression. *IEEE Transactions on Information Theory*, 23(3):337–343, 1977.

[17] J. Ziv and A. Lempel. Compression of individual sequences via variable-rate coding. *IEEE Transactions on Information Theory*, 24(5):530–536, 1978.

[18] N. Ziviani, E. Silva de Moura, G. Navarro, and R. Baeza-Yates. Compression: A key for next-generation text retrieval systems. *IEEE Computer*, 33(11):37–44, 2000.

Compressing Semistructured Text Databases*

Joaquín Adiego[1], Gonzalo Navarro[2], and Pablo de la Fuente[1]

[1] Departamento de Informática, Universidad de Valladolid
Valladolid, España
{jadiego,pfuente}@infor.uva.es
[2] Departamento de Ciencias de la Computación, Universidad de Chile
Santiago, Chile
gnavarro@dcc.uchile.cl

Abstract. We describe a compression model for semistructured documents, called *Structural Contexts Model*, which takes advantage of the context information usually implicit in the structure of the text. The idea is to use a separate semiadaptive model to compress the text that lies inside each different structure type (e.g., different XML tag). The intuition behind the idea is that the distribution of all the texts that belong to a given structure type should be similar, and different from that of other structure types. We test our idea using a word-based Huffman coding, which is the standard for compressing large natural language textual databases, and show that our compression method obtains significant improvements in compression ratios. We also analyze the possibility that storing separate models may not pay off if the distribution of different structure types is not different enough, and present a heuristic to *merge* models with the aim of minimizing the total size of the compressed database. This technique gives an additional improvement over the plain technique. The comparison against existing prototypes shows that our method is a competitive choice for compressed text databases.

Keywords: Text Compression, Compression Model, Semistructured Documents, Text Databases.

1 Introduction

The process of data compression can be split into two parts: an encoder that generates the compressed bitstream and a modeler that feeds information to it [10]. These two separate tasks are called *coding* and *modeling*, respectively. Modeling assigns probabilities to symbols depending on the source data, while coding translates these probabilities into a sequence of bits. In order to work properly, the decoder must have access to the same model as the encoder.

Compression of large document collections not only reduces the amount of disk space occupied by the data, but it also decreases the overall query processing time in text retrieval systems. Improvements in processing times are achieved

---

* This work was partially supported by CYTED VII.19 RIBIDI project (all authors) and Fondecyt Project 1-020831 (second author).

F. Sebastiani (Ed.): ECIR 2003, LNCS 2633, pp. 482–490, 2003.

thanks to the reduced disk transfer times necessary to access the text in compressed form. Also, recent research on "direct" compressed text searching, i.e., searching a compressed text without decompressing it, has led to a win-win situation where the compressed text takes less space and is searched faster than the plain text [12, 13].

Compressed text databases pose some requirements that outrule some compression methods. The most definitive is the need for random access to the text without the possibility of decompressing it from the beginning. This outrules most adaptive compression methods such as Ziv-Lempel compression and arithmetic coding. On the other hand, semiadaptive models —which uses a different model for each text encoded, building it before performing the compression and storing it in the compressed file— such as Huffman [5] yield poor compression. In the case of compressing natural language texts, it has been shown that an excellent choice is to consider the words, not the characters, as the source symbols [7]. Finally, the fact that the alphabet and the vocabulary of the text collections coincide permits efficient and highly sophisticated searching, both in the form of sequential searching and in the form of compressed inverted indexes over the text [12, 13, 9, 8].

Although the area of natural language compressed text databases has gone a long way since the end of the eighties, it is interesting that little has been done about considering the structure of the text in this picture. Thanks to the widespread acceptance of SGML, HTML and XML as the standards for storing, exchanging and presenting documents, semistructured text databases are becoming the standard.

Our goal in this paper is to explore the possibility of considering the text structure in the context of a compressed text database. We aim at taking advantage of the structure, while still retaining all the desirable features of a word-based Huffman compression over a semiadaptive model. The idea is then to use separate semiadaptive models to compress the text that lies inside different tags.

While the possible gain due to this idea is clear, the price is that we have to store several models instead of just one. This may or may not pay off. Hence we also design a technique to *merge* the models if we can predict that this is convenient in terms of compressed file length. Although the problem of finding the optimal merging looks as a hard combinatorial problem, we design a heuristic to automatically obtain a reasonably good merging of an initially separate set of models, one per tag.

This model, which we call *Structural Contexts Model*, is general and does not depend on the coder. We plug it to a word-based Huffman coder to test it. Our experimental results show significant gains over the methods that are insensitive to the structure and over the current methods that consider the structure. At the same time, we retain all the features of the original model that makes it suitable for compressed text databases.

2   Related Work

With regard to compressing natural language texts in order to permit efficient retrieval from the collection, the most successful techniques are based on models where the text words are taken as the source symbols [7], as opposed to the traditional models where the characters are the source symbols. On the one hand, words reflect much better than characters the true entropy of the text [10]. For example, a Huffman coder when words are the symbols obtains 25% versus 60% when characters are the symbols [13]. Another example is the WLZW algorithm (Ziv-Lempel on words) [1].

On the other hand, most information retrieval systems use words as the main information atoms, so a word-based compression easies the integration with an information retrieval system. Some examples of successful integration are [12, 9]. The text in natural language is not only made up of words. There are also punctuation, separators, and other special characters. The sequence of characters between every pair of consecutive words will be called a *separator*. In [1] they propose to create two alphabets of disjoint symbols: one for coding words and another for separators. Encoders that use this model consider texts as a strict alternation of two independent data sources and encode each one independently. Once we know that the text starts with a word or a separator, we know that after a word has been coded we can expect a separator and vice versa. This idea is known as the *separate alphabets model.*

A compression method that considers the document structure is *XMill* [6], developed in AT&T Labs. XMill is an XML-specific compressor designed to exchange and store XML documents, and its compression approach is not intended for directly supporting querying or updating of the compressed document. Another XML compressor is *XGrind* [11], which directly supports queries over the compressed files. Other approaches to compress XML data exist, based on the use of a PPM-like coder, where the context is given by the path from the root to the tree node that contains the current text. One example is *XMLPPM* [2], which is an adaptive compressor pased on PPM, where the context is given by the structure.

3   Structural Contexts Model

Let us, for this paper, to focus on a semiadaptive Huffman coder, as it has given the best results on natural language texts. Our ideas, however, can be adapted to other encoders. Let us call *dictionary* the set of source symbols together with their assigned codes.

An encoder based on the separate alphabets model (see Section 2) must use two source symbol dictionaries: one for all the separators and the other for all the words in the texts. This idea is still suitable when we handle semistructured documents —like SGML or XML documents—, but in fact we can extend the mechanism to do better.

In most cases, natural language texts are structured in a semantically meaningful manner. This means that we can expect that, at least for some tags, the distribution of the text that appears inside a given tag differs from that of another tag. In cases where the words under one tag have little intersection with words under another tag, or their distribution is very different, the use of separate alphabets to code the different tags is likely to improve the compression ratio. On the other hand, there is a cost in the case of semiadaptive models, as we have to store several dictionaries instead of just one. In this section we assume that each tag should use a separate dictionary, and will address in the next section the way to group tags under a single dictionary.

3.1   Compressing the Text

We compress the text with a word-based Huffman [5, 1]. The text is seen as an alternating sequence of words and separators, where a word is a maximal sequence of alphanumeric characters and a separator is a maximal sequence of non-alphanumeric characters.

Besides, we will take into account a special case of words: *tags*. A tag is a code embedded in the text which represents the structure, format or style of the data. A tag is recognized from surrounding text by the use of delimiter characters. A common delimiter character for an XML or SGML tag are the symbols '<' and '>'. Usually two types of tags exist: *start-tags*, which are the first part of a container element, '<...>'; and *end-tags*, which are the markup that ends a container element, '</...>'.

Tags will be wholly considered (that is, including their delimiter characters) as words, and will be used to determine when to switch dictionaries at compression and decompression time.

3.2   Model Description

The structural contexts model (as the separate alphabets model) uses one dictionary to store all the separators in the texts, independently of their location. Also, it assumes that words and separators alternate, otherwise, it must insert either an empty word or an empty separator. There must be at least one word dictionary, called the *default dictionary*. The default dictionary is the one in use at the beginning of the encoding process. If only the default dictionary exists for words then the model is equivalent to the separate alphabets model.

We can have a different dictionary for each tag, or we can have separate dictionaries for some tags and use the default for the others, or in general we can have any grouping of tags under dictionaries. As explained, we will assume for now that each tag has its own dictionary and that the default is used for the text that is not under any tag.

The compression algorithm written below makes two passes over the text. In the first pass, the text is modeled and separate dictionaries are built for each tag and for the default and separators dictionary. These are based on the statistics of words under each tag, under no tag, and separators, respectively. In the second pass, the texts are compressed according to the model obtained.

At the begining of the modeling process, words are stored in the default dictionary. When a start-structure tag appears we push the current dictionary in a stack and switch to the appropriate dictionary. When an end-structure tag is found we must return to the previous dictionary stored in the stack. Both, start-structure and end-structure tags, are stored and coded using the current dictionary and then we switch dictionaries. Likewise, the encoding and decoding processes use the same dictionary switching technique.

3.3   Entropy Estimation

The entropy of a source is a number that only depends on its model, and is usually measured in *bits/symbol*. It is also seen as a function of the probability distribution of the source (under the model), and refers to the average amount of information of a source symbol. The entropy gives a lower bound on the size of the compressed file if the given model is used. Successful compressors get very close to the entropy.

The fundamental theorem of Shannon establishes that the entropy of a probability distribution $\{p_i\}$ is $\sum_i p_i \log_2(1/p_i)$ bits. That is, the optimum way to code symbol i is to use $\log_2(1/p_i)$ bits. In a zero-order model, the probability of a symbol is defined independently of surrounding symbols. Usually one does not know the real symbol probabilities, but rather estimate them using the raw frequencies seen in the text.

Definition 1
(Zero-order entropy estimation with multiple dictionaries)
Let N be the total number of dictionaries. The zero-order entropy for all dictionaries, $\mathcal{H}$, is computed as the weighted average of zero-order entropies contributed by each dictionary ($\mathcal{H}^d, d \in 1 \ldots N$):

$$\mathcal{H} = \frac{\sum_{d=1}^{N} n^d \, \mathcal{H}^d}{n} \tag{1}$$

where n^d is the total number of text terms in dictionary d and n is the total number of terms that appear in the text.

4   Merging Dictionaries

Up to now we have assumed that each different tag uses its own dictionary. However, this may not be optimal because of the overhead to store the dictionaries in the compressed file. In particular, if two dictionaries happen to share many terms and to have similar probability distributions, then merging both tags under a single dictionary is likely to improve the compression ratio.

In this section we develop a general method to obtain a good grouping of tags under dictionaries. For efficiency reasons we will use the entropy as the estimation of the size of the text compressed using a dictionary, instead of actually running the Huffman algorithm and computing the exact size.

If $\mathcal{V}^d$ is the size in bits of the vocabulary that constitutes dictionary d and $\mathcal{H}^d$ is its estimated zero-order entropy, then the estimated size contribution of dictionary d is given by $\mathcal{T}^d = \mathcal{V}^d + n^d \mathcal{H}^d$. Considering this equation, we determine to merge dictionaries i and j when the sum of their contributions is larger than the contribution of their union. In other words, when $\mathcal{T}^i + \mathcal{T}^j > \mathcal{T}^{i \cup j}$. To compute $\mathcal{T}^{i \cup j}$ we have to compute the union of the vocabularies and the entropy of that union. This can be done in time linear with the vocabulary sizes.

Our optimization algorithm works as follows. We start with one separate dictionary per tag, plus the default dictionary (the separators dictionary is not considered in this process). Then, we progressively merge pairs of dictionaries until no further merging promises to be advantageous. Obtaining the optimal division into groups looks as a hard combinatorial problem, but we use a heuristic which produces good results and is reasonably fast.

We start by computing $\mathcal{T}^i$ for every dictionary i, as well as $\mathcal{T}^{i \cup j}$ for all pairs i, j of dictionaries. With that we compute the savings $\mathcal{A}^{i \cup j} = \mathcal{T}^i + \mathcal{T}^j - \mathcal{T}^{i \cup j}$ for all pairs. Then, we merge the pair of dictionaries i and j that maximizes $\mathcal{A}^{i \cup j}$, if this is positive. Then, we erase i and j and introduce $i \cup j$ in the set. This process is repeated until all the $\mathcal{A}^{i \cup j}$ values are negative.

5   Evaluation of the Model

We have developed a prototype implementing the Structural Contexts Model with a word-oriented Huffman coding, and used it to empirically analyze our model and evaluate its performance. Tests were carried out on Linux Red Hat 7.2 operating system, running on a computer with a Pentium 4 processor at 1.4 GHz and 128 Mbytes of RAM. For the experiments we selected different size collections of WSJ, ZIFF and AP, from TREC-3 [3].

The average speed to compress all collections is around 128 Kbytes/sec. In this value we include the time needed to model, merge dictionaries and compress. The time for merging dictionaries is included in this figure, and it ranges from 4.37 seconds for 1 Mb to 40.27 seconds for 100 Mb. The impact of merging times is large for the smallest collection (about 50% of the total time), but it becomes much less significant for the largest collection (about 5%). The reason is that it is $O(vs^2)$ to $O(vs^3)$ time, where v is the vocabulary size and s the number of different tags. Although it depends heavily on s, this number is usually small and does not grow with the collection size but depends on the DTD/schema. The vocabulary size v, on the other hand, grows sublinearly with the collection size [4], typically close to $O(\sqrt{n})$.

In Figure 1 we can see a comparison for WSJ, of the compression performance using the plain separate alphabets model (SAM) and the structural context model (SCM) with and without merging dictionaries. For short texts, the vocabulary size is significant with respect to the text size, so SCM without merging pays a high price for the separate dictionaries and does not improve over SAM. As the text collection grows and the impact of the dictionaries gets reduced and we obtain nearly 11% additional compression. The SCM with merging obtains

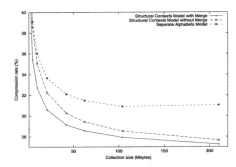

Size	SCM+merge	SCM	SAM
1221659	45.82%	51.34%	51.20%
5516592	35.42%	38.57%	39.09%
10510481	32.73%	35.06%	36.03%
21235547	30.59%	32.23%	33.66%
42113697	29.15%	30.27%	32.10%
62963963	28.58%	29.45%	31.49%
104942941	27.93%	28.54%	30.90%
210009482	27.24%	27.64%	31.03%

Fig. 1. Compression ratios using different models, for WSJ

Table 1. Number of dictionaries used

Aprox.	TREC-WSJ		TREC-ZIFF		TREC-AP	
Size(Mb)	Initial	Final	Initial	Final	Initial	Final
1	11	8	10	4	9	5
5	11	8	10	4	9	5
10	11	8	10	4	9	7
20	11	9	10	6	9	7
40	11	9	10	6	9	7
60	11	9	10	6	9	7
100	11	9	10	7	9	7

similar results for large collections (12.5% additional compression), but its performance is much better on small texts, where it starts obtaining 10.5% even for 1 Mbyte of text.

Table 1 shows the number of dictionaries merged. Column "Initial" tells how many dictionaries are in the beginning: The default and separators dictionary plus one per tag, except for <DOC>, which marks the start of a document and uses the default dictionary. Column "Final" tells how many different dictionaries are left after the merge. For example, for small WSJ subsets, the tags <DOCNO> and <DOCID>, both of which contain numbers and internal references, were merged. The other group that was merged was formed by the tags <HL>, <LP> and <TEXT>, all of which contain the text of the news (headlines, summary for teletypes, and body). On the larger WSJ subsets, only the last group of three tags was merged. This shows that our intuition that similar-content tags would be merged is correct. The larger the collection, the less the impact of storing more vocabularies, and hence the fewer merges will occur. The method to predict the size of the merged dictionaries from the vocabulary distributions was quite accurate: our prediction was usually 98%–99% of the final value.

6 Conclusions and Future Work

We have proposed a new model for compressing semistructured documents based on the idea that texts under the same tags should have similar distributions. This is enriched with a heuristic that determines a good grouping of tags so as to code each group with a separate model.

We have shown that the idea actually improves compression ratios by more than 10% with respect to the basic technique. The prototype is a basic implementation and we are working on several obvious improvements, which will make it even more competitive, especially for small collections. One is the use of canonical Huffman codes, which reduce the size of the dictionary representation. Another is a character-based compression of the vocabularies.

Other improvements would affect the results for every collection size. We can tune our method to predict the outcome of merging dictionaries: Since we know that usually our prediction is 1%–2% off, we could add a mean value to our prediction. With respect to the study of the method itself, we have to investigate more in depth the relationship between the type and density of the structuring and the improvements obtained with our method, since its success is based on a semantic assumption and it would be interesting to see how this works on other text collections.

References

[1] J. Bentley, D. Sleator, R. Tarjan, and V. Wei. A locally adaptive data compression scheme. *Communications of the ACM*, 29:320–330, 1986.

[2] J. Cheney. Compressing XML with multiplexed hierarchical PPM models. In *Proc. Data Compression Conference (DCC 2001)*, pages 163–, 2001.

[3] D. Harman. Overview of the Third Text REtrieval Conference. In *Proc. Third Text REtrieval Conference (TREC-3)*, pages 1–19, 1995. NIST Special Publication 500-207.

[4] H. S. Heaps. *Information Retrieval - Computational and Theoretical Aspects*. Academic Press, 1978.

[5] D. A. Huffman. A method for the construction of minimum-redundancy codes. *Proc. Inst. Radio Engineers*, 40(9):1098–1101, 1952.

[6] H. Liefke and D. Suciu. XMill: an efficient compressor for XML data. In *Proc. ACM SIGMOD 2000*, pages 153–164, 2000.

[7] A. Moffat. Word-based text compression. *Software - Practice and Experience*, 19(2):185–198, 1989.

[8] E. Silva de Moura, G. Navarro, N. Ziviani, and R. Baeza-Yates. Fast and flexible word searching on compressed text. *ACM Transactions on Information Systems*, 18(2):113–139, 2000.

[9] G. Navarro, E. Silva de Moura, M. Neubert, N. Ziviani, and R. Baeza-Yates. Adding compression to block addressing inverted indexes. *Information Retrieval*, 3(1):49–77, 2000.

[10] Ian H. Witten Timothy C. Bell, John G. Cleary. *Text Compression*. Prentice Hall, Englewood Cliffs, N. J., 1990.

[11] P. Tolani and J. R. Haritsa. XGRIND: A query-friendly XML compressor. In *ICDE*, 2002. citeseer.nj.nec.com/503319.html.

[12] I. H. Witten, A. Moffat, and T. C. Bell. *Managing Gigabytes*. Morgan Kaufmann Publishers, Inc., second edition, 1999.

[13] N. Ziviani, E. Moura, G. Navarro, and R. Baeza-Yates. Compression: A key for next-generation text retrieval systems. *IEEE Computer*, 33(11):37–44, November 2000.

Vertical Searching in Juridical Digital Libraries

Maria de Lourdes da Silveira[1,2,*], Berthier Ribeiro-Neto[1,3,**], Rodrigo de Freitas Vale[3], and Rodrigo Tôrres Assumpção[4]

[1] Computer Science Department of the Federal University of Minas Gerais
[2] Prodabel – Information Technology Company for the City of Belo Horizonte, Brazil
[3] Akwan Information Technologies
[4] Central Bank of Brazil

Abstract. In the world of modern digital libraries, the searching for juridical information of interest is a current and relevant problem. We approach this problem from the perspective that a new searching mechanism, specialized in the juridical area, will work better than standard solutions. We propose a specialized (or *vertical*) searching mechanism that combines information from a juridical thesaurus with information generated by a standard searching mechanism (the classic vector space model), using the framework of a Bayesian belief network. Our vertical searching mechanism is evaluated using a reference collection of 552,573 documents. The results show improvements in retrieval performance, suggesting that the study and development of vertical searching mechanisms is a promising research direction.

Keywords: vertical searching, thesaurus, digital library, juridical area, ranking.

1 Introduction

The juridical literature is always expanding. A good part of this literature is now available online and accessible through the Internet. Such accessibility facilitates the access to specialized juridical information, but introduces new problems on its own. Lawyers have limited time for bibliographical searching and frequently have limited access to important information sources. Also they have great difficulty in identifying the most relevant information within the vast juridical collections of today. As a result, people involved with the law and its use are usually unable to take full advantage of computer devices for accomplishing the tasks of juridical analysis and searching.

A standard approach to this problem is to directly apply Information Retrieval (IR) techniques to a full text collection from the juridical domain. We investigate this issue and evaluate its effectiveness. While this approach does provide a solution to the problem of finding relevant information in a large juridical

---

* Partially supported by Brazilian CNPq scholarship grant 141294/2000-0.
** Partially supported by Brazilian CNPq Individual Grant 300.188/95-1, Finep/MCT/CNPq Grant 76.97.1016.00 (project SIAM), and CNPq Grant 17.0435/01-6 (project I³DL).

F. Sebastiani (Ed.): ECIR 2003, LNCS 2633, pp. 491–501, 2003.

collection (or digital library), it does not take into account any specialized knowledge from the juridical arena. That is, there is small effort into using knowledge from the law field to improve the searching for specialized juridical information. This clearly seems to be a strong limitation.

An alternative approach is to combine specialized juridical knowledge, encoded in the form of a thesaurus, with evidence generated by standard IR techniques. In this case, the focus is on building a specialized searching mechanism (or algorithm) for juridical digital libraries. Since the search space is restricted to juridical documents and to the thesaurus concepts, we say that this new algorithm implements a type of *vertical searching*.

Investigating the problem of vertical searching for juridical documents is the path we follow here. We consider a specific form of juridical knowledge, i.e., information provided by a controlled vocabulary of juridical concepts and the relationships among them, encoded in the form of a thesaurus. Given this juridical thesaurus, we study the problem of how to improve the quality of the answers generated by the system, i.e., how to improve retrieval performance.

To combine evidence from standard IR techniques (i.e., keyword-based searching) with knowledge derived from the juridical thesaurus, we adopt the framework of Bayesian networks [10]. Bayesian networks are useful because they allow combining distinct sources of evidence in consistent fashion. Our Bayesian framework leads to a new ranking formula. Through experimentation, we show that this new formula yields improvements in retrieval performance.

The paper is organized as follows. In Section 2, we discuss related work. In Section 3 we present the extended belief network model for juridical digital libraries. In Section 4 we briefly introduce the Federal Justice Council (CJF) Thesaurus, which we adopted, present the reference collection, and discuss our experimental results. Our conclusions follow.

2   Related Work

Traditionally, thesauri are constructed manually for use in a specific area of knowledge. The objective of a thesaurus is to represent concepts and specify their relationships. The more commonly represented relationships are those of equivalence, hierarchy and associativity. In equivalence relationships, the concepts are synonyms, quasi-synonyms, and partial synonyms. In hierarchy relationships, the concepts have a subordination relationship, like broad and narrow terms. In associativity relationships, the concepts have a horizontal relationship, different from the previous ones, defined by specialists in the knowledge domain [6].

A thesaurus can be used both for indexing a collection and for searching information of interest in the collection. In the task of indexing, the thesaurus is used as a list of authorized words that normalize the indexing language. In the task of searching, the thesaurus is used to show to the user associations between its concepts. These associations might lead the user to concepts related to the query concept that were not foreseen by him and that might be useful in the query formulation process [1]. Another use of a thesaurus is as a tool to assist the users with the specification of the query subject [15].

Many authors have used thesaurus in automatic query expansion [2, 3, 5, 7, 11]. Greenberg investigated the use of a business thesaurus for query expansion [2, 3]. The experiments were executed over a collection of business related documents. The queries were real queries selected from questions formulated by business students. The author considered only queries that could be mapped to a concept in the thesaurus. She concluded that, if the focus is on improving precision figures, synonyms and narrow terms should be used for query expansion. Otherwise, if the focus is on improving recall figures, related terms and broad terms should be used for query expansion.

Kristensen [5] studied the use of synonym, narrow and related terms in query expansion in a full text newspaper database. She found enhancements in recall and reduction in precision, and concluded that a thesaurus is "clearly a recall-enhancing tool". Her research showed specifically that synonyms and related terms are equivalent in recall possibilities and that synonyms degrade precision more than related terms.

Mandala et al. [7] used three types of thesauri to select terms for automatic query expansion. The types of thesauri were hand-crafted, generated automatically using co-occurrence patterns, and generated automatically using predicate-argument logic to gather linguistic relations. They developed algorithms to estimate the probability that the terms of each thesaurus are good candidates for query expansion. They showed that the combination of the three types of thesauri yields good results.

Qiu et al. [11] proposed a query expansion algorithm to select and weight the terms to be used in automatic query expansion. They considered the query as a concept and showed how to find good candidate terms for automatic query expansion, using the similarity of the whole query concept to the terms of the collection. They argued that consideration of a query concept is a superior approach.

Ribeiro-Neto et al. [13] used belief networks to combine evidence obtained from past queries with keyword-based evidence. Using four distinct reference collections, they report improvements in precision of at least 59% over keyword-based searching, showing that past queries can be used to improve retrieval performance when combined with keyword-based searching.

Silva et al. [16] used belief networks to combine evidence from the link structure of the Web with keyword-based evidence. The link information is composed of hub evidence (document with a high number of outgoing links) and authority evidence (documents with a high number of incoming links). They report experiments combining keyword-based, hub, and authority evidential information that show gains in precision of 74% over keyword-based searching.

In here, we investigate the use of the concepts and the relationships of a juridical thesaurus as a source of evidential knowledge for improving query results. Contrary to the work in [2, 3], we use the framework of Bayesian networks as a formal underpinning. This provides for modularity and extensibility to naturally incorporate new sources of evidence into the model.

3   Extended Belief Network for a Juridical Digital Library

We adopt the belief network model proposed in [12] as a framework for combining distinct sources of evidential information in support of a ranking of the documents. This network model is extended with new nodes, edges, and probabilities to fit the information encoded in the juridical thesaurus. We say that this expansion is modular in the sense that it preserves all properties of the previous network. Figure 1 illustrates our extended belief network for a juridical digital library. The left hand side represents the original belief network proposed in [12] and the right hand side represents the extension due to the juridical thesaurus.

In Figure 1, the keywords that compose the user query Q are represented by nodes from the set KY. The concepts, which are represented by nodes from the set CC, are obtained automatically by directly mapping the query Q into the concepts of the thesaurus. From the mapped concepts, the thesaurus allows inferring related narrow terms, represented by nodes from the set NT. We defer to represent broad terms, related terms, and synonyms to simplify the model and facilitate comprehension.

The nodes D_{Kj}, D_{Cj}, and D_{Nj}, represent the document D_j in distinct contexts. The node D_{Kj} is used to represent the document D_j when it appears as an answer to a keyword-based retrieval process, i.e., the user query is considered as composed of keywords and is processed using the standard cosine formula of

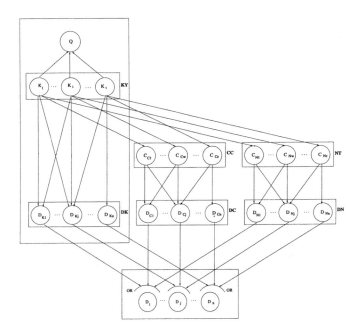

Fig. 1. Extended belief network for a juridical digital library

the vector model. The node D_{Cj} is used to represent the document D_j when it appears as an answer to a concept-based retrieval process, i.e., the document must contain a reference to a concept of the thesaurus related to the user query. The node D_{Nj} is used to represent the document D_j when it appears as an answer to a query composed solely of a narrower concept associated with the original user query, i.e., the document must contain a reference to the narrower concept. We model D_{Kj}, D_{Cj}, and D_{Nj} separately in our network to allow evaluating the impact of concept-based retrieval (versus keyword-based retrieval) in the quality of the results. Evidence provided by the set of documents D_{Kj}, D_{Cj}, and D_{Nj} is combined through a disjunctive operator, as done in [12].

With each node in the belief network we associate a binary random variable. Each of these random variables is labeled with the same label of its corresponding node (because it should always be clear whether we are referring to the node or to its associated variable). The variables are all binary (i.e., each variable is *on* or *off*) because this simplifies modeling and provides enough semantics for modeling the problem of IR ranking. Variable degrees of relationship between any pair of related variables are represented by conditional probabilities associated with the edges of the network.

The documents in the set **DK** are ranked according to the standard vector model (i.e., the cosine formula applied to keywords). The documents in the sets **DC** and **DN** are ranked using the cosine formula applied to concepts. These sets of ranked documents represent additional evidence that can be accumulated to yield a new ranking formula (which, we presume, will lead to higher precision).

In the extended belief network, the rank of a document D_j is computed as follows:

$$P(d_j \mid q) = \eta \sum_{\forall k} P(d_j \mid k) \, P(q \mid k) \, P(k) \tag{1}$$

Assuming that the unique keywords of interest are the query keywords, we define $P(q|k)$ as:

$$P(q|k) = \begin{cases} 1 \text{ if } \mathbf{KY} = k_q \\ 0 \text{ otherwise} \end{cases} \tag{2}$$

where k_q is a state of the variables in **KY** in which the unique nodes that are *on* are those present in the query. This allows rewriting Equation (1) as:

$$P(d_j \mid q) \sim P(d_j \mid k_q) \, P(q \mid k_q) \, P(k_q) \tag{3}$$

where we deleted the normalizing constant η, because it has no effect on the ranking.

We observe that $P(d_j|k_q)$ depends on the evidence obtained from the thesaurus. These evidences are used to enrich the network with distinct representations of the original query. For each such representation, a ranking of documents is generated (D_{Cj} and D_{Nj}). These rankings are viewed as distinct sources of evidence on the final relevance of the documents to the original query. To combine these sources of evidence we use a disjunctive operator because it yields better results [12, 13, 16]. Thus, the document node D_j accumulates all the ranking evidence through a disjunction of the beliefs associated with the nodes D_{Kj}, D_{Cj}, and D_{Nj}. This allows rewriting Equation (3) as:

$$P(d_j \mid q) \sim [1 - P(\bar{d}k_j \mid k_q) \times P(\bar{d}c_j \mid k_q) \times P(\bar{d}n_j \mid k_q)] \times P(q \mid k_q) \times P(k_q) \tag{4}$$

Evaluating each term of this equation in isolation, for example $P(\bar{d}k_j \mid k_q)$, we obtain:

$$P(\bar{d}k_j \mid k_q) = \frac{P(\bar{d}k_j \wedge k_q)}{P(k_q)} \tag{5}$$

As $P(k_q)$ is constant for all documents, define $\alpha = 1/P(k_q)$. Equation (5) can then be rewritten as follows:

$$P(\bar{d}k_j \mid k_q) = \alpha \, P(\bar{d}k_j \wedge k_q) = \alpha \sum_{\forall k_i} P((\bar{d}k_j \wedge k_q) \mid k_i) \times P(k_i)$$

$$= \alpha \sum_{\forall k_i} P(\bar{d}k_j \mid k_i) \times P(k_q \mid k_i) \times P(k_i) \tag{6}$$

where k_i is a state of the set of variables **KY**. We can further write:

$$P(\bar{d}k_j \mid k_q) = \alpha \sum_{\forall k_i} P(\bar{d}k_j \mid k_i) \times P(k_q \wedge k_i)$$

$$= \alpha \sum_{\forall k_i} P(\bar{d}k_j \mid k_i) \times P(k_i \mid k_q) \times P(k_q) \tag{7}$$

Assuming that the unique keywords of interest are the query keywords, we define:

$$P(k_i|k_q) = \begin{cases} 1 \text{ if } k_i = k_q \\ 0 \text{ otherwise} \end{cases}$$

which yields:

$$P(\bar{d}k_j \mid k_q) = 1 - P(dk_j \mid k_q) \tag{8}$$

where k_q is a state of the variables in **KY** where the unique active nodes (i.e., nodes whose associated variables are *on*) are those that correspond to the keywords in the original user query.

The same reasoning can be applied to the other terms of Equation (4), which yields:

$$P(d_j \mid q) \sim [1 - (1 - P(dk_j \mid k_q)) \times (1 - P(dc_j \mid k_c)) \times (1 - P(dn_j \mid k_n))] \times$$
$$P(q \mid k_q) \times P(k_q) \tag{9}$$

where k_c and k_n represent states of the sets of random variables **CC** and **NT**, respectively, in which the only active nodes are those associated with the concepts and narrow terms mapped from the original user query.

We define the prior probabilities $P(k_q)$, associated with the root nodes, as $P(k_q) = (1/2)^t$, where t is the number of terms in the collection, which means that all terms are equally likely.

For $P(q|k_q)$, we write:

$$P(q|k_q) = \begin{cases} 1 \text{ if } \forall_i \ g_i(q) = g_i(k_q) \\ 0 \text{ otherwise} \end{cases} \tag{10}$$

where $g_i(u)$ is a function that returns the value of the i-th variable in the vector u. Equation (10) establishes that the only state k_q of the set K that is taken into account is the one for which the active keywords are exactly those in the query q.

The probability $P(dk_j \mid k_q)$ is defined as:

$$P(dk_j \mid k_q) = \frac{\sum_{i=1}^{t} w_{ij} \times w_{ik_q}}{\sqrt{\sum_{i=1}^{t} w_{ij}^2} \times \sqrt{\sum_{i=1}^{t} w_{ik_q}^2}} \tag{11}$$

where w_{ik} and w_{ij} are *tf-idf* weights [14], as those used in the vector model. This definition preserves the ordering dictated by a vectorial ranking.

Equation (9) is the ranking formula of our Bayesian model for a juridical digital library. Our ranking formula allows combining evidence in several ways. For instance, consider, for a moment, that we are interested only on the results yielded by the vector model. To obtain this effect, we define $P(dc_j \mid k_c) = 0$; $P(dn_j \mid k_n) = 0$. As a result, the ranking $P(d_j|q)$ becomes $P(d_j|q) \sim P(dk_j \mid k_i) \times P(q \mid k_q) \times P(k_q)$ which computes a vectorial ranking.

To consider the combination of keyword-based and concept-based retrieval, we define: $P(dn_j \mid k_n) = 0$. As a result, $P(d_j \mid q) \sim [1 - (1 - P(dk_j \mid k_q)) \times (1 - P(dc_j \mid k_c))] \times P(q \mid k_q) \times P(k_q)$, which yields a ranking that combines keyword-based and concept-based retrieval. Further, the combination of evidences two by two, can be evaluated by properly defining the related conditional probabilities.

4   Experimental Results

In this section, we briefly introduce the CJF Thesaurus and the reference collection used in our experiments. After we analyze the results in two steps. First we show the results for our extended belief network model. Following we compare these results with the procedure of automatic query expansion.

4.1   The CJF Thesaurus

In this work, we use a manually constructed juridical thesaurus, the CJF Thesaurus, to find concepts related to the original query. This thesaurus was designed and constructed by the Brazilian Federal Justice Council in Brazil (CJF), a regulatory institution that supervises the system of Federal Courts in Brazil and their operations [4]. The motivation was to construct a tool to control the vocabulary used by manual indexers when constructing the Indexing Section[1] of the juridical document. The CJF Thesaurus comprises many fields of Law, as for example, Criminal Law, Civil Law, Public Law, Commercial Law, Administrative Law, Constitutional Law, International Law, among others.

The CJF Thesaurus has 8,357 juridical concepts (CC) organized in lexicographical order. From these concepts, 6,103 are classified as Narrow Terms (NT), 891 as Broad Terms (BT), 7,301 as Related Terms (RT), and 1,702 as synonyms (SY). Among the synonyms, 674 are classified as preferred and 1,208 as non-preferred. We note that a concept classified as Narrow Term of a given concept may be classified as Broad Term of another concept and as a Related Term of a third one.

4.2 The Juridical Reference Collection

Our evaluation is carried out using a reference collection composed of Brazilian juridical documents, of a set of real queries, and of a set of relevant documents for each of them, determined by a Brazilian lawyer. The collection is composed of 552,573 juridical documents from the Supreme Federal Court (STF) [17], the Superior Court of Justice (STJ) [9], and the 5 Federal Courts of Appeal [8][2]. The average document size is 164.68 words.

The test queries were selected from a set of real requests made by users of the CJF Internet site [4]. The queries selected, in number of 38, satisfied the following conditions: they had concepts of the CJF Thesaurus associated with them, and these concepts included Narrow Terms relationships[3]. The average number of keywords per query is 8.8.

The relevant document evaluation was done using the well known *pooling* method [18]. The pool of candidate documents was composed of the top-50 ranked documents generated by each of our network rankings. The pool was evaluated by a lawyer, who classified each document as relevant or non-relevant to the query.

4.3 The Results for Our Extended Belief Network Model

We compare the results of a keyword-based (KY) ranking, the baseline of our analysis, with a concept-based (CC) ranking, and with the results generated by a Bayesian combination of them (KY+CC). The results in terms of precision-recall figures are shown Figure 2. The keyword-based ranking yields already a good result, with an average precision of 0.399.

The results yielded by a concept-based (CC) ranking are superior, with an average precision of 0.479. The gain in average precision is of 20.05% and is due

---

[1] After judgment, the juridical document is enriched by a section called Indexing Section created with the purpose to improve information retrieval.

[2] URL's for the other four Federal Court sites can be obtained from [4].

[3] These decisions were made in order to verify the thesaurus contribution.

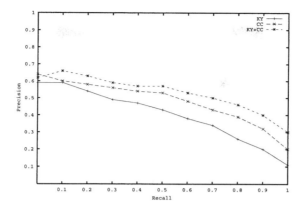

Fig. 2. Results of Bayesian Combination with Keywords and Concepts

to the use of the knowledge encoded in the thesaurus that is related to the test queries.

Finally, we observe that the result generated by a Bayesian combination of keyword-based and concept-based evidences (KY+CC) exceeds the results generated by each of them in isolation. The average precision is 0.529. The gain in average precision is now 32.58%, relative to the keyword-based ranking. This indicates the usefulness of our approach to improve the quality of the results.

4.4 Comparing with Automatic Query Expansion

To illustrate the differences between our extended belief network model and the more common procedure of automatic query expansion (using concepts of the CJF Thesaurus related to query), we consider the usage of Narrow Terms (NT). In the case of the network model, this is done by modifying the ranking to consider Narrow Terms, as described in Section 3. In the case of automatic query expansion, this is done by expanding the original query with Narrow Terms related to it.

Figure 3 illustrate the results. We first observe that Narrow Terms (NT) by themselves yield very poor results. The reason is that the test queries are long (8.8 keywords per query) and have many Narrow Terms related to them (29.5 terms per query generated by 6.1 concepts per query). This generates excessive noise that degrades the results. Despite this negative effect, the extended belief network model is able to filter the noisy NT terms and generate a combined ranking (KY+NT) that is very similar to the ranking produced by keywords only (KY). The ranking generated by automatic query expansion with NT (KYNT), however, suffers the negative impact of the noisy NT terms and yields poor results (relative to our baseline).

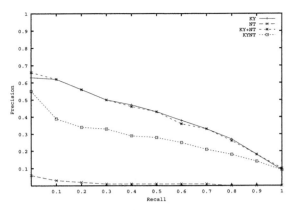

Fig. 3. Comparison of Bayesian Combination and Automatic Query Expansion

5   Conclusions

In this paper, we discussed the design and evaluation of a vertical searching algorithm for juridical digital libraries. Our vertical algorithm allowed combining specialized information obtained from a juridical thesaurus, the CJF Thesaurus, with evidence generated by the classic vector space model. To allow implementing this combination in consistent fashion we relied on Bayesian belief networks.

Our extended belief network model for juridical digital libraries was evaluated using a juridical reference collection of 552,573 documents and 38 real test queries. Our results showed good improvements in retrieval performance. Further, they showed that our model is distinct from the standard technique of automatic query expansion. Such results suggest that the study and development of vertical searching mechanisms is a promising research direction.

References

[1] Alan Gilchrist. *The Thesaurus in Retrieval.* Aslib, London, 1971.
[2] Jane Greenberg.   Automatic query expansion via lexical-semantic relationships. *Journal of the American Society for Information Science and Technology,* 52(5):402–415, 2001.
[3] Jane Greenberg. Optimal query expansion (QE) processing methods with semantically encoded structured thesauri terminology. *Journal of the American Society for Information Science and Technology,* 52(6):487–498, 2001.
[4] Federal Justice Council (CJF) in Brazil. http://www.cjf.gov.br, 2002.
[5] Jaana Kristensen. Expanding end-users' query statements for free text searching with a search-aid thesaurus. *Information Processing & Management,* 29(6):733–744, 1993.
[6] Frederick Wilfrid Lancaster. *Indexing and Abstracting in Theory and Practice.* Library Association Publishing, London, 1991.

[7] Rila Mandala, Takenobu Tokunaga, and Hozumi Tanaka. Query expansion using heterogeneous thesauri. *Information Processing & Management*, 36(2000):361–378, 2000.

[8] Federal Court of Appeals First Region (TRF1). http://www.trf1.gov.br, 2002.

[9] Superior Court of Justice (STJ). http://www.stj.gov.br, 2002.

[10] Judea Pearl. *Probabilistic Reasoning in Intelligent Systems*. Morgan Kaufmann, Los Altos, California, 1988.

[11] Yonggang Qiu and H. P. Frei. Concept based query expansion. In *Proceedings of the sixteenth annual international ACM SIGIR conference on Research and Development in Information Retrieval*, pages 160–169, 1993.

[12] Berthier Ribeiro-Neto and Richard R. Muntz. A belief network model for IR. In *ACM Conference on Research and Development in Information Retrieval - SIGIR96*, pages 253–260, 1996.

[13] Berthier Ribeiro-Neto, Ilmério Silva, and Richard Muntz. Bayesian network models for IR. In Fabio Crestani and Gabriella Pasi, editors, *Soft Computing in Information Retrieval Techniques and Applications*, pages 259–291. Springer Verlag, 2000.

[14] G. Salton and M. J. McGill. *Introduction to Modern Information Retrieval*. McGraw-Hill Book Co., New York, 1983.

[15] Ali Asghar Shiri and Crawford Revie. Thesauri on the web: current developments and trends. *Online Information Review*, 24(4):273–279, 2000.

[16] Ilmério Silva, Berthier Ribeiro-Neto, Pável Calado, Edleno Moura, and Nivio Ziviani. Link-based and content-based evidential information in a belief network model. In *ACM Conference on Research and Development in Information Retrieval - SIGIR2000*, pages 96–103, 2000. Best Student paper.

[17] Supreme Federal Court (STF). http://www.stf.gov.br, 2002.

[18] Ellen M. Voorhees and Donna Harman. Overview of the fifth Text REtrieval Conference. In *Proceedings of the fifth Text REtrieval Conference (TREC-5)*, pages 1–28. National Institute of Standards and Technology, Gaithersburg, MD 20899, 1996.

Corpus-Based Thesaurus Construction for Image Retrieval in Specialist Domains

Khurshid Ahmad, Mariam Tariq, Bogdan Vrusias, and Chris Handy

Department of Computing, School of Electronics and Physical Sciences
University of Surrey, Guildford, GU2 7XH, United Kingdom
{k.ahmad,m.tariq,b.vrusias,c.j.handy}@surrey.ac.uk

Abstract. This paper explores the use of texts that are related to an image collection, also known as *collateral texts*, for building thesauri in specialist domains to aid in image retrieval. Corpus linguistic and information extraction methods are used for identifying key terms and semantic relationships in specialist texts that may be used for query expansion purposes. The specialist domain context imposes certain constraints on the language used in the texts, which makes the texts computationally more tractable.

1   Introduction

Literature on Content-Based Image Retrieval (CBIR) is now stressing the need for using keywords for indexing and retrieving images in addition to the visual features; the latter pose certain practical and theoretical limitations [1, 2]. We have attempted to exploit the use of texts related to images, also known as *collateral texts*, for the indexing and retrieval of specialist images in our recently concluded project – Scene of Crime Information System (SoCIS)[1]. We report on the automatic construction of thesauri from these domain-specific collateral texts. The thesauri can be used for query expansion during retrieval as well as for verifying keywords used for indexing the images.

Earlier image retrieval systems, including search engines, rely almost exclusively on keywords to retrieve images. Manually appending keywords to an image is time consuming: estimates vary from minutes to hours, and the choice of keywords may show the bias of the indexer [3]. This has led to systems that use linguistic features extracted from textual captions or descriptions together with the visual features for storing and retrieving images in databases. A number of systems have shown that retrieval is more effective when both features are combined; Srihari's PICTION system [4], Picard's Four-Eyes System [5], and Paek et al. [6] are good examples here.

---

[1] A three-year EPSRC sponsored project (Grant No.GR/M89041) jointly undertaken by the Universities of Sheffield and Surrey and supported by five police forces in the UK. M.T. acknowledges a doctoral student bursary provided by the EPSRC.

F. Sebastiani (Ed.): ECIR 2003, LNCS 2633, pp. 502-510, 2003.

There are still limitations where keywords or terms are concerned in that the use of related terms such as synonyms, abbreviations and broader or narrower terms is not taken into account. The issue of *inter-indexer variability* [3], the variation in the outputs of different indexers for the same image, has shown a use of such related terms. This issue of related terms can be addressed, to some extent, through query expansion techniques such as the use of thesauri [7, 8]. General-purpose thesauri such as the Longman's Roget's Thesaurus (1911) as well as lexical resources like WordNet[2] are available but inadequate for use in specialized domains due to the fact that neither has much in way of specialized terminology. This establishes the need for domain-specific thesauri. These could be manually built by expert lexicographers, however, handcrafted thesauri face similar problems to those of manual keyword indexing as well as potentially having the additional issue of inadequate domain coverage. One possible solution to this is the automatic generation of thesauri for specialized domains from representative text documents.

Automatic thesauri generation was initially addressed as far back as the 1970s [9, 10] through the use of statistical term-to-term co-occurrence measures for identifying related terms in text documents. This method has a number of drawbacks: many unrelated terms might co-occur if they are very frequently used; synonyms are seldom used together; only single-word terms are considered whereas in a number of specialist domains multi-word terms are used frequently; a cluster of associated terms is produced with no knowledge of the kinds of relationships between the terms. The fact that synonyms were more likely to have similar co-occurrence patterns rather then co-occur in a document or document collection was addressed by associating a term with a phrase based on its contextual information [11]. The SEXTANT system [12] uses weak syntactic analysis methods on texts to generate thesauri under the assumption that similar terms will appear in similar syntactic relationships. Terms are then grouped according to the grammatical context in which they appear. Both the methods above are viable approaches but still do not address the shortcoming of undefined relationships between terms, such as the semantic relationships of synonymy, hyponymy or meronymy.

We have explored a different approach to thesauri construction for specific domains using corpus linguistics techniques; in particular corpus-based lexicography and corpus-based terminology for extracting information about a specific domain. A text corpus, typically a randomly selected but systematically organized collection of texts, can be used to derive empirical knowledge about language, which can supplement, and sometimes supplant, information from reference sources and introspection [13]. The random selection involves either randomly selecting equal amounts of texts from a collection put together by language experts, or by selecting texts randomly from a catalogue of 'books in print'. The systematic organization refers to the selection of different genres of texts – formal and informal types, for example journal and popular science articles; instructive and informative types, for example advanced and basic texts, instruction manuals, and so on. There is much discussion in corpus linguistics about what constitutes a *representative* corpus, but that is more relevant to language as a whole and not as much to specialist languages [14, 15].

---

[2] http://www.cogsci.princeton.edu/~wn/

Specialist languages, considered variants of natural language, are restricted lexically, syntactically and semantically [14]. There is a preponderance of open class words in specialist languages, particularly single and compound noun phrases (NP). These phrases are used to name objects, events, actions and states.   It has been suggested that not only can one extract terms from a specialist corpus [15, 16] but one can also extract semantic relations of hyponymy and meronymy (part-whole relations) between terms from free texts [15, 17].   Our aim is to study the behavior of a specialist language at the lexical, morphological and semantic levels for extracting terms and their relationships.   Section 2 of this paper is about building a representative corpus of collateral texts and subsequently analyzing it to extract terms. The issue of domain coverage has been investigated through the comparison of terms extracted from a *progeny* corpus (representative of a sub-domain) to those extracted from a *mother* corpus.   The extraction of semantic relations between terms based on certain lexico-syntactic patterns in the text is discussed in Section 3. Section 4 concludes the paper.

2   The 'Lexical Signature' of a Domain

An image may be associated in various ways with the different texts that exist *collateral* to it.   These texts may contain a full or partial description of the content of the image or they may contain metadata information.   Texts can be *closely* collateral like the caption of an image, which will describe only what is depicted in the image, or *broadly* collateral such as the report describing a crime scene where the content of an image would be discussed together with other information related to the crime. While closely collateral texts may be used to extract keywords for directly indexing an image, broadly collateral texts of varying genres may be used to extract related terms such as synonyms and hyponyms.

A *forensic science* (FS) corpus of over half a million words has been created.   To ensure that the corpus is representative of the domain, a variety of text types ranging from 1990-2001 were used.   The corpus comprises 1451 texts (891 written in British and 560 in American English) containing a total of 610,197 tokens.   The genres include informative texts, like journal papers; instructive texts, for example handbooks and imaginative texts, primarily advertisements.   These texts were gathered from the Web using the Google Search Engine by keying in the terms *forensic* and *science*. Similarly, we created two sub-domain corpora, *crime scene photography* (CSP) comprising 63328 tokens, and *footwear impressions* (FI) comprising 11332 tokens.

The identification of a *lexical signature* of a domain, mainly comprising frequent single and compound NPs, from a randomly selected corpus will help to initiate the development of a thesaurus for the domain.   A frequency analysis was conducted on the forensic science corpus to determine its lexical signature.   Typically, the first hundred most frequent tokens in a text corpus comprise over 40% of the total text: this is true of the 100-million word British National Corpus (BNC), the Longman Corpus of Contemporary English, as it is of a number of specialist corpora [15]. The key difference is that for the general language corpora the first 100 most frequent tokens are essentially the so-called closed class words (CCW) or grammatical words;

in the specialist corpora, in contrast, as much as 20% of the first hundred most frequent tokens comprise the so-called open-class or lexical words (OCW). These OCWs are used on their own highly frequently, and more importantly, as the head of a compound term or in an inflected (especially plural) or derived form. This frequent use attests to the acceptability of the single and compound words within the domain.

Candidate terms are identified by contrasting the frequency of tokens in the specialist corpus with that of the frequency of the same tokens in a representative corpus of general language. This ratio, sometimes referred to as a *weirdness* measure [15], is a good indication that a domain expert will approve the token or *candidate* term as a term.

$$\text{weirdness coefficient} = \frac{f_s / N_s}{f_g / N_g} \tag{1}$$

where f_s = frequency of a term in a specialist corpus;
        f_g = frequency of a term in a general language corpus;
        N_s = total number of terms in the specialist corpus; &
        N_g = total number of terms in the general language corpus.

The forensic science corpus had 20 OCWs amongst the first 100; the ten most frequent are shown in Table 1 with their frequency, relative frequency and weirdness (calculated relative to the BNC) measures. It can be observed that the term *forensic* occurs over 470 times more frequently in the forensic science corpus as compared to the BNC. Tokens with a high weirdness and relative frequency are usually considered good candidate terms.

These candidate terms are used productively to make compound terms. The compound terms have a nominal head qualified by an adjective or compounded with another noun or noun phrase. English compound terms are usually not interspersed by closed class words, which is the heuristic we have used to extract them. Two frequent compounds, *crime* and *scene* are used to form over 90 different compounds, some comprising up to three (high frequency) tokens, for instance *crime scene investigator*, *crime scene photography*, *crime scene analysis*, and *crime scene photography personnel agency*.

There are a number of tokens that are absent in the BNC; the value of weirdness for such tokens is infinity. Table 2 lists a number of high frequency terms that have *infinite* weirdness. These terms can be neologisms; entirely new words such as *pyrolysis* or extant words joined together like *bitemark* and *earprint*. The terms may also be unusual inflections such as *shoeprints,* the singular of which does exist in the BNC, or unusual derivations such as *rifling*.

Table 1. High-frequency terms in Surrey's Forensic Science corpus. Higher weirdness of a term suggests domain-specificity (N = 610,197)

term	f	f/N	Weirdness	term	f	f/N	Weirdness
evidence	2757	0.0045	20.77	blood	781	0.0013	12.43
crime	2366	0.0038	53.52	dna	676	0.0011	33.05
scene	1605	0.0026	38.18	science	634	0.0010	9.68
forensic	1563	0.0025	471.04	physical	382	0.0006	6.45
analysis	862	0.0014	10.54	homicide	237	0.0004	228.30

Table 2. Candidate neologisms: Frequent terms that are not found in the BNC (N = 610,197)

Single Term	f/N	Compound Term	f/N	Compound Term	f/N
rifling	0.0139%	bitemark	0.0174%	spectroscopy	0.0092%
pyrolysis	0.0124%	earprint	0.0122%	handguns	0.0090%
accelerant	0.0105%	nightlead	0.0105%	shoeprints	0.0070%
polygraph	0.0081%	handgun	0.0105%	toolmark	0.0045%
accelerants	0.0079%	fingerprinting	0.0093%	earprints	0.0040%

Table 3. Most frequent compound terms and their t-values in the Forensic Science corpus

x	y	$f(x,y)/N$ (a)	$f(x)/N$ (b)	$f(y)/N$ (c)	$t(x,y)$ $(a-b*c)/\sqrt{c}$
crime	scene~	0.000912	0.003825	0.002858	23.46
forensic	science~	0.000503	0.002527	0.00124	17.53
workplace	homicide	0.000145	0.00032	0.000462	9.48
crime	lab(orator)~	0.000149	0.003825	0.00167	9.18
cartridge	case~	0.000131	0.000414	0.002656	8.92

Following Church and Mercer [18], we have used the Student's *t-test* to determine whether or not a collocation, or a compound token found in the analysis of a corpus, is due to random chance. They have suggested that 'if the *t-score* is larger than 1.65 standard deviations then we ought to believe that the co-occurrences are significant and we can reject the null hypothesis with 95% confidence though in practice we might look for a t-score of 2 or more standard deviations'. This heuristic certainly appears to work on our corpus in that high t-value (t > 2.0), high frequency tokens are indeed compound terms (see table 3).

The weirdness measure can also be used to determine the lexical signature of a *sub-domain* corpus –the progeny of the mother domain. Here, instead of using a general language corpus as the reference for calculating weirdness we use a (supra-) domain corpus. We used the forensic science corpus as the mother corpus for extracting terms in two emergent sub-domains *crime scene photography* (CSP) and *footwear impressions* (FI). Table 4 shows a comparison of selected high weirdness terms in the two progeny corpora. Note that the highly frequent OCWs in the FI and CSP progeny corpora generally have a much higher weirdness when compared to the FS mother corpus then the weirdness of the same words in the FS corpus when compared to the BNC. The analysis of progeny corpora may yield more specialized terms, their own lexical signature, and these either could be added to the main thesaurus or kept separately as sub-domain thesauri.

Table 4. Comparison of highly weird terms in the two progeny corpora. $r_i = f_i/N_i$, where i refers to the respective corpora

Footwear Impression (FI)	r_{FI}/r_{FS}	r_{FS}/r_{BNC}	CS Photography (CSP)	r_{CSP}/r_{FS}	r_{FS}/r_{BNC}
footwear	126	40	lens	67	8
reebok	55	2	underexposed	49	INF
molding	55	INF	lenses	43	3
gatekeeping	27	INF	tripod	43	12
impressions	25	31	enlargements	39	17

3   Discovering Semantic Relations between Terms

In every language the words, terms or lexical units are grammatically arranged in a certain pattern that conveys a meaning. A range of semantic relations may exist between these different lexical units such as *hyponymy* and *meronomy* [19], which can be used to build hierarchies. The most common type of lexical hierarchies are *taxonomies*, which reflect the hyponymic relationship and *meronomies* which model the part-whole relationship. In this section we discuss the possible elicitation of such semantic relations from texts, which can be used to define broader and narrower terms in a hierarchical thesaurus.

Cruse [19] has discussed the existence of *semantic frames*: recurrent patterns of a triplet of phrases - X REL Y - where X and Y are NPs, and 'REL' is a phrase, typically articulated as IS-A, IS A KIND/TYPE OF, for expressing hyponymic relationships, for example 'A gun <u>is a type of</u> firearm'; or PART OF for expressing meronymic relationships, for example 'A trigger is <u>part of</u> a gun'. More recently, Hearst [17] has suggested that certain enumerative cues may be used to identify hyponymic relationships through the use of lexico-syntactic patterns like Y SUCH AS $(X_1, ...\{or/and\}, X_n)$, Y INCLUDING $(X_1, ...\{or/and\}, X_n)$ and $(X_1, ...\{or/and\}, X_n)$ AND/OR OTHER Y. In all such sentences X and Y are NPs and each X_i in the list $(X_1, ...\{or/and\}, X_n)$ is a hyponym/subordinate of the corresponding Y.

The frame $(X_1, ...\{or/and\}, X_n)$ OR OTHER Y, which is articulated in phrases like 'In the case of shootings <u>or other</u> fatal assaults', appears to be the most productive in that 80% of the sentences found comprising the frame, $(X_1, ...\{or/and\}, X_n)$ and Y showed a relationship of the type – hyponym/sub-ordinate (X_i) and hypernym/super-ordinate (Y), i.e. *shooting* is a type of *fatal assault*. The relationship between the phrases in the frames containing the enumerative cue SUCH AS is reversed: in 'Trace evidence <u>such as</u> fibers, hair, glass and DNA.....', the hypernym is on the left hand side and the hyponyms on the right; *fibers, hair, glass* and *DNA* being types of *trace evidence*. We have analysed over 1200 sentences in the forensic science corpus containing enumerative cues and found that 60% incorporated the frames containing expressions of hyponymic relationship between the phrases, $(X_1, ...\{or/and\}, X_n)$ and Y. Meronymic frames, e.g. X PART OF Y, are not as effective - only 40% of the 60 sentences containing the frame actually did show a meronymic relationship between X and Y. The frames X IS A Y or X IS A KIND OF Y, were the least productive - only 40 out of the 400 sentences incorporating the two frames were actually used to describe a hyponymic relationship.

The sentences containing the frames are extracted automatically from a corpus of free texts with the help of the cues. The sentences are then tagged using a statistical tagger, MXPOST [20]. The output of the tagger comprises part of speech information for the sentences indicating the grammatical category of each word. The conjunctive phrase (REL) that is used as a cue is typically an adjective plus preposition in the case of SUCH AS, or a combination of a conjunction and an adjectival pronominal as in the cases of AND OTHER, and OR OTHER. Regular expressions are then used to detect the tagged sentences that follow the required pattern of the semantic frames discussed above. The correct sentences are parsed to extract the hypernym-hyponym pairs.

Compound words often convey a semantic relationship between the constituent lexical units. Compounding tends to specialize the meaning of the headword, each successive modifier specializing it further. This semantic relationship often signifies the hyponymic relation, for example, taking the compound term *trace evidence*, it can be deduced that *trace evidence* is a type of *evidence*. We have also used this heuristic to extract hypernym-hyponym pairs.

The terms and the semantic relationships between terms in the form of hypernym-hyponym pairs are merged to form (partial) hierarchical structures, which can then be used in (the construction of) a thesaurus. These various hierarchical structures are then marked-up in XML. The content of the thesaurus we built has largely been extracted from the forensic science and progeny corpora discussed in this paper. The SoCIS[3] system, which stores and retrieves Scene of Crime images, uses the XML document to help expand a query to retrieve an image automatically or interactively. In the latter case the XML is parsed to display the hierarchies in a tree structure that can be used interactively by the user to expand the query. Six serving Scene of Crime Officers and Scene of Crime Training Officers have favourably evaluated SoCIS.

4   Afterword

The co-dependence between images and language provides the basis for a significant proportion of human information processing especially in storing and retrieving images. The interest of the information extraction community in retrieving images embedded in texts, especially newspaper texts, is growing. We started this paper by noting that the image retrieval community, under the content-based image retrieval rubric, is increasingly interested in keywords that may be directly or indirectly collateral to images; the latter is key for query expansion. The effective retrieval of images depends significantly upon the existence of thesauri that have good and current coverage of the domain from which the images emanate.

The construction and maintenance of a conventional thesaurus is a labour intensive and expensive task. We have described how this task can be alleviated by the use of domain-specific texts. The domain-specificity of texts is essential for us to use the straightforward frequency metrics and collocation patterns described in this paper, especially the use of semantic frames. No specialist domain remains static: there is a constant flux of new ideas and devices and the revision of extant concepts and artefacts. Subject domains spawn new sub-domains and interdisciplinary research results in newer disciplines. For all scientific and technical endeavours new terms are created, existing terms re-lexicalised, and some terms are purged. Scientists proffer new semantic relations between terms and some succeed whilst others fail. Whatever the endeavours, coinages, retro-fittings, and obsolescence, text is the habitat of terms and the semantic relationships between them. A corpus-based thesaurus construction and maintenance enterprise appears quite logical to us if, indeed, the terms and their relationships inhabit texts in the first place. The analysis of collateral texts could also be considered as a first step towards building multi-media thesauri. Indeed, the interaction between images and texts may be understood better if we understand how to construct and maintain multi-media thesauri.

---

[3] http://www.computing.surrey.ac.uk/ai/socis/. SoCIS has been developed by Bogdan Vrusias and the thesaurus generation program by Mariam Tariq.

References

1. Squire, McG.D., Muller, W., Muller, H., Pun, T.: Content-Based Query of Image databases: Inspirations from Text Retrieval. Pattern Recognition Letters, Vol. 21. No. 13-14. Elsevier Science, Netherlands (2000) 1193-1198
2. Marr, D.: Vision. W.H. Freeman, San Francisco (1982)
3. Eakins, J.P., Graham, M.E.: Content-based Image Retrieval: A Report to the JISC Technology Applications Programme. Image Data Research Institute Newcastle, Northumbria (1999) (http://www.unn.ac.uk/iidr/report.html, visited 15/01/03)
4. Srihari, R.K.: Use of Collateral Text in Understanding Photos. Artificial Intelligence Review, Special Issue on Integrating Language and Vision, Vol. 8. Kluwer Academic Publishers, Netherlands (1995) 409-430
5. Picard, R.W.: Towards a Visual Thesaurus. In: Ian Ruthven (ed.): Springer Verlag Workshops in Computing, MIRO 95, Glasgow, Scotland (1995)
6. Paek, S., Sable C.L., Hatzivassiloglou, V., Jaimes, A., Schiffman, B.H., Chang, S.F., McKeown, K.R.: Integration of Visual and Text-Based Approaches for the Content Labeling and Classification of Photographs. ACM SIGIR'99 Workshop on Multimedia Indexing and Retrieval, Berkeley, CA August (1999)
7. Efthimiadis, E.N.: Query Expansion. In: Williams, M.E., (ed.): Annual Review of Information Systems and Technology (ARIST), Vol.31 (1996) 121-187
8. Foskett, D.J.: Thesaurus. In: Sparck Jones, K., Willet, P. (eds.): Readings in Information Retrieval. Morgan Kaufmann Publishers, San Francisco, California (1997) 111-134
9. Salton, G.: Experiments in Automatic Thesauri Construction for Information Retrieval. In Proceedings of the IFIP Congress, Vol. TA-2. Ljubljana, Yoguslavia (1971) 43-49
10. Sparck Jones, K.: Automatic Keyword Classification for Information Retrieval. Butterworths, London, UK (1971)
11. Jing, Y., Croft, W.B.: An Association Thesaurus for Information Retrieval. In: Bretano, F., Seitz, F.: (eds.): Proceedings of the RIAO'94 Conference. CIS-CASSIS, Paris, France (1994) 146-160
12. Grefenstette, G.: Explorations in Automatic Thesaurus Discovery. Kluwer Academic Publishers, Boston, USA (1994)
13. Leech, G.: The State of the Art in Corpus Linguistics. In: Aijmer, K., Altenberg, B. (eds.): English Corpus Linguistics: Essays in Honor of Jan Svartvik. Longman, London (1991) 8-29
14. Harris, Z.S.: Language and Information. In: Nevin, B. (ed.): Computational Linguistics Vol. 14, No.4. Columbia University Press, New York (1988) 87-90
15. Ahmad, K., Rogers, M.A.: Corpus-based terminology extraction. In: Budin, G., Wright S.A. (eds.): Handbook of Terminology Management, Vol.2. John Benjamins Publishers, Amsterdam (2000) 725-760.
16. Bourigault, D., Jacquemin, C., L'Homme, M-C. (eds.): Recent Advances in Computational Terminology. John Benjamins Publishers, Amsterdam (2001)
17. Hearst, M.: Automatic Acquisition of Hyponyms from Large Text Corpora. In Proceedings of the Fourteenth International Conference on Computational Linguistics (COLING'92). Nantes, France. (1992) 539-545

18. Church, K.W., Mercer, R.L.: Introduction. In: Armstrong, S. (ed.): Special Issue on Using Large Corpora. Computational Linguistics, Vol.9. No. 1-2 The MIT Press, Mass., USA (1993) 1-24
19. Cruse, D. A.: Lexical Semantics. Cambridge University Press, Avon, Great Britain (1986)
20. Ratnaparkhi, A.: A Maximum Entropy Part-Of-Speech Tagger. In: Proceedings of the Empirical Methods in Natural Language Processing Conference (1996) 133-141

Generating Extracts with Genetic Algorithms*

Enrique Alfonseca[1] and Pilar Rodríguez[1]

Computer Science Department, Universidad Autónoma de Madrid
28049 Madrid, Spain
{Enrique.Alfonseca,Pilar.Rodriguez}@ii.uam.es
http://www.ii.uam.es/~ealfon

Abstract. This paper describes an application of genetic algorithms for text summarisation. We have built a sentence extraction algorithm that overcomes some of the drawbacks of traditional sentence extractors, and takes into consideration different features of the summaries. The fitness function can be easily modified in order to incorporate features such as user modelling and adaptation. The system has been evaluated with standard procedures, and the obtained results are very good.

1 Introduction

Automatic Text Summarisation is the task that consists in finding, in a textual source, which information is more relevant for a user or an application, and presenting it in a condensed way. It has received much attention lately, due to its many potential applications. In a broad sense, summarisation systems refer to different problems and can vary largely depending on their aim. For instance, a system that sends summaries of e-mails to mobile phones will be very different from a system that generates summaries of various newswire articles about the same topic. Each of these will have to process different language styles and different domains, and the requirements about the readability and size of the generated summaries will not be the same.

There have been several competitions for automatic text summarisation systems, that have encouraged research in the area, and established common evaluation procedures and metrics. The first one was the TIPSTER SUMMAC evaluation, and the two Document Understanding Conferences [11] in the years 2001 and 2002. The third DUC takes place in 2003.

In this paper, we propose a new procedure for generating summaries from single documents that addresses some of the drawbacks of existing approaches. The algorithm proposed is a sentence extraction procedure that makes use of genetic algorithms. This has several advantages: firstly, Marcu [10] indicates that, when scoring sentences for generating an extract, current search procedures are slow if the weight of a sentence depends on whether other sentences have been selected or not; our approach with genetic algorithms is capable of finding summaries with high scores in a very short time. Secondly, with this approach,

* This work has been sponsored by CICYT, project number TIC2001-0685-C02-01.

F. Sebastiani (Ed.): ECIR 2003, LNCS 2633, pp. 511–519, 2003.

it is very easy to incorporate in the scheme factors such as the suitability of a summary to individual users, and to evaluate the relevance of a sentence in function of the remaining sentences that have been selected for the extract. The system has been evaluated with standard procedures, and the obtained results are very good.

1.1   Text Extraction

Probably the most comprehensive review on Automatic Text Summarisation systems is the one provided by Mani [7]. In it, text summarisation systems are classified in two different kinds: text abstraction and text extraction systems.

Text abstraction consists in summarising the original material, including at least some information that was not present in the original document. Text abstraction usually needs some kind of semantic processing of a text.

Text extraction systems, on the other hand, cite, literally, fragments from the original text. These fragments may be whole paragraphs, sentences, clauses, or words; it may consist in removing the closed class words (prepositions, determiners, conjunctions, etc.), or in extracting the sentences that are judged more relevant. As the compression level increases, more information is discarded from the original documents. Text extraction systems usually suffer from the following problems:

1. They extract single discourse units (e.g. sentences). This may lead to incoherence, for instance, when the extracted sentences contain conjunctions at the beginning of sentences, dangling anaphoras, etc.
2. Sentences should not be evaluated independently beforehand, and next extracted; quite on the contrary, the choice of a sentence should, for example, block the choice of a different sentence that describes the same idea. It may be the case that the top two sentences are each a paraphrase of the other.

In order to improve the readability of the extract, and to mitigate these problems, extracts are usually post-processed. The following are some typical problems:

1. Lack of conjunctions between sentences, or dangling conjunctions at the beginning of the sentences (e.g. an extracted sentence starting with *However*).
2. Lack of adverbial particles (e.g. it would be desirable the addition of *too* to the extract *"John likes Mary. Peter likes Mary"*)
3. Syntactically complex sentences.
4. Redundant repetition (e.g. repetition of proper names, which can be substituted by pronouns).
5. Lack of information (e.g. complex dangling anaphoras, such as *in such a situation*; or incomplete phrases).

1.2   Related Work

Many extraction systems on use nowadays are based on the work done by Edmundson [2], which described a procedure that has later received the name of *Edmundsonian paradigm* [7]. Edmundson summarised papers about chemistry, by ranking the sentences with a function that took into account four variables: the position of the sentence in the document; the number of words from the title that appear in the sentence; the number of words in the sentence that are considered relevant or irrelevant for the domain of chemistry; and the number of words in the sentence that are very frequent in the document being analysed. The weighting function is a linear combination of the values of these variables. Lin and Hovy [6] and Mani and Bloedorn [8], amongst others, further extended this set of features.

This paradigm has often been criticised for the following reasons [7]:

- It does not take into account for the extraction process the compression rate. For instance, if the top two sentences, s_1 and s_2, provide together an idea; and the third sentence in the ranking, s_3, provides alone other important idea, then a 1-sentence summary should select s_3, because it includes a complete idea, than either s_1 or s_2 alone.
- The linear model might not be powerful enough for summarisation.
- Finally, it only uses morphological information.

Other approaches to extraction that try to capture discourse structure in the original texts try to prevent this problem. Mani [7] distinguishes two ways in which discourse can be studied: **text cohesion** [3], studying relations between units in a text, and **text coherence**, represents the overall structure of a multi-sentence text in terms of macro-level relations between clauses or sentences [9].

2   Summarisation with Genetic Algorithms

We have built a *sentence extraction* procedure for producing summaries from single documents. Sentence extractors usually make use of heuristics in order to weight the sentences, and then select the sentences with the higher scores. However, when the score of a sentence depends on whether other sentence has been selected for the summary, then it becomes more difficult to choose the best combination.

In our approach, the selection of the sentences that will appear in the extract is done using a new summarisation method that is based on genetic programming [4]. The procedure is the following: initially, the algorithm starts with a set of random summaries, each of which is considered an individual in a population. The *genotype* of a summary would be the sentences that it has selected to create an extract. For instance, let us suppose that a document contains 47 sentences, and we need a summary with only 13 sentences. Figure 1 shows a possible initial set of five random summaries.

A fitness function has been defined based upon some heuristics. Some of them were previously known to indicate that particular sentences are relevant,

0 2 6	7	9 16 22 24 26 30 38 43 44
0 5 6	12	18 19 21 26 28 31 38 43 46
1 5 6	9	18 24 31 33 35 36 42 44 45
2 3 4	7	20 24 27 29 31 34 38 41 43
2 5 6	8	17 20 25 27 29 32 34 43 44

Fig. 1. Initial population of summaries. Each line is the genotype of a summary, and contains the numbers of the sentences that will be selected for that summary

and we have added some others that help produce summaries adapted to the user's profiles. The objective is that the most informative summaries receive the highest fitness value.

The following are some characteristics of summaries that had been already observed when designing summarisation algorithms:

- Summaries that contain long sentences are better summaries than summaries that contain short sentences [12]. A partial fitness function can be defined as the sum of the lengths of all the sentences in the extract (measured in number of words): $L(\mathcal{S}) = \sum_{i=0}^{N} length(s_i)$.
- Summaries that contain sentences that occur in the beginning of a paragraph in the original documents are better than summaries that contain sentences that occur toward the end [5, 7]: $W(\mathcal{S}) = \sum_{i=0}^{N} 1/position(s_i)$.
- Summaries that contain the sentences in the same order than in the original documents are better than otherwise [10]. This function can be directly implemented in the genetic algorithm, by forcing the sentences to be always ordered: $O(\mathcal{S}) = 1$ if the sentences are ordered, 0 otherwise.
- Summaries that contain sentences from all the paragraphs are better than summaries that focus only on a few paragraphs [10]: $C(\mathcal{S}) = |\{p : paragraph(p) \wedge (\exists s \epsilon \mathcal{S} : s \epsilon p)\}|$.

The following heuristics were also used for the fitness function. Some of them are there for adapting the summary to a possible user profile, and last two try to rule out uninformative sentences.

- $P(\mathcal{S})$: summaries that contain sentences that are more relevant according to the user profile are better than summaries that don't. In our approach, the user profile is defined as a set of documents that the user considers interesting, and a similarity between the sentences and those documents is calculated using the vector model (e.g. the tf·idf metric).
- $Q(\mathcal{S})$: in case that the user has specified a query, then the summaries that contain sentences with any of the user's query keywords are better than summaries that only contain general-purpose terms.
- $V(\mathcal{S})$: summaries that contain complete sentences (with subject and verb) are better than summaries that contain any sentence with any of those constituents.
- $I(\mathcal{S})$: questions are usually low-informative sentences.

Table 1. Summary with the best score at different generations

Generation	Sentences	Fitness
0	1 6 8 13 20 28 29 33 35 41 42 44 46	46.501553
5	1 6 13 20 22 28 29 33 35 41 42 44 46	47.385387
10	1 3 4 6 13 22 29 33 35 41 42 44 46	49.599186
20	1 3 4 6 13 26 29 33 35 39 41 42 44	51.74695
50	3 4 19 24 25 26 29 39 40 41 42 43 44	54.43973

The final score of a summary is a weighted sum of the different fitting functions. We chose a linear combination for our experiments because it has already been used in all the previous approaches that follow the Edmundsonian paradigm, but other approaches should also be investigated. As in his case, the weights for each of the partial fitness functions were set by hand, with the feedback from several experiments.

Once the fitness function has been decided, we applied a standard genetic algorithms, as described here: we start with an initial population of summaries; at every generation, the two less adapted individuals in the population die, and the two most adapted have children. Population changes by means of the *mutation* operator, that changes randomly a sentence number in an individual, and the *crossover* operator, that interchanges a random portion of the genotype of the two parents. After a certain number of iterations, the population becomes homogeneous and the best score does not vary for a certain number of steps. At that point, the evolution stops and the summary with the best fitness function is generated. Table 1 shows the best summary at different stages of evolution for a summary of 13 sentences from a total of 47.

3   Evaluation

The summarisation system has been tested on an adaptive on-line information system about Darwin's *Voyages of the Beagle*. The information shown to the users is dependent on their interest profiles, and they may indicate a compression rate for the texts in the adaptive site. We built a test set of thirty documents from the site, with lengths ranging from 6 to 59 sentences. It consisted of three subsets:

1. A set with 10 documents for a user whose general interest is biology, needing a compression of roughly 29% (the summaries had to be 29% of the original text). Two of the summaries had an additional constraint: that the user wanted specifically to have information about a *carrancha* and about a *bizcacha*, respectively.
2. A set with 10 documents for a user interested in geography, with a compression rate of roughly 39%. Again, some summaries have additional keywords, such as *Siberia*.
3. A set with 10 documents for a user interested in history, with a compression rate of roughly 46%. As before, some summaries will be general, and others have to be focused on specific topics.

Table 2. Agreement between pairs of judges

Compression rate	Judges pair	Agreement
0.29 (10 docs.)	1,2	63.11%
	1,3	62.14%
	2,3	62.14%
0.39 (10 docs.)	1,2	61.26%
	1,3	63.39%
	2,3	62.16%
0.46 (10 docs.)	1,2	65.57%
	1,3	72.95%
	2,3	72.13%

In order to create human-created summaries for testing purposes, each of the three sets of documents was given to three different human judges. Every document carried an explanatory note indicating the preferences of the user, and the number of sentences that had to be selected. The agreement of every pair of judges was calculated for every set of ten documents, as shown in Table 2.

The creation of a summary is something that is not totally objective: different people will probably produce different summaries from the same text, even though they do not have to reformulate the information but only extract sentences. Therefore, for a proper evaluation of the system it is equally important to know how much humans agree on the same task. A widely used metric to measure judge agreement is the Kappa statistic [1], defined as

$$K = \frac{P(A) - P(E)}{1 - P(E)} \qquad (1)$$

where P(A) is the proportion of times that the judges agree, and P(E) is the proportion of times that we would expect them to agree by chance. If all the judges agree, $P(A)$ is 1 and the value of Kappa is 1; on the other hand, if the agreement of the judges is the one that could be expected by mere chance, Kappa takes the value of 0. According to Carletta [1], citing other research works, a value of $K > .8$ can be considered good, and a value between 0.67 and .8 "allows tentative conclusions to be drawn". However, in medical literature values of K between 0.21 and 0.4 are considered "fair".

The values of Kappa obtained from the judges' answers are listed in Table 3. $P(E)$ was calculated in the following way: with a compression rate of 0.46, given a sentence, the probability that three judges randomly choose it as summary-worthy is $0.46^3 = 0.097$. The values obtained show that there is some agreement amongst the judges, as the level of agreement was always substantially higher than the one that could be expected with random summaries, although they are below 0.67. In fact, as [7, pg. 226] notes, in the SUMMAC evaluation four subjects were asked to evaluate some summaries, without explicit criteria. There was unanimous agreement only for 36% of the sentences, leading to a Kappa of 0.24.

Table 3. Level of agreement between judges

Compression rate	P(A)	P(E)	Kappa
0.29 (10 docs.)	0.46	0.024	0.447
0.39 (10 docs.)	0.43	0.059	0.435
0.46 (10 docs.)	0.59	0.097	0.546

The conclusions we can derive from the fact that inter-judge agreement is not very high is that the task was not defined in a very precise way. Indeed, many choices of sentences were left to the personal choice of the judges, as there were not very specific guidelines. In the case of summarisation, even if we know that the user is interested on a topic, such as *biology*, there might be many sentences referring to that topic, and different judges use their own criteria. In any case, the value of Kappa was always well above that of the SUMMAC competition.

After collecting the information from the judges, the *target summaries* used to evaluate the algorithm were calculated with the sentences that had received more votes from them. The agreement between the genetic algorithm and the hand-made summaries was 49.51% for the 29% summaries, 54.95% for the 46% summaries, and 67.21% for the 46%. Considering that the agreement between human judges was between 60% and 70% (c.f. Table 2), the machine-generated summaries can be considered to be at worst around 15% less accurate than human-made extracts, and at best around 5% less accurate.

The readability of the summaries was evaluated in a controlled experiment with 12 people. They were asked to read the generated summaries, and to mark the readability and coherence of the summaries from 1 to 5 (1 meaning very low, and 5 very high). The mean of the answers was 3.42, with a standard deviation of 2.63 (which means that there was substantial disagreement between them).

4   Conclusions and Future Work

This work includes a new approach for text summarisation based on generating extracts of texts with genetic algorithms. The method is very easy to program, and the performance is good considering its complexity, as it takes in average 250 milliseconds to summarise a 20-sentence text in a Pentium III 900MHz machine. In contrast, Marcu [10] states that an algorithm with similar weight functions takes a couple of hours of computation for each document collection in the Document Understanding Conference.

Most procedures for generating a summary by using extraction have one important drawback in that they do not take into account the compression rate for choosing the sentences. The weight of the extract should take into consideration all the sentences that have been selected and the relationships between them. This is specially relevant for multi-document summarisation, when there are sentences with shared meanings. Also, the algorithm does not even restrict the length of the summary. We can easily define the genotype as a boolean vector with zeros and ones, and define that the sentences extracted are those such that the corresponding gene has a value of 1. In this case, we can *evolve* a population of summaries whose length is not fixed beforehand.

The proposed fitness function is only experimental, and most of the future research we are planning concerns it. Apart from introducing new heuristics, we are aware that a linear combination of the different values might not be the best solution, so other possibilities should be explored. The approach presented here is unsupervised, but a future objective is to make the fitness function evolve as well as the summaries, in a supervised environment. The summarisation procedure should also be extended with some kind of linguistic post-processing, such as resolving the antecedents of the pronouns, so that a pronoun whose antecedent has been removed can be replaced by it.

Measures of sentence cohesion and meaning overlapping can be easily encoded in the fitness function, which will guide the evolution of the population of summaries. Genetic algorithms also have the advantage that the search performed is nonlinear, but they can be programmed so the performance is not slow, and they can be built for practical applications. It will be computationally tractable because that function is not called exhaustively for every possible summary, but only on those that belong to the population of summaries at each iteration.

We would finally like to thank Alejandro Sierra and Pablo Castells for the fruitful discussions about future work.

References

[1] J. Carletta. Assessing agreement on classification tasks: the kappa statstic. *Computational Linguistics*, 22(2):249–254, 1996.
[2] H. P. Edmundson. New methods in automatic abstracting. *Journal of the Association for Computational Machinery*, 16(2):264–286, 1969.
[3] M. A. K. Halliday and R. Hasan. *Cohesion in Text*. Longmans, London, 1996.
[4] J. Holland. *Adaptation in natural and artificial systems*. University of Michigan, 1975.
[5] E. Hovy and C-Y. Lin. *Automated Text Summarization in SUMMARIST*. I. Mani and M. Maybury (eds.) Advances in Automatic Text Summarization. MIT Press, 1999.
[6] C-Y. Lin and E. Hovy. Identifying topics by position. In *Proceedings of the 5th Applied Natural Language Processing Conference*, New Brunswick, New Jersey, 1997.
[7] I. Mani. *Automatic Summarization*. John Benjamins Publishing Company, 2001.
[8] I. Mani and E. Bloedorn. Machine learning of generic and user-focused summarization. In *Proceedings of AAAI'98*, 1998.
[9] D. Marcu. *Discourse Trees are good indicators of importance in text. In I. Mani and M. T. Maybury (eds.), Advances in Automatic Text Summarisation*. MIT Press, 1999.
[10] D. Marcu. Discourse-based sumarization in duc-2001. In *Proceedings of Document Undestanding Conference, DUC-2001*, 2001.

[11] D. Marcu. The document understanding conference: A new forum for summarization research and evaluation. In *Aut. Summarization Workshop, NAACL-2001*, 2001.

[12] D. Marcu and L. Gerber. An inquiry into the nature of multidocument abstract. In *Proceedings of the NAACL'01 workshop on text summarisation*, Pittsburgh, PA, 2001.

The ITC-irst News on Demand Platform

Nicola Bertoldi, Fabio Brugnara, Mauro Cettolo, Marcello Federico,
Diego Giuliani, Erwin Leeuwis, and Vanessa Sandrini

ITC-irst - Centro per la Ricerca Scientifica e Tecnologica
38050, Povo, Trento, Italy
federico@itc.it
http://munst.itc.it

Abstract. The rapid growth of the Information Society is increasing
the demand for technologies enabling access of multimedia data by content. An interesting example is given by the broadcasting companies and
the content providers, which require today effective technologies to support the management and access of their huge audiovisual archives, both
for internal use and public services. The Multilingual Natural Speech
Technology lab at ITC-irst has been engaged for several years in developing core technologies suited for audio indexing and retrieval. In this
paper, a news-on-demand experimental platform is presented which integrates several technologies in the area of spoken language processing
and information retrieval. In particular, an overview of the whole system architecture will be given, together with a short description of the
achieved state-of-the-art in each single technology.

1 Introduction

Multimedia digital libraries are becoming a major driving application for the
steady growth of the Information Society. An interesting application area concerns radio and television broadcasting companies, which are rapidly moving
toward digital standards. The availability of huge audiovisual archives will increase the demand of services for the content providers and the public as well.
Consequently, this will give raise to the need for technologies that make the
management and access of audiovisual repositories easier.

In the last years, challenging research problems and innovative applications
have arisen in the broadcast news domain [8, 9, 10, 11, 12]. Automatic indexing of broadcast news by means of speech recognition has boosted interest for
new tasks, such as topic detection and tracking, spoken information extraction,
speaker identification, cross-language spoken document retrieval, etc.

In addition, automatic transcription of broadcast news is itself a challenging
task, both from the acoustic and linguistic point of view. Acoustically, recordings
can be made in studio, with a dictaphone, over the telephone, mobile phone, etc.
Speech segments can be clean, or include background noise, e.g. traffic, music,
other voices, etc.; moreover, background volume can vary gradually or suddenly.
A large number of different speakers typically occurs, even in a small set of

F. Sebastiani (Ed.): ECIR 2003, LNCS 2633, pp. 520–527, 2003.

shows; speakers may be non-natives or have a strong accent; the speaking style may vary from planned to spontaneous.

From a linguistic viewpoint, broadcast news domain is practically unlimited and covers topics that typically change in time. New topics may arise abruptly, survive for some undefined period, and eventually disappear.

The Multilingual Natural Speech Technology lab at ITC-irst has been working for several years in developing and integrating technologies aimed at supporting audiovisual digital libraries, especially for the news domain. In this work a News on Demand experimental platform is presented, which integrates in-house developed technologies, including large vocabulary speech recognition, spoken information extraction, and spoken document retrieval.

The system supports content based retrieval and browsing within a repository of Italian broadcast news shows, thus considerably reducing the time needed to locate relevant recordings.

The paper is organized as follows: in the next section, the overall architecture of the ITC-irst News on Demand system is presented; in the successive sections, single modules are briefly described, by also providing information about their performance and bibliographic references where more details can be found.

2   The System Architecture

The architecture of the ITC-irst News on Demand platform is depicted in Figure 1. The audio/video stream is encoded at a low resolution rate and stored in the archive for future browsing and retrieval. In parallel the audio alone is processed for indexing.

2.1   Indexing

Indexing of broadcast news shows is obtained by means of several processing steps, which are briefly introduced in the following.

Signature Tune Recognition is performed to detect the starting and ending instants of news programs, in order to isolate portions containing only programs of interest.

Audio Segmentation and Classification is performed to detect portions of the signal containing speech and to classify them according to the acoustic content, bandwidth and speaker gender. Only speech segments are processed in the following steps. Classification of segments is used to apply condition-dependent acoustic models during the speech recognition step.

Speaker Tracking aims at recognizing the identity of (few) speakers, which is an important metadata to be added to the archive, and at pooling data of the same speakers. Speaker clustering is exploited by the speech recognizer for acoustic model adaptation.

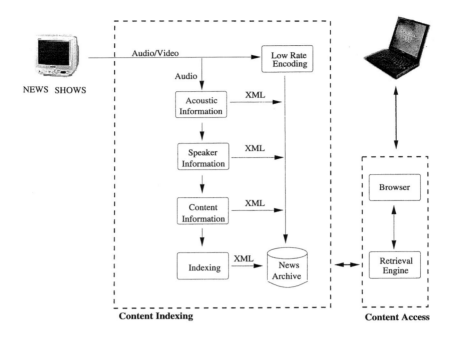

Fig. 1. Organization of the indexing and content-access phases of a news archive

Speech Recognition aims at transcribing segments containing speech. The result is a case-insensitive text with time stamps associated to each word. In this way, each recognized word utterance can be referenced to the video sequence in which it occurred.

Information Extraction is performed on the automatic transcripts to recognize named entities, such as organizations, locations, and persons.

Story Segmentation splits the final transcript into topically cohesive stories. At the moment, segmentation is based only on acoustic features, such as speaker changes or long pauses.

Index Generation is performed by associating to each broadcast news show a compressed video file, a sequence of stories (transcripts) with time stamps and metadata describing the acoustic content, the speaker, and recognized named entities. For spoken document retrieval purposes, an inverted file index is built from the story transcripts.

Fig. 2. The ITC-irst News on Demand system

2.2 Browsing and Retrieval

In Figure 2 a picture of the ITC-irst News on Demand platform is shown. The system supports random access to relevant portions of audio or video documents, reducing the time needed to locate recordings in large multimedia databases. On the left, the user interface of the news browser is given. Starting from the top, we can see the user entered query and a list of retrieved stories, ranked according to their relevance with respect to the query. For each retrieved story, the following information is made available: the matching score, the starting portion of the transcript, information about when the program was issued, and a link to the audio/video encoded file of the story. On the right, the archived data about a story selected by the user are displayed: audio, video, and transcripts augmented with metadata.

The user is given the possibility to play the stories which are contiguous to the one selected. In this way the user can recover the whole news, in case it was split into different stories.

3 Signature Tunes Recognition

This module aims at detecting jingles or signature tunes in an audio stream, among a set of tunes which it was trained on. When a pattern is recognized, it outputs the corresponding label and the time indication of when the signature occurred.

The recognizer relies on a statistical pattern recognition method. Signatures are modeled through 4-state hidden Markov models (HMMs), with left-to-right topology. Actually, only the first few seconds of the starting signatures, and only the last few seconds of the ending signatures are modeled. Other acoustic patterns which are not a signature, like speech, noise and other musical patterns, are also properly modeled. In these cases, a 1-state HMM (i.e. a single Gaussian mixture) is used since no particular temporal structure is assumed.

4   Audio Segmentation and Classification

The most widely used approach to audio segmentation is based on the Bayesian Information Criterion (BIC) [3]. This method is applied to segment the input audio stream into acoustically homogeneous chunks.

To evaluate the segmentation algorithm in detecting the break points, recall and precision are computed with respect to target (manually annotated) boundaries: with half a second time tolerance, the two measures result equal to 82.9% and 85.9%, respectively, on a 75 minutes test set of news programs.

Gaussians mixture models (GMMs) are used to classify segments in terms of acoustic source and channel. Six generic audio classes are considered for classification: female/male wide-band speech, female/male narrow-band speech, music, and silence plus other non-speech events. Classification accuracy, in terms of the six above classes, is 95.6%.

5   Speaker Tracking

Speaker tracking is the process of following who says something in an audio stream. Tracking can broadly be divided into two problems: (i) locating the points of speaker change (segmentation); (ii) identifying the speaker in each segment (labelling/classification).

Speaker segmentation is performed by exploiting the above mentioned BIC-based algorithm. Speaker identification is accomplished by training specific GMMs for a few speakers whose identity is of interest for the digital archive. Statistical models of speakers and of generic acoustic classes, which here play the role of background models, are used to discover if segments contain speech from one of the known speakers.

Clustering of speech segments is done by a bottom-up scheme [3] that groups segments which are acoustically homogeneous with respect to the BIC. As a result, this step gathers segments of the same speakers. Defining the purity of a cluster as the percentage of speech uttered by its dominant speaker, the clustering algorithm provides an average cluster purity of 94.1%.

6   Speech Recognition

Speech segments which are detected by the segmentation and classification module are transcribed by a speech recognition systems which features continuous-density context-dependent HMMs for acoustic modeling, a trigram language model, beam-search decoding, and MLLR acoustic model adaptation [1].

Telephone and wideband speech are modeled separately by triphone HMMs trained, respectively, on 15 and 130 hours of speech. The trigram language model has 64K words and was trained on a large corpus of newspapers and a smaller collection of broadcast news close captions. The language model [4] is compiled into a network structure which embodies both the linguistic and the phonetic descriptions of the task. To reduce the network size, which impacts on the decoder memory requirements, the network compiler exploits a shared-tail topology [4].

The transcript and the output of the speaker clustering procedure are exploited to adapt the acoustic models to any single speaker. In this way, significantly more accurate transcription can be obtained by re-running the recognizer on the segments of that speaker.

Since the language in broadcast news evolves in time, especially with respect to the use of proper names, techniques to adapt the lexicon and the language model have been introduced, which exploit news daily available on the Internet [5].

Recognition performance measured on our benchmark is around 17.9% word error rate (WER). Details can be found in [1].

7   Named Entity Recognition

The named entity (NE) recognition module (see [7]) scans the automatic transcripts looking for proper names corresponding either to locations, persons or organizations. The NE tagger is based on a statistical trigram language model defined on words and NE classes. Each NE class is defined through a probabilistic finite state network (PFSN) which includes a set of known-entries for that class, and a generic NE template model. The template is modeled with a regular expression which allows to cover NEs of different formats and lengths.

Unsupervised training of the NE LM goes through the definition and estimation of simpler intermediate models, which are then used to initialized the final NE model.

The tagger was trained on a large collection of Italian untagged newspapers and a list of a few thousand NEs extracted from the corpus and manually classified. The algorithm has been evaluated on two broadcast news shows. Reference transcripts were manually tagged for a total of 322 NEs.

Results on automatic transcriptions, with 19.8% WER, shows a 75.9% F-score. For comparison, the model achieves a 88.8% F-score on the reference transcripts.

8   Spoken Document Retrieval

In the following, indexing of stories is described, and the ITC-irst approach to cross-language spoken document retrieval is briefly introduced, which permits to query the Italian news archive in English.

8.1   Story Segmentation

The output of the speech recognizer is a text stream. In order to apply information retrieval to spoken documents, the text stream is automatically segmented by introducing story boundaries in correspondence of changes of acoustic conditions and long pauses. Too short stories are not permitted, and joined with the successive ones.

8.2   Cross-Lingual Information Retrieval

A model for cross-language information retrieval has been developed [6], which integrates query translation and document retrieval. Given a query $\mathbf{e}$ in the source language, e.g. English, the relevance of a document d is measured by the following joint probablity:

$$Pr(\mathbf{e}, d) = \sum_{\mathbf{i}} Pr(\mathbf{e}, \mathbf{i}) \frac{Pr(\mathbf{i}, d)}{\sum_{d'} Pr(\mathbf{i}, d')} \qquad (1)$$

The hidden variable $\mathbf{i}$ is introduced to represent Italian (term-by-term) translations of $\mathbf{e}$. The joint probabilities in (1) are computed by statistical models [6] which, through suitable approximations, permit to efficiently compute formula (1). The query document probability $Pr(\mathbf{i}, d)$ is computed by combining the scores of a language model and an Okapi model [2]. The query-translation probability $Pr(\mathbf{e}, \mathbf{i})$ is computed by a hidden Markov model, in which the observable part is the query $\mathbf{e}$ in the source language, and the hidden part is the corresponding query $\mathbf{i}$ in the target language.

A retrieval algorithm is derived which integrates probabilities from both models over a set of N-best translations, which allows an efficient computation of formula (1).

Performance of the IR system was evaluated through a three year participation in CLEF, where it resulted one of the best monolingual systems, and ranked reasonably well in the bilingual tracks.

9   Conclusion

In this paper, the ITC-irst news-on-demand platform has been presented. The goal of the system is to demonstrate potential applications of spoken language technologies in the news domain area. The presented system permits to effectively search and browse broadcast news stories inside a large audiovisual archive on the basis of acoustic and content information automatically extracted from the audio trace of programs. After giving an overview of the whole architecture and of the user interface, technologies employed for the off-line indexing phase and to perform spoken document retrieval are presented. Future work will be in the direction of integrating recent research results on existing modules, and to add novel features to the system, such as text classification, topic detection and tracking. Finally, it is worth to mention that the presented indexing modules are currently deployed by RAI, a major Italian broadcasting company, for internal documentation purposes.

Acknowledgements

This work was carried out within the European projects Coretex (IST-1999-11876) and Echo (IST-1999-11994), the project ProtoRAI sponsored by RAI Radiotelevisione Italiana, and the project WebFAQ funded under the FDR-PAT program of the Province of Trento.

References

[1] N. Bertoldi, F. Brugnara, M. Cettolo, M. Federico, and D. Giuliani. From broadcast news to spontaneous dialogue transcription: Portability issues. In *Proceedings of the IEEE International Conference on Acoustics, Speech and Signal Processing*, Salt Lake City, UT, 2001.

[2] N. Bertoldi and M. Federico. ITC-irst at CLEF 2000: Italian monolingual track. In C. Peters, editor, *Cross-Language Information Retrieval and Evaluation*, volume 2069 of *Lecture Notes in Computer Science*, pages 261–272, Heidelberg, Germany, 2001. Springer Verlag.

[3] S. S. Chen and P. S. Gopalakrishnan. Speaker, environment and channel change detection and clustering via the Bayesian Information Criterion. In *Proceedings of the DARPA Broadcast News Transcr. & Understanding Workshop*, Lansdowne, VA, 1998.

[4] R. De Mori, editor. *Spoken Dialogues with Computers*. Academy Press, London, UK, 1998.

[5] M. Federico and N. Bertoldi. Broadcast news LM adaptation using contemporary texts. In *Proceedings of the European Conference on Speech Communication and Technology*, Aalborg, Denmark, 2001.

[6] M. Federico and N. Bertoldi. Statistical cross-language information retrieval using n-best query translations. In *Proceedings of the 25th Annual International ACM SIGIR Conference on Research and Development in Information Retrieval*, pages 167–174, Tampere, Finland, 2002.

[7] M. Federico, N. Bertoldi, and V. Sandrini. Bootstrapping named entity recognition for Italian broadcast news. In *Proceedings of the 2002 Conference on Empirical Methods in Natural Language Processing (EMNLP)*, Philadelphia, PA, July 2002.

[8] S. Furui, K. Ohtsuki, and Z.-P. Zhang. Japanese broadcast news transcription and information extraction. *Communications of the ACM*, 43(2):71–73, 2000.

[9] J.-L. Gauvain, L. Lamel, and G. Adda. Transcribing broadcast news for audio and video indexing. *Communications of the ACM*, 43(2):64–70, 2000.

[10] A. G. Hauptmann and M. J. Witbrock. Informedia news on demand: Multimedia information acquisition and retrieval. In M. T. Maybury, editor, *Intelligent Multimedia Information Retrieval*. AAAI Press/MIT Press, Menlo Park, CA, 1997.

[11] F. Kubala, S. Colbath, D. Liu, A. Srivastava, and J. Makhoul. Integrated technologies for indexing spoken language. *Communications of the ACM*, 43(2):48–56, 2000.

[12] The SRI Maestro Team. MAESTRO: Conductor of Multimedia Analysis Technologies. *Communications of the ACM*, 43(2):57–63, 2000.

Evaluating Peer-to-Peer Networking
for Information Retrieval
within the Context of Meta-searching

Iraklis A. Klampanos, James J. Barnes, and Joemon M. Jose

Department of Computing Science – University of Glasgow
17 Lilybank Gardens, Glasgow G12 8QQ, Scotland
{iraklis,barnesjj,jj}@dcs.gla.ac.uk
http://www.dcs.gla.ac.uk/~iraklis

Abstract. Peer-to-peer (P2P) computing has shown an unexpected growth and development during the recent years. P2P networking is being applied from B2B enterprise solutions to more simple, every-day file-sharing applications like Gnutella clients. In this paper we are investigating the use of the Gnutella P2P protocol for Information Retrieval by means of building and evaluating a general-purpose Web meta-search engine. A similar project, Infrasearch, existed in the past only to demonstrate the usefulness of P2P computing beyond just file-sharing. In this work, a Java-based Gnutella enabled meta-search engine has been developed and used in order to evaluate the suitability and usefulness of P2P networking in the aforementioned context. Our conclusions concerning time efficiency in different networking topologies are presented. Finally, limitations of this approach as well as future research areas and issues on the subject are discussed.

1 Introduction

During the recent years the Peer-to-Peer (P2P) networking paradigm has become very popular among simple users as well as the corporate sector. As its name suggests it defines equal participation among the nodes in a network. This comes in contrast to the well-known Client-Server networking model which is predominant both on the Internet and on Local Area Networks (LANs).

P2P networking is a subset of distributed computing and it can be seen as one more layer on top of the layers of the various networking protocols like TCP/IP. The fact that it is software based makes P2P solutions very flexible with numerous possible applications. Unfortunately, because of various historical turns, and especially after the Napster incident, most people consider P2P systems simply as file-sharing applications while companies treat them as a tools for enterprise solutions. However, despite Information Retrieval (IR) has been projected as a major application of P2P protocols, no proper investigation has been made into this issue.

F. Sebastiani (Ed.): ECIR 2003, LNCS 2633, pp. 528–536, 2003.

There are countless potential information sources on the Internet nowadays; each of those with its own characteristics, policies, hardware and software architectures. We believe that P2P solutions could help use the Internet in a way never seen before, by building active and collaborating information pools that exchange information regardless of underlying network characteristics and retrieval policies. By distribution of knowledge and technical resources, the retrieval process could also be greatly aided.

In this paper, we will investigate the effects of different networking topologies of a P2P network in retrieval efficiency. This paper is organised as follows. In the next Section we will introduce P2P networking as well as some specifics of the Gnutella protocol. In Section 3 we will briefly describe the experimental meta-searching tool we used and some of the policies we have followed while designing and implementing it. Following that, in Section 4, we will describe the evaluation strategy we used for the aforementioned purpose and finally, in Section 5 we will discuss conclusions and future possibilities of the P2P approach for IR.

2   Peer-to-Peer Networking and the Gnutella Protocol

2.1   Defining Peer-to-Peer

"[...] Instead, machines in the home and on the desktop are connecting to each other directly, forming groups and collaborating to become user-created search engines, virtual supercomputers, and filesystems.[...]" [1, page 3]

As the name "Peer-to-Peer" implies, a P2P network comprises of nodes that are communicating with each other in a predefined framework of equality; the equality having to do with the services each node is *capable* to provide. Because of the various flaws that this description has, it is vital that we precisely define a P2P network before proceeding any further. In order to do so, we first have to define the building blocks of such networks, the *peers* and those aforementioned services will drive our definition.

Definition 1. Peers *are the living processes running on the participating machines in the network that are* potentially capable of *providing and using remote services in an equal qualitative and quantitative manner. Peers, though, may not exhibit equal participation levels. The latter are proportional to the peers' willingness to participate which can be dictated by hardware or other fixed circumstances (eg. limited bandwidth etc.). Peers provide both server and client functionality hence why they are often called servents (**Server** - **Client**).*

We can therefore define a P2P network as follows:

Definition 2. *A* Peer-to-Peer network *is a directed graph whose nodes are represented by* peers *and its edges are represented by abstract communication channels. In such a network, the equality of peers is defined by their potential capabilities while their participation level is analogous to their willingness to participate, as defined above.*

2.2   The Gnutella Protocol

The protocol used for developing our experimental meta-search engine is the Gnutella protocol[1, 7]. Gnutella was the first completely decentralised, genuine P2P protocol, that was born, matured and evolved in the public Internet. Gnutella is a message-based protocol, typically implemented as a distributed P2P application for file-sharing. Some popular Gnutella clients, for instance, are: Limewire[1], Bearshare[2], and GTK-Gnutella[3].

Infrasearch   In the past, the Gnutella protocol, by being simple and elegant, gave rise to new ideas concerning Information Retrieval in conjunction with true decentralised, distributed environments. A P2P meta-search capacity, intended as a demonstration of the adaptability of the protocol, has been developed before.

Known as Infrasearch[1, page 100], the search engine that was pioneered, used the Gnutella protocol to operate over a private Gnutella network, the interface being a standard Web browser and response results being expressed as HTML rendered by the browser. In Infrasearch, each node interpreted the query and supplied results according to its knowledge resources only if it could provide any relevant information.

3   A Gnutella Meta-search Engine

In order to evaluate the suitability of P2P techniques for IR we developed a distributed meta-search engine. Such an engine that uses the Gnutella protocol is described in this section.

3.1   Overview

The main purpose for building such a meta-searching tool was to try to identify the limits of a P2P approach in a well known IR area. The steps of meta-searching are found to be computationally expensive[5], always depending on the algorithms at hand. It would, therefore, be important to make those steps more manageable by distributing the CPU and memory requirements among a set of processing units.

The meta-search engine components, as defined in [5], divide up naturally in a P2P context like Gnutella as it can be seen in Fig. 1. The *Document Selector* component is not applicable for our purposes since we used commercial, general-purpose search engines to retrieve sets of relevant documents, whose most important characteristics and policies are proprietary.

Perhaps the most important feature of such a solution is the distribution of the *Results Merger* component. The reason for that is because, depending on

---

[1] http://www.limewire.com
[2] http://www.bearshare.com
[3] http://gtk-gnutella.sourceforge.net/

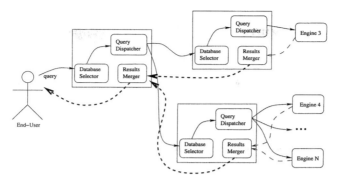

Fig. 1. An example P2P meta-searching network

the re-ranking strategy that we follow and on the desired number of results, its complexity is usually non-trivial. Another reason why such a distribution is an interesting feature is that depending on the different information sources, we would, ideally, be able to apply different recombination procedures at different nodes of the network (stages of the retrieval process).

3.2   Distribution of Meta-search Engine Components

Database Selector and Query Dispatcher The *Query Dispatcher* component is responsible for the modification and routing of the queries in the network. It perceives the rest of the network as a black box. The interface of their interaction is the nodes that a potential query can reach from the current peer.In our prototype, the *Database Selector* was just granting permission to route in an un-informed manner.

Result Merger Probably the most important component concerning the particular experimental system was the *Result Merger*. This component receives results from the nodes its peer has previously sent queries to, re-combines them and routes them back. The re-combination policy followed is discussed in Section 3.4.

3.3   The Components of the System

For the implementation of the system we used the JTella [4] Gnutella library. JTella is written in Java and implements the Gnutella protocol in an intuitive way although it is still at an early development stage. JTella also implements all the Gnutella descriptors described in [7], which constituted an additional convenience factor for information retrieval.

The web meta-searching system developed can be divided into four (4) major components:

PeerFrame This is the main frame of the program. This meta-searcher is a client-based one, even though disadvantages of this kind of systems have been noted [6]. This approach was decided since the system was aimed for experimental purposes and its easy configuration and adaptation was desired.

GUI_Connection This is the main means for the **PeerFrame** to communicate with the JTella classes and the rest of the logic in the application.

Receiver This is actually the peer's listener. It listens for messages arriving at a predefined port and, depending on the kind of message, it performs the analogous actions.

SearchEngineParser This component is responsible for managing the search engines that its peer is responsible for.

3.4 Combination and Re-ranking

For the combination of the results in the system, we used the Dempster-Shafer (D-S) Theory of Evidence Combination as presented in [2].

Suppose that a peer is connected to k information sources and one of those sources, j, returns n_j results in total. Then, the initial score of each of j's returned results would be:

$$S_{i_j} = \frac{[n_j - (p_{i_j} - 1)]}{R_j} \tag{1}$$

where p_i is the proposed, by the information source, rank of the result i (i.e. 1 for the most relevant result, 2 for the next and so on) and R_j is given by $R_j = \sum_{\iota=1}^{n_j} \iota$, which acts as a normalising factor.

Each web search engine has been assigned a positive real number β_j, an untrust coefficient, where $0 \geq \beta_j \geq 1$. Normally, this comes from a trust coefficient which is provided by the user or calculated by a relevance feedback process; on this prototype though each search engine was assigned a constant un-trust coefficient. β_j is assigned to the entire set of documents and is interpreted as the uncertainty of the source of informal evidence. By using β_j and Equation 1, we can evaluate the mass function for each result:

$$m_j(\{d_i\}) = S_{i_j} \times (1 - \beta_j) \tag{2}$$

Finally, the results coming from different information sources (different evidence) can be calculated by applying the Dempster-Shafer theory of Combination of Evidence as follows. For each two information sources 1 and 2, the new mass function of each result d_i of the information provider 1 is given by:

$$
\begin{aligned}
m'(\{d_i\}) &= m_1(\{d_i\}) \otimes m_2(\{d_i\}) \\
&= m_1(\{d_i\}) \times m_2(\{d_i\}) + m_1(\{d_i\}) \times m_2(\Theta) + m_2(\{d_i\}) \times m_1(\Theta)
\end{aligned} \tag{3}
$$

where Θ is the global set of documents.

Additionally, the new un-trust coefficient $m'(\Theta)$ of the combination can be obtained from

$$m'(\Theta) = m_1(\Theta) \times m_2(\Theta) \tag{4}$$

Any new set of results, from a third information source, can be combined further by re-using Equations 3 and 4. This is a simplified form of D-S theory for IR purposes whose details can be found in [2, 3].

4   Evaluation and Comparisons

The retrieval efficiency of a tightly controlled Gnutella P2P network depends highly on the peer topology used. In this section we describe the evaluation procedure we followed in order to measure the effect of various topologies on efficiency. Followed to that, we will briefly present and discuss over the acquired results.

4.1   Evaluation Method and Results

The different topologies that were evaluated can be seen on Fig. 2. For each of these topologies a fixed three-term query was issued to the network from the initiating peer[4]. Also, for each experiment, a standard number of results was required by each participating search engine.

We ran this experiment requesting ten (10), twenty (20) and fifty (50) results from each web search engine in order to observe the difference in retrieval times depending on the number of requested results.

After executing the experiment for each of the topologies of Fig. 2 and for each of the different number of expected results, we obtained the average times presented in Fig. 3. [!t]

As it can be seen from Fig. 3, the centralised approach (Fig. 2(a)) was proven to be worse than all the distributed ones. We believe that this is a strong indication of the potential of distributed P2P IR systems from the retrieval efficiency point of view.

An interesting outcome is that the linear setup with a repeating search engine (Fig. 2(d)) was closely as inefficient as the centralised one (Fig. 2(a)).

The tree structures provided us with useful insight. Firstly, the fact that Balanced Tree 2 (Fig. 2(f)) was significantly more efficient than Balanced Tree 2 (Fig. 2(e)), clearly depicts the advantage of well thought-out distributed systems over the more centralised ones for non-trivial tasks.

Lastly, the most effective approach was the Centralised setup 2 (Fig. 2(b)). We believe that this setup was better than the others because of the small number of search engines used as well as of the fast internal LAN that these experiments were executed over.

5   Conclusion and Future Work

In this paper it was shown that distributed P2P solutions have a clear potential for more efficient IR; in particular that networking topology plays an important role in retrieval effectiveness. This was investigated within the meta-search engine context but, in fact, IR can benefit from P2P solutions in a much more

---

[4] denoted by an asterisk in Fig. 2

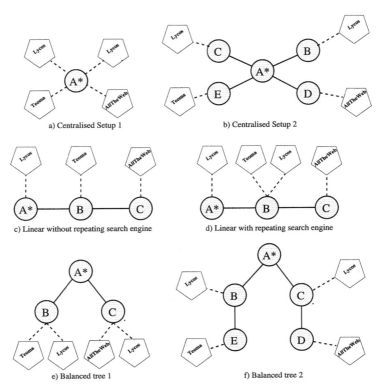

a) Centralised Setup 1

b) Centralised Setup 2

c) Linear without repeating search engine

d) Linear with repeating search engine

e) Balanced tree 1

f) Balanced tree 2

Fig. 2. The topologies used during the benchmarking of the P2P meta-search engine

direct and whole way. The utter aim of the P2P IR approach is that information should be retrieved from a wide variety of information sources, domains and underlying topologies and architectures, seamlessly and transparently to the end user.

We believe there are numerous possibilities for future work in this field so that both efficiency and effectiveness of IR can be significantly increased. Firstly, concerning this particular piece of work, a large-scale evaluation, incorporating more than one queries, of the P2P meta-search system described in Section 3 is being considered to take place in the near future. Additionally, of high importance would be the systematic exploration of suitable meta-data for IR over P2P networks. Another potential research field is the investigation of ways of finding willing and suitable information sources in a dynamically changing network. Such research would aid the IR process in larger and loosely controlled environments such as the Internet.

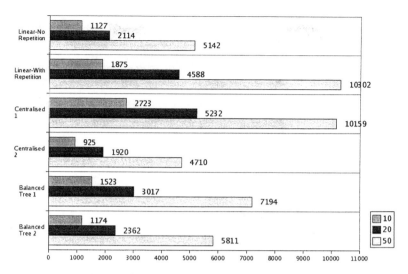

Fig. 3. Comparison of retrieval effectiveness

Acknowledgements

The authors would like to thank Dr. Peter Dickman of the University of Glasgow for his valuable help on practical matters concerning the development of distributed and in particular P2P systems.

The first author would also like to thank the Department of Computing Science of the University of Glasgow for the summer internship opportunity that it provided, thus allowing him to investigate further the field of P2P IR.

References

[1] *PEER-TO-PEER: Harnessing the Power of Disruptive Technologies.* O'Reilly & Associates, Inc., 101 Morris Street, Sebastopol, CA 95472, March 2001.

[2] Joemon Jose and David J Harper. Retrieval mechanism for semi-structured photographic collections. DEXA'97, pages 276–292, Toulouse, France, 1997. Springer.

[3] Joemon M Jose. *An Integrated Approach for Multimedia Information Retrieval.* PhD thesis, The Robert Gordon University, April 1998.

[4] Ken McCrary. The gnutella file-sharing network and java. *http://www.javaworld.com/javaworld/jw-10-2000/jw-1006-fileshare.html*, as viewed on November 20th 2002.

[5] Weiyi Meng, Clement T. Yu, and King-Lup Liu. Building efficient and effective metasearch engines. *ACM Computing Surveys*, 34(1):48–89, 2002.

[6] Wolfgang Sander-Beuermann and Mario Schomburg. Internet information retrieval - the further development of meta-search engine technology. In *Proceedings of the Internet Summit*, Genf, July 22-24 1998. Internet Society.

[7] Clip2 Distributed Search Services. The gnutella protocol specification v0.4. *http://www.gnutella.co.uk/library/pdf/gnutella_protocol_0.4.pdf*, as viewed on November 3rd 2002.

Parallel Computing for Term Selection in Routing/Filtering

Andy MacFarlane[1], Stephen E. Robertson[1,2], and Julie A. McCann[3]

[1] Centre for Interactive Systems Research, City University, London
andym@soi.city.ac.uk
[2] Microsoft Research Ltd, Cambridge CB2 3NH
[3] Department of Computing, Imperial College London

Abstract. It has been postulated that a method of selecting terms in either routing or filtering using relevance feedback would be to evaluate every possible combination of terms in a training set and determine which combination yields the best retrieval results. Whilst this is not a realistic proposition because of the enormous size of the search space, some heuristics have been developed on the Okapi system to tackle the problem which are computationally intensive. This paper describes parallel computing techniques that have been applied to these heuristics to reduce the time it takes to select to select terms.

1 Introduction

This paper describes parallel computing techniques that can be applied to a very large search space for relevance feedback for routing/filtering that has successfully been used on Okapi experiments at TREC [1-4]. The routing task we are considering is the situation where a number of relevance judgements have been accumulated and we want to derive the best possible search formulation for future documents. The filtering task is an extension of this, but a threshold for documents is applied i.e. a binary yes/no decision is made on one document at a time as to whether it will be presented to the user. In [1] it was stated that an alternative to some term ranking methods described would be to "evaluate every possible combination of terms on a training set and use some performance evaluation measure to determine which combination is best". Such a method is very computationally intensive, and certainly not practicable even with parallel machinery. The complexity of one routing session before re-weighting is 2^τ where τ is the number of terms. For just 300 terms, our search space is 2^{300} or 2.04e+90 combinations. Since the term scores also can be re-weighted any number of times, the order for the algorithm's time complexity cannot be stated. Clearly some sort of limit must be set both on the number of times re-weighting is allowed and the total number of combinations inspected for an information need. We use combinatorial optimisation techniques on this search space and apply parallelism to improve the speed of the techniques studied. The methods used by Okapi at TREC

F. Sebastiani (Ed.): ECIR 2003, LNCS 2633, pp. 537-545, 2003.

are briefly described in section 2 and the strategy for applying parallelism to these methods is described in section 3. The data and settings used for the experiments are described in section 4. Section 5 describes the experimental results. Conclusions and further work in the area are outlined in section 6.

2   Methods Used by Okapi at TREC

Okapi at TREC [1-4] applied three algorithms to the term selection problem. Find Best (FB), Choose First Positive (CFP) and Choose All Positive (CAP). With the FB algorithm each term is evaluated in one iteration and the term yielding the best score from the term set chosen: the algorithm stops when a pre-determined threshold is reached. An evaluation in this context is a retrieval followed by the application of some function on the search results to produce a score: for example average precision. Terms that increase this score are retained/removed (see below). The threshold that halts the procedure is reached when there is little or no increase in the score. The other algorithms work in much the same way, but with minor differences. CFP works by choosing the term if it is the first term that increases the score. CAP is an extension of FB/CFP and works by including/excluding all terms that increase the score in an iteration. Each chosen term is accumulated in a *query set*, the final version of which is applied to a test set. Within each algorithm, two operations for choosing terms can be used: add term to the query or delete term from the query. The add term operation can be augmented by reweighing the retrieval selection value: in the case of the Okapi experiments this is either a reduction by a factor of 0.67 or an increase by a factor of 1.5. The Find Best and Choose All Positive algorithms are Steepest-ascent Hill-Climbers while Choose First Positive is a First-ascent Hill-Climber [5].

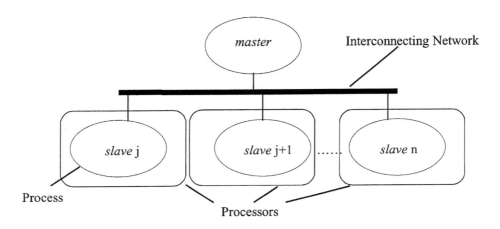

Fig. 1 *Master/Slave* Router Topology

3   Applying Parallelism to the Okapi Methods

An approach to applying parallel computation to term selection is to think in terms of *term set*s and what needs to be done to the Hill-Climber algorithms to reduce their run time. Since the evaluation of operations on terms can be done independently we can distribute the *term set* to a number of slave processes which apply the required Hill-Climber algorithm to each sub-set of the *term set*: an individual term is only evaluated on one processor. Thus by applying inter-set parallelism to the evaluation of terms in the evaluation set, we aim to speed up each iteration. We use a method of parallelism known as the *domain decomposition strategy* [6]: the search space is divided amongst available slave processors, controlled by a master process (see fig 1). One of the advantages of this method is that communication costs are kept to a minimum as processes involved in evaluating terms do not need to communicate to complete their task: however there is an overhead associated with checking stopping criterion in every iteration. This overhead involves both the retrieval of the best yielding term or terms from all slaves by the master and broadcast of the best term data back to the slaves. Each slave has access to the training set on its own local disk in order to increase the flexibility of the parallel algorithms and reduce the overheads of broadcasting term information from the master process to slaves. This method of data distribution is known as *Replication*.

The combinations of algorithms and operations described in this paper are: Find Best, Choose First Positive and Choose All Positive algorithms with *add only*, *add/remove* operations and *add with re-weighting*. It should be noted that the CAP algorithm is a purely sequential algorithm to which inter-set parallelism cannot be directly applied, as the results are the cumulative effect of evaluations in one iteration. However the CAP algorithm can be applied to each sub-set of the term set and we refer to revised version as the Choose Some Positive (CSP) algorithm: we can regard CSP as a compromise between the FB/CFP algorithms and CAP algorithm. In the CSP algorithm the best yielding sub-set of the term set from one process only is chosen. CSP is implemented in terms of CAP. Choose First Positive differs slightly in that it is possible that a better term could be chosen in one inner iteration for each smaller sub-set of the term set (or increasing number of processes). It is possible the terms selected by the Find Best algorithm may differ slightly over runs with varying numbers of processes, possibly affecting the evaluation score. This is because two or more terms may have the same effect when applied to the query and the term that is chosen first amongst these equal terms will be the term used. When the number of processors equals the number of evaluation terms, all term selection algorithms are identical; i.e. they all reduce to Find Best.

4   Description of the Data and Settings Used in Experiments

The database used for the experiments was the Ziff-Davis collection from the TREC-4 disk 3 that is 349 Mb in size with a total number of 161,021 records [7]. Three databases were created for the Ziff-Davis collection: an extraction database, a selection database (both of which form the training set) and a test database. Our focus here is on the training set. We use the extraction database to choose the initial set of terms for the queries using the relevance judgements, and then train the queries on the selection database using the Okapi Hill-Climbers. We used a total of 19 TREC-4 topics on the Ziff-Davis database for these experiments. These topics were chosen on the basis of the number of relevance judgements available for routing/filtering: it was felt that topics with too few relevance judgements (i.e. one or two) would not be of much use in the optimisation process due to excessive overfitting (overfitting can occur when term selection mechanism overtrains). The distribution of relevance judgements for the database was as follows; 1868 (39%) for the extraction set, 1469 (30%) for the selection set and 1483 (31%) for the test set.

The timing metrics we use to measure retrieval efficiency are as follows. For each run we declare the average elapsed time in seconds for term selection over all topics. We define selection efficiency as the improvement in average elapsed time by using parallelism. We use the standard parallel measures:

- Speedup: defined as the increase in speed from 1 to n processors and found by dividing time spent on computation using 1 processor by time using n processors.
- Parallel efficiency: defined as speedup divided by n processors giving an idea of how well processors are being used on a parallel system.
- Load imbalance: we use a metric called LI that is the ratio of the maximum elapsed time over all the processors divided by the average elapsed time [8]: a perfect load balance would achieve an LI of 1.0.

As our focus is on speeding up the algorithms, we do not discuss retrieval effectiveness issues: experiments done by Okapi at TREC have shown that an increase in retrieval effectiveness is available [1-4]. We present runs on 1 to 7 processors: the hardware used for the research was the Fujitsu AP3000 at the Australian National University.

5   Experimental Results

5.1   Elapsed Time for Term Selection

From figs 2 to 4 it can be seen how expensive the application of the term selection algorithms can be, with average elapsed time running into hundreds of seconds and in some cases thousands of seconds. Parallelism has different effects on individual term selection methods which can be either beneficial or detrimental. The FB algorithm is the term selection method which benefits most from the application of parallelism, showing a linear time reduction on all node set sizes. FB also outperforms the other term selection algorithms using more processors (this can be seen from all data presented in figs 2 to 4). Linear time reductions are also found with most parallel runs on CFP using any operation (this is most noticeable with *add only* operation - see fig 2). With regard to CSP using any operation, elapsed times do not follow any trend and vary unpredictably with slave node set size (particularly using *add only* operation - see fig 2). The most expensive operation in the majority of cases is *add reweight*: for example FB run times are roughly four times as slow on *add reweight* as the other operations. It is generally more expensive to use the *add/remove* operation compared with *add only* particularly with the FB algorithm.

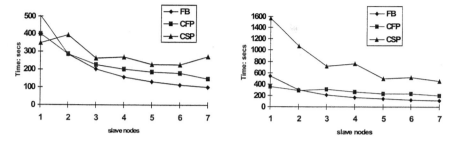

Fig. 2. *Add only* average term selection elapsed time in seconds

Fig. 3. *Add remove* average term selection elapsed time in seconds

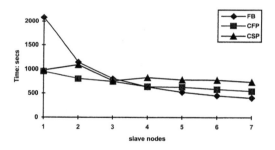

Fig. 4. *Add reweight* average term selection elapsed time in seconds

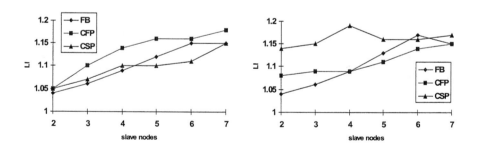

Fig. 5. Add only load imbalance for term selection

Fig. 6. Add remove load imbalance for term selection

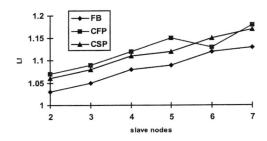

Fig. 7. *Add reweight* load imbalance for term selection

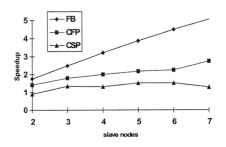

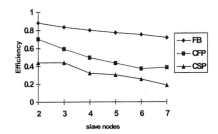

Fig. 8. Add only operation speedup for term selection

Fig. 9. Add only parallel efficiency for term selection

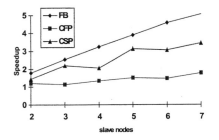

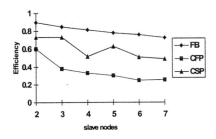

Fig. 10. Add remove operation speedup for term selection

Fig. 11. Add remove operation parallel efficiency for term selection

5.2   Load Imbalance

The imbalance for term selection is low and does not reach a point where load balance is a significant problem for the algorithms: for example an LI of 2.0 would mean halving the effective speed of the machine and the LI figures in figs 5 to 7 are nowhere near that level. However, general trend for load imbalance for most experiments is upwards. The exception is CSP with *add remove* operation which shows a reduced level of load balance over all runs. There is a clear increase in load imbalance as the number of slave nodes is increased, which demonstrates the need for some form of load balancing technique if many more slave nodes were to be used in optimising on a training set of this size. This imbalance contributes in part to the overall loss in term selection efficiency recorded.

5.3   Speedup and Parallel Efficiency

The speedup and efficiency figures are shown in figs 8 to 13. In terms of speedup and parallel efficiency, the FB method shows improvement on all levels of parallelism investigated. Speedup is near linear at 7 slave nodes with parallel efficiency above the 70% mark for any operation. However the speedup and parallel efficiency for CFP is very poor for all three term operations. In most cases a speedup of less than two is registered: a number of factors are responsible for the poor parallel performance. An increase in evaluations with more slave nodes is a significant factor as well as the overhead at the synchronisation point together with load imbalance. For example CFP with *add reweight* increases the evaluations per topic from 3787 on 1 slave node to 5434 on 7 slave nodes: the same trend is found with other operations.

Much the same can be said for CSP, apart from *add remove* operation which does actually show some level of speedup. However, overheads are a much less significant factor for CSP while the increase in evaluations plays a more important part: for example the number of evaluations using the *add reweight* operation increased from 2766 per topic on 1 slave node to 8234 on 7 slave nodes. There are fewer iterations with the CSP method, but individual iterations are much longer. Slowdown for CSP on *add only* and *add reweight* is recorded for 2 slave nodes. It could be argued that using speedup and parallel efficiency to measure the parallel performance of the CSP algorithm is unfair as the parallelism itself imposes an extra workload for the method. However demonstrating that some parallel performance improvement is available while still being able to examine some of the search space is, we believe, worthwhile.

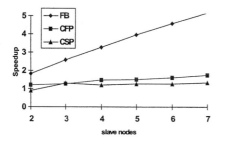 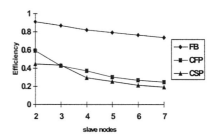

Fig. 12. Add reweight operation speedup for term selection   **Fig. 13.** Add reweight operation parallel efficiency for term selection

6   Conclusion and Further Work

We have found a method of parallelism which by focusing on the main task, namely the evaluation of terms, can speed up the computation of the heuristics and examine more of the search space. We have shown that the speed advantage found with the FB selection method is significant. We believe it is possible to improve the selection efficiency of both FB and CSP using some form of dynamic re-distribution technique for terms in the query. Experiments with CFP are less conclusive and show difficulties particularly with load balance. It may be possible to improve the load balance of CFP but only at a large overhead cost.

We could consider the use of *machine learning* [9] *tabu* search [6] and *pattern recognition* [10] techniques in order to optimise routing/filtering queries. A great deal of research into search space methods has been done in *machine learning* using methods such as genetic algorithms and neural networks that are both very computationally intensive processes. *Tabu* search is a meta-heuristic which can be used to manage other heuristics in order to examine parts of the search space which would not normally be examined with a single search strategy. Some of the selection algorithms used in *pattern recognition* are similar to the Hill-Climbers used in this study [10], particularly Find Best with *add only* and *remove only* operations. We could therefore treat the query optimisation discussed in this research as a pattern recognition problem, treating different combinations of the query as a pattern. The problem would be to find the best yielding 'pattern' in the query. Parallelism could be used to speed up these methods, providing they are able to show retrieval effectiveness benefit on the test set.

Acknowledgements

This work was supported by the British Academy under grant number IS96/4203. We are grateful to the Australian National University, Canberra for the of their Fujistsu AP3000 parallel computer in order to conduct these experiments. We owe particular thanks to Gordon Smith, David Hawking and David Sitsky for their advice on many issues. We would also like to thank David Hawking for suggesting the use of replication for the method of data distribution.

References

[1]   S.E. Robertson, S. Walker, S. Jones, M.M. Hancock-Beaulieu and M. Gatford, Okapi at TREC-3. In: D.K. Harman, (ed.): *Proceedings of the Third Text Retrieval Conference*, NIST Gaithersburg (1995) 109-126

[2]   S.E. Robertson, S. Walker, S. Jones, M.M. Beaulieu M. Gatford and A. Payne, Okapi at TREC-4. In: D.K. Harman, (ed.): *Proceedings of the Fourth Text Retrieval Conference*, NIST Gaithersburg (1996) 73-96

[3]   M.M. Beaulieu, M. Gatford, X. Huang, S.E. Robertson, S. Walker and P. Williams, Okapi at TREC-5. In: Voorhees E.M and D.K.Harman, (eds.): *Proceedings of the Fifth Text Retrieval Conference*, NIST Gaithersburg (1997) 143-166.

[4]   S. Walker, S.E.Robertson and M Boughanem, OKAPI at TREC-6. In: Voorhees E.M and D.K. Harman, (eds.): *Proceedings of the Sixth Text Retrieval Conference*, NIST Gaithersburg (1998) 125-136

[5]   Tuson, Optimisation with Hillclimbing on Steriods: An Overview of Neightbourhood Search Techniques. *Proceedings of the 10th Young Operational research Conference*, Operational Research Society (1998) 141-156

[6]   F. Glover and M. Laguna, Tabu Search, Kluwer Academic Publishers, 1997

[7]   D. Harman, Overview of the Fourth Text REtrieval Conference (TREC-4). In: D.K. Harman, (ed.): *Proceedings of the Fourth Text Retrieval Conference*, NIST Gaithersburg (1996) 1-24

[8]   D. Hawking, "The Design and Implementation of a Parallel Document Retrieval Engine", Technical Report TR-CS-95-08, Department of Computer Science, Australian National University (1995)

[9]   Hutchinson, Algorithm Learning, Clarendon Press (1994)

[10]   J. Kittler, Feature selection and extraction. In: T.Y. Young and K. Fu, (ed.): *Handbook of Pattern Recognition and Image Processing*, Academic Press (1986) 59-83

A Weighting Scheme for Star-Graphs

Jean Martinet[1,2], Iadh Ounis[2], Yves Chiaramella[1], and Philippe Mulhem[1,3]

[1] MRIM, CLIPS-IMAG, Grenoble, France
{jean.martinet,yves.chiaramella,philippe.mulhem}@imag.fr
http://www-clips.imag.fr/mrim
[2] IR Group, Computing Science Department, Glasgow, UK
{jean,ounis}@dcs.gla.ac.uk
http://ir.dcs.gla.ac.uk
[3] IPAL, Singapore
mulhem@i2r.a-star.edu.sg
http://www.i2r.a-star.edu.sg

Abstract. A *star-graph* is a conceptual graph that contains a single relation, with some concepts linked to it. They are elementary pieces of information describing combinations of concepts. We use star-graphs as descriptors - or index terms - for image content representation. This allows for relational indexing and expression of complex user needs, in comparison to classical text retrieval, where simple keywords are generally used as document descriptors. In classical text retrieval, the keywords are weighted to give emphasis to good document *descriptors* and *discriminators* where the most popular weighting schemes are based on variations of *tf.idf*. In this paper, we present an extension of *tf.idf*, introducing a new weighting scheme suited for star-graphs. This weighting scheme is based on a local analysis of star-graphs indexing a document and a global analysis of star-graphs across the whole collection. We show and discuss some preliminary results evaluating the performance of this weighting scheme applied to image retrieval.

1 Introduction

The classical models of Information Retrieval (IR) consider that a document is described by a set of representative index terms. In text retrieval for instance, index terms are keywords extracted from the collection. Because all index terms in a document do not describe it equally, they are assigned numerical weights. The purpose of a weighting scheme is to give emphasis to important terms, quantifying how well they semantically describe and discriminate documents.

When dealing with image documents, we can use keywords to describe main elements appearing on an image, e.g. "MAN" or "SKY". However some information contained in the image cannot be expressed or modeled by keywords themselves [OP98], such as spacial relations between objects, or object attributes. Expression of the spacial relations between objects have been considered in research by Bertino and Catania [BC98] and Di Sciascio and colleagues [SMM02], where the authors define languages to represent shapes and their position on the

F. Sebastiani (Ed.): ECIR 2003, LNCS 2633, pp. 546–554, 2003.

image. This allows for relational image indexing and querying. In order to encapsulate the complex knowledge related to either an image description or a user need, a formalism that supports relations is required. In particular, the knowledge representation formalism of *conceptual graphs*, introduced by Sowa [Sow84], has been used for image representation by Mechkour [Mec95] and image retrieval by Ounis and Pasca [OP98]. We use conceptual graphs to index the images in the collection, assigning some numerical values to elementary sub-graphs in order to represent the importance of a sub-graph in the index.

The work presented here is inspired by the *term frequency* and *inverse document frequency* (*tf.idf*) used in text retrieval[SM83, SB88]. Among the extensions to *tf.idf* in image retrieval, Wang and Du [WD01] introduced the *region frequency* and *inverse picture frequency* (*rf.ipf*), a region-based measure for image retrieval purposes. The images in the collection are segmented into regions, employing several features (e.g. colour components). The *rf* measures how frequently a region feature occurs in a picture, and the *ipf* attaches a higher value to region features that occur in few images, therefore considered good discriminators. All regions are assigned an *rf.ipf* weight, that is stored for the image matching process. Research by Wang is based on signal analysis; it does not imply symbolic meaning of the segmented regions, and no formalism is applied.

In our work, we combine signal and symbolic approaches, using a measure of image region importance which is based on visual parameters determined by the user's perception [Oun99], and an extension of the *idf* using a new definition of a *concept occurrence* in a document. For the classical *idf*, the documents containing an occurrence of a concept c, are counted. The basic idea behind our extension is that a document that contains c', where c' is a specific of c, is somehow *about* c, thereby it should be taken into account in the *idf* definition. The generic/specific relations of the concepts are defined in a lattice.

This paper describes a sound way of weighting elementary conceptual graphs, that are used as index terms within an IR model. The remaining sections are organized as follows: in Section 2 we briefly describe how documents are represented, in Section 3 we examine the elements to be considered in weighting a star-graph. Current experiments are presented and discussed in Section 4.

2   Document Representation

Our image representation model shows the images that were originally represented by conceptual graphs. The conceptual graphs are split into elementary pieces of information, that are considered to be the document descriptors.

2.1   Conceptual Graphs (CGs)

The conceptual graph formalism provides an expressive framework that supports relational image content indexing. A conceptual graph is a bipartite oriented graph, composed with concepts and relations [Sow84]. Concepts and relations are organized in a lattice, which indicates generic/specific relationships. Figure 1

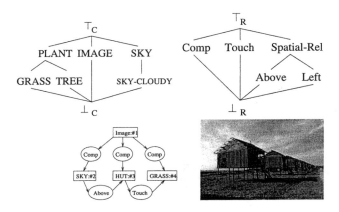

Fig. 1. Example of concept lattice (up left), relation lattice (up right), and a conceptual graph indexing an image (down)

shows example of lattices. We use conceptual graphs to represent images content. Each segmented region of the image is associated with a concept, where the conceptual relations describe relationships between these regions. The conceptual graph, Figure 1, is the index of the picture on the right. This corresponds to the symbolic, structural, and spatial facets of $EMIR^2$, Mechkour's image representation model [Mec95].

We break-up the conceptual graphs into elementary pieces of information. These pieces of information will constitute our indexing terms. For that, we use the *split* operation.

Definition 1. *The* split *operation on CGs is defined as follow [AO00]: let* $[c]$ *be a concept node of a conceptual graph.*

1. *Introduce a new node* $[x]$.
2. *Replace* $[c] \rightarrow (r) \rightarrow [c_1]$ *(or* $[c_1] \rightarrow (r) \rightarrow [c]$*) with* $[x] \rightarrow (r) \rightarrow [c_1]$ *(or* $[c_1] \rightarrow (r) \rightarrow [x]$*), where* $[c_1]$ *is an arbitrary concept in the graph.*
3. *Replace* $[x]$ *with* $[c]$.

This operation introduces a node in the graph, while the number of edges remains constant. It results in two connected, well-formed subgraphs. Let's now consider a graph on which *split* is iterated until each node has exactly one adjacent edge. At each step, the total number of edges remains constant and the number of adjacent edges for one of the concepts decreases. Hence this procedure terminates. A set of well-formed sub-graphs containing only one relation is obtained at the end, which is called a *table of graphs* [AO00]. A table of graphs can be considered a set of star-graphs.

Definition 2. *A* star-graph *is a conceptual graph that contains a single relation. It consists of a single conceptual relation* r, *every arc that belongs to* r, *and every concept* c *that is linked by some arc* (r, c) *that belongs to* r.

We call them star-graph because they are star-shaped conceptual graphs: the relation is the center of the star, and the arcs linking the concepts to the relation form the branches of the star.

2.2   Star-Graphs (SGs) as Index Terms

The set of SGs extracted from the collection of conceptual graphs has a lattice structure. Its partial order relation $\leq$, is the graph projection [Sow84]. This lattice is limited at the top by $\top_{SG}$ and at the bottom by $\bot_{SG}$.

The star-graphs obtained at the end of the *split* iteration are the document building blocks, they are considered document descriptors. From now on, star-graphs will be referred to as *terms*. As for text documents, the weight of a descriptor should represent how important this descriptor is as a part of the document's index and how rare it is within the whole collection. For instance, we want to know how well the term $[SKY] \rightarrow (Above) \rightarrow [HUT]$ describes the document shown in Figure 1 and to what extent this term allows for the discrimination of the documents across the collection. The following section describes a weighting scheme for an SG, based on a combination of a local analysis of elements in a document (a *document-related value*) and a global analysis of the indexed collection (a *collection-related value*).

3   Term Weighting

In this section, we address the extension of the classical *tf.idf* in the context of image retrieval. We define:

- a local analysis for image index terms, that corresponds to the *tf* for text. It consists of determining the importance of a term in a document,
- a global analysis corresponding to the *idf*. Terms are assigned a value according to their distribution in the collection, using some information from the lattice. According to the definition of a lattice, the more specific a term is, the more information it contains, hence the greater it's important to retrieve relevant documents. This global analysis is aimed at emphasizing the impact of more specific terms of the the lattice, while moderating the effect of more generic terms.

3.1   Local Analysis

We define a *Local* value for the index terms. A star-graph consists of a set of concepts with a relation. In order to assign a local value to a star-graph, we need its concepts to be assigned local values. These values are related to a user's perception, that depends on parameters such as the relative surface of the segmented region, its contrast and position on the image [Oun99]. We assume that every concept c of a document d is assigned a value $Local_{c,d}$. The

Local value of an index term t is related to the importance of its composing concepts:

$$Local_{t,d} = f(Local_{c_1,d}, Local_{c_2,d}, \cdots, Local_{c_n,d})$$

where n is the number of concepts in t (i.e the relation is n-adic). For instance, if we assume that the importance of a combination of concepts is the one of the most important concepts in the combination, we can set f to be *max*:

$$Local_{t,d} = \max_{c_j \in t} Local_{c_j,d} \qquad (1)$$

The *Local* value for the term $[SKY] \to (Above) \to [HUT]$ would be the maximum of the *Local* values of $[SKY]$ and $[HUT]$.

3.2 Global Analysis

The objective is to assign a collection-dependent value to a term, depending on its distribution in the collection. The idea is to consider not only the documents in which the term appears, but also the documents containing some terms specific to it. Indeed, the documents that are *about* $[SKY] \to (Above) \to [GRASS]$, are also *about* $[SKY] \to (Above) \to [PLANT]$. Consequently, if a query contains $[SKY] \to (Above) \to [PLANT]$, then the documents containing $[SKY] \to (Above) \to [GRASS]$ are relevant to this query.

Definition 3. *The occurrence of a term t' in a document implies the* implicit apparition *of the terms $\{t|t' \leq t\}$ in this document.*

If $[SKY] \to (Above) \to [GRASS]$ appears in a document, then $[SKY] \to (Above) \to [PLANT]$ appears implicitly. We define the occurrence ratio $p(t)$ of a term t as the number of documents in which it appears implicitly, divided by the the number of documents in which $\top_{SG}$ appears implicitly:

$$p(t) = \frac{card\{d \in D | t' \leq t, t' \in d\}}{card\{d \in D | t' \leq \top_{SG}, t' \in d\}}$$

where d is a document of the collection D. If we call n_T the number of documents in which t implicitly appears and N is the total number of documents in the collection: $p(t) = \frac{n_t}{N}$. Let's interpret $\neg t$ as the union of all the terms *not* below t in the star-graph lattice: $\neg t = \cup_{\neg(t \leq t)} t'$. With this interpretation, $p(t)$ verifies all classical Kolmogorov properties of a probabilistic distribution and therefore is isomorphic to a probability. The *Global* value of a term t, in a collection, is defined as the amount of information held by the term:

$$Global_t = -log(p(t)) \qquad (2)$$

We have defined a local and a global analysis for the star-graphs. Based on the above equations, we can now define the weight of a star-graph.

3.3   Weighting a Star-Graph

The weight W of a term should depend on its importance in the graph and on its distribution in the collection. Based on Equations (1) and (2), a term can be weighted as a combination (e.g. multiplication) of both local and global analysis:

$$W_{t,d} = Local_{t,d} \times Global_t \tag{3}$$

In the section, we have defined a weight for a star-graph (Equation (3)). This weight is the result of a local and global analysis, inspired by the use of the *tf.idf*. In the following section, we describe an implementation and an evaluation for this weighting scheme, on a collection of images.

4   Evaluation

In this section, we present the results of the evaluation for our approach for image retrieval. Instead of using the classical operation to match conceptual graphs (projection operator [Sow84]), we use star-graphs as index terms for the vector space model of IR.

4.1   Image Collection

We used a image test collection [Lim01] providing 498 personal photographs and their indexes according to Mechkour's model [Mec95], as well as the concept and relation lattices. The concept lattice is composed with 104 concepts, such as $[SKY]$, $[BUILDING]$, or $[WATER]$, and has a maximal depth of 6. In this collection, the concepts are weighted only according to their relative surface. For instance, if a building occupies 30% of an image, it will be weighted 0.3. The relation lattice contains 46 relations, such as $(Above)$, or (On_The_Left), and has a maximal depth of 3. A sample of the photographs is given in Figure 2. CGs are composed with an average of 29 SGs. In total, 3854 terms are extracted from the index. This corresponds to the number of dimensions of the vector space model. The test collection provides a set of 38 queries with relevant documents association. Figure 3 shows one of the queries, describing "a person between two buildings". Queries are *propagated* in order to allow a meaningful matching [MCM02]. That is to say, terms specific to the original query terms are added. Indeed, a query containing a term t should match with a document

Fig. 2. A sample of images from the collection

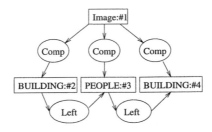

Fig. 3. A query from the test collection

containing a term t', $t' \leq t$, The approach is similar to standard query expansion using a thesaurus, where terms semantically related to the query are added, *except* that instead of synonymy relations, we have typed relations coming from the lattice (generic/specific) that induce a direction for the expansion. The complexity of this operation depends on the size of the lattices. Indeed, the wider and the deeper they are, the more terms are likely to be added.

The system was built on top of SMART [Sal71], that we used as an evaluation kernel. We have evaluated the impact of the weighting scheme defined in the equation (3), in comparison to a boolean weighting scheme.

4.2   Impact of the Weighting Scheme

This experiment is aimed at evaluating the performance of our weighting scheme, that is integrated to the system. We ran four experiments. Our weighting scheme is decomposed, in order to evaluate the effects of individual elements. We also compared the results with the classical *idf*, calculated over the terms. For each run, we used different weighting schemes. The results of the evaluation are presented in Table 1.

We can see that integrating the *Local* value in the document index yields a slight improvement of the average precision across this collection. The use of the *Global* value did improve the average precision as well. In the indexes as in the queries, almost only the most specific concepts (i.e. concepts having no specific in the lattice except $\perp_C$) where used. As the aim of the *Global* value is

Table 1. Average precision for 4 different weighing schemes

Document weights - Query weights		Average precision	Relative change in %-age
Boolean	Boolean	0.4850	0.0
Local	Boolean	0.4893	+ 0.89
Local × *idf*	*idf*	0.4924	+ 1.53
Local × *Global*	*Global*	0.4954	+ 2.14

to moderate the impact of generic terms, while emphasizing more specific ones, the effect of the *Global* value is not as important as we expected, on this test collection. However, we stress that it would be efficient on collections where more generic terms are used in the index as well as in the queries.

5 Conclusion

In this paper, we addressed the problem of weighting elementary pieces of information, the star-graphs. We defined a weighting scheme, that is inspired by the classical *tf.idf* used for text retrieval, employing a *Local* and a *Global* analysis for a star-graph. Our approach introduces a novel framework to combine an expressive knowledge representation formalism with a classical IR model.

We applied our research to image retrieval, in the context of a vector space model. Experiments on an image test collection have shown that integrating our weighting scheme yields improvements in average precision. Further experiments are still being carried out to determine this impact more precisely, especially on the larger FERMI collection [CM97].

Although we have applied the use of SGs as index terms to image retrieval in the context of a vector space model, we think that it could be used in any other media. Moreover, the approach could extend the classical textual IR systems, providing a more powerful indexing language.

References

[AO00]   G. Amati and I. Ounis. Conceptual graphs and first order logic. *The Computer Journal*, 43(1):1–12, 2000.

[BC98]   E. Bertino and B. Catania. A constraint-based approach to shape management in multimedia databases. *ACM Multimedia Journal*, 6(1):2–16, 1998.

[CM97]   Y. Chiaramella and M. Mechkour. *Indexing an image test collection*. Technical Report, FERMI BRA 8134, 1997.

[Lim01] J.-H. Lim. Building visual vocabulary for image indexation and query formulation. *Pattern Analysis and Applications (Special Issue on Image Indexation)*, 4(2/3):125–139, 2001.

[MCM02] J. Martinet, Y. Chiaramella, and P. Mulhem. Un modèle vectoriel étendu de recherche d'information adapté aux images. In *INFORSID'02*, pages 337–348, 2002.

[Mec95] M. Mechkour. *Un Modele etendu de representation et de correspondance d'images pour la recherche d'informations*. Ph.D. Thesis, Joseph Fourier University, Grenoble, 1995.

[OP98]   I. Ounis and M. Pasca. Relief: Combing expressiveness and rapidity into a single system. In *SIGIR'98*, pages 266–274, 1998.

[Oun99] I. Ounis. A flexible weighting scheme for multimedia documents. In *Database and Expert Systems Applications*, pages 392–405, 1999.

[Sal71] G. Salton. *The SMART Retrieval System*. Prentice Hall, 1971.

[SB88]   G. Salton and C. Buckley. Term-weighting approaches in automatic text retrieval. In *Information Processing and Management*, pages 513–523, 1988.

[SM83]   G. Salton and M. McGill. *Introduction to Modern Information Retrieval.* McGraw-Hill, 1983.

[SMM02]   E. Di Sciascio, F. M.Donini, and M. Mongiello. Structured knowledge representation for image retrieval. *Journal of Artificial Intelligence Research,* 16:209–257, 2002.

[Sow84]   J. F. Sowa. *Conceptual Structures.* Addison-Wesley, Reading, MA, 1984.

[WD01]   J. Z. Wang and Y. Du. Rf*ipf: A weighting scheme for multimedia information retrieval. In *ICIAP*, pages 380–385, 2001.

Phrase-Based Hierarchical Clustering
of Web Search Results

Irmina Masłowska

Institute of Computing Science, Poznań University of Technology
Piotrowo 3A, 60-965 Poznań, Poland
irmina.maslowska@cs.put.poznan.pl

Abstract. The paper addresses the problem of clustering text documents coming from the Web. We apply clustering to support users in interactive browsing through hierarchically organized search results as opposed to the standard ranked-list presentation. We propose a clustering method that is tailored to on-line processing of Web documents and takes into account the time aspect, the particular requirements of clustering texts, and readability of the produced hierarchy. Finally, we present the user interface of an actual system in which the method is applied to the results of a popular search engine.

1 Introduction

The problem known as *information overload* becomes particularly obvious to those who use the Internet as their source of information. To support them in their efforts a number of information access tools are offered which have been developed on the basis of information retrieval (IR) techniques. Those techniques can be roughly categorized as intended for searching or browsing.

Automatic search engines are particularly popular information access tools on the Web. Their advantages include: large number of indexed sites, improving accuracy, and relatively good adapting abilities. On the other hand, the number of documents they return is usually overwhelming. Presenting such results in a standard ranked list, without providing the user with appropriate navigation tools can turn the process of finding information into a tedious job. With the ever-growing Web resources and the increasing number of their users the need for new intuitive information access methods becomes even more apparent.

We believe that among various navigation utilities expandable *dendrograms* (i.e. tree-like hierarchies of document groups) are especially well suited for organizing search results because Web users are familiar with such a presentation manner, since it has been used for years in manually crafted Web directories.

The aim of this work is to present a system which employs a novel, fast, fully automatic document clustering technique to produce a navigable hierarchy of Web document groups delivered with meaningful, yet concise descriptions.

The paper is organized as follows. Section 2 gives an overview of document clustering methods. Section 3 describes the special requirements, which have

F. Sebastiani (Ed.): ECIR 2003, LNCS 2633, pp. 555–562, 2003.

to be considered in clustering Web search results. Section 4 presents the proposed hierarchical clustering algorithm and discusses its suitability for the specified requirements. Finally, Sect. 5 describes a system implementing the proposed methodology and gives our conclusions on its performance on Web documents.

2   Related Work

For years document clustering had been extensively investigated in the field of IR [13] for the purpose of the so-called *cluster search*, in which document search is improved by pre-clustering the entire corpus as implied by the *cluster hypothesis*, which states that similar documents are relevant to the same queries [7].

The above described classical paradigm has been recently given the name of *persistent clustering*, as opposed to *ephemeral clustering* in which the grouping process is performed on-line for a dynamically generated input document set [4]. Our study falls within the latter paradigm. It follows such works as [3, 15, 4] where clustering is considered a comprehensive method for accessing information and is applied as a post-retrieval browsing technique.

Clustering algorithms are typically categorized – according to the generated structure – as either flat or hierarchical. And although hierarchical clustering seems most fit for on-line search and browsing purposes, flat methods have been given considerable attention, because of their relatively low time complexity.

Due to space limitations we give only a notion of two recognized algorithms for flat clustering. Scatter/Gather is a clustering method tailored for dealing with large text corpora, and specifically search results [3]. Due to operating on small random samples of documents Scatter/Gather achieves the complexity $O(kn)$[1].

Another interesting algorithm for flat clustering of search results, called Suffix Tree Clustering (STC), has been introduced in [15]. It groups together documents, which share the same phrases. STC not only forms readably described, meaningful clusters, but also scales well to large text corpora due to its linear time complexity. Moreover, it is capable of forming overlapping clusters.

The probably most acknowledged algorithm for hierarchical document clustering is Agglomerative Hierarchical Clustering (AHC) which uses a similarity function to iteratively consider all pairs of clusters build so far, and merge the two most similar clusters. Typically, the processed documents are represented as sparse TF-IDF vectors (which inherently ignore dependencies between words in the documents [5]) with the cosine measure serving as the similarity function [9]. When comparing two clusters, a single-link method is preferred mainly because of its relatively low time complexity $O(n^2)$, as opposed to the at best $O(n^2 \log n)$ time complexity of complete-link method. It has been observed, however, that in the IR applications complete-link produces clusters of higher quality [11].

The commonly recognized shortcomings of AHC when applied to texts, are: its sensitivity to a stopping criterion [6], its greedy manner of choosing the clusters to be merged, and its unsuitability for clustering data of considerably

---

[1] n and k denote the number of documents and the number of considered clusters, respectively. The number of words per document is assumed bounded by a constant.

big size [1]. An additional limitation of the method is its partitioning character (i.e. one document cannot be placed in more than one branch of the dendrogram).

3 Specific Aspects of On-Line Text Clustering

The application of clustering for on-line processing of Web search results imposes specific requirements on the performance of the used techniques, as well as on their outcome. These requirements include: (i) efficiency, (ii) navigable organization of the results, (iii) relevance accompanied by informativeness of the outcome, and (iv) ability to produce overlapping clusters.

Efficiency is the key requirement of any on-line application since the time a user waits cannot be longer than seconds. Thus, the complexity of the clustering method has to be kept as low as possible. Additionally, the method has to be able to operate on snippets returned by the search service, since there is no time to download the whole documents [15].

Navigable organization of the results can be obtained by using expandable dendrograms produced with hierarchical clustering methods. To be really navigable, however, the nodes of the dendrograms have to be supplied with automatically created, yet meaningful descriptions.

Relevance of results is obtained when a clustering method groups documents relevant to the user's query separately from irrelevant ones [15]. In our opinion, the relevance aspect also involves ensuring that the descriptions of the created clusters are informative, i.e. readable and adequate to their content.

The need for *overlapping* in document clustering has been explained in [2]. The fact that a document addresses two or more separate thematic categories implies that it should be placed in two or more branches of the dendrogram.

Taking into consideration the above outlined aspects, in Sect. 4 we propose a hierarchical clustering algorithm aimed at processing Web search results.

4 Proposed Methodology

Of all the clustering algorithms described in Sect. 2 STC seems to be the closest to fulfill the requirements outlined in Sect. 3. Unfortunately, its adaptation for hierarchical clustering is not straightforward. Nevertheless, it constitutes a starting point for the proposed clustering methodology, and thus needs to be sketched out in this section (refer to [14] for a detailed description).

STC is a linear time algorithm that uses suffix trees [10] to identify groups of similar documents based on the phrases shared within each group. A *phrase* is defined as an ordered sequence of words, and a set of documents that share a phrase is called a *base cluster* [15]. The above definitions clearly allow for overlapping or even identical base clusters since several documents may share more than one phrase. Another observation is that the phrase that originated a base cluster can serve as a ready informative description of its content.

Each of the base clusters is assigned a score which is a function of the number of documents the base cluster contains and the number of words (excluding stop-words) that make up its phrase (see [14] for details). An arbitrarily chosen number k of top scoring base clusters is then taken to be processed further.

The STC algorithm performs merging of sufficiently overlapping clusters based on a similarity measure calculated for each pair of base clusters. Base clusters whose similarity equals 1 are merged to form final clusters. The similarity measure $Sim(B_r, B_s)$ for two base clusters B_r and B_s, with sizes $|B_r|$ and $|B_s|$ respectively, is defined as follows [15]:

Definition 1. $|B_r \cap B_s| / |B_r| > \alpha \wedge |B_r \cap B_s| / |B_s| > \alpha \Leftrightarrow Sim(B_r, B_s) = 1$, *otherwise* $Sim(B_r, B_s) = 0$, *where α is an arbitrarily chosen merge threshold.*

The original STC algorithm has been proved to outperform other popular clustering algorithms in the achieved precision and speed even when operating on snippets instead of whole documents [15].

The Hierarchical Suffix Tree Clustering (HSTC) technique proposed herein is based on an observation that the documents grouped in one base cluster can constitute a subset of another base cluster. That reflects a situation when a topic-specific group of documents is a subgroup of a more general group. Naturally, the cluster corresponding to the topic-specific group should be placed in the same branch of the hierarchy but at a lower level than the cluster corresponding to the general group. HSTC provides the methodology for organizing the base clusters identified in Web search results into a navigable hierarchy. It uses an oriented inclusion graph as a representation of the relations between base clusters.

HSTC has the following five logical steps: (i) identifying base clusters, (ii) merging identical base clusters, (iii) constructing an oriented inclusion graph, (iv) eliminating cycles from the inclusion graph, and (v) building the final hierarchy.

The step of identifying base clusters has been taken "as is" from STC. For the sake of speed, we also take the limited number k of best scoring base clusters for further processing. The time complexity of this step is $O(n)$.

The empirical evaluation shows that often whole groups of the identified base clusters are identical (as for the documents contained). We merge identical base clusters into a single cluster labeled with a set of phrases. That improves the efficiency of the consecutive processing. This step is equivalent to the merge phase of the original STC with $\alpha=1$. Its complexity is at worst $O(k^2)$ if there are no two identical base clusters. Due to the transitiveness of the identity relation the complexity decreases when groups of identical base clusters exist.

We define an inclusion relation between two clusters as follows:

Definition 2. C_i *includes* C_j *(denoted by* $C_i \rightarrow C_j$*)* $\Leftrightarrow |C_i \cap C_j| / |C_j| >= \alpha$, C_i, C_j *are clusters of documents, and $\alpha \in (0.5; 1]$ is an inclusion threshold.*

According to the above definition an oriented inclusion graph $G=(V, A)$ is built, where V is a set of vertices corresponding one-to-one to the processed clusters and A is a set of arcs, each representing the existence of inclusion relation between two clusters. The arcs point from the more general to the more specific cluster (just as implied by the symbol of the inclusion relation). It is worth observing that the inclusion relation is not transitive, thus all pairs of clusters have to be considered. The complexity of this step is $O(k^2)$.

If two or more vertices of the inclusion graph are connected within a cycle the HSTC procedure merges their corresponding clusters into a single cluster labeled with a set of phrases. This is reflected in reduction of all the vertices forming the cycle into a single vertex in the inclusion graph. This step of the algorithm profits from the fact that the cycles in the inclusion graph are short and that they are eliminated progressively; its complexity is $O(k^3)$ (it should be remembered that k is a given constant).

The final dendrogram is built top-down starting with the most general clusters. To identify them we need to find the *kernel* [8] of the acyclic graph.

Definition 3. Kernel *of an oriented graph* $G = (V, A)$, *composed of a set of vertices* V *and a set of arcs* A, *is a set* K *of vertices* $K \subseteq V$, *which fulfills the following two stability conditions:*

- Internal stability – *no two kernel vertices are connected by an arc,*
- External stability – *for every vertex from outside the kernel there exists at least one arc from a kernel vertex to the considered vertex.*

The final hierarchy is constructed by putting the kernel clusters at the highest hierarchy level, and adding subclusters accordingly to the arcs of the graph in a depth-in manner, until an end cluster (terminal vertex) is reached. The internal stability of the kernel ensures that the clusters in the highest hierarchy level do not include one another, the external stability of the kernel ensures that every other cluster is placed in at some lower level of *at least* one branch of the dendrogram. The complexity of the kernel finding algorithm is $O(k^2)$.

As it can be noticed, our approach doubly addresses the 'several topics per document' postulate [2]: not only can one document belong to more than one thematic group, but a whole group of documents can also be an adequate subgroup of several more general groups located in different branches of the dendrogram.

5   Implementation

Since the aim of our work is to deliver a navigable hierarchical interface to Web search results we employed HSTC for processing the results of a popular search engine, which intrinsically returns a typical ranked list of snippets. HSTC has been embedded as a module within Carrot [12] – a Java-based system which implements the STC method for English and Polish text repositories.

In the remainder of the section we discuss the user interface, the typical outcome of HSTC, and give our conclusions on some of its performance aspects.

We chose to use the popular tree-control representation of the results, mainly because it is familiar to most computer users, secondly because it is a natural representation for a dendrogram. The included screenshots taken from a working session show that the main system window is vertically split into two panes: the left one presenting the hierarchy of labeled document clusters, and the right one presenting the content of the selected cluster.

The first screen presented to the user after the issued query has been processed contains the top hierarchy clusters (labeled with corresponding phrases).

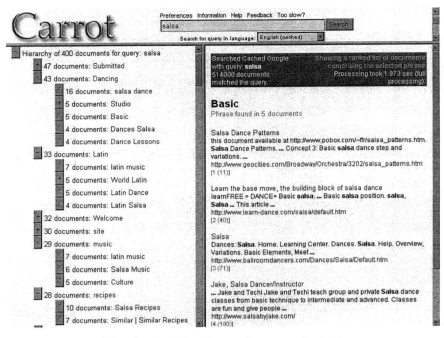

Fig. 1. HSTC outcome for query "salsa"

At the start of a browsing session the right pane contains documents corresponding to the root of the tree (the issued query itself), that is the original ranked list obtained from the search engine. We believe that presenting a user with the form of results he is accustomed to increases the chances that he will not get discouraged at the first glance.

Other aspects of the user interface are also kept intuitive. The "+" button next to the cluster description indicates that this node can be further expanded. If a cluster does not have any subclusters it is marked with a grayed "*" button. An already expanded cluster can be collapsed by pushing the "-" marked button.

For comparativeness with similar systems [4, 15] we chose "salsa" as an example query. Figure 1 presents the hierarchy viewed accordingly to the interests of a user who would rather learn about the salsa music and dancing than cooking. The focus is set to cluster labeled "Basic"; perhaps the user wants to learn about the basics of salsa dancing. She might then go to "Dance Lessons" node.

It can be noticed that HSTC is indeed able to recognize that a group of documents is a subgroup of more than one more general groups – the "latin music" node can be reached as well from the "Latin" as from the "music" node.

The outcome of HSTC for a more systemized input can be seen in Fig. 2. The dendrogram obtained for query "machine learning" seems to achieve higher quality than for the previous query. Also the phrases which label the nodes of the dendrogram are more descriptive. The better organization of search results for this query is probably due to the fact that the pages concerning *machine learning* are themselves better organized.

6   Conclusion

This paper proposes a hierarchical clustering method tailored to the specific requirements of on-line processing of Web search results. It has been designed to provide efficiency, navigable organization of the results, relevance accompanied by informativeness of the results, and ability to produce overlapping clusters.

Surprisingly, although the problem of clustering search results has been addressed in several cited papers, its special aspects have often been suppressed at the evaluation stage. Typically, during evaluation no overlapping is allowed, hierarchical results are transformed into flat, or the existence of cluster descriptions is overlooked. We claim that document clustering needs new evaluation methods considering all their particular requirements. Design of such is part of our planned research.

The experiments performed meanwhile show that HSTC achieves the same high precision as the STC method [15, 14]. This is a straightforward consequence of the fact that both methods use the same underlying concept of base clusters and the highest-level clusters which are placed at the top of the results given by HSTC are the same clusters which achieve the highest score in the STC method.

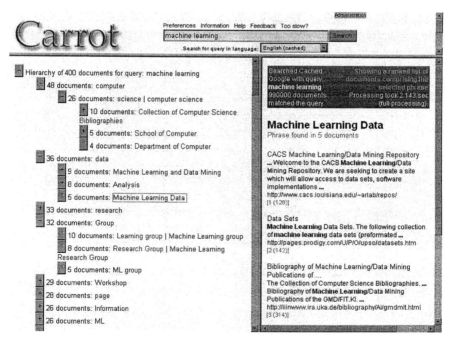

Fig. 2. HSTC outcome for query "machine learning"

Acknowledgements

The author wishes to express her gratitude to Prof. Roman Słowiński for his helpful remarks on this work and to Mr. Dawid Weiss for making his implementation of STC available as open source, thus providing an excellent platform for implementing HSTC. The author also wishes to acknowledge financial support from Foundation for Polish Science, subsidy FNP 16-1.

References

[1] Boley D., Gini M. et al. (1999) Partitioning-based clustering for web document categorization. Decision Support Systems 27 (3), 329-341

[2] Hearst M. A. (1998) The use of categories and clusters in information access interfaces. T. Strzalkowski (ed.), Natural Language Information Retrieval. Kluwer Academic Publishers

[3] Hearst M. A., Pedersen J. O. (1996) Reexamining the Cluster Hypothesis: Scatter/Gather on Retrieval Results. Proc. of the 19th Int. ACM SIGIR Conf. on Research and Development in Information Retrieval, 85-92

[4] Maarek Y. S., Fagin R. et al. (2000) Ephemeral document clustering for Web applications. IBM Research Report RJ 10186, Haifa

[5] Masłowska I., Weiss D. (2000) JUICER – a data mining approach to information extraction from the WWW, Foundations of Computing and Decision Sciences 25 (2), 67-87

[6] Milligan G. W., Cooper M. C. (1985) An examination of procedures for detecting the number of clusters in a data set. Psychometrika 50, 159-79

[7] van Rijsbergen C. J. (1979) Information Retrieval, Butterworths, London

[8] Roy B. (1969) Algèbre moderne et théorie des graphes orientées vers les sciences économiques et sociales, Dunod

[9] Salton G. (1989) Automatic Text Processing, Addison-Wesley

[10] Ukkonen E. (1995) On-line construction of suffix trees, Algorithmica 14, 249-260

[11] Voorhees E. M. (1986) Implementing agglomerative hierarchical clustering algorithms for use in document retrieval. Information Processing and Management 22, 465-76

[12] Weiss D. (2001) A Clustering Interface for Web Search Results in Polish and English. Master Thesis, Poznań University of Technology (http://www.cs.put.poznan.pl/dweiss/index.php/publications/)

[13] Willett P. (1988) Recent trends in hierarchical document clustering: A critical review. Information Processing & Management 24 (5), 577-597

[14] Zamir O. (1999) Clustering Web Documents: A Phrase-Based Method for Grouping Search Engine Results. Doctoral dissertation, University of Washington

[15] Zamir O., Etzioni O. (1998) Web Document Clustering: A Feasibility Demonstration. Proc. of the 21st Int. ACM SIGIR Conf. on Research and Development in Information Retrieval, 46-54

Aggregated Feature Retrieval for MPEG-7

Jiamin Ye* and Alan F. Smeaton

Centre for Digital Video Processing
Dublin City University, Glasnevin, Dublin 9, Ireland
{jiaminye,asmeaton}@computing.dcu.ie

Abstract. In this paper we present an initial study on the use of both high and low level MPEG-7 descriptions for video retrieval. A brief survey of current XML indexing techniques shows that an IR-based retrieval method provides a better foundation for retrieval as it satisfies important retrieval criteria such as content ranking and approximate matching. An aggregation technique for XML document retrieval is adapted to an MPEG-7 indexing structure by assigning semantic meanings to various audio/visual features and this is presented here.

1   Introduction

The challenge for video search is to provide support for the following capabilities:

- Textual queries at different segment levels such as individual frames, shots, scenes, or perhaps whole programmes. Available information for searching should include meta-data, teletext and ASR transcripts.
- Image or video clip queries also at different segment levels. Available support for searching should include various visual and audio features.
- Content-based indexing and similarity comparisons. A video IR system needs to utilise available audio-visual content-based indexing and retrieval techniques. Visual indexing should include techniques like region colour, edge component histogram and face recognition. Audio indexing should use techniques like speech and music recognition. Similarity comparison techniques will vary depending on the indexing technique used.

The above list is representative of what contemporary video IR demands and building systems which realise this means engineering complex systems where interoperability is also desirable and the MPEG-7 video standard delivers an appropriate framework for building this type of video search engine. MPEG-7 is a recently developed international standard for multimedia mark-up where the language describes the syntax and semantics to describe features of multimedia contents at various granularity levels [1]. The challenge for MPEG-7 is supporting video retrieval, allowing a variety features to be indexed on which retrieval can be based.

---

* This paper is based on research undertaken by the first author as a Ph.D.student.

F. Sebastiani (Ed.): ECIR 2003, LNCS 2633, pp. 563-570, 2003.

In this paper we present an initial study of the use of both high and low level MPEG-7 descriptions for video retrieval. Some related work based video retrieval for MPEG-7 will be given in section 2. Since an MPEG -7 description is a standardised XML document, a short survey on current XML indexing techniques is given in section 3 to address their strengths in terms of video retrieval. This shows that IR-based XML indexing provides a better foundation since it satisfies criteria such as content ranking and approximate matching, particularly useful in schema-constrained environments. Section 4 explains the aggregation technique used in IR-based XML indexing. An MPEG-7 indexing framework for video retrieval is given in section 5. This extends the Kazai et al's [2] model to handle audio/visual features as auxiliary evidence to the existing term weight indexing. Finally, we then conclude the paper.

2   Related Work Based on Video Retrieval for MPEG-7

There are a number of related projects that involve searching MPEG-7 descriptions but two are of particular interest. The SAMBITS project has built a consumer terminal that supports the MPEG-7 storage and delivery [3]. Queries to this system are text based and consider content (e.g. keywords) and meta-data (e.g. authors), possibly with an XML structure. The advantage is the ability to integrate content-based, fact-based and structural information.

The second project has designed an MPEG-7 retrieval model based on inference networks and was developed to capture the structural, content-based and positional information by a Document and Query network [4]. Positional information is context-related and contains and the location of content within a document. The MPEG-7 inference network has three layers: Document, Contextual and Conceptual while the Query network consists of concept and context nodes and query operators. Retrieval is done in a bottom-up fashion by accumulating evidence from all layers to find the best shots.

3   Survey of XML Indexing Techniques

Some insights into current XML indexing and retrieval methods are now given as these methods can be tailored for MPEG-7 video retrieval. The methods can be classified into three categories:

- *Information retrieval based indexing* brings the structure of documents together with the content into one unified model. Text indexing methods generally use the traditional tf-idf term weight indexing structure and its variants. Returned items are ranked based on their estimated relevance to a given query and most studies emphasise developing the right ranking formulae such as aggregation-based retrieval within schema-constrained environments [2].
- *Path expression based indexing* regards an XML document as a rooted ordered graph containing a set of nodes (i.e. element ID) and a set of edges (i.e. element name or attribute name). The path index such as Dataguides [5] maintains the

structural summaries of an XML collection. Each entry of the summary is a sequence of edges and attached to a target set of element IDs that are the last node from some path instances in the graph which satisfy the entry. The type of queries used is based on XML structure conditioned on search terms or values. Returned results are the path expression of XML structure rather than the content.

- *Tree matching based indexing* determines whether the query tree approximately appears in the XML data tree and sorts results based on the score of the XML structure rather than content since no term index is provided. *Approximate matching* is measured by the number of paths in the query tree that match against the data tree [6].

The requirements for indexing and retrieval using MPEG-7 are for ranked video segments, textual queries and approximate matching. Three possible types of XML indexing techniques are compared and it shows that the IR-based indexing technique provides a better foundation for multimedia MPEG-7 retrieval since it satisfies most of the listed criteria and is particularly useful in a schema-constrained environment.

4   Aggregation of Term Weights

The aggregation-based XML indexing structure is represented as a graph whose nodes are elements within a document hierarchy and whose edges reflect structural relationships between the connected nodes [2]. Three types of relationships are of interest: hierarchical (parent-child), linear (siblings) and referential (hyperlink). A document component C is not only associated with concept A_j ($1 \leq j \leq n$) within its own content A_j^C but also the content A_j^{si} of its structurally related components S_i ($1 \leq i \leq k$). The assumption of document components being about concepts is interpreted by those containing terms that make a good concept as indicated by $t(A_j^C)$. The aggregation of an overall score for C combines the weights in content A_j^C and A_j^{si} based on three factors: the type of structural relationships, the type of content and the linguistic quantifiers used. The basic model of aggregation is introduced below namely OWA operators and linguistic quantifiers.

4.1   OWA Operators in Structured Document Retrieval

Given a document node C, we have the weight t_0 of a term in its own content A_0^C and the weights t_j in its k structurally related contents A_0^{si} ($1 \leq j \leq k$). Vector $t = \{t_0, \ldots t_k\}$ is the *argument vector* of the term and vector $w = \{w_0, \ldots w_k\}$ indicates the importance value associated with the corresponding term weight of component. An *Ordered Weighted Averaging* (OWA) operation with respect to t is obtained as follows:

1. Sort entries of vector t in descendent order and obtain the *ordered argument vector* $b = \{ b_0, \ldots b_k \}$, where b_j is the j-th largest of t_i. The ordering of the corresponding importance weighting vector w is changed to that of vector b, denoted as $\alpha = \{ \alpha_0, \ldots \alpha_k \}$ where α_j is the importance value of the j-th largest of t_i.

2.   Apply the OWA operator as follows to obtain the overall score t^C of component C:

$$F(t^C) = \sum_{j=0}^{k} \alpha_j b_j \quad where \quad \alpha_j \in [0,1] \quad and \quad \sum_{j=0}^{k} \alpha_j = 1 \qquad (1)$$

4.2   Linguistic Quantifiers

Having obtained the argument vector t, the task left in aggregation is to determine a suitable importance weighting vector w. Words such as „$most$“, „$about$ ¼“ and „at $least$ one“ are called *linguistic quantifiers* describing a proportion of items in a collection. Each quantifier is related to a regularly increasing monotonic function Q to translate natural language terms into a measurable value w_j[7]. Examples of Q are Q = r^p where p ranges $[0,\infty)$, when p = 2 the function implies quantifier *most* which places most of the importance on the lower weights b_j thereby emphasising the lower scores.

In automatic document retrieval, it is possible to determine the ordered importance weighting vector α by some measurable property of the document such as term weights t_j. Each entry of α_j can be calculated based on the formula below to achieve $\alpha_j \in [0,1]$ and $\Sigma_j \alpha_j = 1$:

$$\alpha_j = Q(S_j) - Q(S_{j-1}) \quad where \quad S_j = \frac{\sum_{j=0}^{j} b_j}{T} \quad and \quad T = \sum_{j=0}^{k} b_j \qquad (2)$$

T is the sum of all ordered argument weights b_j of a term and S_j is the sum of j ordered argument weights of the j-th most satisfied components.

5   An Indexing Framework for MPEG-7 Video Retrieval

An MPEG-7 search engine which such as outlined earlier attempts to retrieve video at the shot level limiting its use to high-level evidence such as meta-data and manual text annotation. The goal of this paper is to study the possibility and feasibility of bringing low-level visual features as auxiliary evidence to improve the retrieval results. In trying to achieve this the aggregation technique shows its ability to model textual representations of a component and that of its structurally related components. Our solution is to map a visual feature of a given shot into a term weight vector, or possibly a concept vector based on the assumption that shots in the same cluster present similar visual/audio features and are designed to capture a similar semantic meaning. The dialogue (e.g. ASR transcripts or teletext) of the shots in the cluster will most likely exhibit similar patterns of term occurrences. Linking audio/visual features to term weights can provide auxiliary evidence to the existing shot dialogue. A crucial concern is that the language variations used in the dialogue and pure term occurrence patterns may not be enough. Our future work will attempt to map audio/visual features to a higher-level concept representation via the characteristics of dialogue term usage.

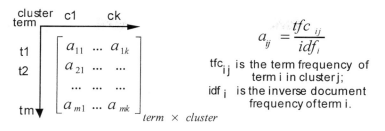

Fig. 1. The Term-by-cluster matrix A

5.1   Cluster Semantic Assignment: Term-by-Cluster Matrix

Clustering is intended to identify structures hidden in data sets using an unsupervised learning approach. A k-means clustering technique can be applied to shots for each audio/ visual feature [8] and having obtained shot clusters, we can estimate the extent $P(C_k|S_j)$ to which a given shot S_j falls into cluster C_k by Eq (3):

$$P(C_k \mid S_j) = \frac{P(C_k)P(S_j \mid C_k)}{\sum_{k=1}^{n} P(C_k)P(S_j \mid C_k)} \tag{3}$$

where $P(S_j|C_k)$ is the distance measure between shot S_j and the centre of cluster C_k., $P(C_k)$ is the accuracy of cluster C_k being correctly classified, n is the total number of clusters, and $P(C_k|S_j)$ is the probability that a given shot belongs to a cluster.

Cluster semantic assignment is used to connect the feature cluster with a semantic representation, and as previously mentioned this could be a term weight vector. A term-by-cluster matrix, similar to term-by-document matrix, is used to record the degree of association between any clusters and terms in the MPEG-7 collection including titles, program abstract and dialogues. This matrix has k columns and m rows, where k is the total number of clusters and m is the total number of indexed terms (Figure 1).

A Singular Value Decomposition technique can be used to derive semantics from matrix A. SVD was originally developed for text retrieval to provide term similarity information based on document co-occurrences [9]. The same can be applied to the term-by-cluster matrix, decomposing A into a diagonal matrix and two orthogonal matrices to obtain an approximation by choosing the number of singular values j:

$$A'_{term \times cluster} = U_{term \times j} S_{j \times j} V_{j \times cluster}^{T} \tag{4}$$

where S is the diagonal matrix with only the first k non-zero singular values in descending order. U and V are matrices consisting of the first k columns corresponding to the singular values in S and each column is with unit-length. We can have the following by observing the matrix A':

- A *Term-cluster* comparison is the individual cell of matrix A': a'_{ij} .
- A *Cluster-cluster* comparison is the dot product of two vector rows of matrix A'.
- A *Term-term* comparison is the dot product of two vector columns of matrix A'.

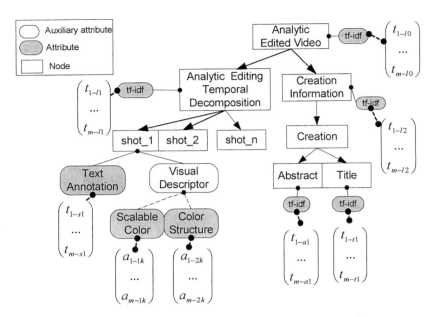

Fig. 2. Before indexing MPEG-7, a tree structure representation

5.2   The Overall Structure

An MPEG-7 document can be regarded as a tree whose nodes are the *retrievable* points from which users can then start video browsing or playback and whose edges represent hierarchical relationships (Figure 2). Each node has an attribute represented by a term weight vector based on the content, which can be directly obtained from the MPEG-7 documents such as a document abstract and ASR transcripts. There exists special types of attributes that are calculated from a term-cluster mapping function which we call *auxiliary attributes* to shots, namely they are various visual features originally indexed by pre-computed feature vectors.

The video indexing task is to first obtain the overall representation of a shot by combining the weight of Text-Annotation and those of auxiliary attributes. We can then use the aggregation method to compute the overall representation of the non-leaf nodes. The completed index structure is shown in Figure 3. Retrieval can be done in a straightforward manner by converting any given query into a term weight vector, obtaining the dot products between query vector and the overall term weight vector of all the nodes in the MPEG-7 tree, and finally sorting the dot product values in descending order for result display.

5.3   Combining Weights of Auxiliary Attributes

Aggregation can be used in situations when there exists a *direct* dependence relationship between an attribute and a node such as the *Text-Annotation* attribute and *Shot* node. It is not suitable for combining weights of an *auxiliary* attribute such as visual features because the relationship between a shot and a term is conditioned upon the shot's feature clusters. A simplified Bayesian approach can be used to obtain the belief value $P(t_l|S_l)$ of an index term t_l within a given shot S_l conditioned upon the corresponding visual feature clusters (i.e. the degree of belief that shot S_l supports term t_l via clusters). This helps summarise the visual features based on some concrete textual words rather than the abstract colour or shape information. It is somewhat implicit representing the semantic of the visual features in a quantitative way.

The Bayesian inference net model assumes that random variables take up two values {true, false}. To simplify the computation, we approximate the belief by using only true values. The strength of the relationship is given in principal by a conditional probability. The task is to find the degree of belief $P(t_l \mid S_l)$ shown below:

$$P(t_1 \mid s_1) = P(t_1 \mid c_1)P(c_1 \mid s_1)P(s_1)$$
$$+ P(t_1 \mid c_2)P(c_2 \mid s_1)P(s_1) \qquad (5)$$
$$+ P(t_1 \mid c_3)P(c_3 \mid s_1)P(s_1)$$

where $P(C_j \mid S_1)$ is the probability that a given shot belongs to a cluster C_j (see Eq.3); $P(t_1|C_j)$ is the probability that that a given feature cluster is implicitly expressed by term $t1$ (see term-by-cluster matrix in section 5.1).

6   Conclusion

This paper describes a study of an MPEG-7 indexing framework for video retrieval extended from the aggregation based indexing model of structured document retrieval. The main thrust of this paper focuses on mapping visual/audio features into term weight vectors thereby providing auxiliary evidence to the overall representation of a shot. The cluster semantics assignment helps to find semantic meanings (i.e. a term weight vector) for each feature cluster based on the assumption that programmes such as news and documentarys provide a rich set of words and have a consistent and structured language style.

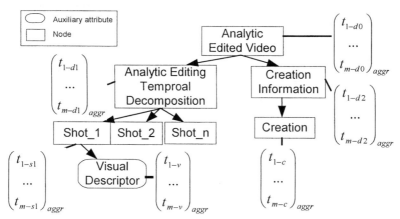

Fig. 3. After indexing MPEG-7 : each node has its corresponding aggregated term weight vector, as indicated with light yellow background

Our future work will implement our framework to evaluate its effectiveness in retrieving video shots based on various query types: textual, image and video clip. To aid evaluation our experiments will be carried out on the TREC2002 video search collection. This search collection consists of 40 hours MPEG-1 video and 25 queries addressing users' information needs in various types. It also provides a set of MPEG -7 descriptions for shot boundary and ASR transcripts. To facilitate clustering assignment, we need to generate low-level visual/audio MPEG-7 descriptions based on our own feature extraction tools since those of TREC2002 only give information on whether a given feature is present in a given shot or not. The experiments will provide us with an insight into retrieval effectiveness by combining visual features in video search.

References

[1]   Day, N. and Martínez, J.M. (ed.): Introduction to MPEG-7 (v4.0), working document N4675, (2002). Available at: http://mpeg.telecomitalialab.com/working_documents.htm, last visit on 29th Oct, 2002

[2]   Kazai, G., Lalmas, M. and Rölleke T.: A Model for the Representation and Focussed Retrieval of Structured Documents based on Fuzzy Aggregation. In: String Processing and Information retrieval (SPIRE 2001) Conference, Laguna De San Rafael, Chile. Nov (2001)

[3]   Pearmain, A., Lalmas, M., Moutogianni, E., Papworth, D., Healy, P. and Roelleke T.: Using MPEG-7 at the Consumer Terminal in Broadcasting. In: EURASIP Journal on Applied Signal Processing, Vol.2002, No.4, April 2002, 354-361

[4]   Graves, A. and Lalmas, M.: Video Retrieval using an MPEG-7 Based Inference Network. In: Proceedings of SIGIR'02, Tampere, Finland, August 2002, 339-346

[5]   McHugh, J., Widom, J., Abiteboul, S., Luo, Q. and Rajaraman, A.: Indexing Semistructured Data. Technical Report, January, (1998)

[6]   Chen, Z., Jagadish, H.V., Korn, F., Koudas, N., Muthukrishnan, S., Raymond Ng, and Srivastava, D.: Counting twig matches in a tree. In: Proceedings of IEEE International Conference on Data Engineering, Heidelberg, Germany, April 2001. 595--604

[7]   Yager, R.: A Hierarchical Document Retrieval Language.   Information Retrieval, Vol.3, No.4, December (2000), 357-377

[8]   Buhmann, J.M.: Data clustering and learning. In: Arbib, M. (ed.): Handbook of Brain Theory and Neural Networks. Bradfort Books, MIT Press, (1995)

[9]   Deerwester, S., Dumais, S. T., Furnas, G. W., Landauer, T. K., & Harshman, R.: Indexing by latent semantic analysis. Journal of the ASIS, 41(6), (1990), 391-407

Document Retrieval in the Context of Question Answering

Christof Monz

Language & Inference Technology, University of Amsterdam
Nieuwe Achtergracht 166, 1018 WV Amsterdam, The Netherlands
christof@science.uva.nl
www.science.uva.nl/~christof

Abstract. Current question answering systems rely on document retrieval as a means of providing documents which are likely to contain an answer to a user's question. A question answering system heavily depends on the effectiveness of a retrieval system: If a retrieval system fails to find any relevant documents for a question, further processing steps to extract an answer will inevitably fail, too. In this paper, we compare the effectiveness of some common retrieval techniques with respect to their usefulness for question answering.

1   Introduction

Document retrieval systems aim to return relevant documents to a user's query, where the query is a set of keywords. A document is considered relevant if its content is related to the query. Question answering (QA) systems, on the other hand, aim to return an (exact) answer to a question.

Since 1999, the annual Text REtrieval Conference (TREC) organized by the National Institute of Standards and Technology (NIST) features a question answering track. Given a large number of newspaper and newswire articles, participating systems try to answer a set of questions by analyzing the documents in the collection in a fully automated way.

Most, if not all, current question answering systems first use a document retrieval system to identify documents that are likely to contain an answer to the question posed. This pre-processing step, also referred to as pre-fetching, is mainly motivated by feasibility considerations. Question answering requires a deeper analysis of the documents, e.g., syntactic parsing, synonym linking, pattern matching, etc. It is impossible to do this for a complete collection of documents of reasonable size in an efficient manner. Therefore document retrieval is used to restrict the whole collection to a subset of documents which are probable to contain an answer, and then the actual process of answer selection is carried out on this subset.

The information needs for ad-hoc retrieval and document retrieval as a prefetch for question answering are quite different, viz. finding documents that are on the same topic as a query and documents actually containing an answer to

F. Sebastiani (Ed.): ECIR 2003, LNCS 2633, pp. 571–579, 2003.

a question, The issue at this point is whether techniques that have proved to be effective for ad-hoc document retrieval are equally effective for retrieval as pre-fetching for QA.

The importance of this questions lies in the strong impact of the effectiveness of a document retrieval system on the overall performance of the answer selection module: If a retrieval system does not find any relevant documents for some question, even a perfect answer selection module will not be able to return a correct answer. The PRISE retrieval system [9] was used by NIST (for TREC-10 and TREC-11) to provide participants in the QA track with potentially relevant documents, in case a participating group did not have a retrieval system. For example, using a cut-off of 20, which is in the vicinity of the cut-offs used by many participants in TREC QA tracks, PRISE failed to return any relevant documents for 28% of the questions of the TREC-11 data set. This affected not only questions which can be considered difficult by the current state of the art in QA, or questions which did not have an answer in the collection, but also relatively 'easy' questions such as (1) and (2).

(1) *What year did South Dakota become a state?*   (topic id: 1467)
(2) *When was Lyndon B. Johnson born?*   (topic id: 1473)

Our objective is to investigate what retrieval techniques allow for an optimization of document retrieval when used as a pre-fetch for QA.

To the best of our knowledge, there is hardly any systematic evaluation of document retrieval as pre-fetching for question answering. Which is somewhat surprising considering the number of QA systems employing document retrieval in one form or another. The only work focusing on this issue is [6], where the impact of passage-based retrieval vs. full document retrieval as pre-fetching is investigated.

The remainder of this paper is organized as follows: The next section explains the test data and retrieval techniques that are investigated. Section 3 presents the results of the experiments. Finally, section 4 gives some conclusions.

2   Experimental Setup

2.1   Test Data

We used the TREC-9, TREC-10, and TREC-11 data sets consisting of 500 questions each with 978,952 documents for TREC-9 and TREC-10 from the TIPSTER/TREC distribution and 1,033,461 documents for TREC-11 from the AQUAINT distribution. At TREC-9 and TREC-10, participants were required to return up to five answer-document-id pairs for each question, where the answer can be any text string containing maximally 50 characters, and the document-id refers to the document from which the answer was extracted. At TREC-11, participants were required to return one answer-document-id pair for each question, where the answer had to be the exact answer.

In addition, we used the judgment files which were provided by NIST as a result of their evaluation. A judgment file, which is comparable to a qrel file in

Table 1. The median number of relevant documents and the corresponding median absolute deviation (mad)

	TREC-4 ah	TREC-7 ah	TREC-8 ah	TREC-9 qa	TREC-10 qa	TREC-11 qa
median	74.0	55.0	68.5	7.0	5.0	3.0
mad	89.2	62.8	60.1	8.9	6.6	3.0

ad-hoc retrieval, indicates for each submitted answer-document-id pair, whether the answer is correct and whether the document supports, i.e., justifies, the answer. The justifying documents form the set of relevant documents against which we evaluate the different document retrieval approaches for pre-fetching. If none of the participants returned a supported answer, that topic was discarded from our evaluation. This also included questions that did not have an answer in the collection, which can be the case since TREC-10.

The final evaluation sets consist of 480, 433, and 455 topics for TREC-9, TREC-10, and TREC-11, respectively. The original question set for TREC-9 actually contained 693 questions where 193 questions were syntactic variants of 54 of the remaining 500 questions. Here, we did not use the variants, but if a relevant document for a variant was included in the judgment file, it was added to the set of relevant documents of the original question. Variants were removed to avoid repetition of topics, which could bias the overall evaluation. We also included 10 topics of the TREC-11 question set, where, although none of the participants found a relevant document, NIST assessors 'coincidentally' recognized a document containing an answer during their evaluation.

One of the traits of the question answering data sets, compared to earlier ad-hoc retrieval data sets, is the much smaller number of relevant or supporting documents. Table 1 displays the statistical distribution of relevant documents over several data sets. As will be seen later on, this property does affect retrieval performance.

2.2   Document Retrieval Approaches

All retrieval techniques discussed in the remainder of this article use the FlexIR retrieval system [7]. FlexIR is a vector-space retrieval system with several features including positional indexing, blind feedback, and structured querying.

In this subsection we introduce some techniques which are known to have a positive impact on the effectiveness of document retrieval, and which have also been used by participants in TREC's question answering tracks. Of course, this is only a selection of retrieval techniques that can and have been applied to pre-fetching. Nevertheless, we aim to discuss some techniques that are commonly used.

Stemming. Stemming has a long tradition in document retrieval, and a variety of stemmers are available, see [3] for an overview. Here, we use the Porter stemmer [8], which is probably the most commonly used stemmer. Since the Porter stemmer is purely rule-based, it sometimes fails to recognize variants, e.g. irregular verbs such as *thought*, which is stemmed as *thought*. Therefore, we decided to also use a lexical-based stemmer, or lemmatizer [10]. Each word is assigned its syntactic root through lexical look-up. Mainly number, case, and tense information is removed, leaving other morphological derivations such as nominalization intact.

Some QA systems do not use stemming to avoid compromising early precision [2], while others use a hybrid approach where the index contains both, the original word and its stem, and matching the stem contributes less to the document similarity score than matching the original word.

Blind Relevance Feedback. Blind relevance feedback analyzes the top n (usually $5 \leq n \leq 10$) documents from a preliminary retrieval run to add new terms, and to reweight terms that were part of the original query. Blind feedback has become a standard technique in document retrieval because of its consistent and strong positive impact on retrieval effectiveness, cf. [11]. On the other hand it is not used in the context of question answering, which might be because there is only a small number of relevant documents, see table 1, and it is known that blind feedback performs rather poorly under those circumstances. Nevertheless, we wanted to confirm this empirically in the context of question answering. Our blind relevance feedback approach uses the top 10 documents and term weights were recomputed by using the standard Rocchio method. We allowed at most 20 terms to be added to the original query.

Passage-Based Retrieval. Passage-based retrieval splits a document into several passages, where passages can be of fixed length or vary in length, start at any position or at fixed positions, and overlap to a certain degree, see [4] for a comprehensive overview. Passage-based retrieval has proved particularly useful for document collections that contain longer documents, such as the Federal Register sub-collection of TREC. Using passages instead of whole documents emphasizes that the information sought by a user can be expressed very locally. This probably also explains its appeal to question answering, where answers tend to be found in a sentence or two, and it is not surprising that many QA systems use passage-based retrieval instead of document retrieval.

From the broad spectrum of available passage-based retrieval techniques, we used the approach described in [1], where all passages are of fixed length and each passage starts at the middle of the previous one. The first passage of a document starts with the first occurrence of a matching term. Given a query q and a document d which is split into passages $pass_d^1, \ldots, pass_d^n$, the similarity between q and d ($sim(q, d)$) is defined as $max_{1 \leq i \leq n} sim(q, pass_d^i)$. This mapping of passages to their original documents is mainly for evaluation purposes, as the NIST judgments are made with respect to document ids. When using a passage-based retrieval system in the context of an actual QA system one would probably

Table 2. Comparison of the ratios of questions with at least one relevant document (a@n) using lemmas vs. porter stemming

a@n	TREC-9		TREC-10		TREC-11	
	lemma	+porter	lemma	+porter	lemma	+porter
a@5	0.6687	0.7000 (+4.6%)	0.6443	0.6490 (+0.7%)	0.4813	0.5231 (+8.6%)
a@10	0.7396	0.7854 (+6.1%)	0.7298	0.7344 (+0.6%)	0.6066	0.6264 (+3.2%)
a@20	0.8042	0.8458 (+5.1%)	0.7875	0.8014 (+1.7%)	0.6659	0.7055 (+5.9%)
a@50	0.8729	0.9146 (+4.7%)	0.8568	0.8753 (+2.1%)	0.7516	0.7956 (+5.8%)

like to return passages instead, as this allows the answer selection procedure to analyze smaller and more focused text segments.

3 Experimental Results

3.1 Stemming

The first retrieval technique we investigated is stemming. In the literature stemming is sometimes described as recall-enhancing, e.g., [5], and the question is whether retrieval as a pre-fetch to a question answering system can profit from stemming, in particular, since pre-fetching should opt for early precision. Table 2 shows the a@n scores for lower cut-offs, where a@n is the number of questions with at least one relevant document up to rank n.

One can notice that the improvements for TREC-10 are much lower than for the other two collections. This could be due to the much larger portion of definition questions in the TREC-10 question set. Questions asking for a definition often contain foreign or technical terms, see (3), or proper names, see (4), where in both cases morphological normalization does not apply very well, if at all.

(3) *What is amitriptyline?*   (topic id: 936)
(4) *Who was Abraham Lincoln?*   (topic id: 959)

Summing up, one can say that applying stemming consistently improves a@n scores, although the extent depends on the question type (e.g., definition questions show lower improvements) and the specificity of the question, i.e., if there is only a small number of documents containing an answer. For these reasons, and because stemming has become a standard technique in document retrieval, stemming is applied to all experiments discussed below, including the Lnu.ltc baseline run.

3.2 Blind Relevance Feedback

Similar to stemming, blind feedback has become an established technique in ad-hoc document retrieval throughout the years. The experimental results for blind feedback compared to plain retrieval are shown in table 3.

Table 3. Comparing simple and blind feedback retrieval

a@n	TREC-9 Lnu.ltc	+feedback	TREC-10 Lnu.ltc	+feedback	TREC-11 Lnu.ltc	+feedback
a@5	0.7000	0.6125 (-12.4%)	0.6490	0.5289 (-18.4%)	0.5231	0.4000 (-23.5%)
a@10	0.7854	0.7125 (-9.2%)	0.7298	0.6028 (-17.3%)	0.6264	0.4923 (-21.4%)
a@20	0.8458	0.7833 (-7.3%)	0.7875	0.7067 (-10.2%)	0.7055	0.5824 (-17.4%)
a@50	0.9146	0.8604 (-5.9%)	0.8568	0.8199 (-4.3%)	0.7956	0.7077 (-11.0%)

These results confirm our suspicion that blind feedback is not appropriate in the context of question answering. All runs dramatically decrease in performance. The bad performance of feedback is most likely due to the small number of relevant documents per topic. This could also explain why the results decrease from TREC-9 to TREC-11, as also the average number of relevant documents decreases, see table 1.

3.3   Passage-Based Retrieval

Passage-based retrieval is widely used in QA systems and is therefore worth analyzing in more detail. As mentioned in section 2.2, we chose to define passages in terms of windows, where each window is of fixed length and overlaps 50% with the previous one. Defining windows this way, exhibited rather consistent improvements in earlier work on ad-hoc retrieval [1]. We experimented with 11 different window sizes: 10, 20, 30, 50, 70, 100, 150, 200, 250, 350, and 500 words. In all cases, the overlap ratio of 50% remained fixed.

The similarity between a query and passage was computed with the Lnx.ltc weighting scheme, which is similar to the Lnu.ltc weighting scheme except that document length normalization is not applied. Normalization was left out because all passages are of fixed length and therefore normalization is expected to make little difference.

Figure 1, shows the a@n scores for the three TREC collections, with $n \in \{5, 10, 20, 50\}$. In addition to the passage-based runs, also the results for the base runs, using full-document retrieval, are shown.

Contrary to what one might expect, all runs using passage-based retrieval perform worse than the respective full-document retrieval run, at any cut-off. In none of the cases, passage-based retrieval provides more questions with at least one relevant document than full-document retrieval. We expected passage-based retrieval to improve early precision by preferring documents that contain matching terms closer to each other and rank lower documents that do contain terms in the query but the terms are more spread. To analyze whether precision increased, we measured the p@n score and some of the findings are shown in table 4. Unfortunately, due to space restriction, we can not display the results for all passage sizes, but we tried to select some window sizes that show the overall characteristics.

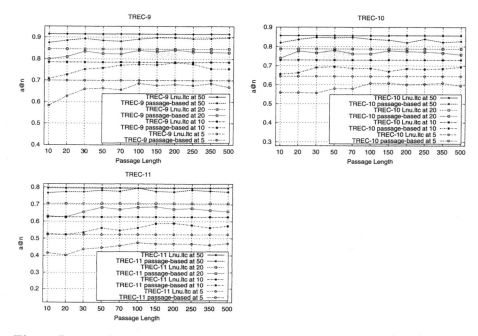

Fig. 1. Ratios of questions with at least one relevant document (a@n) for different passage lengths and cut-offs (5, 10, 20, and 50). For each cut-off, the a@n score of the corresponding Lnu.ltc full-document retrieval baseline run is plotted as a straight line

Table 4. p@n scores for different passages sizes compared to full-document retrieval

| | p@n | full | Passage Length | | | |
			30	70	150	250
TREC-9	p@5	0.3104	0.2721 (12.33%)	0.2750 (11.4%)	0.2767 (10.85%)	0.2750 (11.4%)
	p@10	0.2388	0.2085 (12.68%)	0.2210 (7.45%)	0.2196 (8.03%)	0.2221 (6.99%)
	p@20	0.1717	0.1617 (5.82%)	0.1644 (4.25%)	0.1637 (4.65%)	0.1631 (5.0%)
	p@50	0.1023	0.1021 (0.19%)	0.1023 (0.0%)	**0.1029 (+0.58%)**	0.1010 (1.27%)
TREC-10	p@5	0.2707	0.2259 (16.54%)	0.2411 (10.93%)	0.2480 (8.38%)	0.2494 (7.86%)
	p@10	0.2127	0.1841 (13.44%)	0.1885 (11.37%)	0.1880 (11.61%)	0.1892 (11.04%)
	p@20	0.1542	0.1389 (9.92%)	0.1386 (10.11%)	0.1450 (5.96%)	0.1417 (8.1%)
	p@50	0.0886	0.0856 (3.38%)	0.0851 (3.94%)	0.0849 (4.17%)	0.0843 (4.85%)
TREC-11	p@5	0.1675	0.1415 (15.52%)	0.1451 (13.37%)	0.1508 (9.96%)	0.1473 (12.05%)
	p@10	0.1237	0.1068 (13.66%)	0.1086 (12.2%)	0.1147 (7.27%)	0.1097 (11.31%)
	p@20	0.0845	0.0802 (5.08%)	0.0788 (6.74%)	0.0791 (6.38%)	0.0787 (6.86%)
	p@50	0.0475	**0.0491 (+3.36%)**	**0.0487 (+2.52%)**	**0.0477 (+0.42%)**	0.0468 (1.47%)

Although precision does increase in a few cases, in general, also precision score drop when applying passage-based retrieval. Here, an increase in precision does not mean that more question are provided with relevant documents, as can be seen in figure 1, but that for some questions more relevant documents are found by passage-based retrieval than by full-document retrieval.

It is not obvious why passage-based retrieval performs worse than document retrieval. Especially since Llopis et al. [6] report significant improvements for passage-based retrieval when used for question answering: a@5 +11.26%, a@10 +14.28%, a@20 +13.75% and a@50 +9.34%. These improvements are with respect to the results of AT&T's version of SMART on the TREC-9 data set. It is hard to compare their results directly to ours for two reasons: First, the AT&T run is significantly worse than our baseline, and, secondly, it is not clear how they dealt with question variants, as discussed in section 2.1. Nevertheless their improvements are so large, that it is not unlikely that they also apply to our experimental setup.

In the approach by Llopis et al., documents are split into passages of n sentences ($n \in \{5, 10, 15, 20\}$), and each passage starts at the second sentence of the previous passage. Their improvements are probably not so much due to the fact that they use sentences instead of words to identify passage boundaries, but the fact that their passages have a much larger overlap ratio than the passages used here. Their best results are reported for passages containing 20 sentences, yielding an overlap ratio of approx. 95%—*approximately*, because sentences can differ in length—compared to an overlap of 50% used in our experiments.

Combining our results with the findings of Llopis et al., it can be concluded that passage-based retrieval can yield better results for document pre-fetching, but that passages should significantly overlap with each other.

4 Conclusions

In this paper, we evaluated the performance of three retrieval techniques with respect to question question answering: stemming, blind feedback, and passage-based retrieval. Applying stemming resulted in consistent improvements in precision and recall. Blind feedback performed rather badly, and should be discarded as an option for question answering.

Passage-based retrieval did not live up to the expected improvements. In fact, our approach resulted only in a few cases in minor improvements in precision, and overall performed worse than the baseline. This is in contrast to some other results in the literature and shows that the way passages are formed is an important issue.

Acknowledgments

The author was supported by the Physical Sciences Council with financial support from the Netherlands Organization for Scientific Research (NWO), project 612-13-001.

References

[1] J. Callan. Passage-retrieval evidence in document retrieval. In B. Croft and C. van Rijsbergen, editors, *Proceedings of the 17th Annual International ACM SIGIR Conference on Research and Development in Information Retrieval*, pages 302–310, 1994.

[2] C. Clarke, G. Cormack, D. Kisman, and T. Lynam. Question answering by passage selection (MultiText experiments for TREC-9). In E. Voorhees and D. Harman, editors, *Proceedings of the Ninth Text REtrieval Conference (TREC-9)*, pages 673–683. NIST Special Publication 500-249, 2000.

[3] D. Hull. Stemming algorithms—a case study for detailed evaluation. *Journal of the American Society for Information Science*, 47(1):70–84, 1996.

[4] M. Kaszkiel and J. Zobel. Effective ranking with arbitrary passages. *Journal of the American Society for Information Science and Technology*, 52(4):344–364, 2001.

[5] W. Kraaij and R. Pohlmann. Viewing stemming as recall enhancement. In *Proceedings of the 19th Annual International ACM SIGIR Conference on Research and Development in Information Retrieval*, pages 40–48, 1996.

[6] F. Llopis, A. Ferrández, and J. Vicedo. Passage selection to improve question answering. In *Proceedings of the COLING 2002 Workshop on Multilingual Summarization and Question Answering*, 2002.

[7] C. Monz and M. de Rijke. The University of Amsterdam at CLEF 2001. In *Working Notes for the Cross Language Evaluation Forum Workshop (CLEF 2001)*, pages 165–169, 2001.

[8] M. Porter. An algorithm for suffix stripping. *Program*, 14(3):130–137, 1980.

[9] Z39.50/Prise 2.0.
www.itl.nist.gov/iaui/894.02/works/papers/zp2/zp2.html.

[10] H. Schmid. Probabilistic part-of-speech tagging using decision trees. In *Proceedings of International Conference on New Methods in Language Processing*, 1994.

[11] J. Xu and B. Croft. Query expansion using local and global document analysis. In *Proceedings of the 19th Annual International ACM SIGIR Conference on Research and Development in Information Retrieval*, pages 4–11, 1996.

A Study of the Usefulness of Institutions' Acronyms as Web Queries

Sándor Dominich, Júlia Góth, and Adrienn Skrop

Department of Computer Science
University of Veszprém, Veszprém, Hungary 8200, Egyetem u. 10
{dominich,goth,skrop}@dcs.vein.hu

Abstract. Many people in Hungary use the Web to obtain information from public institutions and organizations. Because these users typically do not know the URL of the desired institution's home page, they use a Web search engine to get there. Institutions' names are usually difficult to recall exactly, thus they are not being used as queries in search engines. Instead, the acronyms of institutions are being used: they are easy to remember and are extensively used in media and by people in everyday life. The paper is concerned with studying the usefulness of the acronyms of Hungarian institutions and organisations present on the Web. The study shows that the majority of acronyms lack this ability. Causes are presented, and possible remedies are suggested. Because the method used in the paper is language independent, it can be used to carry out a similar study in another country too.

1   Introduction

As it is well-known, the World Wide Web (briefly Web) has become one of the most popular and important Internet applications both for users and information providers. The information stored in Web pages can be categorised in several generic categories being used by typical target user group. For example, the research/academic category includes pages containing papers which report on research results; this category is primarily used by academic users.

Another important category is the generic category of institutions, which includes the Web pages of institutions and organisations of interest to a large mass of users such as state departments or ministries, financial institutions, public transportation companies, libraries, civil organisations, political parties, public health institutions etc.. The primary aim of a user wanting to obtain information from a specific institution is to get to the home page of that institution as easily and quickly as possible. On the other hand, the primary aim of an institution is that its home page be easily found by users. Because most users do not know the URL of the home page they want, the typical scenario is as follows: (i) select a Web search engine, (ii) enter

F. Sebastiani (Ed.): ECIR 2003, LNCS 2633, pp. 580–587, 2003.
© Springer-Verlag Berlin Heidelberg 2003

the acronym (or full name) of institution as a query, (iii) examine the first page (or two) of the hit list.

Users prefer using acronyms because they usually do not know the full names of the institutions exactly. There are many studies on evaluating the effectiveness of Web search engines, for example [1], [2], [11], [12], to quote just a few. Acronyms as a topic are present in research and applications, but in a different way. In [3], one can find the expansions of many acronyms; [9] offers a biomedical acronyms database for specialists; [10] reports on an acronym server that builds an acronyms database using Web data; whereas [13] is a study of the effect of abbreviations on retrieval effectiveness.

However, to the best of our knowledge, a practical study on the usefulness of institutions acronyms is lacking: is the acronym of an institution able to identify its own institution? Therefore, the aim of this paper is just this. The usefulness of the acronyms of Hungarian institutions present on the Web is studied, a list of useful acronyms is given, causes of uselessness are presented, possible remedies are suggested.

2   Usefulness of Acronyms

Nowadays, it is a common phenomenon that people turn to the Web to get information. Users' information needs vary to a great extent, and are related to different areas of everyday life. A very important application of the Web is to obtain information related to institutions, e.g., financial, public administration, educational, etc.. Institutions usually have long, multiple words official names. Also, every institution has got its own official acronym that uniquely identifies it. An acronym usually consists of the initials of name's words which may be expanded with extra-letters to ease pronunciation such that: MEH (Magyar Energia Hivatal), GVH (Gazdasági Versenyhivatal), MABISZ (Magyar Biztosítók Szövetsége).

Because acronyms of institutions' names are commonly and very often used in both media and by people in everyday life, the aim of this paper is to investigate the ability of the acronyms of Hungarian institutions' names to find the home page of their own institutions when being used as queries in Web searching (or briefly: usefulness of acronyms).

There are many acronym finders on the Web (e.g., [3]), these are not in Hungarian, and their primary aim is to give indications on possible meanings of an acronym. These are only used by a few people mainly because of language difficulties.

3   Experimental Setting

A number of 120 institutions in Hungary that have acronyms and are present with their own Web site on the Web were identified [4], [5], [6], [7], [8]. A list was compiled containing the full name, home page URL, and acronym for every institution. The list is not included in this paper because of size restriction; Table 1 shows a fraction of it.

Table 1. Full name, home page URL, and acronym of institutions in Hungary

Full Name	Home Page URL	Acronym
Budapesti Közlekedési Vállalat	http://www.bkv.hu/	BKV
Magyar Energia Hivatal	http://www.eh.gov.hu/	MEH
Országos Meteorológiai Szolgálat	http://www.met.hu/	OMSZ
Országos Közoktatási Intézet	http://www.oki.hu/	OKI

Six Web search engines:

- Heuréka: http://www.heureka.hu
- Altavizsla: http://www.altavizsla.hu
- Ariadnet: http://www.ariednet.hu
- Google: http://www.google.com
- Metacrawler: http://www.metacrawler.com
- AltaVista: http://www.altavista.com)

were used to evaluate the usefulness of the acronyms.

Heuréka, AltaVizsla and Ariadnet are the most frequently used Hungarian search engines (they are hosted and operated in Hungary) in Hungary which primarily index and search Hungarian Web pages. They are preferred by most Hungarian users, who are lay people and have language difficulties when trying to use search engines in another language. However, three well-known general search engines (Google, Metacrawler, AltaVista) were also used because, on the one hand, they are preferred by the computing society, and, on the other hand, non-Hungarian speaking people might want to find out information on Hungarian institutions (for example, when they plan to travel to Hungary, or if they live in Hungary).

When users look for an institution, they usually enter its acronym to a search engine, and, ideally, expect to get a link to the appropriate home page among the first ten hits returned. Thus, an experiment was carried out during September-October 2002 by entering each acronym to each of the six search engines, and evaluating the first ten hits according to usefulness measures as defined below.

4   Measures

Only the first ten hits returned, i.e., the first page of hits, were evaluated (because users typically do not examine more links) for every acronym and search engine. Every link was assigned to exactly one of the following two categories:

- Category one: link to the home page of the institution. This is the Web page that is desired to be retrieved when the institution's acronym is used as query.
- Category two: link to a page or site page (i.e., it is not the home page) that contains a site map or a navigational link to the home page.

Thus, some eight thousand hits were examined, because there were category 2 links as well. As the aim is to have a measure for the usefulness of acronyms rather than for search engine effectiveness, the following measures were defined and used.

4.1   Pseudo-Precision

For every acronym a, a measure called *pseudo–precision*, denoted by Π_a, is defined as follows:

$$\Pi_a = \frac{r_a}{N} \qquad (1)$$

where N is the total number of search engines used ($N = 6$ in our case), and r_a is the number of search engines that return category 1 links. Pseudo-precision is an analogue of the classical precision measure, and means the proportion of search engines for which the acronym proves useful. The value of pseudo–precision is normalized, it has values between zero and one. The more search engines retrieve a home page, the most useful the acronym is. The pseudo-precision of an acronym is directly proportional with the number of search engines that retrieve the home page.

Example 1. The home page of *"Magyar Tudományos Akadémia"* (Hungarian Academy of Sciences), having the acronym *MTA*, was found by Ariadnet, Google and AltaVista, and was not found by Heuréka, AltaVizsla, and Metacrawler. Thus, the pseudo–precision Π_{MTA} of *MTA* is $3/6 = 0.5$.

4.2   Mean Reciprocal Rank

While pseudo-precision is a measure of the usefulness of an acronym, a more articulate and combined measure should give an indication of how easy it is for the user to get to the home page looked for from the hit list. Thus, another measure is defined as follows.

For every acronym a and every search engine i, a measure called *reciprocal rank*, denoted by RR_{ia}, is defined first as follows:

$$RR_{ia} = \begin{cases} \dfrac{1}{r_{ia}} & \text{category 1\_link\_in\_position\_}r_{ia} \\[2mm] \dfrac{1}{\kappa r_{ia}} & \text{category 2\_link\_in\_position\_}r_{ia} \\ & \text{and\_no\_category 1\_link} \\[2mm] 0 & \text{no\_link\_in\_categories 1\_2} \end{cases} \qquad (2)$$

where r_{ia} is the rank of the link in the hit list, and κ is a penalty factor. In our experiments, the rank is taken as being the sequence number of the link in the hit list, but it could also be taken as the relevance value, if this is known, of the link given by the search engine. The penalty factor is set to two in our experiments, but it could be taken as being equal to any other positive integer.

Example 2. The home page of *"Magyar Tudományos Akadémia"*, having the acronym *MTA*, was found by Ariadnet, and was ranked in the 7th position. Thus, the *reciprocal rank* $RR_{Ariadnet,MTA}$ of *MTA* at Ariadnet is $RR_{Ariadnet,MTA} = 0.14$.

The higher the reciprocal rank, the easier it is for the user to get to the desired home page, i.e., the reciprocal rank and the number of links to be examined are inversely proportional with each other.

Because we want a measure for the usefulness degree of acronyms regardless of the search engines used, an average of the reciprocal rank is defined as follows.

A *mean reciprocal rank*, denoted by MRR_a, for every acronym is defined as follows:

$$MRR_a = \frac{1}{N} \sum_{i=1}^{N} RR_{ia} \qquad (3)$$

where N is the number of search engines used.

Example 3 For the acronym *MTA* ("*Magyar Tudományos Akadémia*") the following rankings were obtained:

Search Engine	Category	Ranking
Heuréka	2	4
AltaVizsla	2	5
Ariadnet	1	7
Google	1	1
Metacrawler	0	0
AltaVista	1	1

Thus, $MMR_{MTA} = 0.39$.

5   Results and Discussion

Figure 1 shows a pseudo–precision histogram for acronyms for all search engines. It can be seen that the majority of acronyms are useful (above 0.5; as perhaps expected), a few are very useful (value 1), and about 17% can hardly be judged as being useful.

Figure 1 also shows pseudo–precision histograms separately for Hungarian and general search engines. It can be seen that the majority of the acronyms perform better in general search engines than in the Hungarian ones. While the average pseudo–precision is 0.44 in Hungarian search engines, it is much higher, 0.78, in general search engines. This result is perhaps unexpected in that one would have thought that the acronyms should perform well in Hungarian search engines as well, or better. The differences in performance of acronyms may be due to the fact that each individual search engine uses its own unique formula (algorithm) to index and rank Web sites, and the algorithms use various factors to rank pages in their search results. Search engines may provide basics of their indexing and page ranking policies, however the Hungarian search engines used do not provide the same.

Figures 2 and 3 show the mean reciprocal rank histograms for all search engines, for Hungarian search engines, and for general search engines, respectively. A 0.1 step is used on the horizontal axis.

It can clearly be seen that, as expected on the basis of meta-precision, the degree of usefulness of about half the acronyms is much higher in the case of general search engines than Hungarian ones.

Average values of the mean reciprocal ranks are shown in Table 2.

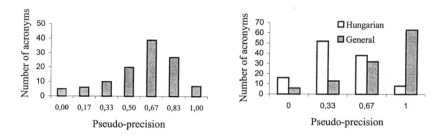

Fig. 1. Overall pseudo–precision histogram and Pseudo–precision histograms for Hungarian and general search engines separately

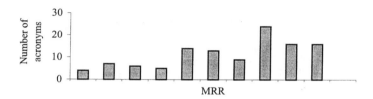

Fig. 2. Mean reciprocal rank histogram for all search engines

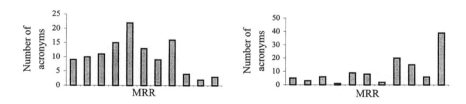

Fig. 3. Mean reciprocal rank histogr am for Hungarian and for general search engines

Table 2. Average mean reciprocal ranks

	Average *MRR*
Over all search engines	0.53
Over Hungarian search engines	0.38
Over general search engines	0.68

Table 3. The useful Hungarian acronyms on the Web

ÁNT	ND	MK	matáv	OEP	MK	KÉ
FVF	BG	MK	MKGI	OF	IS	SO
GVH	AP	MO	MGY	OM	TÁ	SZ
MAB	DO	MO	NIIF	KS	MS	Z
MFB	MG	MS	NIOK	ME	SZ	

Based on our results, there are 34 acronyms that identify their institutions in Hungary (Table 3).

This poor performance of acronyms can be seen as a noteworthy situation. Analysing possible causes, the following two causes were identified.

Poor Web page design of home pages and sites is one of the causes. Apart from content information (using the acronym as content or meta-data) also page–related factors (format, placement of the title tag, frequency of keywords etc.) and overall Web page design contribute to search engine ranking. The usage of title tags, fonts, character sizes, colours as well as of content need be considerably revised and improved by webmasters.

Another cause is that quite a few acronyms have multiple meanings. For example, the acronym *MNB* (which identifies the Hungarian National Bank) also stands for the following institutions: Magyar Nemzeti Bibliográfia, Magyar Nemzeti Bizottság, Moffat, Nichol & Bonney INC., Moody National Bank, Malvern National Bank, which, due to a much better web page design, are retrieved more easily (ahead of the Hungarian *MNB*).

6   Conclusion

The usefulness of the acronyms of Hungarian institutions to identify institutions was evaluated on the Web using Hungarian as well as general search engines. Evaluation measures were defined to judge usefulness. The results show that the majority of the acronyms are not effective in identifying their institutions. This means that (i) they fail to fulfil their roles of identifying their institutions, (ii) webmasters should seek ways to improve on the situation by a more careful design of home pages taking into account the different ways in which different search engines index and rank Web pages, (iii) the acronyms should be revisited as regards their uniqueness and identification property (although it is very improbable that, for example, the Hungarian Academy of Sciences (MTA) or Hungarian National Bank (MNB) would even consider changing their acronyms).

It is planned to make the results in this paper available for the webmasters of Hungarian institutions in order to draw their attention towards enhancing their Web pages.

The method proposed and used in this paper is language independent, and it can be used for carrying out similar experiments in other countries, too, where acronyms are being used.

Acknowledgements

The authors would like to acknowledge the support of grants OTKA T 037821 (National Foundation fro Scientific Research, Hungary), NKFP OM-00359/2001 (Ministry of Education, National Research and Development Program, Hungary), and AKP 2001-140 (Hungarian Academy of Sciences).

References

[1]   Chu, H. and Rosenthal, M. (1996). Search Engines for the World Wide Web: A Comparative Study and Evaluation Methodology. *Proceedings of the American Society for Information Science Annual Meeting*, 33, pp: 127–135

[2]   Gordon, M., and Pathak, P. (1999). Finding information on the World Wide Web: the retrieval effectiveness of search engines. *Information Processing and Management*, 35, pp: 141–180

[3]   http://acronymfinder.com

[4]   http://www.lap.hu/temakor.html

[5]   http://katalog.index.hu

[6]   http://index.hu/catalog

[7]   http://www.wahoo.hu/index

[8]   http://www.webmania.hu

[9]   http://www.lethargy.swmed.edu/argh/ARGH.asp

[10]   Larkey, L.S., Ogilvie, P., Price, M.A., and Tamilio, B. (2000). Acrophile: An Automated Acronym Extractor and Server. *Digital Libraries – ACM Conference on Digital Libraries*, San Antonio, TX, June 2-7, ACM Press, pp: 205-214

[11]   Leighton, H. V., and Srivastava, J. (1999). First 20 Precision among World Wide Web Search Services (Search Engines). *Journal of the American Society for Information Science*, 50(1), pp: 870-881

[12]   Oppenheim, C., Morris, A., and McKnight, C. (2000). The evaluation of WWW search engines. *Journal of Documentation*, 56(2), pp: 190-211

[13]   Ruch, P., and Baud, R. (2002). Evaluating and reducing the effect of data corruption when applying bag of words approaches to medical records. *International Journal of Medical Informatics* (Articles in Press) (full text online: http://www.sciencedirect.com)

Building a Hierarchy of Events and Topics for Newspaper Digital Libraries

Aurora Pons-Porrata[1], Rafael Berlanga-Llavori[2], and José Ruiz-Shulcloper[3]

[1] Universidad de Oriente, Santiago de Cuba, Cuba
[2] Universitat Jaume I, Castellón, Spain
[3] Institute of Cybernetics, Mathematics and Physics, La Habana, Cuba

Abstract. In this paper we propose an incremental hierarchical clustering algorithm for on-line event detection. This algorithm is applied to a set of newspaper articles in order to discover the structure of topics and events that they describe. In the first level, articles with a high temporal-semantic similarity are clustered together into events. In the next levels of the hierarchy, these events are successively clustered so that composite events and topics can be discovered. The results obtained for the F1-measure and the Detection Cost demonstrate the validity of our algorithm for on-line event detection tasks.

Keywords: Topic Detection and Tracking, Text Clustering.

1   Introduction

Starting from a continuous stream of newspaper articles, the *Event Detection* problem consists in determining for each incoming document, whether it reports on a new event, or it belongs to some previously identified event. One of the most important issues in this problem is to define what an *event* is. Initially, an event can be defined as something that happens at a particular place and time. However, many events occur along several places and several time periods (e.g. the whole event related to a complex trial). For this reason, researchers in this field prefer the broader term of *Topic*, which is defined as an important event or activity along with all its directly related events [4].

A *Topic Detection System* (TDS) is intended to discover the topics reported in newspaper articles and to group them in terms of their topics. In this paper we will consider *on-line* systems, which incrementally build the topic groups as each article arrives. Current on-line TD systems have in common that use both the chronological order of articles, and a fast document-clustering algorithm. For example, the system presented in [9] uses the *Single-Pass* algorithm, a moving time window to group the incoming articles into topics and it defines a similarity function that takes into account the position of the articles in this window. In [5], the *Single-Pass* algorithm is applied to a set of document classifiers whose thresholds take into account the temporal adjacency of articles. The *UMass* system [1] uses an *NN* algorithm, which has a

F. Sebastiani (Ed.): ECIR 2003, LNCS 2633, pp. 588–596, 2003.

quadratic time complexity. One limitation of current TD systems is that they make irrevocable clustering assignments. As a consequence, the set of events detected by the system could depend on the arrival order of the documents.

In this paper, our main concern is to discover the temporal structure of topics and events, that is, to identify not only the topics but also the structure of events they comprise. For example, Figure 1 presents part of the event structure of the „Kosovo War" topic. In the first level of the hierarchy, incoming documents are grouped into small events (the number of documents of each event is indicated between parenthesis). In the upper levels, composite events as well as topics are successively built from them.

Current TD systems cannot deal with event structures, whereas traditional hierarchical clustering algorithms are not appropriate for on-line event detection because they are not incremental. Moreover, the levels of the generated hierarchies do not correspond to the different abstraction levels of events and topics.

The remainder of the paper is organized as follows: Section 2 presents the representation of documents taking into account their temporal and place components, Section 3 proposes a new document similarity function for these documents, Section 4 describes the clustering algorithm, and Section 5 describes our experiments. Conclusions and further work are presented in Section 6.

2   Document Representation

The incoming stream of documents that feed our system comes from some on-line newspapers available in Internet, which are automatically translated into XML. This representation preserves the original logical structure of the newspapers. Nevertheless, in this work we will use only the publication date and the textual contents of the articles. From them, the system builds three feature vectors to represent each document, namely:

- *A vector of weighted terms,* $T^i = (TF_1^i, \ldots, TF_n^i)$, where the terms represent the lemmas of the words appearing in the text, and TF_k^i is the relative frequency of the term t_k in the document d^i. Stop words are disregarded from this vector.

- *A vector of weighted time entities,* $F^i = (TF_{f_1^i}, \ldots, TF_{f_{m_i}^i})$, where time entities are either dates or date intervals, and $TF_{f_k^i}$ is the absolute frequency of the time entity f_k in d^i. These time entities are automatically extracted from the texts by using the algorithm presented in [3].

- *A vector of weighted places,* $P^i = (TF_{p_1^i}, \ldots, TF_{p_{l_i}^i})$, where $TF_{p_k^i}$ is the absolute frequency of the place p_k in d^i. These places are automatically extracted from the texts by using a thesaurus of place names. Places are represented by their paths within the thesaurus, where each level indicates a geographic region (country, administrative region, etc.).

Fig. 1. Event Structure for the Kosovo War topic

3   Document Similarity Measure

Automatic clustering of documents, as in event detection, relies on a similarity measure. Most of the clustering algorithms presented in the literature use the cosine measure to compare two documents. In our case, we consider that two articles refer to the same event if their contents, places and time references approximately coincide.

To compare the term vectors of two documents d^i and d^j we use the cosine measure: $S_T(d^i, d^j) = \cos(T^i, T^j)$.

To compare the time vectors of two documents we propose the following distance:

$$D(d^i, d^j) = \min_{f^i \in FR^i, f^j \in FR^j} \left\{ d(f^i, f^j) \right\}, \text{ where:}$$

i) $d(f^i, f^j)$ is defined as follows:

- If f^i and f^j are dates, then $d(f^i, f^j)$ is the number of days between them.
- If $f^i = [a, b]$ and $f^j = [c, d]$ are date intervals, then

$$d(f^i, f^j) = \min_{f_1 \in [a,b], f_2 \in [c,d]} \left\{ d(f_1, f_2) \right\}.$$

- If one of them is a date and the other is an interval, then

$$d(f^i, f^j) = d([f^i, f^i], f^j).$$

ii) FR^i is the set of all dates f^i of the document d^i (not necessarily unitary) that satisfy the following conditions:

- Each f^i has the maximum frequency in d^i, that is, $TF_{f^i} = \max_{k=1..m} \left\{ TF_{f^{ik}} \right\}$.
- Each f^i has the minimum distance to the publication date of d^i (this condition is not considered when comparing cluster representatives instead of documents).

To compare the place vectors of two documents we propose the following function:

$$S_P(d^i, d^j) = \begin{cases} 1 & \text{if } \exists\, p_q^i, p_t^j \text{ such that they have a common prefix} \\ 0 & \text{otherwise} \end{cases}$$

Finally, the overall temporal-semantic similarity measure is defined as follows:

$$S(d^i, d^j) = \begin{cases} S_T(d^i, d^j) & \text{if } S_P(d^i, d^j) = 1 \wedge D(d^i, d^j) \leq \beta_{time} \\ 0 & \text{otherwise} \end{cases}$$

where β_{time} is the maximum number of days that are required to determine whether two articles refer to the same or to different events.

This measure tries to capture the idea that two documents reporting a same event should have a high semantic similarity, time proximity and place coincidence.

4   Hierarchical Clustering of Documents

Traditional hierarchical clustering algorithms are intended to build a hierarchy of document classes. However, the levels of the generated hierarchies correspond to the steps of the clustering algorithm, but not always to the required abstraction levels of our application. Instead of that, in our algorithm each level of the hierarchy consists of a set of clusters of *abstract* documents, which are the representatives of the clusters generated in the previous level. As a consequence, each level of the hierarchy represents a different abstraction level of the original document collection.

In the following section we describe how cluster representatives are obtained, and afterwards we present the proposed clustering algorithm.

4.1   Cluster Representatives

The representative of a cluster c, denoted as $\bar{c}$, is a tuple $(T^{\bar{c}}, F^{\bar{c}}, P^{\bar{c}})$, of terms, temporal and place component, respectively. In this work, it is calculated as the union of the cluster's documents:

$T^{\bar{c}} = \left(T_1^{\bar{c}}, ..., T_n^{\bar{c}} \right)$, where $T_j^{\bar{c}}$ is the relative frequency of term t_j in the sum vector of the cluster's documents.

$F^{\bar{c}} = \left(F_{f_1}^{\bar{c}}, ..., F_{f_s}^{\bar{c}} \right)$, where $F_{f_j}^{\bar{c}}$ is the absolute frequency of the time entity f_j in the cluster, that is, the number of documents in the cluster that contain this time entity, and s is the total number of time entities that describe the documents of this cluster.

$P^{\bar{c}} = \left(P_{p_1}^{\bar{c}}, ..., P_{p_l}^{\bar{c}} \right)$, where $P_{p_j}^{\bar{c}}$ is the absolute frequency of place p_j in the cluster

and, l is the total number of places that describe the documents of this cluster.

In order to reduce the length of the cluster representatives, we truncate their vectors by removing the terms (res. dates, places) whose frequency is smaller than the tenth part of the vector maximum frequency.

4.2   Incremental Hierarchical Clustering Algorithm

The hierarchical algorithm we propose (see Figure 2) uses a clustering routine that should satisfy the following requirements:

- It must be incremental.
- It should not depend on the order of the incoming documents.
- It must use a similarity measure that takes into account the temporal-spatial proximity of documents.

Input: Similarity measure S and its parameters; Clustering routine and its parameters.
Output: Hierarchy of document clusters representing the identified events and topics.
Step 1. Arrival of a document d and *Level* = 1.
Step 2. Apply the clustering routine in the first level of the cluster hierarchy.
Step 3. Let RS the set of clusters that are removed when applying the clustering routine.
         Let NS the set of the new clusters that are formed.
         Increment *Level*.
         Let Q be a queue with the documents to be processed in this level, $Q = \varnothing$.
Step 4. Remove all the representatives of the clusters belonging to RS in *Level*.
         Put into the queue Q all the elements of the clusters in *Level* where at least one
         representative was eliminated. Remove these clusters from the list of the existing
         clusters.
Step 5. Calculate the cluster representatives of NS and put them into the queue Q.
Step 6. For each document in the queue Q apply the clustering routine.
Step 7. If *Level* is not the top level in the hierarchy then Go to the Step 3.

Fig. 2. Hierarchical incremental clustering algorithm

Some examples of clustering routines are the algorithm GLC [7] and the Incremental Compact Algorithm [6]. The algorithm GLC finds incrementally the connected components in a graph based on the β_0-similarity, whereas the incremental compact algorithm is based on the incremental construction of β_0-compact sets.

Since the proposed algorithm is incremental, it is assumed that a hierarchy of documents already exists, where the first level consists of a partition of the document collection, and the next levels contain the cluster representatives of each previous level. When a new document arrives at the system, the clusters in all levels of the hierarchy must be revised. Firstly, the algorithm applies the clustering routine in the first level of the hierarchy, which can make new clusters to appear and other existing ones to disappear.

When clusters are removed from a level of the hierarchy, their representatives must be removed from the clusters in which they were located in the next level. Similarly, when new clusters are created, their representatives must be calculated. The members of the clusters where changes took place (that is, some cluster representatives were eliminated) as well as all new representatives, must be queued in order to incorporate them to the set of existing clusters in this level of the hierarchy. For that purpose, we apply the clustering routine again. This process repeats until the top level of the hierarchy is reached. It is worth mentioning that in each level of the hierarchy different parameters of the similarity measure and of the clustering routine, and even different clustering routines can be used.

In the Figure 3 (a) an example of a hierarchy of clusters is shown. When the new document d arrives, a new cluster is created with some documents of the cluster 2 and all the documents of the cluster 3. The Figure 3 (b) shows the changes that take place in the second level of hierarchy. As it can be noticed, the representatives $\bar{c}_2$ and $\bar{c}_3$ are removed and two new representatives $\bar{c}_2'$ and $\bar{c}_{11}$ are created. The representatives $\bar{c}_1$, $\bar{c}_4$, $\bar{c}_5$, $\bar{c}_2'$ and $\bar{c}_{11}$ are placed in the queue of documents in order to incorporate them to the set of clusters in the second level of hierarchy.

The main advantage of the proposed algorithm is that the generated set of clusters at each level of the hierarchy is unique independently on the arrival order of the documents.

5   Evaluation

The effectiveness of the proposed clustering algorithm has been evaluated using a collection of 452 articles published in the Spanish newspaper "El País" during June 1999. We have manually identified 68 non-unitary events, being their maximum size of 16 documents. From these events we have identified 48 topics, whose maximum size is 57 documents. The original collection covers 21 events associated to the end of the „Kosovo War" along with their immediate consequences. These events have a high temporal-semantic overlapping, which makes difficult their identification.

In this work we only deal with the two first levels of this hierarchy, called the *Event Level* and *Topic Level* respectively. For the evaluation, we have applied the Incremental Compact Algorithm [6] as the clustering routine in all the levels of the hierarchy. This algorithm uses a threshold β_0 to decide when two documents are considered similar.

To evaluate the clustering results we use the overall *F1-measure* [2] and the *Detection Cost* [4] to compare the system-generated clusters with the manually labeled events in each level of hierarchy.

Figure 4 shows the results for the F1-measure and Detection Cost at the *Event Level* with respect to the threshold β_0. Each curve represents a different document similarity measure, namely: *Terms* represents the cosine measure where only the document term vectors are considered, *Place+Time* represents the similarity measure proposed in the Section 3, and finally *Time* is similar to the previous one but disregarding the place component. In the last two cases the number indicated between parenthesis represents the best threshold β_{time} obtained for each case.

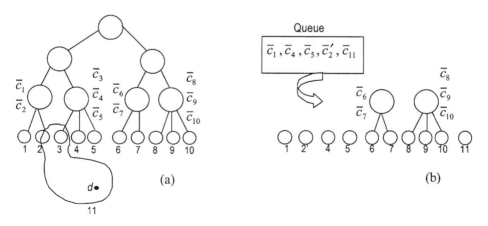

Fig. 3. A hierarchy of clusters

As it can be noted, the best results are obtained when considering the temporal component. As a consequence, we can conclude that the time component improves the quality of the system-generated events. Surprisingly, the worst results are obtained when including the place component in the document representation. We think that this negative results are due to two main reasons. Firstly, the current implementation does not detect all the relevant places from texts, and many of the detected ones are ambiguous (i.e. they have several paths in the thesaurus). Secondly, many events involve multiple and disparate places, which makes even more difficult to find a representative place for them.

With regard to the *Topic Level*, Figure 5 shows the results for the F1-measure and the Detection Cost. A similar behavior of the system effectiveness with respect to the similarity measures is observed at this level. Notice that the separations between the different approaches are much greater at this level.

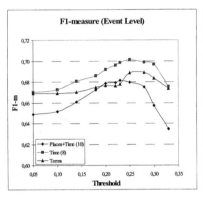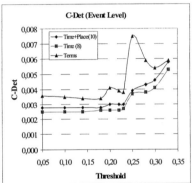

Fig. 4. F1-measure and Detection Cost for the Event Level

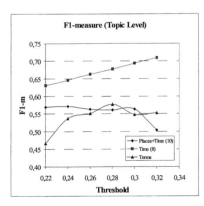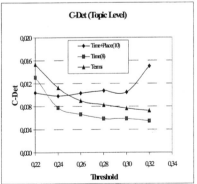

Fig. 5. F1-measure and Detection Cost for the Topic Level

6   Conclusions

In this paper a new similarity measure between documents considering the places, the temporality and contents of the news has been introduced. Unlike other proposals, the temporal proximity is not just based on the publication date, but it is calculated using a group of dates automatically extracted from the texts of the news [3]. This temporal component characterizes the time-span of events and topics, which can be used in a similar way to the Timelines [8] to browse the whole document collection.

A new algorithm for determining a hierarchy of clustered articles is also introduced. In the first level the individual events are identified. In the next levels, these events are successively clustered so that more complex events and topics can be identified. Its main advantage is that the generated set of clusters is unique, independently of the document arrival order. The hierarchy obtained by our algorithm allows users to discover the temporal structure of topics and events, that is, to identify not only the topics but also the possible smaller events they comprise. This hierarchy can be very useful for specialist that analyze unknown collections of documents. Our experiments have demonstrated the positive impact of the temporal component in the quality of the system-generated clusters. Moreover, the obtained results for the F1-measure and the Detection Cost also demonstrate the validity of our algorithm for event detection tasks.

As future work, we will analyze the conceptual description of the obtained groups at any level of the hierarchy. Additionally, we will compare the system effectiveness at each level of the hierarchy to the events identified by other Topic Detection systems of the literature. In [6], we have already compared our system with other Topic Detection systems regarding just the events at the first level of the hierarchy. There the results showed that our system clearly outperforms these other systems.

References

[1]   Allan, J.; Lavrenko, V.; Frey, D.; Khandelwal, V.: UMass at TDT 2000. In Proc. *TDT 2000 Workshop*, 2000.
[2]   Larsen, B.; Aone, C.: Fast and Effective Text Mining Using Linear-time Document Clustering. *In KDD '99*, San Diego, California, pp. 16-22, 1999.
[3]   Llidó, D.; Berlanga R.; Aramburu M.J.: Extracting temporal references to automatically assign document event-time periods. In Proc. *Database and Expert System Applications 2001*, 62-71, Springer-Verlag, Munich, 2001.
[4]   National Institute of Standards and Technology. The Topic Detection and Tracking Phase 2 (TDT2) evaluation plan. version 3.7, 1998.
[5]   Papka, R.: *On-line New Event Detection, Clustering and Tracking*. Ph.D. Thesis Report, University of Massachusetts, Department of Computer Science, 1999.
[6]   Pons-Porrata, A.; Berlanga-Llavori, R.; Ruiz-Shulcloper, J.: Detecting events and topics by using temporal references. *Lecture Notes in Artificial Intelligence* 2527, Springer Verlag, 2002, pp.11-20.

[7]   Ruiz-Shulcloper, J.; Sánchez Díaz, G.; Abidi, M.A.: *Heuristics & Optimization for Knowledge Discovery, Chapter VI. Clustering in mixed incomplete data,* Editors H.A. Abbass, R.A. Sarker, C.S. Newton, Idea Group Publishing, USA. pp 88-106. January 2002.

[8]   Swan R. C.; Allan, J.: Automatic generation of overview timelines. In Proc. *ACM/SIGIR 2000*, pp. 49-56, 2000.

[9]   Yang, Y.; Pierce, T.; Carbonell, J.: A Study of Retrospective and On-Line Event Detection. In Proc. *ACM/SIGIR 1998*, pp. 28-36, 1998.

A Machine Learning Approach for the Curation of Biomedical Literature

Min Shi[1], David S. Edwin[1], Rakesh Menon[1], Lixiang Shen[1], Jonathan Y.K. Lim[1],
Han Tong Loh[1,2], S. Sathiya Keerthi[2], and Chong Jin Ong[2]

[1]Design Technology Institute Ltd, Faculty of Engineering
National University of Singapore, 10 Kent Ridge Crescent, Singapore 119260
[2]ME Department, National University of Singapore, 10 Kent Ridge Crescent, Singapore
{dtishim,dtidsaej,dtirm,dtislx,dtilykj,
mpelht,mpessk,mpeongcj}@nus.edu.sg

Abstract. In the field of the biomedical sciences there exists a vast repository of information located within large quantities of research papers. Very often, researchers need to spend considerable amounts of time reading through entire papers before being able to determine whether or not they should be curated (archived). In this paper, we present an automated text classification system for the classification of biomedical papers. This classification is based on whether there is experimental evidence for the expression of molecular gene products for specified genes within a given paper. The system performs preprocessing and data cleaning, followed by feature extraction from the raw text. It subsequently classifies the paper using the extracted features with a Naïve Bayes Classifier. Our approach has made it possible to classify (and curate) biomedical papers automatically, thus potentially saving considerable time and resources. The system proved to be highly accurate, and won honourable mention in the KDD Cup 2002 task 1.

1   Introduction

The explosion of information technology has given rise to an exponentially increasing amount of data being created and stored in large databases. These databases contain a rich source of information. There has been growing interest in the application of information extraction [1, 2, 3] to help solve some of the problems that are associated with information overload. However, due to their sheer volume an enormous amount of manual effort is needed to analyse them. Many of these databases are used for archival purposes only.

With the advent of efficient and reliable computational methods many of these databases are being analysed in view of extracting useful information from them. One such database that the authors have analysed belonged to the biomedical domain. This database, which focused on the Drosophila Fly [4], was provided as competition set in the Eighth ACM SIGKDD International Conference on Knowledge Discovery and

F. Sebastiani (Ed.): ECIR 2003, LNCS 2633, pp. 597-604, 2003.
© Springer-Verlag Berlin Heidelberg 2003

Data Mining. The authors' team participated in the competition and was awarded a honourable mention.

The focus of this competition was to automate the work of curating (archiving) biomedical databases by identifying what papers need to be curated for Drosophila gene expression information. This competition was an attempt to use automated technology to try to filter relevant papers from such vast archives. It examined the work performed by one group of curators for FlyBase [5] (A Database of the Drosophila Genome), a publicly available database on the genetics and molecular biology of Drosophila (fruit flies).

In this work, we implemented a computational method to extract features and relevant statistics from the free text in the papers and made use of Naïve Bayes Classifiers [6] for classification of papers.

Although the accuracy of our system might be less than what could be possible by manual classification by a human, experts can verify the information against the paper. This will serve as assistance because they are able to process large quantities of text quickly in batch.

2   Problem Description

In this work, we focused on learning models that could assist genome annotators by automatically extracting information from scientific articles. The task was elaborated as follows; [7]

For a set of papers, given:

1.   A paper on Drosophila genetics or molecular biology
2.   A list of the genes mentioned in that paper

Produce the following output:

1.   Provide a YES/NO determination of whether any experimental results of interest for this task are reported in that paper on any molecular products (transcript and/or polypeptide) of those genes; we called it doc-level in this paper.
2.   Indicate for each gene (in the list) the product type(s) (transcript (TR) or polypeptide (PP) or both) for which there are experimental results of interest. It is called doc-gene-level in this paper.
3.   Provide a RANKING of the papers in the test set in an order so that the papers more likely to require curation (i.e. contain experimental results of interest for some gene product) are ranked higher than the papers that will not require curation (do not contain experimental results for some gene product).

In the following paragraph, the data given in training set and testing set will be elaborated. It includes the text paper(paper in text format), gene list, evidence file, the gene synonyms database and so on and so forth.

There were 862 text papers and 249 text papers in the training and testing data sets respectively. The text papers were derived from the HTML version freely available in the public PubMed system. An extraction of typical paper is shown in Fig. 1.

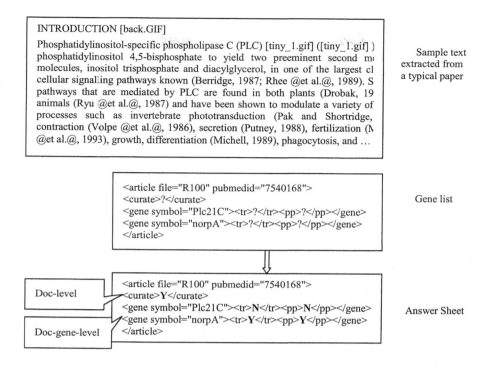

INTRODUCTION [back.GIF]

Phosphatidylinositol-specific phospholipase C (PLC) [tiny_1.gif] ([tiny_1.gif]) phosphatidylinositol 4,5-bisphosphate to yield two preeminent second me molecules, inositol trisphosphate and diacylglycerol, in one of the largest cl cellular signalling pathways known (Berridge, 1987; Rhee @et al.@, 1989). S pathways that are mediated by PLC are found in both plants (Drobak, 19 animals (Ryu @et al.@, 1987) and have been shown to modulate a variety of processes such as invertebrate phototransduction (Pak and Shortridge, contraction (Volpe @et al.@, 1986), secretion (Putney, 1988), fertilization (N @et al.@, 1993), growth, differentiation (Michell, 1989), phagocytosis, and ...

Sample text extracted from a typical paper

```
<article file="R100" pubmedid="7540168">
<curate>?</curate>
<gene symbol="Plc21C"><tr>?</tr><pp>?</pp></gene>
<gene symbol="norpA"><tr>?</tr><pp>?</pp></gene>
</article>
```

Gene list

Doc-level

Doc-gene-level

```
<article file="R100" pubmedid="7540168">
<curate>Y</curate>
<gene symbol="Plc21C"><tr>N</tr><pp>N</pp></gene>
<gene symbol="norpA"><tr>Y</tr><pp>Y</pp></gene>
</article>
```

Answer Sheet

Fig. 1. Samples of some source files provided

For each paper in both the training data and testing data, there was a template called a 'gene list' as shown in Fig. 1. The question marks (for each gene product), had to be replaced by either a 'Y' or a 'N', thus forming a corresponding 'answer sheet'. The answers ('Y' or 'N') for papers in the training data were given while the answers for the testing data were to be filled up by the system to be developed.

In the answer sheet, it was decided that two levels had to be considered. One was the doc-gene-level which indicated whether or not there was experimental evidence for a particular gene. Another was the doc level. Any of the 'Y's at the doc-gene-level would lead to a 'Y' at the doc-level. A 'Y' at the doc-level meant that the paper had experimental evidence of interest and should be curated.

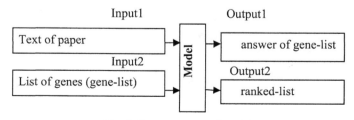

Fig. 2. Input, output and model

There were 283 curated papers out of 862 papers in the training data. For each of the curated papers, there was a corresponding evidence file provided by Flybase. Each file contained the experimental evidence of interest mentioned in the corresponding paper. The evidence was in the form as it appeared in the FlyBase database, as opposed to always being direct passages from the paper. An example of experimental evidence of interest listed for a paper was that in the file for one paper, one line was: <EVIDENCE GENE="Phm" PRODUCT="Phm-RA" PTYPE="TR" EVTYPE="TRL"> 1.7 (northern blot)</EVIDENCE>. This line indicated that an experimental result found in the paper was for "Phm-RA", a "TR" transcript of the gene with the symbol "Phm". The result was that the transcript length ("TRL" field in FlyBase) was 1.7kb, which was found using "northern blot" analysis. According to Flybase, any evidence that fell into the 15 types for TR and 12 types for PP was considered sufficient evidence for the presence of the corresponding gene product. The evidence files played an important role in the training of a model. These files are discussed in greater detail in a later section.

Lastly, a gene synonyms database was also given because a common complication of reading papers on Drosophila was that different papers could refer to a gene by some name other than the gene symbol. For example, one paper used the name of "guf2" for the gene with the FlyBase symbol "SmD3". This gene was also referred to as CG8427. To help deal with this, FlyBase maintained lists of these alternate names (synonyms) that were updated as the curators read more papers. The database given in training data also was also applicable in testing data.

Based on the problem description and the training and testing data, we were required to build a system in the manner as shown in Fig. 2.

3   Approach Taken

In building the system, we took three steps - data pre-processing, data preparation for the classifier, and model building.

3.1   Data Pre-processing

The original articles were formatted as raw text files. The text in these files contained large amounts of noise. In addition, the formatting of these original articles was irregular and inconsistent. As mentioned before, many synonyms were being used to refer to the different genes, which increased the complication. As such, extensive pre-processing and data cleaning needed to be carried out so that the articles could be represented in a manner by which features could be properly extracted and relevant statistics about these features generated.

Noise Removal. The first step in pre-processing the data was the removal of certain control characters in the raw text that would otherwise interfere with the detection of gene symbols within the text. More specifically, these characters are '@' and '-'. These characters, in many cases, appeared at either the beginning or end of a gene symbol (or a synonym for a gene). In order to carry out the synonym replacement or statistics generation, these control characters had to be removed. Otherwise, modules that scanned the text for these words would not be able to locate them. This output from noise removal was then passed into the module that performed the synonym replacement.

Synonym Replacement. Using synonyms to reference a particular gene is very common in biomedical papers. To find out the occurrence of a gene, it is necessary to replace all the synonyms with the original gene symbol.

Formatting. Document formatting was included as part of the pre-processing. It took the pre-processed article files as input to generate a corresponding file that was formatted in a consistent manner, with special tags to indicate the location of different sections and paragraphs in the text.

Feature Extraction. Extraction of features from the articles involved searching for gene symbols and various evidence keywords from the text. According to the task documentation, there were tens of evidence types. We managed to use 12 types in building the model. We generated two types of keywords in which one type was from evidence files themselves (e.g. the phrase "northern blot" was picked as one keyword for an evidence of a transcript) and the other type was manually extracted from the training texts by domain experts. When the two sets of keywords were ready, the statistics generation was carried out. We were interested in the distance between a gene symbol and the keyword. For instance, if the gene and the keyword were in the same sentence, the distance was 0. If keyword is in the next sentence, the distance was 1. Within a single paragraph, the distances were calculated and recorded in an output file that was generated for each evidence type.

To find the needed yes/no (Y/N) answers, we decided to split our system into 2 levels. One level determined whether experimental evidence existed for a product (transcript (TR) or polypeptide (PP)) of a particular gene within a particular paper or document (doc-gene-level). The other level determined whether such evidence existed for any gene in a particular paper (doc-level). A 'Y' for any gene product at the doc-gene-level would lead to a 'Y' at that paper's doc-level, which meant that the paper should be curated .

3.2   Data Preparation for Classifier Building

After the final stage of text processing, a list of doc-gene examples is produced. This list contains some examples where all the attributes contain no values. This happens where none of the keywords being searched for is present, especially for the negative examples. Before the data is imported into the classifier, all these doc-gene combinations are removed.

Condensation of Paragraph. For each doc-gene combination, if there are several times in which a gene occurs within one paragraph, there are several repetitive representations for this doc-gene example. However, only one example is necessary. As such, we removed the redundant examples.

In essence, the doc-gene example that had the minimum distance between a particular gene under consideration and the other keywords was chosen as the representative example. All ties were kept. This was done to both the positive and negative examples.

Manual Checking. This step is only applied to the training set. Upon removing the repetitive doc-gene examples found within the same paragraph, the positive examples to be given to the classifier were manually chosen. Once the positive examples are manually selected, they are combined with the other negative examples. Because the answers are an abbreviated form of the evidence files, these files were not available for the test set.

Final Input into Classifier. The data generated from the text are transformed to the final format. For the nth keyword, the minimal absolute distance (KWn) is kept and the count (KWn_count) of its appearance around the gene under consideration is listed as a feature. Hence, for each keyword two features are created. The section in which the particular example occurs is also used as a feature. After this preprocessing, the data is ready for classifier building.

3.3   Model Building

The Naïve Bayes Classifier (NBC) has been used as an effective classifier for many years [8]. The use of NBC facilitated quick running time. This was essential for our system, which required building multiple classifiers, each with a large number of input records. The ROC curve [9] and the F-measurer were used as scoring mechanism.

Building Classifiers. There are two-stages for model building (each having a classifier). In the first stage, the doc-gene examples (statistics of KWn, KWn_count) are given as input to the first classifier. An initial classifier model is built. The output of the classifier was probabilistic estimates of whether a 'YES' class (for Evi) is obtained for a given doc-gene example which was done by 5-fold cross validation. As such, there was a probability estimate for all doc-gene examples. The doc-gene examples are not unique because some ties were kept. There could be more than one example for a particular doc-gene. Since the final scores are computed for distinct doc-gene examples, it was necessary to finally compute a F-measure based on distinct doc-gene examples. This was carried out by picking the example with the highest probability for similar doc-genes so that only one of them was used as the representative example. At the end of the first stage, a set of distinct doc-gene examples was available for input into a second classifier.

In the second stage, distinct doc-gene patterns are used to train the classifier. The probabilistic output is used to compute the ROC curve and F-measure at the doc-gene level. In plotting the ROC, the number of true positives was taken to be the actual number of positively classified documents in the entire set of training documents. In this way the model was built for each evidence type.

Figure 3 shows the model.

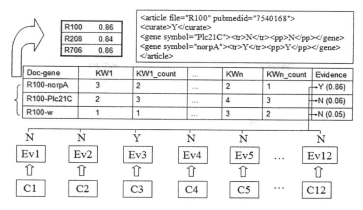

Ci is the ith part of the first classifier; Evi is the ith Evidence type

Fig. 3. Model

Evidence at Doc-Gene-Level and Doc-Level. For each gene listed with each paper, steps were carried out to answer the doc-gene-level Y/N questions by determining whether experimental evidence existed for that gene's TR products and similarly for PP products. For example, let the scores for the three genes in paper R100 be as follows: gene R100-norpA is 0.86, R100-Plc21C is 0.06 and R100-w is 0.05. Then 0.86 will be chosen as paper R100's representative score.

A threshold was set by maximizing [ROC + F-measure].The score of a paper was not only critical for curation of a single paper. It also determined the position of the paper in the ranked list. The higher the score is, the higher the paper is ranked.

4   Results

The following table was provided by KDD cup 2002 committee, showing the results from all submissions.

Each of our scores was within the corresponding first quartile. Our approach performed quite well on the "ranked-list" (81%) and "yes/no curate paper" (73%) subtasks.

Table 1. Comparison with the overall score

Evaluation Sub-Task	Best	1Quatile	Median	Low
Rank list	84%	81%	69%	35%
Yes/No curate paper	78%	61%	58%	32%
Y/N gene products	67%	47%	35%	8%
Overall:	76%	61%	55%	32%

5   Conclusion and Future Work

In this work, an approach has been provided for detecting evidence of gene-product formation in biomedical papers. In particular, a document collection on Drosophila was studied. The biomedical articles were initially pre-processed to remove noise and to provide for standardization between articles. Important features were then extracted and used as input into a Naïve Bayes Classifier. We found that domain knowledge was essential for the feature extraction task. A classifier was built for each evidence type, the results from which were finally combined for evidence detection of gene-product formation.

Acknowledgements

This work was supported by the Design Technology Institute Ltd. management. We would like to thank the graduate students K. B. Siah, B.L. Lim and W. Chu from the National University of Singapore ME Dept. for their contributions to this work. Thanks are also given to P. Long, P. Kolatkar from the Genome Institute of Singapore.

References

1.   Sekimizu, T., Hyun S PARK, Tsujii Junichi Constructing Title Identifying the Interaction between Genes and Gene Products Based on Frequently Seen Verbs in Medline Abstracts. (1998) Genome Informatics. Unviersal Academy Press, Inc.
2.   Thomas, J., Milward, D., Ouzounis, C., Pulman S. and Carrol. M., Automatic Extraction of Protein Interactions from Scientific Abstracts in Pacific Symposium on Biocomputing 5, Honolulu, (2000) 538-549
3.   Craven, M., Kumlien, J. Biological Knowledge Bases by Extracting Information from Text Sources Proceedings of the Seventh International Conference on Intelligent Systems for Molecular Biology (1999)
4.   Roberts, D.1998, Drosophila: A Practical Approach, IRL Press
5.   Flybase Website-A Database of the Drosophila Genome: http://www.flybase.org
6.   Michie, D., Spiegelhalter, D. J., and C. C.Taylor Machine learning of rules and trees. In Machine Learning, Neural and Statistical Classification. (1994). 50-83, Ellis Horwood, New York
7.   KDD CUP 2002 WEBSITE: http://www.biostat.wisc.edu/~craven/kddcup/
8.   Cheng, J., Greiner, R. Learning Bayesian Belief Network Classifiers: Algorithms and System, (2001), Proceedings of the fourteenth Canadian conference on artificial intelligence) AI'2001
9.   Bradley, A. P. The use of the area under the ROC curve in the evaluation of machine learning algorithms. Pattern Recognition, 30(7), (1997). 1145-1159

Automatic Construction of Theme Melody Index from Music Database for Fast Content-Based Retrievals

Chang-Hwan Shin, Kyong-I Ku, KiChang Kim, and Yoo-Sung Kim

School of Information and Communication Engineering
Inha University, Incheon 402-751, Korea
yskim@inha.ac.kr

Abstract. In traditional content-based music information retrieval systems, users may face with longer response time, since the traditional systems mostly do syntactic processing to match query melody and whole melodies of the underlying music database. Hence, there has been a growing need for theme melody index that can support to quick retrieve the relevant music to user's query melody. In this paper, we suggested an automatic mechanism for constructing the theme melody index from large music database and also showed how the theme melody index can be used for content-based music retrievals by implementing a prototype system.

1   Introduction

Although music information retrieval is a relatively new area of investigation, there are great needs for efficient content-based music information retrieval systems that can quickly retrieve the relevant music on demand from very large music database with low storage overheads and fast response time. As content-based music information retrieval systems, several systems have been developed([1,2,3,4]). However, the previous systems have two major problems. First, these systems do not have the indexing mechanism that is helpful to improve the retrieval performance. Hence these systems need time-consuming syntactic processing for retrievals. Second, these systems do not use the full primitive features that are essential to represent the semantics of music. In some traditional systems[1,2], music information is represented by only the pitch variation patterns with 3 alphabets. Other systems[3,4] use the variation degree between two continuous musical notes to represent the retrieval feature of music. However, representing music by either only the pitch variation patterns with three characters or only the degree of pitch values of musical notes is not enough to include the semantic of music information.

To solve the first problem, previous researches([5,6]) proposed theme melody index schemes in which the theme melodies extracted from a song are included. However, in these works, they consider only the exactly repeated patterns within a music object as a theme melody of the music. That is, the previous extracting mechanism can

F. Sebastiani (Ed.): ECIR 2003, LNCS 2633, pp. 605–612, 2003.
© Springer-Verlag Berlin Heidelberg 2003

not extract the approximately(not exactly) repeated patterns as the theme melodies. In general, however, theme melodies can be repeated more than once with some variations within a song. In our previous work([7]), we proposed a theme melody extraction mechanism in which a graphical clustering algorithm is used for grouping the approximately repeated motifs into a cluster and a theme melody is extracted from each cluster. However, we have not showed how the theme melody index is automatically built and used for content-based music retrievals in detail.

In this paper, we show how the theme melody index is constructed automatically with the theme melodies extracted from a MIDI file as the semantically representative melodies for the music. That is, first we determine which features of theme melody should be used for distinguishing the theme melody from others. Then, we also show how the theme melody index is used for content-based music information retrievals.

The rest of this paper is organized as follows. In section 2, we briefly introduce the extraction mechanism of theme melodies. In section 3, we show how the theme melody index is constructed and also how the theme melody is used for efficient content-based music information retrievals. Finally, section 4 concludes this paper.

2   Extracting Theme Melodies

Music listeners get the semantics of music from the sequence of notes. And music composed as the continuous musical notes has three characteristics: rhythm, melody, and harmony. Among the above characteristics, we adopt the melody as the primitive feature of music for supporting content-based music information retrieval because melody can be a decisive component for representing music([7,8]).

A motif is the minimum pattern that has some meaning by itself in the music's hierarchical structure. The theme is one of the important motifs that have the characteristic, "*theme reinstatement*" that means the theme must be repeated more than once with some variances in a music object([5,7,8]). In general, therefore, music listeners may remember the theme melodies of a music object as the main meaning of the music.

In [7], we proposed a theme melody extraction mechanism in which a graphical clustering algorithm is used to classify the repeated similar motifs into one cluster. In this system, when a MIDI file is submitted, it is decomposed into the set of motifs each of which is the minimum meaningful unit. From motifs, pitches and lengths of musical notes are extracted. Then the mechanism computes the similarity values between all pairs of the motifs and a fully connected similarity graph is constructed. By using the proposed graphical clustering algorithm in [7], the motifs of the music are clustered based on the similarity values between motifs. Finally, a representative melody from each cluster is selected as the theme melody based on the locations of the melodies in the music and the maximum summation of the similarity values concerned to the melody in a cluster. However, in this paper, we change the selection strategy of the theme melody from each cluster to allow the selected theme melody having center position of the cluster in metric space of M-tree([9,10]).

3   Automatic Construction of Theme Melody Index

3.1   Representation of Theme Melodies in M-Tree

As well known, M-tree represents data objects into the multi-dimensional space for indexing and retrieval, and uses the similarity that is measured by a distance function. Hence, the metric space composed by a M-tree can be represented as (D, d), where D is the domain of data objects and d is the distance function.

To place an extracted theme melody into the metric space of M-tree, we choose the average length variation and the average pitch variation of the theme melody as the key features. Hence, the metric space of M-tree is a 2-dimension space of *(average length variation, average pitch variation)*.

If we assume that a theme melody of n/m times has k continuous notes, $[(l_1, p_1), (l_2, p_2), \ldots, (l_k, p_k)]$, where l_i and p_i are the length and pitch of i-th musical note in the melody according to the value of Table 1 and the pitch value of MIDI file, respectively. The average length variation $\bar{l}$ and the average pitch variation $\bar{p}$ are computed by Equation (1) and Equation (2), respectively. In Equation (1), the first term denotes the average length difference of k musical notes in the theme melody to the dominator m of the times of the music and the second term denotes the average value of k-1 length differences between continuous k musical notes. Similarly, in Equation (2), the first term denotes the average value of pitch differences between the first musical notes and the following k-1 ones and the second term is for the average value of k-1 pitch differences between k continuous musical notes. And the distance $d(v, u)$ between two theme melodies $u(\bar{l}_u, \bar{p}_u)$ and $v(\bar{l}_v, \bar{p}_v)$ is computed by Equation (3) as the Euclidean distance in 2-dimensional space.

$$\bar{l} = ((\sum_{i=1}^{k} | m - l_i |)/k + (\sum_{i=1}^{k-1} | l_{i+1} - l_i |)/(k-1))/2 \tag{1}$$

$$\bar{p} = (\sum_{i=1}^{k-1} (\frac{| p_1 - p_{i+1} | + | p_{i+1} - p_i |}{2})) /(k-1) \tag{2}$$

$$d(v,u) = \sqrt{| \bar{l}_v - \bar{l}_u |^2 + | \bar{p}_v - \bar{p}_u |^2} \tag{3}$$

Table 1. Length Values for Musical Notes and Rests

Index	0	1	2	3	4	5	6
Note	𝅝	𝅗𝅥	𝅘𝅥	𝅘𝅥𝅮	𝅘𝅥𝅯	𝅘𝅥𝅰	𝅘𝅥𝅱
Rest	▬	▬	𝄼	𝄽	𝄾	𝄿	𝅀
Value(2^{index})	1	2	4	8	16	32	64

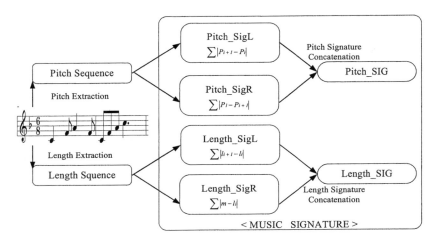

Fig. 1. Composition Procedure for Length Signature and Pitch Signature

If we use only the average length variation and the average pitch variation of a theme melody to place the theme melody in 2-dimensional metric space of the theme melody index, there might be two melodies that have same $\bar{l}$ and $\bar{p}$ values even if they are mainly different in melody patterns to each other. To distinguish these melodies, we use the length signature and the pitch signature of theme melody each of which summarizes the length variation pattern and the pitch variation pattern of continuous musical notes within the theme melody, respectively. As shown in Fig. 1, these signatures are composed during the calculation of the average length variation and the average pitch variation. That is, the length signature consists of two parts, *Length_SigL* and *Length_SigR* which come out from the first term and the second term of Equation (1), respectively. Similarly, the pitch signature in which *Pitch_SigL* and *Pitch_SigR* are concatenated is composed from Equation (2). In section 3.3, we will discuss how these signatures are used for ranking the retrieval results.

3.2   Construction of Theme Melody Index

For the simplicity to describe the procedure of automatic construction of the theme melody index for music database, we will use an example, a Korean children song of Fig. 2.

The song is divided into 8 motifs each of which is labeled with the circled number in Fig. 2. As the final result of the graphical clustering algorithm([7]), two candidate partitions (1,3,7) and (2,4,8) are returned and the 1st and 8th motifs are extracted as the representative from each cluster, respectively, since the 1st and 8th motifs place the centric positions of their clusters. From the music score of the song in Fig. 2, we can recognize the first and last motifs have exactly or approximately repeated several times to give users the impressions as the main melodies of the song.

Fig. 2. The Music Score of a Korean Children Song "Nabi Nabi Hin-Nabi"

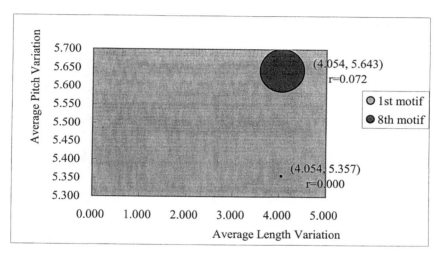

Fig. 3. Logical View of Two Theme Melodies in Theme Melody Index

After two motifs are inserted into the theme melody index, the logical view of the theme melody index is shown in Fig. 3. The cluster that includes the 1st motif as the centric point of (4.054, 5.357) with radius = 0 is figured as a point in Fig. 3.

Since motifs 1, 3, and 7 have the exactly same values of *(average length variation, average pitch variation)*, the radius of the first motif becomes 0. And, the cluster of motif 8 is shown as a circle of the centric point (4.054, 5.643) with radius = 0.072, the maximum distance between motifs, in Fig. 3.

To compare the efficiency of the theme melody index against the whole melody index, we do experiments with an experimental music database of 47 Korean children songs. We extract 96 theme melodies at total by the theme melody extraction mechanism([7]), whereas the total number of melodies from the database is 343. After inserting 96 theme melodies, the theme melody index consists of 10 nodes with height 2 levels, while the whole melody index consists of 41 nodes with height 3 levels. This means, the theme melody index can reduce the retrieval time since it has lower height than the whole melody index.

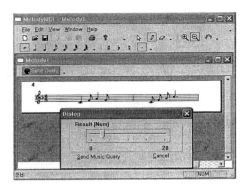

Fig. 4. Query Interface

3.3   Content-Based Music Retrieval Using Theme Melody Index

In our study, for making user's query melody, we use a query interface as shown in Fig. 4, by which users can draw some part of melody on a music sheet. With user's query melody, users should specify the number of expected retrieval results.

As an example, let us consider that user gives the first part of Fig. 2 and the user also specify the expected number of retrieval results to 3 as shown in Fig. 4. First, from the user's query, the times, the number of musical notes, the pitch sequence, and the length sequence are extracted. Then, the feature information such as the average length variation L, the average pitch variation P, the length signatures LSL and LSR, and the pitch signatures PSL and PSR of the query melody is composed.

With the average length variation and the average pitch variation of the query melody, we retrieve the similar theme melodies to the given query melody from the theme melody index by using the k-nearest neighbor search algorithm of M-tree, here k is the expected number of retrieval results specified. However, since we retrieve the related theme melodies based the distance in 2-dimensional metric space which consists of the average length variation and the average pitch variation, some melodies which have different shapes in music score but have similar values for the average length variation and the average pitch variation to the query melody given might be retrieved as the results. To rank them, we use the signatures that summarize the variation patterns of continuous musical notes within a melody with respect to the length and the pitch.

If we perform a k-nearest neighbor search for the query melody given of Fig. 4 in the theme melody index, we get the retrieval result as shown in Table 2. In Table 2, we can recognize that Result 2 has smaller distance(0.156) from the given query melody than that(0.286) of Result 3 even though Result 3 is more similar to the query melody than Result 2.

To rank appropriately, we use the difference between signatures of query and those of retrieval results. For the retrieval results of Table 2, we can calculate the difference of signatures between each retrieved melody and the query melody as in Table 3. And according to the difference of signature, $\sum |s_q - s_r|$ between the signature S_q of query melody and the signature S_r of melody retrieved, we can decide the ranks for the melodies of retrieval result. In Table 3, the final rank is denoted in the last column.

Table 2. Theme Melodies Retrieved by The Query Melody of Fig. 4

	Distance	Music Score
Result 1	0.000	
Result 2	0.156	
Result 3	0.286	

Table 3. Ranking Retrieval Result with Signature Difference

	Distance	PSL	PSR	LSL	LSR	$\sum |s_q - s_r|$	Rank
Query		30	45	17	13		
Result 1	0.000	30	45	17	13	0	1
Result 2	0.156	26	70	18	19	36	3
Result 3	0.286	23	56	17	13	18	2

Therefore, we can get the first retrieved result ranked based on the signature difference. From the final result, we can do relevance feedback phase to get more relevant melody to what they want and finally to improve the satisfaction of users to retrieval results. As the relevance decision of user for retrieved results, users choose one melody that is the most similar result to what they want with user's confidence from 0% to 100%. Then, we can make a revised query from the relevance decision of user, and we use the range search query of M-tree with the revised query for relevance feedback. The revised query has the average length variation and the average pitch variation of the selected melody and radius r_q. The radius r_q is either an increased value or a decreased value from the distance r_s between the selected melody and the previous query melody according to the user's confidence C by Equation (4).

$$r_q = r_s \times (1 - \frac{C - 50}{50})$$ (4)

4   Conclusions

In this paper, we proposed an automatic construction mechanism of the theme melody index for very large music database by using the theme melody extraction mechanism and M-tree indexing scheme. In the proposed mechanism, a set of theme melodies is extracted from a music file based on the similarity, and the extracted theme melodies are placed into the 2-demensional metric space by their average length variation and average pitch variation values. By using the theme melody, we can reduce the index size for underlying very large music database and the response time to user's query melodies. We also proposed the content-based music retrieval mechanism using theme melody index. In the retrieval mechanism, to improve the quality of retrieval result, we include the ranking scheme in which we use signatures that summarize the variation patterns of melodies and the relevance feedback scheme by which users can get more or less retrieval results according to user's relevance decision.

Acknowledgements

This work was partially supported by grant No. 2000-1-51200-009-2 from the Basic Research Program of the Korea Science & Engineering Foundation and also supported by Korea Research Foundation for the 21st Century.

References

1. Ghias, A., Logan, J., Chamberlin, D., Smith, B. C.: Query By Humming Musical Information Retrieval in an Audio Database. ACM Multimedia, (1995)
2. McNab, R. J., Smith, L. A., Witten, I. H., Henderson, C. L., Cunningham, S. J.: Towards the Digital Music Library: Tune Retrieval from Acoustic Input. Digital Libraries, (1996)
3. Jee, J., Oh, H.: Design and Implementation of Music Information Retrieval System Using Melodies. The Journal of Korea Information Processing Society, Vol.5, No.1, (1998) (in Korean)
4. Kornstadt, A.: Themefinder: A Web-based Melodic Search Tool. Melodic Comparison: Concepts, Procedures and Applications, Computing in Musicology 11, (1998)
5. Liu, C. C, Hsu, J. L., Chen, L. P.: Efficient Theme and Non-trivial Repeating Pattern Discovering in Music Databases. Proceedings of the 15th International Conference on Data Engineering, (1999)
6. Chou, T. C., Chen, L. P., Lie, C. C.: Music Databases: Indexing Techniques and Implementation. Proceedings of IEEE International Workshop on Multimedia Database Management Systems, (1996)
7. Kang, Y., Ku, K., Kim, Y.: Extracting Theme Melodies from Music by Using a Graphical Clsutering Algorithm for Content-based Music Retrieval. Lecture Notes in Computer Science, Vol. LNCS 2151, Springer-Verlag, Berlin Heidelberg New York (2001)
8. Lee, B., Paek, G.: Everybody Can Compose Songs If They Read Three Times It. Jackeunwoori Pub. Co. Seoul (1989) (in Korean)
9. Ciaccia, P., Patella, M., Zezula, P.: M-tree: An Efficient Access Method for Similarity Search in Metric Spaces. Proceedings of the 23rd VLDB, (1997)
10. Patella, M.: Similarity Search in Multimedia Databases. Ph. D. Thesis, Dipartimento di Electtronica Informatica e Sistemistica, UNIVERSITA DEGLI STUDI DI BOLOGNA, (1999)

A Personalized Information Search Process Based on Dialoguing Agents and User Profiling

Giovanni Semeraro[1], Marco Degemmis[1], Pasquale Lops[1],
Ulrich Thiel[2], and Marcello L'Abbate[2]

[1] Dipartimento di Informatica
Via Orabona 4, 70125 Bari, Italy
{semeraro,degemmis,lops}@di.uniba.it
[2] Fraunhofer IPSI
Dolivostr. 15, 64293 Darmstadt, Germany
{thiel,labbate}@ipsi.fraunhofer.de

Abstract. The amount of information available on the web, as well as the number of e-businesses and web shoppers, is growing exponentially. Customers have to spend a lot of time to browse the net in order to find relevant information. One way to overcome this problem is to use dialoguing agents that exploit user profiles to generate personal recommendations. This paper presents a system, designed according to this approach, that adopts a query refinement mechanism to improve the search process of an Internet commerce web site.

1 Introduction

Nowadays enterprises are developing new business portals and provide large amounts of product information: choosing among so many options is very time consuming for customers. Electronic commerce has become a domain where the full potentiality of intelligent agents [3] can be demonstrated in an attempt to solve the *information overload* problem: the management of huge amounts of information requires solutions that show a certain degree of *autonomy* and *personalization*. Agent technologies fit these requirements since they represent a paradigm for the implementation of autonomous and proactive behaviors. Our solution is based on *intelligent agents* (chatterbots) which represent virtual assistants able to dialogue in natural language with customers. The agents learn a user's preferences during the interaction and store them in a profile exploited to formulate *"personalized"* queries in order to generate individual recommendations. This paper proposes an *"intelligent"* retrieval process founded upon chatterbot technology, user profiling techniques, and a query expansion mechanism which uses the profiles in order to refine the original query assumed by the chatterbot. In the COGITO project [12], we used this approach to enhance the search function of the BOL web site, an on-line media shop specialized in books.

Among systems using natural language to interact with users, NLA (Natural Language Assistant) [4] supports users in finding relevant products on PC

F. Sebastiani (Ed.): ECIR 2003, LNCS 2633, pp. 613-621, 2003.

e-commerce sites. NLA combines classical rule-based AI technologies with statistical parsing techniques, based upon decision trees induction to generate queries. The decision tree contains a model of a conversation used to generate SQL queries in a transparent way for the user. Conversely, the COGITO agent refines the user's queries, expanding them with the knowledge stored in his/her personal profile.

Various learning approaches have been applied to construct profiles useful to retrieve relevant items in large repositories. In [7] it is presented an evolutionary method to build a customer's profile for DVD film recommending. The profile is used to recognize whether the customer is interested in a specific item or not. Our profiling system does not adopt a binary decision that categorizes the products into the classes of customer-likes and customer-dislikes, but it infers the product categories preferred by a user. Data mining methods are used by the 1:1Pro system [2] to build profiles that contain rules describing a customer's behavior. Rules are derived from transactional data, representing the purchasing and browsing activities of each user. Using rules is an intuitive way to represent the customer's needs. Moreover, the rules generated from a huge number of transactions tend to be statistically reliable.

2   Learning User Preferences to Build Personal Profiles

A user profile is a structured representation of the user's interests which can be exploited by a retrieval system in order to autonomously pursue the goals posed by the user. The Profile Extractor (PE) is a module that employs supervised learning techniques to discover user's preferences from data recorded during past visits to the e-commerce web site. It builds profiles containing the product categories preferred by a buyer. The system was tested on the German virtual bookshop of the Bertelsmann Online company (www.bol.de). The user's preferences inferred by the system are the ten main book categories the product database is subdivided into: *Belletristik* (Fiction), *Computer_und_Internet* (Computer and Internet), etc. The input to PE is represented by an XML file containing all the details of users (Figure 1). The *XML I/O Wrapper* extracts the data required to set up the training examples (number of searches and purchases for each product category, number of connections, etc.). This information is arranged into a set of unclassified instances, each instance representing a customer. Instances are pre-classified by a domain expert (each customer is associated with a subset of book categories) and processed by the *Rules Manager*, which induces a classification rule set for each book category.

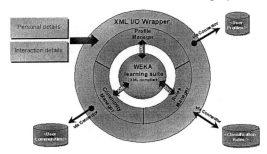

Fig. 1. The architecture of the Profile Extractor

The learning algorithm is PART [6], implemented by the WEKA learning suite [13]. After training, the *Profile Manager* uses the rule sets to predict whether a user is interested in each book category. Classifications and transactional data are gathered to form the user profile. It is composed by two frames: *factual*, (personal and transactional data), and *behavioral*, containing the learned preferred book categories, ranked according to the degree of interest computed by the learning system (Figure 2). An empirical evaluation of the added value provided by PE to learn interaction models for the users of a digital library service is available in [10]. Profiles can be used to improve the quality of the results of retrieval processes. In standard retrieval situations, it is the user's responsibility to formulate a query. In our case, the agent has to generate a query automatically, starting with the current dialogue topics. We employ a number of strategies to refine this initial query.

Profile of user 119

CONNECTIONS_NUM	23		Belletristik	0.9902
SEARCH_NUMBelletristik	3		Computer_und_Internet	1.0
SEARCH_FREQBelletristik	0.2		Kinderbucher	0
PURCHASE_NUMBelletristik	23		Kultur_und_Geschichte	0.7982
PURCHASE_FREQBelletristik	0.35		Nachschlagewerke	0
SEARCH_NUMComputer_und_Internet	1		Reise	0.0038
SEARCH_FREQComputer_und_Internet	0.2		Sachbuch_und_Ratgeber	0.6702
PURCHASE_NUMComputer_und_Internet	13		Schule_und_Bildung	0
PURCHASE_FREQComputer_und_Internet	0.24		Wirtschaft_und_Soziales	0
...			Wissenschaft_und_Technik	0
Factual			**Behavioural**	

Fig. 2. An example of user profile

3   User Profiles as Part of a Unified Query Expansion Model

We distinguish three different cases in which a conversational agent may generate a query to a background database during an on-going dialogue: explicit user requests, unrecognized user input during metadialogues and proactive product recommendation. An explicit user request starting with "I am searching for..." or "I would like to buy...." causes the chatterbot to move into a specific internal state, in which rules for the generation of a query can be triggered. The rules in this context generate questions eliciting attributes to be included in a SQL query. When the user inputs some text that is not recognized by the agent, while talking about transaction issues or site handling mechanisms, the user is usually asked to rephrase his last input. This may be achieved by moving into a particular context, in which dialogue management rules for the output of standard ELIZA-style sentences are contained. Given a text retrieval facility, however, the terms appearing in the problematic sentence can be instead included be posted as a query to external knowledge sources like help texts or FAQ documents kept in an IR-system. The set of attributes of the query also takes contextual data into account, like other so far discussed topics or user-specific properties [1]. Finally, the last case applies when a chatterbot recognizes the prerequisites for proactively recommending a product. General search strategies for recommending an eventually interesting product can be construed in form of logical predicates generally referring to the users' likes and dislikes (e.g. *"likes_to_read (book_genre)"* where *"book_genre"* is set to a specific genre according to information extracted from the dialogue) or to more specific product-relevant features (e.g. *"favourite_book(title, author, publisher)"* where some of the variables are set to values). Depending on the chosen search pattern, the query will consist of a generic template, updated with the values of the variables coming from the fulfilled predicates. In each of the above-mentioned cases, the generated query may lead to unsatisfying results, e.g. because too few or too many items are retrieved. Therefore, once the system evaluated the result set, it may be necessary to refine the query in order to enhance the quality of the set of results. For the query refinement task we introduce a set of query expansion methods relying on information to be systematically extracted from external sources. A query expansion process consists of an improvement of the criteria used for the specification of a query. This is usually achieved by adding search terms to an already defined query. The intent is to improve precision and/or recall which are well known and commonly used measures to evaluate the performance of information retrieval systems [9].

The additional terms are usually taken from a thesaurus, but not necessarily, as we will see in the following. As depicted in Figure 3, different expansion mechanisms can be applied. The decision on which source to use for the expansion depends on the kind of search strategy both user and agent intend to follow and also on the current context. Before explaining how the expansion is realized for each search strategy, we will characterize each kind of used information source in the following.

Both user and agent utterances are stored within a special kind of log file called Structured Dialogue History (SDH). It usually consists of a sequence of mappings between a sentence and a dialogue act according to a generic dialogue model called COR [11]. In this way, it can be avoided to repeat asking questions for specific information, which have already been asked in previous dialogue steps. The answer to these questions can be used for the refinement of a query. Another relevant information stored into the SDH is a reference to the context of the utterance providing evidence on its relevance to the expansion process.

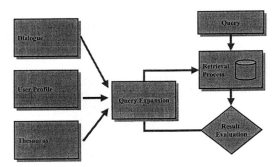

Fig. 3. Query Expansion Model

Another context parameter which influences relevance judgments for a given query is the collection on which the search is performed. Products like books or other kinds of media are usually characterized by a textual description. The most relevant words contained in these descriptions can be clustered according to their relation to the most frequently appearing ones, with the aim of generating a "thesaurus" of terms. In this way, it is possible to look up, for a given term, a set of probably related other terms, to be used for expanding a query. For instance, if a query is intended to retrieve manuals about a given topic expressed by a sequence of terms (e.g. "Java Programming"), the result quality can be improved by adding also the terms resulting from the intersection of the determined sets of related terms. The generation of clusters can be kept more successful if applied to previously defined product categories, in order to be able to assign different relevance values to terms appearing simultaneously in different categories. The categorized descriptions of books are passed through a 3-phase process in order to build the thesaurus. In the first phase, a vocabulary is constructed. Appearing terms are normalized (i.e. "stop-words" are removed, and general stemming procedures applied), and the equally distributed ones are removed, since they are not relevant for the thesaurus. In the second phase, three similarity measures s0, s1, and s2 are computed between every couple of terms:

s0:   cos $(t1, t2)$
s1:   #of Docs containing both terms/#of Docs containing t1
s2:   #of Docs containing both terms/#of Docs containing t2

where t1 and t2 are terms, represented by their "document vector" [9].

These similarity values are used during phase 3 of the construction process, in order to determine relationships between terms. For instance, the "broader" relation between term t1 and t2 is set if $s1(t1,t2) > s2(t1,t2)$. By choosing a threshold the related relationship can be determined for a term if its frequency is above that threshold. During phase 3 the vocabulary is structured by applying the so-called "layer-seeds" clustering procedure. It consists of the following processing steps: for each defined category the most frequent term, called "seed" is selected. The similarity values between the seed and all other terms within the category are calculated. A cluster will contain the seed as well as all "narrower" terms, i.e. terms tx with $s1(ts,tx) < s2(ts,tx)$, where ts is the seed. The narrower terms are grouped together in a new layer, and the whole procedure is repeated for this new layer. The process is terminated if there is no seed found within a layer (for a more detailed discussion about the "layer seeds" procedure cf. [5]).

In addition to the information need expressed in current the dialogue the user will certainly have interests, skills, and habits which determine her search behavior but are not explicitly mentioned in her utterances. They might, however, be issues in past dialogues, or can be inferred from the system's knowledge about similar users. Chatterbots with personalization facilities collect user properties gathered during the dialogues within internal archives. The generated user profiles are accessed in case of users visiting the site at different times and in different sessions. In this way the recurrence of some basic questions can be avoided, and the dialogue kept more interesting and up-to-date for the user. The profiles contain both generic user attributes like age, country of provenience and gender, as well as details about her hobbies, activities, likes and dislikes. In the next section, we show how a conversational agent can exploit the knowledge stored in a user's profile in order to support him/her in searching for products of interest.

4   Exploiting the Profiles to Search for Interesting Products

The COGITO chatterbot (Susanna) accesses the profile of a user for identifying the preferred book category, which can be enclosed in the original query submitted to the search engine of the BOL web site, as demonstrated in the following scenarios.

Scenario 1: A *user without a profile* asks Susanna for a book by the author *King*: it finds several books through a remote call to the search engine, and displays them as shown in Figure 4. Notice that the books that rank at the top are authored by Stephen King. Books by other authors are found further down the list, which means that the user must scroll down a long list if he/she is not looking for a book by Stephen King.

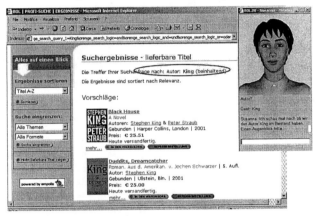

Fig. 4. Susanna offers a long list of books belonging to several categories

Fig. 5. List of books written by authors whose last name is "King" belonging to the book category "Computer & Internet"

Scenario 2: A *profile of the user is available* to the system. Consider that the profile of such a user is the one presented in Figure 2 and the query is the same as in the previous scenario. Now, the first book displayed is a book about Windows 2000 co-authored by Robert King (Figure 5). This result is due to the fact that the original query about King has been automatically expanded into "King AND Computer & Internet" (Figure 5), since *Computer_und_Internet* is the category with the highest degree of interest in the profile of the user. In all dialogue examples discussed so far the system supported the user in formulating a precise query by determining the characteristical properties of potentially relevant information items. Some users might not pursue this search strategy, but exhibit a different search behavior, e.g. by looking for items similar to objects they know. In the following section, we outline how our approach can be extended to cope with a wider spectrum of search strategies.

5   Search Strategies

In e-commerce applications in which users will search for information about products as well as for the product itself, an intelligent conversational agent can play a valuable role supporting some or all of the mental search strategies that users may apply while visiting the site. A set of five mental search strategies (empirical search, analytical search, browsing, search by analogy and bibliographical search) were originally identified in the "Book House Project" [8], but have been empirically verified in several other domains since users utilize identical strategies for seeking and retrieving information about various subjects. The conversational skills of the COGITO agent enable the system to support these strategies in very natural way. The standard behavior of the agent intends to keep the dialogue going on. Its major purpose is to gather relevant data about the user, in order to achieve its profile, which will be mainly used for the implementation of empirical search strategies. Age, gender and language, for instance, can be used for characterizing a specific category of products, which the assistant will take into account, while generating suggestions or answers to explicit user requests as we have outlined in the previous section. Other rules support analytical search as a search strategy. At this time the agent would output the following sentences:

A: We have a lot of interesting books in our stock. What sort do you prefer?
A: Do you have a favourite Author?
A: Do you prefer a hardcover format for your books?

The answers to these questions are used by the system as constraints (i.e. attributes and parameters) to a product retrieval process, as they can be seen as representations of the user's needs. Once a sufficient amount of search parameters are available, the system autonomously starts a background retrieval process looking for products that can be recommended. In case of an unacceptable number of results (i.e. too few or too many), the query is expanded by looking up the product thesaurus. Related terms can be added to the initial set of attributes and a new generated query can be posted again.

In the continuation of the dialogue the agent may have recognized a specific user interest, like the preference of reading horror stories featuring chainsaw murders.

After being recommended related products, the user may input the following sentence:

U: I already know enough stories about chainsaw murders. Isn't there anything else?

This imprecise formulation of the user's wish can be regarded as a prerequisite for browsing the category of horror literature with the aim of discovering new interesting items. In this case, the query expansion can be based on the dialogue history; already mentioned unwanted terms (for instance the term "chainsaw") can be used for filtering out the result set. Moreover, the product thesaurus can be invoked again, with the aim of suggesting other related terms to use for the browsing step. At this point consider the case in which the recommended book is topically relevant to the user but fails to meet further relevance criteria:

U: I already own that one.

This case appears to be now the right prerequisite for applying a search by analogy strategy. The system can use the suggested book, and therefore its main features, as a model document for searching for similar books. Exploiting the features of the COGITO system, we can modify the similarity search if needed: the user profile can be taken into account in order to identify some other attributes to include into the query. For instance, by considering the user's age, the result set can be restricted (there may be horror books not suitable for a younger audience). The model book may have some properties expressed by representative keywords. Looking up these keywords in the thesaurus may provide some related terms, to use once again as additional attributes for the query.

Finally, a bibliographical search strategy can be carried out when the user selects a specific book out of the presented list and asks for detailed information about it.

References

1. L'Abbate, M., Thiel, U.: Chatterbots and Intelligent Information Search. In: Proceedings of the BCS-IRSG 23rd European Colloquium on Information Retrieval Research (2001) 200-207
2. Adomavicius, G., Tuzhilin, A.: Using Data Mining Methods to Build Customer Profiles. IEEE Computer 34(2) (2001) 74-82
3. Bradshaw, J. M.: Software Agents. AAAI/MIT Press, Menlo Park (1997)
4. Chai, J., Horvath, V., Nicolov, N., Stys, M., Kambhatla, N., Zadrozny, W., Melville, P.: Natural Language Assistant. A Dialog System for Online Product Recommendation. AI Magazine 23(2) (2002) 63-75
5. Chen, L., Thiel U., L'Abbate, M.: Konzeptuelle Query Expansion auf der Basis des Layer-Seeds Clustering Verfahrens. In: Hammwöhner, R., Wolff, C., Womser-Hacker, C. (Hg.): Information und Mobilität - Optimierung und Vermeidung von Mobilität durch Information. Proceedings of the 8th International Symposium on Information Science. Konstanz: UVK Verlagsgesellschaft mbH (2002)

6. Frank, E., Witten, I.H.: Generating Accurate Rule Sets Without Global Optimization. In: Proceedings of International Conference on Machine Learning, Morgan Kaufmann, Menlo Park (1998) 144-151

7. Lee, W.-P., Liu, C.-H., Lu, C.-C: Intelligent Agent-based Systems for Personalized Recommendations in Internet Commerce. Expert Systems with Applications, 22(4) (2002) 275-284

8. Pejtersen, A. M., Jensen, G., Steen, W., Jensen, H.: Visualization of Database Structures for Information Retrieval. ALT-J Association for Learning Technology Journal 2 (3) (1994)

9. Salton, G., McGill M. J.: Introduction to Modern Information Retrieval. McGraw-Hill, Singapore (1984)

10. Semeraro, G., Ferilli, S., Fanizzi, N., Abbattista, F.: Learning Interaction Models in a Digital Library Service. In: Bauer, M., Gmytrasiewicz, P.J., Vassileva J. (eds.): Proceedings of 8th International Conference on User Modelling, Lecture Notes in Artificial Intelligence, Vol. 2109. Springer, Berlin Heidelberg New York (2001) 44-53

11. Stein, A., Gulla, J. A. and Thiel, U. User-Tailored Planning of Mixed Initiative Information-Seeking Dialogues. User Modeling and User-Adapted Interaction 9(1-2) (1999) 133-166

12. Thiel, U., L'Abbate, M., Paradiso, A., Stein, A., Semeraro, G., Abbattista, F., Lops, P.: The COGITO Project: Intelligent E-Commerce with Guiding Agents based on Personalized Interaction Tools. In: Gasos, J. , Thoben, K.-D. (eds.): e-Business Applications: Results of Applied Research on e-Commerce, Supply Chain Management and Extended Enterprises. Section 2: eCommerce, Springer-Verlag (2002)

13. Witten, I.H., Frank, E.: Data Mining: Practical Machine Learning Tools and Techniques with Java Implementations. Morgan Kaufmann, San Francisco (1999)

Author Index

Lecture Notes in Computer Science

For information about Vols. 1–2539

please contact your bookseller or Springer-Verlag

Vol. 2580: H. Erdogmus, T. Weng (Eds.), COTS-Based Software Systems. Proceedings, 2003. XVIII, 261 pages. 2003.

Vol. 2581: J.S. Sichman, F. Bousquet, P. Davidsson (Eds.), Multi-Agent-Based Simulation II. Proceedings, 2002. X, 195 pages. 2003. (Subseries LNAI).

Vol. 2582: L. Bertossi, G.O.H. Katona, K.-D. Schewe, B. Thalheim (Eds.), Semantics in Databases. Proceedings, 2001. IX, 229 pages. 2003.

Vol. 2583: S. Matwin, C. Sammut (Eds.), Inductive Logic Programming. Proceedings, 2002. X, 351 pages. 2003. (Subseries LNAI).

Vol. 2585: F. Giunchiglia, J. Odell, G. Weiß (Eds.), Agent-Oriented Software Engineering III. Proceedings, 2002. X, 229 pages. 2003.

Vol. 2586: M. Klusch, S. Bergamaschi, P. Edwards, P. Petta (Eds.), Intelligent Information Agents. VI, 275 pages. 2003. (Subseries LNAI).

Vol. 2587: P.J. Lee, C.H. Lim (Eds.), Information Security and Cryptology – ICISC 2002. Proceedings, 2002. XI, 536 pages. 2003.

Vol. 2588: A. Gelbukh (Ed.), Computational Linguistics and Intelligent Text Processing. Proceedings, 2003. XV, 648 pages. 2003.

Vol. 2589: E. Börger, A. Gargantini, E. Riccobene (Eds.), Abstract State Machines 2003. Proceedings, 2003. XI, 427 pages. 2003.

Vol. 2590: S. Bressan, A.B. Chaudhri, M.L. Lee, J.X. Yu, Z. Lacroix (Eds.), Efficiency and Effectiveness of XML Tools and Techniques and Data Integration over the Web. Proceedings, 2002. X, 259 pages. 2003.

Vol. 2591: M. Aksit, M. Mezini, R. Unland (Eds.), Objects, Components, Architectures, Services, and Applications for a Networked World. Proceedings, 2002. XI, 431 pages. 2003.

Vol. 2592: R. Kowalczyk, J.P. Müller, H. Tianfield, R. Unland (Eds.), Agent Technologies, Infrastructures, Tools, and Applications for E-Services. Proceedings, 2002. XVII, 371 pages. 2003. (Subseries LNAI).

Vol. 2593: A.B. Chaudhri, M. Jeckle, E. Rahm, R. Unland (Eds.), Web, Web-Services, and Database Systems. Proceedings, 2002. XI, 311 pages. 2003.

Vol. 2594: A. Asperti, B. Buchberger, J.H. Davenport (Eds.), Mathematical Knowledge Management. Proceedings, 2003. X, 225 pages. 2003.

Vol. 2595: K. Nyberg, H. Heys (Eds.), Selected Areas in Cryptography. Proceedings, 2002. XI, 405 pages. 2003.

Vol. 2597: G. Păun, G. Rozenberg, A. Salomaa, C. Zandron (Eds.), Membrane Computing. Proceedings, 2002. VIII, 423 pages. 2003.

Vol. 2598: R. Klein, H.-W. Six, L. Wegner (Eds.), Computer Science in Perspective. X, 357 pages. 2003.

Vol. 2599: E. Sherratt (Ed.), Telecommunications and beyond: The Broader Applicability of SDL and MSC. Proceedings, 2002. X, 253 pages. 2003.

Vol. 2600: S. Mendelson, A.J. Smola, Advanced Lectures on Machine Learning. Proceedings, 2002. IX, 259 pages. 2003. (Subseries LNAI).

Vol. 2601: M. Ajmone Marsan, G. Corazza, M. Listanti, A. Roveri (Eds.) Quality of Service in Multiservice IP Networks. Proceedings, 2003. XV, 759 pages. 2003.

Vol. 2602: C. Priami (Ed.), Computational Methods Systems Biology. Proceedings, 2003. IX, 214 pages. 20

Vol. 2604: N. Guelfi, E. Astesiano, G. Reggio (Eds.), S entific Engineering for Distributed Java Applications. P ceedings, 2002. X, 205 pages. 2003.

Vol. 2606: A.M. Tyrrell, P.C. Haddow, J. Torresen (Ed Evolvable Systems: From Biology to Hardware. Procee ings, 2003. XIV, 468 pages. 2003.

Vol. 2607: H. Alt, M. Habib (Eds.), STACS 2003. P ceedings, 2003. XVII, 700 pages. 2003.

Vol. 2609: M. Okada, B. Pierce, A. Scedrov, H. Toku A. Yonezawa (Eds.), Software Security – Theories a Systems. Proceedings, 2002. XI, 471 pages. 2003.

Vol. 2610: C. Ryan, T. Soule, M. Keijzer, E. Tsang, Poli, E. Costa (Eds.), Genetic Programming. Proceedin 2003. XII, 486 pages. 2003.

Vol. 2611: S. Cagnoni, J.J. Romero Cardalda, D.W. Cor J. Gottlieb, A. Guillot, E. Hart, C.G. Johnson, E. M chiori, J.-A. Meyer, M. Middendorf, G.R. Raidl (Eds Applications of Evolutionary Computing. Proceeding 2003. XXI, 708 pages. 2003.

Vol. 2612: M. Joye (Ed.), Topics in Cryptology – CT-RS 2003. Proceedings, 2003. XI, 417 pages. 2003.

Vol. 2614: R. Laddaga, P. Robertson, H. Shrobe (Eds Self-Adaptive Software: Applications. Proceedings, 200 VIII, 291 pages. 2003.

Vol. 2615: N. Carbonell, C. Stephanidis (Eds.), Univers Access. Proceedings, 2002. XIV, 534 pages. 2003.

Vol. 2616: T. Asano, R. Klette, C. Ronse (Eds.), Geometr Morphology, and Computational Imaging. Proceeding 2002. X, 437 pages. 2003.

Vol. 2617: H.A. Reijers (Eds.), Design and Control Workflow Processes. Proceedings, 2002. XV, 624 page 2003.

Vol. 2618: P. Degano (Ed.), Programming Languages an Systems. Proceedings, 2003. XV, 415 pages. 2003.

Vol. 2619: H. Garavel, J. Hatcliff (Eds.), Tools and A gorithms for the Construction and Analysis of System Proceedings, 2003. XVI, 604 pages. 2003.

Vol. 2620: A.D. Gordon (Ed.), Foundations of Softwar Science and Computation Structures. Proceedings, 2003 XII, 441 pages. 2003.

Vol. 2621: M. Pezzè (Ed.), Fundamental Approache to Software Engineering. Proceedings, 2003. XIV, 40 pages. 2003.

Vol. 2622: G. Hedin (Ed.), Compiler Construction. Pro ceedings, 2003. XII, 335 pages. 2003.

Vol. 2623: O. Maler, A. Pnueli (Eds.), Hybrid Systems Computation and Control. Proceedings, 2003. XII, 55 pages. 2003.

Vol. 2625: U. Meyer, P. Sanders, J. Sibeyn (Eds.), Al gorithms for Memory Hierarchies. Proceedings, 2003 XVIII, 428 pages. 2003.

Vol. 2626: J.L. Crowley, J.H. Piater, M. Vincze, L. Paletta (Eds.), Computer Vision Systems. Proceedings, 2003 XIII, 546 pages. 2003.

Vol. 2633: F. Sebastiani (Ed.), Advances in Information Retrieval. Proceedings, 2003. XIII, 546 pages. 2003.